SOLVING MONA LISA

SOLVING MONA LISA

THE DISCOVERY OF MY LIFE

Ron Piccirillo

Ron Piccirillo
P.O. Box 18701
Rochester, NY 14618-9998

Hardcover edition, grayscale illustrations, May 2019

For special discounts on bulk purchases, or to book an event, email solvingmonalisa@yahoo.com.

Cover design by Ernie Roszkowski and Ron Piccirillo
Interior book design by Ron Piccirillo
Copy editing by Dusty Fox
Cover art and any other original art copyright © 2019 Ron Piccirillo
Back cover photo by Katie Cassara Photography

The events and conversations in this book have been set down to the best of the author's ability, although some names and details have been changed to protect the privacy of individuals.

www.RonPiccirillo.com

ISBN-13: 978-1-7330372-4-2

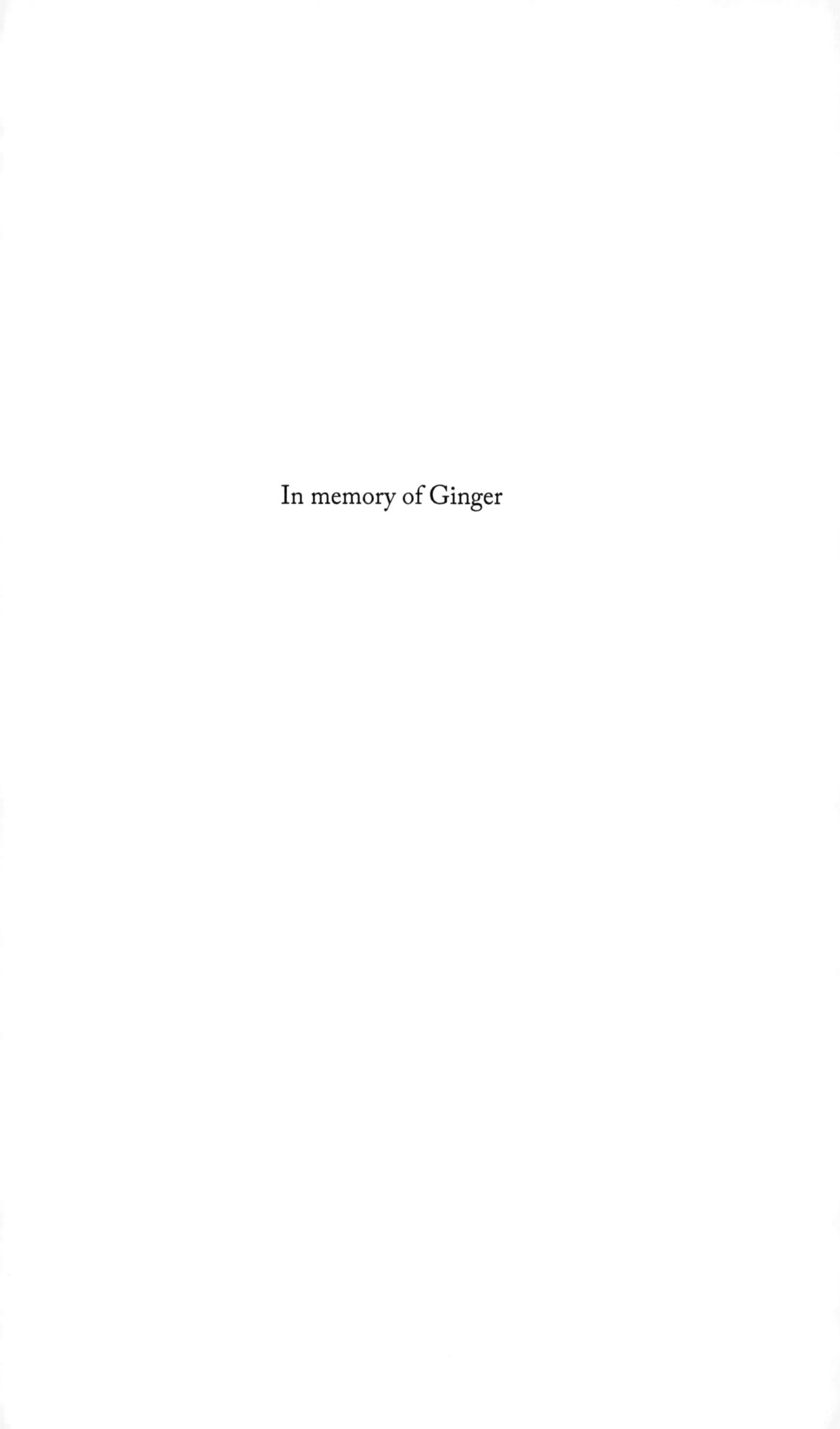

In memory of Ginger

Contents

Author's Note

In 2011, while referencing a copy of Leonardo da Vinci's *Mona Lisa* for one of my own paintings, I made an accidental discovery. I was studying her this way and that, as I did with all kinds of art, when I spotted something no one had ever pointed out before. It was an optical illusion that, when viewed correctly, revealed hidden imagery. As I looked closer, I realized other images were hidden in the art.

Eventually, news reports of what I found spread internationally. Some questioned whether the images were real or just a figment of my imagination, while others simply passed the images off as insignificant. I had no idea why Leonardo placed them there, but hoped that scholars would come forward with an explanation. And although I found similar images in other Renaissance art, almost all the news reports focused on *Mona Lisa*, which created the impression that the secret images were isolated to that one painting. In addition, the complexity of the illusions caused some inaccurate reports, making the controversial discoveries even more difficult to accept.

Still, no one could explain what the images meant. And though Leonardo had a reputation for being oddly clever in his artwork, and was known to create picture puzzles and riddles, scholars didn't seem to take my findings seriously. I assumed art historians were either unable to see the images, since it required an artist's eye, or that they were skeptical from the start—surely they had become annoyed with the overabundance of theories from art enthusiasts trying to solve Mona Lisa's identity or explain the reason for her smile. If that was the case, I couldn't blame them. I had read enough theories on the subject to realize how ridiculous those ideas could be.

Nevertheless, I considered my findings to be significant to the Renaissance, if not only to Leonardo's art. Since *Mona Lisa*'s creation centuries before, there had been constant debate over the painting's enigmas. Even if my discoveries were deemed meaningless, I thought it was in the best interest of the art for historians to further research my findings and confirm any possible connections to the painting's mystique.

Through my own expertise as an all-around artist, oil painter, and illustrator, with a profession in graphic design, I eventually interpreted the meaning of the secret images without the help I initially sought from experts. The challenge I suddenly faced was that my conclusions about Leonardo and his art contradicted what historians believed about *Mona Lisa.* Demonstrating what I found would not be easy, since there was already such strong disagreement among art historians about the painting.

One issue they had always faced was the lack of evidence supporting any of the discussed theories. Few historical writings seemed to provide any explanation of *Mona Lisa*'s mysteries. And each one was questionable at best: a vague note written by Agostino Vespucci in 1503; a 1517 journal entry by Antonio de Beatis, describing a meeting allegedly involving the *Mona Lisa*; and a description of the painting by Giorgio Vasari, who first used the name *Mona Lisa* years after Leonardo's death, though Vasari was thought by some to be describing a different version of the painting.

While I was sure I had uncovered the answers historians had been looking for, I was equally confident they would pay no attention to what I had to say since I wasn't one of *them*. One agreement among them was that Leonardo never mentioned anything about the painting anywhere in his thousands of pages of writings. What sets the secret images apart from previous speculations is that the specific clues about the painting come directly from Leonardo's writings—evidence that can be seen in his art with the naked eye.

One passage I came across linked directly back to *Mona Lisa*—missed by experts only because it referenced the secret images that I found, making the passage appear irrelevant otherwise. It would become a key that would open up a world of knowledge about the art.

I knew that writing a book was the best way for me to explain everything. Doing so, in my own words, would allow me to convincingly make sense of everything the world had questioned about *Mona Lisa,* from the location depicted, to the subject's identity, to the meaning of that mysterious smile. The process of researching and writing was slow and tedious. I was constantly making one breakthrough after another, the discoveries becoming vast and complex. Answering some of the oldest mysteries about the portrait presented new questions. It struck me as the most important artistic revelation in Renaissance art—and maybe even of all time.

The initial thought of creating a scholarly book didn't appeal to me. That wasn't my style. I wanted something that was readable. Plus, I had a story to share. A story that would connect with readers, as I believed Leonardo intended *Mona Lisa* to connect with viewers. The years I spent studying the portrait had changed me forever. So I knew I had to write *Solving Mona Lisa*, a mystery memoir of sorts. Leonardo's work constantly left me astonished and euphoric with what I kept finding, and I wanted readers to experience making the discoveries as I had while solving what I considered the greatest puzzle of the art world.

The project became so important to me that I was ready to sacrifice everything for it. I was passionate about creating art in my free time, but gave that up to focus my attention on my memoir. I abandoned most of my social life. I quit my job as a graphic designer, putting my career on hold in order to research and write full time. My financial resources dwindled. My relationship with my fiancée suffered. At times, the discoveries would feel like a curse, because nothing seemed more important than a book that finally provided answers to so many unanswered questions about Leonardo's art. I couldn't walk away without completing what I set out to do, no matter what. I was too determined, too inspired for my own good by what Renaissance artists had accomplished. And I couldn't ignore the sense of destiny and faith that seemed to poke at my shoulder.

Eight years would be, by far, the longest I'd spent on an art project. I wrote *Solving Mona Lisa* as a memoir, but must point out that it is unlike a typical book of that genre. At times, I did tear my skin open, spilling my guts onto the pages. But I don't dwell in the depths of my personal life as much as the typical memoir. My focus, priority, or theme, is mostly on figuring out *Mona Lisa*'s mysteries along with those of other related works of art. But I do touch on the effects it has on my personal views on life.

Occasionally, pages may read as if pulled from an art history lesson—less memoir-ish than I would have liked—something that couldn't be avoided in setting out to provide a revolutionary understanding of *Mona Lisa*. But I'm proud to say that I don't regurgitate old information into unoriginal theories as many books about *Mona Lisa* have done.

Solving Mona Lisa presents the *why*, *how*, *when*, *where*, and *what* to some famous art mysteries. Though *Mona Lisa* may be the most famous, she is not the only painting I discuss in detail. The characters and meaning of Sandro Botticelli's *Primavera* and the meaning of Hans Holbein's *Ambassadors* have also been puzzling experts for centuries. All will be resolved in *Solving Mona Lisa*, including the story behind the woman, details of her identity, the meaning and exact reason for her smile, and many other previously unknown details. One other important exploration in the book—I also discuss connections and revelations in Michelangelo's Sistine Chapel art in detail.

No matter your expectation or artistic knowledge, *Solving Mona Lisa* provides a greater understanding of *Mona Lisa* and many other works of art. It will make you question how answers so obvious were able to hide in plain sight for so long, and will present innovative ways to look at art as Renaissance artists intended for us to do.

Before letting you go, there are some people I must first thank. My family and friends, for supporting my work, and for the constant reminder to finish my memoir and get on with my life. My dog Pinch, for keeping me company over the years through many drafts of this book—the writer's life can be lonely without the companion of a best friend. Hope and Joshua, for all the informative library critiques. Paul, for that second pair of eyes, and pointing out some illusions even I had missed. "Pasquale," for all those great conversations on art and how truly dark Italian Renaissance life was. Heather, for your patience through the years, and for convincing me to leave my job to pursue writing the book full time. Ma, for believing so strongly in me, not once questioning why I quit my job, but instead offering to provide anything I could have asked for. Jen, for providing writing space and a place to stay while I wrote. Ernie, for your brilliant graphic design skills. Dusty, for copyediting—aka adding clarity and livening up my words. Marta, for your feedback. Brian, for your thoughts, along with your legal assessments. The Rochester Institute of Technology, University of Rochester, and Rochester public libraries for use of your space and beautiful book collections.

A final note—the chapter, "What You See Isn't What You Get," combines several events and sets of dialogue into the scene. It's the only chapter in which I use this style, having decided that it would be the best way to set the tone of the story. The events and experiences in the rest of the book are true and told to the best of my memory, as is the dialogue—which in many cases is not verbatim. Whenever memory has failed me (considering I can barely remember yesterday's lunch), I have paraphrased dialogue to provide clarity and maintain the overall tone. Chronology of some events has been modified and some descriptions changed to protect the privacy of certain individuals.

—Ron Piccirillo
March, 2019

Mona Lisa by Leonardo da Vinci (c. 1503-c. 1517).

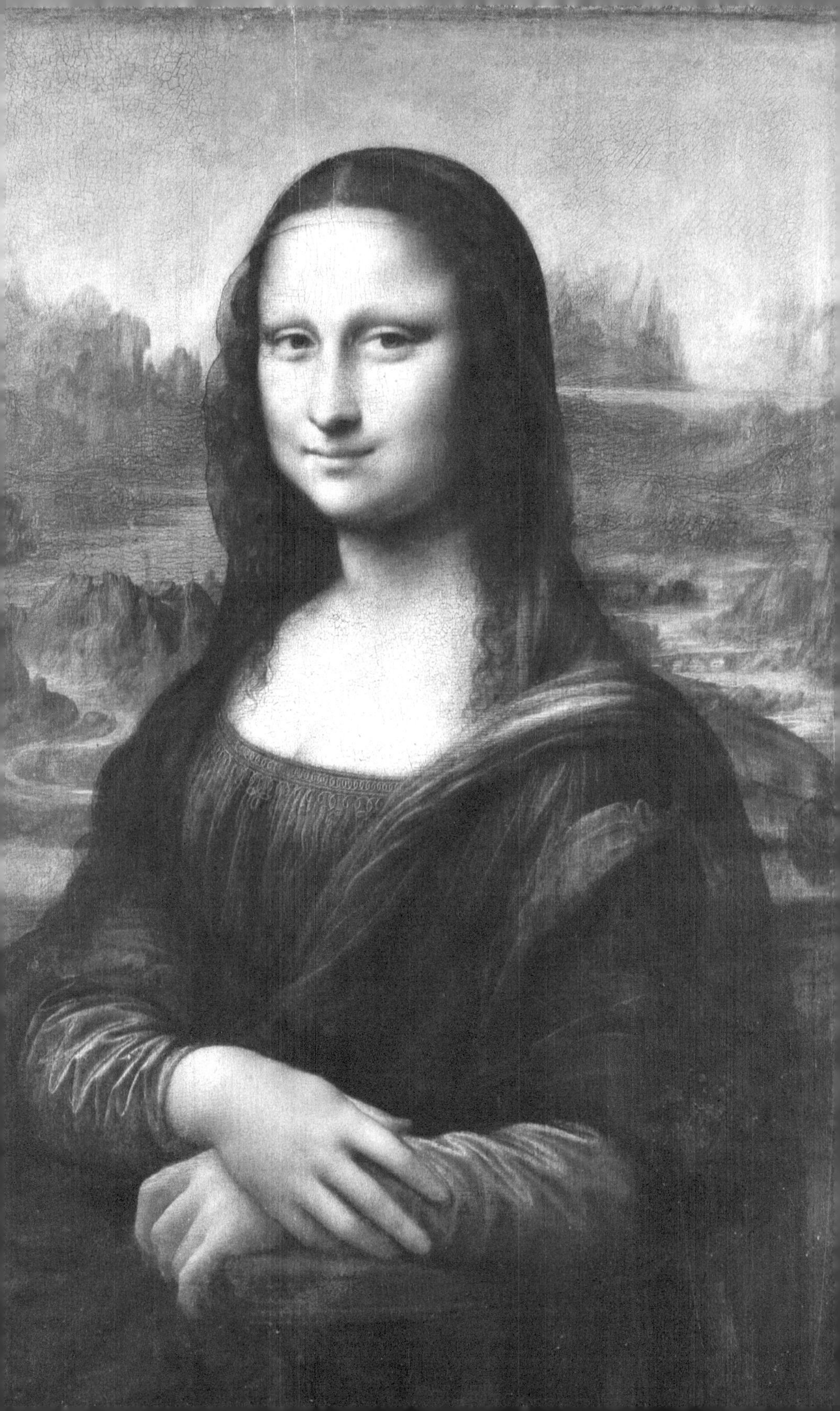

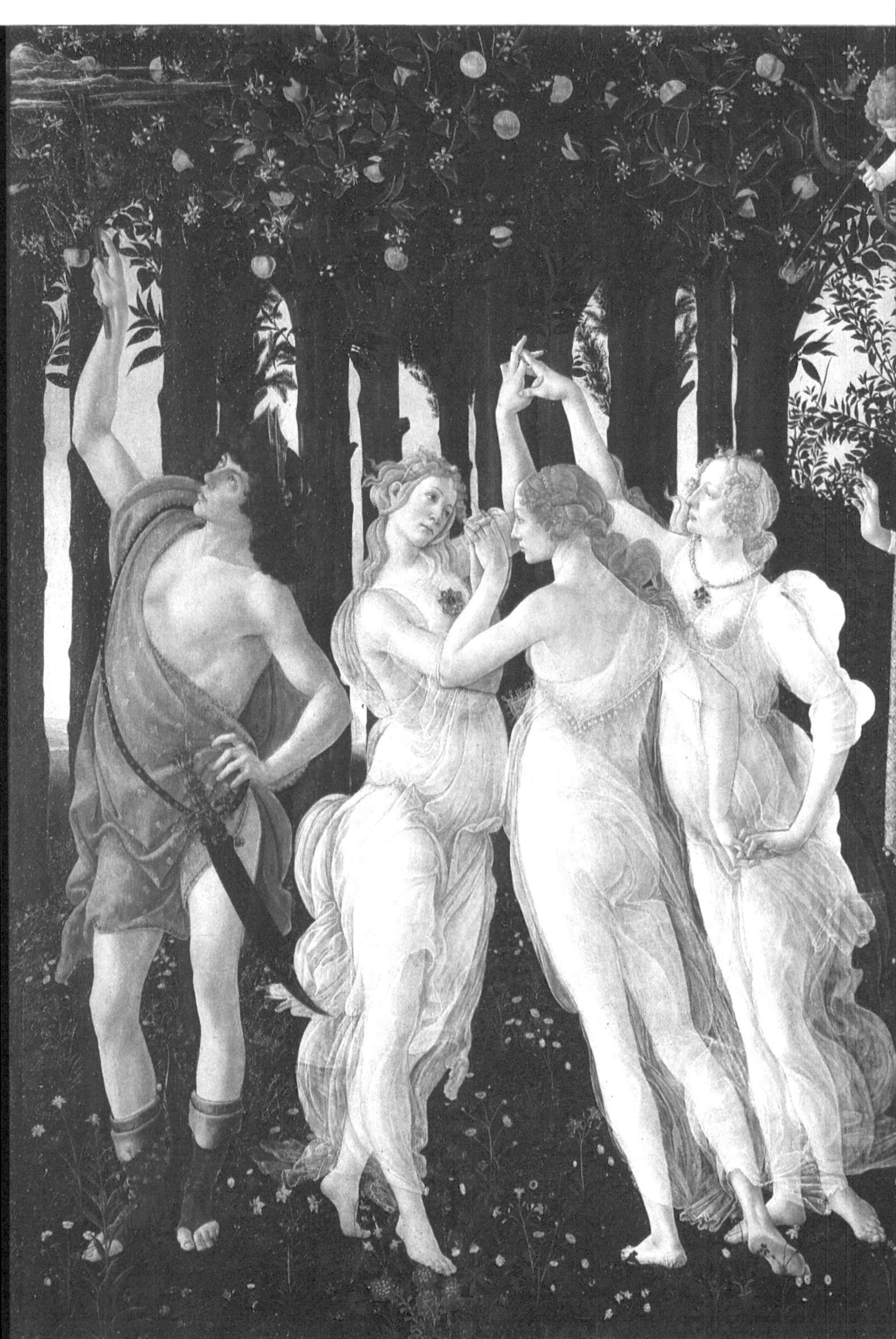

Primavera by Sandro Botticelli (1470s-c. 1480s).

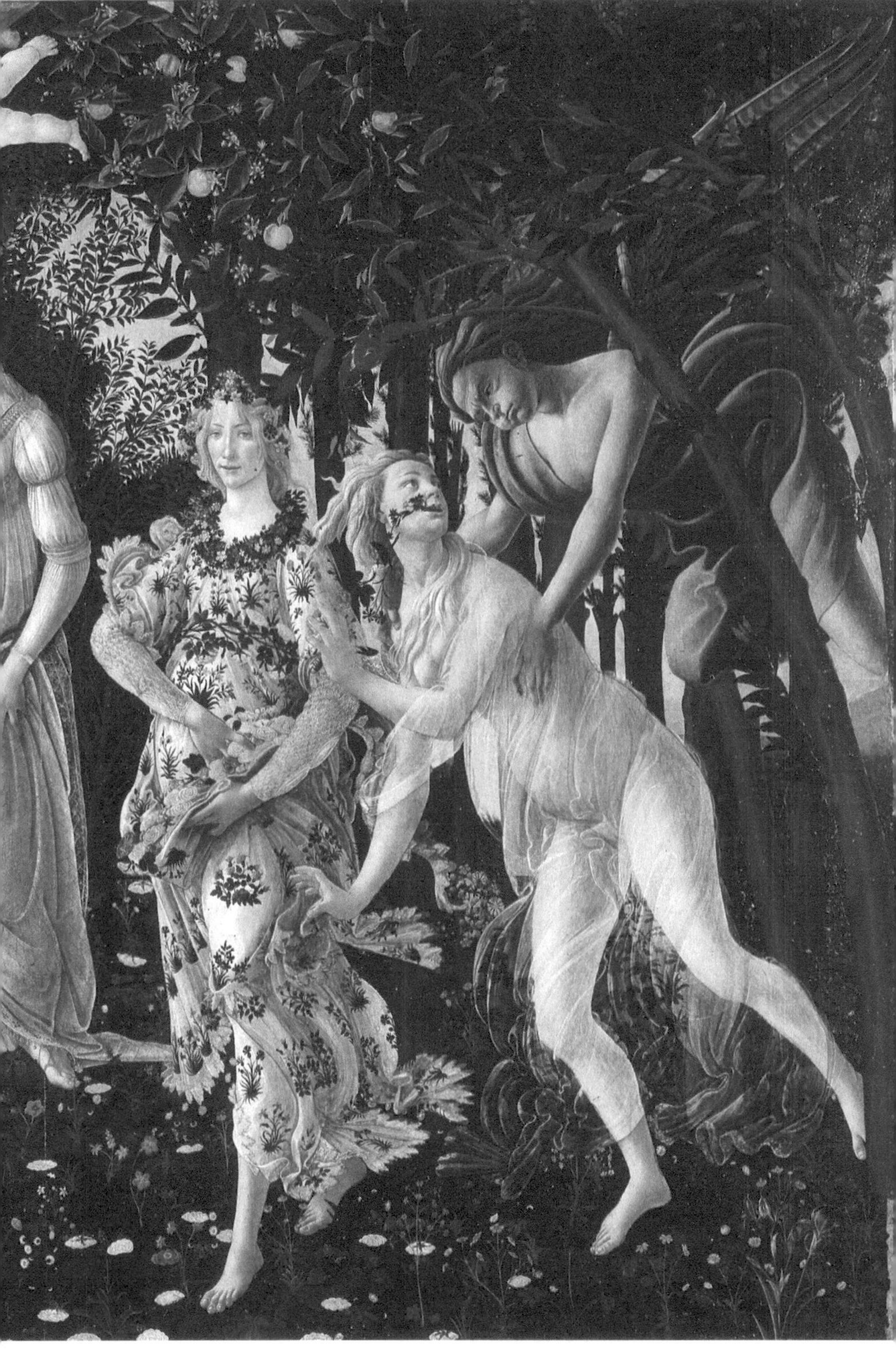

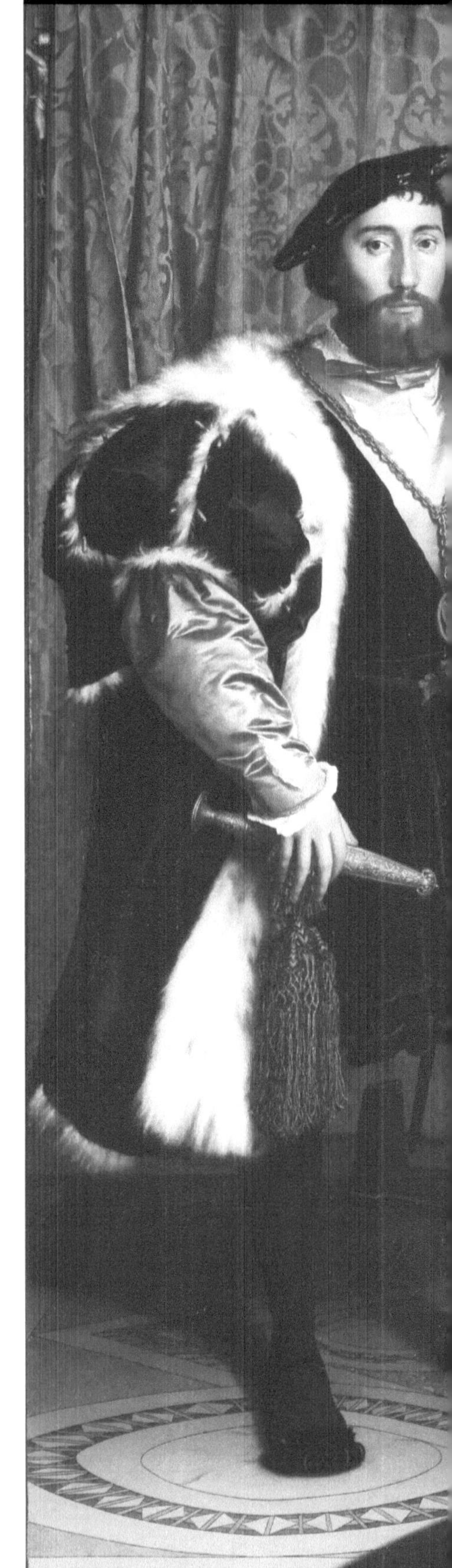

The Ambassadors
by Hans Holbein the Younger (1533).

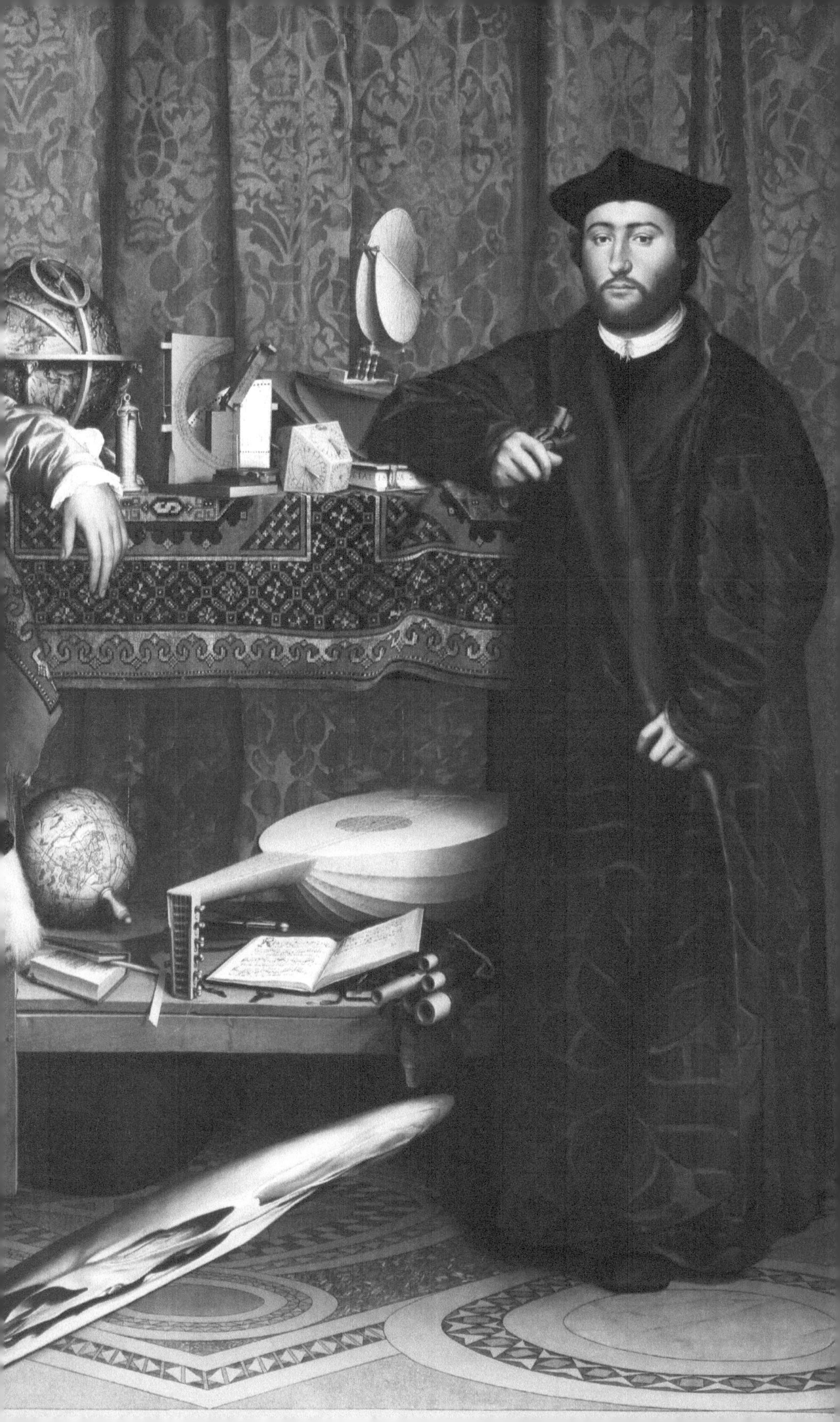

The Mysteries

For more than 500 years, the identity behind Leonardo da Vinci's *Mona Lisa* has remained unknown. It has been argued that the portrait could be one of several possible women, while a few questionable sources have led some experts to believe it is a portrait of Lisa Gherardini. The painting was in the artist's possession until his death in 1519, but Leonardo left no explanation about the art.

The reason for her enigmatic smile, which has intrigued both experts and art enthusiasts alike, has also remained a mystery.

In an effort to learn about the art's meaning, attempts have been made to track down the actual location of the background depicted in *Mona Lisa*. Yet, no one can say where it is, if it even exists ...or if it was simply an invention of Leonardo's mind.

Another Renaissance painting that has been a huge subject of controversy is *Primavera*, a painting by Sandro Botticelli. No one can explain its characters or setting with certainty.

Also puzzling is *The Ambassadors* by German artist Hans Holbein the Younger. The large portrait of two men is known for being one of the first of its kind to contain a strange style of optical illusion known as an anamorphosis, but the reason for it has not been explained.

No one has ever considered that the mysterious meanings behind *Mona Lisa*, *Primavera*, and *The Ambassadors* were linked in any way.

anamorphosis | ˌanəˈmôrfəsəs |
noun (plural **anamorphoses** | -fəˌsēz |)
1 a distorted projection or drawing that appears normal when viewed from a particular point or with a suitable mirror or lens.[1]

What You See Isn't What You Get

"Her name was *Envy*."

That's what I told the reporter, who scribbled in his pad while interviewing me from across his desk. Like the rest of the world after I first went public, he wanted to know exactly what I discovered in *Mona Lisa*—what I *saw*.

Until recently, I didn't understand why anyone wasted time trying to figure out who the woman in *Mona Lisa* was, or where she was sitting, or why Leonardo da Vinci secretly worked on the painting for years.

Art historians previously identified her as one of several women—Isabella of Aragon, Cecilia Gallerani, Caterina Sforza, to name a few—yet, new details in recent years led them to believe it was now a portrait of a lady named Lisa Gherardini.

But I had proof she was someone else.

Leonardo's art has been studied as if religious relics, but no one has ever been able to decipher that vague portrait of the haggard-looking woman.

"*Envy* is what Leonardo called her," I said.

Skepticism was practically dripping from his smirk.

"Mr. Piccirillo," he grinned, "experts state the artist never mentioned the painting."

"They do say that. But they were fooled by Leonardo's illusion. He described the painting very clearly in his writings."

He twiddled his pen between his fingers before writing something down.

"What makes you such an expert?" he asked with squinting eyes.

He had a point. And as I tried to think of an answer, Francisco Goya's *Third of May 1808* came to mind—a painting of a scared man in front of a firing squad with his arms raised in surrender. But in my mind, the figure suddenly had my face.

Was I an expert? In addition to a career as a graphic designer, I spent my life studying, creating, and deconstructing art—from comic books as a child to magazine ads in my teen years to oil paintings when I fell in love with the medium in my thirties. But considering the unanswered questions we still had about Leonardo's life and art, was anyone truly an expert?

"Leonardo was an artist," I said to the reporter. "And so am I."

"But art's subjective, is it not? Especially art like *Mona Lisa*?"

"Only until someone can prove otherwise."

Whenever I listened to experts try to explain her famous smile, I'd roll my eyes. Sigmund Freud once wrote that the smile was based on Leonardo's memories of his mother.[1] A Harvard professor suggested that one had to *look away from her mouth to see her smile*.[2] Another scholar explained how our mind sees a smile about to form, so we subconsciously picture her already smiling.[3] Many experts expressed their own reasons for the smile. At times, they would speak with such certainty, as if *their* opinions were irrefutable. Of course, none ever presented real proof to back up their theory of why Leonardo included the smile.

Why couldn't they admit that no one knew why she was smiling? And why did some speak as if it were some beautiful painting? Did no one else find her appearance unattractive? Leonardo obviously didn't set out to paint an attractive-looking woman. Anyone could see that just by how pretty some of the women in his other paintings and drawings were—especially the angel in both the Paris and London version of his *Virgin of the Rocks*. (Although no one is sure if the angel is male or female, to me the angel's feminine qualities were dominant.) Every time I see her, I feel a sense of joy as my mind became free of every other thought in the world. She is truly angelic.

And why was there such an infatuation with *Mona Lisa*'s smile anyway? When he was younger, Leonardo made several clay heads of women smiling. In other words—there's no reason the painting's smile would appear so strange. Was it because we knew nothing else about her, and her smile was something that allowed people to feel connected to the painting? There were other puzzling elements, but I never understood why any of them mattered so much. Sometimes artists like to come up with vague pieces just to get people thinking and talking—which is what I used to think Leonardo had done. Regardless, there were questions no one had answers to.

Who was she?

Where was she?

What bridge was in the background?

Why did the left half of the horizon not line up with the right?

After all, it was painted by one of the most brilliant minds to ever walk the Earth, a man whose ideas were hundreds of years ahead of his time. A genius among geniuses. Everyone knew that painting was impossible to figure out.

Then one day …the impossible happened.

And it happened to me.

My story already caught the attention of NBC, ABC, *The Daily Mail*, *The Sun*, and many other media outlets, including *The Today Show*. All the focus was on the first images I uncovered, which I decided to go public with in an attempt to find out their meaning.

Considering how bashful I was, the international publicity was ironic. And if anyone had said that I would one day write a book about it, I would have thought they were crazy. But I had an obligation to publicize what I stumbled upon in Leonardo's art. The discoveries that came after the publicity were significant enough to change art history as we knew it. I knew I had to share everything I found, especially as an artist. *Despite what everyone would think.*

It all started with that first clue I spotted: a secret image. A discovery that was purely accidental, which led to all the other clues, and eventually, to the answers that explained it all ... that *proved* who *Mona Lisa* really was. The problem was that it felt more like a curse than an achievement. And publicizing it was like opening up Pandora's box.

I thought no one would believe an unknown artist in Rochester, New York—instead of a renowned art historian somewhere in Europe—had deciphered *Mona Lisa,* that I had solved the art world's greatest riddle by outwitting history's most brilliant minds. The seven-year quest would put me in a battle of wits against thinkers like Leonardo, Michelangelo, Plato, Ovid, and Dante. I didn't think I had a chance in hell. Yet, something kept driving me forward. I couldn't walk away, although at times that's exactly what I wanted to do. But more clues kept appearing, each one gripping at me with a force that may as well have been Leonardo's own hand. It made me feel alive. I became focused on finding meaning to it all. I suddenly felt—*knew*—that figuring out answers to the mysteries was my purpose in life.

So I had to tell my story, even if no one would believe it. The reporter asked his questions, and I gave him my answers, his writing hand scribbling down notes as if it had a mind of its own.

"You said there's a secret image in the painting?" asked the reporter.

"The painting is an optical illusion," I said. "*Mona Lisa* is secretly a double portrait."

He looked at me as if I was joking. The room felt like it was shrinking. Thankfully, I had brought a large printout of the famed painting with me to show him.

"I'm not sure how everyone missed it," I said. "Holbein painted a well-known optical illusion in *The Ambassadors*. But no one knew that Leonardo was painting similar optical illusions decades before because his were camouflaged within the paintings—invisible unless you knew the secret to seeing them."

He stared at me intently, looking a little unsure. "How did someone like you figure this out?" he carefully asked.

"It was all in his writings, ciphered as double meanings. Leonardo secretly described *how* to view the illusion. He left *Mona Lisa* behind as a riddle before he died—except that he called her Envy."

"Envy? You're sure?"

"That's what he wrote."

"Assuming it's true, what else did you find out?"

"I can point out her actual location on a map."

"No one's been able to figure that out. But you can somehow prove this?"

I nodded.

Yes. Yes, I could.

He bit his lower lip, briefly keeping his pen still against his writing pad and shook his head gently as if shaking off a thought. His confusion was almost comical. Then he continued asking questions, and I continued giving answers.

"Anything else?" he asked when the interview was through.

I thought back to the three main points my public relations agent had advised me to focus on. My first revelation had been that Leonardo da Vinci's writings led me to the discoveries. My second was the hidden imagery in *Mona Lisa* that no one ever noticed before. And the third had been mentioned in every news report, book, documentary, and commentary. The great mystery fascinated everyone because of the supposed impossibility that anyone could ever solve its meaning. And unlike anyone else, I had proof.

"I can show you why she's smiling."

"Here all suspicion needs must be abandoned,
All cowardice must needs be here extinct.
We to the place have come, where I have told thee
Thou shalt behold the people dolorous
Who have foregone the good intellect."
And after he had laid his hand on mine
With joyful mien, whence I was comforted,
He led me in among the secret things.

—Dante Alighieri,
The Divine Comedy
(*Inferno*, Canto 3.14-21; Longfellow)

1

The First Clue

In the fall of 2011, I was working as a graphic designer in the marketing department of a jewelry store, creating every type of graphic for all of our ad campaigns. The work was different from the advertising agency I came from. It was a smaller business—something I appreciated. Instead of trying to please teams of multimillion-dollar clients, I had only two people to present my work to—the marketing director and one of the owners. Both had a great sense for design solutions.

But I was 37, and my career had exhausted me over the years. With the holiday season approaching, we were pressed for time, as usual. I was accustomed to tight deadlines and the stress it caused. I hated it, of course, but I'd learned to create some of my best work under pressure. Still, I daydreamed about being home with my bins of oil paints and brushes.

I decided to spend Friday night at a quiet bookstore, studying famous paintings to spark inspiration for a portrait of my dog Ginger—a small, 10-pound Miniature Pinscher the color of a copper penny. She was younger than Pinch, my other Miniature Pinscher—whose fur was instead charcoal black, but otherwise looked like her twin. My plan was to create a separate portrait of Pinch after I finished Ginger's.

As a child, there was nothing I loved more than art. My earliest memory from growing up in a quiet neighborhood in Western New York, not far from the Great Lakes, was when I was perhaps 11, scribbling in a coloring book. I remember the feel of the crayons, pressing against the pages on top of the formica table in our home. A humid, summer breeze was blowing through the open windows, causing the drapes to slow-dance like ghosts.

Ma worked at a cast iron sewing machine next to me that shook the room like a passing train. Long pins radiated from her lips like toothpicks. In the room were spools of thread, which I'd carefully feel, wondering why the different colors felt the same.

The cut fabric pieces came alive as she sewed them together, magically turning them into a dress.

"Where did you learn that?" I asked.

"In Italy. Before I came to *A-me-ri-ca*." She sang the word in four large syllables in her thick Italian accent, then told me how our family moved here from the old country before my siblings or I were born. My grandfather's brother, who had already settled here, convinced my parents to move to America in search for a 'better future.' As farmers, their shoes were constantly mud-ridden, and the chance at better jobs appealed to them. "We wanted clean shoes," Ma later told me. She came here first. Papa came later after "he got his papers."

"Speak of the devil," she said—her favorite saying. "I gotta make some food for your daddy." Then she hurried down the hall toward the kitchen, the short curls of her hair bobbing and her clogs slapping the wood floor as she disappeared to make his lunch.

It wasn't long after Papa came home that the arguing started. Ma was short in height, and with her usual pink apron, didn't look intimidating, but her wailing echoed off the walls like small explosions while the sounds of utensils clanged against each other whenever she slammed kitchen drawers shut. Papa wasn't much taller, and with his soft, wavy James Dean-like hair, resembled St. Thomas from Leonardo's *Last Supper.* Like the saint in the painting, Papa would point his finger when he spoke, waving it around like a wand.

I never knew what they were arguing about since their Italian became very quick, making it difficult to tell where the sounds of words ended or began, but hearing them fight always caused a tightening feeling in my chest. There was something hypnotic about the stark contrast between Papa's calmness and Ma's chaotic movements when they fought. The feeling was like watching a lion overtake a baby elephant on *Wild Kingdom* as it bit down and clawed into the gray, leathery skin with unemotional ease.

I huddled over my coloring book, putting every bit of concentration into the world drawn on those pages, fueling my imagination and forgetting about the real one around me. Whenever Papa was around, I became even more introverted than I already was. I never talked back to him the way I sometimes dared to with Ma. Physically, I had no reason to be scared of him. Although he would never spank me, that would have been easy to deal with. It was his look of disappointment that I feared, the way his eyes darkened and a cryptic smile appeared as he shook his head ever so gently with disapproval.

My parents' arguing would end just as quickly as it started. But the action of coloring madly afterward would continue, as if the crayon could erase the emotional strain. Yet the anxiety could only be tucked away, never really disappearing at all. I'm not sure if that had any connection to my desire in being an artist, but I eventually knew I would spend my life as one. It always felt as natural as swimming is to a fish.

Originally, I wanted to be a comic illustrator, and dreamt of penciling issues of *The Amazing Spider-Man.* As a child, drawing pads and pencils kept me content for years. But I never felt that my illustrations were good enough, and so I turned to graphic design as a more practical route. My concern was only in feeding my artistic passion. Materialistic things and climbing corporate ladders never meant much to me. For most of my career, I enjoyed hiding behind a computer monitor, doing what I loved. But over the years, through the course of several jobs, office politics, tight deadlines, and what I felt was a lack of appreciation for the creative—as if it were an assembly line meant to quickly pump out work in large quantities—caused my inspiration and determination to fade. My life began to feel like it was missing something.

Just a year before, at 36, I discovered oil painting, and my passion to create began to bloom again. So there I was in the bookstore, darkness creeping through the windows, the smell of coffee fading, along with the number of people whose attention was lost in the books they held. Barely anyone around to interrupt my time with *Mona Lisa*, lying flat at my feet on the floor.

I had seen images of her countless times. There was a creepy, nightmarish quality about her that I never liked, as if she had climbed out of a Stephen King novel. The soil-colored cloak, crimped hair, the sheer veil, and a landscape resembling that of another planet. She looked like a corpse with its eyes open.

I did my usual thing, turning her upside down to face away from me. To fool my mind into forgetting all the times I'd seen her, to see her as if for the first time. It was an artist's technique I learned when I was young—something to do with how the mind recognizes imagery—and I had regularly used the technique with my own graphic design work and paintings, but it was the first time I ever tried it on someone else's art. There was no room on the shelves, so I used the floor, stepping away to see her from a distance. Another technique—distancing my view to eliminate details from my vision so balance and basic composition stood out.

I compared her to a photo on my phone of my painting of Ginger—cleverly entitled, *Ginger*. A close-up of my dog staring up at the camera. A red chew toy rested by her paw.

Like *Mona Lisa*, I rotated *Ginger* upside down. Something about it was off. It's why I came to the bookstore, where I usually looked to artists like Van Gogh, Matisse, Picasso, and many others to provide solutions. But *Ginger*'s composition was simple, so I decided to compare it to *Mona Lisa*.

Not that my art could ever compare to Leonardo's.

I continued inching backward, focusing on general masses of shapes in the art. Like a sculptor, I had to solve the problem of general shapes first, details last.

For a long moment I was still, allowing myself to get lost in a gaze at the harmony of earthy browns and melancholy blues.

It was then that I realized I had placed Ginger's head too close to the painting's center. *Boring! Mona Lisa*'s head was in the upper third portion of the canvas, horizontally centered, but turned to the left, her eyes still on the viewer; her hands in the bottom third, slightly off center to keep it interesting. Her chest was placed in the middle third portion, showing Leonardo's use of *The Rule of Thirds:* a focal point—head, chest, hands—in each of the three sections, as if a grid divided the image both horizontally and vertically into thirds, with the focal points placed near the crossing of the imaginary lines.

Leonardo also used his *sfumato* technique—soft edges and hazy forms as we *actually* saw objects, rather than hardened edges common in earlier art, the background softer-looking than the sitter in the foreground. Artistically, *Mona Lisa* was perfect.

Ginger lacked all those qualities. The wood floor planks in *Ginger*'s background had a hard-edged look, and it didn't help that its perspective drew focus off the canvas and away from what should be the focal point.

I sighed and shook my head at the mistakes I made, knowing I had to start the painting over. With all my experience as a graphic designer, I should have known better. But I continued to compare both paintings for other improvements I could make. I took a few more steps back—far enough to fit Leonardo's *Last Supper* between me and *Mona Lisa.*

How I wish I could have watched Leonardo paint her with all those layers of colored oils over each other. Like translucent paper-thin panes of stained glass that made the canvas come alive. I would have given anything to learn his techniques firsthand. Studying the art from across the room, I wondered: Did he use a model? Did he first begin painting her face? How much time was spent planning and sketching? *And why were there no clouds?*

With *Mona Lisa* appearing so small, the lights and darks dominated the art. The details were gone. The mountains were bumps, her cloak just a smear of dirty brown. She resembled an old ceramic doll in the distance, balancing on its head.

And as I took one last step back—something appeared.

I did a double take. Then tried to squint the confusion from my eyes.

I knew I was only seeing what I was seeing because I stood so far from it, in the same way a cloud's shape could only be seen from far away. And if it hadn't been upside down, I probably wouldn't have noticed it at all.

But ...despite everything I knew about the painting, it was nothing I had ever heard about. Not in school. Or any book. Or any art documentary. Not even in any of those countless theories scholars had discussed.

The formation I saw, spanning the height of the painting was

...a question mark?

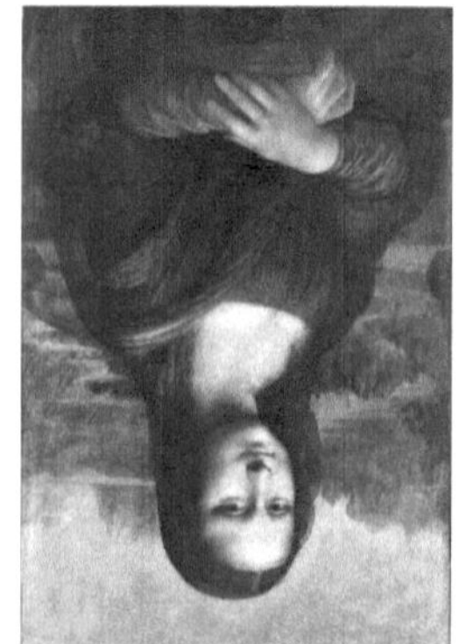

Mona Lisa, upside down, undoctored.

"A question mark?" a college friend asked as we got into his car outside the bookstore.

"In the most mysterious painting on Earth. You don't find that strange?" I asked, holding up to him the upside-down book showing *Mona Lisa*.

But he just looked at me and chuckled lightly.

"Look at how the highlights form the question mark," I said, ignoring his reaction as I began to run my pinky finger along the series of highlights forming the punctuation mark's shape. I started at her left forearm near the elbow at what was now the top left of the painting.

"Follow this path along her arms and hands," I said, trying to guide his view as I moved the point of my finger across the painting rightward, through her overlapping hands, then bending slightly downward.

"...and curl over her elbow," I went on, making an invisible curved line over her right elbow,

"...then straight down the center of her chest," I continued, motioning my point downward-left, falling through the figure's abdomen and toward the bare part of her chest.

"...and dipping at her collarbone and stopping at the shadow on her neck." I pulled my pointing finger away from the dark shadow dividing her neck from her chin—where the stroke of the question mark ends.

He just sat there, ignoring the book's image altogether, instead studying me, his eyebrows raised in an amused look, and his car keys still in his hand.

"Look at her face," I said, ignoring his mocking expression as I motioned a circle around her head. "The circular highlight of her face forms the dot—the dot of the question mark. The shadow of her jaw separates the stroke from the dot. Don't you see it?"

"Why are you holding her upside down?" he finally said.

"Because sometimes I look at art that way. Just pretend there is no upside down and just look at it."

He looked at it.

"Sorry," he snickered, "I don't see it."He put the key in the ignition and pulled out of our parking spot to head home.

"Seriously, man," I said. "It's strange."

I realized early on in my life that I observed art differently from most people, that I perceived details others might find uninteresting or odd—so I wasn't bothered by his reaction. There were times when my artistic views sounded weird to others, but I learned to embrace my way of thinking—a reminder that I had a mind only an artist could have. It was also a reminder of why I kept many thoughts to myself.

What might be a simple pencil drawing to someone else would be to me a complex and captivating graphite life form, waiting to be explored. I may spend way too long studying the architecture of a specific line in an image, for how it curves in such a way, that I'll be more fascinated with that detail than the whole image itself. To me, all images, even photographs, are finished puzzles

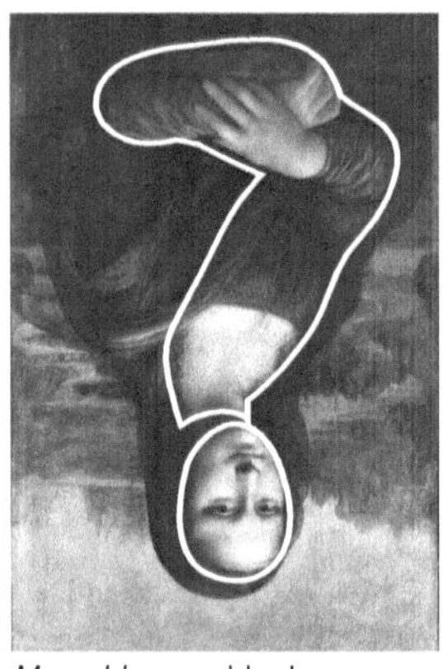
Mona Lisa, upside down, showing the location of mark.

waiting to be taken apart by their elements. And the size of the puzzle pieces depend on the complexity of the art.

So while my friend drove us back home, I sat quietly in the car, holding the book away from me, tilting it one way then another. What came to mind as I studied her was the question of her mysterious identity. But there were other unsolved problems scholars had been unable to answer, such as the portrait's meaning, and the actual location of the background, or the reason for the crooked horizon line. And—of course—the mystery of her smile. Mysteries Leonardo only left in this one painting. It made the question mark I saw hard to ignore.

A short while later, my friend pulled in front of my house to drop me off. Then, after a slight hesitation, he said with a curious look, "Show me that again."

I'd usually lay in bed in the dark at night, contemplating ways to improve current art projects. That was my routine before falling asleep. There was a sense of therapeutic satisfaction in solving those visual problems. And it was my way to decompress in the way someone might enjoy Sudoku or reading a novel and forgetting everything else in the world.

Since I began oil painting, I had taken to studying the great masters. Just seeing images of their art transported me to the artist's world. It wasn't the feeling that I had entered the painting's image. It was more like I had entered the artist's studio, able to experience their thoughts as that specific painting was being made, able to see their technique, wondering what inspired them, what they were trying to express, and if they created the painting just for themselves, or for everyone else to see. In the same instant, I'd feel jealous, envious, awe, and intrigue, wishing I could paint as well as them. Those emotions would quickly turn to inspiration and determination to create my own work of art.

Different artist's styles gave me slightly different feelings, as if they were like different flavors for my soul to taste. I would feel more passionate and infatuation with Sandro Botticelli's female figures than with those from any other artist. I was in awe over Albrecht Dürer's ability to make the simplest illustration look like a masterpiece—like his *Great Piece of Turf* (an amazingly beautiful section of grass) and *Study of a Hare* (a simple image of a rabbit). Images of Leonardo's paintings made perfection seem like a tangible item that could be touched and felt. Picasso's art provided me with a greater sense of freedom than any other artist. His work constantly reminded me to just have fun brushing the paint on, that all I had to do was cover the canvas with colorful imagery. Then there was Salvador Dali, an artist whose work I avoided because of the depressing feelings it caused.

That night, the comforting scent of oil paints—usually a scent that helped lull me to sleep—permeated my house. But instead, I was wide awake. I couldn't get my mind off of *Mona Lisa*. And the question mark. I turned on the lamp. A minute later, I was hunched over my bedroom desk, examining her again.

All those mysteries. Still unsolved after 500 years.

Leonardo did something unusual with *Mona Lisa*. Artists of the time told stories with their work by including recognizable details, such as depicting Christ's last supper with twelve apostles seated around him, Judas usually holding the bag of coins from his bribe to betray Jesus. Leonardo's version includes allusions, such as St. Thomas pointing a finger toward heaven—a prelude referencing him later touching Christ's side wound. Other revealing details in Renaissance works of art included the angel wings of Gabriel, a fruited tree where Adam and Eve stand, the cross Christ carries on his back, or the small reed cross carried by St. John the Baptist.[1] Even portraits of unfamiliar figures might include revealing details, which are not always obvious. Hans Holbein included a squirrel in *A Lady with a Squirrel and a Starling*, alluding to the woman's family crest.[2] A portrait of a mathematician might include geometric tools. The juniper bush Leonardo placed in the portrait of *Ginevra de' Benci* is believed to be a word play on the woman's name.[3]

All of Leonardo's paintings had something—details and clues that told a story beyond the scene of the painting.

Except for *Mona Lisa*. Every part of it was vague: the indistinct mountains and rocky terrain, including a bridge that looked like any other bridge, her unidentifiable clothing and face, and a smile that almost seemed to mock the viewer for knowing nothing about her.

Leonardo broke tradition by going out of his way to make the woman and the scene around her undetectable. *But why?*

The smile was at the center of every international news story about her. Yet, no one knew the meaning behind it. New theories turned up constantly, overpriced at a dime a dozen, and always lacking evidence. Everyone seemed to be on a wild goose chase to nowhere.

And then there was the puzzle of the background's location. And the crooked horizon line—which no theory could explain. An artistic flaw equal to a mathematician failing a count to ten.

Or was it intentional, Leonardo?

The Renaissance was a time in which paintings contained clues about their meaning and figures. So why did Leonardo create such a vague painting?

His *Last Supper* was an obvious representation of Jesus and his disciples before his crucifixion. In *St. John the Baptist*, the religious figure points toward heaven while holding a cross made from reed—cluing us to his identity. *The*

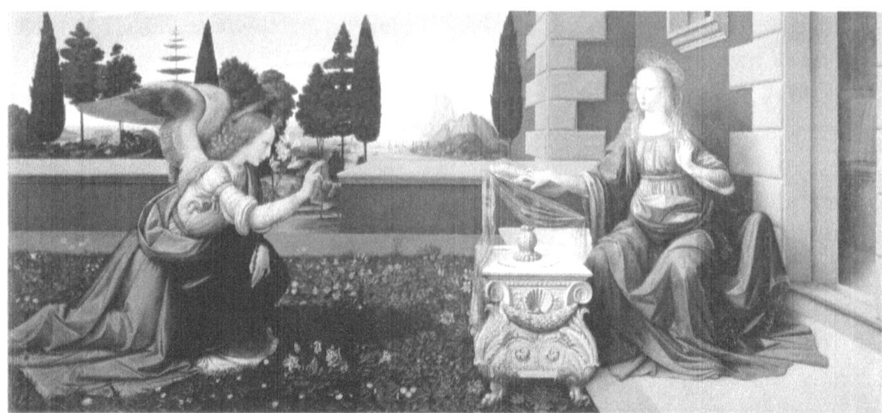

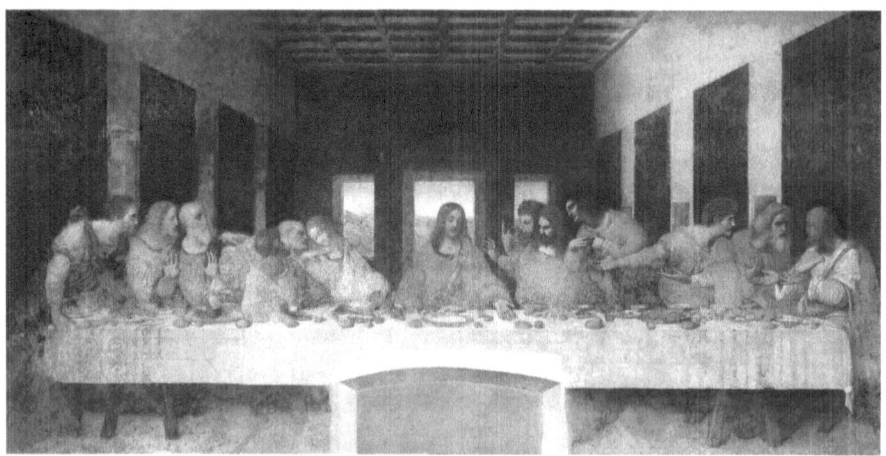

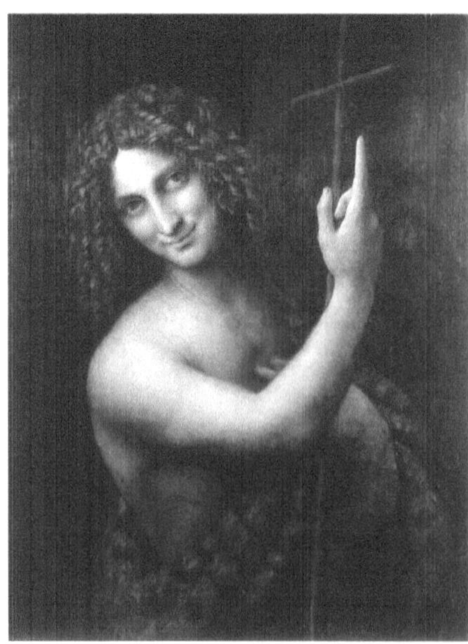

TOP: *The Annunciation* (1472-75).
CENTER: *The Last Supper* (1495-98).
LEFT: *St. John the Baptist* (1513-16).

Annunciation depicts the moment Gabriel announces to the Virgin Mary that she would conceive a child. The Virgin's halo is just one of many details verifying the biblical scene.

Contracts were also kept on file in the public records system established at the time, detailing commission work of the artists. Francesco del Giocondo was said to have hired Leonardo to paint the portrait of his wife, Lisa Gherardini, believed to be the subject in *Mona Lisa*. Yet, no records of this transaction exist.

In fact—apart from a few questionable notes that later surfaced—no contractual third-party proof of *Mona Lisa* existed at all. It was as if he had secretly created the painting for himself.

I stood the hardcover upside down on my desk and backed up to my bedroom's far wall. Then I unfocused my vision, like so many times before. Both my dogs—Ginger and Pinch—followed my movement with their eyes. I expected the mark to be gone, thinking that maybe the bookstore's lighting tricked me into seeing it. Or that I had a bout of overactive imagination.

The question mark appeared instantly. Like a giant typewritten character. Clear, unarguable, purposeful. For a moment I stood there, my eyes not wanting to leave the image. Especially as I considered the painting's mysterious nature.

I crossed the room back to my desk and sat in the old, wooden chair to study her. On the page opposite *Mona Lisa* was *The Last Supper*. Leonardo was the first to paint the exact moment Christ revealed that one of His disciples would betray Him. But Leonardo was not the first to portray the scene at that infamous dinner. Many depictions of the event were created by other artists before his time.

It made me think of *Mona Lisa*'s replicas from other painters. Replicas were characteristic of important figures like the Virgin Mary, Christ, and God. So why would a bunch of different artists paint Lisa Gherardini, an unimportant figure? And why had Leonardo kept the painting such a secret?

And why did you put that mark there, Leonardo?

I closed the book and got into bed.

Ginger jumped up and curled herself next to me. I hit the light switch and the room went dark.

Then I just stared at the ceiling, envisioning the *Mona Lisa*.

2

The Mountain

At work the next day, I should have been concentrating on designs for our newest promotion. But when no one was looking, I searched online, Googling the words MONA LISA QUESTION MARK to see if anyone else had seen it before. I had such a strong feeling about that mark.

But there was no mention of it online. Just endless pages of results discussing theories about her smile.

When I finished my work, I made up an excuse in order to leave early.

What I really had to do was satisfy my growing curiosity.

The drive home seemed to take forever.

I let the dogs out and went straight to my bedroom.

She was waiting there, on my desk. Posed. Upside down.

"Hello, Mona."

Even up close, I was able to see the question mark. There was no way to unsee it. But what did it mean?

I was quickly becoming obsessed with it, a feeling I recognized and knew would be something I wouldn't let go of until I found an answer. It wasn't an unusual sensation for me when it came to art.

My biggest obsession came to me when I was young. I froze the first time I came across a rack of comics and saw Spider-Man's huge, white eyes outlined in those thick, black lines. On the cover, he was holding a mask belonging to a villain called Hobgoblin who was being escorted away by police. In the foreground, in that iconic comic lettering, Spider-Man's word balloon read: "*NO!* IT CAN'T BE TRUE*!* I'VE FINALLY MANAGED TO UNMASK THE *HOBGOBLIN!* BUT, IT CAN'T BE...*HIM!!*"[1]

I had never even heard of Hobgoblin before then, but with those four sentences, I had to take home that comic book and learn who he was.

I found out who Hobgoblin was. And that was when I found out something about myself, too: I wanted to spend my life as a comic illustrator.

For the next ten years, I didn't miss a single issue of *Amazing Spider-Man* as I became submerged in the comic world. On television, I'd watch reruns of *Batman,* the old 1960s TV series. One of the usual villains was the Riddler, dressed in green spandex with a large question mark on his chest. "Riddle me this," he would say to the Dynamic Duo before leaving behind a riddle to solve, his maniacal laugh blasting from the television speakers.

Throughout the shows, the Riddler left them many corny riddles:

When is a person like a piece of wood?
When he's a ruler.
How many sides has a circle?
Two: inside and outside.
What won't run long without winding?
A river. [2]

Leonardo was himself a mysterious figure. He wrote backwards, right to left: his writings had to be viewed in a mirror to be read.

So what was your riddle, Leonardo?

There were rumors he had been part of a secret society. Some stories involved hidden symbolism in his art. Yet, why did *Mona Lisa*, unlike his other art, have no clues, no details at all to explain its meaning?

Except, there *was* something: a symbol, when turned upside down.

Slowly, I rotated *Mona Lisa* upright, the book making a brushing sound against the desk of the quiet bedroom. I wasn't sure what I was looking for, but still spent a few minutes examining her closely.

I rotated the book again. Even slower.

Was it possible *other* marks would appear?

I analyzed the art as if there was no actual upright position. Ignoring how I'd been *taught* to see. Forgetting the image before me was of the world's most famous painting.

I stood back, pushing the book around with my finger, assessing each side, watching it the way I used to watch wooden horses on a merry-go-round, studying their intricate details as they passed, round and round. Continuously guiding the book's rotation with my finger, I moved closer.

I didn't know what I was looking for specifically, but kept my eyes open for something that didn't belong, like another symbol or even a detail to debunk the question mark somehow. I didn't have much expectation to find anything, but I had to make sure in order to satisfy my curiosity. I continued to search for something, anything. Yet, nothing new revealed itself.

I stopped and stepped back to the other side of the room, using the technique of distance that made the details disappear. Then I moved in again, hovering close enough to see the painting's *craquelure*—the tiny cracks from the aged paint resembling a desert floor that hadn't seen rain for a long time. I almost felt rude being so close, as if she were uncomfortable with my intrusion into her personal space. I paused at the details.

I never had much patience for things like being stuck in a traffic jam, or small talking with strangers, or watching the microwave counter zero out (I would impatiently open the door with only seconds left), but when it came to art, I could gladly take all the time in the world.

I repeated the process with each side. Turn the painting. Step back. Move forward. Repeat. Every bit of rotation showed nothing. Until my eyes spotted something *there,* along the horizon.

Something that wasn't …right.

The area of mountains on the painting's left side looked like …something more. As if an image were superimposed over it.

I moved closer and tried to touch it, as if I could scratch it away. But it wasn't a superimposition, not another layer: it looked like the image was really part of the painting. My years of experience with Photoshop taught me the telltale signs of an image that had been doctored. Up close, I didn't see any kind of interruption in the paint strokes, or to the fine cracks of the craquelure, or color. The image had not been altered at all, despite what I was seeing. The ghost image I saw took planning. It *had* to be part of the painting.

I stepped back to reset my vision.

That was when the image revealed itself with clarity.

The mountain was alive.

3

The Lion

I was looking at the shape of an eye.

And there was also a mouth. Open, like a dog biting at the empty air.

Upright, it was a mountain of rock. Just as it was supposed to be.

But when the painting was turned 90 degrees clockwise, that same mountain—the one closest to *Mona Lisa*'s eyes—resembled some kind of head, as if carved from the stone.

I could make out the shape of a thick jaw. Not a canine's, but more like that of a more powerful animal. The cheek was far too high on the head to be human. The skull was wider and more exotic. A tongue was sticking out from it. The nose was not a nose, but a snout.

I brought the book downstairs where there was better lighting.

But the image didn't disappear. It could not be unseen.

Just a mountain?

No. It was something more. The tuft of hair wrapping around its head could not be denied. The fur covered everything except for its pointed ears. Like a cat. A large and powerful cat.

The image seared itself into my mind. *What was it doing there?* On the horizon next to *Mona Lisa*'s head, almost touching her hair, a lion was roaring like only a lion could.

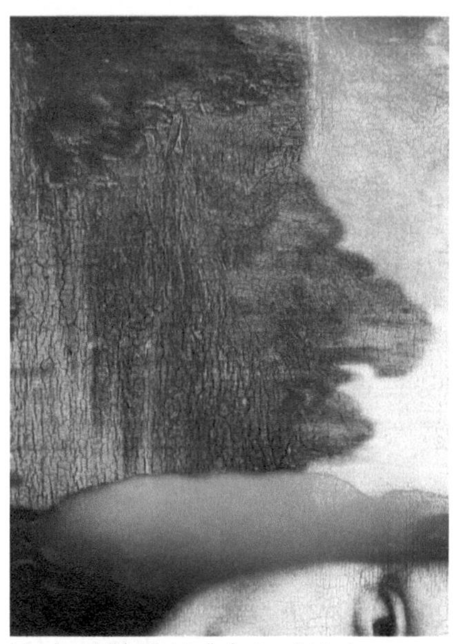

Lion head (highlighted), facing right when *Mona Lisa* is rotated 90° clockwise.

A question mark? And now a lion's head?

Leonardo did sketch lions. He even built a mechanical lion that moved. But I never heard of a lion in his paintings. I studied it, processed its look, its style, noting its subtlety, observing how practically invisible it was when the painting was upright, and recognizable only when on its right side.

I rotated the art a quarter-turn

clockwise and counterclockwise, over and over, switching views, watching the characteristics that allowed it to be seen one way but not the other.

The painting consumed me. I was in a world where only the two of us existed, as if there was no substance to anything else around me. Staring at the lion's head, I scanned and zoomed—focusing and unfocusing over the rest of the art like a detective, searching for other lurking creatures, for any other secret imagery as the smiling figure in the painting watched me.

The painting was again on its right side. That's when something else appeared: a *second* image. It sat to the left of the lion's head, above the woman's chest, in the landscape closer to the foreground. Its chin touched the figure's shoulder.

Like the lion, it faced the smoky, bluish-green sky.

But the new creature resembled the head of a man.

It was larger than the lion's head, but smaller than that of the figure's. Its misshapen face emerged from the contours and shadows in the landscape. It had dark eyes that were close together and high on its head. It made me think of an African tribal mask.

Its face was split in two sections by the backward S-shaped trail along the valley, just as the section of fur is separated from bare skin on a baboon or ape. I could see the eyes, nose, nostrils, mouth, a cheek, all formed from the details in the mountain. The ear was shaped by the flat valley of reddish earth.

The ape's mouth was open, as if about to screech.

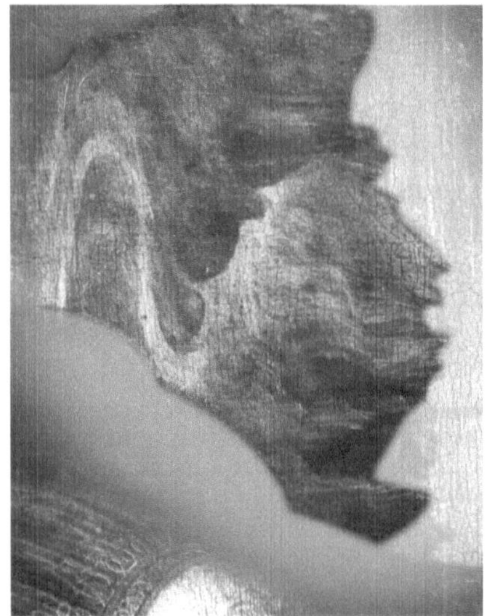

Primate's head (highlighted), facing right when *Mona Lisa* is rotated 90° clockwise.

Then, on the right side of the painting, opposite the lion, a third animal emerged.

It was formed from the mountain on the water's horizon, touching the back of *Mona Lisa*'s head. It also faced the sky.

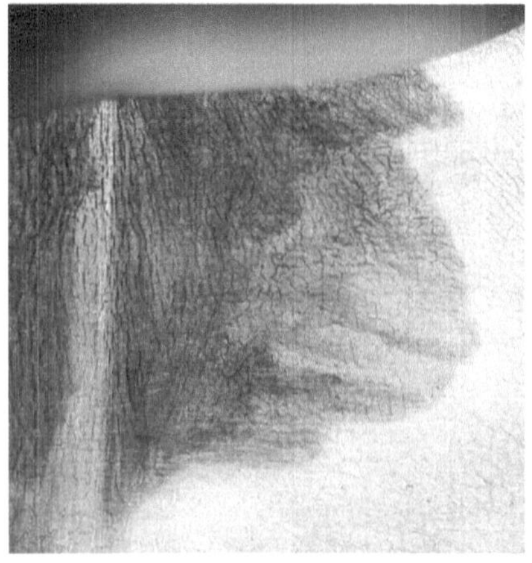

Third animal head (highlighted) facing right when *Mona Lisa* is rotated 90° clockwise.

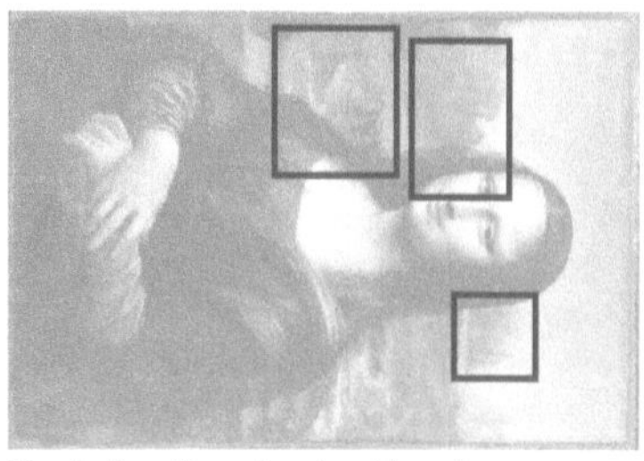
Key to location of animal heads.

I rubbed my brow.

The third creature was not as easy to make out as the lion and ape. But in profile I could see some sort of mouth and eyes.

A cow? A bear, or ram? Or some other animal?

What looked like lips were large and smooth. Because of the lion and ape, I assumed it to be a mammal. And there seemed to be textured fur, thick-looking and woolly, around its stocky head and neck. The only conclusion I could come to was that it was a buffalo.

Or was it a mountain goat?

It was difficult to tell, but if it had horns, they were probably concealed behind the figure's head.

4

Animals

The month I turned 14, an artist named Todd McFarlane started illustrating *The Amazing Spider-Man.* Although comic book cover art was usually a lot better than the rest of the book—a marketing gimmick that always left me disappointed—I'd still race my bike to the comic shop, with an inevitable fear that the issue would miss its delivery date and I would be left empty-handed.

The quality of the inside pages of comic books sometimes seemed like a rushed afterthought. McFarlane changed that. His drawing style was rich in intricate detail, and the attention he gave his covers continued onto his inside pages—each page was a work of fine art. His style become more daring with every issue. The limbs of his characters more dramatic. More alive. Darker. His art would break from panels, no longer confined by them as comics had always been. And he reinvented Spider-Man's look. *His* Spider-Man could hyperextend his body into swinging positions like a muscled yogi—more spider than human. It was as if he rebelled against the unwritten rules of comic illustration that artists had been following. In fact, his style ignited an explosion of creativity from other artists.

One thing was for sure: I wanted to be the next Todd McFarlane.

I would recreate McFarlane's drawings in my journey to become a better artist. Even though I had been copying art out of coloring books long before I discovered comic books, it wasn't easy to recreate McFarlane's art. Even in my best attempts, the style was slightly off. His lines looked smooth and natural like the work of someone who had many years of experience, while mine—because they were drawn slowly as I calculated positions of lines and anatomy—looked a little forced and amateurish.

Still, to be like Todd McFarlane, I had to think like Todd McFarlane. I looked for patterns in his art, studied the way he positioned figures, or how he controlled the reader's focal point, his use of camera angles, two-point and three-point perspective, vanishing points, foreshortening, *bird's eye* and *worm's eye views*—techniques, I would later learn, that were first developed by Renaissance artists.

Until then, I never studied someone's work so obsessively.

That was how I first learned how well artistry could *hide* art.

While reproducing a splash page from *Amazing Spider-Man,* I noticed the head of a cartoon cat McFarlane had placed on a figure's T-shirt. It was Felix the Cat. I thought I had seen the cartoon character before.

I went to a box of comics in my collection and sorted carefully through some older issues. And I realized I *had* seen him before. *A lot.* More and more, I found images of Felix, hidden throughout different issues, randomly placed in McFarlane's art. As a logo on a jar of jelly. On the side of a taxi. As a stuffed animal in a pile of toys. Felix was even in some old issues I had of *The Incredible Hulk* McFarlane had penciled.

I wasn't sure if anyone else caught it, but it became a sort of game for me: *Find Felix.*

Years later, I read an article in which McFarlane explained the story. Someone he knew carried around a Felix the Cat doll to cope with Post-Traumatic Stress. Because the guy didn't purchase the comics McFarlane drew, McFarlane offered to put Felix the Cat in his art if the guy agreed to buy them.[1] Even though I didn't know the story behind it until later years, as a kid I knew there had been some connection to McFarlane's personal life.

Finding those cartoon cats was the first time I realized how an artist could place something personal from their life into their work. All the while, I began looking at art differently, and learning to look for things hidden in plain sight. Drawings and paintings took on a deeper meaning. Like a frame taken from a movie roll. I began looking for the story in each art piece.

So what was the story behind Leonardo's animals? Did he hide them just for fun? Or was it something more? And was it just an odd coincidence that *Mona Lisa*'s letters could be rearranged to spell out ANIMALS with only the letter O leftover? I knew I was being overly suspicious, so I passed it off as coincidence.

As *Mona Lisa* sat upside down on my bedroom desk, I wondered why I never heard of the animals before. But their presence became obvious. Besides his mirrored writing and *Mona Lisa*, I wasn't aware of any other great enigmas in his art.

He never left any clues about the *Mona Lisa*'s meaning, so I wondered if there was any connection between the animals and the question mark that dominated the painting when upside down?

I had read a story about a 700-year old fresco by Giotto di Bondone in the Basilica of St. Francis of Assisi in Italy. Camouflaged in the clouds of *Death and Ascension of St. Francis* was a face of a devil. Art restorers recently discovered the devil face, which had been missed for centuries as it was too difficult to see from the floor. Giotto painted the fresco two centuries before *Mona Lisa*'s creation. And like her animals, Giotto's demon was facing the sky.

Strangely, both Giotti and Leonardo were Florentines.

Were the animals that much different from the demon? The first were hidden in a mountainous landscape; the other was in the clouds.

I didn't consider hidden images to be an unusual concept in art. And it didn't surprise me that Leonardo did this. I was more amazed that no one spotted them before.

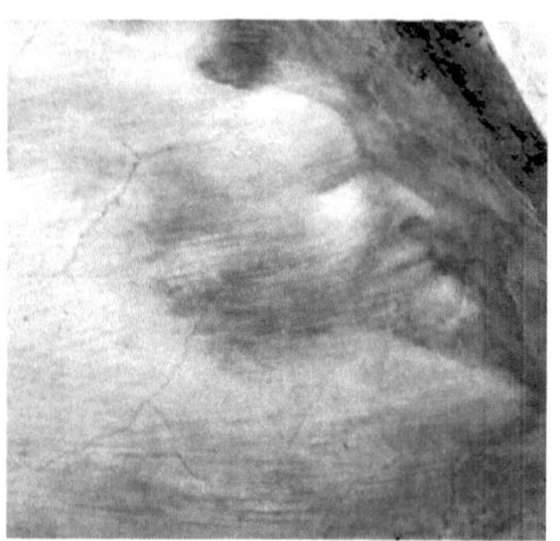

Face hiding in clouds of Giotto's *Death and Ascension of St. Francis* (1300).

I hooked my fingers behind my head and leaned back, gazing to the ceiling as I thought of times I hid imagery in my art, but usually it involved details that had a reason to be in my art. In fact, the more I considered secret imagery, the more I realized how normal it was in the ad world. In the FedEx logo, the negative space between the E and x forms an arrow, symbolizing its transport speed. The Toblerone Swiss chocolate hides a silhouette of a bear in the mountain of its logo. *Something Leonardo would appreciate.* The NBC logo is camouflaged as a multi-colored peacock.

Academicians like Dr. Bryan Wilson Key and Marshall Mcluhan even wrote controversial books on the subject.

I wondered if scholars knew of the hidden objects in *Mona Lisa*, but refused to acknowledge them for some reason. If so, there had to be some mention of them in art books, even though I found nothing online. So I headed back to the bookstore.

In the art section, I took a few books on Leonardo to a couch nearby, spending a good stretch of time with each. I meticulously searched indexes, scanned chapter titles and checked pages. When those books offered nothing, I searched through another pile, until no more books on Leonardo's art were left. I moved on to books on the Renaissance. Then ones on illusions and symbolism. Even books on artists like M.C. Escher and Salvador Dali, known for optical illusions in their art. Still, there was nothing.

The only books left were a few I deliberately skipped over because of their hefty length: an extensive collection of notes and comments by the artist himself; Leonardo da Vinci's notebooks.

Leonardo made various notebooks—more than 7,200 pages survived,[2] filled with sketches and writings in Italian in his backwards penmanship. Over time, they were collected and grouped into manuscripts like the *Codex Atlanticus*, *Codex On the Flight of Birds*, *Codex Forster*, then translated into books.

In 1994, Bill Gates purchased Leonardo's *Codex Leicester* for $30,802,500. At the time, it was the largest amount ever spent on a manuscript.[3] It contained scientific studies on subjects like astronomy, the movement of river water, plate tectonics, and the moon's glow.[4]

I had assumed that Leonardo's writings would be poetic and hard to understand, like tackling the writings of Shakespeare or Chaucer. But it *was*

Leonardo. And there was nothing left to check. I pulled the only two books from the shelf, knowing they were too small to contain *all* his writings. The larger book had images of Leonardo's originals—dirty, cream-colored paper with sketches intermixed with lines of ancient-looking script. Some of Leonardo's pages contained small amounts of notes and drawings, others so cramped with text that barely any space was left to write.

Sighing, and with the same feeling I used to get in school before taking a written test, I chose the smaller book, took a seat, and began. I expected to be put to sleep, but was surprised to find how absorbed I became in Leonardo's writings. Page after page, I found myself gaining interest. But there was also something more. Something personal that I couldn't quite explain.

I kept searching.

There were studies on the human body's movement. How it should be represented. Anatomical drawings. Painting advice such as how landscaping should look grayer in the distance and water should be more reflective. How the atmosphere causes parts of the horizon to look paler—I took a photography book down from the shelf to see for myself and saw that it was true!

There was an entry on how some rainbows are not produced by the sun. And also a description of an earthquake that caused the sea's bottom to open and briefly swallow its water. Leonardo had arguably been the first to study plate tectonics.

There were aphorisms, like "He who thinks little makes many mistakes,"[5] and straightforward observations: "A man at three years will have reached the half of his height."[6]

I was surprised to find myself thinking of him as practical rather than mythical like some god. But one passage (which I now call *Checking Your Work*) almost shocked me because he suddenly seemed relatable:

> … When you are painting you should **take a flat mirror and often look at your work within it,** and it will then be seen in reverse, and will appear to be by the hand of some other master, **and you will be better able to judge of its faults** than in any other way.
>
> It is also a good plan every now and then to go away and have a little relaxation; for then when you come back to the work your judgment will be surer. …
>
> It is also advisable to **go some distance away, because then the work appears smaller, and more of it is taken in at a glance,** and a lack of harmony or proportion in the various parts and in the colors of the objects is more readily seen (Codex Leicester, emphasis added).[7]

The advice of using a mirror to check your work was given to me by an art teacher and was a technique I'd been using for years. As was my practice of time spent away from my art so I was "better able to judge of its faults" when I returned to it later. And especially my stepping some distance away so it appeared smaller—just as I did in spotting the question mark. Had I been using Leonardo's techniques all those years?

There was a sudden connection with the artist I never felt before, and a slight sense of enlightenment, causing the corner of my mouth to rise.

But my smirk quickly disappeared when I came to a suspect passage. What I call the *Anamilia* passage describing groups of animals.

The first group included apes.

The second included the lion.

The last included the buffalo:

> Man. The description of man, in which is contained those who are almost of the same species just as the baboon, **the ape** and others like these which are many.
>
> **Lion** and its followers, such as panthers, lions, tigers, leopards, lynxes, Spanish cats, *gannetti* and ordinary cats and the like.
>
> **Horse** and its followers such as the mule, the ass and the like which have teeth above and below.
>
> Bull and its followers which are horned and without upper teeth, such as the **buffalo**, stag, fallow-deer, roebuck, sheep, **goats**, ibex, milch cows, chamois, giraffes (Codex Leicester, emphasis added).[8]

I made my way to the cashier with the two books.

But I had a feeling it was going to be a late night, so I took a detour to the bookstore's café for a coffee to go.

On the way there, as I reflected upon the animals and the question mark, a thought began to form. At first I thought the punctuation mark represented a question to be answered, and that the animals were some sort of clue to help clarify the question. But was that necessarily so? Images could be misconstrued. I'd seen it happen regularly in playing *Pictionary*, in which players shouted out words, rapid fire, as they had to guess what their teammates were communicating, using only drawings, no words. The object was to shout the correct answer before time ran out.

Rarely was the correct answer guessed on the first try. Even simple images could be interpreted different ways. It's what made the game so fun. The sketch of a cell phone could be interpreted as "call" or "cell phone" or "dial." Fire can fetch screams of "hot" or "burn" or "bonfire." A waterfall could mean "water" or "gravity" or a specific place like "Niagara Falls."

Communicating a complex sentence through images instead of words would be a nightmare. At an art exhibit, a lady once approached me about one of my paintings. She told me how clearly she could see "the representation of a young generation's struggles." Her description sounded so much better than the truth: I only wanted to replicate a cool photo of me and my friends. It was easy to see how an artist's work could be interpreted differently. Leonardo must have thought of that. So what was his question? And how could it be *verified?*

Whatever it meant, my gut was beginning to tell me that Leonardo would only communicate a question that could be taken with exact meaning. Something that was foolproof.

As I thought of the *Pictionary* example, another game came to mind: *Jeopardy!*

A game's objective was usually to figure out the answer to a given question. But *Jeopardy!* was different. What made the game unique was that its players started with the answer.

The object was to figure out the question.

Could it be that I already had the answer?

Could it be that the *animals* were the answer?

Was it the question that I was supposed to figure out, Leonardo?

5

Those Who See

Leonardo mentioned nothing about *Mona Lisa* in his writings.

That's what I was taught. But was that true?

After seeing the *Animalia* passage, I began to question everything I had learned. But there was something else. Three of the four groups of animal references were present. That couldn't be a coincidence.

And if so, then, logically, I had missed the fourth group—"horse and its kindred."

At home, I examined the art more carefully. But, no matter how hard I looked, there was no sign of a horse. Maybe there was something more in Leonardo's writings I hadn't noticed yet. Something that would explain things.

So I moved on for the moment.

I plopped the book onto the floor and got into a comfortable position and continued reading. I sank into his writings. Every word seemed to push me closer to feeling like I was understanding Leonardo. One passage, especially with the sarcasm of its last line, made me realize that Leonardo took issue with those who knew nothing about art—something I had experienced throughout my career as a graphic designer:

> I know that many will call this useless work, and they will be those of whom Demetrius said that he took no more account of the wind that produced the words in their mouths than of the wind that came out of their hinder parts: men whose only desire is for material riches and luxury and who are entirely destitute of the desire of wisdom, the sustenance and the only true riches of the soul. … And often when I see one of these men take this work in hand I wonder whether he will not put it to his nose like the ape, or ask me whether it is something to eat (Codex Atlantico).[1]

I always had an issue that *Mona Lisa* got all the attention when there were paintings at the Louvre in Paris that had more beauty. Art like Ingres's *Une Odalisque,* Bosch's *Ship of Fools,* and especially Leonardo's *Virgin of the Rocks.*

I found Leonardo's writings to be mostly objective, with a precise and indisputable quality. He was able to write with perfect clarity, which puzzled me more when I came across an odd, almost cryptic entry I call *Point-of-Sight*: "The point of sight must be at the level of the eye of an ordinary man, and the farthest limit of the plain where it touches the sky must be placed at the level of that line where the earth and sky meet; excepting mountains, which are independent of it."[2]

What exactly was Leonardo trying to point out? He was describing the horizon, but did he mean the viewer should *look* at the painting with their sight level at the horizon incorporated into the art? Or that an artist should portray the view *from* that point?

I thought of the murals from his time, trying to get an idea of his meaning. But murals were usually positioned high on walls. In his *Last Supper,* the horizon line lies behind Christ's head, high above the top of the doorway that was later cut into the wall and the painting.

Leonardo knew that art would be seen from the floor. If *Point-of-Sight* was to be followed, a ladder would be needed to reach the height of the horizon in *The Last Supper*.

I also thought of paintings where the horizon was not visible. And even some of the ceiling paintings with views looking straight up into the sky.

If he meant the artist should paint a view level with the horizon, then *Mona Lisa* contradicted this. Her perspective was from a point looking downward onto the landscape and its horizon. To top it off, Leonardo placed the sitter's eyes *above* the horizon line. So it couldn't be referring to the figure's view either.

There was another strange entry that stuck out: *The d-Point*. Leonardo included a diagram with the description:

> Supposing *a b* to be the picture and *d* to be the light, I say that if you place yourself between *c* and *e* you will not understand the picture well and particularly if it is done in oils, or still more if it is varnished, because it will be lustrous and somewhat of the nature of a mirror. And for this reason the nearer you go toward the point *c*, the less you will see, because the rays of light falling from the window on the picture are reflected to that point. But if you place yourself between *e* and *d* you will get a good view of it, and the more so as you approach the point *d*, because that spot is least exposed to these reflected rays of light.[3]

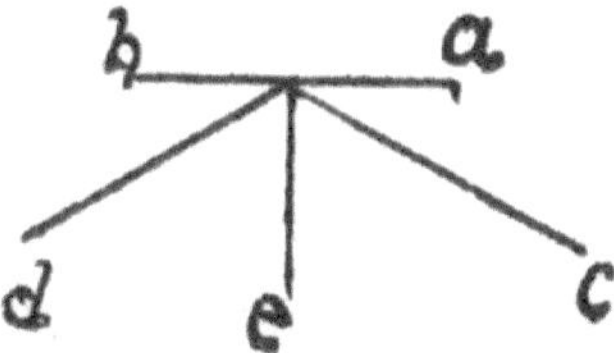

Why the advice on avoiding the glare on a painting in order to better see a picture? No, not *see*, but *understand.* An odd word choice, I thought, since a glare prevents one from *seeing* the art. The glare had an indirect relationship.

Yet, the point was obvious. *Too obvious.* Why waste the time to write that down at all? Was Leonardo referring to something else, something other than "reflected rays of light?"

From a shelf, I took down a book containing his paintings and drawings. Upstairs, I placed them next to each other on my bed. His art side by side with his writings. I wanted to understand what Leonardo was thinking before he hid the animal images. I wanted to get inside his mind by literally reading his thoughts, imagining myself as him, while in front of his art.

I knew a little about symbolism, that in art from other eras, a dog could symbolize royalty or fidelity, and that felines could symbolize craftiness or promiscuity. But what were Renaissance animals supposed to mean?

As a starting point, I knew the lion was *King of the Jungle*. But that phrase may have come after Leonardo's time. And I knew American settlers fed off of buffalo, but that was also long after the artist's time, and on a different continent.

Apes were sometimes associated with humans. The famous diagram of evolution from ape to man came to mind.

So what was the connection between the three species?

I needed some kind of specialist. An art historian. But I couldn't just turn over what I found to a stranger. I wanted to keep it secret. At least for a while. Because *Mona Lisa* was so famous and so widely studied, I knew that would be like trusting wolves to guard a package of raw beef.

Then I thought of my friend Charles from the ad agency I had worked for. Before becoming a copywriter, he taught art history at a local high school. We worked together for years on the same account and occasionally met for drinks.

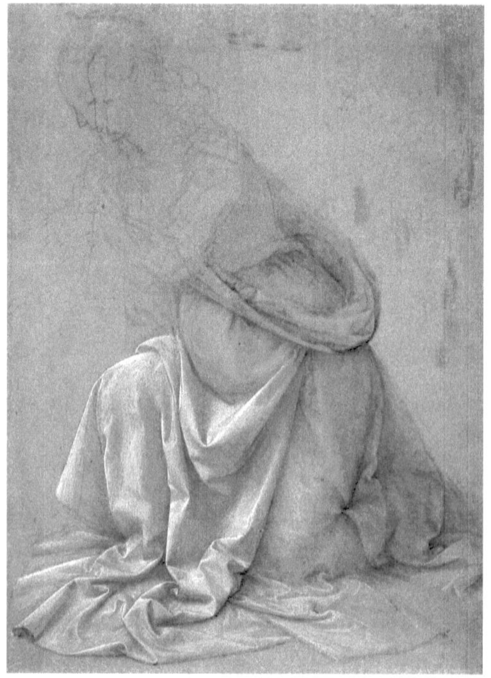

Drapery Study for a Kneeling Figure (c. 1475-c. 1480).

I knew I could trust him to keep things quiet, so I decided I'd give him a call. But I would wait until after I finished sorting through Leonardo's writings.

In bed that night, I couldn't stop yawning. It was well past my bedtime, but I wanted to finish reading about Leonardo's drapery studies. The art book in front of me showed his *Drapery Study for a Kneeling Figure Turned to the Left*—one of his studies on drapery folds. While reading about his technique, I pictured him forming a small clay model, draping a small cloth over it like a dress so he could practice sketching the shadows and highlights of the folds.

But I eventually became too tired, sliding the two books aside without closing them, and pulling the cool pillow under my face. The book with the drapery study sat open to my right, practically in front of my nose, touching the pillow. I didn't close my eyes right away and instead let them gaze over the image and onto the far wall, tranquility keeping me from moving any more to turn off the bedside lamp. Any thoughts melted into a blur.

Waiting for sleep to take me away, I glanced at the drapery image on the nearby page without focusing my vision. Not really looking at it as much as in its direction. But something odd appeared from it, startling me out of my sleepy state.

I must have fallen asleep, because I swore an image of a horse head appeared like it was floating on the page over the sketch of drapery. It was a fuzzy image. But for some reason it didn't feel like a dream.

I pushed up onto my elbows and rubbed the confusion from my eyes. As I looked down onto the image again, I saw nothing odd.

Of course it was a dream, I thought to myself. Yet, I couldn't fight off how real it felt. I must have been so intent on finding the fourth group in *Mona Lisa* from the *Anamilia* passage—the horse—that it caused me to dream seeing it.

I looked around the room, for some reason with the odd sense that I'd just been tricked, which made no sense.

I touched the book's image, as if there were something invisible resting on top, like a wrinkled plastic wrap that somehow made its way onto the page, warping the art into the shape of a horse's head. But I couldn't hear the crinkle of plastic and didn't see anything of the sort.

When I lowered my head back onto the pillow, a horse's head appeared a second time.

Although I felt my jaw loosen, I didn't move, afraid that the horse would disappear before I figured out what it really was. The confusion of that ghost-like image kept me there for a few minutes. There was no logical explanation, so I was sure that my mind was playing tricks. But the image didn't go away.

... You will get a good view of it. ...

The words worked their way through my confusion, coming to the front of my mind like a neon sign, flashing its brightness as I tried to figure out where I had read those words. And why I was getting a strong sense from them.

My eyes wouldn't let go of the horse head. And after a moment of stillness, I recalled where I had seen the words. *The d-Point.*

... If you place yourself between e and d you will get a good view of it, and the more so as you approach the point d. ...

As I pictured myself on the bed where I lay, I thought of the diagram associated with *The d-Point*. Then I realized my head was to the left of the book and slightly raised on the pillow, just like in the diagram. And that I was looking rightward, at the horse head that appeared to be superimposed on the book. What took place finally hit me.

An optical illusion!

It took a moment to register that my view was in the exact position Leonardo described in *The d-Point,* where I would "get a good view of it."

Whatever *it* was had me staring wide-eyed.

The d-Point wasn't just advice on avoiding a painting's glare. I was quickly becoming sure there was something more to what he wrote.

Are they some kind of instructions, Leonardo?

My eyes stretched wide open, cartoon-like as the answer came to me, molding itself from the question.

I reached over to try and touch the horse carefully with a finger, breathing out the words: "The fourth animal." *The horse head.*

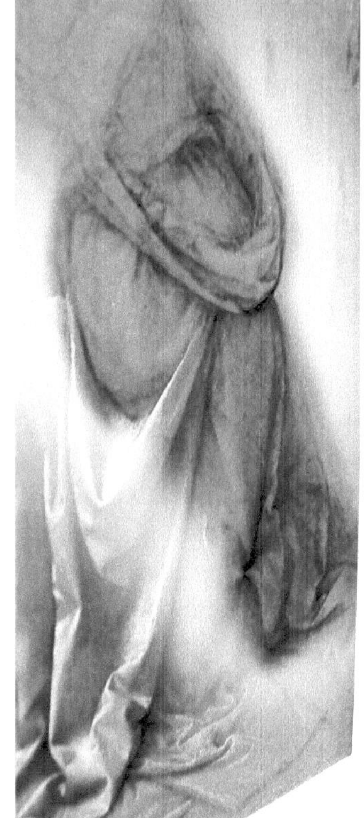

Drapery Study for a Kneeling Figure showing horse head (highlighted) when viewed from Leonardo's d-point.

Clarity came to the details of the long, bony skull that took shape. I practically felt Leonardo in the room, as if he had risen from his grave and was floating on a bed of air beside me, his long, soft beard brushing my neck and his mouth inches from my ear, filling it with the warmth of his breath, causing goosebumps along my skin to rise as he whispered: "Sì. Sono istruzioni."

Yes, they are instructions.

6

Secrets of the d-Point

I placed myself again at the d-point, and there was the horse head. *Was I only imagining it? Did its shape only seem to fit because I was looking for it?*

But it wasn't just a horse head in any random position. It resembled horse heads Leonardo drew in his studies.

I searched through his other works, wondering if their d-points would reveal other creatures. Sure enough, they did. Another drapery study—*Drapery Study for a Standing Figure Seen from the Front*—seemed to be showing a horse head also. More hidden creatures began showing up in many of his drawings. I could only spot them from the d-point: viewing each one from the left side. Not all were mammals. In some of his landscape drawings, I came across three hidden reptiles. In *Tempest over Horsemen and Trees with Enormous Waves*, I spotted what looked like the top of a crocodile head, as if it were moving along the water's surface toward the viewer.

In *Bird's-eye View of the Region around Arezzo, I spotted* the profile of another reptile that again looked like a crocodile, but with its mouth open. The texture of its scales were cleverly represented by the bumpy topography, its eye constructed from the inhabited part of the landscape, a village perhaps, at the top of the pentagon-shaped area of negative space.

In *Bird's-eye View of the Landscape, Showing the Tuscan Cities of Arezzo, Perugia, Chiusi and Siena*, the cream-colored negative space seemed to form a bird head with a large beak, which it used to hold a man down by his torso. The man, lying horizontally, even showed a surprised expression. He was formed by the blue-colored water, and his left hand clutched the top of the bird's beak as if to pry himself from its grasp.

Why the heck was it showing a bird attacking a man?

It confused me more. How could I be sure about what I was seeing? Some images were unmistakable, others ambiguous. Trying to decipher some of their shapes was like trying to spot a polar bear in a blizzard. At what point could I be sure the ambiguous images were put there?

I had to walk away to clear my head.

When I came back to see if they were still there, I saw that they never left. In fact, they stood out even more. It was as though I were *unable* to unsee them. Once the d-point helped point out the images, it was almost no longer needed.

Were they simply pranks? Images Leonardo created to entertain himself?

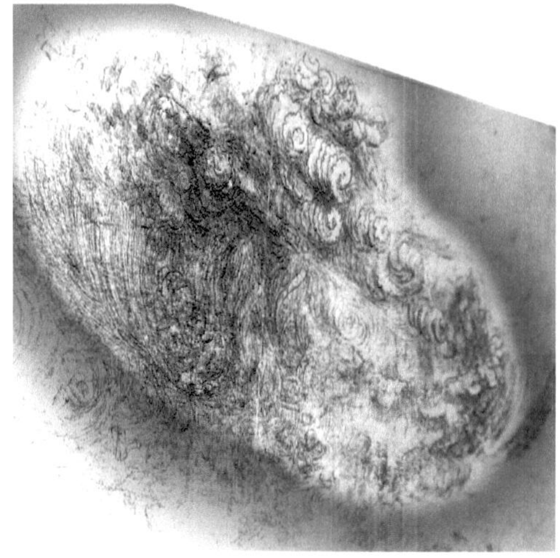

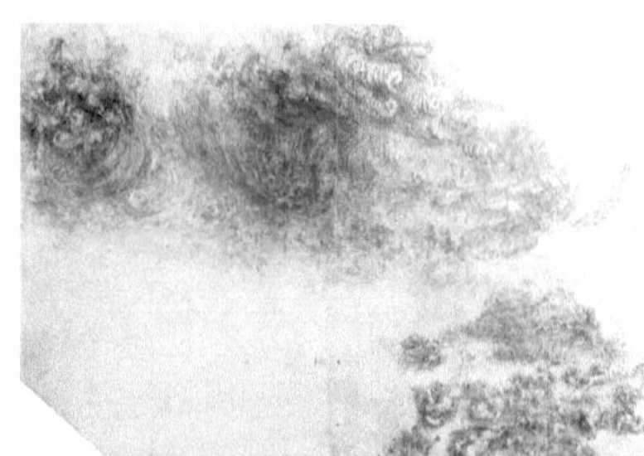

LEFT: Section of *Tempest over Horsemen and Trees* (c. 1514)—d-point view showing reptile (highlighted). **RIGHT:** Traditional view.

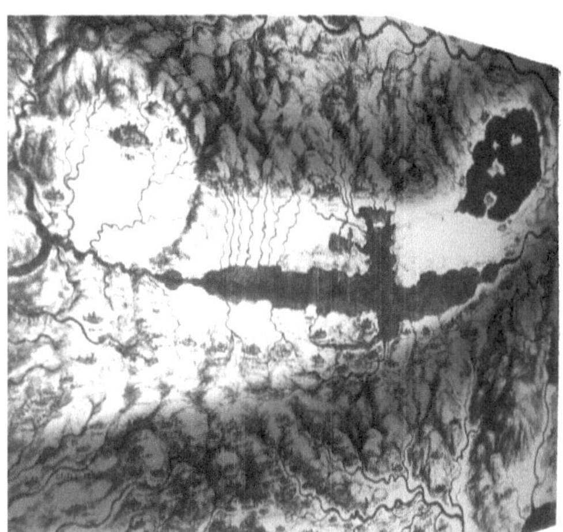

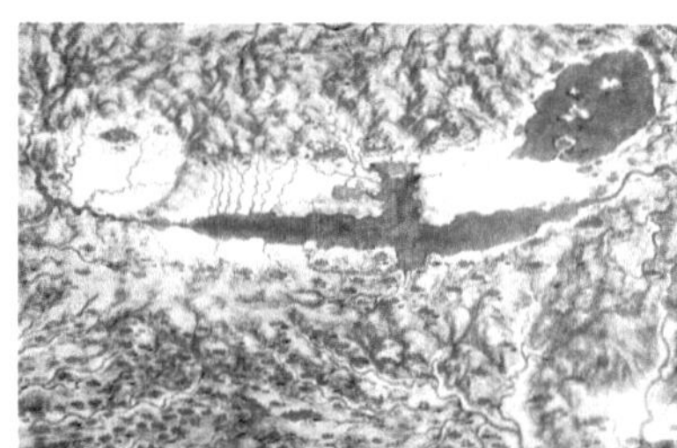

LEFT: *Bird's-eye View of the Region around Arezzo* (c. 1502)—view from d-point of bird head holding a man with its beak (highlighted). **RIGHT:** Traditional view.

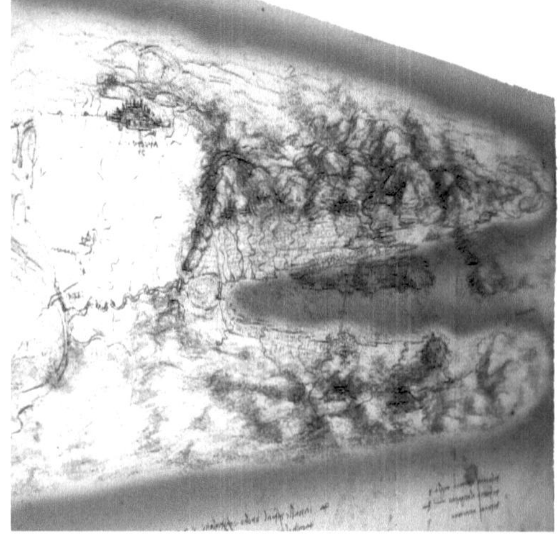

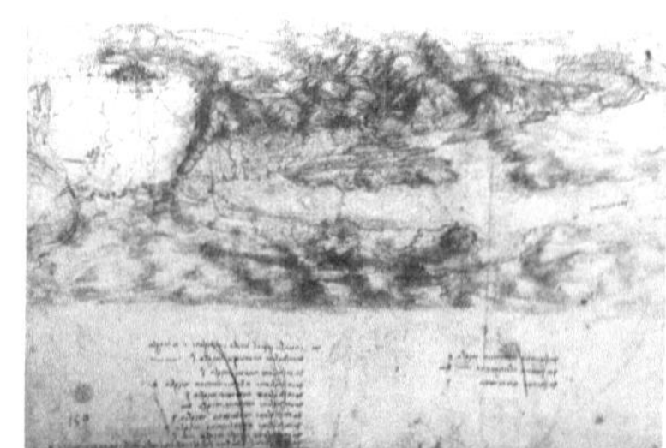

LEFT: *Bird's-eye View of the Landscape, Showing the Tuscan Cities of Arezzo, Perugia, Chiusi and Siena* (c. 1502)—view from d-point showing reptile (highlighted). **RIGHT:** Traditional view.

Did he slip these figures in, waiting to see if anyone noticed as he showed them the art?

Maybe I wasn't as surprised as I should have been. I had seen optical illusions before as early as the fourth grade, when I created some myself. I was fascinated by library books I came across that were filled with all kinds of optical illusions. I'd stare at the psychedelic geometric patterns that remained stationary, but appeared to move on the printed page. I was entertained by the funny image of the elephant that either had four or five legs, depending on how you looked at it. And I would stare at those lines that didn't look parallel even though they were, due to their surrounding patterns, as I tried to train my eye to fight through the illusions' attempt to twist my mind's perception.

I remembered seeing M.C. Escher's never-ending stairs for the first time, and the two hands that were drawing each other. I examined it for a long time, many times trying to find some clue revealing which hand started drawing first. A class troublemaker saw me gawking at a book of illusions one day and told me that the logo of the heavy metal band Dio was an illusion. That upside down, the intricate details spelled out DEVIL.

I began drawing my own illusions whenever classes bored me, which was often. I drew vulgar words and made each letter look so very tall and skinny—the height of my notebook paper—that they looked like an innocent set of lines. Only when I placed my head on the desk and looked across the paper lying flat on my desk, *shortening the image, like Leonardo,* did the lines suddenly make sense and form recognizable words.

I thought I had invented a secret way of writing. Of course there was nothing new at all about it. It was the same technique every town or village used when it spray-painted words like SCHOOL or STOP in lengthened letters on the roads so approaching drivers could read them more easily from an oncoming angle. And suddenly I could see that Leonardo used the same technique. Masterfully.

What first intrigued you, Leonardo?

Too excited to sleep, I spent part of the night focusing on the first horse head to see what more I could learn. Or maybe just to marvel at it. What detail! Looking across at the *Drapery Study for a Kneeling Figure Turned to the Left*, I could see the horse's lips, its large nostrils, eye sockets and lashes, even the bridle around its head, all of it formed from folds of cloth in the drapery study. Certain lines were thicker and darker so they stood out from the d-point angle, while less dominating lines seemed to disappear. They *guided* you to see the hidden image. Or fooled you, depending on the degree of the angle.

I turned the image around and upside down, I slanted and tilted, I used the d-point on every side. But the horse head only appeared when I followed Leonardo's written instructions—when I looked from just the point to the left—its d-point. But why put an illustration of a *horse* in a drawing that was totally unrelated? And why *hide* it?

Was it a game, Leonardo? Pure fascination with technique? Or something more?

A friend of mine once commissioned me to do a pencil portrait of his two baby daughters—a present for his wife. I worked from a photo he gave me. One daughter was a newborn, swaddled tightly in a blanket. The problem was that there was no way of knowing if his newborn was a boy or a girl just by the photo. Of course, anyone who knew them would know, but as an artist, I needed to suggest her gender in a way so even a stranger looking at the art piece would know. Because the drawing was done in black pencil, I couldn't solve the problem with a pink blanket or a rosy complexion. And her ears were not yet pierced, which might have helped suggest her gender.

Eventually, I got the idea to use the folds of her cloth to reveal her gender with a subtle clue. It would have to be beautifully understated, like the way Mary Cassatt had painted nude babies in an elegant way that showed and deserved respect. I left the secret to her gender right there in the open, even if most viewers would not realize it unless it was pointed out. As an artist, my job was to include that important detail, not throw it in the viewer's face.

My friend barely said a word when I showed him the drawing. His eyes and his smile told me how he felt. He gave me a hug and said his wife would love it.

"I had to leave a clue about her gender," I admitted to him, "so I worked some subtle folds into her blanket, to represent the female anatomy. It's done in the art world all the time," I added, pleased at my own ingenuity.

His smile shrank as he studied the folds between the newborn's legs, subtle lines I had placed as blanket folds that just barely mimicked the anatomy of the female body part. Until I pointed it out. "You drew my baby's *vagina*?" he then gasped.

Maybe I was a little over-optimistic about his understanding of art. It wasn't like I had shown him Gustave Courbet's *The Origin of the World*, a painted close-up of an unkempt vagina, once described in the art world as "having escaped pornographic status." But from the expression on my friend's face, I realized he wouldn't be looking at the portrait quite the same way again.

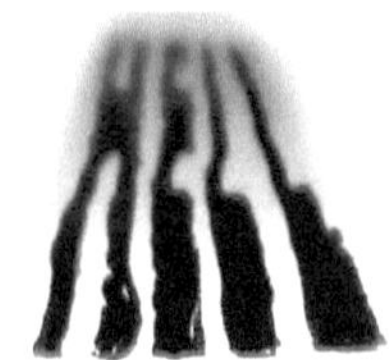

ABOVE: Formation of the word HELL when Piccirillo's childhood illusion on **RIGHT** (direct view) is seen from extreme angle below art.

I should have known that it was something only an artist might have understood. I knew that next time I would keep something like that to myself.

"Maybe you shouldn't tell your wife about that part," I said to him.

There could have been a good reason Leonardo hid the animals. And if he hid things in his drawings, I wondered if he also hid anything in his paintings.

But I doubted it.

If Leonardo was playing, or experimenting, surely he'd restrict that sort of thing to sketches. He *planned* his paintings to a meticulous degree, and sometimes spent years executing them. Drawings were done quickly. So an illusion here or there wasn't a big waste of time. It was probably just something to add a little fun to his drawing studies. Paintings were taken too seriously to incorporate illusions. *I thought.*

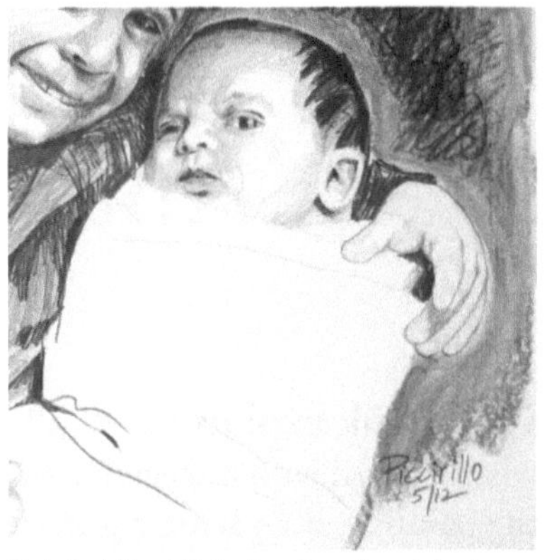

Detail of Piccirillo's drawing of an infant.

I figured drawings would allow for better concealment of the illusions– they'd be much harder to pick out if they were the same color as the surrounding scenery. I would have guessed that separate colors would make it stand out. I wasn't even sure it were possible to conceal an illusion in a painting the way the horse head was hidden.

The mountains in *Mona Lisa* were an entirely different kind of illusion. The view had to be rotated to reveal them as animals, but the images *themselves* weren't stretched or otherwise distorted. Stretching a colored image across a flat, colored canvas so it remained *un*-noticed except from a secret angle? The idea seemed too complex. Granted, the mind of Leonardo was nothing *but* complex. But I couldn't think of a single example of an artist doing something like that.

Or ...was there one such example?

I ran downstairs and scanned the art books on my shelves. I had forgotten the artist's name and painting, so it took me a moment to find. But I had a vague memory of the art. It was a large portrait of two men standing, leaning on either side of some kind of table or shelves. And the green curtain background they stood against. It was mostly known for its large, *unhidden* illusion.

And there it was, in one of my college art history books. The page I stopped on showed it: *The Ambassadors*, a painting by German artist Hans Holbein the Younger, painted in 1533—fourteen years after Leonardo's death. It *explicitly* presented the kind of optical illusion I had seen in Leonardo's drawings. An *anamorphic* illusion.

7

Anamorphosis

One book explained the illusion as "a distorted image recognizable only when viewed with a special device, such as a cylindrical mirror, or by looking at the painting at an acute angle."[1]

Although *The Ambassadors* is well known to showcase the illusion, the technique of anamorphosis may have been used as early as the prehistoric cave paintings at Lascaux—specifically on the figure of a bull to "maintain its dimensions" and prevent the art from looking distorted because of the shape of the cave.[2] It was similar to what Michelangelo would later do on the curved ceiling of the Sistine Chapel so the art would look proportionally correct to viewers below.

Like *Mona Lisa*, *The Ambassadors* was a mysterious creation. Scholars debated the meanings of both masterpieces for centuries. At first glance, *The Ambassadors* was a portrait of two men. Standing between them was a set of shelves filled with scientific tools and musical instruments.

But what draws the viewer's attention is the distorted image of a human skull that stretches like a rubber band across the entire bottom of the painting. In plain view. *Impossible* to miss. So startling that it actually interrupts the beauty of Holbein's painting, giving it a distressing quality. It practically slaps the viewer in the face.

Only in the anamorphic view—a specific point—does the skull appear in perfect proportion, no longer stretched. Unlike the images I found in Leonardo's drawings, *The Ambassadors* skull had to be viewed from the right side of the painting, instead of the left.

I thought about Leonardo's left-handedness having something to do with

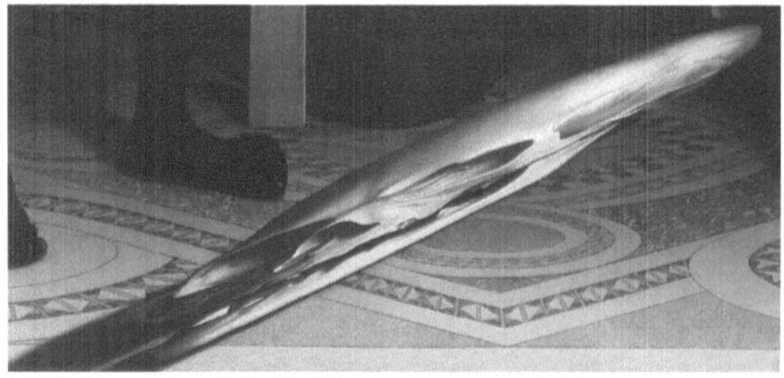

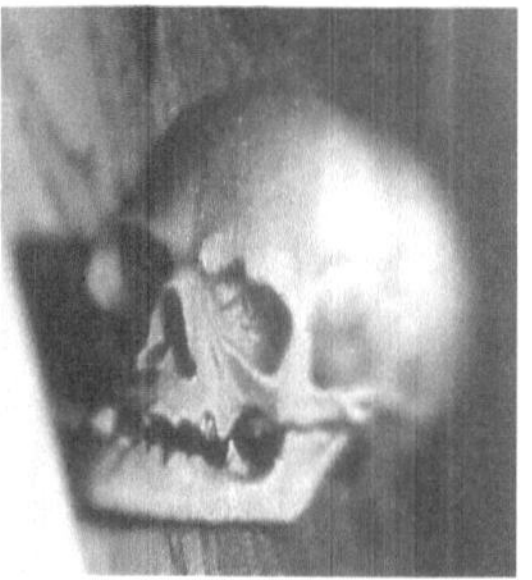

LEFT: Direct view of skull in *The Ambassadors*. **RIGHT:** Anamorphic view.

that. But after some deliberation, I tossed the irrational idea away.

Was there no attempt to hide the skull because Holbein figured it was impossible to do in colored oils?

In any case, a lot of skill was needed to pull it off. Maybe Holbein *could* have concealed it better. And maybe Leonardo valued the beauty and integrity of his paintings much more than Holbein, and in turn would never compromise them for an illusion that poked the viewer in the eye with the tackiness of Holbein's skull.

But no one knew the reason why the skull was there.

I remembered other illusions from that art period. Some time after Leonardo, artist Giuseppe Arcimboldo created specialized human-looking portraits made from a collage of painted objects.

I pulled out an image of *The Librarian*, a portrait created from an array of library items. A stack of large books formed the body. Small ones for the head. Ribbon page holders placed for eyebrows, an ear, and fingers. A nose was created by tilting one of the smaller books over the lips. In *Spring*, a variety of flowers, plants, and leaves were painted to create the head and bust of a female figure. *Earth* was made of an elephant, boar, cheetah, lion, ram, monkey, and other land animals grouped together to form a male figure's portrait.

But Arcimboldo's paintings didn't need to be viewed at special angles to see the illusions. The concept of the portraits were their illusions.

Yet, there was *The Gardener.* When turned upside down it became another painting: *Vegetables in a Bowl.* The illusion of a face wearing a bowl for a hat rotated to become a still life of a bowl of vegetables—related items grouped to form one large image.

In fact, for the jewelry store I worked at, I had once used Arcimboldo's technique to create an ad for a fashion show. For the ad, I repositioned a pile of jewelry so it elegantly formed a woman's face. It took a while to get the stones and pieces just right so the face looked subtle enough, yet was easy to make out. The design was so well received—even one of the attendees at the fashion show (a woman in her sixties, wearing an expensive set of earrings and designer clothes) asked to meet me. It was an odd request (as if I were a well-known artist), and the only one I ever got from a stranger. Introducing myself to her was a little awkward, but I was also flattered. I couldn't say no. Her simple request was one of the best compliments I ever received, and for the rest of the night, I held my chin high.

Even in the ad world, illusions were not unheard of.

The more I searched back in history, the more I realized illusions were not such a strange concept for Leonardo's time, which made the illusions in his drawings easier to accept. *The Ambassadors* (1533) was considered one of the earliest known anamorphic *paintings* during the Renaissance period. But the earliest illusion of that kind from the same period was a drawing made around

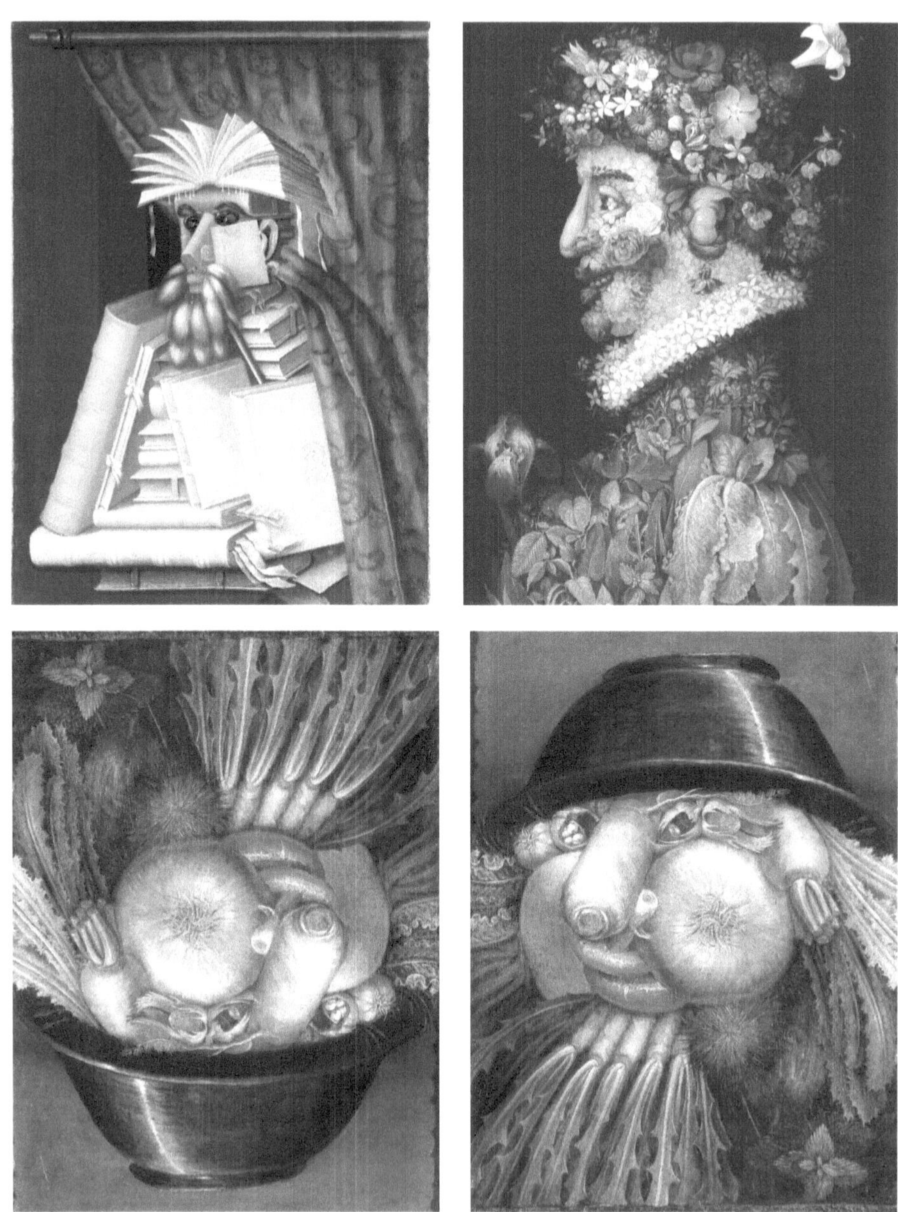

TOP ROW: Arcimboldo, *The Librarian* (c. 1566) and *Spring* (1563).
BOTTOM ROW: *Vegetables in a Bowl* and *The Gardener* when rotated (c. 1587-90).

1485. The name itself was revealing enough that it left me a little bewildered.

The drawing was of an eye, made of just a few stretched lines that probably took the artist just a few minutes to create. Like Holbein's skull, it was easy to see the eye shorten into its correct proportion from the anamorphic angle. Named after the artist that created it, *Leonardo's Eye* was the earliest known illusion of its kind to display anamorphosis so that its presence was obvious to the viewer.

After spending time to process what I just learned, I took out a pen to recreate the drawing. My sketch may have not turned out as perfect as Leonardo's, but it took less than a minute to make. And since those childhood days in elementary school when I drew my own illusions, it reminded me of how simple some optical illusions were to create.

To hide them in a drawing would obviously have taken longer. Still, I was convinced that hiding an anamorphosis in a painting would be difficult, if not impossible to pull off. I almost didn't bother looking, but I knew I wouldn't be

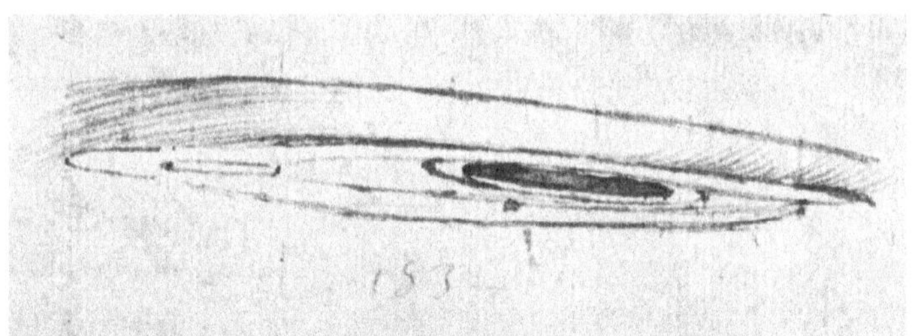

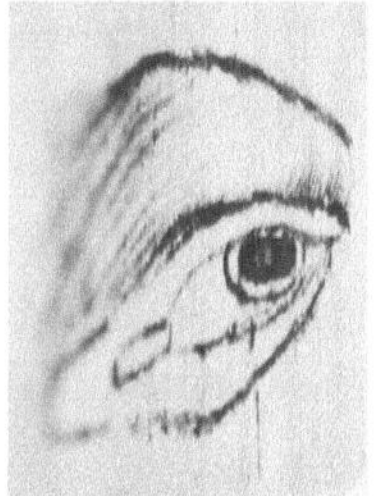

LEFT: *Leonardo's Eye* (c. 1485). **RIGHT:** Anamorphic view of eye.

satisfied until I made sure Leonardo's paintings weren't hiding anything.

As far as I knew, no one had ever looked for such images in his art. Or *seen* them hidden in another artist's work. Just the thought of looking at Leonardo's art from a different angle made it feel as if I were about to see his art for the first time again. It was tempting enough.

As I pulled open a book of his art, I suddenly had a strange and heavy feeling, taboo-like, as if I were opening Pandora's Box.

Still. It didn't matter. Because I had to see.

8

Ah, You See?

It was at The Farm that I experienced seeing land differently in a way that changed the perception I had of my father.

The Farm was just what we called it. But there were no animals, except for the occasional pet dog Papa kept there. It was just a desolate piece of land. Papa called it "an investment," with the idea that our family would live there someday, away from the neighborhood I didn't want to leave. I was glad when Ma secretly told me we would never move there.

In my teens, he brought me down to help restore the house on the land. Papa and I never saw eye to eye. To him, jobs were simply about making money. To me, it was about chasing dreams, and doing something I was passionate about (while hopefully making enough money to survive on). So although I wanted to stay home and work on improving my comic illustrations, I didn't think he would understand how important those drawings were to me. How they helped make me a better artist. He had been pushing for me to get a job like he had, in some factory for General Motors. But I knew I could never be happy at a factory job. I'd be happy working as an artist, even if it meant making less money.

It later reminded me of Michelangelo, and how his father opposed his wanting to be an artist. And although Papa would never do so, Michelangelo's father and uncle would beat him, believing his profession as an artist would disgrace the Buonarroti-Simoni family name.[1] But like Michelangelo, my mind couldn't be changed. Art was in my blood.

That passion wasn't something I expected Papa to understand. But I didn't want to disrespect him by denying him the help he wanted at The Farm.

On one of many visits, it was just him and I. The soot-covered house, with its cobblestone-wrapped base, sat on a plateau that dipped down to a large plain before ending at the distant woods—Papa's private hunting ground during deer season. But I never saw a single animal there except for passing birds. It looked as lifeless as the background in *Mona Lisa*.

I was working all day at clearing out items left behind by the previous owner. Stacks of aged newspapers, rusted containers, and other random junk. I carried everything to the pile of garbage outside as if it were hazardous, holding it far from my body while holding my breath.

At lunchtime, I sat out in the sun, on the slope behind the house, overlooking all the land, bordered on one side by a creek. I bit at my sandwich as I took in the view.

It was the first time I really examined the scenery and noticed that it wasn't as grim as I always had seen it before. In all the times I helped my father there, I had missed many of its details. The gentle sway of the patches of wild grass along the field, the undisturbed look of the terrain, as if no one had ever stepped foot on it. How the sky was so open that it felt like I had gone back in time.

There was a mysterious, yet peaceful quality to all of it, as if I was sitting in front of the world's largest painted landscape.

I was lost in a gaze, chewing on my food in a trancelike state when Papa approached quietly from around the front of the house, where he had been working. "Ah, you see?" he said, as if he had known how I failed to see the land before then.

I gave a slight nod.

"This was all water many, many years ago," Papa said, gesturing his hand in the air at the distant past. "Before you were born. Before Jesus Christ."

It was then that I realized how the land's shape resembled a beach shore without water. And why I occasionally found sea shells buried up near the house.

I sat there for a bit, losing myself to the scenery, with Papa.

9

Transfiguration

I began with *The Baptism of Christ*—a painting Leonardo first worked on in his early twenties as an apprentice to Andrea del Verrocchio.

Using the same simple steps in which the horse head illusion seemed to work, I placed the book's image flat on my bed. Then my head to the extreme left of it, at the position Leonardo described in *The d-Point.*

It helped me to use one eye, as if looking through a microscope.

I settled on a point roughly three inches off the plane of the canvas and three inches away from the image's left edge, since that's what appeared to work best with the drawings, looking across the painting's surface. But I drew back now and again, playing slightly with distance, since I wasn't really sure from how far to view it, the whole time still maintaining the d-point angle.

I unfocused my vision slightly to blur out the weaker details so bolder ones stood out, which appeared to reveal the hidden images.

Although I wasn't sure what to look for, I figured if there was something hiding, it would pop out the way those first images did. I thought maybe the head of some creature would appear, if anything at all. But I was open to the idea that my preconception was totally off.

There were two angels in *The Baptism of Christ.* Since Leonardo was known to only paint one of them, I focused my concentration to that area. As I searched over the art, I scanned the painting as a whole and in bits.

What appeared was ...nothing ...absolutely nothing.

What would I do, anyway, if I did find something? I still hadn't considered what I would do about the animal heads in *Mona Lisa*, but I knew that couldn't be kept a secret for long. Sooner or later, it had to be shared. Art was an integral part of my life. Art *was* my life. And I would owe it to the art world to provide them with anything I discovered. Plus, historians would want to know what I found, even if it turned out to be meaningless.

But I didn't believe Leonardo would paint anything meaningless.

Regardless, it was my duty to share the information. Even if the last thing I wanted was the attention from finding those animals, which I was sure I'd get, considering how much attention any story involving *Mona Lisa* usually received. In a way, I was already beginning to regret seeing them. But I tried to push that thought from my mind.

The bright side was that I wasn't going to waste too much time looking through Leonardo's art since he only created about fifteen paintings. I had a good feeling they would all turn up empty, which meant I'd be in bed within the hour.

The next image in the book was *The Annunciation*, a painting in which Gabriel announces to Mary that she's been chosen to give birth to Jesus.

Again I positioned my head to the extreme left of it, and repeated the same steps. And again I waited for something to appear.

But again, there was nothing.

I spent a little less time with *Portrait of a Musician*, feeling that I would find nothing there either. I was right, nothing showed up there. And there was nothing whatsoever in *Lady with an Ermine*.

Portrait *Ginevra de' Benci*? Not a thing.

Madonna of the Carnation? Zilch.

St. John the Baptist? Nada.

The d-point revealed nothing in any of them.

"So much for opening Pandora's Box," I said to myself, flipping pages to the next image, which turned out to be *Mona Lisa*.

And although no anamorphosis showed up in the previous paintings, there was something that made me nervous as I prepared myself to examine her. Maybe I thought that if any of his paintings contained an anamorphic image, *Mona Lisa* would be the one, because those three ambiguous animal heads were already hiding there. Or maybe it was her mysterious nature.

I had been laying on my bed, and there was a long hesitation as I rose to my hands and knees. For some reason, I couldn't lie down for that painting. Maybe it was the sudden tension. And anticipation. But I had to reset myself. I had a sudden desire to ask her permission to peek at her differently than she was used to, as if she were alive. Like proper etiquette, it seemed rude to approach her otherwise.

Mona Lisa was no longer just a painting I respected for historical reasons. Since finding the animals, I was developing a personal connection to her. Or to Leonardo. Or both. There was something different about the figure's eyes as I hovered over her, preparing myself to view her from the d-point. No doubt she was growing more fascinating to me every minute.

Who are you, really?

Although some believed her name was Lisa Gherardini, no one really knew the answer for sure. That question would remain a mystery forever.

So I thought.

It was so quiet in my bedroom that rubbing my temple sounded to me like sandpaper scratching stone.

Before examining her, I spent a few seconds staring off at the white of the pillow to clear my mind, forgetting what I was *supposed* to see, and ignoring everything I knew about the painting. I pretended it was a picture I had never seen before. So I could look at her objectively.

Holding my breath, I put myself in position to view her from her extreme left. Like a sniper crouching to look down the scope of a gun.

From that angle, I took in the portrait's scenery, patiently looking up and down the art, the way I would look for letters in a word search puzzle, except that I was searching for unseen images and from an extreme angle. I took in the bluish, cold-looking mountains, jagged in the far distance. Then the rocky background closer in the foreground—smooth, waving, warm-looking stone in one area, and gloomy, unleveled terrain in another, with a mishmash of landscape filling the space all around the female figure. I scanned the bodies of water—what could have been lakes, or rivers, and even an ocean at the horizon. Then the empty, hazy sky above, a whitish glow bouncing off the deadness of the earth.

But, nothing happened. There was nothing there. Nothing at all.

I let out a breath and kept my position, trying to figure out why I had the feeling I was missing something. It was impossible not to notice her eyes. *Mona Lisa* was one of those paintings in which the eyes appeared to follow the viewer around the room no matter where they stood. I was surprised that even from the extreme angle of my position, it still looked as if she could see me.

And there was something else. From that angle, I noticed that the broken horizon line experts were unable to explain looked *worse*—more slanted, like it was really off. I just stared at it. It was then, because of the horizon line, as I racked my brain wondering what Leonardo was thinking, that I thought of the *Point-of-Sight* passage. My view was from a level around the top of her shoulders—the middle of the painting. But a sudden inkling froze me in place, making me feel as if I were floating over a cliff's edge, just then realizing where I had taken a wrong step.

It couldn't be.

I suddenly had a strong feeling the d-point was just one step to seeing the illusions; that there was something else I needed to do. I almost didn't want to move, too scared to do it, as if in a way, I didn't want to know the answer. But that thrill made me even more curious to know if my inkling was correct. Slowly, I rotated the image around slightly as I continued investigating.

It only had to rotate a few degrees …and that's when *everything* changed.

The woman appeared to transform. It was as if her eyes came alive, her whole body reversing in age, her skin tightening, her demeanor morphing, like time was suddenly reversing itself in the picture. The woman became *someone else*. The haggard-looking lady disappeared. And in her place was someone younger and more petite.

Every thought I ever had about that image ricocheted across my mind at what felt like extraordinary speeds, like heated atoms bouncing off each other. In an instant, everything I knew about that painting imploded into one simple formula.

The answers appeared right in front of me, in the artwork's transformation. Her identity. The crooked horizon. Leonardo's strange passages. And that smile. It all made sense: *The whole painting is an optical illusion.*

It was too much to take in all at once. I couldn't take my eyes off her. My senses could barely handle what I was seeing. If a feather floated onto my bed, it would have sent me jumping.

The complexity of *Mona Lisa*'s illusion went *way* beyond what Leonardo did with his drawings. What I began to realize was that *The d-Point* was only half of a set of instructions. Or *coordinates.*

The *Point-of-Sight* was the other half. Sight "must be placed at the level of that line where the earth and sky meet; excepting mountains."

In other words—*the horizon.*

At first, as I examined *Mona Lisa*, I had been too far below the painting's horizon line, which is why I didn't notice the illusion. Only when I rotated the image so my eyes were aligned with the horizon did it appear.

I should have known from Holbein's skull image that *two* coordinates were needed. It had to be viewed from one side of the painting at a specific angle. In *The Ambassadors* case it was from the right side. But it also had to be looked at from the correct *height.* Holbein used an imaginary line horizontally crossing the middle of the painting. Where that line crosses the angle of the painting's own d-point, is the point from which the skull could be seen correctly.

Leonardo's illusions needed to be seen from the left. But the principle was the same. With *Mona Lisa*, a certain height was also needed to see the illusion. That's when *Mona Lisa* began to reveal her secrets.

The biggest difference from Holbein's art was that Leonardo's illusions were hidden.

I wasn't sure how much time I spent gazing at her from that secret perspective, but I didn't want to let go of what I saw.

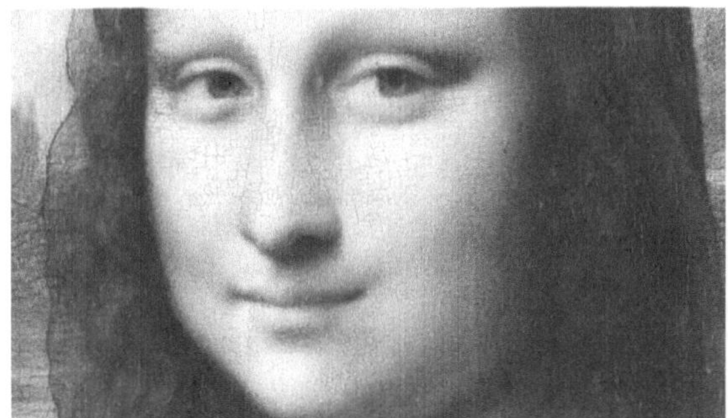
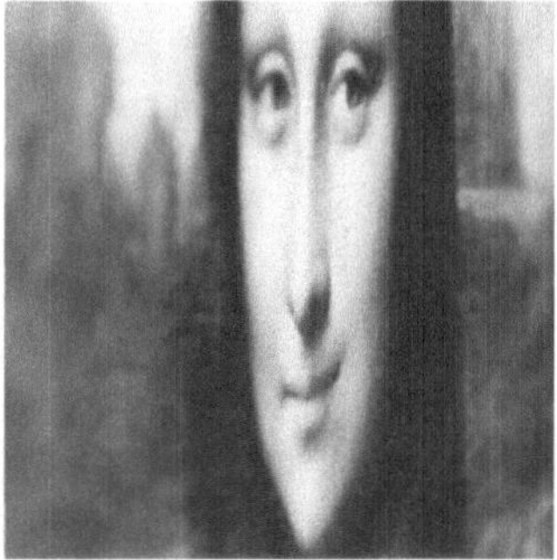

LEFT: Traditional view of smile. **RIGHT:** Anamorphic view of smile.

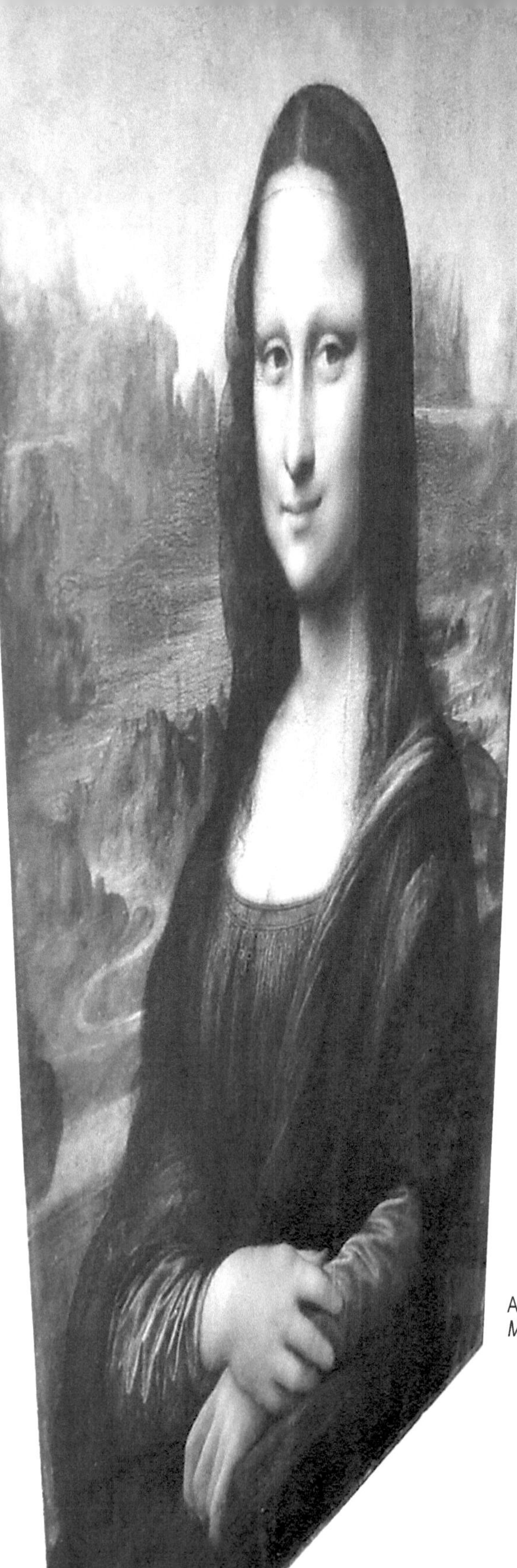

Anamorphic view of *Mona Lisa.*

From the d-point, her hands—described by art experts as bulky—became more delicate.

And her smile—the expression of her smile actually *increased!*

Yet, the most magical part of the illusion was the rocky landscape behind her. *I'll be damned.* It seemed to morph entirely into a different image. It changed into a body of water.

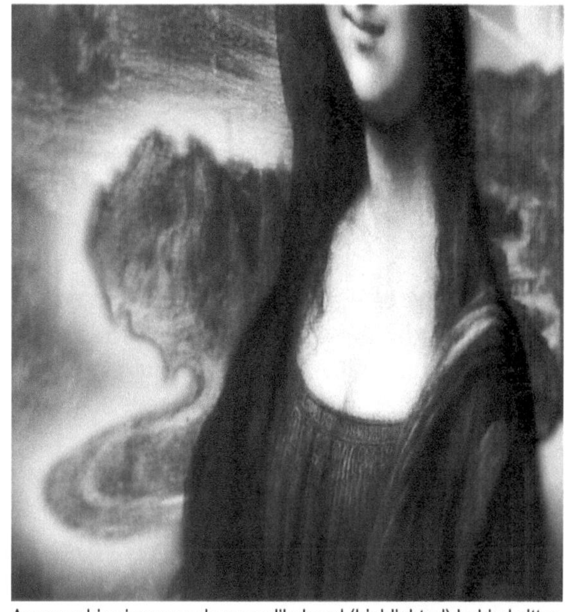
Anamorphic view reveals crocodile head (highlighted) behind sitter.

But there was something directly behind the woman that I could not believe. Even though I had spotted reptiles in his drawings, it seemed impossible for it to show up in an oil painting.

I couldn't deny what I saw because I was staring it straight in the eye as it appeared to be coming toward me. In the background—which became an illusion of being water-flooded, resembling something closer to a swamp—was the gigantic head of a crocodile.

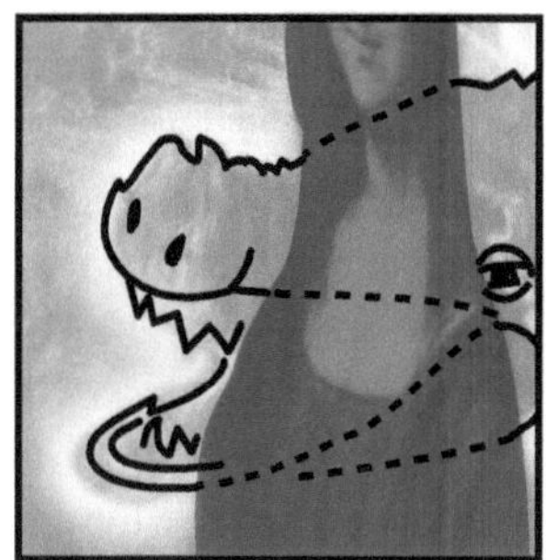
Reptile's approximate position.

And it looked as if it was about to attack *Mona Lisa* from behind.

10

Crazy?

A couple weeks after discovering that Leonardo painted the optical illusion, I picked up the phone and called my friend from the agency I once worked for. I mentioned *Mona Lisa* without giving much detail, so he wouldn't be surprised by the topic when we got together, but I also didn't want him to think I had lost my mind.

Charles was not only someone I could trust to keep what I found quiet. His years of teaching provided him a bit of knowledge about art—a topic we discussed many times during his later years as a copywriter while working together at the agency. But I could tell he sensed something strange when I brought up her name.

I needed him as a second pair of eyes, another person to tell me if what I was seeing was real. I didn't expect him to believe what I was about to show him. In fact, I had started wondering if I was nuts because of what I was finding.

Does a crazy person know they're crazy?

He showed up to my house wearing a sport jacket, as usual, and holding a trilby—a hat he always took off before entering someone's home.

As we made small talk, I placed a book of Leonardo's writings and one with his art on the living room coffee table, next to the beer I fetched him.

I held up a small recorder. "You mind if I record our conversation?" I asked, "So I could reference it later?"

"Be my guest," he said. "What's all this about?"

"How much do you know about *Mona Lisa*?"

We had enough conversations on art in the past that such a question out of the blue wasn't unusual. Humoring me, he leaned forward from the couch, resting his elbows onto his knees as he looked down to think. A small glare bounced off his smoothly shaven head, and for a moment, he looked like Rodin's sculpture, *The Thinker*.

"I spent entire classes discussing that painting," he said with a certain pride. "I think I can say I know it pretty well."

"Tell me what you know."

"Well ...it's painted on poplar wood, in his famous *sfumato* technique—smoky edges to represent how we really see distant objects. It took Leonardo *years* to complete, and it was with him when he died.

"The big question is, *Who is in the picture?* They say Lisa Gherardini, but there have been many candidates. Some think it's a self-portrait, which would explain why she looks sort of mannish."

I nodded without saying anything to interrupt him, impressed at what he knew and remembered.

"There's also the unbalanced horizon, making the mountains look uneven. What's *that* all about?" Charles said with a puzzled look. "And nobody can tell where that background came from. You would think with over five hundred years of tourists crawling around Florence, where Leonardo lived, someone would recognize the spot. *What is she smiling about?* Of course that's the biggest mystery. No one knows." He shrugged. "That's pretty much everything I know. Why the sudden fascination with *Mona Lisa* anyway?"

"I know this sounds crazy, but I may have discovered something about the picture."

"What do you mean?"

I began to explain everything to him, beginning with the question mark. He knew me well enough to know I wasn't kidding, but he still looked unsure. So I showed him the illusions so he could see them with his own eyes.

"Well ...huh," was all he said at first, then twisted his head looking at them from various angles. "How about that? I mean ...it's *possible*. But, why would there be a question mark?"

"I don't know. But, it led me to the other images. Don't you think he had to leave the answers to her mysteries around *somewhere?*"

"Like I said, there are a lot of unanswered questions about that picture. Leonardo didn't leave any clues, as I recall."

"The more I thought about it, the more I believed he did. His writings were filled with wisdom. But he clarified everything he wrote about. So I didn't think he would leave no explanation behind."

"How do you mean?"

"I'm not sure if you ever read them, but Leonardo left *thousands* of pages of notes. He wrote about philosophy, science, his reflections on nature, and some of the best painting advice there is. He wrote in a way that left no room for confusion. For the most part, he explained everything meticulously. Somewhere in his writings, I believe he explains the painting's mysterious nature. Even if the explanation wasn't obvious.

"I know that question mark means something more. It's got to be a challenge, Charles. He's asking something: *What do you see?* That mark isn't accidental. Leonardo didn't do accidental. In fact, I think he left us clues to her identity in plain sight."

"If they are in 'plain sight,' why hasn't anyone managed to see them?"

"Maybe no one has been looking at her the right way. Charles, have you ever heard anything about animal heads?"

I showed Charles the animals along with Leonardo's *Animalia* passage.

He held the book up sideways as he examined *Mona Lisa*'s image. From where I stood, it looked like he was studying a nude centerfold in a magazine.

He then slouched back on the couch.

"I guess I sort of see them," he said. "Now that you've shown me where to look. But don't you think ...I don't know ...that it could just be kind of chance resemblance?"

"A coincidence? Matching the *Animalia* passage in his notebooks?"

"Yeah, that might be stretching it," he said, then chewed on his bottom lip. "But why paint them on their sides?"

I shook my head. "No idea."

"And what about those other two things you showed me?"

"*The d-Point* and *Point-of-Sight*? They're suspicious, right?"

"Tell me again why you say that," he asked, lowering the book.

"Because he painted *The Last Supper* up high on a wall. Too high to use the d-point and point-of-sight on without a ladder."

"So what's the connection to *Mona Lisa*?" Charles asked.

"One night I dozed off with one of his drapery studies next to me," I said, explaining the first anamorphic illusion I saw: the horse's head.

"Strange. It's like what you said about Leonardo's writings, or at least the d-point and point-of-sight things. They seem to have double meanings."

I nodded. "At face value they mean one thing. But on a deeper level they have another meaning. Which helped point me to seeing them."

"Like a *double entendre*. A play on words."

After showing Charles how to view the secret images in Leonardo's art, I gave him some time to search others on his own as I watched quietly. He hunched closer and closer to the pictures on the pages, one image after another, scrunching his face, eventually spotting some of the hidden images without my help.

I took a moment to enjoy watching Charles discover the images for himself. There was an air of excitement that was electrifying.

"Is that its *snout?*" he asked, looking at one of the images. "Oh, *now* I see it."

"It gets easier with practice. Some are more difficult than others."

"It's like the-profile-and-the-vase illusion," he said.

"Right. But some of these are *anamorphic* illusions."

"You mean like that painting, *The Ambassadors*?"

"Exactly. Holbein's painting."

And a realization suddenly hit me. Before I saw the illusions, no one had probably seen them since ...*you created them, Leonardo.*

To be the first to have seen these since Leonardo himself caused a slight stinging sensation behind my eyes. I was standing, but suddenly had to sit.

"The big question is," Charles said, turning away from the book to look at me, "are we imposing a horse head onto the picture because we *want* to see it? Or is it really there? And did Leonardo intentionally put it there?"

I took a breath and told him "I already considered that. Remember looking for images in clouds as a child?"

"Sure. I still catch myself doing it."

"Clouds form spontaneously. These paintings were formed *intentionally*. We know when we're seeing something with the help of our imagination, and when we're seeing what's really *there*. Our minds can tell the difference." I pointed to the book in his hands. "*These* are real."

"You think he deliberately hid images of horses—*anamorphic* images—in his art?"

"Yes. I do."

"Well," said Charles after a pause. "Why not? He was noted for being a trickster." He paused a moment. "You know, he even created pictograph puzzles—images and symbols that form sentences. Worth checking out."

"Pictographs?" That I didn't know, but it sounded like something I had to look into.

"Still. What would a horse head have to do with *Mona Lisa*?"

"I was sort of hoping you could tell me. See, I applied Leonardo's instructions to *Mona Lisa*. And what I saw …well, it wasn't a horse head. There was no horse head."

"What you saw?"

"Take another look at her, Charles. This time, look from the extreme left side—the d-point. *And* keep your eyes at a height level with the horizon—as the *Point-of-Sight* explained."

"What am I looking for?"

"You'll have to see it for yourself, but the whole painting transforms."

"Transforms to what?" he said, wrinkling his forehead.

"The landscape changes. The background begins to resemble a swamp. All at once, the woman becomes surrounded by water, as if she's sitting in the middle of a lake. It's a whole new painting.

"Best of all, you'll see her smile like never before."

Charles looked at me suspiciously. *Yeah, right.*

"You have to see it," I said.

He shrugged and turned to the book. As he squinted and adjusted his focus, he blinked once, and squinted again.

"Tell me I'm not imagining it," I said.

For a moment he said nothing. I could see him adjusting his focus onto the picture, the suspicious look on his face slowly beginning to fade. "I've seen that painting a million times," he said in a very quiet voice. "But never like *this*. The woman looks different from this perspective. It's astonishing."

"What do you see exactly?" I asked, curious to compare what we each saw.

"Well, not the usual, chunky, out-of-shape *Mona Lisa* I've been used to all these years. From *this* angle, she's thinner, younger, …*happier*. Even that large hand of hers is more feminine. So much about her changes. Even her face."

"The question mark makes sense now, doesn't it?"

He lowered the book flat onto his lap, leaned back on the couch, and seemed to get lost in thought.

"You've caught things I've missed. That *lots* of people missed, Ron. How could that have been overlooked for so long?"

"I really don't know. Maybe for all sorts of reasons. Some people are colorblind; others are blind to certain types of illusions. I'm sure all the years I spent studying, creating, and meticulously breaking down images in Photoshop gave me an advantage to seeing it. We all see things differently," I said to Charles. "I know *that* from my experience with clients. Some focus on the whole picture, others on unnecessary details. And it's not like these illusions are easy to see. Hell, they look like they're designed not to be seen! Not only are they a trick to the eye, but they're hidden. *And* they have a secret viewing point."

"But why hidden?"

"I don't know." *But I needed to find out.*

"I have to admit," he said, shaking his head slightly. "I have no idea what they could symbolize."

"There's something else. *Two* things, actually."

"I'm still trying to wrap my head around what I've *already* seen."

"I've spent the past couple weeks reading Leonardo's writings. There's a passage that didn't seem like much at first. I'm sure no one thought much of it. But after stumbling upon *Mona Lisa*'s illusion, I was reminded of it. It mentions God and death and torment. It sounded kind of satanic. Not the kind of thing that's easy to forget."

"I'm listening."

"Experts said Leonardo never wrote a word about *Mona Lisa*. Maybe he never wrote about the image we see on the *surface*. But details in that piece of writing matched what I found in the painting—at least, when I looked at her from the angle Leonardo described: the *hidden* portrait in the secret, anamorphic illusion."

"He *described* what you found?"

"Not only that. You know the *Mona Lisa* name was given to the painting after Leonardo died. They've been trying to figure out who she is. But in that writing I mention, Leonardo *named* the woman in the painting."

I pulled out a copy of Leonardo's strange notebook entry and slid it across the coffee table to Charles.

> Envy must be represented with a **contemptuous motion of the hand towards heaven**, because if she could she would use her strength against God; **make her with her face covered by a mask of fair seeming**; show her as wounded in the eye by a palm branch and by an olive-branch, and wounded in the ear by laurel and myrtle, to signify that victory and truth are odious to her. Many thunderbolts should proceed from her to signify her evil speaking. **Let her be lean and haggard** because she is in perpetual torment. **Make her heart gnawed by a swelling serpent**, and make her with a quiver with tongues serving as arrows, because she often offends with it. Give her a leopard's skin, because **this creature kills the lion** out of envy and **by deceit**. Give her too a vase in her hand full of flowers and scorpions and toads and other venomous creatures; make her ride upon death, because Envy, never dying, never tires of ruling. **Make her bridle**, and load her with divers kinds of arms because all her weapons are deadly. Toleration. Intolerable. No sooner is Virtue born than Envy comes into the world to attack it; and sooner will there be a body without a shadow than Virtue without Envy (emphasis added).

"Or I should say," I continued, "that Leonardo named the woman hiding in the illusion. I highlighted parts of the description that seemed to match. Leonardo called her Envy."

11

Not Alone

I realized I had to make my discovery of *Envy* public. But I dreaded the idea. The thought of standing before a camera, answering whatever questions reporters would ask, brought back old memories of stage fright and humiliation.

I was once at a team event with ninety coworkers in which each of us had to read from a handout in front of the group. I grew nervous watching the microphone get closer as it was being passed around the conference hall. My heart began to race as I became flustered. When the microphone was finally handed to me, I lost all ability to make out the words on my printout. The letters had turned into meaningless shapes, scrambled chaotically in my mind as I failed to process them—the way a baby might look at them for the first time without knowing what they were. Just feeling the microphone's cold handle made me feel naked and nauseous in front of everyone. My throat clenched shut as my coworkers stared, and all I could do was to nervously pass the microphone on to the person next to me. My legs were so numb I had to look down to make sure I didn't wet myself.

But would things have gone differently if I had to speak about something I was truly passionate about? Something I didn't have to pretend to enjoy, such as team building events?

"Ron," Charles said, "You've discovered something really special. You've *got* to make this public."

I knew I would. Scholars would want—*need*—to know what I had found. It was new information about one of the greatest works of art ever created; the images visible from the new perspective Leonardo described could have some important connection to many of the *Mona Lisa* mysteries.

But I was out of my league. I was an artist. A good one. A successful one. I wasn't an art historian, or visual psychologist, or Renaissance scholar. I was someone who stumbled over something no one noticed before. Or had noticed but forgotten. Or concealed.

After watching Charles' reaction to the images he had seen from the new perspective, I knew they were really there.

But why were they there, Leonardo?

Why hide such *masterful* technical artistry, something with such subtle complexity?

I couldn't come up with a reason. I knew what I had uncovered needed to be shared with the public. But I wasn't the right person to do it.

"The camera *likes* you, Charles. Why couldn't you be the one to publicize my findings?"

"You made those discoveries, Ron. Not me."

"I've seen you speak in front of crowds. You seem to thrive off it."

"Look, I'm still not even sure if I really saw what you showed me. Only you can describe what you see. And it's no big thing to give a talk. Maybe you could do some kind of lecture."

"I'm not a speaker, Charles, and I can't entertain an audience."

"You had *me* enthralled."

"That's different."

"Is it?"

I was already beginning to regret what I had found. Working for ad agencies taught me long ago that well-received stories were few and far between. I watched enough public figures get trashed or outed. I've seen what negative publicity could do to a person. What I found was not something I expected others to take lightly. Added to my inexperience and fear of public speaking, the fact that I had never done a single newspaper interview made this a recipe for disaster. It would likely leave me looking like some kind of nutjob.

I had devoted my life to art. In return, it gave me everything—a life in which I was able to have a career I was passionate about. Would my reputation be worth the sacrifice?

"You know," Charles said, putting on his sport coat to leave, "back when I was teaching, my students discovered something tucked away in the public library. A box of letters George Custer wrote to an aunt here in Rochester." He placed the trilby back on his head. "The letters covered the weeks before he died, revealing major historical notes. I was interviewed about the discoveries. *Major* discoveries. It was published in an antique collectors journal. A *very* big deal." He paused, looking a little disappointed. "You know what I got out of it?"

I shook my head.

"Twenty newspaper copies. That was it."

I tried to paint that night.

Creating art always took me away from the problems in the real world. But I could barely find the strength to hold a brush, because deep down I knew if I didn't do something about the discoveries, I could never move on.

I decided to revisit everything I found, hoping it would lull me to sleep and also give me a better idea of what I should do. I even found Leonardo's puzzle pictographs that Charles had mentioned. There were two sheets I came across. Each showed lines of small drawings placed neatly in rows like words forming sentences. Each image of each line had to be said out loud in Leonardo's Italian language, then deciphered to sound out sentences.

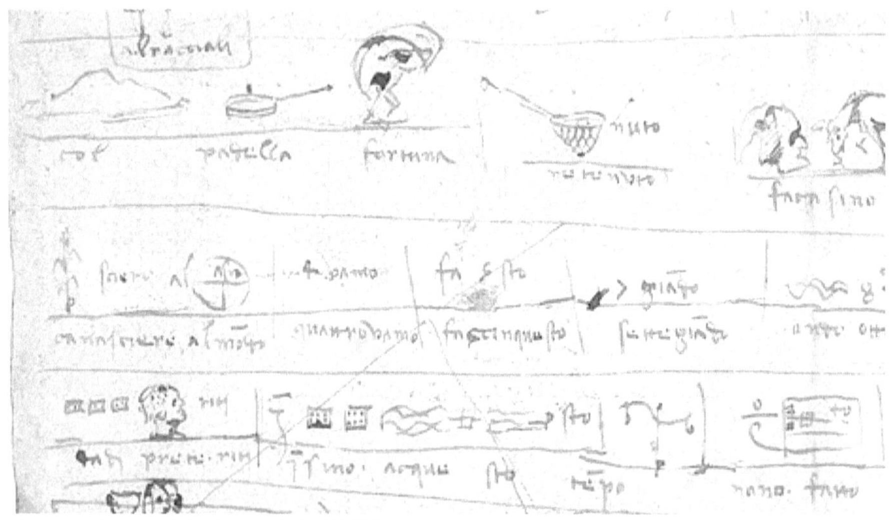

Section of Leonardo's pictograph (1487-90).

One line showed a picture of a *colle*, or hill, *patella*, a frying pan, and a figure with a clock over his face, representing "fortune." Read out loud, the phrase sounded out the words *col padella fortuna*, or *colpa della fortuna*, or "a stroke of luck."[1] *Exactly what I needed.*

But if I was going to get anywhere in finding a meaning to the animals, I would need more than luck. It would take determination and wit to figure out what the most brilliant genius of all time had been hiding in his art.

Applying the pictograph concept to the "lion head, ape head, buffalo head," I came up with *testa di leone, testa scimmia, testa di bufala.* But it didn't seem to mean anything. Neither did any other possible arrangement of words like *leone scimmia bufala* or *bufala scimmia leone.*

The sounds of the words meant nothing to me at all.

At least it helped convince me again that I wasn't just imagining the images I was finding—wouldn't I imagine hearing things also, like the sounds of words making sense when they really didn't?

But the information Charles gave me turned out to be useful. The pictographs showed that Leonardo *had* used pictures to represent words. Still no clue why they were there, but they *were* there. I had no doubt of that. Even if others would. There was too much to think about, and it left me a bit confused.

I was up late that night, pondering ideas as I examined Leonardo's art over and over, hoping something would come to me. Another clue. Another idea. A possible answer.

A new image did appear.

Although it was in a book of Leonardo's works, it was the first time the image of a whole animal revealed itself to me, rather than just the animal's head. From the anamorphic angle on the left, a horse showed itself. Head,

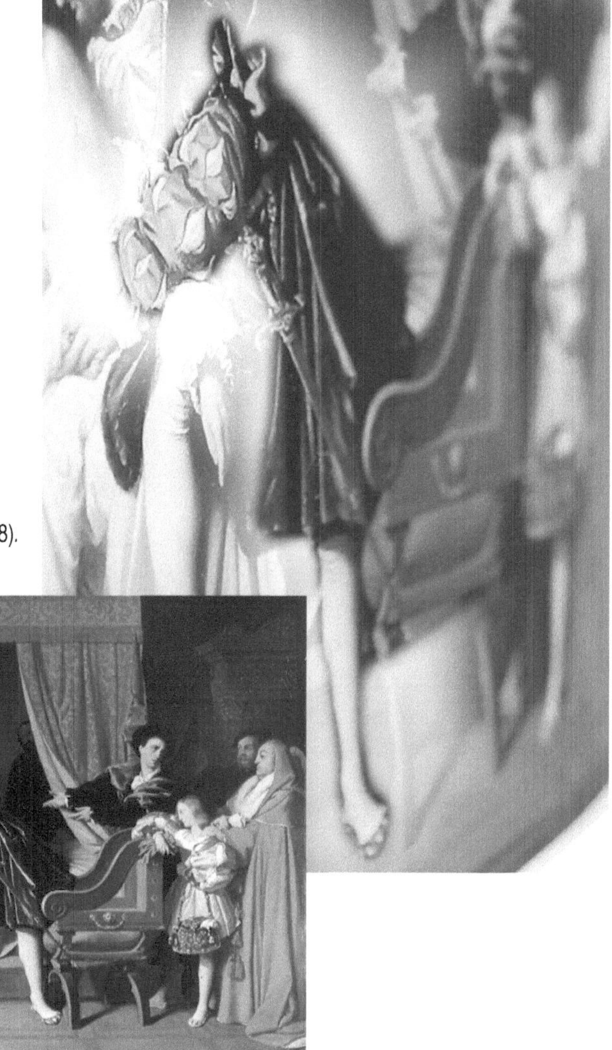

RIGHT: Anamorphic illusion of horse (highlighted) in *Death of Leonardo da Vinci* by Jean Auguste Dominique Ingres (1818). **BELOW:** Traditional view of art.

body, and all, from its muzzle to its skirt.

The painting was called *The Death of Leonardo da Vinci.* Because I'd been so absorbed in what I had found throughout Leonardo's art, I hadn't considered if other artists hid anything. The problem appeared when I remembered that *The Death of Leonardo da Vinci* was painted by French artist Jean Auguste Dominique Ingres.

Not Leonardo da Vinci.

12

Invidia

From that point on, my pastime consisted of searching through images from the Renaissance, using Leonardo's instructions from *The d-Point* and *Point-of-Sight*. In the living room around me rested images I had carefully cut out and pages I had neatly torn from their bindings. They covered the rug where I sat, the coffee table next to me, and the seats of the couch. Colored page markers peeked from the books like confetti, each one indicating a newly discovered illusion.

Countless illusions of animals were hiding everywhere. The hours I spent searching added up to days; the days to weeks. During the month of October 2011, sleep and my day job felt like interruptions. But even at work, I searched images online when no one was around to see.

However, the habit didn't last long. I found I could only look at the images in the privacy of my own home, where I didn't feel so paranoid about anyone else learning what I had found. I had a strong urge to keep it all secret, at least until I could figure out what the images meant. Although I had no idea why they were there, my intuition told me there was something special about them. And I wanted the chance to first figure them out on my own.

I spent extra time hunting through more popular works of art, centering myself in front as I rotated pictures of the paintings and checked from all four sides for any ambiguous images—ones like *Mona Lisa*'s mountains that looked like animals when they were rotated.

As for any hidden anamorphic objects, I checked those from the left side as per Leonardo's instructions, making sure to level my eyes at the height of the horizon whenever possible.

One well-known painting, Titian's *Venus of Urbino,* showed no horizon, but through a window in the background a sky could be seen, so I guesstimated the horizon's position to be just below the window frame.

From there, under the main nude figure, in the folds of the bed sheet, a crocodile head appeared. Its long jaws with teeth formed by smaller wrinkles created a head as large as the reclined figure. A flower falls from her hand to form the eye. I wasn't sure how I didn't notice it when looking directly at the art, because once I saw it from the d-point, I was able to easily see it when I looked away from the d-point and directly at the art, just as I had been looking at it all my life.

One great thing about seeing the secret images was that it felt like I was looking at every art piece for the first time, as if I had been blind up until then, and was now able to awe over the art like never before. The downside was that I would never see the art the same way again.

But nothing could have stopped me from searching for more.

In Titian's *Pastoral Concert*, I spotted the heads of an elephant and ape in the trees, a crocodile in the grass, and a lion in the folds of the central figure's red garment. Its tongue sticks out mockingly, as a child's would. But I wondered why Titian's animals could be seen straight on when the painting was upright, without having to turn the painting around or use any special anamorphic angles? The elephant and ape head in the trees had to be studied intently to realize they were there, made from the shadows and shapes of the leaves. It seemed so obvious once I saw them, so I wondered how I missed them up until that point.

I couldn't help but notice that each artist's illusions had a personal style to them, just as their art did. In a way, it gave the art a unique signature. Titian's animals had a slight comedic quality to them, while Leonardo's looked darker and more mysterious.

Nevertheless, if the images were supposed to be secret, as it seemed, why did Titian not turn them on their sides? Was he so confident viewers would miss them? That observers would be too distracted by the painting's main content that they'd look past what was hiding in plain sight? Or were they not supposed to be so secretive? I wasn't sure, but I wanted to know.

I continued on to Raphael's work. In his *La Velata*, a wrinkled-looking pig's head is concealed inside the folds of the woman's sleeve. She had been the artist's mistress, so I wondered if Raphael was implying what I thought he was by placing the pig there, since she also seemed to be pointing at herself.

But then in another portrait of his mistress—*La Fornarina*—there was a horse head. Its eye is formed from her belly button. The shape of its ears are suggested from the shape of her hand, which holds her breast.

In *St. Jerome*, by Sandro Botticelli, the scene's rocky landscape forms the profile of a large human head when viewed straight on.

His *Birth of Venus* shows anamorphic images of two human-like heads—the view as if behind them and looking over their shoulders. A male on the left. And a green-skinned female on the right. Both are almost as tall as the figure of Venus.

Some illusions appeared so clearly that I wondered how amazing they would look in real life.

I had only searched a small fraction of Renaissance art, yet I had found so much. I couldn't fathom the amount of illusions that must have existed. It was as though the most brilliant artists to have ever lived were in cahoots, and now I was in on the secret.

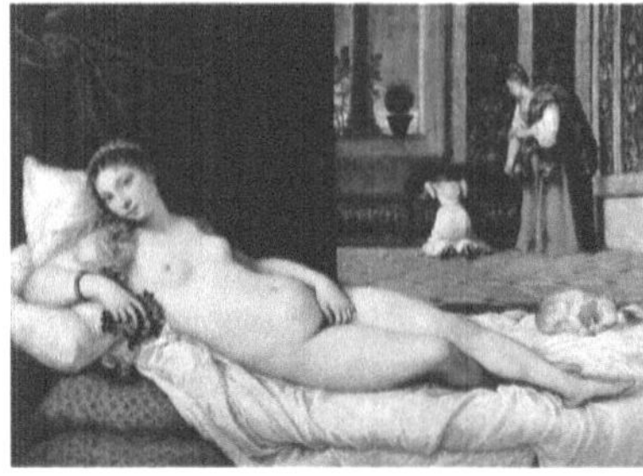

LEFT: Traditional view of Titian's *Venus of Urbino* (1534). **MIDDLE:** Anamorphic view of crocodile (highlighted). **BOTTOM:** *Clockwise from left*—the (highlighted) heads of a lion, elephant, ape, and crocodile in Titian's *Pastoral Concert* (c. 1509).

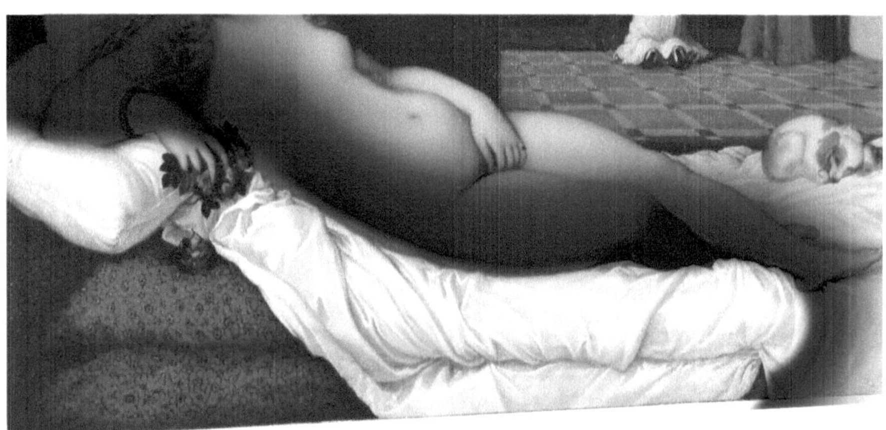

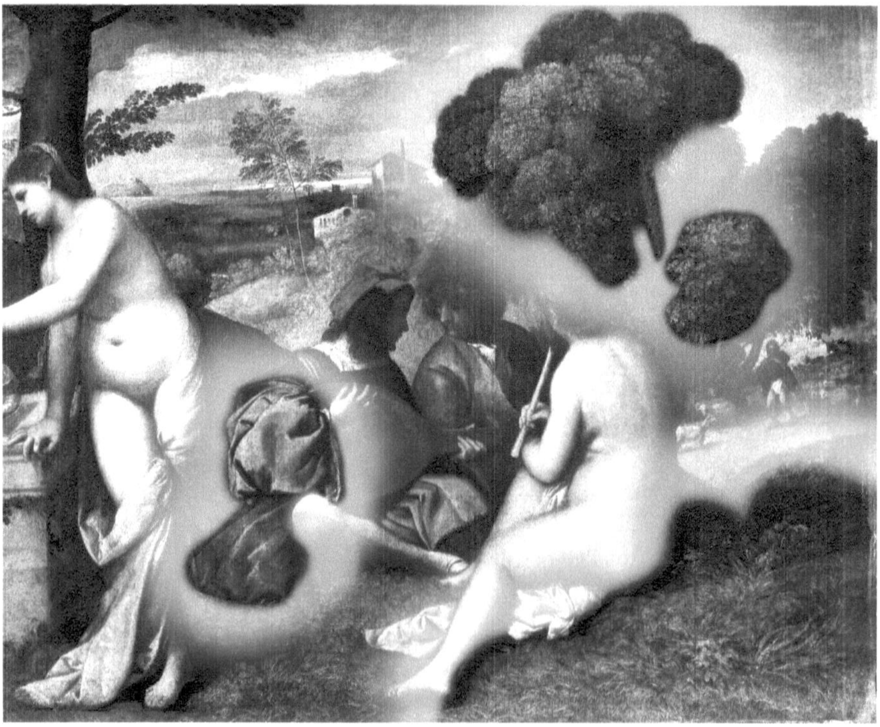

One painting threw me off. It was *The Battle of Alexander at Issus* by Albrecht Altdorfer, portraying a scene from 333 BCE. In the clouds of the painted sky, a large skull can be seen from the anamorphic angle, which immediately made me think of the impossible-to-miss skull in Holbein's *Ambassadors.*

It also made me think that sometimes images did really appear in clouds.

And like Holbein, Altdorfer was German.

Initially, I thought the illusions were limited to Leonardo's art. Until I saw that other artists hid them—including artists from non-Italian origins. When I spotted the horse in *The Death of Leonardo da Vinci* by French artist Jean

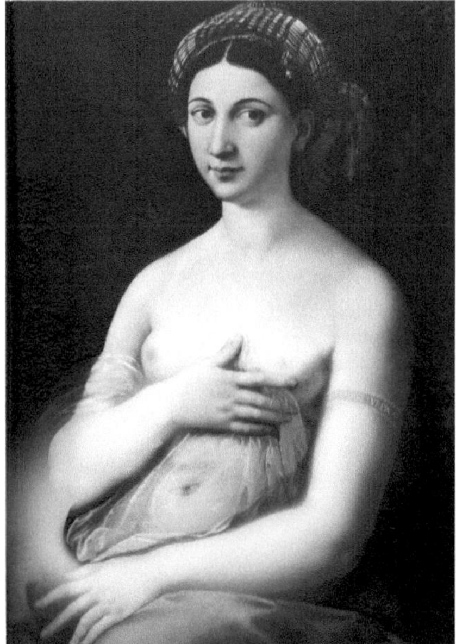

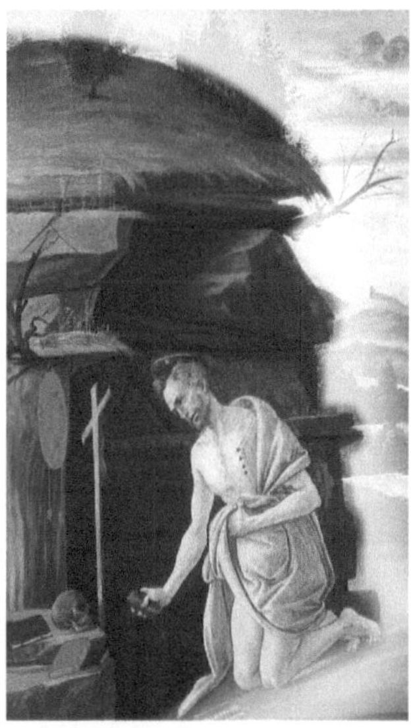

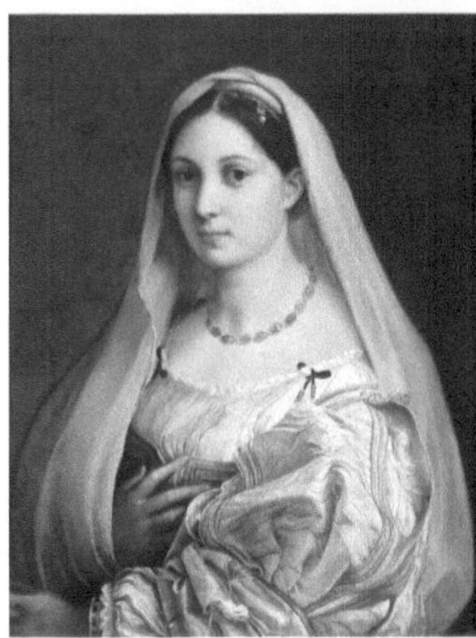

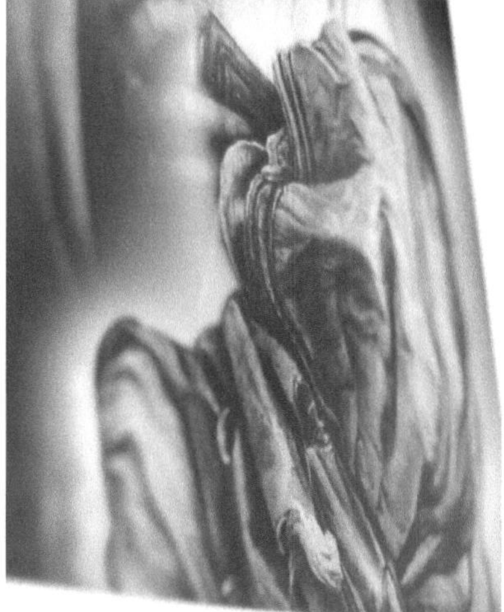

TOP: Horse head (highlighted) in Raphael's *La Fornarina* (1518-19). Human head (highlighted) in Botticelli's *St. Jerome* (1498-1505). **BOTTOM:** Traditional view of Raphael's *Woman with the Veil* (1514-15), and section showing anamorphic view of boar head (highlighted).

Auguste Dominique Ingres, I realized artists from other countries were part of this puzzle. But seeing that two German artists each hid an anamorphic skull in their art told me that there had to be some specific meaning to the images. I knew a depiction of a skull wasn't the strangest thing. But it still felt very suspicious. Any possibility the hidden images were chosen at random began to disappear from my thoughts.

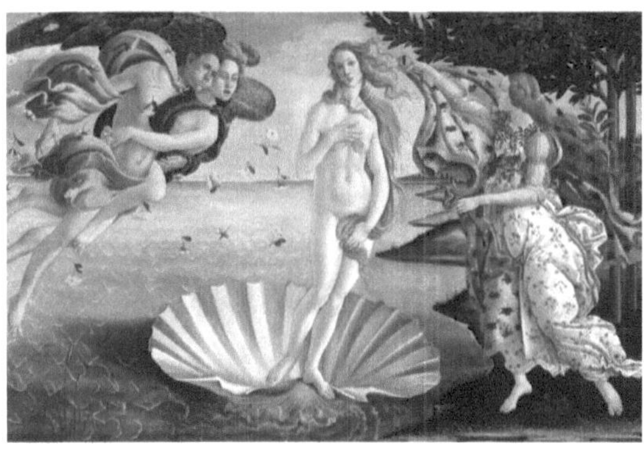

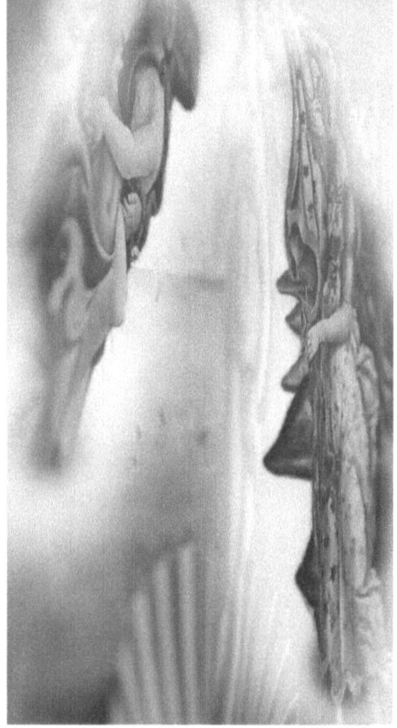

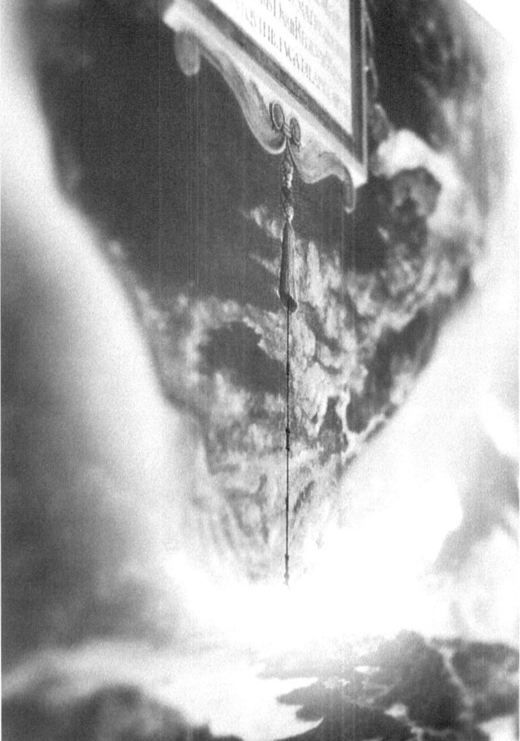

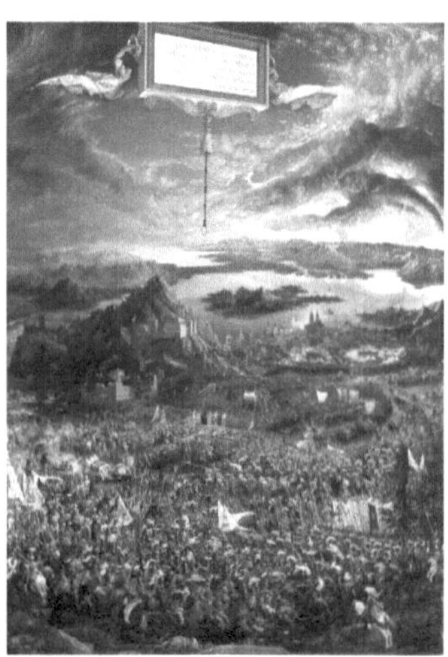

TOP: Traditional view of Botticelli's *Birth of Venus* (c. 1484-1486), and anamorphic view of hidden faces. **BOTTOM:** Anamorphic view of large skull (highlighted) hidden in Altdorfer's *Battle of Alexander at Issus* (1529), on right.

More strange was the pattern of numbers I also began to notice. The *333* BC Battle of Issus. Holbein's *Ambassadors*, painted in 15*33*. *The Death of Leonardo da Vinci*, painted *300* years after Leonardo's passing. Even *Mona Lisa* seemed to like the number 3: she was *30* inches tall, and it's believed that Leonardo started painting her around 15*03*. What was believed to be a self-portrait that Leonardo created in red chalk was 33.3 centimeters tall. I thought maybe I was looking too deep into everything, but even in his will, Leonardo requested "three high masses" and "thirty low masses," followed by "three masses."

What was so special about the number 3?

Though I didn't have an answer, I kept those numbers in the back of my mind.

The more I found, the more baffled I became.

If Ingres got his idea from seeing *The Ambassadors*, why did he use a horse? And why hide the image?

That made me think—*believe*—that Ingres knew about the secret images from the Renaissance. But what connection was there between the German artists, Italian artists, and Ingres, a Frenchman?

I used to study the shapes of passing clouds in my childhood, imagining creatures such as dragons or dinosaurs. On cloudless days, I would look to the thickly grouped leaves of trees. I was even able to use the irregular patterns of wood grain from the wall panels of my parents' house whenever I napped on the couch. My ability to imagine objects got stronger the more I used it.

But I always knew it was just my imagination. There was never any confusion about it.

The images I found in the paintings and drawings were different. They felt real. They were real. I was sure of it. Despite my bewilderment of their unknown meanings, there was a consistency to them. The regulars seemed to be the lions, the apes, the horses, and the crocodiles.

Those animals had no special meaning to me. Seeing them in places like zoos never left much of an impression. No traumatic experience in my life ever involved those animals. So there was no reason I would be imagining them. I considered the possibility that I was using the paintings to replace the clouds from my childhood as a gateway to my imagination, through some psychology I couldn't explain. But that just sounded silly. Plus, Leonardo described the animals in his *Animalia* passage.

It didn't take long for me to develop an eye for spotting the images, so I went back and rechecked and restudied everything from the beginning, knowing I might have missed some.

I was right. Something I didn't previously see appeared in Leonardo's version of *The Last Supper*, a scene of Christ and His Twelve Apostles, painted on the wall of the Santa Maria delle Grazie in Milan.

From the very left, in the wrinkles of Bartholomew's robe, I caught the features of what could be the face of an ape, or maybe it was that of a horse if I were correctly seeing two ears that seemed visible.

There's also the face of a lion. Third from the left, the apostle Andrew, looking surprised, raises both hands to form the cat's mane. Peter, seated fourth, holds a knife that creates the split of its jaws.

At the other end of the table a horned bull's head was hiding. Next to it was a fourth animal, but I couldn't tell whether it was a horse because it seemed to have a sort of silly expression more characteristic of a mule.

In all my previous findings, the animals I spotted came across very clearly. But I could barely discern the animals in *The Last Supper*. It made sense why I missed them the first time. I couldn't tell if it also had to do with the illusion itself or the deterioration of the painting—which began chipping off a few years after Leonardo applied the paint.

He used an experimental technique so he could rework the art at his leisure instead of restricting his painting time to a day or two per section: the short amount of time fresco allowed after it was applied. Not having the freedom to later rework imperfections probably didn't appeal to the artist who spent years on the much smaller *Mona Lisa.* His technique failed, and restorations were done in later years. I despised the idea of art restorations. Hearing about them left me feeling like someone needed to be punished for the crime. Restorations were no more than an accepted form of vandalism because at times it involved repainting the original work by someone other than the original artist. Even if they made an art piece *look* as it originally did, painting over the original artist's work technically was the process of covering up the original artist's creation.

A friend once asked me why I had such a problem with that.

"This obviously never happened," I told him over beers, "but if Michelangelo restored a damaged Picasso by repainting over it, and he did it perfectly, would it still be a Picasso?"

I said, of course, that the scenario "was impossible, since Michelangelo was long dead before Picasso was even born." But I wouldn't consider it a true Picasso. Maybe I'd consider it a Picasso vandalized by Michelangelo. Or a replica of the original artist's work.

In the case of Leonardo's *Last Supper,* I wondered if the faded illusions I almost missed were a result of the botched restorations, which basically amounted to other artists repainting over the flaking art. In one of the restorations, the wrong kind of paint was mistakenly used. The next restorer that came along stripped off the paint and repainted over it again. More restorations later followed. So little is left of Leonardo's original that some considered *The Last Supper* more of a full-size reproduction of what Leonardo left behind rather than his own original work.

I considered it the world's most expensive "paint by number."

Experts later realized that inexperienced restorers had altered some of the faces of the apostles. If that was true, then how altered were the unknown illusions that I almost missed seeing?

I was confident restorers had no idea what was hiding there, even as they stood inches away, brushing their own paint layers over it.

But probably by the same miracle, during World War II (when the church was bombed and that painted wall was still left standing), traces of the illusions remained. Luckily, I was able to make what looked like a connection between the unidentified figure in *Mona Lisa* and that church wall. Both paintings showed an ape and lion—if the one in *The Last Supper* was an ape and not a horse. *Mona Lisa* has a buffalo whereas *The Last Supper* shows a bull. But Leonardo categorized the buffalo and bull together in *Animalia*.

Oddly, the animal heads in *The Last Supper* seemed to be positioned as main courses of food. I had to wonder what that was all about.

If they existed in an obvious painting of Christ, did it mean *Mona Lisa* had some religious significance? Before art historians believed she was Lisa Gherardini, some thought the figure represented the Virgin Mary.

I wasn't sure what to think just yet. But I took a moment to lean back and cross my arms as I sometimes did when contemplating an idea or realization. I didn't know why I had a sudden warm feeling at the thought of her being some divine figure since I didn't believe in that stuff.

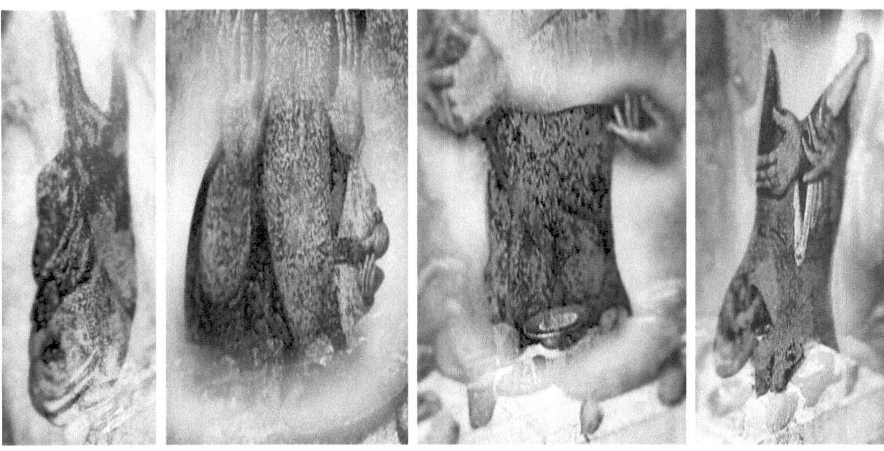

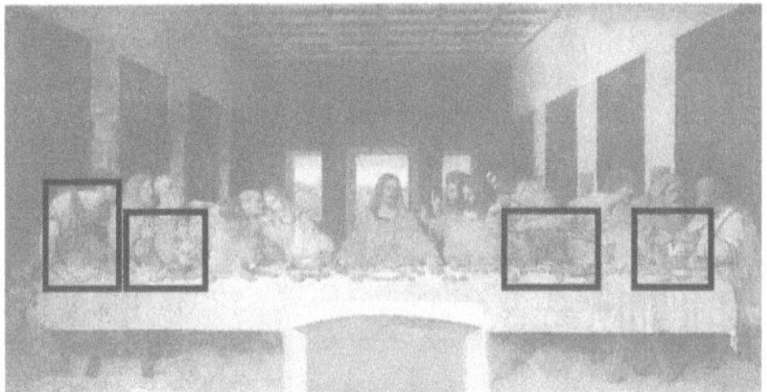

ABOVE: Anamorphic view of what looks like a horse head, lion head, bull head, and what looks like the head of a mule (all highlighted) in Leonardo's *The Last Supper.* **LEFT:** Key to location of images.

I continued looking where I left off—going into other periods of art.

With some of the heavier books, rather than holding them up vertically as I liked, I laid them on the table, having to hunch over and bend my neck, squinting for long periods of time until I had to straighten myself up again as soreness crept into my neck and back and eyes. It reminded me of what Michelangelo must have felt as he crooked his head upward during those years he worked on the ceiling of the Sistine Chapel.

I knew of the many illusions later created by Salvador Dali, such as the double image that showed a face from a distance, but up close, depicted a different scene altogether. They were intended to be looked at like Giuseppe Arcimboldo's in-your-face double imagery portraits: no special viewing angle needed. The focus of his art were the illusions themselves, which he made in the sixteenth century. Dali's illusions were also out in the open, meant to be seen.

To the contrary, the optical illusions remained hidden in the Renaissance period, until Holbein was the first to present his skull in full view. I decided to concentrate my focus around the time Leonardo lived and the years before—the Middle Ages—since Giotto had hidden the devil's face that art restorers had found in one of his frescos.

In fact, I thought to return to Giotto to learn more about him. There had to be some connection between Giotto and Leonardo, who were both Florentines, even though Giotto lived more than 100 years before. If there was a connection between the devil face and animal heads, I wasn't seeing it. At least, not until I came across some frescos Giotto painted.

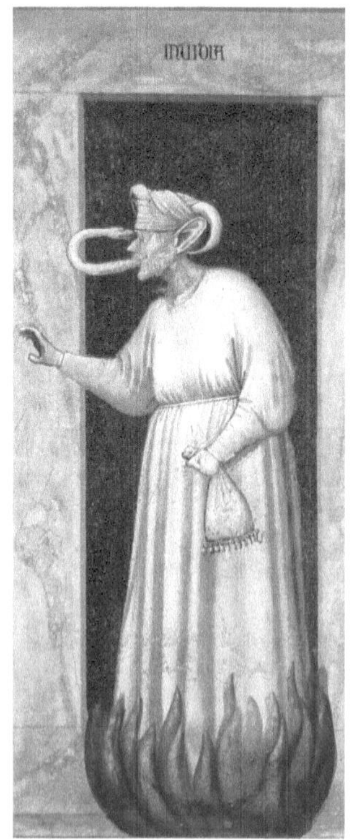
Giotto, *Invidia* (c. 1306).

In Padua, Italy, on the south wall of the Scrovegni Chapel, Giotto portrayed each of the seven virtues. On the north wall, he placed their corresponding vices, better known as the seven deadly sins. One of Giotto's figures depicts an old, monstrous woman in profile. Her ears are large and elongated like that of a gargoyle, with sharp horns curling downward. A snake slides outward from her mouth and curls back around to meet her face, eye to eye. Above her, in capital letters, is the Italian word *INVIDIA.*

Leonardo had used the same word in his passage to describe *Mona Lisa*. Translated into English, *Invidia* is the word for *Envy.*

13

The Art Museum

Charles recommended contacting one art museum in the city that could help, but I was hesitant. It was difficult enough to tell Charles my secrets. And he was someone I had known and trusted for years. They were the only art museum in the city I thought could help, but I knew nobody associated to that museum, and I didn't know if I could trust anyone there with my secrets before publicizing them. If I showed them what I had discovered, would they claim the findings as their own and deny my part in them? Would they be any help in figuring out what it all meant? Would they even take anything I had to say seriously?

I wasn't sure why I found it hard to trust people, but I had always been suspicious of everyone's intent. Maybe it traced back to that childhood Christmas when Papa warned me to hide upstairs so Santa could drop off presents. Wondering why *he* didn't have to hide, I snuck back downstairs to catch Papa placing a present at the tree. From that point, not only didn't I believe there was a Santa, but I also started to pick apart everyone's words for hidden lies. Maybe it was a few years later when an older kid from up the street convinced me to trade my old Star Wars comics for his box of baseball cards, just before his family moved. A friend of mine later explained how valuable Star Wars comics had become and how worthless my box of cards were. Maybe my distrust for others came in high school: I came back from the bathroom and saw that someone had gone through my belongings and taped to the lunchroom wall drawings I had made of women posed in nightgowns. (I didn't draw them completely nude since the comic books I read avoided nudity.) My high school class applauded mockingly as I made my way back to my seat. I knew it was my friend Jason who had done it since he was laughing and clapping louder than anyone else.

So it was going to be difficult for me to trust the art museum. All I thought of was how they would take advantage of me once I revealed to them what I had found. I was confident that any new information on *Mona Lisa* would get a lot of attention, but I didn't think anyone would believe that some unknown artist had found it.

Still, I had no choice—if I was going to figure out why the illusions were there, I needed to seek help publicizing my findings.

I had three objectives. The first was to get official verification that the images existed, even though I was already sure they were real. Verifying what I found would add a sense of credibility and set my second goal into effect. That goal was to publicize the new clues—if that's what they were. I was hoping the publicity would trigger a chain reaction of art historians and other experts to gather and provide detailed knowledge of the illusions and why animals were being represented.

The third goal was to have my name placed at the center of it all. I felt that might open up more doors for me in the art world. To where? I wasn't sure. But I knew that I loved painting more than anything. And a chance at my own exhibit one day at the MoMA or The Guggenheim—regardless of how unlikely my chances were—was worth a shot. There was also the possibility of working a number of jobs in the art world I otherwise would never be given the chance to do. In other words, it could provide better opportunities for me as an artist.

Although it would never be good enough for me to simply guess the meaning of the animals without finding concrete proof of their significance, I took stabs at it.

The lion had a reputation of being powerful and brave. But I once watched a documentary in which a threatened buffalo used its horns to tear a lioness apart as it tossed her up in the air over and over again like a weightless mass of meat. I didn't remember ever seeing either animal interact with horses—which were mostly used for transportation, racing, and farm work. I thought specifically of warfare since Leonardo had sketched soldiers riding horses in combat. None of the images I found resembled zebras, so I didn't believe that species had any specific connection to their meanings. As for apes, they were always compared to human beings in reference to evolution.

The crocodile felt more important somehow—it had to represent some kind of devil since the *Envy* passage described the "creature" as a "swelling serpent."

I purchased *The Penguin Dictionary of Symbols* for help, but each creature had a number of possible meanings. It didn't give me the bulletproof explanations I needed, but it did give me some ideas. A lion generally symbolized a positive trait such as justice, divine energy, that it was a destroyer of evil and ignorance. It could also symbolize resurrection.

A roaring lion was something completely different. With jaws spread open, it could be similar to Underworld deities such as the crocodile. *Mona Lisa* showed a roaring lion, but not all of the paintings did. And what did it mean anyway if it did? The problem was that some lions I found were roaring and some were not. Some were placed in religious paintings and others were not. There was no consistent context to pull answers from.

The entry for *Serpent* ran fourteen entire pages of various meanings, explaining how it could symbolize anything from Satan to one's libido.

It only complicated things since multiple creatures were placed within the same artworks, therefore multiplying the combinations of meanings to consider.

Plus, different combinations of animals were used throughout.

Most were just the *heads* of animals. A *head* had its own meaning. Context also determined symbolic definitions. Many of the meanings seemed plausible, but none jumped out at me. It felt impossible that I would ever pinpoint it with certainty.

Crocodiles had numerous meanings also. Regarded as a "negative symbol," the crocodile controlled "forces of death and rebirth" or it could be "lord of the Underworld." Just two of many meanings. Interestingly, "the connection of crocodiles and jaws is associated throughout the world with their role in initiation."

Death and rebirth? Initiation?

"In Ancient Egyptian mythology," *The Dictionary of Symbols* explains, "the crocodile Sobek … was called 'the Devourer.' [Sobek] would swallow the souls who were unable to plead their cause and who would become mere excrement in his bowels."[1]

The book seemed to hold some sort of answers, but there were too many possible meanings. With so many contexts to choose from, it was difficult to pinpoint.

I knew I wouldn't be satisfied without an unquestionable explanation that fit perfectly, like a missing puzzle piece. But it was all as vague as *Mona Lisa* herself.

And wasn't it possible that Leonardo meant something completely unique? Something no one had thought of or written about?

I was more lost than when I started.

I had visited the local art museum many times, always pausing at the Monet and Cassat that hung on the walls. But the painting I always spent the most time with was *The Fox and the Heron* by Frans Snyders, a Flemish painter who created the art around 1630-40. It illustrates the fable of a Fox who invites a friend, the Heron, over for dinner. The Fox serves soup, which the Fox could easily consume, as a dog can with liquid, but the long-beaked Heron could not. So when the Heron later had the Fox over for dinner, it was served in a long-necked jar with an opening too small for the Fox to reach inside, but was no problem for the Heron.

It was with seeing that painting for the first time years before that I realized art was not only about appearance, but the story that pulls a person in, making it memorable.

What I would learn years later was that animal fables—like the one in Snyder's painting—originated with Aesop, a Greek slave who lived around 620 BCE to 564 BCE. His stories consisted of animals with human traits that presented a moral to be learned. "In Greece, during the epoch of the Tyrants, when free speech was dangerous, the Fable was largely used for political purposes."[2]

I'd also learn that Leonardo had a book on Aesop in his possession.

On my visit to the art museum the day before calling them, I stopped at a painting by Jean Auguste Dominique Ingres, who had also painted *The Death of Leonardo da Vinci.* I didn't spot anything out of the ordinary, but, of course, I wasn't able to take the item off the wall in order to rotate it and check all its sides.

I asked for the curator when I finally called. The curator, who sometimes selects the art pieces to display, was the only position I knew a bit about. I was hoping she would know of an art historian or some kind of symbolism expert with whom I could connect.

I introduced myself on the phone to the curator, a nice-sounding lady, and said that I wanted to talk about a discovery I made.

"You may want to talk to our director," she told me. "He can help you more than I."

"What did you discover?" I waited for her to ask, with some excitement. Surely anyone working at an art museum would be interested to know, I figured.

She wasn't.

"Do you want to know what I found?" I asked.

"That's okay," she said, sounding more interested in being left alone. "I'm in the middle of a project …with only a few seconds to spare."

So I called the museum director after she gave me his direct line. He didn't pick up, so I left a message mentioning a "small discovery" I wanted to discuss. I wanted it to sound less important than it was, realizing how crazy the message might otherwise seem.

He called me back minutes later with a cheery voice. "How can I assist you?"

Unsure how to explain myself without sounding like a nut, I told him I uncovered something and needed his help.

"What is it? You find a Van Gogh or something?"

I faked a polite chuckle. "No, nothing like that," I said.

"What's your discovery, then?"

"I sort of have to show you," I said, and asked if he had time to meet. I was sure he would understand once I showed him.

"My schedule's kind of full right now," he said with a less cheerful tone.

"It would be worth your while."

"How so?"

"It has to do with Renaissance art. And your museum has a few Renaissance paintings." On my visit the day before, I examined them. I couldn't get too close because of the guard that hovered there, but I had a good enough view. It was the first time I had real live paintings instead of just a picture from a book. One was of a Madonna and Child, and the other, a painting of St. Paul. I felt the hairs on my arms and neck rise as I positioned myself to their left.

There was no question of the horse head illusion that appeared in one and the group of faces in the other.

"What did you say you do again?" the director asked.

"I'm a graphic designer. …and painter."

He wasn't just *asking* a question. He was questioning me.

"Well, I have a meeting to run to," he said. "Why don't I call you this afternoon and we could chat more about this?"

Two days passed without a call, so I left him a message.

A few days later, I left another message, but I never heard from him again.

It wasn't like me to give up so easily. But because I never had a good feeling about contacting them to begin with, I looked at it as a sign. And I knew I was avoiding the inevitable: that I would have to publicize what I found on my own. Without anyone's help. Even so, I couldn't help but wonder if the reaction I got was something I would have to get used to. It wasn't a surprise, but it still left me disappointed.

What could I have expected? I wouldn't have returned my calls either. I had made as prestigious a find as I could ever make. But how could I, or anyone, explain the hidden animal heads and optical illusions in *Mona Lisa* without sounding a little nuts?

Through the years, *Mona Lisa* had the effect of the full moon. It attracted so many silly attempts from those claiming to be able to explain her mysteries. Art historians were probably overwhelmed with emails and letters from those offering new ideas about her mysteries, some who likely considered their theories to be "groundbreaking information" on the world's most famous painting. Even credible academic sources occasionally presented their own theories, which sometimes sounded just as foolish.

Too many theories had developed over time. Of all the ones I'd heard or read, none were convincing enough. The media would report these stories purely for entertainment value, but the art community seemed to have heard enough speculation about *Mona Lisa* long before. If academic sources like college professors weren't being taken seriously for their theories, what chance did I have as an artist?

Then again, they only had theories.

I had proof.

14

The Advice

I went to go see an old boss of mine for some advice.

Saul had a successful career in advertising and owned an agency I once worked for. His specialty was public relations. And I needed to know how to go about publicizing what I had found. I thought publicity would cause someone who might know the meanings of the hidden illusions to come forward.

Saul agreed to meet me one night after work. He answered the door dressed in a tuxedo as if just returning from a gala. He pulled off his bow tie and welcomed me in. Accentuated by a goatee and slick black hair, there was never anything other than a smile on his face. He always looked ready to tackle the day.

His wisdom tended to be a little philosophical. "Likability is just as important as talent and passion," he once told me. "You have to be someone others *want* to work with."

In my early twenties, my art appreciation for the comics I read and drew inspiration from turned into a passion for graphic design. I found myself examining advertisements, noticing how movie posters could move me, and I would see and feel the beauty in a good-looking letterhead. I was so focused on my art that I didn't even start dating until after I graduated. In fact, I didn't have a girlfriend until I was twenty-two.

The decision to give up my dream of illustrating comics, and instead become a graphic designer, came after I submitted some sketches to both Marvel Comics and DC Comics. Each sent me a rejection letter. The content of those letters determined the direction I took in life; they were the most fascinating letters I had ever received. One letterhead showed Superman, Flash, Batman, and other superheroes standing on each other's shoulders to form a totem pole. The art filled the height of the paper. It took me a minute to realize that holding the paper to the light revealed that the DC Comics logo from one side of the paper fit perfectly in Wonder Woman's outstretched hands on the paper's opposite side. The images on both sides came together to create the illusion that she was holding it high above her head as she stood at the peak of the totem pole.

The Marvel Comics letterhead was much simpler—a large Spider-Man about to swing off the page—but just as impactful.

Visual design was a language I understood intuitively. I realized that was my calling. It was Saul's advice that helped me stand out in future job interviews. I acted cheery, concentrating on being friendly with potential bosses instead of trying to impress them. I lacked the confidence to talk about myself because I didn't think I was impressive in any way, which usually lead me to fumble over my own words.

I was in my early thirties when Saul's agency hired me, but I struggled to fight through the intimidation I felt from those around me. Everyone seemed so pleasant. At the time, I was trying to ground myself, while seeking some sort of happiness. My marriage had recently ended, which left me heartbroken and full of resentment. I didn't relate to happy people the way I could to art. Around others, I felt almost alien. I only pretended to be cheerful, donning a fake smile in an attempt to fit in.

It took me a long time to get used to working in such a friendly workplace. I would wander the building, fearing that coworkers would see right through my fake cheerfulness. I took precautions to avoid Saul by choosing longer routes instead of passing by his office whenever I had to deliver printed art pages to my account executive. Office politics was my kryptonite. But when left alone to create, I was usually beaming on the inside.

The challenge in developing art in such a demanding industry satisfied me. It forced me to create my best work. The pressure I hated from that fast-paced world actually gave me a high that I oddly craved. And it also helped to keep my mind off my outside life after my divorce.

My experience at the agency played a big part in my professional development.

Eventually, I was laid off with a bunch of other employees from different accounts. The client offered me a job to work for them directly, but five years at the agency without making time for a social life had left me feeling burnt out. I needed something new.

Years later, as I began making those Renaissance discoveries, that past life no longer seemed to matter.

A month passed since first seeing the images, and I was desperate for direction on publicizing what I had uncovered.

After Saul signed a non-disclosure agreement, I didn't waste much time in pulling out my art books to show him some of the illusions.

Eventually, I showed him the animal heads in *Mona Lisa*. And the anamorphic ones in *The Last Supper*.

Without moving his eyes from the picture of Christ and His disciples, Saul told me how he once stood in that monastery in Milan, looking up at that painting. That even in its poor condition, he had so much admiration for what Leonardo painted.

"You think that might be Mary Magdalene?" he asked casually. He was referring to the identity of the figure directly to the left of Christ. After Dan

Brown's *Da Vinci Code*, some believed the figure known as John the Apostle was actually Mary Magdalene. I hadn't read the book, or seen the movie, but I had read articles about it. I felt the question was somewhat patronizing, and I told him I wasn't sure what to believe.

Although he couldn't see some of the more complicated illusions I pointed out, like the ones in *The Last Supper*, Saul still understood the significance of what I had found.

I pulled out the *Envy* passage, explaining the matching descriptions to the details in *Mona Lisa*'s optical illusion. I tried to give him a strong sense of what I had discovered, so he would have a better idea on how I could go about publicizing the findings.

There were parts that still made no sense to me. And there were obvious references to the painting. But I didn't understand Envy's anger toward God. If *Mona Lisa* was Leonardo's *Envy*, I had to wonder if she portrayed a religious figure.

In the time since discovering the illusions, I learned what to look for in spotting them. The details were not always clear, but the animal heads were there. In *The Last Supper*, the hidden illusion was like bad reception on a television screen—blurred by static, yet it revealed enough for me to make out the images.

"No one knew about the optical illusions," I told Saul. "So restorers must have disfigured them. But they haven't disappeared completely."

"I can see some of the optical illusions you pointed out," Saul said.

Early in his career, Saul had been a creative director. He had the eye of an artist, which helped him to see some of the things I pointed out.

"Leonardo's idea about the d-point is intriguing," he said, "Why do *you* think they hid these?"

"I don't know. But if I could get the media to put this out there, the news might reach someone who can figure it out. I just didn't know where to start."

"What about the art museum?"

"I tried. They didn't seem to take me seriously."

"Have you tried presenting this to art historians?"

"I'm worried about them stealing credit for the discoveries. Who knows if I can trust them?"

"No, no, no," he said. "Present it publicly. You never meet the guy who wants to murder you in private. You meet in the public square, where everyone can see it happen. Then let the story fall where it will." He thought for a moment. "There are two stories here. First, *The d-Point*. And then the *Envy* passage. The media might only care about *Mona Lisa* and *Envy*. That's your lead story."

"Everyone will think I'm crazy," I said, saying it more to myself.

"It doesn't matter if they do think that, Ron," Saul said. "It's like you said to me—'The world needs to know about this.'"

15

Ginger

In October of 2011, shortly after talking with Saul, Ginger died.

It was after I took the dogs for a walk around the neighborhood, the fallen leaves crunching under our feet. At an empty baseball field, Ginger playfully chased Pinch.

I didn't have a care in the world at that moment as I enjoyed watching them play. When we got home, a confused look entered Ginger's eyes as she stood there resting, her tongue bouncing from her mouth after running around. She looked as if she had forgotten where she was. In a strange motion, she drooped down onto the grass, as if sedated. Something was wrong, so I hurried to get to her. She only moved her eyes as I slipped my hands through the sharp blades of grass under her to carry her limp body to the car, where I wrapped her in a blanket.

I put Pinch in the house and raced Ginger to the closest animal hospital. With one hand on the wheel and the other caressing her head, I told Ginger that everything would be okay. I was careful in passing through any red lights.

She swung her eyes to me, and an uncomfortable pain hit my gut. *Hurry,* her eyes seemed to beg.

I put more weight on the gas pedal as a sudden memory came of the first time I saw her, sitting there like an Egyptian sphinx in her cell-like room at the shelter. Dog howls echoed around us, but Ginger just looked at me quietly with curiosity. While I signed the adoption papers, I learned the previous owner had left her when she was only one, and I didn't know why. But I swore to Ginger that I'd never abandon her.

A few years before that, I had agreed to getting Pinch in order to please my then wife. But toward the end of my marriage, I felt unlovable and worthless, and Pinch was there whenever I wept in secret. I never expected her simple presence to ease my pain. But she became the one thing I was most determined to keep from my broken marriage.

After my divorce, I set out to "find myself." I bought a house where Pinch and I lived. I never realized how a pet could fill the void I felt. Two years later, I adopted Ginger so Pinch wouldn't be alone at home. My schedule at the agency was hectic. I didn't think I could care for another dog as much as I did for Pinch, who kept me feeling sane, and in a sense, alive, in the years after my divorce.

It was impossible not to love Ginger. She would curl up next to me on the couch and rest her head on my leg whenever I sat to watch a movie. I like that she made me feel needed.

I cared for my dogs more than I did for any human. And although I knew I would never abandon either of them, my love and care for them came in knowing that they would never abandon me.

I tried to control my emotions as I carried Ginger through the glass doors of the animal hospital, still wrapped in the blanket. Stringy saliva had formed at the corners of her mouth.

The veterinarians brought her to the back room for immediate testing as I sat in the waiting area.

After a while, Anny, the vet in charge of Ginger, recommended keeping her overnight while I waited at home. I hesitated, but wanted to cooperate, so I trudged back to my car, fighting the urge to turn around and head back to the building to wait there.

Still, it felt wrong to leave without Ginger.

Over the next two days, I visited before work and after. Anny allowed me to spend some time in the back room with Ginger. I knew how expensive it was to keep my dog there, but it didn't matter.

On the third night, Anny took me aside and shamefully admitted that they couldn't figure out why Ginger was extremely sick—and that blood had started to exit her rear end. When I pushed for an answer, Anny said Ginger might only last for three or four days. I felt my weight shift like I was going to fall, then it was as if a pallet of bricks had been lowered onto my chest.

"Can anything be done?" I begged.

She talked about "exploratory surgery," but it sounded to me like a shot in the dark, and no guarantee of helping. There was also the chance of Ginger not making it through the surgery at all.

I asked for a moment alone to think it over. Abby tended to the other animals. Ginger watched me sit down, cross-legged, on the hard linoleum floor in front of the open crate where she rested. IV tubing was taped to the lean muscles of one of her bony legs.

I wasn't sure why she began scratching at the crate's plastic floor in a sort of unsuccessful army crawl. She was obviously too weak to move, but then I realized, dumbfounded, what she was doing. She had turned herself just enough to face me, then was barely able to pull herself closer to me. It was just enough for her to rest her snout on my knee with the lightest touch, yet my emotions were crushed by its weight.

I petted her as everything became blurry through my tears.

I wanted nothing more than to just be near her.

As I contemplated the surgery, time was running out. The likelihood of Ginger dying during the procedure was something I couldn't bear. I would stand by my promise to never abandon her, or even let her *feel* that I deserted her. I was her best friend. Her master. Her family. If she were to pass, I wanted it to be in my arms, not on some cold, metal operating table, or in an animal hospital that was unable to help her. I wanted Ginger to feel that I would be there to comfort her until the very last moment. At least, I could provide her the comfort of her own house.

Against Anny's advice, I said I'd return in the morning to bring Ginger home. There was the feeling of vice grips tightening around my insides. I would have taken her home right then, but it was already late at night, and Ginger had IV needles connected to her leg.

Back home that night, I thought of how consumed I had been over the discoveries in the previous weeks, which gave me the sense that I had been neglecting Ginger. That I gave her barely any attention except to feed and occasionally walk her. The portrait of her I had started remained untouched since I saw the question mark in *Mona Lisa*.

Had it not been for Ginger's portrait, and comparing it to the upside-down *Mona Lisa*, I may not have uncovered anything at all. Would I have noticed a sign of Ginger's sickness earlier if my face were not buried in all those art books, obsessively searching for images of lions and apes and crocodiles and other animals?

The discoveries suddenly felt of no importance to my life. In fact, my resentment toward them increased throughout the night.

Unlike the animals in the paintings, I knew what Pinch and Ginger meant to me. They symbolized a loyalty I could never feel with any human. They represented the perfect trust. I would be there for them. And they would be there for me.

In my bedroom, I prepared a pile of blankets and pillows and all her toys. Then, for the first time in years, I knelt and prayed, hoping I had been wrong about God's existence, because I needed Him to be real, and to hear me begging for Ginger to get well. I swore to Him that I would never lose faith again if she regained her health.

With barely any sleep, I got up the next morning to go get her. As I left the house, the hospital called. I answered, expecting them to say that Ginger was ready to be picked up. Instead, a male vet on the other end said that Ginger was doing her "stretches."

"What do you mean?" I asked, frightened of whatever *stretches* meant.

"It's what they do just before passing on," he said.

My despair couldn't feel any different from *seppuku* as I leaned forward from the tightness in my stomach. Like the meat of it was being sliced open for my organs to slither out.

"I'm on my way," I managed to say, as if something could be done to make Ginger wait. I never looked at the speedometer on the way there. All I could picture was Ginger, struggling to hold on, waiting for me to get there so I could say goodbye.

Anny met me at the front counter. "I'm so sorry."

Ginger had died several minutes before I arrived.

She was placed in front of me on a table in a private room where I was left alone to tell her goodbye. The blanket I had carried her in days before was underneath her. I pushed a fist against my chest where agony overpowered me. I petted her lifeless body, placing my head on her chest, and began to cry like a little boy. The vets still didn't know what had made her so sick. But a part of me died with her. And the mystery of her death would haunt me forever.

I didn't care about *Mona Lisa* after Ginger died.

At work, I pushed through jobs with only the intent of getting them done quickly. Motivation had seeped from my soul.

At home, I moped. I tried to paint, attempting to ignore my sadness, but holding the paint brush felt different, useless. So I spent a lot of my time sitting on the couch, watching movies, mostly just staring past the screen.

The discoveries fell away from my mind. At the same time, I couldn't completely forget them—as much as I tried. At times I became upset about the precious time I should have spent with Ginger instead of Leonardo's art.

I thought of how short Ginger's life had been. That thought mixed with the memory I had of witnessing the horrible death of a coworker many years before, which got me thinking about my own life. If I were to suddenly die, what contribution would I leave behind? Did I make any kind of difference in the world?

And would I regret anything?

I hated that last question because the answer was obvious.

Slowly, the itch came back. I realized it was inevitable. I'd open up one of my art books, barely glancing at a page before closing it again. Each day, the books seemed to stay open for a longer period. My glances became scans. The scans turned to close examinations. Examinations triggered contemplations. With each day, the need to reveal what I had discovered grew stronger.

After staring at my computer one morning, I emailed a short message to a public relations professional Saul had recommended. With the path I felt I was about to choose, I was going to need a public relations rep. Still, the simple thought of potential news interviews filled me with stage fright.

16

Kristine

The PR rep's name was Kristine. After a phone conversation, she invited me over to her house to talk further.

We sat across from each other at the kitchen table. Kristine pushed aside a vase of black-eyed Susans and baby's breath. The arrangement reminded me of Sandro Botticelli's *Primavera* painting, known for the many flowers illustrated in the art, and also showing one of the figures gathering them.

"How are you in front of a camera?" Kristine asked.

The distorted look on my face said it all.

"Well, we can work on that. Have you told me everything?" she asked in a voice that was comforting and caring—one I felt I could trust. "The more I know, the better I can plan."

I barely knew where to begin. So I began to spill out everything about what I'd discovered about *Mona Lisa*.

After some discussion, she said we should consider that the connection between Leonardo's animal writings and the animal heads in *Mona Lisa* were just coincidence. She was sure others would bring that up. "We should cover all questionable points," she said. "I've seen enough press releases to expect objections to whatever we present."

I said there were too many animal heads, and they were just too obvious for anyone to think it a coincidence.

She asked to see a few.

I pulled some printouts from my backpack. I had glued them to foam board to keep flat—it made it easier to recognize the illusions and avoid the reflective glare that the curved pages of books sometimes presented. I pointed out some of the simpler, more unmistakable images, like Titian's *Venus of Urbino* crocodile.

Kristine came from a family of artists and had studied art in college, so she found them easy to see.

"This is so odd," she said, as if witnessing something paranormal. "You're right. There they are. But they're slipped into the art in ways that make them so easy to miss."

"At first, yes," I said, "but after a while, they sort of jump out at you."

"Why would the artists hide them like that?"

I told her I wasn't sure.

"This one that Botticelli did," Kristine said, pointing to the face-shaped landscape in the image of *St. Jerome*. "Are you *sure* no one's seen this before? It's so obvious."

"Maybe someone did. *We* have. But as far as I know there isn't a single mention of these anywhere."

She sat back in her chair, tapping her bottom lip with her finger tips.

"The media will want to know *why* no one spotted them before. And I don't want to sound skeptical, but ...there's something that's bothering me."

"Kristine, I'm expecting skepticism. I'd rather hear those kinds of questions from you first instead of being surprised by the media."

She looked down at the image she held of *Mona Lisa*, then back to me. "These three animals—the ape, and lion, and the one we're not sure of that you think may be a buffalo—I just don't see the sense in why Leonardo would paint them sideways."

That puzzled me initially as well. At first I thought it was just a better way for Leonardo to hide them. But he might have had another reason also.

"The animal heads only *appear* to be on their sides," I said. "They're actually drowning in another image—the secret image of a swamp with a gigantic crocodile. The crocodile is killing off the animals."

She looked at me distantly. Then she took off her reading glasses, which gently tugged at some strands of hair, and rested them on the table. And she placed her pen down on her yellow writing pad, as if we were suddenly out of time.

17

The Crocodile

Kristine's eyes lit up when she examined *Mona Lisa* from the anamorphic d-point, which showed her features reverse in age. "Incredible," she said.

"Her smile changes," I said. "It's rounder. More expressive. Like a smirk."

For a moment, Kristine seemed lost in the painting, as if I wasn't even there. Her reaction brought me back to the awe I felt when I first saw *Mona Lisa*'s figure turn younger, thinner, more feminine, and even more graceful as her smile grew brighter. But there was also the unmistakable evil lurking behind her, seemingly unknown to the woman sitting with her back to the crocodile.

I had a sense that my uncovering of the anamorphosis would impact how some people looked at the world. Regardless of their meanings, the illusions presented a way to see things differently, to open one's mind and peer past the surface in search for what otherwise could be missed.

Artists such as Van Gogh and de Kooning had fueled my desire and motivation by exhibiting through their art the unique ways in which they viewed the world. So to see Kristine get lost in what I had found and shared with her, and to see her inspired, made me blissful. Maybe the hidden creatures wouldn't mean much to the rest of the world. But to me, they were extraordinary. I was told on several occasions that I never gave myself enough credit. Maybe I rarely felt that I had done anything worth crediting. But as I thought of all those experts around the world who had unsuccessfully attempted to decipher *Mona Lisa* over the years, and how I believed I'd gotten further than anyone had ever come, a strong sense of self-respect came to me. It was something I had felt very few times in my life.

Mixed in that emotion was also a sense of destiny—something I never before thought existed. And as scared as I was of going public and facing the criticism I expected, it was that faint feeling that made me realize that I had to go through with it, no matter what.

There were other factors that began to push me forward. *Mona Lisa*'s illusions were significant all on their own. But seeing the same creatures in *The Last Supper* made it something more. Although I was born to a Catholic family, I questioned the existence of a higher being. Events in my life strengthened the doubt I had—the most recent being Ginger's unexplainable passing.

My faith was in art, the one thing I wholeheartedly believed was my purpose in life. My spiritual connection was with history's great artists. But the hidden wildlife in the sacred *Last Supper* offered *Mona Lisa* a religious connection. So I began to wonder if I'd been wrong to doubt God's existence. Was my connection to the discoveries His doing? An attempt to regain whatever faith I once had? Using art—the only way He knew He could ever reach me?

I shook off the crazy thought. But to help answer those questions, I had to figure out the hidden creatures' meanings.

"How did you even figure out the crocodile was there?" Kristine asked.

"Through Leonardo's writings."

"Lots of people have read what he's written. Why didn't they see it?"

"Maybe they didn't see how misleading his writings are. That there are double meanings to his words. Like *Mona Lisa:* two paintings in one. Maybe they've been looking in the wrong place, using X-ray machines to study layers of paint *under* the surface for clues about the painting. But it's not like Leonardo knew we'd be able to X-ray his art. So, assuming *Mona Lisa* has some kind of message he wanted us to figure out, why would he hide clues where they couldn't be seen by the naked eye? Leonardo was far too brilliant for that. Like a magician, he tricked us by putting the answers right in front of our eyes."

"Can you show me what you mean?"

I took printouts of Leonardo's writings from my bag and placed them on the table. "Ok. Paintings used to look flat, like a coloring book," I began to explain. "The Renaissance changed all that. It was a time of artistic experimentation. The understanding of shadows and how distant imagery appeared blurry and less detailed, the sense of dimension and realism with the help of linear perspective."

Kristine nodded. "Like train tracks fading off into a spot on the horizon."

"Yes, the *vanishing point*. We knew anamorphic illusions existed. In paintings like *The Ambassadors*, they're impossible to miss. But we didn't ever expect them to be hidden. And for some reason, that's what Leonardo and the others did.

"It's like the animal heads. In some of the art, you can see them straight on if you know how to look, but sometimes you have to turn the image on its side. In others, they can only be seen by angling the art away from your view—as Leonardo's *d-Point* explains."

"So she has both."

"Yes. The mountains that also form animal heads are ambiguous illusions—one object that can be seen as two different objects. In *Mona Lisa*'s case, the mountains have to be rotated to see the heads. In addition, there's the anamorphic illusion that changes the whole painting. But you can't tell any of it is there unless you know how to look."

"Or follow Leonardo's cryptic instructions."

"Exactly." I slid a printout across the table to Kristine. "Take a look at this *Envy* passage Leonardo wrote."

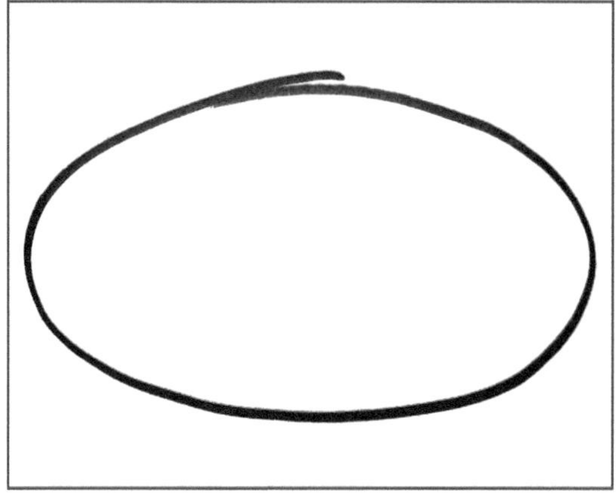

"Okay," she said, after scanning it.

"Now,"I flipped the paper over and drew a simple egg shape, "...imagine looking at this oval. Does it look like I'm hiding anything?"

"Of course not."

"Because it's just a simple shape. No need to look further, right?"

"Correct."

"But if I angle the oval *away* from you, like this, so you're looking across the length of it instead of straight on, from your angle, the long curves of the oval shorten to reveal what you didn't realize—*couldn't* realize—I was hiding. ...A circle."

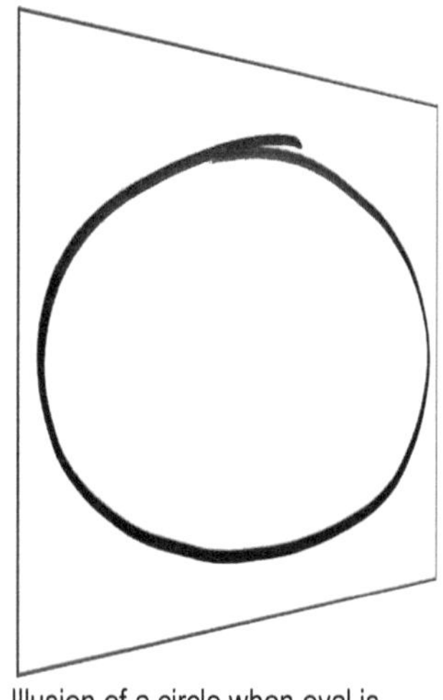

Illusion of a circle when oval is viewed from an anamorphic angle.

"A secret anamorphic image," her voice grew with excitement.

"Yes, a simple example. The same trick can make a trapezoid form a square. Who would ever think to look for it? And if I showed that oval to a hundred different people ...if I showed it to a hundred *thousand* people ...not one person would think to look for a hidden circle."

"And *millions* have seen the *Mona Lisa*."

"Leonardo knew no one would look for a hidden illusion. That we'd all be too busy awing over the actual art, looking at it straight on. I think that's what those artists were counting on."

"But why hide one image inside another?"

"I don't know. But you don't have to know *why* an image is there to *see* that it's there."

"And this *Envy* writing?" Kristine said, pointing her pen to it.

"If I wrote about an illustration of a perfect circle I created and named it *Circle*, I'm sure nobody would realize I was describing the egg shape I drew for you. Not unless they figured out that I was talking about the circle that could only be seen in the *illusion*.

"*Mona Lisa* was the name given to the painting after Leonardo died. But he never called it that. Come to think of it, I don't think the words *Mona Lisa* exist anywhere in his writings. And art historians always believed he never wrote about the painting. But he did. His *Envy* is a description of the painting we named *Mona Lisa.* Except, it only describes the imagery in the anamorphic scene."

"For example?"

"You saw how a younger woman appeared in the picture. But a different background materializes also."

Kristine's look of surprise was subtle as she picked up the picture to examine again.

"The rocky terrain turns into a swamp," I said "…Or maybe it's a lake. But it's definitely flooded with water. In the middle of it all appears the gigantic head of a crocodile, in the water behind her. You can see it facing left with its jaws open." I pointed it out to her. "Look at how the mountains form the armored texture of its scales. And over here on the left is the snout. And see this? The trail shaped like a backward *S* forms the open mouth, just as crocodiles sometimes keep their upper jaw open above the water's surface. The bridge over her on the right forms the eye. One picture within another.

"*Envy* isn't some kind of random prose poem. It's describing all of this. Even the animals facing the sky. But it took me a while to realize that they're not painted sideways."

"What do you mean?"

"I thought the lion was roaring and the ape screeching because their mouths are open. But now I think they're gasping for air with their heads above water, trying to keep from drowning in the crocodile's swamp—the way prey does when a crocodile attacks. Crocodiles tend to pull their prey under water to drown them."

"So the crocodile is killing the animals?"

"It looks that way," I said, then pointed to one of *Envy*'s lines. "Right here, Leonardo wrote 'Give her a leopard's skin, because this creature kills the lion out of envy and by deceit.' But I'm confused because Leonardo's 'creature' refers to the woman in the painting. She's Envy. She's the creature. The serpent is a separate character in the prose poem: the crocodile." I ran a finger along the line as I read. "'Make her heart gnawed by a swelling serpent.' *Her* refers to the woman. *Serpent* refers to the crocodile."

"But wouldn't *serpent* mean a snake?"

"I thought of that, but wasn't sure if a crocodile may have been considered a serpent back in Leonardo's time. Both *Mona Lisa* and *The Last Supper* show a lion, and possibly an ape and bull, and we already know one painting is a biblical story. *Envy* mentions heaven and God, so I have the impression *Mona Lisa* might be a religious painting. In the Bible, a serpent represents the devil. But there's some belief the reference for 'serpent' was mistranslated in the original Hebrew writings, which tells of Moses's staff turning to a crocodile—not a snake—when he faced Pharoah. One documentary explains that it can be traced back to Sobek—a god the Egyptians worshipped. A human with a crocodile head."[1]

"It sounds plausible."

"Look at the illusion again," I said. "With its wide-open mouth, the crocodile looks like it's getting ready to bite down. And look at the shape of the highlight of the woman's chest, which happens to be positioned within the croc's jaw. The highlighted area is shaped like a heart. Which fits the line that reads, 'Make her heart gnawed by a swelling serpent.' There's also the possibility Leonardo simply preferred to use a crocodile instead of a snake to represent Satan."

"Can a crocodile represent Satan?" she asked.

"Leonardo described his method of creating imaginary creatures." I read from one of his writings:

> ...You cannot make [an imaginary] animal without it having its limbs such that each bears some resemblance to that of some one of the other animals. If therefore you wish to make one of your imaginary animals appear natural—let us suppose it to be a dragon—take for its head that of a mastiff or setter, for its eyes those of a cat, for its ears those of a porcupine, for its nose that of a greyhound, with the eyebrows of a lion, the temples of an old cock and the neck of a water-tortoise.[2]

"He obviously never saw Satan," I said, "so maybe he represented the devil with existing creatures from nature, just as he explains in his writings."

Kristine noted something on her pad.

"Other details can be matched between the painting and *Envy* poem," I said.

"Like?"

"*Mona Lisa*'s veil." I pointed to a line. "'Make her bridle.' But I have to admit that many of the lines don't make sense to me, like the 'thunderbolts' proceeding from her, and her 'evil speaking' and 'leopard's skin.'"

"Leopard's skin? ...Could he mean a panther? It's a leopard, and black like her clothing."

"A panther? I didn't even think of that, but yeah, it could."

"It's like a puzzle," Kristine said enthusiastically.

"Whoever Leonardo painted, it can't be a portrait of Lisa Gherardini. She has to represent someone bigger. Which is why I need help from the experts."

"I think it's time we create a press release, Ron. To let everyone know what you found."

I was suddenly a little lightheaded. "Yeah, I'm ...sure the media will have a field day with all this."

18

Pre-Press

I thought a press release meant I'd be standing behind a podium and making an announcement to a crowd of reporters, but maybe I had watched too many episodes of *Law & Order*. Kristine explained that it would simply be a formal written statement she would upload to a site where "millions and trillions" of reporters fish out stories they found interesting enough to cover. Sort of like shouting out to the world what I had done, then waiting for someone to approach and ask for me to explain.

We ping-ponged emails back and forth, trying to word the press release just right for our November 29 upload date. We couldn't ignore the fact that I was making some large claims, so we had to be strategic in making the statement *sound* genuine, regardless of the evidence I could present.

As we got closer to our release date, I was both electrified and scared shitless. I didn't like being the center of attention. Even my childhood birthday parties made me uncomfortable, especially the part where everyone gathered to sing me "Happy Birthday." It would feel like I was suddenly thrown onstage without an act. I considered myself too uninteresting to have any self-confidence about it. If *Mona Lisa* was any less of a big deal, I might have talked myself out of doing the story altogether.

I wondered about the reaction I'd get. In the past, I watched as less notable stories about *Mona Lisa* played out in the news. So I had no doubt my story would catch the attention of the world. Just as a story about a massive train wreck would. But how long before my story would draw attention? A month? A year? And how much scrutiny would there be? Would the publicity reach anyone able to explain the animal heads? And if they believed I spotted something millions of others had missed, would they even take the secret images seriously? Or would they consider it to be some joke the artists played? I was open to the idea that the animals were just that, but *Envy* was no joke.

I considered it to be a real break in the case of *Mona Lisa*'s identity.

Despite all I had found, I still had questions of who she was. Was Envy her real name? I didn't believe so. It was another mystery to pile on top of the others.

The press release was only the beginning. Kristine recommended we "attack from every angle." So the moment it would upload to a site connected to what she described as the "sites-portals-hubs," a set of blog posts and a YouTube video I planned on creating would also go live. The video would tease viewers about the illusions, hopefully hooking them to visit my blog, which would show and explain them, focusing mostly on *Mona Lisa.* I would also post my discoveries on social media. My goal was to figure out the meanings of the animals and secret illusions, and also to claim credit to what I found before anyone else figured it out—even though 500 years had already passed without anyone else seeing the illusions or realizing *Envy*'s connection to *Mona Lisa.* Maybe it was out of greed, but I couldn't help being worried about it—even if it seemed unlikely that anyone else would uncover what I had found.

There was no question my story would seem crazy at first. Hopefully, the attention would cause *Mona Lisa*'s mysteries to unravel. It was too unusual a story for Kristine to say what to expect. We tried to prepare ourselves. She had her job to do. And I had mine. So like a hermit, I hid in my house—away from the outside world—working away on the video, which I titled *Making the Mona Lisa Smile.* I called the blog *The Hidden Horse Head*—named after the first anamorphic image I saw of the horse's head. The first post was, of course, on *Mona Lisa.*

As I started the projects, actually putting what I saw down in writing, I couldn't help but see that my revelations sounded even more far-fetched. I knew it was all real. In a way, it was difficult for me to believe it had gone unnoticed for so long. I was sure many would find it hard to believe—especially after all the silly theories that appeared over the years in the art world. I'd shake my head at times, sure that I would end up as a kind of joke in the end. But reading what I had written did help make sense of it. And it added a layer of reality. And that increased my need to figure out the reason for the illusions.

I began imagining how reporters would jump at a story about optical illusions that were never seen before. But I realized that no press release or news interview could possibly cover all the details. It involved too many illusions, too many works of art. Even a multi-episode documentary running a whole season would have its hands full. I realized that only a book could explain it all and give the discoveries some kind of sense.

Kristine said to stick only to facts, but I found myself speculating and coming up with theories that I would later realize were incorrect. The problem was that I became a little too enthusiastic and incorporated my theories into the blog and YouTube video. There was simply too much commotion inside my head. I was barely getting any sleep and overthinking everything. My judgement was slightly blurred.

Fortunately, all that commotion kept me from worrying about how I would handle being in the limelight, if it came to that.

19

Giving Thanks

By Thanksgiving, I had completed the video and blog, and Kristine had finalized the press release. We just had to wait a few more days. Inside me was a pit of emptiness formed from curiosity, anxiety, worry, relief. I needed answers to fill that void. I couldn't tell if I was more interested in getting those answers about the paintings or in seeing how the public would react to my news. I was always fascinated by human behavior, which explained my ability to watch hours of *Forensic Files*, trying to figure out the criminal before the end of each episode. I was curious about who would be able to see the optical illusions and what they would think of them.

At our family get-together, I picked lightly around my Thanksgiving dinner, my uncertainty about the upcoming press release—just days away—subduing my appetite.

Two years prior, there was a news story of a father claiming that his son was inside a large weather balloon he released into the atmosphere. It turned out that the father made up the hoax in order to seek fame. And I remember thinking what it probably did to the family's reputation. The story stuck out to me, maybe because it sounded far-fetched from the start, as I believed mine would seem to others in the beginning.

From the very first thought of going public, I knew my reputation would be on the line. As an artist and graphic designer, I learned to deal with criticism. But how would it affect my family because of their association to me? Would my sister and brothers suddenly be "the siblings of that wacky *Mona Lisa* guy?" Would my story change the way Ma was treated by her neighbors and friends? That worried me more than anything.

I had a discussion with Ma weeks before, when I first decided to go public. She saw the worried look on my face when I stopped by to tell her how I learned of Leonardo's secrets. I wasn't sure if she understood the importance of the discoveries, but I knew she saw how important *I* considered them to be. Before that day, I don't think she ever saw the look that must have shown on my face. I certainly had never felt that kind of responsibility and determination before.

"I met with a PR agent," I told her.

"What's that?" she asked.

"Someone to help me publicize a story."

"What kind of story?" she asked, with growing interest.

"Something that might be on the news. Sort of a big discovery."

I watched her face balloon with excitement. "*What kind* of discovery?"

"Do you know *Mona Lisa*?"

"Yeah," she puffed out a breath of surprise.

"I found some things no one has seen before."

She sat quiet for a moment, taking in what I said. "*My* son made a discovery?" she exclaimed. She threw her hands up and in her Italian vernacular screamed out a blessing of good fortune toward the ceiling—a reaction one would expect from a lottery winner.

I laughed lightly, at the same time pushing away my rising emotions. I didn't remember ever feeling such an intense sense of pride for myself.

"I don't think everyone will believe me," I warned her. "Some people may say some bad things about me. But it's something I have to do."

She scrunched her face into an angry look. "You know what? To *Hell* with what people say," she said, making a rude hand gesture to the empty room around us. She also said something in Italian I didn't understand, yet I could tell it wasn't something anyone would ever say in church.

Then she hopped from her chair and leaned over to bear-hug me while I was still sitting. Even though she's shorter than me and had just turned 71, she had surprising strength.

20

Release

The following Tuesday I sat at work, watching the clock on my monitor screen change to 9:00 a.m.—the time of the press release, and the minute the video and blog went live. The moment of no return.

I felt like I had just dropped a match over a lake of gasoline, bracing myself for the explosion, but also fascinated to see how far the flames would reach.

Weeks before, I told a couple coworkers I worked closely with that I had done something they wouldn't believe, and that it would probably be all over the news. When they asked what it was, I only hinted that it had something to do with Leonardo da Vinci, and said that I couldn't tell them anything else. They bombarded me with questions, promising to keep it under wraps, but I was too paranoid the secret would leak before I could claim the discoveries as my own, starting with the press release. It was hard not to scream out what I had done, but I wasn't going to break. Still, they took wild guesses every day, which I responded to each time by saying that what I had done was bigger than what they were guessing, which intrigued them even more.

On that same Tuesday, I finally told them the news. Keeping such a secret from everyone had been a test to my commitment. But knowing my findings were finally out there—at least, in press release form—deflated a lot of the pressure I had felt. I planned to take it easy for a bit, and prepare mentally for whatever reaction might come next. Or might not come at all. I was partly sure I'd be contacted for a story. But being in the center of it made everything surreal in a way that made me partly unsure of anything.

I expected weeks to pass before anyone contacted Kristine or I, so I thought I'd be getting back to a normal sleep schedule, and spend some time painting to relax. The next morning was the first time I was able to focus on my work at my job since first seeing *Mona Lisa*'s question mark. Usually, I would almost be hypnotized by the shapes, images, and colors filling my computer screen from the designs I created. At times, the sensation of such focus was like meditation.

That morning, I worked on holiday ads for our new campaign, which always challenged me since I wasn't allowed to use the word *Christmas*. We didn't want those with non-Christian beliefs to feel excluded. Even in my previous job at the agency, Christmas-specific symbols, such as Santa or a Christmas tree, or even reindeer, were rarely allowed—we didn't want to exclude certain demographics. I understood the issue, but was always still irked by it. It had nothing to do with my feelings for Christmas. It was the idea of beating around the bush with my art, forced to be suggestive when my job was to clearly communicate using visuals. Apparently, the first amendment didn't seem to apply to graphic designers. It made me wonder if Renaissance artists were limited in showing certain imagery so as not to offend others. But what could anyone possibly have against lions and apes and crocodiles?

I closed my eyes and took a deep breath, telling myself to get back to work and to try not to think of what Leonardo hid.

Before noon, I presented three concepts to my marketing director. First, a cropped image of a snowman with a carrot nose, sapphire rings for eyes, and jewelry pieces for a mouth. My second concept showed a stack of presents piled twenty feet high on our company's iconic taxicab. The third was of a married couple embracing, our branded jewelry box exposed in the woman's grip as she kissed him.

My marketing director suggested that I try a collage of jewels positioned to form one large snowflake. She pointed to an earlier design I had made for a fashion show in which my inspiration came from Renaissance artist Giuseppe Arcimboldo—an artist who used everyday objects to create illusions of portraits.

That was the norm: creating several ideas, each one different from the others. So I started on the fourth concept—the snowflake, submerging myself in my art. But every so often, I found myself gazing at the monitor, wondering if deciding to go public was a huge mistake. And also if I would even be able to handle it. It would be a disappointment if no one picked up the story. But it would also give me a sense of relief to have tried, and that I would have faced my fear of being put in the spotlight, that I would have followed through with interviews no matter how scared I may have been. But I liked being anonymous to the world. It was always my art that I wanted everyone to notice, not me.

I was deep into my work when Kristine called.

"You're not going to believe this," she calmly told me over the phone. "Ray Levato from Channel 10 wants an exclusive interview. On *live* TV."

There was a rush of unease, like I was suddenly on a rollercoaster without a seatbelt, about to enter the section of loops.

"Can you be at the news station in an hour?" she asked.

"But the press release just went out," I said, having expected to warm up with some small newspaper articles at first, slowly working up my courage as I made my way to a camera interview later.

"This would be a great opportunity to get your story out there."

There was no question that she was right, but as I tried to think of some excuse, the word "okay" snuck its way from my mouth.

"Wonderful. Just to warn you, his on-air sobriquet is *Skeptic Ray.* He's a little doubtful about your claims."

21

The First Interview

I told my boss I had to leave for a couple hours, then raced home to gather some images of paintings I'd cut and matted in preparation a week before.

I changed my clothes and took a sport coat with me. But only to make myself look more like a serious college professor instead of the eccentric, t-shirt wearing artist I was. It was the same reason I had not shaved for the past couple weeks. It was one thing to know what I was talking about, another to *look* like I knew. And I wanted all the help I could in convincing everyone.

I didn't expect good things to come from an interviewer who went by the name of Skeptic Ray. But I wasn't sure if I'd get another opportunity for an interview. Or if anyone else would be any less skeptical than I guessed a man named Skeptic Ray would be.

Pulling into the Channel 10 WHEC parking lot was like a chariot ride into an arena. I felt like a gladiator with no weapon to fight off lions waiting to claw my insides out.

"Hey, Ron!" a man in the distance yelled out just as I got out of my car. He was holding open the glass doors of the building entrance. He looked like a reporter, especially with the papers he held in one hand flapping in the wind.

Skeptic Ray?

I was too far away to recognize him, but I knew who it was. I waved a hand to let him know that I heard his call. Because I was so tense, I wasn't sure if my voice would even carry across the distance. Plus, I didn't want to look like a fool, shouting across the parking lot.

I grabbed my bag from the back seat and closed the car door.

"Over here!" he yelled.

I stopped and stared at him for a moment, trying to fake my confidence as if it should be him who was scared of me. My nerves were buzzing, and I was hoping that if I ended up puking, it would be at that moment outside instead of during the live interview when the cameras were recording and when, potentially, the whole city was watching.

Just present the story, I kept telling myself on the drive there. *Pretend you're talking about art to a friend*—just as I had a million times before.

I tried to focus on my breathing.

Kristine parked her minivan near me and walked over, her eyes as wide as her smile. *So exciting,* the expression on her face said.

"I hate being in front of the camera," I said.

"You'll do *fine*. Remember, bring everything back to Leonardo's writings like we talked about. *He* wrote about the illusions. You're simply presenting them."

She didn't seem as worried as I thought she should have.

Ray was taller than I expected. Because of where he stood, I had to walk under his outstretched arm holding the door.

I couldn't tell if he was squinting from the bright sun or if he was carefully examining me. He was also smiling, but unlike Kristine's, his crossed me as the kind of smile a surgeon would use with a patient before an operation for an incurable disease.

"So, you're an artist?" he asked with a deep newscaster's voice once we all entered the building.

"All my life," I said, trying not to sound nervous by being short with him. I didn't want him to think I was naive in any way, just because I had never done an interview before—if he even knew that.

We passed a large room of reporters, which struck me like a movie scene. The room was filled with metal desks and outdated monitors and spiral telephone cords crisscrossing everything. It sounded like rain on a tin roof from all the typing taking place.

When we entered a conference room, I placed my bag on the floor next to a large table surrounded by fake leather chairs.

Ray took a moment to talk to a cameraman who was already there tinkering with his equipment. Then he turned to inform us that the interview would no longer be live, that they would pre-record and edit it later.

Kristine and I looked at each other as I let out a deep breath, somewhat relieved, but I was still a little rubbery in the legs.

"Make sure the camera's always rolling," Ray then told the cameraman. From the moment Kristine mentioned Skeptic Ray's name, I had a dislike for him. But hearing his words to the cameraman made me think he was out to get me. Maybe it was common practice to tell a cameraman that, but it sounded to me like he wanted to catch me fumbling with my words in hopes of discrediting me. I instantly wanted to hate him, and a small portion of my anxiety made way for anger.

Kristine sat at the table—off-camera—as Ray and I stood in position to start.

He explained that he wanted to end up with a ninety-second shoot. But how was I going to demonstrate my findings in such a short time? It was impossible, because there was so much to explain.

Once he was ready to start, Ray guided me to stand and face him in a specific way, and told me to focus on him, not the camera. He nodded to the cameraman, then turned to me and proceeded with the first question. "So tell me, what makes you think your discoveries are real?"

As I began to answer, Kristine suddenly chimed in: "*Excuse* me, Ray." Her interruption surprised me as much as it surprised Ray, who turned to her with a look. Then ever so politely, Kristine said, "I think you want to ask Ron what the discoveries are."

It took Ray a moment to look back at me. "Let's start again," he said, composed. "How are you qualified to make these discoveries?"

"*Excuuuse* me, Ray!" Kristine called out with a hint of frustration, just as I was about to explain my art background to Ray.

Her raised voice practically shook me from my nervous spell as I realized why she was shouting. I was naive and too nervous to see that Ray's questions were worded in a way that I suddenly felt were intended to discredit me before I could even answer. Kristine, who I didn't think possessed a rude cell in her body, was sabotaging the recording, making Ray's question and my answer in that clip unusable with her scream, saving me from potential embarrassment.

Although I wasn't sure what she would have done if the interview were live, I was thankful that she was there. She sat there in her chair, her hands folded together with a queen's mannerism as she gave me a motherly smile. Like a fox protecting her cub.

I suddenly had the sense that I was there only to play the role of a clown in Ray's circus. And it wasn't just that I felt disrespected. It was as though he was disrespecting what I was so passionate about. My blood began to boil.

I knew not to expect everyone to take me seriously, but I thought I would at least have the chance to present my case.

Ray pushed his chin forward as if his collar was too tight, and reworded his question: "So, tell me *what* you found in *Mona Lisa*."

I waited a second to give Kristine the chance to interrupt. When she said nothing, I answered Ray's question.

Through the interview, I began to relax. It was like I'd expected an extremely difficult test, sure that I would fail, but then realizing I had been prepared to answer every question, the answers even coming to me very easily. Ray and I flowed into a rhythm after a while, almost as if we were simply having a conversation about art.

And in a flash, an hour of answering questions had passed.

As I prepared to leave, grateful it was finally over, I caught Ray looking at the image of *Mona Lisa* I had left on the table. At first, I didn't believe Ray had any genuine interest in the painting—except to do a story on a subject that was sure to get viewers' attention. But as he looked at *Mona Lisa*, I noticed a glimmer of real curiosity. I could see it in his eyes.

"You know," he said, "In all honesty, I don't get the big deal with this art."

"The world's fascinated with that painting," I told him. "And these discoveries—the animals—could help answer her mysteries."

"I still don't get it."

I thought for a moment, wanting him to understand.

"You ever collect comic books, anything like that?" I asked.

"Coins."

I told him about the first time I came across a buffalo head nickel. "It was in the change a cashier handed to me. Sort of magical because I never heard of a buffalo head nickel before that, but I could tell the nickel was real even though it was different from what nickels were supposed to look like. It showed me how things that we can be so unaware of can still exist. Made me wonder what else was out there.

"As far as *Mona Lisa*, not everyone will understand the discoveries. But they're still important. That kind of stuff inspires people."

Kristine and I thanked Ray for the interview and headed for the parking lot. When we reached our cars, she stopped to give me a hug. "No matter how the segment turns out," she said, "I want you to know you did great."

"I hope he doesn't butcher me too badly."

She got into her car and left. I climbed into mine. And just sat there holding the wheel, not moving from my parking space.

A chilling rush of emotion unwound inside me, and all at once my energy was gone, leaving me feeling weak, but also satisfied. Even though it had not been live, I had in a way, faced my fear, regardless of how I did. It was very frightening, but also empowering.

I wondered if that was just the beginning of what was to come. And if the interviews would only get more difficult. The idea of giving up came to me, but I knew that it wasn't an option I'd accept.

I couldn't shake the eerie sensation that the painting had a message more important than I could ever guess. Though no one else had ever succeeded in doing so, something inside me right then and there told me that I was meant to decipher that portrait, one way or another. Even if it took me the rest of my life.

Is that what you wanted, Leonardo?

I looked around at the parking lot of empty cars surrounding me, thinking of the long journey I was likely facing. And in that instant, I felt like the loneliest man in the world.

I was never one to believe in destiny, but I couldn't ignore the connection I kept feeling to that painting. I just wasn't sure what it was about it that was drawing me in. It felt personal, like everything from my life was meant to lead me to that point, like *Mona Lisa* had somehow been waiting for me. And I suddenly knew that with or without anyone's help, I would figure her out and uncover all her secrets.

Maybe I felt I owed it to Ginger. Or to myself. But either way, it wasn't a choice. It was something I had to do.

22

Fame

I returned to work after leaving the news station.

"How did it go?" my marketing director asked.

"Okay," I lied.

"When will we see the interview?"

"Possibly tonight. . . . If they run it."

I was so spent from the interview I almost didn't care if they ran it at all.

I sat at my desk and pretended to work, but could only think of the criticism I was about to endure from Skeptic Ray's report—if he did decide to run the story. I imagined the news editors gathered around in the editing room, their eyes rolling while they watched the recording and telling each other how the story was not newsworthy at all.

And if they did run it, how would Ray treat the story? Would I be the joke of the news hour? A few seconds of coverage—just long enough to poke fun at? I was pretty sure I would be.

I tried to tell myself that it didn't matter what anyone else thought. "To *Hell* with what people say," Ma had said.

I learned from her long ago that sometimes you had to do what you believed was right—and to ignore what other people thought. That I had to do what I had to do. At one time in our family, divorce wasn't an option. The word itself was taboo, causing gasps and expressions of sorrow in family gossip. It was a thing that happened to "those American families," not traditional Italian families like ours. In our large circle of family and friends, especially with the older generations, it seemed to me that it didn't matter how miserable Italian couples were, they stayed together, no matter what.

So when Ma decided to divorce Papa, family members came to talk to her to try and convince her otherwise, telling her that they should stay together for the sake of the family. I would hear her voice rise against the opposing views she received. She stood her ground. I remembered how she and I talked about what other family members might say. I had been the one to tell her that she couldn't worry what other people thought. That she had to do whatever was needed to make herself happy. At the same time, I decided that I would no longer care what others said either. That I would stand behind Ma's decision, no matter what.

Of all the many family members and cousins and friends that came from

Italy long ago, and the generations that came after, Ma had been the first that I knew of to get a divorce. Despite everyone else's view, she did what she needed to do.

I *knew* what I saw in those paintings was real. And if no one else could see it, so be it. I had done my part in publicizing it. And I would stand my ground and accept that there would be opposing views.

As difficult as it was, I tried to concentrate on my art at work.

I looked at the clock around 4:00 p.m.—an hour before the evening news report. Since I hadn't yet heard anything from Channel 10, I figured that they decided not to run the story. Just then, I received a text from Kristine. I had to read the message a couple times, not believing what I saw.

"Channel 10 editor called. Making you the lead story!" I was still staring at my phone screen when a second text came through: "…and giving you four minutes of airtime! Congrats!"

"They're putting my story on the news," I told Ma over the phone. I had to pull the receiver away from my ear when she screamed.

"Should I tell everyone?" she asked. But I knew she already had her finger ready to dial other family members with the news.

A few minutes before 5:00 p.m., a bunch of us at work gathered in front of the store's television. When the News 10 NBC jingle came on, everyone hushed. The main news anchors appeared and immediately introduced Skeptic Ray for that night's lead story.

"Art from the Renaissance is noted for its hidden images and meanings," he began. His voice was compelling, and he had the demeanor of someone delivering groundbreaking news. In a way, he appeared like a different person from the one who interviewed me. "*Mona Lisa* has been noticed for her mysterious smile," he continued, "[and] she apparently is not alone on the canvas. So says Ron Piccirillo." I was thrilled to hear him say my name. He listed the animals I pointed out and how I found them using "an old artist's trick of looking at the work from a different perspective."[1]

I was then shown explaining to Ray how I turned the painting on its side and spotted the images. Seeing myself on television was like watching someone else who just happened to look like me.

"Piccirillo poured over the writings in Da Vinci's own notebooks," Ray said, "where he found passages Da Vinci referred to animals and other clues."

I watched myself standing in front of a projection screen during the interview, pointing out the details of the ape's face, stating that it faced right as I pointed a thumb in the same direction, then moving on to indicate the lion's head. I was a little surprised to see how calm I looked on TV. I was aware that nervous shaking could get lost on camera unless seen close-up, so I felt somewhat lucky about it. In fact, I looked perfectly calm.

The camera sure can fool you.

"But there are more hidden images," Ray continued, "including a crocodile that could refer to a passage Da Vinci wrote. He mentioned a serpent gnawing at *Mona Lisa*'s heart. Piccirillo says he hid the heart in *Mona Lisa*'s cleavage."

My jaw dropped when he used the word *cleavage* to describe, arguably, the most important painting in the world. Although I did describe a heart-shaped highlight that was visible on her chest in the illusion, and how it was strategically positioned between the crocodile's long jaws—even though the crocodile is in the background and the woman is in the foreground—I never used the word *cleavage.*

On TV, I was indicating the eye and snout of the crocodile as a photo of the reptile's head from my blog appeared on screen, shown from the secret angle. "Its jaws are open," I said in front of the camera.

"Piccirillo was led by the notes Da Vinci wrote down 500 years ago," Ray said.

When Ray had asked me to show him the *Envy* passage from a book during the interview, I thought he was only looking to quote from the passage. But the newscast showed me reading the *Envy* passage at a point when I thought the cameraman was no longer recording. I had forgotten that Ray had told him to make sure the camera was always rolling, even when I thought the interview was over. Ray asked me to clarify Leonardo's use of the word *serpent,* which he understandably took to mean snake. I took it to possibly include crocodiles also, and theorized that "five hundred years ago, the crocodile may have been considered a serpent." It was a question I was hoping to avoid until researching it further, but had no choice but to answer on the spot.

Asked if the animals were really there or if I were just seeing shapes that only resembled animals, I pointed out that I consistently found many of the same animals spread over countless artworks by different artists. "There's a point where everything stops becoming coincidence and you have to think a little more about it," I told Ray. But I wish I had phrased it differently, like "give it some serious consideration" instead of "think a little more about it."

I'm not sure if I would have gotten them, but I should have asked for a list of questions Ray was going to ask me so I could have thought more about my wording beforehand.

"This is *the most* studied portrait of the last 500 years," Ray was saying to me on TV. "How is it that *you* are the first to see this?"

It was a question I really had no answer for because I was still astounded no one else had seen it. How could five centuries have passed without a single person noticing? But since I had no choice but to answer, I gave him the only explanation I could think of: that it was "an accidental discovery."

Ray went on to tell to tell viewers where *Mona Lisa* was currently located, then in closing, briefly talked about me, like how I "studied the *Mona Lisa* in art history class" and that my "parents are from Italy, which, of course, is the heart of the Renaissance."

Then finally, one of the main news anchors appeared. "Ray, for years people have speculated as to who *Mona Lisa* really is," she said. "Who does Piccirillo think she is?"[2]

"Ron points to a passage by Leonardo da Vinci that speaks directly to the painting," Ray said. "It teases us that it may not be a real person after all, but the persona of a trait. And that trait ...is *Envy.*"

I felt a couple coworkers pat my back as I stood there, staring at the television, a little shocked at how well the report turned out, all things considered. I had expected a bashing from Skeptic Ray. Instead, he presented the story as though I had achieved something praiseworthy.

I wasn't sure if I had somehow persuaded Ray to present the story in a positive light or if I had just misread him, or if it was something else, but I was grateful for his presentation.

The morning after the broadcast, Kristine sent me another request for a local interview. Then another. And another. I was bombarded with requests that day. She recommended accepting every one I could. Some reporters scheduled a video interview. Others asked me questions over the phone.

That night, friends posted comments on my social media pages.

"What an amazing discovery!"[3]

"Nicely done, Ron! Truly."[4]

"Congrats on the media coverage!"[5]

"Have you Googled yourself today?" one person asked. "Close to 500 references to your story out there!"[6]

By that Friday, Kristine, following the story, told me it posted on national websites like Bing and MSN.com, where it made the Editors' Picks.

I began tracking the story geographically with Google Analytics, watching it begin to pulsate over the web. Finally, after months of anxiety, the story was time-stamped in cyberspace, impossible for anyone else to steal credit for—something I no longer had to worry about.

All I had to do was wait for someone to come forward and explain what the animal heads and hidden illusions meant since I still had no clue. There had to be a scholar out there somewhere with the answers. Since I was too impatient to wait, I would continue researching on my own, but I was losing hope in figuring it out. I had to remember that it all started by accident with that question mark, so maybe I'd accidentally stumble upon their meanings also.

That night, I went out for a few drinks with Brian—a lawyer and long-time friend.

When first making the discoveries, I met with Brian to see what legal rights I had. Was I entitled to publicize them first? What rights did I have if I decided to write a book about them? With all the time I had invested searching and uncovering, I didn't want someone else reaping the rewards of my work. I knew I'd never get another chance to do something I considered prestigious that also had to do with art. I also thought it might open up doors to opportunities I otherwise would not have, so it was important to me to be credited for what I had done.

It turned out that I had no rights, so I had to protect what I knew until the right time came to publicize the story.

If anyone had found out about my discoveries beforehand, there was nothing I could have done about it. That was one reason I was paranoid and therefore kept it secret until the official press release. It was also a reason why I went public, "where everyone can see it happen," as Saul had advised.

At the bar, packed wall to wall with drinkers and loud conversation, Brian and I joked about my fifteen minutes of (local) fame. Back in high school, neither of us were ever considered one of the popular kids. We were dorky and shy, and the only place I would have ever felt popular enough to end up with a cheerleader was in my dreams. An accidental glance from them in the school's hallway could cause a movie reel of fantasies to play out in my mind. I didn't know what it was like to be wanted by a girl like that. Back then, I didn't even know how I would recognize it.

In my late 30s, I was used to being somewhat invisible to girls whenever I went out drinking. Tom Cruise, I wasn't. But on a good day, I might pass for John Travolta's distant cousin—one with slightly crooked teeth and a big nose.

So when a cute girl rudely brushed between me and Brian—taking a place at the bar so she could order her drink first—I gave the back of her head an eye-rolling.

"You know who you just cut in front of?" Brian said to her jokingly.

She looked confused and partially annoyed.

"A famous man," he told her.

I shook my head at his banter as the girl turned to me, like I suddenly appeared out of thin air. "Really?" she said, smiling with curiosity, but unconvinced.

"No," I said, suddenly feeling a little light on my feet. "Not really."

"This guy is all over the news," Brian said.

"Shut up," I said.

"I'm Sarah," the girl said.

"That's Mr. Mona Lisa," Brian said.

"You jerk," I said.

When she asked, I explained why I was on the news, sort of giving her pieces of the story as I babbled about Leonardo da Vinci when I really thought she would rather me talk about what kind of car I drove. But I didn't think a Scion

TC would've impressed her either. It always felt silly to attempt to impress a girl, yet I didn't stop myself from trying. She pretended to be interested. And I pretended to believe she was.

After she got her drinks, she returned to her group of female friends nearby, and I turned to Brian. "Mr. Mona Lisa?"

He just laughed.

Glancing at the group of girls minutes later, I noticed a couple of them looking up at me, down to their phones, and back to me, as if comparing something. There was a shimmer of what I thought it would feel like to be the popular kid. It was wrong to abuse what I was passionate about just to lust after a girl's attention. But I still liked it.

It wasn't too late when I got home, and I was still a little light on my feet from the alcohol and slight attention I received. Before going to bed, I spent some time preparing a couple canvases with gesso so they'd be ready when I decided to start painting again.

The next morning, I was awakened by my phone ringing.

"*Mister* Piccirillo!" a familiar man's voice said when I answered. Still half asleep, and with a slight headache, it was as though only a few minutes had passed since my night out. I looked at the time, not believing that it was already morning. "I just caught you on *The Today Show,*" he said, although it didn't quite register.

"Is that you, Rick?" I asked, rubbing my eyes awake. He was a friend I had not spoken to in a few months. "What are you talking about?"

"You didn't know about it?"

"What show?"

"*The Today Show*? Al Roker. Matt Lauer. National broadcast, buddy."

"You're kidding, right?"

"Not joking."

It wasn't that I didn't believe that the news made the show. I just couldn't see how the story could have spread so fast. And to reach *The Today Show*?

"What did they say?" I asked, suddenly too anxious to even be astounded or exhilarated or whatever I was supposed to feel.

"They talked about the animals you found."

"They say animals? Or animal *heads*?"

"I don't remember. It aired from some Da Vinci exhibit in London."

"London? Rick, that's not national. That's *inter*national." I jumped out of bed, stumbling toward the laptop on my desk. "How was the report? Good? Bad? Terrible? You are kidding me, aren't you?" My computer wouldn't turn on fast enough so that I could watch the report online.

"Eh, not really sure how well the report went, but they played a scene from *The Da Vinci Code.*"

"You mean with Tom *Hanks*?"

Before he could respond, my phone began ringing with another call trying to get through.

"Hold on, Rick," I said and answered the other call.

"Is this Ron Piccirillo?" a polite, British-sounding voice asked.

"Yes, but …" I was about to tell him that I didn't want to buy whatever he was selling. But then he introduced himself as Daniel Bates from the *Daily News* in London."

"You're calling from London?"

He explained that he saw my story on *The Today Show* and was writing an article on a Leonardo exhibition in London. He wanted to ask me a few questions. "I'd like to congratulate you. It's quite the discovery."

He began asking questions without wasting any time. And he didn't sound skeptical about what I had found. It felt a little surreal, but I went along, not having time to overthink it. We discussed *Mona Lisa*, of course.

"Very good. *Very* good," he repeated after several of my answers.

Just as Skeptic Ray had, Daniel wondered if a serpent and crocodile were one and the same. I told him that I thought they were. At least, when referencing the *Envy* passage, it seemed that way. "Leonardo's *Envy* poem describes details seen only in *Mona Lisa*'s illusion. The description of the serpent in the poem matches the crocodile. So yes, I thought they were the same."

I had pulled a book to reference the painting to better explain details to Daniel, and found myself still mesmerized by the green, ghostly image of the crocodile.

Even as I talked to Daniel, I thought of how eerie the crocodile head looked, as if waiting to snap its jaws down on its victim. It felt as though its evil presence seeped into the room with me. The image was also beautiful, practically pulling me into a wicked trance.

My need to know the painting's meaning grew stronger at that moment.

When asked what the serpent represented, I said "It could represent a demon. Or Satan himself. Maybe Leonardo just used the features of a crocodile to represent the serpent, as Leonardo wrote about in reference to creating imaginary creatures. He wrote that features of existing creatures in nature, such as a crocodile, should be used to create imaginary ones, such as a serpent, or devil. But I'm still researching it."

I didn't want every interview to focus on just Leonardo and *Mona Lisa* since there were so many other important artists and works of art involved. Including more pieces of art in reports would be more convincing to readers and viewers. So, pulling images from my mind, I introduced illusions not covered in the first report: "Another crocodile head in Titian's *Venus of Urbino.* An ape, lion, and elephant head in his *Pastoral Concerto.* An elephant head on Michelangelo's *Fall and Expulsion from Garden of Eden* on the Sistine Chapel ceiling. Botticelli and Raphael also hid images."

I pointed out that Botticelli's art contained mostly anamorphic illusions of human-like faces where other artists focused on animal heads. It was yet another layer of mystery to what it all meant.

As I mentally scrolled through the endless list of paintings and drawings, I realized that it would take a book to mention them all. I also found it odd that I wasn't nervous at all after a bit of talking. I wasn't sure if it was because I felt so comfortable talking about art, or that I was on the phone and in the safety of my own home, or if Daniel's unexpected call gave me no time to overthink the interview, thus giving me no time in which to build up worry and become nervous about it. The combination of all three may have helped. (In the process, I forgot all about Rick on the other end—who had probably hung up by then.)

The experience of my first interview with Skeptic Ray seemed to capture what I had felt all my life. It was always the same scenario. I'd become so worried about all the things that could go wrong in giving a class presentation, or speaking in a microphone at a team building event for work, or being interviewed on live TV, that I drove myself crazy with worry.

The events themselves weren't the cause of my stage fright, I realized. Although I had been so scared about the publicity, the first interview turned out fine. And the one with Daniel wasn't going bad. In fact, it was enjoyable. I actually liked challenging my own fear, and more so as I found myself thriving in the situation. Maybe I'd never be able to avoid stage fright altogether, or the anxiety of an interview, but I knew for the first time in my life that I could deal with it, maybe even learn to ignore it.

"Daniel, it's important to realize *The Last Supper* and *Mona Lisa* basically show the same hidden animal heads."

"Brilliant. And these 'anamorphic illusions' exist in the Sistine Chapel ceiling also, you say?"

"Yes. They're very subtle."

"Very good. *Very* good."

"It's also important to note that all these were created before 1533 when Hans Holbein painted *The Ambassadors*, because art scholars thought it was one of the first Renaissance paintings, if not the first, with this kind of illusion. It's just that, before 1533, artists like Leonardo camouflaged the illusions into the art."

"Remarkable."

It sounded like he meant it, which filled me with pride.

"What do you think the images mean?" he asked.

"I was hoping someone would come forward with that answer. It's part of the reason I'm publicizing what I found."

23

Distorting the Picture

After my call with Daniel, I kept waiting for the latest episode of *The Today Show* to appear on their home page, anxiously hitting my browser's reload icon for what seemed like hours until the story was finally uploaded. There was *Mona Lisa*—a thumbnail image next to a piece on Brad Pitt. I couldn't click the play icon fast enough. I had no idea what to expect, despite Rick's reaction.

Lester Holt opened with the story. He noted her famous smile, and described how I was looking past her smile and finding hidden images. But he referred to me as an art historian. Not sure where he got that idea, but I never implied to anyone that I was an art historian—because I wasn't.

I also didn't know how *The Today Show* found out about the story or got hold of the news footage. Was it the press release? Did the local news channel contact them? I figured they were maybe an affiliate. And I don't know why I wasn't contacted to verify any of the information or answer questions.

Lester then introduced NBC's Keir Simmons, who was reporting on the story from London. How did it make news in another country so quickly? And on a major network at that? It made the world suddenly seem like a small place—as if the United Kingdom was just across the street, and not on the other side of the ocean. It felt like everyone in the world was about to learn just who I was. Whatever was going to be said about me would be perceived as fact. I was at the mercy of Lester and Keir. My discoveries and reputation were in their hands.

Keir, who reminded me of a younger Pierce Brosnan, told the camera that experts have studied *Mona Lisa*'s every brushstroke, but wondered how we could all have missed something "that one man in Rochester, New York, stumbled upon?"

Creepy violin music from Italian Composer Gaetano Donizetti that I had used on my YouTube video sounded in the background.

"Mystery is never far from the name Leonardo da Vinci," said Keir.

Tom Hanks appeared in a scene from *The Da Vinci Code* as Keir commented. I grew up watching Hanks in *Bosom Buddies*—one of my favorite 80s sitcoms. Hanks played the role of a single man struggling to survive in the advertising industry. I watched it then, and lived it later. (Minus the part where he wore women's clothing, pretending to be a girl.)

"For look a little closer," said Kier. "…Isn't that the face of an animal?" The camera zoomed onto one animal head and then another.

He was correct. It was the face of an animal. You couldn't miss it. And I was in the middle of trying to uncover why. Yet, his voice had a note of mockery.

I was glad my story reached a major news show, but also slightly annoyed at the overtone of amusement I was detecting. But was it my story? Or was the program taking it in another direction—the wrong direction? The report interspersed clips from my interview with Skeptic Ray. I thought of all the hundreds of thousands or millions of people across the country—across many countries—watching on television. I'd hoped that what I'd discovered would be presented fully and fairly, but it didn't sound like it was going in that direction.

Keir explained how I was researching an art project when I found "writings in Da Vinci's own notebook referencing the beasts." His use of the word *beasts* gave a bizarre feel to what I found. (As if it wasn't bizarre enough already.)

Maybe the spin they were putting on the story would help. Maybe it would give it the controversial feel that would bring it more attention.

"In London," he continued, "where an exhibition of Da Vinci's five-hundred-year-old art is drawing large crowds, experts agree that Leonardo da Vinci liked his pictures to be more than a little cryptic, but are yet to be convinced about this latest discovery."

The image of a prestigious-looking man seated in an antique-style office came on, making the MacBook he was using on his desk seem out-of-place. The name MARTIN KEMP, ART HISTORIAN floated onto the screen.

I recognized Kemp from books and articles I had read and documentaries I had watched. He was considered one the world's leading experts on Leonardo da Vinci, if not the leading expert, so I was a little shocked at his presence. I thought my publicity would inspire people to come forward and help explain the animals' meaning—scholars, historians, amateurs, anyone who had a reasonable answer to the mystery—but I never expected the world's leading expert on Leonardo da Vinci to weigh in.

Still, maybe Kemp could explain why the images were hidden? Why had the artists not mentioned them? Why were some images visible only from certain angles—distorted and anamorphic—and other images ambiguous? Why were so *many* major artists doing it, and in so many of their paintings? Why did images seem to be limited to specific animals and sometimes human-like faces? Why were Leonardo's writings coded with double meaning?

So I held my breath. Kemp was the one person who could add credibility to my findings or squash them completely—and with just a few words. If he found what I was saying plausible, or even just interesting, surely the opinion of the world's leading expert would mean that *some* scholars would take my findings seriously enough to look further for answers. If he didn't, I would end up an object of ridicule, and have to continue searching on my own. If that became the case, I'd likely never find them.

I leaned forward in my chair, waiting for Kemp's next words.

Kemp's laptop showed two images of *Mona Lisa*. Even though the images were only visible when the painting was on its side or viewed from the d-point, the images on Kemp's screen were in the upright position. And he was looking at them straight on. That wasn't a good sign. If Kemp were investigating my claims, the image would not appear to him that way. One *Mona Lisa* looked like it had either been color-corrected or was a picture of the painting after a cleaning, much more bluer and truer to its original color. Seeing two of the same images together made me think of the Prado version of *Mona Lisa*. The Prado version was a replica—practically a twin of the original. Experts thought that one of Leonardo's students may have painted it. Replicas were not unusual. Multiple portraits from various artists were usually created of royal figures and religious ones, like Christ or the Virgin Mary. To me, the Prado was another piece of evidence that Leonardo's version was likely someone other than Lisa Gherardini, who was neither royalty nor divine. And the Prado version wasn't the only replica. There was the *Isleworth Mona Lisa*—another version some scholars believed Leonardo painted. But there was no evidence to prove that he had. It wasn't common for artists to sign their works at the time. (Michelangelo carved his name into his *Pietà* after hearing a crowd mistakingly credit the sculpture to another artist, but found it to be an act of vanity. He never signed another work of art again.) And I had checked the replicas for hidden imagery—there was nothing to be found in the Prado or *Isleworth Mona Lisa* when examined from Leonardo's d-point. No ambiguous or anamorphic images.

In fact, as I watched, it occurred to me that the presence of hidden or anamorphic imagery could be used as a tool. Artworks had different characteristics based on which artists painted them, and these characteristics were clues that helped distinguish the creators of some of the world's greatest artworks from copies or disputed works. The presence and handling of hidden or anamorphic imagery was another defining mark of some artists. What I had discovered could help narrow down the identities of artists of disputed works of art. The images Leonardo hid had a dark and serious tone. Titian's had more of a comical appearance. The hidden imagery was a signature that could help prove that the work in question was genuinely theirs.

But to see those images, you had to look at the artwork from particular angles. That's not what Kemp was doing. It worried me that Kemp wasn't looking at them that way. Instead, he was viewing them straight on, so nothing would show up from his point of view. I had a sinking feeling.

"There *is* deeper meaning in his paintings," Kemp responded with a British accent, "but there are not [some] kind of hidden objects. They're not some kind of visual puzzle in that sense."

He seemed to sigh in frustration. I took the look on his face to say: *Here*

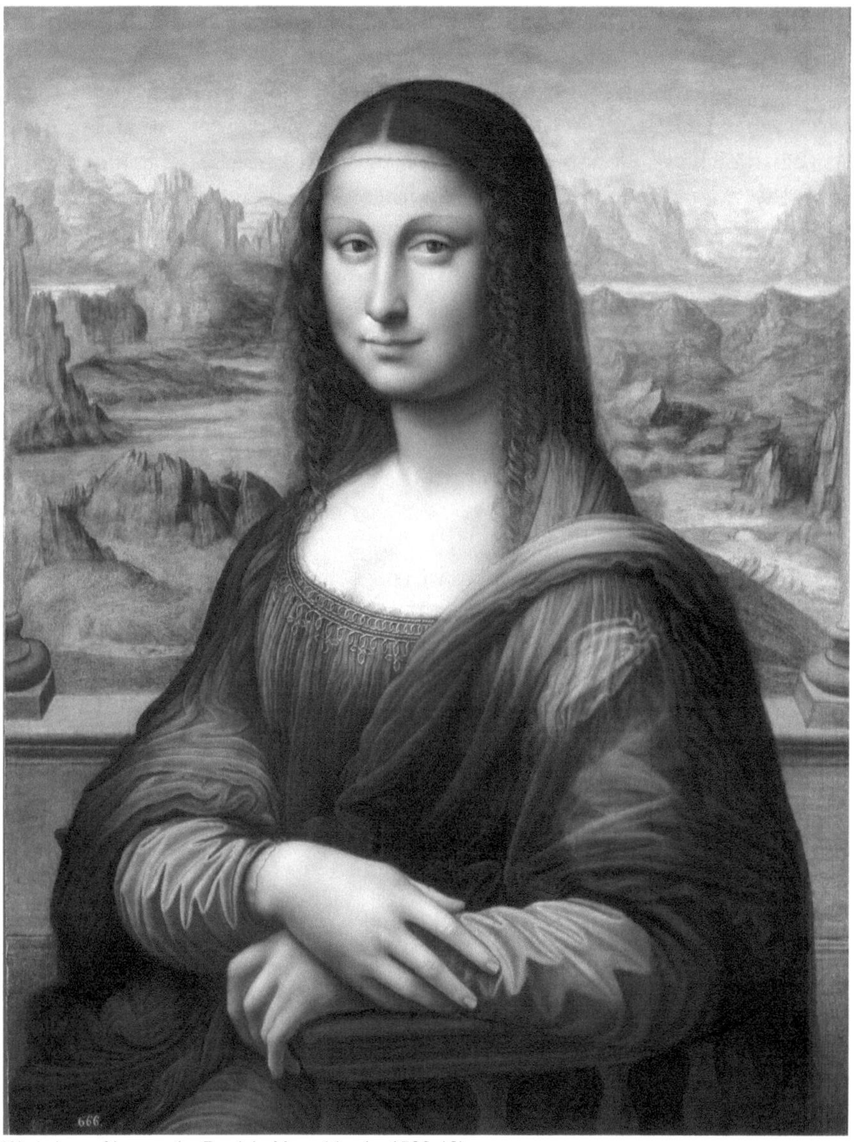

Workshop of Leonardo, Prado's *Mona Lisa* (c. 1503-16).

we go again, another silly Mona Lisa *theory!*

I leaned back in my chair and blew out a breath.

But I couldn't blame him. I found myself sympathizing.

I had done so much research into *Mona Lisa* since seeing that first hidden image. I had read many, many theories about the portrait over the years. Some were beyond ridiculous. Art historians were probably exposed to silly, unconvincing, even crazy, theories all the time. They had to be sick and tired of them. If I were in Kemp's place, I'd roll my eyes at the mention of a new theory.

"But this is different," I wanted to yell at the screen. "It's not a theory. The images are *there. Just look!*"

I wished I could have been there to show and explain to him what I found. But I wasn't. And, based on the upright images he was viewing on his computer, and that they had called me an art historian when I had never made any such claim, I wondered if anyone had even bothered to explain to Kemp *how* to see the images? Had he simply just been asked *if* there were images hiding?

Maybe the biggest distorted picture was the one journalists had presented to Kemp. But, it no longer mattered. My claims had just been shot down by Kemp. By the world's leading Leonardo expert. On a show with worldwide coverage.

Keir reported that "Experts do, in all honesty, doubt [Leonardo] intended to hide the shapes of animals in his work," but I wondered if he talked to any other historians besides Kemp. Toward the end of his report, Keir commented that

> The *Mona Lisa* is on display in the Louvre in Paris, and perhaps, from now on, those visiting that famous museum might take a little more time and step just a touch nearer. But whether there really are animals hidden in DaVinci's paintings or whether Ron is simply seeing things that aren't there—that, perhaps, is the real riddle.[1]

I replayed the video a few more times, amazed *The Today Show* had covered my discoveries internationally, but also noting that scholars who saw the report might simply agree with Kemp and not bother to take the initiative to investigate any further.

I wondered if the mysteries would remain unsolved forever.

And if I had made the biggest mistake of my life.

24

Deeper Distortions

A few days later, Daniel's article came out. Not in the *Daily Mail*, as he originally mentioned. Instead, it was in *The Sun*—the largest paper in the entire United Kingdom. When I read the article, I almost choked. Even though I had called the sitter *Envy*, I was pretty sure I didn't say anything about the seven deadly sins. But Daniel referred to it that way. He also wrote that I "noticed the lion's head hovering in the air ..." and then I saw "the buffalo and I thought, 'Oh my God.'"[1]

I didn't remember saying those things either. *Oh my God* wasn't an expression that naturally came out of my mouth. If words *had* slipped from my mouth, the phrase would likely have been closer to "Holy shit, there's a freakin' lion right there."

The article also said I had "discovered what looked like a crocodile or snake coming out of the left-hand side of [*Mona Lisa*'s] body." *Coming out of her body?* How could anyone take me seriously after reading that? I read over it a few times, hoping I had read it incorrectly. I thought I had been clear on explaining that "serpent" referred to the crocodile. Where did he get the impression it was bursting out of the woman in *Mona Lisa* like the creature in the *Alien* movie that broke out of the guy's chest? I was sure I had also described it being *behind* her, and that the crocodile's snout could be *seen* to her left and the rest of its head to her right.

The article didn't mention any other artists. Maybe I was overreacting, but didn't anyone care about paintings from artists like Michelangelo or Botticelli? The attention was all about *Mona Lisa, Mona Lisa, Mona Lisa.*

I was learning a lot about the media world, such as the big difference in what was actually said and what was reported—especially in-between quotation marks. One thing I didn't want to deal with was rude criticism from any reporters.

Daniel, at least, had been polite and enjoyable to talk to.

One morning at work I got a call from a journalist who said she was from the *Toronto Star.* I snuck into an empty meeting room for some privacy. She seemed nice as she asked questions about how I became so interested in *Mona Lisa*—an assumption I continuously corrected: I was indifferent about the painting until *after* I came across the strange animals. As soon as I listed the specific mammals, though, her mood changed.

"Wait," she protested. "A *buffalo*?" Her voice rose, killing any objective tone she had. I wasn't sure if she thought I was joking. "How would Leonardo da Vinci know what a buffalo looked like?" she said. "Why would he paint a buffalo? Don't you know there *are* no buffalo in Italy?" She threw me the questions in an annoyed tone without giving me time to answer. It suddenly felt like an interrogation. All that was missing was the bright, hot lamp pointed at my face.

"I ...don't know," I said, "but the buffalo is in his painting."

I heard the light slam of something over the phone. It sounded like a notebook closing or maybe a hand slapping a pencil onto the desk. I stood there feeling like an idiot, desperate for a good answer to give her. I thought of Leonardo's drawings. He sketched images of dragons and the apocalypse and Jesus and His apostles, but he never saw those either. He probably saw drawings and paintings of them by other artists. I've never seen Leonardo da Vinci for that matter, but I knew what he looked like enough to draw him based on drawings and paintings I'd seen. Why was it hard to believe Leonardo created something that could have been based on someone else's illustration, perhaps by someone who had been to a place where buffalo actually roamed?

"I have all the information I need," she then told me. *Interview over.*

I asked when the article would publish, unsure what else to say in the awkward moment.

"I don't know, I'll have to run it past the editor," she told me. But it sounded like a response just to get me off the phone.

Right after the interview, frustrated and unable to let it go, I looked up the buffalo's history. Wasn't that part of her job anyway, something the reporter should have done before criticizing me? Although some species of European bison became extinct before the 1900s,[2] the Bufala Mediterranea Italiana (water buffalo), introduced to Italy during the Barbarian invasions, was indigenous to the region.[3] I wish I had known that before.

There were other possibilities to Leonardo's ability to paint a buffalo. Among many things, he was a zoologist. And during that time, royalty sometimes displayed their wealth by showcasing their exotic animals. Leonardo spent some time around royalty.

Each day following, I waited for the story to appear, but as far as I could tell, the *Toronto Star* story never saw the light of day.

Many journalists, including Daniel, really were a pleasure to talk to. More and more, I found myself feeling comfortable talking with them. But was it helping me understand what I discovered? Was I *learning* anything, or just getting exposure that took time away from my job, my life, and my search for the truth about *Mona Lisa*'s mysteries? Eventually, I began to look forward to the publicity coming to an end.

25

Betrayal

As a commercial graphic designer, my job was to catch the attention of viewers and convey a specific message with my art. A design's success was impossible to calculate since there were too many factors, such as how and where and when to place ad campaigns through different media. There were too many things to consider. Not only where and how to place an ad, but whether in a magazine, social media, a billboard? Snail mail, email blast, or television commercial? Saturday, Tuesday, or the second Thursday of the month? The 9:00 p.m. slot or mid-morning? Could the client afford to do all of the above?

Nothing made me more enthusiastic than creating a billboard. Seeing my work hovering over different parts of the city was like having the biggest exhibit in town. One with the most viewers by far since many stood over the busiest expressways in the city.

To maximize publicity, a client might be assigned a team of experts. It could include account executives, creative directors, art directors, web designers, publicists, media experts, and artists, to name a few. It wasn't cheap. A national campaign, such as a Super Bowl commercial, might cost millions just to air a 30-second spot, plus the cost of making the commercial. So when *The Today Show* spent three minutes covering what I found, a story viewable to millions and spreading to other countries, and having done it with only Kristine to help me, it felt like I could accomplish anything.

Although I was sort of disappointed by how *The Today Show* story turned out, the story was out there at least. That was something. Maybe experts would look into the mystery of the images despite the media piece. My fingers were crossed regardless.

The publicity also gave me a sad sense of isolation from the world. I was on my own in the spotlight, feeling like Neil Armstrong when he left Earth's atmosphere and first stepped onto the moon, unsure what those steps might bring and likely thinking of everything that could go wrong.

I knew that no matter how other reports would portray me, I'd be able to handle it, to shrug it off if I had to. It wouldn't be the end of the world. I learned that about myself many years before, in my relationship with Paige.

In my twenties, more than a decade before, I met Paige. We dated a few years, and talked about marriage and kids. I was envious of other people my age who already had families of their own. So, on a beach in the Bahamas, I proposed to her. A year later, we were married at a private country club.

We loved each other, but, over time, our arguments became disastrous. We lacked the proper skills to communicate. She would yell. I would use hurtful words. Yet, no matter how angry I got, I never screamed, as if that made it okay.

After one of our more furious episodes, I caught my reflection in the bathroom mirror and was frozen by how enraged I looked. Paige had mentioned my cruel look when I argued, but I never saw it with my own eyes until then. The man in the mirror had the snarl of a wolf and the stubbornness of a mule.

It reminded me of how my father sometimes looked when arguing with Ma, and it made me hate myself for how I was.

Over time, Paige became distant, her words short.

One morning, I stepped out of the shower as she stood in front of the mirror brushing on her makeup, wearing only a bra and panties. Despite our fights, I saw her as beautiful and desirable, and I loved how the curves of her skin glowed. As I reached for a towel, I saw three odd, reddish marks on her back—what looked to me like scratches. In our most intimate moments, we never clawed at each other like animals, so I didn't think they could be mine. And they looked too wide to have been made by her own fingers. I pointed them out. She said it was just dry skin. Her eyes seemed to tell me something different. I felt my stomach free-fall, and I became enraged with jealousy, imagining Paige embracing another man in the dark.

Trying to deny what my gut screamed, the room became a blur of red. A vision entered my mind the next moment with calculating detail of me slamming her head against the mirror, broken shards of glass shattering against the floor. The vision continued with her trying to regain focus as I returned from the kitchen with a long chopping knife—the one I used to slice raw chicken with ease. Then the image of me pulling back her hair, tightening the tendons of her neck as I moved the knife in a few quick swipes. Drops of blood speckled the white tile, then a widening spill of dark merlot as Paige fell limply to the floor.

The vision passed as quickly as it appeared, and I left the bathroom without saying another word. Based on relationships I had before Paige, I knew I was prone to jumping to conclusions, that my jealousy sometimes caused me to imagine the worst, and I knew how damaging such a false accusation could be.

Still, I was devastated, and I fought with the idea of what to do. Had Paige been with someone else or was I imagining it, making it all up in my head? It was hard to ignore what was real. The hardest thing to consider was giving up our marriage and the chance at having kids—a future my heart had been set on.

Weeks passed after seeing those marks on my wife's back, and I still wasn't sure what to do. Leave her? Forgive her? Go on pretending I didn't know what

I felt sure was going on?

I was hopeless. I'd look in the mirror and see only a failure, barely able to look myself in the eyes, sickened by my own reflection. Divorce was the only option I saw. In a way, there was something strangely comforting about the idea. Maybe because, in a crazy way, it would finally give me and my dad something in common.

But I struggled to work up the courage to tell her. We were sitting next to each other on the couch one evening. She was watching television. I was just staring at the screen, going over the words I had been practicing to tell her. But every time I readied myself to say them, my throat would turn to stone. The idea of putting it into words seemed so heinous. I hated her so much, and yet I still loved her. For a while we quietly sat there. She was gently fidgeting with her cuff when she turned to me with a troubled look. She touched her hand to my knee, and I thought I was going to vomit. The unexpected touch was like an excruciating poison. *Did you touch* his *knee like that before he made love to you?* I wanted to scream at her. I put a hand on my stomach to steady my sudden nausea.

"I'm pregnant," she then told me.

I must have looked confused because she repeated the words. It was like being stung by giant wasps.

I don't remember how we decided it, but days later it was decided. I didn't know the decision would haunt me forever. Yet I wondered if it was even mine. I didn't know if I would be able to take knowing that it wasn't. Feeling like I had failed to keep my wife happy and that I lacked control over my own life, the idea that it had been *me* who had gotten her pregnant seemed like the only piece of dignity I had left to cling onto.

We drove to a clinic. Neither of us said anything on the way there. We pulled into the parking lot in back of the building—so no one could see us go in. I didn't exactly understand the effect of what we were about to do. I didn't know how I was *supposed* to feel. But I felt it was my job to escort her there. Like a guard walking a death row inmate to the chair.

They called her to the back room. I sat in the waiting area up front, confused about the whole thing. I couldn't figure out how I was going to act or what I was going say when she returned. When they were done with her, I could tell that the woman I had brought there was gone. As if they had secretly given me a clone of Paige instead. She looked and acted like she was someone else. Her eyes were different. Her body language was different. She seemed lost.

I didn't have the heart after that to divorce her. I thought maybe the new version of her would never stray, as if she had been reset, and that we would be able to start over. Hope was all I had, and at the time, I didn't believe life could get any worse. But it would get worse, and after that part of my life was over, I'd realize I was capable of handling almost anything.

26

Exposure

The Monday after that Saturday episode of *The Today Show* aired, I turned on my computer at work and saw a message on my Facebook wall that a friend had posted: *Guess what's trending on Yahoo!? You are!*[1]

I thought she was kidding until I saw my story on the *Yahoo!* home page. It was almost fake-looking, surreal, like someone had played a joke on me.

It wasn't a joke.

In addition, over the next few days, my YouTube video—which I expected might get 5,000 views—received more than 400,000 views. The count was nothing compared to other viral videos out there, but it surprised me nonetheless, especially since it was the first video I ever uploaded to the site. My blog averaged 10,000 visitors a day. Previously, a few likes on social media would have made my day.

Facebook friend requests trickled in from all over the world—Istanbul, Greece, Ghana, Serbia—and other places I had never heard of. Using Google Analytics, I followed the story's geographical reach online with amazement. The news of *Mona Lisa*'s animals had circled the Earth, hitting every single country in the world. Immediately after my press release, 200 reports mentioning my name had shown up in Internet search results. That increased quickly to 500. Then 2,000, climbing to 10,000 and rising in just days. Like an explosion of aerial waves across the Earth's surface, my name showed up all over the Internet in all sorts of languages. But it wasn't until I saw an article about me from China, *written in Chinese,* that reality hit me on how far the story had spread. It felt incredible, like I had made contact with some alien planet I thought would be impossible to reach.

But something else was just as incredible. With all those countless eyes all over the world seeing what I had found, still, not one person contacted me with any explanation to the animal heads. I thought surely someone, somewhere, had been puzzled by the same mysteries as I had and would come up with answers, or even just speculations. But there was nothing. No one. I was no closer to the answers than before. Journalists continued asking their meanings, and yet, I could only tell them I was still researching for answers.

I had no control in what the reports said. The journalists controlled the story. Some were enthusiastic, some skeptical, others objective. I welcomed every perspective, and so I continued answering their questions. No publicity was necessarily bad. I expected, hoped even, that the range of views would cause controversy—the most powerful kind of publicity.

I was getting so comfortable with being interviewed that I began expressing my theories instead of sticking to what I knew for sure. It was a way to keep the information fresh—to give them new material. I suggested a possible religious connection to the hidden images. Plus it made sense. After all, the *Envy* passage—which described *Mona Lisa*—mentioned God. But it was only a theory.

Yet, plenty of non-religious Renaissance art contained the images. Even sketches Leonardo made during his scientific studies had them.

By then, my living space was filled with books on Renaissance artists, biographies, symbolism, and history. I had to buy extra shelves to keep them from sitting in piles on the tables and floors.

I also brought home books specific to the time period and the Medieval one immediately before, since I noticed that some images appeared earlier, like in Giotto's art and other artists that came way before Leonardo.

I thought that if I could learn as much as possible about life back in Renaissance Italy, maybe I'd have a better idea on what the artists were thinking back then, which would help me get an idea of what they may have been trying to hide. Or maybe it would help me realize whether it was all just some gigantic joke.

I didn't think that post-Renaissance history mattered (in relation to *Mona Lisa* anyway), so I stuck to what happened before and during that period. My reading list included all sorts of books that seemed significant for the time—copies of Leonardo's notebooks; *Signs & Symbols in Christian Art*; *Mona Lisa: Inside the Painting*; *How to Read a Painting*; *How to Read Bible Stories and Myths in Art*; *Masters of Deception*; *The Divine Comedy*; *The Canterbury Tales*; *The Holy Bible*; *Vasari's Lives of the Artists*; *Man and the Renaissance;* and many other references.

New books arrived every few days at my door. I even read fictional books like Dan Brown's *The Da Vinci Code* for the first time and watched the movie, looking for ideas that might point me in a direction I hadn't yet thought of or to a piece of knowledge unknown to me—double-checking of course for actual facts whenever sources were fictional. I was desperate for a lucky break, and wasn't going to rule anything out, so I looked everywhere I could think of.

To make things more difficult, I was a slow reader. Time and again I wished I had a team of specialists to help me research. But there was also something about working alone that I liked. I thought maybe an answer would never be found. That maybe it had something to do with some previously known event forgotten about over the centuries, or had been kept secret to begin with, or was never recognized as important enough to be written about in art history books.

If centuries of experts couldn't figure out *Mona Lisa*'s riddles, what chance did I really have? Especially without help. I felt like David against Goliath, except without his sling and stones.

Still, I kept at it. Maybe it was because I was an artist. I enjoyed learning all I could about the great artists, the ancestors of my craft, even if I didn't know if I'd ever find my answers. Like a sponge (as one creative director had compared me to), I soaked in the knowledge I collected as I tried to understand what I saw in their paintings. There was even something very therapeutic about it. Like sailing the ocean on a calm day with no destination in mind.

My years as an artist provided me with a trained eye. Artists learn to see art, and visualize images, in special ways. Even dealing with clients teaches you things about what artists can and can't put into or leave out of their work. I had spent years studying art in college, in galleries, in books, and on the job. That experience gave me an edge non-artists, however well-read, might not ever have.

Artists have unique ways of seeing things and putting art together. It's what made a Picasso so different from a Monet. So while I didn't expect every artist to see the images I saw, I expected that some would. And some did. So it was an especially pleasant surprise to see how many messages I received from people from all walks of life who saw the heads. I suppose I shouldn't have been that surprised. It's hard not to see what's there, especially when someone points it out.

What I didn't like were the rude comments posted to my video and blog: "Worst bullshit ever," "This guy's a real attention whore," "A load of tosh. Your imagination equates to a runaway train!" and "A theory based on a question mark? Cut off your ear and send it to your mother, you're insane!"[2]

They're just closed-minded, I'd tell myself. To me it seemed that they couldn't see the illusions; therefore, in their minds, the illusions didn't exist. I didn't think they considered the possibility of being wrong.

Kristine suggested I reply to everyone to keep them engaged and help keep the story traveling and also to defend what I found. It wasn't a matter of arguing. "Remember, you're just presenting what's there," she told me.

So that's what I did. Keeping up with replies was a lot of work, and it was draining. Sometimes I wanted to lash out at those leaving rude remarks. I told myself I wouldn't take the comments personally, but it was difficult not to. It made the discoveries more personal too. And it also made me more intent on searching for the truth.

The problem was, unless they read my blog, most people were unaware of all the other discoveries I'd made. No one wanted to report the *whole* story. There were hidden images in hundreds if not thousands of other paintings, but because most reports focused only on *Mona Lisa*, many people who criticized me were unaware of all the hidden symbolism in the other artists' works unless they had read my blog posts—which many had not, but were still quick to jump to their conclusions.

I kept making a point of mentioning new illusions in each interview, hoping reporters would talk about more than just *Mona Lisa*, but it didn't seem to work.

Growing tired of getting nowhere, I began to miss working on my own oil paintings. Art was the love of my world. There were times it kept me preoccupied when it was what I needed most to forget about a problem in my life. It was also my most therapeutic activity, but the discoveries seemed to compromise that since they caused more frustration than enjoyment at times.

With each passing day, I wanted the interviews to be over more and more. I wanted to get back to working with my pencils and paints and brushes. Back to my normal life, and putting the discoveries behind me.

27

Dear John

As I thought more about the religious connections the images might have, I again found myself confronting my own religious beliefs—or lack there of. At times in my life, I had blamed God for the outcome of certain events. That was until I became sure that the reason my prayers were never answered was because there was no one there to answer them.

Every so often, I'd think back to my time with Paige. In struggling to deal with what I believed was her infidelity, it felt like my life was collapsing around me. I also struggled with my relationship with my father, and found it easier to distance myself from him when what I craved was to be closer. We just didn't seem to have anything in common—and neither of us put forth the effort to pretend that we did. My outside life affected my work as a graphic artist at the screen printing shop where I was employed. I barely had the strength to move through each day. I felt like I was stuck in an Edvard Munch painting.

One bitterly cold day in February of 2005, as snow quietly fell outside, I was shaken from my chair by the sound of a truck crashing against the side of our building—an old barn that had been renovated. The truck's impact caused the floors and walls and everything attached to vibrate as if from an earthquake.

I heard my coworker Katie scream John's name from outside. Katie, a fifty-year-old mother of two, was our customer service person. John—who was quite open about his strong Christian faith—was still in college, was working part-time while studying to become a graphic designer.

I ran to the exit door, looking out on the parking lot where the sound of the explosion came from. Katie hurried back inside, passing me with a look of terror. More coworkers rushed inside through the doorway where I stood, but hesitant to go through. Minutes before, everyone had stepped outside to help with a large delivery—everyone except for me and the customer I was working with at my desk. Of the six of us in the building, I accounted for everyone stepping back inside except John.

The February air bit at my face when I stepped out through the door and onto the elevated platform overlooking the parking lot. A short distance away was a man—the driver—in a kneeling position on the ground, cupping his face with his hands like a crying child who had just fallen and scraped his knee. His truck was parked behind him. I could see how he had backed it up way too quickly, smashing its rear into the building (later learning he had mistaken the gas pedal for the brake). Its back wheels were still up on the incline of the grass as it leaned forward.

"*John.* Oh *John*," Katie yelped behind me.

I don't know how long I stood there before stepping awkwardly down each stair toward the pavement. It was like I had lost some control in my legs, and I fought the terrifying urge to turn back, petrified of what was down there, as if I were stepping into a pool of starving crocodiles.

As patches of ice cracked under my feet, I saw something that took a moment to register—an arm peeking out horizontally from the rear of the truck still in contact with the building. Five curled fingers hung lazily from the arm. It looked like someone had jammed a life-size Jesus crucifix in the inches of space where the truck smashed into the wall. My approach took enormous effort. The kneeling man was a short distance between us. His face was as pale as the snow.

"What happened?" I managed to ask as I approached, despite my throat feeling clamped shut.

He lifted his eyes up to mine and tried to speak, but his mouth just opened silently. I could see strands of saliva stretched between his tongue and teeth. Everything was in slow motion but also spinning uncontrollably fast. Flakes of snow fell around us like tiny angels coming to collect a soul.

When the scene finally registered, I hollered with all my might: "Move the truck! Get it off him!"

My voice seemed to shake some part of him awake, and he rose as if it hurt every part of his body to do so. Time was crucial, and I knew it was John behind that truck, pinned between it and the exterior wall. The shock of it didn't allow me to see what I otherwise would have realized—that the loud crushing sound was a result of the truck slamming into the outside wall, with John being slammed against it just as hard.

The truck moved forward seconds later, and something, someone, dropped to the ground behind it. No question that John would be hurt. Would he have some broken bones? A crushed lung? A horrible concussion? I stepped carefully, distancing myself from the truck, as if it were possessed and capable of losing control a second time, knocking me from my feet.

The rest of the memory came to me in bits and pieces over the following weeks. My mind (I later realized) disconnected itself from its recording device as if to protect itself. Automatic shut-off. Silence came, like everything was under water. I wanted to scream for help at what I saw, but there was no sound. Just like in those nightmares I used to have as a child, where I was being chased and couldn't call out for help. Until then, that had only taken place in my sleep.

When I reached the back of the truck, John's feet came into view. Then his legs. They formed the shape of the letter P. One straight, one bent at the knee. Patches of grass peeked through the snow around him, framing him like a picture of a tossed rag doll. Just minutes before, he had walked past me on his way outside. So he *had* to be alive, I thought. Really, really hurt, but alive. I waited for his chest to rise and fall, or an arm to twitch in pain. But he just laid there, as still as Christ being held by the Virgin Mary in Michelangelo's *Pietà* sculpture.

I drew up the courage to look at his face. It didn't quite look like him anymore. His head was deformed, oblong and cone-shaped like that of a newborn baby. It had cracked open, and from the back of his head, vapor was escaping into the winter air. Strangely, not a single hair was out of place.

His right pupil, the size of a pencil dot, stared up past me. His left eye was gone from its empty, pink socket. It hung on the side of his head against his cheek, facing his ear. I couldn't help studying the large orb shape, as if he were just some bizarre art exhibit. His lower jaw had split from his skull, the skin stretched over it.

I forced myself to look away, yet even then it felt rude to do so, as though I would offend him by not being able to accept his new appearance. But then I was looking at the wall next to me where he had slammed his head. Stuck there to the wall was a circular pattern of chicken-like pieces, but bloodless.

I managed to pull out my phone.

"He's gone," I told the 911 operator, too terrified to say the word *dead.*

"Can you feel for a pulse?" She asked.

"He's *gone*," was all I could say, again.

"We need to make sure," she said more sternly. "Do you know how to perform CPR?"

I closed my eyes without responding to the question.

Then came the sound of the first siren in the distance. It shocked my body like a jolt of electricity. A fire truck appeared. Then an ambulance. Then a tidal wave of police cars. An unsynchronized orchestra of CB radios crackling helter-skelter.

I didn't want to leave John alone with all those uniformed strangers. But the crowd of police, firemen, and medics surrounding his body slowly pushed me aside.

Some time later, I was sitting outside, zombie-like, cold and numb under the darkened sky, floating in a sea of red and white strobes, overlooking the snowy parking lot trampled with footprints. There was yellow barricade tape. The image of the truck and John's tarp-covered body next to it froze itself into a very deep part of my memory. A part of me had also died at that scene.

Paige came to pick me up, and as we drove away, I slowly turned to catch the dreadful scene, its mirrored reflection spread across the water of the canal hugging the road. And I knew right then that our life together had to end.

I doubted God's existence more than ever during that period of my life. At

John's funeral, I stood in the pew, holding Paige's hand, even though I decided I would end things between us. But just for that moment, I needed to hold someone's—*anyone's*—hand, desperate to touch something that felt real and alive. I remember standing there, wishing that God were real and would appear to me face to face, just so I could tell Him how much I hated Him. I didn't care about any consequence it would bring. I was too shattered to care.

From that day on, I wondered what it all meant. Everyone at one point in their life wonders what their purpose is. That day, I wondered about mine. What was the meaning of my life? I was determined to spend time alone until I figured it out. I was independent by nature, and liked to keep to myself anyway, so I embraced my time alone. Paige and I filed for a divorce and sold our house. For months afterward, I felt so alone, unwanted, and broken. And for the next couple years, I kept to myself, to heal.

One day, I came across a cheap oil painting kit, out of place on a shelf in a department store. I never had the urge to paint with oils. Yet something would not allow me to leave the store without it. I took it home and instantly fell in love with the process. It helped fill some of the emptiness I felt. Then came *Mona Lisa*, and the discoveries a few short years later. And, though I found it hard to accept, I felt, deep in my soul, that I was meant to solve *Mona Lisa*'s mysteries. I knew it in a way that made no sense to me, but still I was sure.

There was a strange feeling that my past and present were connected in a way that defied logic. It was no secret that I wanted to be an artist from the very beginning, and that I was determined to make it my career.

Yet, the discoveries were different. For the first time in my life, I had a sense of purpose—more than a sense—it was closer to a knowing. But who was I to think I could find the answers on my own? Was I kidding myself? I wasn't an art historian, nor a detective. What chance did I have of figuring out who Envy really was? Or what the painting was supposed to mean? And what about its other mysteries, such as the reason the left and right sides of the horizon didn't line up? And where Leonardo got that background from? Was it imaginary, as some art historians thought?

I assumed he created the background from imagination since the animal heads were carved out of the mountainous landscape. Though I couldn't be sure. There was the possibility that he altered an existing background by adding the heads. It was all a bunch of riddles. Riddles no one had ever solved.

And what about the expressive smile the woman presented in the anamorphic perspective. What was *that* all about? I needed to know.

If my purpose in life really was to solve *Mona Lisa*, then why was it that the deeper I looked, the more puzzling she appeared to be?

28

Pride

Ma was really proud about the discoveries. "*My* son did that?" she would say out loud every so often, unable to get over the fact that the same news channels she watched for years, covering stories like the Kennedy assassination and the fall of the Berlin Wall, had presented stories on her own son.

Since my elementary school days, she would brag to her friends and family about my art, sometimes borrowing drawings from my room to show them when I wasn't around—which always left me embarrassed, because I didn't consider my art to be good enough to show.

At the first family gathering since the press release, everyone had something positive to tell me about what I'd done. My family would never see my news stories as good or bad. To them, being on the news was simply a proud moment for the whole family.

"The teacher talked about you in class, Uncle Ron," said my ten-year-old nephew as family members gathered around the kitchen island for appetizers before dinner. "He said how you found stuff in *Mona Lisa*."

"How did your teacher find out about it?" I asked, curious how the publicity found its way to certain demographics—like that of a high school teacher and students. It was interesting to see how the reports made their way through the Internet, or in newspapers, or TV, or simply by word of mouth.

"In the paper, I think."

I wasn't aware that any local paper had written an article about me, which I found odd since the story already reached other countries. But hearing my nephew's comment was more wonderful than making *The Today Show*.

I thought of all the historic figures I learned about when I was his age, and wondered if my name would ever be included on a school test one day.

> *What Italian artist discovered optical illusions in Renaissance art such as* Mona Lisa*?*
>
> *a. Danny DeVito*
> *b. Ariana Grande*
> *c. Ron Piccirillo*
> *d. Pablo Picasso*

"Uncle Ron," my six-year-old niece chimed in. "You're popular."

Hearing that made my heart melt. "I've always been popular," I joked.

I thought back to my dorky high school self, never once thinking that I would ever be called popular. One of my own friends regularly called out *Travolta* whenever he saw me, claiming that I styled my thick, fluffy hair like Tony Manero from *Saturday Night Fever*. (My older brother David referred to it as a bouffant, usually in front of his friends.)

"Has dad seen any of the news?" I turned to David and asked as I took an appetizer from one of the trays.

"You joking?" he snickered. "Sure. He saw your TV interview."

I could tell by his tone and expression that I was about to be disappointed.

Dad and I had not been on good terms, which made get-togethers a little awkward between us. We both greeted everyone else except each other at family gatherings. It wasn't that we hated each other. In what I considered an attempt to make me feel guilty, dad had been ignoring me. My brothers went through similar situations with him in the past, but eventually reconciled.

The previous year, I held out my hand to greet him and wish him a Merry Christmas. "I'm not going to wish you Merry Christmas," he told me, refusing to shake my hand, "because you never come visit me." I was hurt, and I was also ashamed as a son.

It was true that I rarely visited him. He voiced the concern quite a few times to me. In retaliation, I assumed he was ignoring me to teach me some kind of lesson, to make me guilt-ridden.

Up until my thirties, I pretended to agree with everything he said in order to avoid confrontation, and also out of respect, since he was my father. "You only get one father," Ma would joke, sometimes adding "...and you can't trade [him in] for another."

For years, I listened to my dad bad-mouth my mom. It were as if he expected me to hate her because of how he felt. "Should hang them all with a rope," he would growl to me about women, usually on our ride down to work at The Farm during my teenage years, "especially your mother, that son of a bitch"—which always came out as "you mudder, dat sonna-ma-bitch." His Italian accent made it more threatening, and sent waves of anxiety through me, especially since he would do his venting in the van as we rode, leaving me no escape. Years of him repeating that phrase over and over to me (along with other ideas on decreasing the female population) left me bitter and wanting to stand up to him. But I never did. My few attempts always backfired and left me feeling worse.

All my life, I craved my father's approval, so for the most part, I dealt with the torment. Maybe that made me a weak son. Or maybe it just made me a son. I wasn't sure. I'd convince myself that his temperament was a result of his upbringing in Italy and its culture at the time, justifying why he would voice his opinion without care for any repercussions. Still, I didn't think I could ever please him. Just before Paige and I had sold the house during our divorce, I invited dad over for coffee to break the news to him, sure that of all people, he would understand because of his own divorce. We sat at the kitchen table drinking cups of espresso when I told him. He was surprised, but showed little compassion. Instead, he criticized me, jumping to the conclusion that it was because I hadn't pleased my wife often enough in bed. He asserted this while making pumping motions at me with his fist. His reaction stung.

Months later, after moving into a rental property I had purchased in a desirable up-and-coming part of the city, I again invited him over, wanting his blessing. But he could only berate me about what a mistake it was to buy a house in the city.

There were other incidents that chipped away at my concern for our relationship. One day I realized I just didn't have the energy to deal with him anymore. It saddened me because I had become disconnected enough to be okay with the idea of not having him in my life. And I hated myself for that. I didn't think it was possible to resolve anything by talking with him. It was after that Christmas when he refused to shake my hand that I became irrational toward him, and decided to show him that I could be just as stubborn as I considered him to be, believing that it was the only way to prove to him that I was not some coward that would put up with his lack of respect.

When I made international news about *Mona Lisa*, I thought my father would put our differences aside for a moment to acknowledge what a terrific thing his son had done. A faint sliver of pride was all I wanted from those dark eyes of his. It would have given me the hope I once had in being able to live out some dysfunctional relationship with the man I used to call Papa.

"So did dad say anything when he saw me on the news?" I asked David.

He raised his eyebrows and gently shook his head: *No*. "I tried to explain it to him. With his English being so rusty, I'm sure he didn't understand the story because he started to talk about this and that. You know how he gets—he turned the conversation back to himself."

"How can he see me on the news and not even ask why I was on there?" I said with frustration, but with no surprise. The disappointment came to me in a way a retired boxer might find a scratch of comfort in getting punched—it was a reminder of how capable he was of easily handling the pain.

"He's impossible to impress," I said.

I didn't get any attention from dad, but journalists continued to call. Students from other countries sent me questions for papers they were writing. Some film grads asked me to come down to New York City for a low-budget documentary, but since I couldn't drop everything at work on such short notice to be there the next morning, they decided on another project.

I never thought I'd like the attention, but I was thrilled about the ripple in the art world I had caused. As a painter, I enjoyed having people discuss my work, whether constructive criticism or a plain liking for what I'd done.

Every so often I'd give some thought to the sense of purpose that was developing. But what did it really mean? Considering what I found, it became clear that we would have more insight into the lives of Renaissance artists. And because it contradicted what historians believed, it meant a possible change to what was written in history books. *Me, changing history*—it sounded so strange.

I received plenty of skepticism. While some applauded my findings, others challenged them. A search for *Mona Lisa blogs* returned over 3,760,000 online results. So of course there were bloggers who wanted to discuss my findings. *Why not?* I thought. But it became apparent that some of them didn't believe any of the things I had found. It was as though I were disrespecting the *Mona Lisa* by presenting new information about it. But I still exchanged emails at some of their requests, curious as to what they might point out that I could have missed. I wanted to know everyone's perspective on the painting. Maybe I'd learn something that could put me closer to figuring out the animal heads.

Of course, a few didn't agree with how I used the words *serpent* and *crocodile* interchangeably in reference to Leonardo's *Envy* passage. "Leonardo clearly knew the difference," they argued, insisting that serpent could only mean snake. But I wasn't easily convinced on what bloggers *believed* Leonardo knew. I considered the possibility, but preferred proof.

But they did have a point, so I wanted to get to the bottom of it. Taking serpent's correct usage, I knew it could mean "a large snake," or "a sly or treacherous person ..." or even "a bass wind instrument made of leather-covered wood ..." as the dictionary describes.[1]

Another possibility was that centuries ago—as I mentioned in my first interview—*serpent* could have had a different meaning, and that it might have been considered to be a *crocodile*. Just as Pluto was once considered a planet until it was not.

Since the *Envy* passage referenced God, I had to consider the possibility that Leonardo's use of the word *serpent* was biblical. So the first thing I looked up was its use in the Latin Vulgate Bible—a common version in Leonardo's time, and one he had in his possession. Of the 96 times I counted it used, one verse stuck out more than the others—"And he laid hold on the dragon the old serpent, which is the devil and Satan, and bound him for a thousand years" (*Douay-Rheims*, Apoc. 20:2).[2] It references the serpent as being five things: a dragon, the devil, Satan, male, and having been in existence for a long time—none of which stick to the presumed meaning of a snake. So if a serpent could be a dragon, why not a crocodile? (I would later find a definition by author George Ferguson, in *Signs & Symbols in Christian Art*, that "the dragon, or serpent, was selected by the painters of the Renaissance to symbolize the Devil."[3])

Since Leonardo wrote that characteristics of existing creatures in nature should be used to create imaginary ones, it made sense that he possibly used a crocodile head from nature to represent the devil, or serpent, which is imaginary.

One blogger accused me of *pareidolia*: seeing images that don't exist. That was a significant objection, and I thought seriously about it. Maybe I *was* seeing things. It was possible. But then why did Charles and Saul and many visitors to my blog comment about seeing the same things? Besides, can't someone with pareidolia also see things that *are* there? We may see a face in a cloud, but when we see a friend's face we're not making it up. It's really there. Plus, when we see a face in a cloud, we *know* we're making up the image in our mind. Most of us can tell the difference between a horse we sort of see in a cloud and a painting of a horse. We *know* the horse in the painting is intentional. And the images are consistent throughout the canvases, and described and referenced in the combinations as Leonardo wrote. Would pareidolia include seeing writings that were not there also?

How could anyone believe Leonardo *himself* missed seeing the animal heads that *thousands* of people could see in his paintings once you pointed them out? He worked on *Mona Lisa* alone for years—until the very end of his life. Would he *not notice* that parts of the painting looked like animal heads?

That argument wasn't enough for some critics who insisted the lion and other beasts in the paintings didn't exist just because *they* couldn't see them. I pointed out to them that some people can't recognize certain images. They introduced the idea of pareidolia. I brought up *prosopagnosia*: the *inability* to see faces. I couldn't explain why some people couldn't see the images in Leonardo's paintings anymore than I could explain why some people loved optical illusions and others couldn't see them at all. Some have a gift for image recognition, and others don't, just like some can follow a melody and others can be tone-deaf. Some can clearly see things others can't. Sometimes another person has to point the images out. There's always someone who first has to point something out that was previously unnoticed. Wasn't it possible that I was that person?

"How do you *know* Leonardo created a lion?" wrote one person, who admitted he was an artist. After reading a blog post of his about Marcel Duchamp's *Nude Descending a Staircase, No. 2*, I wrote back that it looks nothing like its title, that it looks more like "an explosion in a shingle factory," as one critic described it. "So how come you don't express any doubt in your blog post about what Duchamp's painting shows?"

"It's the name of the painting," was his response.

"But Leonardo described the lion in words, and you don't see that?" I rebutted.

"You primed everyone into seeing the lion."

"So if I said Duchamp's painting looks like a lion, would you suddenly be convinced that it did? Because that would be silly."

We went back and forth with emails, which turned nasty. I didn't mind a debate with an open-minded individual, but I didn't expect to argue. I knew what I found was real. I didn't feel that I had to convince anyone if they weren't going to be open-minded to a new idea. I realized that with some critics, I just couldn't win. And even though there were more positive responses than negative, the cynics began to weigh me down. Having to continuously defend my discoveries to those determined in not believing what was right in front of them was tiring.

Interview requests decreased just after Christmas of 2011. I looked forward to being a nobody again and getting back to my normal life. Especially my art. But I was no closer to the meaning of my findings. No one yet came forward with any kind of help. Even those who could see the animals didn't seem to think much of them. But I still felt there was something more to it. Why else would it involve so many paintings and so many artists with such secrecy? And without knowing the answers, I wasn't going to end my search.

One thing that fascinated me about all the coverage was how each newsperson presented the story in a different perspective with a different style. It varied as much as the style between artists of different periods and even those from the same. A report like *The Today Show* may have suggested I have an overactive imagination, where another might show me as somewhat scholarly. One might use a comical tone. Another, more humble. One, artistic. Another straight forward.

Instead of focusing on *Mona Lisa*, Chris Coffey from the local YNN channel focused his story on me, *the man behind the discoveries*, and how my passion for painting led to them. He showed up to my home with a handheld camcorder to film me painting. Trying to make the footage more exciting, I moved the brush dramatically around the canvas like I was channeling William de Kooning.

In a live radio interview on Talk Radio Europe airing in Spain, host Lisa Grant described the discoveries as *The Da Vinci Zoo Code*. Focusing on the animals themselves, she showed no doubt in their existence. But I wasn't sure what to think about the reference to Dan Brown's fictional book, since Brown's controversial story was considered far-fetched by some. (I always defended Brown, stating that he wrote and labeled his story as fiction, so people were taking it too seriously.)

Brother Wease, a local DJ I listened to growing up on *The Brother Wease Morning Circus*, and the man who had introduced me to bands like Led Zeppelin and Def Leppard, also interviewed me on the air. From all the years I listened to him on the radio, I knew it would be more of a fun interview that likely wouldn't be taken seriously, so I was able to let my guard down.

"So, what artists are we talking about here?" he asked.

"Renaissance artists," I said. "Guys like Michelangelo, Leonardo, Raphael."

"The Teenage Mutant Ninja Turtles?" he joked.

"Right," I said, laughing with the show members.

Assuming I was working on a book, Wease asked if it were out yet. I told him that I didn't have one, but suddenly thought back to all the publicity I received and how all that valuable time spent on television and radio, along with the countless articles online, could have been spent publicizing a book detailing everything I found instead of trying to squeeze it all into interviews that lasted minutes, usually feeling like I was leaving audience members with doubt due to the lack of an explanation. I knew I had to get a book out. If I didn't, the illusions would never be taken seriously enough, and neither would I. Instead of depending on journalists and newscasters, the book would at least be in my own words, explaining things exactly as I wanted to explain them. Even my blog—which revealed some of my findings—didn't cover everything fully, since blog posts had to be kept short.

The problem was that I didn't consider myself a writer. The blog had been a feat in itself, but writing a book would be a whole different ball game. Like the difference between a pencil sketch and a painting masterpiece. English class was never a favorite subject of mine. I never took any kind of creative writing class. Or typing class, for that matter. But I did have something to say. And all the attention I received told me one thing: there were people interested in hearing about it.

One day while I was walking Pinch, an acquaintance I once worked with (who was also an artist) and who lived in my neighborhood, pulled up in his car, next to me. "So, Ron. You solved *Mona Lisa*, huh?" he scoffed, sticking his head out the window, a grin on his face.

I shrugged. "I think I found a few things other people missed, yeah," I said.

"Yeah, *if* Leonardo really did hide those things."

What stung me wasn't his skepticism, but the fact that it came from someone I knew well and considered somewhat friendly.

"Look for yourself," I said.

I knew right then, that if I didn't come out with a book that presented my case, I was never going to live it down.

"Now that you're in the history books, you going to move on?" he said in a patronizing voice.

"There's more to figure out. Way more."

"No kidding. Tell me."

"I'm saving it for my book," I told him.

It didn't matter if I had to do it all alone. Or that *Mona Lisa* was considered an impossible puzzle. I would find the answers I sought. And I knew it would be the biggest art project of my life.

29

Religious?

By February of 2012, since nobody had come forward to suggest what the animals meant, I decided to pull the plug on the publicity and get back to my normal life. Besides, there was a book I needed to start writing.

I returned most of my focus to my graphic design work. There were plenty of projects to do and deadlines that couldn't wait. Coworkers joked about the imaginary lions or crocodiles hidden in the ads I created, and I'd politely laugh and change the topic.

"I thought of you this weekend," one of the salespeople said one day as she held a large book in her arms. She explained that her mother recently passed away and she had been collecting her belongings. "I found an old book that you're welcome to have if you want it. It's about Michelangelo." She placed one of the largest art books I'd ever seen onto my desk. "I want it to be with someone who will appreciate it."

"I'd love to have it," I told her.

One of the jewelers, Joseph, later stepped into my office as he continued polishing a piece of jewelry with a cloth. He glanced down at the book. "The guys in back were telling me about the *Mona Lisa* thing," he said. Joseph had a brawny voice, and a body like a bulldozer, with hands delicate enough to put together intricate jewelry. There were times during our discussions that he reminded me of Doctor Ian Malcolm—Jeff Goldblum's character in *Jurassic Park* who talked about chaos theory.

"You know," he said, always willing to talk religion or culture or human nature, "the economic foundation of modern society owes a lot to the Medicis. They controlled Italy's economy in Leonardo's time. It's the basis for our economy today."

"You don't say."

"I do say. So why were you on the news discussing *Mona Lisa* anyway?" (Joseph told me once that he barely watched television.)

"Believe it or not, there are images in *Mona Lisa* no one has ever spotted before."

"Are you joking?"

"I'm serious." I told him briefly about the creatures I found.

"Animals, huh?" He said indifferently. "How did you come across this?"

"My dog." I laughed at the amused look on his face. "An accident, really."

He looked down and rubbed the back of his head with his palm. "I was very intrigued when I studied that stuff years ago."

"What do you mean, *studied that stuff*?" I asked, a little confused by his statement.

"In college."

"You studied animal symbolism?"

"Theology. Two classes short of getting my major. But I knew my Bible. Full of symbolism. Lions, lambs, scorpions. It's really something."

"What …exactly did you learn about?"

"Let's see," he said, still polishing the jewelry in his hand. "Biblical stories and folklore that passed through generations but was never really written down. All animals represent something. The lion with its power and dominance. There's more meaning to it than *king of the jungle*. At least biblically. Read the Old Testament sometime."

"I think I will."

The second I left work, I went straight to the bookstore, for the first time passing the Art section as I headed to the section on Religion, where the bibles were kept.

A week later, Joseph and I were sitting in my kitchen.

"Anything to talk theology," Joseph said. "Symbolism always fascinated me."

"Coffee while we talk?" I asked.

After finding out Joseph had studied theology, I needed to pick his brain. So I invited him to my place one night to talk privately.

"Wow, is that a percolator? You *are* Italian," he chuckled.

"I'm kind of picky about coffee. It has to be strong."

We talked about art for a bit. And also about religion. Joseph was a dedicated Catholic, aware of my belief that God didn't exist. We had discussed it before. We respected each other's views, and had the discussion more out of curiosity as to why we had such different religious beliefs when we seemed to agree on everything else.

Eventually, I asked what he knew about possible meanings behind a lion.

"Okay, the coming Messiah was called the Lion of Judah," he said. "And Satan, the dark one, is said to be like a roaring lion."

"A roaring lion?"

"*Like* a roaring lion."

"What about an ape?"

"I'm not sure if there's a biblical reference, but an ape might represent mankind itself."

"Like the diagram of the human evolution of man?"

"Perhaps. Something like that."

"What about a buffalo, or bull?" I was still unsure what the third animal in *Mona Lisa* was, but *The Last Supper* seemed to contain a bull head.

"Not sure about buffalo, but a bull in the Old Testament may represent one of the accepted sacrifices for removing sin. In the New Testament, a winged bull symbolizes the Apostle Luke, and a winged lion the Apostle Mark."

Could the animals represent certain figures?

"And an elephant?"

On Michelangelo's Sistine Chapel ceiling was an elephant head, on the panel called *The Downfall of Adam and Eve and their Expulsion from the Garden of Eden,* just like one that appeared in Titian's *Pastoral Concert.*

"I don't believe elephants were known by the Hebrews when the Old Testament was written. But they did trade. And with trade came ivory, so they might have *heard* about elephants. But I can't be sure about that one."

That made the idea of religious symbolism seem less plausible. (Interestingly, though, I later came across an article announcing excavations in an ancient synagogue in Israel that uncovered a mosaic depicting elephants.[1])

"What about a horse head?"

"God fashioned the horse," Joseph said. "Scholars debated why Jesus would ride to Jerusalem on a donkey instead of a horse. After all, he's claiming to be a king. You'd think a conquering king would appear on a warhorse. In the Roman world, a king might represent his control of a city by riding in on a donkey, showing everyone how safe they are, that a warhorse wasn't needed. In general, horses appear all throughout scripture."

As they do in Renaissance art.

It made me wonder about *The Last Supper*, which showed a mule head instead of the more common heads of stallions I found elsewhere. The mule had a slightly comical characteristic—pronounced ears and a tongue sticking out through buckteeth-like features.

"Was Jesus the only one associated with a donkey?" I asked.

In Leonardo's charcoal drawing of *The Virgin and Child with St. Anne and St. John the Baptist,* the Virgin Mary and St. Anne sit on what looks to be a rock. Yet, from the d-point, they look as if they were suddenly positioned sidesaddle on what I guessed to be a donkey because they seem to be sitting on something bulkier and lower to the ground.

"There's reference to the Virgin Mary using a mule on her journey to where the Christ child would be born," Joseph said.

Hidden in the drawing's background is a crocodile. What makes it stand out is how the art seen on the surface appears to interact with the hidden image of the crocodile. St. Anne is shown pointing her finger upward. Just inches away on the drawing, in the far background of the rocky landscape, is a whole crocodile. It is formed by the unfinished line art. I could see its upper and lower jaw with textured scutes riding along its back and up its tail. There are subtle, but clear markings for eyes and nostrils. I called it the *creeping crocodile* because of how it seemed to be sneaking up on the figures in the foreground.

And St. Anne is pointing right at it.

Her expression, directed at Virgin Mary, looks like a warning: "Watch out—it's on its way," she seems to be saying. It made me more confident that the crocodile was something evil.

And yet, the Virgin Mary looks calm. *No big deal.*

"What does this mean to you?" I asked Joseph as I passed him a copy of the *Envy* passage. "A poem Leonardo wrote. Translated, of course."

He adjusted his glasses, rubbing his temple as he read.

"Very intriguing," he said when he was through.

"How so?"

"Well, this line here—'Wounded in the eye by a palm branch.' When Christ came, instead of letting him ride over dust and dirt, people threw their cloaks and palm branches down as a carpet for him to walk on, symbolizing his power and importance. The olive branch often symbolizes an offer of peace. The olive tree is representative too, since the olive was used to make oil, which was used in anointing—symbolic of the spirit of God."

He placed the paper back down. "Okay. This other line—'Give her a leopard's skin, because this creature kills the lion out of envy and by deceit.' The lion almost always represents Jesus, the coming Messiah. This seems to describe God being worshipped in his dwelling."

"But if the lion and crocodile could represent Hell, how can they also represent Heaven?" I asked.

"Lucifer was considered the greatest of all the angels, right? He's called the morning star, the most glorious of all beings. But he doesn't receive any of the

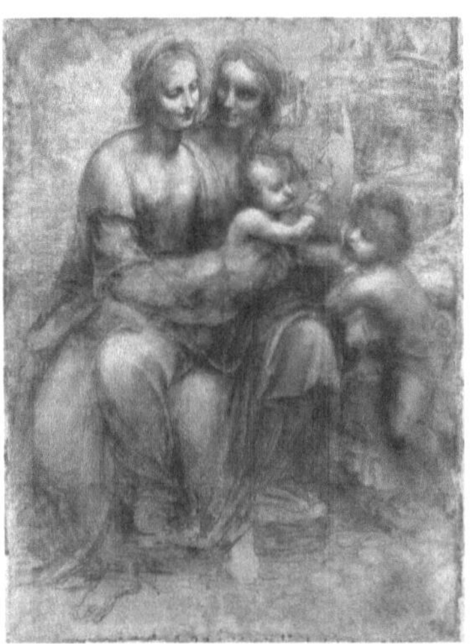

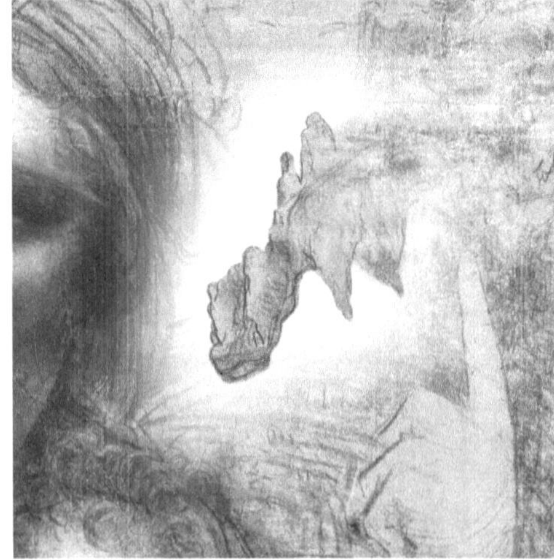

LEFT: *Virgin and Child with St. Anne and St. John the Baptist* (c. 1499-1500).
RIGHT: Close-up of crocodile near St. Anne's head.

worship. The serpent, Lucifer, wishes to be worshipped. Since he can't be, he goes on to ruin the most precious of all things because he was envious of God."

"So Lucifer is the serpent?"

"Right. A serpent. Satan."

As I thought about it, I realized that their had been no greater envy than that from Satan—so great that it caused God to banish him from Heaven.

Is your crocodile Lucifer, Leonardo?

"So what does Lucifer do?" Joseph continued. "Well, he goes to God's creation, the Garden of Eden, to mess things up."

Joseph points down at a line. "In reference to 'Give her a leopard's skin,' the question is who does *'her'* refer to? Now I don't know that *'her'* is a specific person, but I do know this: it resembles what happens in the Garden of Eden."

"How?"

"Satan is bound to Earth. No longer can he roam the heavens as he pleases. So after God forms the perfect man, Adam, the pinnacle of creation, he fashions Eve, and Satan comes and offers her fruit from the Tree of Knowledge. You know the rest of the story."

"The same Tree of Knowledge Michelangelo painted on the Sistine Chapel ceiling?" *Where I found a hidden elephant head?*

"Correct. Against God's advice, Eve is influenced by Satan, and she takes fruit from the Tree of Knowledge, since knowledge can make her God-like. She does so out of envy. This eating of the fruit represents the beginning of the mixture of good and evil. The implication is that Adam, enticed by Eve, also eats the fruit."

"So you think Leonardo's poem is about Eve? *She's* Envy?"

Joseph ran a finger along more text. "It could also be a description of how Envy corrupted man. 'Make her bridle, … all her weapons are deadly.' Maybe we should ask ourselves if this is about the human condition."

"Could the ape represent mankind? …Mankind *corrupted*?" I said, more to myself.

As we tapped into what artists like Leonardo and Michelangelo might have been thinking, and their possible messages about God, the room began to have a ghostly feel. It was almost as if a séance were taking place, like Leonardo were alive in another world and listening to our conversation. The air was electric.

For the umpteenth time, I contemplated the heads in *The Last Supper*: an ape or horse, a lion, bull, and donkey. And *Mona Lisa*: an ape, lion, and buffalo.

A painting of Jesus. And a painting of Envy.

But how did they connect?

"Jesus and Eve," I said. "What symbolic connection do they have?"

"In simple terms? Some believe Jesus was sent to pay for the sins that began because of Adam and Eve."

"You don't sound sure that Envy and Eve are the same."

"Well, it's only a possibility."

"Can *Envy* be the Virgin Mary?" I asked, fishing for other possible explanations. "…Or Mary Magdalene?"

Joseph shook his head. "I don't think so."

"But this part of the line here," I pointed, "'… a contemptuous motion of the hand towards heaven, because if she could she would use her strength against God. …' Some woman is upset with God. Didn't the Virgin Mary and Mary Magdalene have reason to be upset? Didn't God take Jesus from them? Isn't that a good cause for anger? …Defiance?"

Joseph chewed the tips of his glasses. "It's a possibility."

"But you're not convinced?"

I thought I was getting somewhere, but adding more possibilities to the equation made it more difficult to figure out. Every option was just speculation. The answers were moving farther out of reach.

If you were trying to say something, Leonardo, why didn't you make it easier to understand?

"What were they trying to hide?" I asked. "Some alternate faith? Views that made them heretics to the church? …Which they advertised to other artists?"

"I don't know. Maybe they were just thumbing their noses at the Church."

"Mocking the Church?"

"Sure. Through hidden symbols. The Church was pretty rough."

"Especially with the Spanish Inquisition," I added.

"In Italy?"

"I think it was in Southern Italy at the time," I said. "The Kingdom of Naples, run by the Spaniards, I believe."

"Didn't the Church force Michelangelo to paint the Sistine ceiling?"

"It was a friend of Raphael—Donato Bramante—who convinced the Pope to make Michelangelo paint the ceiling. Bramante wanted him to look inferior to Raphael. Ceilings were 'usually allotted to assistants or lesser-known artists,'[2] so it may have felt insulting to Michelangelo, who tried to decline so he could carve the sculptures he had already been commissioned to do. Raphael, who was jealous of Michelangelo, was sort of the brat of the Renaissance artists. He and his contemporaries wanted to shame Michelangelo, and expected him to fail miserably since he had no experience with fresco, or barely much painting for that matter. They actually thought he would do a shitty job."

"Looks like the joke was on Raphael."

"Right. But the Pope did threaten to toss Michelangelo from the scaffolding for taking longer than expected."

Moving on, I showed Joseph a printout of Holbein's *Ambassadors*.

"You familiar with this painting?" I asked.

"Not so much. Looks cool though." He looked closer. "What the hell is *that*?"

"It's considered one of the first anamorphic paintings in Western art. Painted years after Leonardo died. No one's sure about its meaning. That distorted skull you're looking at is what they call anamorphic. Unlike the illusions I've been finding, this one's in plain sight. Impossible to miss."

He took a closer look, tilting the paper until the skull compressed into its correct shape—from its anamorphic viewpoint.

For centuries, the painting has baffled historians. Some think it symbolizes the unification of capitalism and the Church; others believe it represents religious strife. The wooden shelves the two men in the portrait are leaning against hold astrological gadgets like a sundial, a celestial globe, a compass, tools, musical instruments, mathematical tools. Two-thirds of the background is taken up by a silky green curtain with a darker, velvety, irregular pattern. The floor contains an odd pattern of large circles conjoined by a central square, over which the stretched image of the skull looks as if it had been slapped onto the canvas like a bumper sticker.

"Notice the item peeking from behind the curtain," I said, pointing to it.

He pulled the printout close to his eyes. "Part of a crucifix?"

"Yeah. But all the scientific tools are out in the open."

"So he's trying to say these are men of science who don't *completely* lack faith in God? Or that no matter what their belief, His presence will always be known?"

"They aren't scientists. One man on the right is dressed in clerical clothing. The other is not."

"Who are they?"

I looked down at my notes.

"Their names are Jean de Dinteville and Georges de Selve. Dinteville was a French ambassador when King Francis ruled—the king who invited Leonardo da Vinci to France to work near his castle during his last few years."

"Interesting connection."

"Leonardo was given use of Clos Lucé—a chateau near Château d'Amboise, the king's residence. He spent three years there and died in 1519. It's possible Leonardo worked on *Mona Lisa* during that time. Fourteen years later German painter Hans Holbein creates the world's first anamorphic painting—or what is *believed* to be the first. Because the Italians had been creating them secretly for years, I realized."

"That doesn't sound like a coincidence."

"No. It doesn't."

There had to be a connection to King Francis, but I couldn't put my finger on it. Francis bought the *Mona Lisa* when Leonardo died. But did that mean anything? Could Holbein's skull represent death? Or the end of something? The end of whatever Leonardo and the others were putting in their art? Was

Holbein showing the illusion in plain sight to reveal the secrets of the artists that came before him?

"Why do you think a German painter didn't have to hide his beliefs when Italians did? Politics? Religion?"

Joseph scratched his head. "Was Holbein one of the Reformation artists?"

"I think he illustrated Martin Luther's translation of the Bible."

"So no Pope giving orders there then?"

It was the first time I wished I had paid more attention to art history in college. I loved the visual aspect of art, but was never interested in its relationship with religion and politics—in the Renaissance or any other time, including my own lifetime. I wish I knew more. Still, I remember reading that Leonardo influenced Holbein. So Holbein couldn't be attacking Leonardo's beliefs. Or was he? Or was he passing on information, like an apostle to Leonardo? Could Holbein have seen *Mona Lisa* while it was in the king's possession? Could King Francis have known about the illusions from Leonardo, and showed them to Holbein?

Leonardo had lived with King Francis, and they became good friends. It later sparked several artists to depict paintings of Leonardo dying in the king's arms. Several years after Leonardo's passing, Holbein painted *The Ambassadors.* One figure in the portrait was an ambassador for the king.

My attempts to figure out anything about the secret images seemed to lead me into an endless pit of countless questions. And no one had a single answer.

All Joseph could conclude was how "completely mind-blowing" it all was.

What I didn't mention to Joseph was that although Holbein's skull illusion appeared in plain sight, Holbein hid other images in *The Ambassadors.*

Holbein's use of the right-side d-point view to create the skull illusion, when Italian artists stuck to Leonardo's left-side d-point view, made me realize that no side of the painting was safe from hidden illusions. *The Ambassadors* caused me to begin checking every side, more carefully than I had at the beginning of my discoveries, when I didn't yet have the practice of spotting some of the more intricate illusions.

As if the amount of illusions that I found from the anamorphic view on the left side wasn't enough to deal with, I realized that anamorphic illusions could appear from any side of a painting. It all depended on how and when the artist decided to hide them. There didn't seem to be a consistent rule to how they did so.

The Ambassadors was one of the first in which I carefully checked the anamorphic angle from each side, and also for ambiguous illusions that could be seen straight on.

From the angle where the skull can be viewed correctly, I could also see the head of a dragon or lizard in another part of the painting. I wasn't able to tell what kind of beast exactly, but it was gnashing its teeth. And the way Holbein put it together made me immediately think of Arcimboldo's art style in which he used objects to form images in his portraits. The beast's eye is the blue globe, the top and bottom shelf are the jaws, it has a lute for a tongue, and bottom fangs form from the white pages of the open book. It reminded me of Leonardo's roaring lion in *Mona Lisa*, only very mechanical looking and toy-like.

From the d-point above the painting, a snake- or toad-like creature seemed to be swallowing the religiously dressed figure. From the painting's left side, the folds of the red sleeve of the other figure showed the sad-looking face of a man with a white goatee and thin strands of brown hair.

On the other side of his coat was a rat or mole, hanging lifelessly from his left shoulder, tan and white in color and concealed into its fur trim. Or was it a mink?

And while every history book mentioned the anamorphic skull, I was still astounded that no one saw or mentioned the other anamorphic images. Why hadn't anyone spotted them after seeing the skull? Was I really the first to see them? And if the skull had historians debating its meaning, along with the meaning of the painting, how would the new images affect scholars' opinions on the art?

"Have any historians contacted you about your findings yet?" Joseph asked.

"No. Not yet. I'm not sure if I want them to at this point. I don't think they'll take me seriously. And I don't blame them. The news reports have made the images look pretty crazy. And they're already hard to believe to begin with. But the more I find, the more surprised I am that no one discovered these illusions before I did."

"Why do you say that?"

"*The Ambassadors* is one of the first *painted* illusions of its kind. But there's

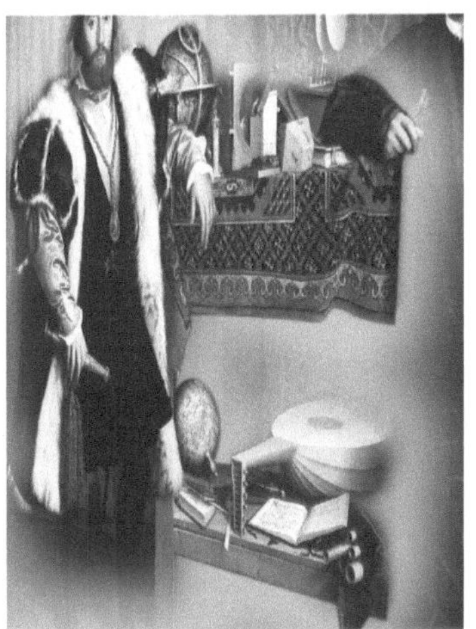

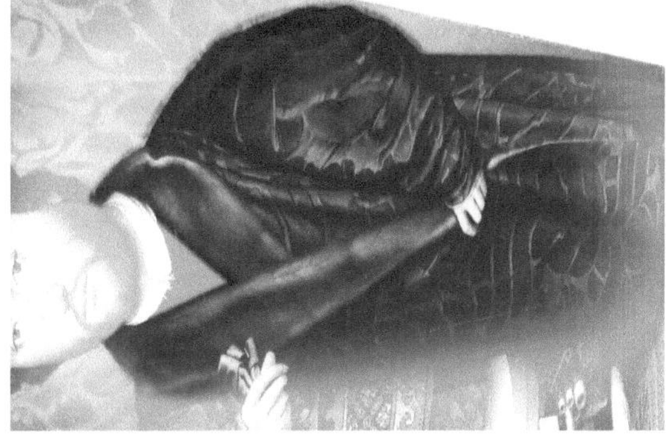

Anamorphic view of a beast's head (highlighted) and what could be the head of a toad in *The Ambassadors*.

a drawing that's older, considered the first anamorphic image historians knew of. Just a few lines that look kind of like a water puddle until you use the anamorphic perspective. Then it becomes a human eye.

"And that's not all. The eye lies next to another anamorphic line drawing of a child's face. When I printed out the eye image, I didn't realize the printout was upside down as I examined it. I saw the eye that historians talked about, but none of them seemed to spot the *second* illusion in the image. Upside down, the face of a screaming child appears in the drawing of the eye. Two illusions in one image. An eye that also hides an infant's face. And next to it is a separate drawing of a child's face"

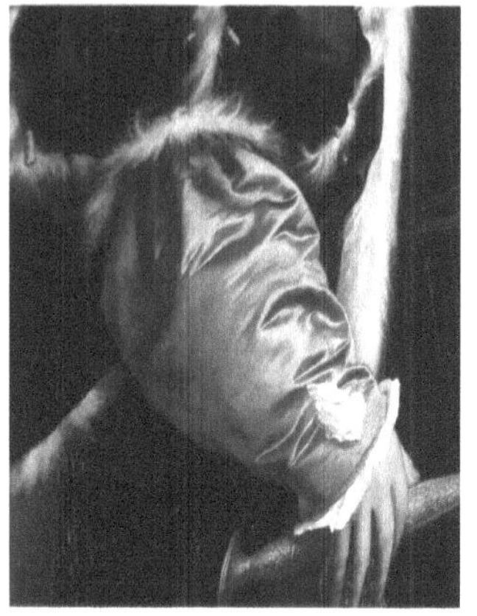

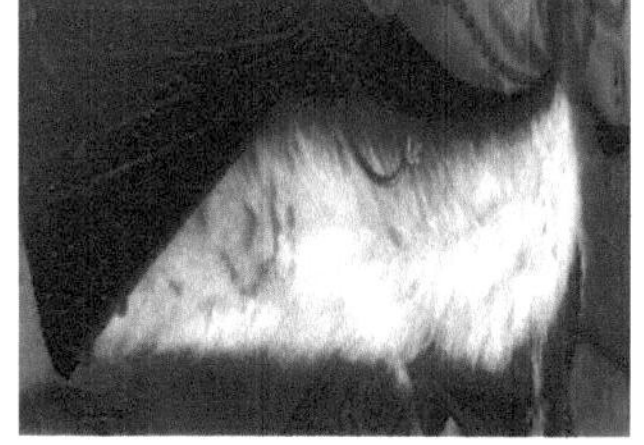

FROM TOP: Anamorphic view of male head and rodent.

"And the artist?"

"The same one who painted *Mona Lisa.* Experts call it *Leonardo's Eye.*"

"Well, how much more obvious could it be?" Joseph leaned back and rubbed his temples. "So you have to break your mind to see the illusions?"

"You have to push your mind into looking at them in a different way."

"Can I point something out to you?" he said, slowly shaking a pinkie at me.

"Sure."

"Have you considered that maybe there's a reason you dedicated your life to art when you had no faith in the Church?"

"What do you mean?"

"If God were to speak to you, Ron, how would he do it?"

I chuckled and shook my head. "God's not trying to speak to me through Leonardo's art," I said.

"I'm talking about you. Not God. Could all this matter to you because it's more than just an intellectual pursuit? Maybe a spiritual pursuit?"

"Maybe," I said, but only out of respect for his belief. I knew it didn't have anything to do with divinity. No more than spotting a four-leaf clover in a park

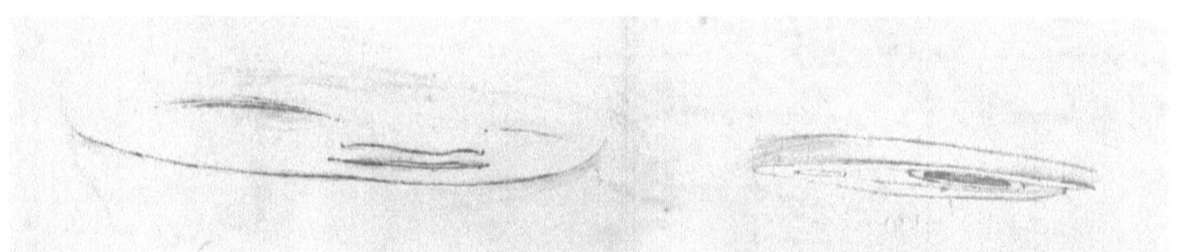

Anamorphic face of infant and *Leonardo's Eye* when viewed straight on (c. 1485).

that plenty of people walked by before someone sees it. It's not that the person was looking for it. Seeing it was just an accident. For others, maybe blades of grass blocked their view. Or they were too far away. Or they were paying more attention to the nearby trees or birds. One day someone happens to be at the perfect angle, close enough to see all four leaves in the shape of a cross, and are paying enough attention to recognize it. They see what everyone else missed. But not because they're chosen by some higher being.

"Out of hundreds of thousands of people—*millions and millions* of people," Joseph continued, "who have seen or seriously studied and contemplated these paintings over time, you're the one chosen to have the right tools and the right mind-set to see all this. From my theistic view, that's how it seems to me. He gave you a gift, Ron."

Joseph and I never came to a sure conclusion on who *Envy* was. I thought his knowledge in theology would help. It did in a way. But I had more questions than I started with. Could *Envy* also be Eve? The Virgin Mary? Mary Magdalene? How would I be sure?

The placement of crocodiles in Leonardo's work was confusing. If it represented something biblical, like Satan, it made sense that a dark-looking painting like *Mona Lisa*, whose figure had been described by Leonardo as haggard, had one. It made sense that *The Virgin and Child with St. Anne and the Infant St. John* did too. But a lot of non-religious works of art had hidden pictures of crocodiles also.

And why is *Mona Lisa* dressed in such dark clothing? Was she mourning? For Christ?

After Joseph left, I sat and flipped mindlessly through art books, contemplating our conversation.

So many hidden images. So many to count. So much to figure out.

On one of the pages I came across was a carving by Donato di Niccoló di Betto Bardi. Better known as Donatello. His sculpture of a lady was made from the same kind of poplar wood *Mona Lisa* had been painted on. The book described Donatello's carving as *haggard*. The same word Leonardo used to describe Envy, which described the illusion in *Mona Lisa*.

The carving, made fifty years before the painting, was over six feet tall, and of a very lean-looking woman, practically skin and bones, like a homeless person who barely sees any food. The woman, standing, touches the tips of her fingers together as if about to pray.

I thought back to a line in Leonardo's poem: "Let her be lean and haggard because she is in perpetual torment." Could it be that the woman in Leonardo's painting and in Donatello's carving were the same? Were *Mona Lisa* and *The Penitent Magdalene* both representing Mary Magdalene?

30

Scene From Above

Joseph's question wouldn't go away: *If God were to speak to you, Ron, how would he do it?*

I sat on my living room couch, staring at the television. It was turned off. Outside the window, as they did every night at that time of year, crows called out in the distance. I pictured the sky filled with their silhouettes, gliding their way to perch onto the towering trees all around the neighborhood. So many had been appearing that winter that the local neighborhood association considered them a nuisance and had been working to scare the birds out of the area. But I found their numbers fascinating—how so many could practically block out the dark blue sky around sundown. I also found their appearance ironic. I had read that crows could represent intelligence or trickery. *Like the geniuses of the Renaissance and their secrets.* But crows could also symbolize the mystery of creation.[1]

A breeze rattled one of the storm windows.

Was Joseph right? Could God (*if* He existed) be trying to win back my faith? Through art, the thing I was most passionate about?

I just couldn't accept the idea.

Science explained things. *God?* God was just a character in a story.

I could tell that the images I found were real. All I had to do was look in order to see they existed. When I had looked for God, even spoken to God, no one answered. Nothing was there to answer.

Joseph's belief in God stumped me. He was smart. Not just book-smart, but able to formulate ideas objectively and logically. He understood science and scientific thinking. I had learned that about him from many of the conversations we had. His faith in God contradicted all that. There was no logic to it, no scientific proof or explanation. How could someone ignore the lack of evidence, just throw logic and science out the window to believe something so improbable? More than improbable: *impossible.*

But it didn't surprise me either. Faith was something human beings seemed to accept naturally, maybe because it gives us a sense of purpose. It didn't have to make sense. I remembered a movie—*The Gods Must Be Crazy*—about an African tribe that thought a Coca-Cola bottle that fell from the sky had been sent by God. If it made people happy to consider that something that was unexplainable could be a message from God, who was I to judge?

But sometimes you couldn't help judging.

Back in December of 1996, when I was 22, my friend Mike and I spent a week in Clearwater, Florida to visit his sister, Sue, who was living there. We spent our time playing basketball at the beach. Mike and I ate corndogs and gazed at girls as they sauntered by in their swimsuits. One day Sue picked us up from the beach. The three of us had lunch at a diner that looked like something out of the 50s. Afterwards, we had our picture taken posing against a classic black '52 Pontiac hot rod in the parking lot. Flames were painted along its sides.

On the way back, we noticed that traffic was unusually slow, and many of the cars were pulling off to park to the side of the road. People were exiting their cars and walking toward a nearby parking lot where an office building covered in mirrored glass panels stood.

"What's going on over there?" I asked.

"The Virgin Mary's ghost," Sue said.

"Are you serious?" Mike asked.

"No joke. People are coming in from all over to see it," Sue said.

While Mike and I had been at the beach that day, unbeknownst to us, local news stations began reporting of the Virgin's apparition emerging on one of the darkly mirrored sides of the building.

We pulled off to the side of the road to see for ourselves.

What looked like a crowd from a rock concert had gathered at the side of the building where the apparition supposedly appeared. There were thousands of people, all looking like they were waiting for something to happen. We moved in closer.

I was sure there was some logical explanation for whatever we were about to see. But whatever it was, I expected it to look at least *something* like the Blessed Virgin—the kind eyes, pale skin, gentle mouth, and flowing robes I had seen so many times in films and paintings. Something impressive. Or maybe a little spooky.

But when the "apparition" came into view, I felt like a complete idiot for having expected so much. On the surface of the mirrored glass panels was a warped reflection like the shaky outline of a bowling pin, a smudge of slightly colored swirls like I had seen on fresh oil spots on driveways. It looked less like the Holy Virgin than someone wearing a black bedsheet over their head while standing in the dark.

I looked at everyone around me, feeling a little pity for them. How could anyone be fooled into thinking that distortion across those panes of mirrored glass was the Mother of Jesus? I was embarrassed for them the way I would be for an adult who still believed in Santa Claus. If it really was a sign from the Virgin, why did she show up outside a financial office instead of a church or some other sacred place?

But I kept my thoughts to myself. A few months before, Mike's mom lost her battle to cancer. Like a second mother to me, she used to put out an extra dinner plate whenever I stopped by, and regularly invited me to their campsite to spend the weekend with their family. When she became really ill, her family brought her home from the hospital, knowing there was nothing more the doctors could do. I remembered her sitting on her porch, as still as the trees around us, zombie-like, staring out at nothing specific, her mind lost to whatever thoughts the drugs and chemotherapy allowed to remain. Mike's family had put their faith in God, praying for Him to save her.

But He never did. Just as He had always ignored my prayers.

We all wanted to believe in Him. Some of us did believe. Yet, it didn't matter. Just like the people trying to convince themselves that they were looking at the Virgin's apparition: we were lying to ourselves. Because it appeared in December, they considered the image on the building to be a Christmas miracle. To me, it was a lie. And I wanted the truth. But I said nothing, not wanting to offend anyone who truly believed it was a sign from the Virgin. I had no right to destroy anyone's hope of her existence.

Weeks later, back home, as I went through photos of my visit to Florida, something about the image of us with that '52 Pontiac tugged at me. The colors and the nostalgic feel made me want to recreate the image as a painting. I had done that before with photos, turning them into pencil drawings, but a pencil didn't seem right for replicating that photo. There were too many beautifully colored details for a pencil drawing to do them justice.

I had never used acrylic paints before. I had never even had an interest in painting until seeing that photo. I didn't know where the sudden urge came from, but something made me want to give it a try. I spent a day preparing a canvas. First, I sketched the image onto it with a pencil, and then I applied the first layers of paint. I used a technique I found in a library book, painting on the dark layers first, then gradually working in lighter ones. Even though it was my first attempt to paint, I expected it to be as good as the ones hanging in galleries, with a shiny surface and illusion of depth so convincing that I would feel like I could reach my hand into the scene as if it were real and three-dimensional, and not some flat, two-dimensional canvas.

After hours of work, I stepped back to check my progress. I was instantly disappointed. The painting looked amateurish, muted and dull. I realized my enthusiasm and confidence had outweighed my experience and skill. I thought it looked so bad it was comical. Worse than comical. Having lacked painting experience, I had expected the art to look good even in its beginning stages. So instead of pushing myself to continue working on it—which may have improved the art if I had added more layers of details and depth, massaging the stiff-looking canvas figures into more natural-looking postures—I cleaned up my work area and repackaged the brushes and paints and stored them away in the basement. And I didn't touch a paintbrush again for thirteen years.

I was sure Joseph was wrong. My discoveries had nothing to do with God. No one and nothing was trying to speak to me through art.

If there was a God to speak to me, He would have spoken to John: He would have told John to stay inside, so that a truck would not end up crushing him to death. God would have told me to take Ginger to the veterinarian sooner, before she had gotten really sick, or He would have told me to leave a few minutes earlier that other morning so I had time to say goodbye. God would have saved my friend's mom from cancer.

There were many things God could have fixed. But He never said a thing. How could He say anything? He wasn't there. He wasn't real. What happened, happened, and that was the end of it.

And there I was, sitting in my living room, thinking about Joseph's remarks. So why did it bother me so much? For some reason I thought back to the acrylic painting I tried to create from the Florida snapshot. Thirteen years had passed, and then, one day, I picked up a brush again, and began painting for the first time with oil paints instead of acrylic paints. I started on a different photo—a portrait of me and a few friends stuffed in a photo booth, which I cleverly named *Photo Booth*. That time—the second time—I fell in love with painting instantly. Maybe it was the switch from acrylic to oils. Or the years in between. Time had changed me. I thought of the paintings I made later, then eventually the one of Ginger that I started before the discoveries began.

I put my feet up between the books stacked on my coffee table. Underneath them was the book my co-worker had given to me: *Michelangelo, The Painter*—an ironic title, since he considered himself a sculptor. I put my headphones on and filled my ears with the sounds of Pink Floyd singing about being comfortable and numb. I closed my eyes and relaxed. Yet, I couldn't help picking up the book a few minutes later and placing it on my lap, then flipping through the heavyweight pages, made yellow along the cracked edges by time.

I stopped at a caption that read *The Fall and Expulsion from the Garden of Eden*—one of the painted panels on the Sistine Chapel ceiling, where the gray rocks grouped behind Adam and Eve resembled an elephant head and part of its body. It seemed to be lying on the ground, like it had collapsed, or maybe died. A small tree stump that looked out of place behind Eve formed the elephant's tusk. Eve's closed hand formed the animal's eye.

And there—though I wasn't one hundred percent convinced—two panels away, in *The Great Flood*, was an image that looked to be a crocodile head.

I shook my head. Why were these artists, the greatest masters of one of the most celebrated cultural periods of all history, putting *crocodile heads* in their paintings? It was exasperating. I wanted to find some simple explanation for it all. I even tried my best to see some *impossible* image, like a space capsule, so I could pretend to myself that I was just seeing things and go see a therapist and be done with it.

Though I kept finding images hidden throughout Renaissance art by different artists working at different times, the images always seemed to be the *same*—lions, apes, crocodiles, horse heads, and mules, among others. Like there was some kind of common visual code or language or symbolic references known to those Renaissance artists in on the gag. Why were the same images being repeated, and why only in some paintings? After all, many, even most, paintings from the Renaissance hid absolutely nothing at all. Nothing *I* could find, anyway. The images in *Mona Lisa* were brilliantly concealed. The *Isleworth Mona Lisa*, a copy, contained absolutely nothing.

In cases where illusions didn't appear, I simply moved on. I didn't have time to go over the whole of Renaissance art in detail. Entire teams of scholars would be needed to do what I was trying to accomplish alone. I was overwhelmed enough by the amount of research that needed to be done. There were too many images waiting to be seen, too many angles and perspectives that needed to be explored, for me to expose them all. I didn't need to waste my time trying to excavate images that were not there, or took me off the trail of understanding *Mona Lisa*, and why Leonardo had given her the levels, the *depths*, of imagery that he had.

It was obvious Leonardo had a way of adding imagery that was clever, technically challenging, and could introduce entirely new levels of subtlety and meaning to visual art. He was one of the most admired and imitated artists of his time. But I whizzed through most of those other works of art as if they were on a conveyer belt.

I had already filled several binders with images of animal heads I had outlined or otherwise marked up. Maybe I would never know what they meant or why they were there. But they *were* there. Anyone could see that just by looking. Maybe I'd never have all the answers, but if finding and cataloguing the images was as far as I would ever get, so be it. I'd write a book describing whatever I saw. Let other people continue the search. Maybe they could explain it while I got on with my life.

I flipped another page, and then another of the large Michelangelo book. Then my page-flipping stopped.

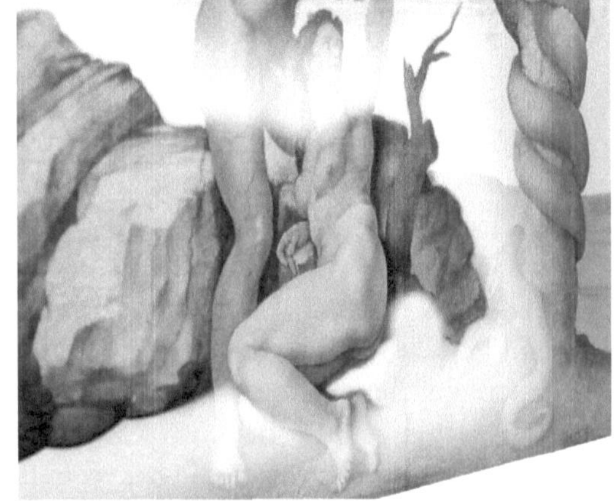

Elephant (highlighted) in *Fall and Expulsion* (1508-12).

I came to a poem Michelangelo wrote. I wasn't aware that he, like Leonardo, wrote many pages of notes, letters, and poems. As I read the poem on that page, one line took hold of me:

In front my skin grows loose and long; behind,
By bending it becomes more taut and strait;
Crosswise I strain me like a Syrian bow:
Whence false and quaint, I know,
Must **be the fruit of squinting brain and eye;**
For ill can aim the gun that bends awry.
Come then, Giovanni, try
To succour my dead pictures and my fame;
Since foul I fare and painting is my shame. (emphasis added)[2]

That fifth line—"the fruit of squinting brain and eye"—I was sure was no coincidence. When I considered the supporting lines—"By bending … / Crosswise I strain me … / … that bends awry"—I knew he was referring to anamorphosis in his poem.

Ambiguous images sometimes only needed to be rotated to be seen, the way *Mona Lisa*'s mountains revealed animals. But *anamorphic* illusions—especially those camouflaged within the art—required more skill, a sort of shaking-free of preconceptions. Some people may only see what they expect to see—the conventional imagery they're already aware of. To forget the art on the surface you *expect* to see, you need to open up your mind and be willing to see what is actually *there*, even if it's something completely unexpected. It takes practice—a *strain*, a *squinting* of the *brain and eye*. Just as an archer squints when he draws his bow, or a hunter learns, through the slivers of space between the trees in a forest, to spot the subtle movements and textures of animal fur.

"So you have to *break* your mind to see the illusions?" Joseph had asked.

But it was just the opposite. You have to *open* your mind and allow yourself to see the shapes and lines that are there, without automatically pushing them out of your mind if they don't seem to make sense in the context of the rest of the picture.

It was like making a change from seeing the crowd of a stadium to focusing on a few select people in that crowd. Or seeing a galaxy of stars at night, but changing one's perception, bending the mind to focus on a constellation like Orion or Hercules, which otherwise would be lost in the star-filled sky.

"You know," Joseph had said, smiling, "I remember seeing a psychology video on YouTube. The teacher showed his students a video of basketball players shuffling around a room and asked them to count the number of times the ball was passed between them. While the students concentrated on the ball being passed, a guy in an ape costume walked through the disarray of moving players. When the teacher asked about it afterwards, many of the students admitted being so focused on the movement of the basketball that they failed to notice the person in the gorilla costume. But even the ones who saw the gorilla failed to notice the color of the background change in the middle of the scene!"[3]

"But the ape was there," I said, "whether they saw it or not."

He nodded. "Yeah. The ape was there."

He got it. It wasn't a matter of making yourself see something. It was about letting go, and seeing what was right in front of you even though you couldn't figure out why the artist put it there, even if it didn't make sense.

Michelangelo was not just talking about how to see in general. He was referring to *his* own art.

Had I missed something in the Sistine Chapel art? Was there more than the two simple images of the elephant and crocodile I spotted?

No—it *couldn't* contain anamorphic illusions too. The ceiling was too large. Too high. The art was too complex. There were more than 45 panels up there, each facing in eight directions, toward one of the four walls or the four panel corners. On top of that, the ceiling was curved like the top of a rounded tunnel. Not *just* curved, but uneven. *Bumpy.* It wasn't like having the luxury of distorting an anamorphic image on a nice, flat canvas—the canvas itself was distorted.

Technically, the art on the Sistine Chapel ceiling was already known to be anamorphic. It was no secret that Michelangelo had warped his figures and images along the ceiling's curvature so they would appear in proportion from below. He *had* to warp them to correct for the ceiling's existing distortion so they would appear normal from the floor. The stone-like dividers he painted throughout were also obvious distortions of perspective.

But with all the labor of distorting the surface imagery to worry about, surely Michelangelo wouldn't try to *also* place hidden anamorphic illusions up there too. The technical demands on the artist's ability to visualize would be superhuman. And besides, no one would be able to see them from the ground anyway. There was no access to the height that would be needed to see them. There would be no purpose in hiding them there.

And if all *that* wasn't enough, it was the first time Michelangelo had painted fresco. It was such a hard technique to handle, some artists refused to take jobs that required it. The plaster had to be applied in small sections and while still wet, painted over in a day's time before the base layer dried and would no longer allow the paint to adhere. Michelangelo already had to deal with painting over 130 feet of ceiling. Even he couldn't be crazy enough, or talented enough, to attempt to slip hidden, anamorphic imagery into his titanic frescos. Could he?

Yet, part of his poem hammered away at me. *Must be the fruit of squinting brain and eye.*

Had I been so engrossed in *Mona Lisa* that I failed to give Michelangelo's supreme masterpiece its due? Had I not *seen*? His poem wasn't just some random piece of writing, was it? If he did put illusions up there, what purpose would they have? To see them, you would have to be positioned near the ceiling.

They would be seen only by you, Michelangelo. From your scaffold, but never again once the scaffold was taken down. So why paint them at all? Or did you expect that some day, someone would see them? ... Someone like me?

I sat up, searching the pages for an image of the ceiling. Included in the book was a large foldout poster. It was black and white, but it would do. I unfolded and cut it out carefully, then flattened it on top of the coffee table with my hands.

Then I stopped, and closed my eyes. *What did any of it have to do with* Mona Lisa*?* Did I want to go down that road? *Just put what I've found so far into a book and get on with your life,* I told myself. Let everyone else do the searching.

Finding the answers would require too much research for one person working on their own. There were too many artists, too many questions, and too many masterpieces to examine. I would only end up pulling myself away from the one reason I started in the first place.

It was the mystery of *Mona Lisa* that opened a door, and inside that room were many other mysteries. But finding all those puzzles didn't explain any of them. I had to solve that first puzzle before moving on to the rest. Yet, ignoring all those other mysteries was torturous, like ignoring a building full of victims trapped inside a growing inferno.

I opened my eyes, the Sistine Chapel still spread out in front of me. There, in the center of the ceiling, was the story of Genesis: The Creation of Man, the Temptation, the expulsion from the Garden of Eden.

The art was created on orders from the Vatican, the most powerful institution in Michelangelo's world—an institution that exiled, excommunicated, tortured, and executed critics and heretics. Michelangelo was forced to paint that ceiling at the Pope's mercy. And they both knew it. The artist had stood on a high platform while he worked. He arched his back with his chin pointed to the sky, like someone staring at the stars, drips of paint splashing onto his face for years. *Years*. And after he finished the project—probably the greatest single work of art ever created—the Church, upset about some of the nude religious figures, had another artist paint cloth over the offending body parts.

The art on the Sistine Chapel ceiling had its own mysteries. Why did Michelangelo include the *Putti* (naked children) in the painted stone pillars, and the *Ignudi* (nude male figures)? The assumption was that they served as decoration. But assumptions, like *Mona Lisa* being a portrait of Lisa Gherardini, never sat well with me.

It was silly to think the images in *Mona Lisa* were put there just for laughs. I had to think that Leonardo put them there to add extra meaning to the painting—to say something more about what was there on the surface. Or maybe to say something else entirely, but surely something else that *mattered*. No artist would set himself such steep technical challenges as a joke. Michelangelo was just as serious about his art. If there was additional hidden imagery there, he put it there for a reason.

I began with the panel containing the elephant head—*The Fall and Expulsion from Garden of Eden*. I positioned my eye almost level with the paper's image, looking across the art as Michelangelo would have seen it up close from his scaffold, rather than directly at it, as the clergy and church visitors would from the floor.

I had noticed that whenever illusions were present, something in the art seemed off. An overabundance of clothing wrinkles was a telltale sign, which looked to be a favorite spot for artists to hide pictures—like the horse head Raphael hid in the sleeve of *La Fornarina* or Bartholomew's robe in Leonardo's *Last Supper* that hides the head of what is either an ape or horse (but difficult to tell because of the damaged surface). An overdramatic gesture looked to be another sign. Sometimes figures were positioned in certain ways that helped form the shape of an image—like the knife Peter holds in the same painting, creating the split of the lion's jaws, or like the two leftmost figures in Botticelli's *Birth of Venus* forming the likeness of a man's face. For the same reason, an oddly placed object could be a clue—like the flower in Titan's *Venus of Urbino* that falls onto the bed, creating the eye of the crocodile. Imperfect compositions, considering the artists who created them, also served as a clue. (That reminded me of Michelangelo's *Last Judgement*, which I still had yet to check—it always seemed a little *too* chaotic.) And *Mona Lisa*'s misaligned horizon—how could a scientist like Leonardo make that mistake? There had to be a reason for it.

In Michelangelo's *Doni Tondo*, the Virgin Mary sits in front of St. Joseph. The painting looks more like a family photo rather than a biblical scene. She hands off the Christ child to the saint, or maybe the saint is handing the child to the Virgin, but whichever it is, she sits in an uncomfortable, strangely hyperextended posture. Why such a clumsy pose?

Looking more closely—"squinting brain and eye"—I saw why Michelangelo had done it: he did it for the illusion of a large horse head. Formed from the three figures posing closely together, the image spanned the height of the frame.

Were those kinds of odd, hyperextended poses and puzzling gestures also present in the Sistine Chapel ceiling art? Instead of wondering about it, I looked, kneeling onto the floor with my head close to the foldout, angling my view across the paper. Pope Julius II and countless future visitors wouldn't see any secret images from the floor looking up, but Michelangelo would be able to from where he worked on the art.

I imagined myself as the Italian sculptor, angry and frustrated, in regular physical pain, forced by Julius—"The Fearsome Pope"—to spend years up on the scaffolding, threatened for not working quicker and finishing sooner (something my career as a graphic designer made easy to imagine). I imagined the knots of my arched back, the ache in my twisted neck, painting by candlelight as globs of paint fell into my straining eyes.

If Michelangelo wanted to slip hidden images into his work that could only be seen from special angles, close-up, then he could put whatever images he wanted there. No one would be able to tell. No one would be able to see them except, possibly, his assistants. Michelangelo didn't know that his art would be photographed and printed in books or digitized and studied up close. He didn't picture a future artist finding them in Leonardo's work, and becoming so suspicious of the Sistine Chapel ceiling that he'd examine it closely on a coffee table.

But he knew painted fresco could eventually fade and crumble. And he knew the value of his work, and that it wouldn't be left to fall apart. Other artists would climb future scaffolding for repairs and maintenance to his work. They'd see his images from the same angles he did when he painted them. Was that how he thought his messages would eventually get through? Did he think restorers would be astute enough to notice any distorted images he hid there? Or by other artists who might possibly repaint over the ceiling?

Restoration work had been done several times. No one had mentioned any kind of hidden imagery. Had the restorers overlooked it? Had they been so technical in their mentality that they didn't see it as an artist would? Had the restorations been so extensive that they altered any anamorphic illusions, almost past the point of recognition, as they likely did on Leonardo's *Last Supper*? I was afraid and angered by the thought.

Or had the restorers seen things, but pretended not to in order to avoid ridicule or controversy? Had they rejected what they saw as a trick of the mind? Was it possible Church officials had seen things, but *concealed* what they saw? Could the artists that were sent up there later to cover the offensive parts have been secretly told to destroy any illusions?

I loosened my mind and squinted my view against each individual panel from its d-point as I had done weeks before. Then I checked large areas at a time, grouping and testing different amounts of panels together from every direction, as if there were no left, no right, no top, no bottom. Next, I tried to forget the individual panels completely and just looked at the entire ceiling as one whole image.

Then I remembered Leonardo's *St. John The Baptist.* With a curled arm, the saint points his finger upward. The gesture was suggestive, seeming to be important, but pointing to nothing. It confused me, and what also confused me was the way pointing gestures seemed to be everywhere in Renaissance art. I'd always noticed it, but no one ever explained why it was all over the place in art from that period.

The assumption was that St. John, just like St. Anne in Leonardo's sketch, is pointing toward heaven. But why should we assume that? Especially when so many oddly pointing fingers in Renaissance art point in so many other directions? *The Last Supper* was famous for its gesturing figures, each apostle's hands positioned differently from each other, alongside those of the centered Christ.

Leonardo wrote extensively on how to portray unique gestures and positions to make figures appear in natural-looking poses. One way he described doing this was to study the movements of the deaf: "Let your figures have actions appropriated to what they are intended to think or say, and these will be well learnt by imitating the deaf, who by the motion of their hands, eyes, eyebrows, and the whole body, endeavour to express the sentiments of their mind."[4]

But sometimes the figures were pointing at nothing at all. Not that I had seen anyway.

Leonardo's notebooks, and my own eyes, had shown me a deeper way of looking. And once again, his writings seemed to hint at what it was I was supposed to see:

> The action by which a figure points at anything near, either in regard to time or situation, is to be expressed by the hand very little removed from the body. But if the same thing is far distant, the hand must also be far removed from the body, and the face of the figure pointing, must be turned towards those to whom he is pointing it out.[5]

But what was I supposed to see exactly?

St. John's expression was just a little too coy. Many pointing figures seemed to be saying, "Look at this" or "Look at that." But the *this* or *that* was never explained. I had no clue what the pointing was all about.

Then, with a chill brushing my neck, I realized that maybe I *did* have a clue. The clue came from *The Virgin and Child with St. Anne and St. John the Baptist.* St. Anne was pointing to an ambiguous image of a crocodile. The clue was in

. . . the pointing,

. . . the point,

"*. . . The action by which a figure points. . . .*"

Again, Leonardo had provided instructions. Not only did he hint that "The action by which a figure points at anything . . . is to be expressed by the hand . . ." but also that "the face of the figure pointing must be turned towards those to whom he is pointing it out," and that "the motion of their hands, eyes, eyebrows, and the whole body, endeavour to express the sentiments of their mind."

And in *St. John The Baptist*, St. John was looking right at me.

I pushed Michelangelo's art aside, and found a large, crisp, full-color reproduction in one of the many art books on Leonardo I had collected. I examined it from the left-side d-point, except ...there wasn't anything there. It looked like Leonardo hadn't hidden anything at all in *St. John The Baptist.*

I leaned back, still looking at St. John, but thinking of the anamorphic images in *The Ambassadors* that were visible from various directions. Although Leonardo described the d-point view as being from the left, it didn't seem to mean there was an iron law requiring every artist to place every last image from the left side. Holbein certainly hadn't followed the rule, instead placing the anamorphic point from the right of the painting.

So what would happen if I looked at it from *another* side? From the bottom of the image, looking upward, in the direction the saint was pointing? As if he were saying, "Look at that." So I checked.

Again, there was nothing.

Then I turned St. John's portrait around, and looked from the top downward. Maybe the saint was pointing in the direction to look *from.*

The image appeared instantly. But it wasn't like the animals I had been seeing. In fact, it was the first time I'd seen an illusion of the creature. St. John's arm formed the body of the reptile. His hand formed the shape of its head. His curled arm made it look like the creature was coiled and ready to strike. And from the look of its fangs, I got the impression it was something deadly, possibly a viper.

Maybe it was no coincidence that he was pointing upward, from where the snake could be seen.

Art historians would say the saint was pointing toward heaven. Maybe so. Maybe that was the conventional meaning Leonardo was commissioned to present—what he was expected to show. But what if he was *also* pointing at something besides heaven?

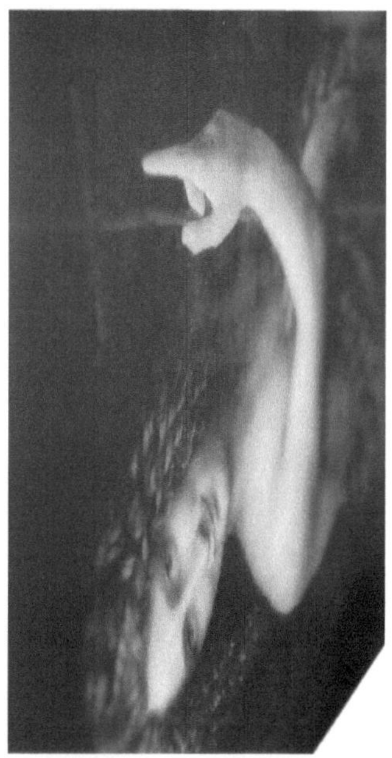
Anamorphic view of snake in *St. John The Baptist* (1513-16).

Leonardo was considered to be an agnostic, or possibly an atheist. So what was he saying by showing a figure pointing toward heaven with the hidden symbol of a deadly snake? That the idea of heaven was no different from a vicious viper? That God was no different from a serpent ...from Satan? Or maybe that the Church was evil? Was that why St. Anne, sitting beside the Virgin Mary, was pointing to a crocodile? Were Leonardo's religious masterpieces just clever expressions of his *contempt* for religion?

Or was he expressing something more complicated? Was the saint genuinely pointing toward God, but secretly presenting the snake to the Almighty as some sort of biblical vision or message? And if so, was that the case in all the pictures?

Was Mona Lisa*'s upside-down question mark meant for Him, Leonardo?*

A question for God?

But Leonardo didn't believe in Him. And neither did I. Although, there had been times I ...*questioned it.*

Was that what it meant, Leonardo—a sign you were questioning His existence?

I slowly lowered the book with the image of St. John to the floor next to the coffee table as I considered a belief Leonardo and I may have shared. His knowledge and studies put him hundreds of years ahead of his time. He was a genius who seemed to know everything. His discoveries covered subjects like anatomy, science, astronomy, and nature. He would prove or disprove common beliefs by studying them and writing down his conclusions. But was there something even the brilliant Leonardo could not determine with certainty?

After some time, I returned to the Sistine Chapel ceiling art, finding an updated color version and placing it flat against the coffee table like the monochrome one I had before. I positioned a row of books along one side, and then the opposite, raising the two edges while the surface down the center of the art still touched the table, so its curve replicated that of the actual ceiling in the Vatican City. Careful not to overlook anything I might have missed the first time, I checked colors, forms, and shapes from every direction, every angle.

To slip a small number of hidden images on a small scale onto a small canvas was one thing. Especially if an artist could take all the time he wanted. Leonardo had years to do it with *Mona Lisa*. Perhaps he did it with no one watching. For Michelangelo to create that kind of magic on an enormous curved ceiling, with figures that were larger than life, with fresco that didn't allow retouching—all while deceiving powerful Papal officials below as they observed and criticized—would have been close to impossible.

I closed my eyes, and imagined myself in Michelangelo's place on that high platform. I emptied my mind of expectations and assumptions and let my eyes adjust themselves and prepare to see whatever they showed me, whether complex anamorphic symbols or normal simple shapes and colors, as I had so many times before.

I took my time sweeping my eyes back and forth along the panels, balancing myself with my hands along the edges of the foldout as I crawled around the images of the Sistine Chapel ceiling on the table, waiting for something, anything, to appear.

Soon, panels seemed to begin morphing. And as new images registered, I could see what had been hiding there all along.

Good God.

31

Research

Whatever I had found, it was an entire new world of Renaissance art hidden alongside the Renaissance art everyone knew on the surface. I thought it had the potential to change the whole meaning of what we saw, just like the new imagery in *Mona Lisa* changed how I looked at that painting. And there was no way around it. If I wanted answers I would have to read many books. Art history books usually put me to sleep, but I knew I couldn't guess what the Renaissance artists were up to unless I knew more about how they lived, their politics, their history, and their culture.

I continued reading from the grocery list of books I had, taking plenty of notes. But it seemed that the more I learned, the more I had to investigate in order to narrow down possibilities behind *Mona Lisa*'s meaning. I kept adding more books to my reading list—books like Shakespeare's *Romeo and Juliet*, Machiavelli's *The Prince*, and Leonardo's *Treatise on Painting*. Newer books too, like Ross King's *Michelangelo and the Pope's Ceiling*, Thomas Cahill's *Mysteries of the Middle Ages*, and Christopher Hibbert's *The House of Medici*. Plus all the papers I came across, like Martin Kemp's *Navis Ecclesiae*, in which he wrote, "The interpretative problem posed by Leonardo's most splendid allegorical drawing, the *Allegory of the Nautical Wolf and Imperious Eagle*, is not that we possess too few clues in deciphering its various symbols but that we are embarrassed by too many alternatives."[1]

Too many alternatives. *And how!* With all those hidden symbols there seemed to be so many possible meanings. So how was I going to figure out what they mean exactly?

I kept a list of other unsolved Renaissance art mysteries taped to my desk—in the off-chance that the mysteries were somehow related. Included were ones I considered questionable, like the belief that *Mona Lisa* was Lisa Gherardini.

- Identity of *Mona Lisa*—Lisa Gherardini?
- Landscape from Leonardo's imagination? Or does it exist?
- Why doesn't left half of horizon line up with right half?
- Why is she smiling?
- Precise meaning of Holbein's *Ambassadors*? Significance of skull?
- Why Michelangelo's *Last Judgement* includes scene from Dante's *Inferno*?
- Precise meaning of Botticelli's *Primavera*?
- What are the words "CERCA TROVA" supposed to mean in Giorgio Vasari's *Battle of Marciano*?

I kept the mysteries in the back of my mind as I started to write my book.

I also put together a binder of images with notes about the illusions and descriptions of what the paintings themselves meant. Maybe I'd get lucky and something would click into place.

Every so often, I wanted to give up looking for *Mona Lisa*'s answers. But then I felt like I couldn't put out a book unless it explained everything. I continued researching as I wrote, but I wasn't getting anywhere. Plus, I had a job, friends, a social life, and a girlfriend I was very serious about. I also had my *own* art I wanted to work on.

I'd swear to be done trying to figure it out. Yet, every so often over the next few years, I'd glance at my bookshelves, but try to continue with whatever I was doing—eat dinner, sort laundry, watch a movie. I couldn't help opening up a book, promising myself one last look, just a quick peek at an illusion that had boggled my mind. Hours would pass before I had to force myself to close whatever books were open around me and place them back on the shelves, telling myself to stop searching for the answers I could not find.

At times, a possible theory would come to me. I'd have to research whatever it was right then and there. Before long, a poster of the Sistine Chapel ceiling or one of *Mona Lisa* would be spread across the coffee table or floor as I hovered inches over the art. It took over my life. The more I tried not to examine the illusions any farther, and only write about what I had already found, the stronger the urge became to continue looking.

The book would explain things I never had a chance to explain during past interviews. It would answer many questions scholars had no answers to. But it would never feel like I had done enough, because it wouldn't answer *all* the questions I wanted it to.

It became difficult to focus on my job as a graphic designer. The projects I worked on began to feel meaningless. The illusions were all I could think about. I constantly calculated theories in secret, wondering just what it was that I was missing. Anything that was said to me in everyday conversation would trigger a new thought, such as a simple comment about politics or life or even the weather. I knew how obsessed I had become, but I didn't fight it because it made me feel so alive, so significant. But I was still just one artist—scratch that, one *writer*—working alone, feeling like I had used up all my resources.

And why did Michelangelo's ceiling seem to affect me most? Was it that I had been familiar with the art all my life, but suddenly saw proof of something I never would have believed existed? Or was it that I was no longer sure what to believe in? Was there something bigger out there, something I haven't seen proof of—yet?

The same art history that had bored me to sleep in college became fascinating to me as I researched information for my book.

Ross King's *Michelangelo and the Pope's Ceiling* helped me better understand the artist's frustration over the ceiling he painted. How Michelangelo not only lacked any experience painting fresco, a medium so difficult to work with even Leonardo avoided using it on *The Last Supper* and *Battle of Anghiari* (even though his techniques were disastrous failures), but that there was also the hazard of working on a high scaffold. A fall from the ceiling's height meant death. And he did some of his painting during the freezing cold winter months.

Giorgio Vasari, the world's first art historian, drew me into the world of the artists. A great painting master himself, he wrote *Lives of the Most Excellent Painters, Sculptors, and Architects* during the lives of many of the artists he covered. He was friends with some of them, including Michelangelo. Vasari's stories made me feel as if I were actually there with the artists. In one, he tells of Michelangelo putting the final retouches on *David* while the Gonfalonier, looking on, said to the artist

> … that the nose of the figure was too thick. Michelangelo noticed that the Gonfalonier was beneath the giant, and that his point of view prevented him from seeing it properly; but in order to satisfy [the Gonfalonier] he climbed upon the staging, which was against the shoulders [of the statue], and quickly took up a chisel in his left hand, with a little of the marble-dust that lay upon the planks of the staging, and then, beginning to strike lightly with the chisel, let fall the dust little by little, nor changed the nose a whit from what it was before. Then, looking down at the Gonfalonier, who stood watching him, he said, "Look at it now." "I like it better," said the Gonfalonier, "you have given it life." And so Michelangelo came down, laughing to himself at having satisfied that lord, for he had compassion on those who, in order to appear full of knowledge, talk about things of which they know nothing.[2]

I never realized that in their own time, even the greatest artists in history had to deal with obnoxious critics. How often had I been frustrated by a client's need to change an art piece, their revisions sometimes ruining my work. Vasari allowed me see Michelangelo and Leonardo as colleagues, not just unapproachable masters.

Vasari's biography on Leonardo interested me most of course. But when I read Vasari's description of *Mona Lisa*, I became disappointed:

> For Francesco del Giocondo Leonardo undertook to execute the portrait of his wife, Mona Lisa. He worked on this painting for four years, and then left it still unfinished; and today it is in the possession of King Francis of France, at Fontainebleau. If one wanted to see how faithfully art can imitate nature, one could readily perceive it from this head; for here Leonardo subtly reproduced every living detail. The eyes

> had their natural lustre and moistness, and around them were the lashes and all those rosy and pearly tints that demand the greatest delicacy of execution. The eyebrows were completely natural, growing thickly in one place and lightly in another and following the pores of the skin. The nose was finely painted, with rosy and delicate nostrils as in life. The mouth, joined to the flesh-tints of the face by the red of the lips, appeared to be living flesh rather than paint. On looking closely at the pit of her throat one could swear that the pulses were beating. Altogether this picture was painted in a manner to make the most confident artist—no matter who—despair and lose heart. Leonardo also made use of this device: while he was painting Mona Lisa, who was a very beautiful woman, he employed singers and musicians or jesters to keep her full of merriment and so chase away the melancholy that painters usually give to portraits. As a result, in this painting of Leonardo's there was a smile so pleasing that it seemed divine rather than human; and those who saw it were amazed to find that it was as alive as the original.[3]

The belief that *Mona Lisa* is a portrait of Lisa Gherardini has been based mostly on Vasari's description of the painting, even though Vasari never mentioned the name Gherardini. Even so, I always had the impression from what I had been taught that Vasari's description clearly described Gherardini as the woman in the portrait, if not by name, then by description. But that's not how I felt after reading what he wrote.

In fact, I felt like I'd been fooled my whole life.

Maybe I was being skeptical, but my instinct told me something was off. I wanted to know how the Louvre's *Mona Lisa* compared to Leonardo's other female portraits, so I created a chart. On one axis I placed the details Vasari used to describe the painting. On another axis, I listed the portraits the artist made. I was curious to see how well each portrait fit or didn't fit Vasari's description. Not because I believed Vasari was describing some other portrait Leonardo made, but because I needed to know how credible current beliefs were.

I listed the *Ginevra de' Benci*, *Lady with an Ermine*, *La belle ferronnière*, the Louvre's *Mona Lisa*, and also the *Isleworth Mona Lisa* (whom some critics think is the actual version Vasari described). Next to each painting I drew twelve empty boxes, one for each detail Vasari wrote down. In each box I placed a checkmark if the painting matched verbatim what Vasari described.

I didn't consider myself an art historian, but I was a lifelong artist who studied art in college and worked professionally for more than twenty years, not to mention that I spent most of my free time during my life studying and making art. My critique had to count for something.

It was not an obvious description of *Mona Lisa*, whose lips don't show much red as Vasari describes. *Her* smile is more mysterious than pleasing. Her eyebrows? There's nothing natural about her eyebrows. She barely has any! It's been argued that the color in the painted eyebrows vanished over time, but it's hard to believe the *thickly* painted areas would have vanished when more delicately painted ones still appear in his other portraits. Especially if a dark pigment matching her head of hair had been used. It's not like he used some experimental technique like in his wall murals.

Vasari describes a painting with lustrous eyes. Yet, that doesn't describe the painting we know. And what part of the *Mona Lisa* do experts consider unfinished? The *Isleworth* version is obviously unfinished, but the one we all know in the Louvre looks finished to me. And no way is the woman in the portrait beautiful as per Vasari's description. Maybe the definition of beauty was different in Leonardo's time, but looking at other women he painted or even those other artists like Botticelli illustrated, such as the women in *Primavera*, Vasari had to be describing another woman in a different painting.

After splitting his description into twelve specific details and going over each portrait, I ended up with a surprising tally. *Ginevra de' Benci* matched 6 of the 12 details. *La belle ferronnière* matched 3. *Lady with an Ermine* matched 10, but one I didn't credit her with was arguable, so she might have matched 11. *Isleworth Mona Lisa* matched 8, or possibly 9 since I didn't credit her with a detail that was arguable also. The biggest surprise was that *Mona Lisa* matched only 2. Four were arguable, which at best, would have matched her with only 6 of the 12 details. Of all the female portraits Leonardo created, *Mona Lisa* matched Vasari's description *the least*.

The *Isleworth* version matched four times as many details. The best match was his *Lady with an Ermine*. In fact, *Lady with an Ermine* could have arguably matched every single detail. I didn't credit her rosy and delicate nostril because she only shows one, while (in the English translation at least,) Vasari uses the plural form: nostrils. Plus, there was one last thought I couldn't get over. It's the mention of Leonardo's use of singers, musicians, and jesters to entertain the model. Might that kind of entertainment possibly have brought—an ermine?

I didn't know if Vasari was describing *Lady with an Ermine*, but I wasn't convinced that he was discussing the painting we call *Mona Lisa*. In *The Three Mona Lisas*, author Rab Hatfield points out that Italian painter Giovanni Paolo Lomazzo (1538-92) "implies in his *Trattato dell'arte della pittura* that a picture showing 'la Gioconda' and another showing 'Mona Lisa' were different paintings."

Vasari was known to be inaccurate with facts. He wrote that Leonardo passed away at age 75, when experts pointed out that he was actually 67. He also wrote that Botticelli died at 78, when he was really 65.[4]

But the case of Lisa Gherardini wasn't built wholly on Vasari. There was also a 1503 marginal note written by Agostino Vespucci that some believe confirms that Leonardo worked on a portrait of Gherardini at the time. But Vespucci's note (like Vasari's) never mentioned the name Gherardini:

	Vasari's Description of Mona Lisa	1 Isleworth Mona Lisa	2 Portrait of a Lady in Profile	3 Mona Lisa	4 Lady with an Ermine	5 Ginevra de' Benci	6 La belle ferronnière
1	Eyes "natural lustre and moistness"			□	■	■	
2	Delicate lashes				■	■	
3	Rosy and pearly tints around eyes	□	■		■	■	
4	Eyebrows: "thickly in one place" "lightly in another"		■		■		■
5	Finely painted nose	■		□	■		
6	Rosy and delicate nostrils	■					
7	Mouth joined to flesh tints of face by red of lips	■		□	■	■	■
8	Pit of throat seems to pulse	■			□	■	
9	"Very beautiful woman"	■	■		■	■	■
10	"full of merriment" (seems entertained)		■	□	■		
11	no melancholy like other portraits	■	■	■	■		□
12	"Smile so pleasing", "divine rather than human"	■	■	■	■		
13	Left unfinished	■			■		

Comparison of Vasari's 1550 description to Leonardo's paintings (Leonardo's *Mona Lisa* not pictured).

> Apelles the painter. That is the way Leonardo da Vinci does it with all of his paintings, like, for example, with the countenance of Lisa del Giocondo and that of the holy Anne, the mother of the Virgin. We will see how he is going to do it regarding the great council chamber, the thing which he has just come to terms about with the gonfaloniere. October 1503.[5]

Maybe I was missing something, but why was "Lisa del Giocondo" mentioned in relation to "Anne, the mother of the Virgin?" Could Lisa del Giocondo have been the model for Anne in another work of art, not *Mona Lisa*? The note could also be read as describing paintings that were yet to be created. Or maybe Lisa del Giocondo and Anne, the mother of the Virgin, are only being referenced as styles in relation to Apelles the painter—after all, Vespucci seems to only call attention to them as an "example." And what is he referencing in "the thing" that "he has just come to terms about?" And why do we assume that anything he says *at all* is correct? Who knows what Vespucci was told, and by whom? Or how reliable his source was? After all, it was just a note quickly scribbled in the margin of a book.

Maybe the Apelles mention was a reference to Sandro Botticelli's *Calumny of Apelles* painting. Wasn't that a possibility? (I later read one of the nine figures represented envy, and that Botticelli was inspired by a story of Apelles, who was falsely accused by a jealous painter of encouraging a revolt against the Egyptian King, who then imprisoned Apelles temporarily. In revenge, he created a painting mocking the foolish king.[6])

There were too many possible interpretations to Vespucci's note. Yet, art historians seemed sure it all pointed to Lisa Gherardini. It made me skeptical about everything I was ever told.

Experts couldn't even agree on when Leonardo painted *Mona Lisa.*

The banking system kept track of artist's transactions with buyers. The same cataloging system lacks any evidence supporting the claim that Leonardo painted a portrait of Francesco del Giocondo's wife. During 1503, Leonardo worked on several paintings, including *Virgin of the Rocks*, *The Madonna of the Yarnwinder*, and possibly *The Virgin and Child with St. Anne*—the same St. Anne that Vespucci referenced in his note. But none of them were portraits of only a female figure as per the assumption from Vasari's description.

Could Vasari have been describing the recently discovered *Isleworth Mona Lisa*? It's a second version some have attributed to Leonardo that was only revealed to the public in 2012, after sitting away in a Swiss bank vault for forty years. Unlike the Louvre version, the sitter is younger and more attractive, and the painting shows large areas that are unfinished.

Maybe I still didn't have the right answers. But I was beginning to spot the ones others got wrong.

32

The Dark Renaissance

The anamorphic illusions I found were sheer artistry. So why weren't Leonardo and Michelangelo and other artists pointing them out and bragging at the top of their lungs? They were in competition with each other for commission work. They were glorified for their art, and that glory was one reason an artist would be asked to do a commission. So why weren't they showing patrons the ingenious illusions they created since it could lead to more work?

Why keep it all so secret, Leonardo?

It wasn't a question I could answer just by looking at the pictures. I could see *what* was there. Almost anyone could. But what I saw didn't explain *why* it was there. Was it some social thing, like the Victorians never talking about sex? There had to be a reason. I was hoping that the person I was on my way to see would have some kind of answer.

Joseph recommended that I speak to an old buddy of his, someone he said probably read hundreds of books on the Renaissance. He explained that his friend used to teach Renaissance history at the college level, but had since retired.

"He didn't put you to sleep like other professors, either," Joseph explained. "He's very down-to-earth. You'll like him."

After an email exchange, the professor and I decided to meet at a coffee shop at the nearby university. I wasn't sure what he looked like, but I knew he was in his sixties. I entered the café to see students reading their school books or hiding behind their laptops, but I thought I had spotted him. The man was holding a book, but not so much reading it as dripping IQ all over it. Gray hair, distinguished wrinkles, a tie, and a tweed jacket with patches at the elbows. He looked as dignified as one of the statues standing in the quad.

"Professor Pasquale?" I asked, approaching the table where he was sitting.

He looked up at me, then made a face and jerked his thumb questionably over at a guy in the corner, sitting by a chalkboard decorated with student graffiti. He looked like a farmer in his red plaid and jeans. He lifted a hand and waved me over.

"You must be the *Mona Lisa* guy," he said, sticking out his hand for me to shake.

"Thanks for meeting me out here," I said to him.

"No thanks needed. I enjoy chattering with a fellow Renaissance man. Now *scholars*," he stealthily glanced at the guy in the tweed and lowered his voice. "...all *they* want to talk about is academic piss politics, or some obscure nonsense they write papers about. I'm always gratified when I see someone from the real world showing interest. Besides, I hear you're an artist."

"I am," I said, snickering at his comment.

"Then maybe I'll learn something too. Artists can have a unique perspective historians don't usually possess. So what can you tell me?"

"As I said in my email, I'm working on a book, but my knowledge in Renaissance politics is not as strong as my knowledge in art history."

"I get you. What would you like to know?"

"Well, as I explained, I wanted to keep our discussion confidential, but have you ever heard anything about Leonardo hiding images in his art?"

"Can't say I have. I mean, I've heard crazy stuff ...like tiny numbers in Mona's eyes. Some people have too much time on their hands. *Pish posh.*"

I had sent Pasquale a couple links to news reports of me pointing out *Mona Lisa*'s animals, and brought with me a book to show him to refresh his memory. "Why would Leonardo hide images like this?"

He shrugged. "Maybe because it was intricate and complicated, and he wanted to show how talented he was."

"I don't think he was showing off since he was definitely hiding them."

"Hmm. He might have done it just to prove to himself that he could do it. Like a private joke, I guess. Leonardo could be pretty secretive. He liked to conceal things in his writings. Easy to imagine he'd do the same in his art. We could never be completely sure."

"I figured Leonardo and other artists that slipped in these kinds of images were trying to say something. With this kind of technical achievement, why didn't they publicize this stuff?"

Pasquale signaled at my notebook. "May I?" So I flipped to a blank page and slid it over along with my pen.

"Look," he said, "Here's the timeline:"

He wrote "1227" at the top, practically pressing the pen through the paper.

"1227. Genghis Khan dies. Khan came close to taking over and tearing down all of Europe."

"Genghis Khan?"

"Ruler of the Mongol Empire."

"Oh."

Pasquale wrote down a list of dates on my pad, explaining their significance while writing key words under each.

> "1307—Dante challenges the Pope, and is sentenced with fourteen others to death in absentia. He can't return to Florence, where he was born.

1307—Friday, October 13. With the backing of the Pope, the Knights Templar—the Catholic religious order—are rounded up and murdered by Philip the Fair of France. His fairness is arguable.

1337—Hundred Years' War begins. England, France fight for *116 years* to see who is Europe's top dog.

1347—The Black Death. It ravages 40% of Europe. By the second year, 50% of Europe dies.

1378—The 'Western Schism.' Three rival claimant popes are elected simultaneously. The political leadership is in chaos. It's the 'infallible' spiritual leadership. Who's running the show?

1431—May 30. A 19-year-old Joan of Arc burns at the stake in Rouen for heresy.

1453—Constantinople falls to Sultan Mehmet II and Islam.

1454—Wars of the Roses—Another European War—between the House of Lancaster and the House of York: the red rose against the white.

1479—Ferdinand of Aragon and Isabella of Castile become the 'Catholic Monarchs of Spain. One year later, the Inquisition begins and Jews are expelled. Keep in mind, the Kingdom of Naples covered the bottom half of Italy and was owned by the Spaniards.

1492—Rodrigo Borgia becomes Pope Alexander VI. Considered *the* most brutal and corrupt leader of the entire period.

1494-95—Friar Savonarola takes control of Florence. Thousands of books, paintings, other works of art, destroyed in his famous Bonfires of the Vanities. He even condemned works by Ovid and Dante. Sandro Botticelli is seen tossing some of his own paintings into the fires. A year later, Savonarola is tortured and burnt at the stake for heresy.

1513—Machiavelli, greatest political theorist of the era, friend to Leonardo da Vinci, is arrested, charged with conspiracy, imprisoned, tortured. These were fun times.

1517—The start of the Reformation. Entire Western nations break with Catholicism totality and start their own forms of Christianity. Not only does this divide Europe spiritually, but starts an entirely new cycle of wars and internal persecutions, each faith going to war with the others."

He tapped the pen on the paper.

"*Look* at this, Ron. It's a *mess!* The Mongol hordes sweep over Europe. The entire Eastern Roman Empire falls to the Muslims. Half the people in Europe drop dead. Over a hundred years of war, then *more* wars, the Inquisition, corrupt popes and the Borgias cutting throats left and right. The Knights Templar slaughtered like pigs. Joan of Arc burnt at the stake. Savonarola burning entire museums-worth of Florentine art. Finally, Catholic Europe falls apart and in its place you have fanatically religious Protestant states battling fanatically religious Catholic states and each other. And creative geniuses like Dante and Leonardo and Michelangelo are in the middle of it! You get what I'm saying?"

"Yeah, sounds like a wild party," I said, even though I wasn't perfectly familiar with all the political details he mentioned. But I understood his point.

"You want to know why an artist would hide something? These were scary times. Opinions got people killed. So they're going to keep their heads down and their mouths shut. Or at least, appear to. That's why."

He popped the pen onto the table with a sharp snap.

"Sorry," he said. "Each year I have to explain to a new bunch of students—usually artists ...no offense—that the Renaissance was not some big happy-dappy art fest full of humanist liberals like themselves. It wasn't like that at all. Those were hard Goddamned times, Ron." He leaned in and lowered his voice. "Everyone sees all those cute women Botticelli painted, and the popes and princes looking fat and sassy and everything looks so classic and beautiful. Pish-Posh. You can bet those artists had their own private opinions about it all. They had every reason not to put it out there. So they didn't put it out there."

I knew artists had it tough back then, having to take commissions they didn't always like, and for clients they didn't always like, sometimes threatened into completing those jobs they didn't want in the first place. And I completely understood—I had gone through that during my career too. But I didn't realize *how* bad it was. What Renaissance artists had to deal with was a whole other dimension. I didn't recall reading how horrible the times were in Leonardo's notebooks. Maybe there was a reason he didn't talk about it. Looking at the dates Pasquale wrote down (and making a mental note to double-check them later), I had a real sense of how much danger and pressure the greatest artists in history faced.

But Pasquale was wrong. They did find a way to put their thoughts and feelings *out there*—just not in a way everyone could easily see.

33

A Walk Through the Woods

Leonardo's notebooks, Vasari's *Lives*, and other writings such as Dante's *Divine Comedy* opened up a whole new world to me.

Dante's story of traveling through Hell, Purgatory, and Heaven before returning to his normal life made me wonder if the unfortunate events in my past were needed for me to understand true happiness. Like understanding the taste of sweet without knowing sour. Was there a balance between the two? A sort of yin and yang, love and hate, summer and winter. Did the level of one's suffering in life equate to the amount of joy they could experience?

As I wrote my memoir, placing that imaginary microscope over my own life, I poured my soul onto the pages, thinking of how I got to where I was, examining my life from a perspective I had never used before, as if I were suddenly watching a biography of myself. It gave me the chance to see the person I had been and the person I had become.

The more I wrote, the more I learned about the Renaissance artists who had come to mean so much to me. Not only did I learn more about myself, but also why many of the painters I loved wrote too.

And so, secluding myself like a hermit, I spent every available minute writing, reading, and learning. A lot of it took place on my porch at a folding table and chair, where the chirps of birds darting by caused me to lift my head from my laptop or a book with a sense of wonder and tranquility.

In 2012, a year into working on the book, I met Heather.

I was upset about the sudden tax hike on my home. So one day in the middle of landscaping my yard, I felt entitled to help myself to the large pile of mulch the town had conveniently dropped off for the neighborhood victory garden a few plots down from me. I figured that, indirectly, the taxes on my home contributed to paying for that mulch. I felt that justified me taking some for my own yard.

Heather (who I had never met), was in charge of overseeing that victory garden. She was passing by when she caught me pushing my wheelbarrow down the sidewalk, away from the mulch pile, a trail of wood chips connecting it to my yard.

I had no idea who she was as she got out of her car and approached me, but I was immediately struck by her short blond hair, smile, and amazing blue eyes (once she removed her sunglasses). She also seemed a touch amused. Through the hours I spent carrying loads of mulch back in a wheelbarrow, I had forgotten about the tax increase on my house, and was having such a good time working in my yard (or happy about all the money I saved from the free mulch) that the wide grin on my face must have looked comical to Heather.

After I explained myself, she laughed and invited me to take more once they were finished with what they needed.

Every so often after that day, when she visited the garden, she would stop by to say hi whenever she saw me working outside. I was glad when she did. Heather wasn't just pretty—her smile beamed as if the world were a perfect paradise. Every now and then, I would find myself thinking of her.

One sunny day, she asked if I wanted to walk with her to nearby Highland Park, and if I wanted to bring Pinch. Highland Park had the world's largest collection of lilac trees, and was also home to the annual Lilac Festival, where the aroma of sugar-fried dough would overtake the scent of lilac blooms. It was like sticking your nose in a vase of flowers in the middle of a pastry shop.

There was something special about Heather. She introduced me to the beauty of walking the paths inside the park on the most quiet days, when no one was around. From one of the park's highest points we could see the city skyline, framed on one side by trees and by a descending field of green on the other. There were also plenty of squirrels to make Pinch tug on her leash, wanting to chase them all.

Heather and I took walks there often as we talked about life and our dreams. She talked about the importance of living in the moment. It was something I always took for granted, always worried about the future instead of what was right in front of me. "Live in the moment" became her words of guidance for me, helping me to see the important things in life. When we talked, she had a way of looking through my eyes, as if studying my thoughts as I spoke them. The blue of her eyes were as intense as the special blue Leonardo mixed into his art. Heather and I had immediate chemistry. We dated for two years, then decided to buy a house together on the other side of the Genesee River. She was understanding of all the time I spent on the book, and could tell I had lost the passion I once had as a graphic designer. That my need to accomplish such a time-consuming project filled that void.

The book was always on my mind—I just couldn't get away from constantly thinking about it.

"Why don't you quit your job to finish writing your book?" Heather said one day. She was fully supportive, and would bring up the idea every so often. A year passed before I finally decided to take that leap of faith. I considered it a huge gamble to quit what I was good at in exchange for writing a book, which I barely knew anything about or considered myself good at. But I believed in what I had found and that it needed to be shared with the world. More importantly, I had someone who believed in me, and someone who I could also share all my secrets with.

Many of my past relationships seemed to fail partly because I prioritized my artistic goals over my relationships. And I had always been a workaholic. But Heather made me want to prioritize my relationship above everything else. It helped that I was burnt out in my career as a graphic designer, which made it easier to quit without any regrets.

Ironically, the importance of finishing the book and figuring out all I could about *Mona Lisa* only increased in time, especially as I got closer to the answers. And the closer I got to finding answers, the more it drew me away from living my life.

34

Dante

I wasn't originally planning on reading *The Divine Comedy* since it was written during the Middle Ages, before the Renaissance, and didn't seem important enough in relation to Renaissance artists. Art history books usually mentioned Dante, the poem's author, as more of a side note, so I thought at first that it would be useless. But Dante had been a big inspiration to Michelangelo. Michelangelo had used a scene from *Inferno* in his fresco on the Vatican wall, the *Last Judgement*. The artist strayed from the biblical stories in more ways than that. He'd added the scene of Charon and King Minos from *The Comedy* into *The Last Judgement*. He also wrote poetry in praise of Dante, words that caught my eye: "What should be said of [Dante] cannot be said; / By too great splendor is his name attended. … // … Ne'er walked the earth a greater man than he. "[1] I was learning that Renaissance artists found ways to say things that couldn't be said. Something about Dante resonated with them more than anyone realized.

Botticelli, who Vasari described as having "wasted much of his time, bringing infinite disorder into his life by neglecting his work" by drawing over 90 pictures for *The Comedy*,[2] also painted a portrait of Dante. Years earlier, he even created a *Mappa dell'Inferno*, a detailed map of Dante's Hell.

So maybe *The Comedy* was worth a quick read …but I never expected it to change my life. Yet it would, just as it changed the lives and art (as I would later learn) of Michelangelo and Leonardo and many others.

Years before making any of my discoveries, I had picked up a copy of *The Comedy*. I wanted to read it because of all the times I'd heard the book referenced online and in movies. But I wasn't able to get past the first few pages—Dante's poetry was difficult to understand. So it sat on my bookshelf for years, collecting dust.

But after seeing the images in Michelangelo's frescos, and realizing how important Dante was to him, I took down my copy, brushed away the dust, deciding to give it another try. I thought I was nuts to even attempt reading it—a whopping 700 pages of medieval poetry! But I was determined to learn all I could about the Renaissance and what people living at the time read and thought about.

Dante was considered one of the world's greatest poets, and, like most of the painters I'd been studying, he was a Florentine. His masterpiece, *The Divine*

Comedy, was even credited with establishing the Italian language.

Dante wrote other works. There was *La Vita Nuova* (*A New Life*), written before *The Comedy*. In *A New Life*, he tells the story of his falling in love at first sight with Beatrice Portinari—another Florentine—when he was nine. Although pledged to an arranged marriage, Dante becomes so intoxicated at the sight of Beatrice the second time he sees her that he has to rest, but falls asleep and has a vision. Afterwards, he is haunted by the dream in which a spirit carries Beatrice in its arms while feeding Dante's heart to her. Dante explains that Beatrice had died at an early age, but that he is never able to let go of his love for her, and how friends would see him in pain and grieve for him.

In *The Comedy*, Dante makes Beatrice the thread that leads him from Earth into Hell, Purgatory, and, finally, Heaven. *Inferno* is the first of the three books that make up *The Comedy*, and also the most popular. Second is *Purgatorio*, where souls and their sins are purified, and also where Beatrice eventually enters the story. Last is *Paradiso*—Heaven, where Beatrice leads Dante through the Nine Celestial Spheres and eventually to God Himself before Dante returns to Earth.

Beginning with *Inferno*, the story starts on Good Friday of the year 1300.[3] Dante, thirty-five,[4] is lost in the woods—explained by books as allegory of sinning, or being lost from the righteous path. He wanders until he reaches the foot of a mountain, but cannot ascend. The way is blocked by a leopard, a lion, and a she-wolf. He meets the spirit of the Roman poet Virgil, and learns that the only way to make it back home is to take a direct route through the afterlife. Virgil guides Dante through the first part of his journey.[5]

Unable to put *Inferno* down at first, I walked around the house with my eyes glued to its pages, fascinated by Dante's unique and meticulous description of the hell-world. The rhythmic prose felt like a favorite song. It was far from the typical fires-of-hell cliché. Others portray Hell as a mob scene of burning bodies, but Dante takes the reader on a tour of a well thought-out world with actual rules.

As the two poets pass the Gate of Hell, they enter the Ante-Inferno, where the souls of those uncommitted to God or Satan reside. I found myself reading the section carefully since it was probably where my own soul would eventually end up—*if* the story were real. Souls there spend their time continuously chasing a blank banner (symbolizing their meaningless lives on Earth) as wasps continuously sting them and maggots eat their dripping blood. I pictured myself naked in Dante's Ante-Inferno, chasing this banner while being stung by wasps on parts of my body I didn't want to think about, trying to shake off the maggots as they pulsated and squirmed from the sucked blood, which I found more disgusting than anything else described. The punishments aren't something Dante came up with casually. They're symbolic, but well thought out. Every image Dante describes contains meaning.[6]

Dante's Hell isn't just a spiritual place. It's an actual location, directly underneath Jerusalem—in a way, upside down from the holy city. Architecturally, it's a large, funnel-shaped pit, just as Botticelli illustrated in his *Mappa dell'Inferno*. In the story, its border is marked by the Acheron River, where souls wait to be ferried across by the ferryman Charon—the scene Michelangelo illustrated in *The Last Judgement*.

Traveling through each of the nine levels of Hell, the poets encounter souls tormented by worsening punishments designed to fit the sins they committed back on Earth when they had lived. Hell has levels—like a skyscraper, only the floors go deeper into Earth with each different level. Minos, a grotesque-looking sort of doorman, assigns each sinner to the appropriate level by the number of times he coils his tail around himself.

I paused to take a look at how Michelangelo illustrated Minos in *The Last Judgement*. He painted the creature with his tail wrapped twice around himself—the Second Circle of Hell, reserved for Lustful Souls. Was Michelangelo suggesting that Lust was the main sin of the Sistine Chapel-goers likely to see his work? Or was he maybe saying that Lust was his own main sin before God? Who knew?

In the Second Circle there are Lustful Souls being forever whirled in a hellish wind. It reminded me of the promiscuous life I lived after Paige and I divorced, how I was unable to let anyone into my world while I tried to heal. Craving to feel wanted, I sought only carnal moments with women I met. The relationships I eventually had felt meaningless. I was numb to any feelings of affection, until I was eventually able to heal.

Each level in Hell has its own unique clientele. There are the Gluttonous Souls who lived life stuffing themselves like wild dogs, as if their God-given bodies were meant only to produce waste. They soak in a freezing storm of feces and slushy filth as the three-headed dog Cerberus flays and quarters them with its claws. Wasters and Hoarders are forced to roll huge weights at one another. The Wasters scream criticism at the Hoarders, and the Hoarders scream criticism at the Wasters. Wrathful Souls fight with each other while submerged in the River Styx. Heretics who believed that their bodies contained no souls burn painfully in tombs.

Did bodies have souls? I was sure God didn't exist, but I wasn't sure what to think about the idea of a soul existing in a physical body. Dante seemed pretty sure that souls did exist, body or not. Some souls in *The Comedy* spend eternity in a crimson river of boiling blood and flames, surrounded by hundreds of Centaurs—half man, half horse—shooting arrows at any of the tortured souls trying to rise from the boiling river. Depending on the severity of their sins, some souls are partially immersed while others are completely under the surface.

Those who committed malice or fraud are in the eighth circle of Hell.

A Geryon—a creature with a human head, a reptile body, lion paws, and a scorpion stinger on its tail—guards them. The creature made me think of a painting Vasari described about Leonardo's childhood. Piero, Leonardo's father, once asked the young Leonardo to paint a shield for him. Leonardo assembled parts he took from reptiles, insects, bats, and other creatures and fashioned a creature that looked like a dragon "emerging from the dark cleft of a rock. ..." Piero saw the image and was startled at how lifelike it looked, not realizing at first that it was a painting.[7]

Dante showed no mercy to the mighty and powerful, or those in positions of political or religious authority. Corrupt popes have the soles of their feet perpetually burned. The fate of false prophets is to walk in reverse with their heads twisted on backwards. Corrupt politicians are boiling in tar.

I couldn't help wishing that some of it were real.

In the ninth and last circle of Hell is a frozen lake called Cocytus. The extent to which souls had sinned determines how deeply they're submerged in the ice. Traitors are submerged up to their chins. Others lie frozen, flat on their backs with only their faces protruding from the ice. Some are completely submerged. I thought of the animals hidden in *Mona Lisa*, and how only their heads were showing, but knew it might only be coincidence.

In the center of the icy lake is a gigantic Lucifer, cast down by God to suffer forever in the center of Hell. His flapping wings freeze the lake around him as his three heads chew on the three worst sinners in history. Two of Lucifer's jaws chew on Brutus and Cassius, who murdered Julius Caesar. Only their heads stick out of Lucifer's mouths as he chomps on their bodies. Lucifer's middle head chews on Judas—the betrayer of Christ. Unlike Brutus and Cassius, Judas is in head first. Only his feet stick out between Lucifer's gnashing jaws, flailing in excruciating pain that never ends, since everyone in Hell continuously heals, so the pain from being tortured is also continuous.

During his journey, Dante doesn't go unnoticed by the damned. Many of the *shades*, or dead souls, he encounters can tell by his shadow that he's still alive, since shades don't cast shadows.

Leaving Lucifer to enjoy his snacks, Dante and Virgil next stroll into *Purgatorio*. It's not as gory, but I'm still fully engaged in the poem. Most any place looks good after visiting *Inferno*.

Purgatory is a mountain located in the middle of the sea on the exact opposite side of Earth from Jerusalem. But its entrance is at the mouth of the Tiber River, where Rome is said to be founded. Souls in Hell are forced to be there, unable to ever leave. But in Purgatory, souls are there voluntarily—and temporarily—to pay for their sins on one of seven mountain terraces. Each terrace is dedicated to one of the seven deadly sins. In order to travel through Purgatory, Dante has to pay penance also. Upon entering Purgatory, an angel inscribes seven *Ps* on Dante's forehead with a sword. Each one is wiped clean as Dante pays penance on each terrace.

The poets climb the rocks along a zigzagging path toward a flat ledge, the first terrace, occupied by souls who are guilty of pride. Carved on the side of the mountain in white marble is the Virgin Mary in the Annunciation. Dante is so stricken by the heavenliness of the carving that he feels she can speak and move. So Virgil has to urge him to continue on. There are two more carvings Dante must see: one of the Ark of the Covenant with King David prancing around it, and another of the Emperor Trajan surrounded by knights on horses and a weeping widow.

Throughout *The Comedy*, Dante interacts with souls he personally knew or who may have been well known at the time. On the terrace of those paying penance for pride, he encounters Italian painter Oderisi da Gubbio, placed in Purgatory for his vanity in artistic genius, even though he was eventually exceeded by his pupil, Franco Bolognese. Dante uses the scene to reflect specifically on artistic pride, pointing out that one artist's glory will always be eclipsed by another.[8] The example given is his old acquaintance Cimabue, whose glory was overshadowed by his pupil Giotto:

> O thou vain glory of the human powers,
> How little green upon thy summit lingers,
> If't be not followed by an age of grossness!
> In painting Cimabue thought that he
> Should hold the field, now Giotto has the cry,
> So that the other's fame is growing dim. (*Pur.* 11.91-96; Longfellow)[9]

Giotto's mention stood out to me since some of the earliest ambiguous illusions of animal heads I found had appeared in his art, and also because of the devil's face researchers discovered in his 700-year-old fresco, *Death and Ascension of St. Francis*, positioned in the clouds, facing the sky, just as Leonardo's lion head faced the sky.

Giotto painted a portrait of Dante, who was his "dear friend. ..."[10] Maybe it was another coincidence, but I began to wonder if Giotto's use of hidden imagery had anything to do with the idea of allegories Dante used in *The Comedy*, which was known for its hidden meanings.

Either way, the concept of artistic pride made me think of Verrocchio and Leonardo—master and pupil. Leonardo's talent had surpassed that of his master to the point that Verrocchio vowed never to touch a paintbrush again.

I considered my own skill as an artist. At the agency where I had worked, many times clients chose my designs over those of other artists on the account. It was a boost of confidence, and in those moments I took great pride in my hard work, but I never felt that my skills would last, that there would always be better, younger graphic designers out there. In fact, soon after I quit my job at the jewelry store to work on my book full time, I wondered if that career had come to an end. I was sure the time off would affect my work as a graphic designer if I ever decided to go back to that kind of work.

I also thought of all the unsuccessful relationships I had. Just as there would always be a better artist out there to replace me, did the idea also apply to the women I had dated in the past? Would my relationships always be temporary, just as they proved to be up to this point? The idea made me glum. The worst part of a relationship going bad was always the *unknowing*—that unsettling feeling of whether the end was near or if I was just experiencing a bump in the road—each bump feeling like its own purgatory. Breakups at times left me feeling rejected, depressed, and, worst of all, like a failure. Enough experience taught me that there would always be someone better to come along. But the same was true for the women I dated—there would always be someone out there that could replace me. Yet, there was an odd sense of relief in thinking that maybe I wasn't as big a failure at relationships as I thought, that maybe each of my relationships was supposed to be temporary.

After the mention of Cimabue and Giotto, Dante and Virgil continue on to the second terrace where they encounter the envious souls paying penance. The envious spirits are huddled and seated against the dark rock of the cliff, barely visible at first since their clothing color camouflages them against the identically colored rocks behind them.

For a moment, I thought of the envious souls and of Leonardo's *Envy* writing. The seven deadly sins had been referenced in so many stories that I figured any similarities were likely just coincidence.

The poets continue on through the terraces of the wrathful, then the slothful, the avaricious and prodigal, the gluttonous, and finally the lustful, meeting souls along the way while it's explained that all acts of good and evil stemmed from love. As I thought of arguments from past relationships, I had to agree—some fights stemmed from jealousy, or the idea of a threat to the love we felt for one another. Even fights about money that I had were explained by this, as I viewed it as a threat to the financial protection to those relationships. If not for the love I felt, I would have been indifferent rather than angry.

As I reached the end of *Purgatorio*, something strange was occurring to me. Although I'd never read *The Comedy*, some of the scenes felt sort of familiar. At first, I thought it was like déjà vu, but then it got stronger, as if I had read some of the scenes in *The Comedy* before. But I was sure I had never done so. One of the scenes that gave me that sensation took place just before Dante reaches the Garden of Eden, where he is surrounded by a forest full of fruits and flowers. He has a dream about a beautiful girl named Leah, who is gathering flowers, walking and singing along the way. She explains to Dante that she weaves garlands from them, and adds that her sister Rachel does nothing but stare into the mirror all day, admiring her own eyes.

It was like I'd seen the description before, right down to the details. But where? It was like seeing a stranger I was sure I'd met before. Maybe I had seen the description in a movie. Or in a picture.

Or ...a *painting*.

For a long moment I sat there and thought about it, trying to squeeze the blurry image from my mind. *A forest of fruit and flowers? A beautiful girl gathering the flowers?* Where had I seen that before?

With a sudden inkling, I rushed across the living room to get one of my art history books from the shelves. I flipped quickly through pages, unsure of what exactly I was looking for. Every image was familiar in some way: Giotto's *Lamentation*, Masaccio's *Tribute Money*, Weyden's *Descent from the Cross*, Donatello's statue of *David*, an image of Gutenberg's printing press—many I knew very little about, yet I had seen them all in my research.

I stopped searching when I came to one of Botticelli's most famous paintings.

I sank to a sitting position on the floor, mesmerized as I took in its details, slowly pulling the open book closer to me, feeling practically paralyzed by a sudden realization.

Mysteries didn't only exist in *Mona Lisa*. Botticelli's *Primavera* (also called *Allegory of Spring*) offered many recognizable details, but its meaning was a mystery to scholars. They were unable to agree on its subject matter. I put the book with *Primavera*'s image aside, but kept it close as I continued reading *Purgatorio*. Every so often, I'd look from the poem to the painting, and back again.

Botticelli's female figures were the most beautiful and majestic of his time. Different from any other women I'd seen on canvas. Each one looked so alive, so complex, yet modest, as if the figures themselves were unaware of their own beauty. There was something about their faces, especially their eyes, that made them look as if Botticelli knew each figure in real life. Or maybe Botticelli's style made me feel more connected to his figures.

Botticelli was a part of Andrea del Vercocchio's circle of artists, which included Leonardo da Vinci. Because of Botticelli's gentle looks and wavy, flowing hair, I always pictured him as a sort of pretty-boy artist—until I read his biography in *Lives of the Artists*. Vasari describes Botticelli as "a man of very pleasant humour ... [who liked] playing tricks on his disciples and friends," such as when the artist "accused a friend of his own of heresy before [a clergy member]" for writing a commentary on Dante and taking the poet's name in vain.[11]

In another anecdote, a cloth weaver moved in the house next door to Botticelli along with eight looms that were so loud Botticelli's house would shake when they were being used, and so the artist was unable to get any work done. (It reminded me of Ma's sewing machine, which shook the room as if a train were passing by in the distance.) Botticelli repeatedly asked his neighbor to end the noise, but he responded that he "would and could do what he pleased in his own house. …" So Botticelli—whose house stood taller—cleverly balanced an enormous stone on his own house, which "threatened to fall at the slightest shaking…" onto the cloth weaver's house, and also smashing his machines. He complained to Botticelli, who responded that he "would and could do what he pleased in his own house. …"[12]

The story gave me a better appreciation of Botticelli, whose most famous work is *The Birth of Venus*. It shows the nude goddess floating to shore on a scallop shell, pushed by the current of air the winged wind god Zephyr produces from his mouth as he flies toward her. With an arm, he carries another female figure. And a third female, on the right of the painting, stands on shore, ready to cover the approaching nude Venus.

Aside from the woman in *Mona Lisa*, no other figure in art was more familiar to me than Botticelli's Venus. Since the 1980s, Adobe—the computer software company—had been using Botticelli's image of Venus as their main branding image for their Adobe Illustrator software. As a graphic designer, I used the program multiple times a day throughout my career, and saw her face every time the startup screen appeared. And I never got tired of seeing her beauty, especially her auburn hair flowing across my computer screen.

Although *Primavera*'s meaning has caused disagreement among scholars, at first glance, it looks like a scene from a hippie party in the woods. The painting is both peaceful and disturbing. *Primavera*'s central figure holds up a hand and looks outward, as if addressing the viewer. The female figure to the right of her is wearing a wreath around her neck and head and is carrying flowers. The girl next to her seems to have dark flowers coming out of her mouth and is being pulled out of the scene from some flying male figure that looks like an evil angel or spirit. With their eyes locked on each other, she looks entranced with him. And no one else in the scene seems to have a problem with her abduction. Or maybe everyone is celebrating—as if the girl is being sacrificed to an evil spirit like in many horror movies I've seen. The trees around him bend with his sweeping movement toward the girl while all the other trees around the painting, filled with what could be peaches or oranges or apples, stand still. The ground is filled with many flowers.

Three women dressed in white gowns are grouped on the left, holding hands and dancing in a small circle. They interlock their fingers and gesture with their hands as if communicating silently to one another. Their movements are beautiful and carefree, and they seem so entranced with each other that along with the central figure looking out from the painting, they seem to have a sort of witchcraft characteristic to them.

I spent hours examining the painting's details, trying to make sense of what Botticelli had done. Despite what had been written about it in books, I

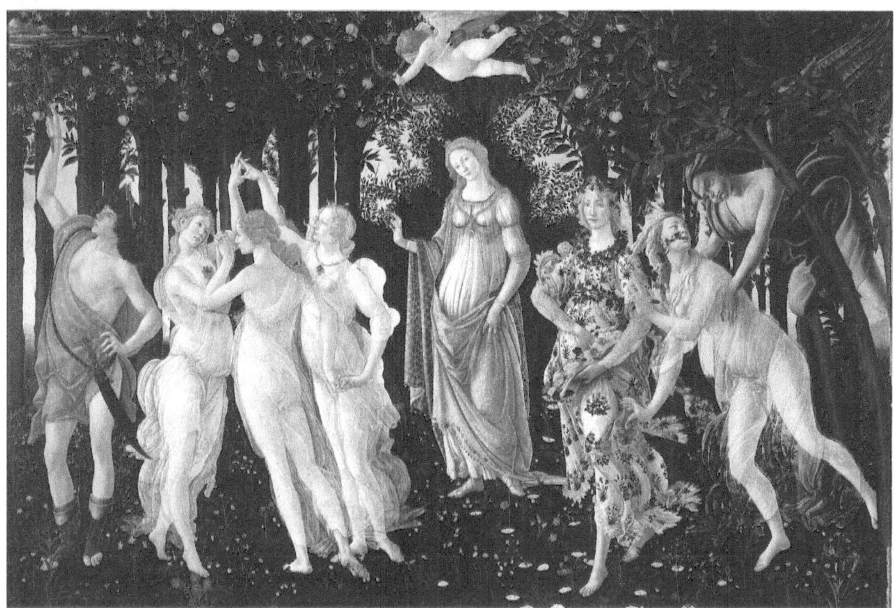

Primavera by Sandro Botticelli (1470s-c. 1480s).

felt there was more to be discovered.

To the left is a man poking at something above him—some odd-shaped smoky substance that looks like it's supposed to be a cloud. It didn't make much sense to me. (Leonardo mocked Botticelli for his amateurish landscapes. Botticelli considered landscapes "a vain study, . . ." to which Leonardo mockingly describes Botticelli's technique as "throwing a sponge impregnated with various colours against a wall, [and leaving] some spots upon it, which may appear like a landscape."[13]) He wears a protective sword and helmet, yet the rest of his half naked body is covered only in a red cloth that won't protect him from any kind of attack. It appears to be there just for show, like a costume. Historians haven't been able to agree on who he is. Some believe he is Mercury, and that the center figure is Venus, with seven other mythological figures throughout the composition showing an allegorical painting of spring. One of Botticelli's most famous artworks, *Primavera* was painted over 160 years after Dante's poem, but the references and similarities were becoming unmistakable.

Botticelli knew Dante's work, illustrating over 90 scenes from *The Comedy*. So was it possible he placed elements from Dante's poem into his art?

Art historian Frank Zöllner, in his book *Sandro Botticelli*, writes that *Primavera*'s "figures are difficult to identify without a precise knowledge of the text on which the painting is based." He explains the male figure to the left poking at the odd, cloud-like substance is Mercury, since the god is "associated with banishing the winter winds and heralding the arrival of spring." There seems to be some general agreement among art experts that Botticelli worked from this and several other classical texts. Another is Virgil's description of Mercury in *Aeneid*, "… shepherding the winds before him with his wand, he swam through the murk of the clouds" (IV, 242-246).[14] Another is of the winged cherub at the top, described by Apuleius in *The Golden Ass* as the "most indiscreet youth whose own bad habits show his disregard for public morality. He goes rampaging through people's houses at night armed with his torch and arrows, undermining the marriages of all. He gets away scot-free with this disgraceful behaviour, and nothing that he does is worthwhile" (IV, 28-V, 24).[15]

As I read the examples, I was slightly frustrated, and wondered if I was missing something, lacking understanding, or justifiably unconvinced about Botticelli's use of those classical writings as historians believed. I felt the texts were too abstract in describing the art. I needed something concrete in the way Leonardo's *Last Supper* clearly fit details from biblical texts, such as "… supper was done …" (*Douay Rheims*, John 13.2), Jesus "was troubled in spirit …" when he said "one of you shall betray me" (13.21), then Simon, the rightmost figure, "beckoned to him … Who is it of whom he speaketh?" (13.24), when then "Jesus answered: He it is to whom I shall reach bread …" (13.26)[16] as He and Judas reach for bread at the same time in Leonardo's art along with other matching details.

Of the samples Zöllner presented, it was text from Ovid's *Fasti*, which he called "the most important source … " to explain *Primavera*'s composition because *Fasti* not only names the figures, but describes the events in the picture.[17] Zöllner pointed out specific lines, like "… As she talks, her lips breathe spring roses …" (V, 194)[18] which could describe the girl holding a flower in her mouth, with that part of the scene described in the following lines:

> It was spring, I wandered; Zephyrus saw me, I left.
>   He pursues, I run; he was the stronger;
> And Boreas gave his brother full rights of rape
>   By robbing Erectheus' house of its prize.
> But he makes good the rape by naming me his bride,
>   And I have no complaints about my marriage.
> I enjoy perpetual spring: the year always shines,
>   Trees are leafing, the soil always fodders.
> I have a fruitful garden in my dowered fields,
>   Fanned by breezes, fed by limpid fountains.
> My husband filled it with well-bred flowers, saying:
>   "Have jurisdiction of the flower, goddess."
> I often wanted to number the colours displayed,
>   But could not: their abundance defied measure.
>
> (V, 201-14; Boyle and Woodard)[19]

I wasn't convinced about *Fasti*'s connection, nor was I unconvinced. It just wasn't a strong enough argument to me. It wasn't *concrete*. If Ovid's writings were the main source for the imagery, only a portion of *Primavera* was described by it.

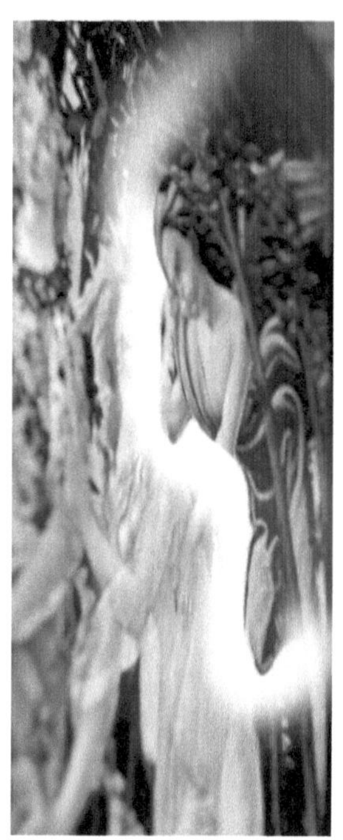

Anamorphic illusion of bluish, witch-like profile in *Primavera.*

Early on, I had spotted a large, blue anamorphic head that looked like that of a witch because of its long, pointy chin and menacing grin. The head was formed from the blue male figure thought to be Zephyrs, god of the west wind, and could be seen from the d-point on the painting's left. The head made no sense to me at the time, but years later, I'd get a chance to read Ovid's *Metamorphoses*, and the poem's first two lines, "My mind leads me to speak now of forms changed / into new bodies" (1.1-2; Martin),[20] would make me think back to the blue figure's *form* changing into a new anamorphic *body.*

But those connections wouldn't appear to me until later. All that was known was that classical writings like those of Horace, Ovid, and Virgil were thought to be the sources of some Renaissance works by the artists very familiar with the writings. Yet, Dante was, if anything, *better* known to those artists because the poet had been a fellow Florentine, a countryman writing in their own language and using scenes and themes from their own history, their own religion, their own personal connections. How could they *not* make use of his work? And more so than any classical author distant from them in time and culture?

As I continued to compare *The Comedy* to *Primavera*, I began to find even more similarities between the two. One item after another ...I wondered more and more how it had all been missed.

35

Between the Lines

I spent weeks scanning *Purgatorio* and *Paradiso* again and again, checking each scene closely against the art. I regularly held the books next to each other, flat, reading one while studying the art of the other, using a marker to highlight written details in *The Comedy* matching those in *Primavera* and circling details in the picture of the painting, making notes pointing to specific *cantos*—or passages—written by Dante.

It was a painstaking task. Time and again, I'd shake my head, finding it hard to believe what I was finding.

Botticelli was known to create illustrations for *The Divine Comedy*. He even painted a portrait of the poet in 1495. Giorgio Vasari wrote that Botticelli wasted away his time on the drawings, making it sound as though the artist was obsessed with Dante. So I wasn't surprised to find that *Primavera* seemed to originate from *The Comedy*. But why wasn't this obvious to everyone, particularly experts?

Art was often created from existing texts such as those from the Bible or Greek mythology. Why would *Primavera* be any different? Were art experts simply not that aware of Dante's work? It was possible, since the poet was born over a century before many Renaissance artists. He was considered more of a highlight of the late Middle Ages rather than the Renaissance.

Was Florentine artist Giotto the bridge between Dante's symbolism and ideas, and the painters of the high Renaissance? He was a good friend of Dante's, and is mentioned in *The Comedy*. Surely someone as deeply interested in Dante as Botticelli knew of Giotto's connection.

But that was for historians to figure out. I was a painter trying to understand the work of another painter. And it was clear to me that many of *Primavera*'s details were inspired by scenes and symbols from *Purgatorio* and *Paradiso.*

I wondered whether or not I was beginning to get as obsessed as Botticelli had been. After poring for weeks over *Purgatorio* and *Paradiso*, I was able to see elements and scenes from those poems in almost every part of the painting, not just a tiny percentage or a single element like experts claimed to spot from Ovid's writings. Dante's writings seemed to permeate every detail in *Primavera*.

The details began appearing in a scene when Dante dreams of a beautiful girl singing and gathering flowers for garland. It had to be the same figure in *Primavera* that Botticelli painted, walking and gathering flowers.

Youthful and beautiful in dreams methought
 I saw a lady walking in a meadow,
 Gathering flowers; and singing she was saying:
"Know whosoever may my name demand
 That I am Leah, and go **moving round**
 My beauteous hands to make myself a garland.
To please me at the mirror, here I deck me,
 But never does my sister Rachel leave
 Her looking glass, and sitteth all day long.
To see her beauteous eyes as eager is she,
 As I am to adorn me with my hands;
 Her, seeing, and me, doing satisfies."

(*Pur*. 27.97-108; Longfellow; emphasis added)[1]

In the dream, Leah tells Dante that her sister Rachel spends the day admiring her own eyes in the mirror, so I studied the female figure on the right of the painting since her trancelike eyes were locked with the spirit who is taking her away. As if she committed a sin for admiring herself in the mirror, and was being taken away to be punished. Could that have been her sister Rachel?

The next morning Dante wakes up and explores the Garden of Eden and sees another beautiful figure. Her name is Matilda, and he compares her eyes to those of Venus. Matilda is the real version (in the story) of Leah from Dante's dream. Like Leah from his dream, she's picking a bouquet and singing and dancing as she steps over red and yellow flowers.

As turns herself, with feet together pressed
 And to the ground, a lady who is dancing,
 And hardly puts one foot before the other,
On the vermilion and the yellow flowerets
 She turned towards me, not in other wise
 Than maiden who her modest eyes casts down (*Pur*. 28.52-57)[2]

Dante questions the existing breeze in the Garden of Eden since he didn't expect there to be any kind of weather there. Matilda explains that the breeze instead comes from the motions of the heavens. She says this to Dante in order to "purge away the cloud that smites upon thee" (*Pur.* 28.90),[3] which may be why the male figure on the left of *Primavera*—which begins to seem more and more like Dante himself—is poking at a cloud. And like a slight clue referencing the breeze, Matilda is the only figure whose clothing is reacting like fabric in the wind. The clothing on the other figures only seems to be reacting from their movements. And although Matilda is walking (or dancing)—"one foot before the other, / On the vermilion and the yellow flowerets ..." (28.54-

55)[4]—she certainly isn't running, as the tail end of her gown would suggest. In fact, only around that figure are there a concentration of red and yellow flowers near her feet.

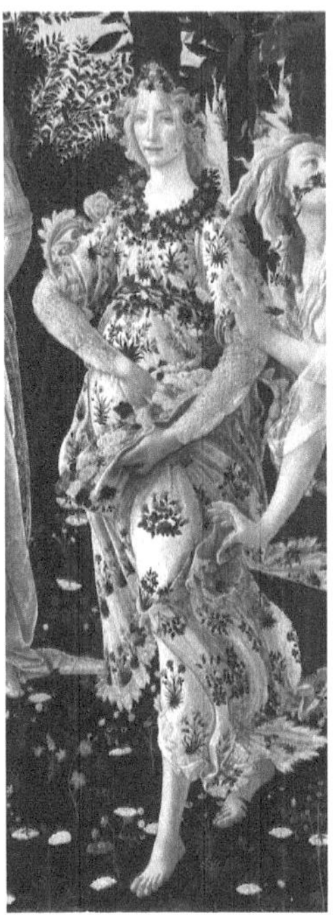

Primavera figure, possibly Leah, gathering flowers.

(I later read that Martin Kemp and Giuseppe Pallanti, referring to a Leonardo sketch of a pointing lady that may be Matilda, seem to pick up on her Dantean roots almost intuitively in *Mona Lisa: The People and the Painting*: "[the drawing] ... precisely captures the spirit of Dante's vision of feminine grace in the idyllic grove beside the river. In this case we may think that the image is more directly illustrative of Dante's vision. In any event, Leonardo is as much a Dantesque painter as Michelangelo. ..."[5])

In *The Comedy*, three dancing maidens soon appear: "Three maidens at the right wheel in a circle / Came onward dancing; ... // ... one of them with three eyes in her head" (*Pur.* 29.121-22, 132).[6]

Three eyes in her head? It was a detail I didn't catch until I looked closer. Because of the angle, I couldn't see the face of the auburn-haired maiden with her back toward the viewer. But Botticelli illustrated the maiden next to her on the left with three fingers pointing directly at the unseen face of the middle maiden. The left maiden looks quite puzzled also, tilting her head like she's looking at something she's not used to seeing. A woman with three eyes, perhaps?

It was suggestive at most. But that was all it needed to be. I was very well aware of how sly and subtle Leonardo had been when it came to presenting images and symbols. Exactly why, I still couldn't entirely say. But I knew Botticelli could have been just as sly in representing Dante's writings.

The main female figure was holding up her hand as if conducting their movements—"And now [the maidens] seemed conducted by the white, / Now by the red, and from the song of her / The others took their step, or slow or swift" (*Pur.* 29.127-29)[7]—and she was wearing colors of white and red.

Riding on a chariot in a procession, Beatrice comes into the story: "... Over her snow-white veil with olive cinct / Appeared a lady under a green mantle, / Vested in color of the living flame" (*Pur.* 30.31-33).[8] She rises and, like a parent condemning a child for misbehaving, accuses Dante of going off the righteous path back in the world of the living.

I remembered Dante first seeing Beatrice wearing a lily white gown in *A New Life*. Botticelli's central figure does have a white veil and a white gown and is vested in red ("color of the living flame"), though I didn't see a green mantle ("olive cinct"). But the surrounding scenery is filled with lots of green. Could the artist have used that to represent her green mantle?

At the end of the scene, Beatrice tells Dante to bring word back to the living, so others could learn what is pleasing or offensive to God. "... And bear in mind, whene'er thou writest them," she says, "Not to conceal what thou hast seen the plant, / That twice already has been pillaged here" (*Pur.* 33.55-57).[9] That detail brought me back to the blue spirit abducting Rachel (or the goddess Chloris, as some believe her to be, on the right side of the painting). As the god takes Rachel away to have his way with her, pieces of chewed flower fall from her mouth—a possible connection to something Beatrice says elsewhere: "For biting that, in pain and in desire / Five thousand years and more firstborn soul / Craved Him, who punished in himself the bite" (33.61-63).[10]

There were so many of these small, distant links that kept me suspicious of their connections. *Primavera*'s image was burnt into my mind as I searched for written details, simultaneously comparing and reading, comparing and reading. Every so often, another illustrated detail would match what I read, such as the cherub's *broken crossbow* at the top of the painting. I had to look closely to see that the top part of the bow does not retract as the cherub pulls the string back.

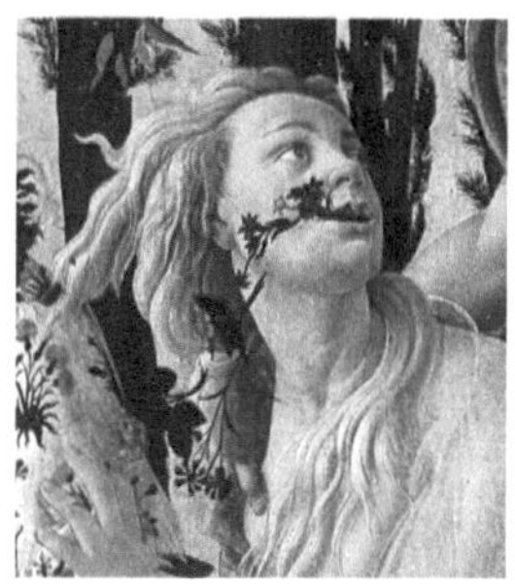
Figure biting a flower stem.

Sure enough: one side of the string isn't even there, as if it had snapped off. "Even as a cross-bow breaks, when 'tis discharged / Too tensely drawn the bowstring and the bow, / And with less force the arrow hits the mark ..." (*Pur.* 31.16-18).[11]

I found many other details in the painting matching those in *The Comedy*. Some were literal, and others allegorical, like the gloomy sun rising in the horizon behind Beatrice. The areas of blue sky that can be seen through the leaves in the background directly behind Beatrice are wing-shaped, but are also contained within the shape of a circle, as if it is a sunrise that is "overshadowed," as Dante describes Beatrice when she appears, at the moment that her hand had "angelical ascended."

> ... And **the sun's face, uprising, overshadowed**
> So that by tempering influence of vapors
> For a long interval the eye sustained it;
> Thus in the bosom of a cloud of flowers
> Which from those hands **angelical ascended,**
> And downward fell again inside and out,
> Over **her snow-white veil with olive cinct**
> **Appeared a lady under a green mantle,**
> **Vested in color of the living flame.** (*Pur.* 30.25-33, emphasis added)[12]

No, it wasn't a bright sunrise, but Dante had described it as *overshadowed*, so suddenly the blue-filtered sunrise shape became a possible match.

Paintings of Dante usually portrayed him in red clothing, so I had a feeling the left male figure in *Primavera* was Dante. But why would he be wearing a sword and helmet? I remembered that he had been a soldier in the 1289 Battle of Campaldino against the Roman Emperor-supporting Ghibellines. That was one possible explanation. The sword could also tie back to a line from Beatrice, when she tells a saddened Dante that "… For by another sword thou need'st must weep" (*Pur.* 30.57).[13]

Seeing how Renaissance masters created these paintings made them more intriguing than ever. It was as if Botticelli created *Primavera* as a sort of movie poster—a collage of referenced details from different scenes placed into one frozen moment.

During college, I spent a couple years working in a VHS movie rental department. I awed over some of the promotional posters. As a future graphic designer, I liked to study the movie posters, and even the VHS movie covers, whenever I had the chance. I was curious as to why I favored certain designs and disliked others. Good movie posters sometimes highlighted parts of different scenes into one powerfully concentrated image, like an overview of the story, sometimes showing characters more than once on the same poster. One of my favorite poster artists, Drew Struzan, had done this with a *Raiders of the Lost Ark* poster, not only showing the large face of Indiana Jones with his iconic fedora as the main focus, but also incorporating a smaller image from a scene where Indiana Jones faces his fear of snakes (the poster shows deadly cobras).

Details in *Primavera* consisted of a mash-up of key characters and moments from *Purgatorio* and *Paradiso*. And with each pass through *The Comedy*, I kept finding more.

Primavera certainly had its share of hidden imagery. In the upper left corner, in the only existing cloud (or whatever it really was), the shape of a crocodile head appeared from the left d-point. Dante pokes at it with a caduceus. I knew I'd seen that same crocodile head-shaped cloud before because Botticelli created them in other paintings. The *Dictionary of Symbols* explained that it could symbolize a number of things including greed or chaos, and was "capable of destroying human life."[14]

When I looked at Primavera from the d-point above the art—just as Leonardo's portrait of St. John showed a viper that could be seen from above the art—I could see the three dancing maidens combine into some wild creature's head. Its jaws were wide open. *Roaring*.

I thought it might be a lion's head. Its features, like its wide jaws, were certainly close. And if it was, I was sure the resemblance to *Mona Lisa*'s roaring lion was no coincidence. I no longer believed in coincidences when it came to Renaissance art.

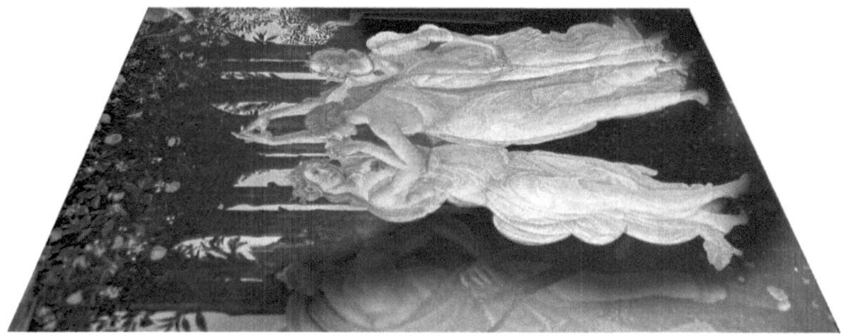
Anamorphic view of lion head (highlighted) in *Primavera.*

The more similarities I found between *Primavera* and *The Comedy*, the stronger my belief became that the painting represented the poem. What really stuck out was a discussion between Dante and Beatrice about whether Plato's writings were intended to contain hidden, symbolic meanings. I wondered if Renaissance artists like Leonardo and Botticelli took this idea from Dante's writings? That Dante included the Plato discussion, *at the very least*, suggested that the poet contemplated using hidden meaning. Of course, it was already considered an allegorical poem—which was another way of saying that it contained hidden meanings. Even conventional art historians regarded *Primavera* as an allegory. Their only problem was the strange habit of attributing all the allegorical meaning to classical writers instead of Dante. What *really* made the paintings complicated was that everything appeared to have more than one meaning. I had no doubt that the three figures in the painting holding hands were inspired by Dante; the thing was, that didn't mean they couldn't stand for the Three Graces of the classical world too.

Maybe the painting did represent material from Ovid's *Fasti*, as experts said. Maybe the experts were not as wrong as I first thought they were. Maybe they were also right that *Primavera* represents Mercury and Venus as well. And if Botticelli included details from *Fasti* and *The Comedy*—two different stories by two different poets, then why couldn't Botticelli have represented a third, or fourth, or fifth story within the painting also?

Why was art always discussed as if to have just one meaning? It wasn't a secret that artists created art with more than one meaning. Raphael's famous *School of Athens* fresco, portraying philosophers such as Apelles, Pythagoras, and even Plato—who happens to be centered in the painting with Aristotle—is believed to use the likeness of more than one real life figure. Raphael used Leonardo da Vinci's image to represent Plato, since Raphael favored Leonardo. He used Michelangelo's image as the figure of the philosopher Heraclitus. He used his own image to portray Apelles. There had to be specific reasons why he chose certain companions to represent historic philosophers. Maybe Leonardo favored Plato's ideas, while Michelangelo favored Heraclitus, and Raphael favored Apelles. Or maybe Raphael associated the artists with certain philosophers through his own opinions.

Renaissance paintings seemed to have multiple layers of meaning. Was one layer meant to be understood as a completely different painting? Or was one layer intended to be a commentary on the other? Did one layer mock the other—was one layer the "official" version, and another layer the artist's true thoughts and feelings? How could we be sure?

I was beginning to see connections and meanings not just between things that *could* be seen, but also between what *couldn't* be seen, because they were deliberately hidden, almost invisible—until one knew how to look for them, which made me think of some of the other mysteries. Were they mysteries? Or had we simply failed to see what was right in front of us?

The idea of God came to mind. He was something I didn't believe in because, aside from a written story, there was never any proof. But was the real truth only that I couldn't see the proof? Was the anamorphic god folded away everywhere throughout my life, and was I only failing to see Him because I was not looking from the right angle? Would He suddenly spring out of nowhere one day, like the question mark on Leonardo's canvas, and would my life be totally changed yet again? Did it even matter—did His non-existence have as much impact on my life as His existence would?

Either way, His existence would have defied logic. All I knew was that He had managed to hide himself a lot more skillfully than Leonardo's brush could do. I looked, but nothing was there.

Maybe acting as if God existed mattered more than whether He did or not. Maybe, as *The Comedy* seemed to show me, staying along the righteous path shouldn't be done out of fear of a higher being, but out of the goodness of our hearts. That was the real blessing.

For those who opposed my view, maybe my lack of faith was part of His plan. Maybe there was something greater He wanted from me first. Moses didn't have complete faith until he experienced his journey. Was I on some journey too? Was there something I had to do, some message I had to deliver, before I could finally succumb to faith in Him? And why couldn't two opposing views about God both be correct? The way I saw it, that wasn't any less logical than the idea of His existence.

Dante's writings were causing me to see things differently—with a truly open mind. Everything began to seem possible once I realized how much I was missing that had always been right in front of me—specifically in those famous works of art I always thought I knew.

Dante was no longer just a guy I only knew through a mention in movies that referenced *Inferno*, or as an author whose poetry I had guessed (incorrectly) to be boring. The more I read, the more his writings became translucent. And the multiple translations only made his poetry deeper, more interesting, more beautiful. I was no longer reading one simple translation with one simple message on the surface. Each translation had its own special added layer of insight. There were multiple layers of meaning, like Leonardo's writings. I was beginning to read the same way I was looking at paintings: I was developing a kind of x-ray vision, learning to see through the first layer on the surface, then dig deeper down to the harder-to-reach meanings.

I developed a passionate attachment to Dante's writings. To Dante himself. I was even beginning to look up to him.

My quest wasn't just about figuring out the connection between Dante and Botticelli and possibly Leonardo; it became a quest about understanding Dante's connection to me. I felt like his story could have easily been mine. His Hell, although different in detail, touched on one thing after another that reminded me of different parts of my life—experiences that changed who I was.

A transformation was taking place inside me.

But I still needed to understand the connection between Dante and Botticelli. If I felt connected to Dante, I felt connected to Botticelli even more. He had caught the Dante bug, too. Dante inspired him. Dante *mattered* to him. Dante's works shaped his own art. It was obvious. It was all over *Primavera*. So why wasn't it talked about?

Why did Botticelli want everyone to think he painted Venus and Mercury instead—*if* that's what he wanted everyone to think? Why was that how people looked at the painting up until now? Why had Botticelli not stepped up and pointed out the Dante elements? Were Dante's writings considered taboo? Would Botticelli have been called a heretic? Was there any connection to Savonarola's bonfire of the vanities that came two decades later in 1497, when Botticelli would be seen throwing his own paintings into the fires? Perhaps something he saw as inevitable? There had to be a reason for all the secrecy.

I had personal references in some of my paintings too. I didn't need to write an entire book to explain every brushstroke. Not everyone might know what every item in those paintings meant to *me*, but I knew, and that was enough. And if a buyer liked what they saw without me having to explain it all, that was okay too.

Still, something fishy was going on during the Renaissance. But I had too many other things to figure out, so I could only wonder for the time being.

36

Venus and Mars

Three years after first discovering the question mark in *Mona Lisa*, I was sitting in an old school chair in the attic office of the house Heather and I had purchased. I was going through art books on Botticelli. At times, my research into Renaissance art would focus for weeks or months on stories from Vasari or on the Medicis or certain popes, then I would emerge to go over Leonardo and *Mona Lisa* again—always with deeper understanding and insight. Michelangelo's art would loom in the background, like an unknown continent I would have to eventually explore. Less well-known painters of the time, like Arcimboldo or Crivelli, would catch my eye and distract me for days.

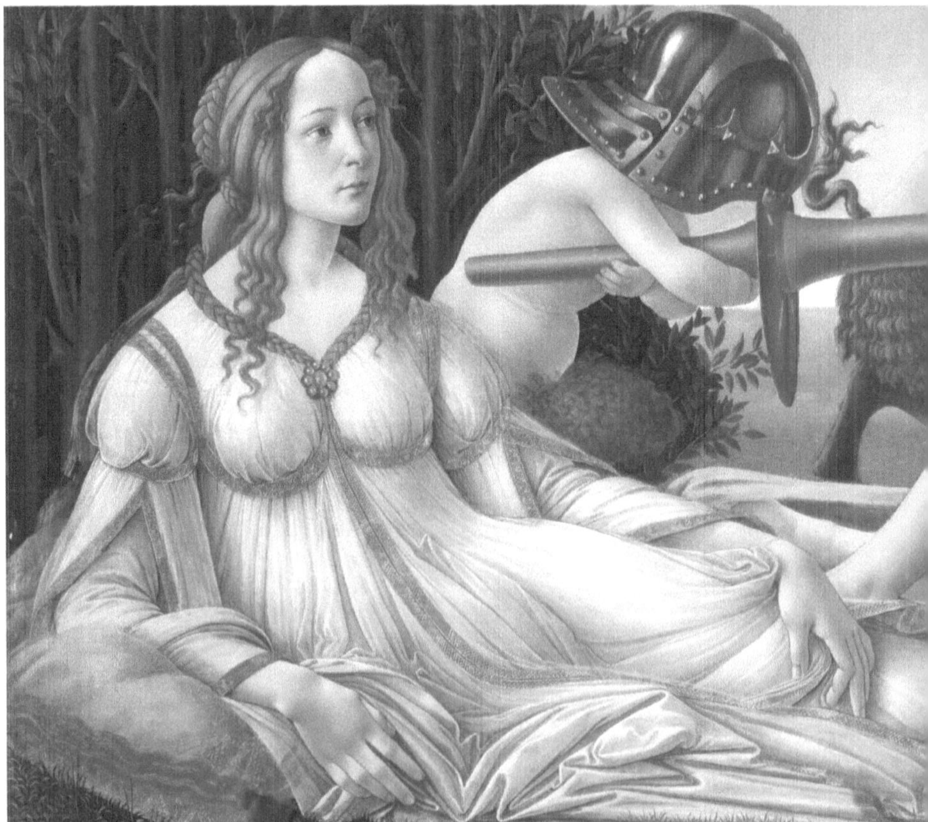

Venus and Mars by Sandro Botticelli (c. 1485).

But I couldn't stop returning to Botticelli.

As I stood over a table of images of paintings and sculptures and other old art I'd cut out, my eyes stopped on *Venus and Mars.* His paintings were generally painted in tempera—watercolors mixed with egg yolk that produced vibrantly beautiful colors. Colors almost as beautiful as the womanly figures Botticelli created—slim, strong, lovely creatures that made me think of actress Uma Thurman.

I had studied *Venus and Mars* plenty of times over the years. Each time something made me pause. Each time I had a hunch I was missing something big. Unlike *Mona Lisa*, no big mysteries existed in *Venus and Mars.* Not that anyone knew, anyway. It was just a picture of a goddess and a god picnicking. The goddess was a perfect example of Botticelli's ability to paint women more beautifully than anyone else. The god looked like he'd passed out after drinking too much wine.

Technically, the painting is as good as tempera gets. But it was puzzling. There were questionable details experts hadn't been able to explain. What was the meaning of the frantically buzzing wasps near the god's head as he lies

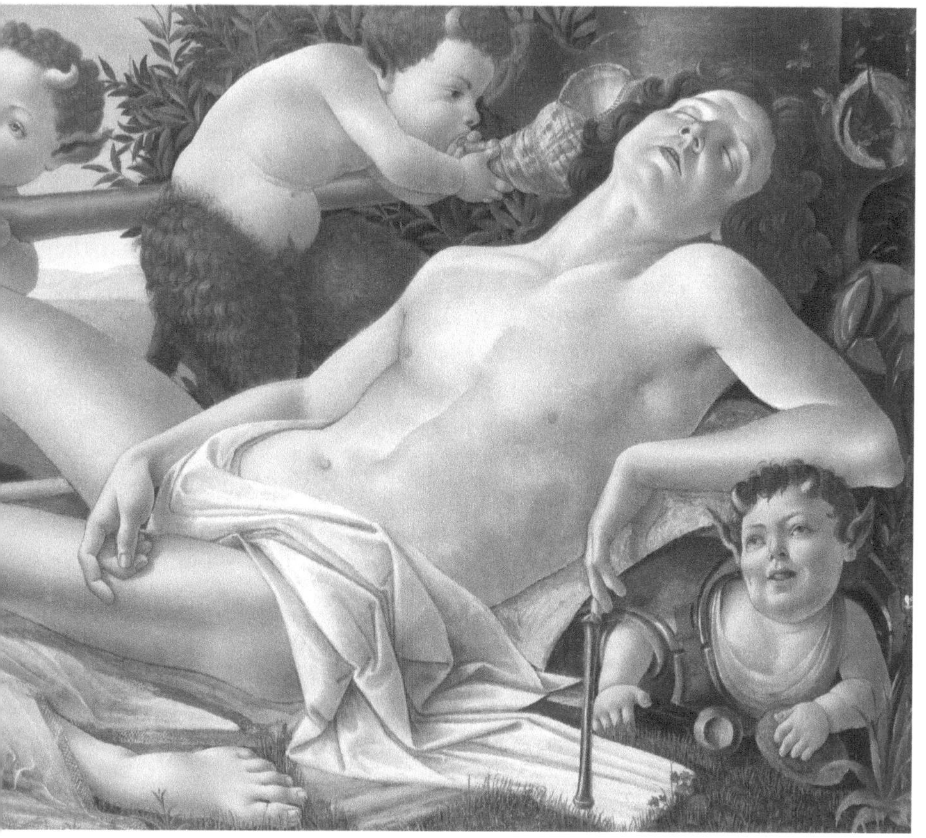

sleeping along the grass against a tree stump? Why does he seem unaffected by the sound of the conch one satyr blows into his right ear? And if he was the god of war, why was he just lying there? I was getting used to the idea of finding double meanings and meaningful gestures in Renaissance art. *Venus and Mars* didn't show much gesturing. Mars is out like a light as Venus is reclined along the grass, just watching him while four dopey-looking satyrs lark about. She seems to contemplate something as Mars sleeps. But what exactly?

One oddity is that Venus is usually portrayed in the nude, like Botticelli had done with *Birth of Venus.* He portrayed the goddess wearing nothing at all. Not even a hint of her owning any clothes. Yet, in *Venus and Mars*, she wears a long white gown trimmed with gold. Mars is the one who is practically naked, covered only at the waist by a white loin cloth. What made experts think she was Venus? It nagged at me.

No one could explain with certainty why Mars is almost nude and Venus is fully clothed. That alone made me question if the painting was really showing the two deities as historians believed—especially after finding that *Primavera* portrayed figures from *The Comedy.* It always bothered me when art information was presented as fact when it was questionable at best. Like a high school rumor. I always trusted that what I read in art history books were facts—never did I realize that alternate points of views existed between art experts to what those books taught me.

So why were the figures considered to be Venus and Mars? Because someone said so? If we were seeing the painting for the first time, and knew nothing about it, who would the two main figures be? That's how I looked at it.

What nagged at me was that, except for slight differences in what they wore, the female in *Venus and Mars* looked like the same girl in *Primavera*—who I was pretty sure was Beatrice. It was the same with the male figure I thought might be Dante. Experts state that the male character in *Primavera* is Mercury, and that the male figure in the other painting is Mars. Yet, except for their armor, the two gods look like the same exact person. *Mercury in one? Mars in the other?* It didn't make sense.

I had found animal heads within the folds of clothing in *Venus and Mars*, but I had never examined the painting too closely beyond that to look for illusions. I printed off four large quartered sections of the art and taped them together to form one large poster. As I read more about the painting, I studied each detail on the printout and also on my computer. I put down my own notes and thoughts on the paper version and in my notebooks.

From what I read, the wasps were the most mysterious detail in the painting. I wondered about that. The wasps were explained to be a representation of the pains of love in reference to Venus, but that made no sense to me—why aren't they stinging him then? Another explanation suggested the wasps may have been the result of wordplay on the Vespucci name, the family who may have commissioned the art, since *vespa* was Italian for wasp, which was also depicted on their coat of arms.[1]

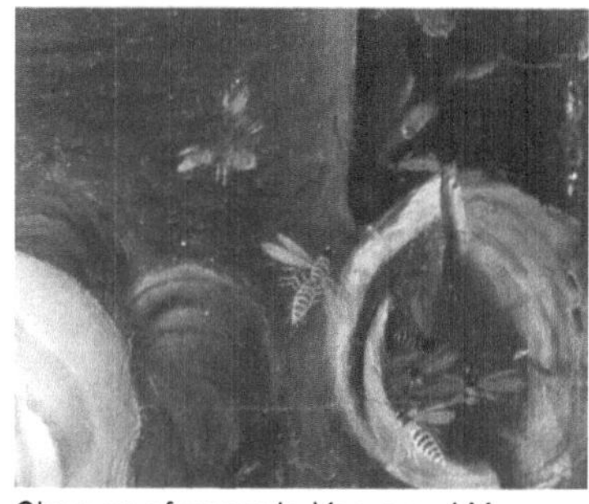
Close-up of wasps in *Venus and Mars.*

My discoveries about the way artists like Botticelli incorporated items in their paintings was *multi-layered*: so maybe the wasps were a surface reference to the Vespuccis, but I also thought they might be a metaphor for something else.

I knew a bit about insects. Not only did I research whenever I found a new bug around the house or garden, but on summer days, I liked watching bees working back and forth between the periwinkle-colored, lilac-shaped flowers on two of my favorite shrubs in the backyard. Bees are gentle by nature, stinging only if threatened. They had no reason to sting me as I watched them. I could get close enough to see the pollen they had walked through clumped around their hairy little legs. I'd even pet them with the tip of my finger. Heather and I even looked into the idea of beekeeping in the backyard to produce our own natural honey.

On the other hand, wasps were a different insect altogether. Those long-bodied devils and their dangly legs are very protective of their hive, very territorial. They'll attack with a rapid succession of vicious stings for getting too close. Even noise, such as the sound of a lawnmower, as I have experienced, bothers them. I've been stung enough around the house to know. So the picture of dormant wasps puzzled me. They don't seem bothered by Mars, whose head was way too close to the tree hole where they nested. Add the sound of the conch and you have the right conditions to irritate wasps into attacking.

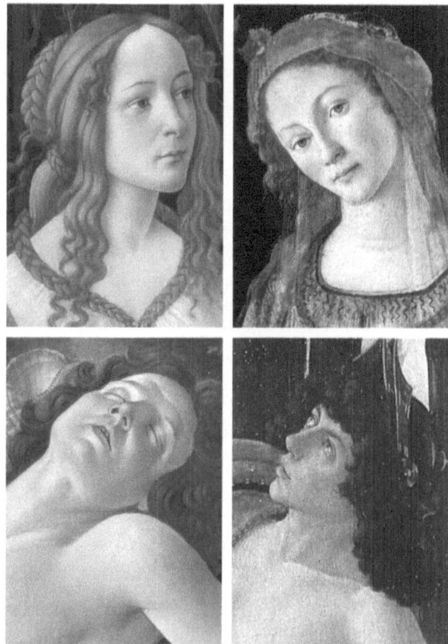
TOP ROW: Female comparison in *Venus and Mars* and *Primavera.* **BOTTOM ROW:** Male comparison in *Venus and Mars* and *Primavera.*

Because Botticelli seemed to pay careful attention to details in *Primavera*, incorporating scenes from stories like Ovid's *Fasti* and Dante's *Comedy*, I knew I couldn't leave any of the details in *Venus and Mars* to chance. In fact, the wasps reminded me of something I read. Hadn't I already come across some reference to wasps in Dante's poem, in the part of Hell I thought I'd find myself in one day?

I made my way around the painting, gathering more notes, pausing at the loin cloth—something I was used to seeing represented on Christ—bouncing my eyes back and forth between the cloth and the wasps, beginning to realize the male figure was really Dante!

Botticelli, you sly dog.

The white loin cloth, and my sudden understanding that the wasps were harmless to Dante were strong clues. I needed to double-check my hunch in *Inferno*, but continued on, intensely noting every questionable part of the art, such as the satyrs playing with the armor, especially the one sounding the conch at the figure's right ear.

Frank Zöllner explains the playful satyrs "represent the aggressive and base drives of humankind" and "embody sexual desire. …" Zöllner also points out that Italian Renaissance scholar and poet Angelo Poliziano commented that "the conch shell produces a sound so shrill that sleep becomes impossible," signifying that Mars will inevitably awaken to Venus's sexual pleasures.[2]

I didn't have a strong reason to doubt Zöllner. Though I didn't agree with everything I read, I found his book enjoyable and informative. He showed how Botticelli could have combined and represented different stories and references into one single work of art. Yet, I began to believe that in addition to Mars and Venus, the figures represented Dante and Beatrice. Maybe even *principally* Dante and Beatrice. If the painting may have combined unrelated material from those such as Ovid, Lucretius, Lucian, and even Ficino,[3] then why not Dante and his *Comedy* as well? Wouldn't someone as saturated in Dante's writing as Botticelli was have references from Dante also?

It's not that I believed historians to be wrong, just that they weren't entirely correct. They couldn't be, because they didn't have access to the entire painting—the hidden images and revealing perspectives and subtle anamorphic distortions that provided valuable clues allowing it all to fall into place. That's why the art always looked so suspicious to me, because the complete story was just out of reach, under the surface. Renaissance paintings came to look to me the way a crime scene looks to an experienced investigator. To unexperienced eyes, the scene looked ordinary, but to an investigator spending long amounts of time examining each detail, sifting through each clue, brooding over each puzzle, uncovering material evidence that casual glances miss, the scene was a revelation.

The answers didn't reveal themselves all at once. I wasn't part of an investigative team, and it would have been good to have had scholarly help, but I had to work alone. So I was left with questions to which I couldn't find ready answers. Why, for example, is Dante, or Mars (or whoever else the sleeping figure may be), unresponsive to the conch? Why are his toes covered by the blanket? Why does he look to be pointing to his leg?

Some scholars claimed the two figures had just made love. But, if something intimate happened, why aren't they *both* nude?

Did Mars fall asleep while disrobing, before making love? Or was it only lust? Perhaps he was too tired from playing with his lance? Did Mars even *have* a lance? Didn't jousting originate during the Middle Ages—Dante's time? And what was the reason for the tree stump's missing branches that looked like they had been cut?

Over the next several weeks, I did exactly what I told myself I wouldn't do if I was ever going to finish my book—I looked for answers to paintings that didn't seem related to *Mona Lisa.* I couldn't let it go. So many things bothered me about that painting. Maybe I was weak, but it was impossible to ignore. Maybe I was too involved. I loved pondering the art. I was constantly preoccupied by it, even at work when I should have been focused on my job instead of sneaking a few minutes here and there whenever no one was looking to examine paintings online.

I knew an artist like Botticelli wouldn't paint something without a reason. If the figures were Beatrice and Dante, as I suspected, the scene itself could not have been taken from any point earlier than the end of *Purgatorio*, since that's when Beatrice enters into the story to guide Dante.

Of course, the art could have been made from a free-floating associative combination of details from different parts of *The Comedy,* like Botticelli had done with *Primavera*, treating it like a movie poster that incorporated different elements from different scenes.

I thought back to Drew Struzan's iconic *Star Wars* debut poster with Luke Skywalker standing He-Man-like, holding a glowing lightsaber, in the background a squad of Rebel fighters attacking the Death Star—a scene in which Skywalker pilots one of the X-wing starfighters. So Skywalker technically appears two times on the poster. One character, shown twice, used to represent two different scenes. Did the movie poster artists just hit on their approach instinctively, and had Renaissance artists also? Or had the influence of the Renaissance artists somehow trickled down through the centuries to Hollywood movie posters?

Matching Dante's writing to Botticelli's art was no easy task—which is probably why it went unnoticed for so long. It wasn't like connecting two straightforward descriptions. *The Comedy* is an allegory.

Originally written in Italian, I used multiple translated versions to better figure out its meaning. I mainly used translations by Henry Wadsworth Longfellow, and also by John Ciardi. But the poem took time to comprehend. In many ways, it was like a Renaissance painting itself, only worse: worse because while a painting might have dozens of hidden meanings and symbols, *The Comedy* stretched nearly seven hundred pages. There were symbols and hidden meanings popping out on every page. Matching details could be deceptively subtle. I had to decipher possible alternative meanings in nearly every sentence, and then try to catch places and ways that Botticelli might have incorporated any of it in his art, which, in addition, might be incorporating other symbols too. It was like a crazy new sport where following all the clues was like rushing downhill while details flashed by at breakneck speeds: *Extreme Allegoric Painting.*

I noted a line describing one of Dante's fainting spells:

> I **never heard,** nor here below is sung,
> The hymn which afterward that people sang,
> **Nor did I bear the melody** throughout.
> Had I the power to **paint how fell asleep**
> Those **eyes compassionless,** of **Syrinx** hearing,
> Those **eyes to which more watching** cost so dear,
> Even as a painter who from model paints
> I would **portray how I was lulled asleep;**
> He may, who well can **picture drowsihood.**
>
> (*Pur.* 32.61-69, emphasis added)[4]

At times, Dante is unable to perceive sound during these spells. It wasn't hard to see how that line could tie back to *Venus and Mars.* The male figure is sleeping ("paint how fell asleep") and unaffected by the sound of the conch ("Nor did I bear the melody"). But the satyrs threw me off because they appeared nowhere in *The Comedy*, causing me some doubt about the painting's connection. I felt I needed to be able to explain every part of the painting in order to be sure of its connection to *The Comedy*, and I was asking too much. Botticelli could well have derived only the major images in his painting from Dante, and, feeling he had made his point, relaxed. Using material from Dante to inspire scenes in one's painting didn't commit an artist to connect *every last image* in that painting to Dante. Maybe the forest of trees behind Venus is a reference to Dante entering the Dark woods. Or maybe they're just trees. It wasn't enough to see a connection: there had to be multiple connections that worked together. And that looked like the case: the passage references certain words or actions Botticelli represents in *Venus and Mars*—"melody … paint … asleep … drowsihood"; Botticelli, the "painter who from model paints"; "nor did [Dante] bear the melody," and so is "lulled asleep" by the sound of the satyr's shell; and I, the viewer, "who well can picture drowsihood"; while Beatrice's "eyes [are] compassionless … watching. …"

Alongside all that, Dante mentions a *Syrinx*—a nymph from Greek mythology. The seven Nymphs, guarding Beatrice's chariot, are also involved in the scene. Nymphs and satyrs are commonplace images in the classical world, which led me to believe it was the reason for the satyrs. The connections were not hard evidence, but they were becoming evident. Yet, I wasn't completely satisfied.

Dante awakens with Beatrice near him, "[seated] upon the very earth. ..."

> ... **"Behold her seated** underneath
> The leafage new, upon the root of it.
> Behold **the company that circles her**
> . . . .
> **Alone she sat upon the very earth,**
> **Left there** as guardian of the chariot
> Which I had seen the biform monster fasten.
> Encircling her, a cloister made themselves
> **The seven Nymphs** (*Pur.* 32.86-88, 94-98; Longfellow, emphasis added)[5]

"*Left* there"—Botticelli placed Beatrice on the left side. A line a few pages later reads, "... When Beatrice towards the left-hand side / I saw turned around, and gazing at the sun ..." (*Par.* 1.46-47).[6] Later, souls are seated in the heavens so that on one side are those who always believed in Christ—which included Beatrice. On the other side sit those who believed only after Christ came, which could explain Dante sitting opposite Beatrice:[7]

> **Upon this side, where perfect is the flower**
> With each one of its pedals, **seated are**
> **Those who believed in Christ who was to come.**
> **Upon the other side, where intersected**
> With vacant spaces are the semicircles,
> **Are those who looked to Christ already come.**
> . . . .
> ... In equal measure shall this garden fill.
> (*Par.* 32.22-27, 39; Longfellow, emphasis added)[8]

Because Dante's original text was in Italian, I wondered how different translations of *The Comedy* would affect the imagery I was matching up, but realized it wouldn't make a difference, no matter which translation I used. The object being discussed in each scene and the action pertaining to it would be the same no matter what language described it. It didn't matter whether it said "behold her seated upon the root of it" or "she was seated on the tree's roots" or "she rested her butt down on the part of the plant buried in the earth." The object—*Beatrice*—and the description or action—*sitting*—would still fit the imagery Botticelli painted.

Either way, one of the reasons for Botticelli's placement of the figures on the left and right seemed to come from those seated in *The Comedy*'s Heaven.

Botticelli seemed to make another crafty reference when positioning Dante at Beatrice's feet, his head turned to his left, unable to sense sound or sight.

> … That **all my other senses were extinct,**
> And **upon this side and on that** they had
> Walls of indifference, so the holy smile
> Drew them unto itself with the old net
> When forcibly **my sight was turned away**
> **Towards my left hand by those goddesses**
> . . . .
> Thus Beatrice, and I, who **at the feet**
> **Of her commandments** all devoted was
> (*Pur.* 32.3-8, 106-07, emphasis added)[9]

I dug deeper into the scene, becoming more attentive to every word and possible meaning. The similarities I found mostly took place in *Purgatorio*, after the events describing *Primavera.* Descriptions matching painting and poem kept popping up. In one place Dante compares his slumber to the Transfiguration of Christ—a miracle the apostles witness when Moses and Elias suddenly appear next to Christ, then vanish. "… Moses and Elijah vanished from them; / And saw the Master's robe change back to cloth" (*Pur*. 32.80-81; Ciardi).[10] The reference left me wondering about the loincloth Dante (or Mars) wears.

Is that why he's practically nude?

The scene was one of many key points in which Dante experiences a divine transformation. At first, I suspected his nudity might represent the uncommitted souls in Hell, since he had been on the path to becoming one of them before his journey. It was a scene I remembered well, because if Dante's Hell were real, I knew I'd likely end up with those uncommitted souls—nude, and continuously surrounded "by gadflies and by hornets …" (*Inf.* 3.66; Longfellow).[11]

> And I, who looked again, **beheld a banner,**
> Which whirling around, ran so rapidly,
> That of all pause it seemed to me indignant;
> And after it there came so long a train
> Of people, that I ne'er would have believed
> That ever Death so many had undone.
> . . . .
> These miscreants, who never were alive,
> **Were naked, and were stung exceedingly**
> **By gadflies and by hornets that were there**.
> These did their faces irrigate with blood (*Inf.* 3.52-57, 64-67, emphasis added)[12]

I thought the white cloth Botticelli dressed him in symbolized Dante's new commitment to God. Instead of chasing an empty banner, he had, in a way, caught it, and used it to cover his naked soul—a metaphor Botticelli painted in literal form. Some humor from Botticelli, perhaps? I also figured that was the reason the wasps were leaving Dante alone, since he's no longer on his way to becoming an uncommitted soul, a fate that included being stung by wasps.

The banner could also double as a loin cloth. Following a hunch, I spent time researching Jesus: His Crucifixion, Resurrection, the Five Holy Wounds.

It was then that I realized how ingenious Botticelli really was.

My admiration for the painting gradually turned into awe. Not long before, I'd been blind to so many details Botticelli scattered throughout his masterpiece. After studying each and every detail, the religious allegory grew larger and more profound. It was pretty clear.

The second time Dante encounters Beatrice in *A New Life*, she's dressed "in a dazzling white gown …" and gestures to him in greeting. Dante feels so intoxicated that he's "overcome by a gentle slumber …" while thinking of her a short while later.[13] The white gown could be pointing to the White Rose of Paradise: "In fashion then as of a snow-white rose / Displayed itself to me the saintly host …" (*Par.* 31.1-2)—where souls happen to be flying around like "a swarm of bees …" (31.7).[14] Her white gown alone was barely any proof, but it was another possible reference to Dante's writings. And it could explain why she was fully dressed—because she was Beatrice, not Venus.

At one point during his visit to the heavens, Dante is instructed to look into the eyes of the Virgin Mary to receive grace and be granted the vision of God, able to see the faces of spirits: "Look now into the face that unto Christ / Hath most resemblance; for its brightness only / Is able to prepare thee to see Christ" (*Par.* 32.85-87).[15]

The words caused me to pause with suspicion: … *The face that unto Christ hath most resemblance? … Prepare thee to see Christ?*

I stared at *Venus and Mars* as if I had never seen it before. In a way, I realized I hadn't. Not the way it suddenly appeared to me then, for the first time.

I turned my large printout of the painting counter-clockwise, slowly—just as I had with *Mona Lisa.* But then I stopped before it was on its side as I took in Dante's pose. It wasn't an illusion. Instead, I was looking at an allusion.

He no longer looked like he was asleep. Instead, he resembled a figure I had seen in many other paintings.

The loin cloth. His lifeless-looking body.

Practically standing on its bottom-left corner, the painting showed a completely different story. A completely new, higher, layer of meaning.

… *Prepare thee to see Christ.*

With the painting turned, it seemed to show Jesus, as if hanging from the cross, more specifically, his descent from the cross after his crucifixion. In fact, I was sure of it.

I flipped back and forth through *The Comedy*, searching and searching over and over. The same lines, the same scenes. I'd read them so often, but noticed details I had missed or forgotten. It was easy to see why no one made the connections between Botticelli's painting and Dante's writing. And who would have thought to look at it from a rotated position? Or maybe Botticelli was making a point to look at art in untraditional ways. Still, every time I reread a scene, I'd find something I had missed. Seven hundred pages of ambiguously written poetry was too much to recall perfectly.

At night, I'd barely get much sleep. Heather would ask me to come to bed, but there was always "one more thing I had to look up" or "just a few more minutes" that I needed. Two or three hours later I'd finally force myself to bed, but only to lie there reading, the whole house dark except for the lamp next to me, the only place in the world that felt awake and alive to me. Just me and ghosts from Italy's past. If I wasn't reading Dante, I was leafing through some other book about Italy's art history. I couldn't read fast enough, couldn't take in enough knowledge. There was not enough time in the world and not enough books to satisfy my curiosity. I needed to learn everything I could, needed to get my hands on anything with words, anything that hinted at Italy's past. Maybe it would lead me to new information about *Mona Lisa*, about *Venus and Mars*, about Botticelli, or Lisa Gherardini. I needed to know about it all, every little detail. Every piece of information was suspicious until I saw otherwise. Especially with *The Comedy*, I'd pass over each word, considering each possible definition and context my brain could come up with, until Heather eventually awoke just enough to ask me to click off the light. I'd silently pout to myself, as if her request was unreasonable. Then I'd reluctantly switch off the lamp and stare into the darkness, my mind spinning with different theories and possibilities. I'd wake up the next morning feeling like I didn't sleep at all, preoccupied with the idea that there was so much to check out, so much to read, and so much to write about.

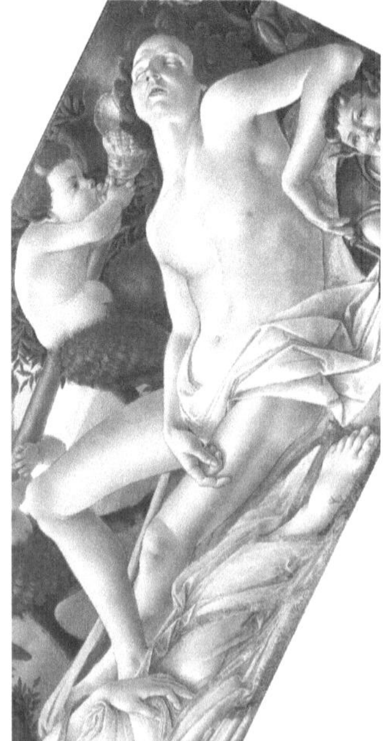
Venus and Mars, rotated, alluding to image of Christ.

Following the scenes Botticelli painted in *Venus and Mars* is a climactic fable witnessed by Dante and Beatrice. An eagle sweeps down and attacks the Tree of Knowledge of Good and Evil, stripping it of foliage and branches. The eagle then attacks Beatrice's chariot, representing the holy ark. The chariot "reeled, like [a] vessel in a tempest / Tossed by the waves, now starboard and now larboard" (*Pur.* 32.116-17),[16] rocking it like a ship in a storm. A fox jumps onto the chariot, which suddenly transforms into a seven-headed monster representing the seven deadly sins:

> So changed, the holy ark began to sprout
> heads from its various parts: **three from the pole,**
> **one from each corner**. Seven in all grew out.
> The **three were horned like oxen,** but the **four**
> **were each armed with a single evil horn.**
> **No one had seen the monster's like before.**
>
> (*Pur*. 32.142-47; Ciardi, emphasis added)[17]

I continued underlining sentences that matched details in *Venus and Mars*. The monster's horns—were they being represented by the satyrs? In the poem, three of the heads have two horns like oxen, and the other four heads have a single horn. Botticelli painted four satyrs, but only three of their heads are visible, each with two horns (assuming the one at top right has another horn on the left side of his head). Yet, the fourth head is concealed under a helmet, so no one can say how many horns it has. It could possibly be one of four "armed with a single evil horn." In fact, "no one had seen the monster's likeness before." *Clever, Botticelli.*

Or was I wrong? The fable didn't mention any satyr, much less seven of them—only a seven-headed monster. But did the monster need to be present to make a connection to the tale? Were paintings like Leonardo's portrait of St. John the Baptist null because he didn't include any other apostles? The reed cross he held seemed to be enough to symbolize St. John's identity. How about a painting of thirteen men around a dinner table—was that enough to conclude it was Christ's Last Supper? Or was it simply a matter of including enough surrounding details to fit the figures to their story? If Botticelli included seven satyrs, would it have been enough to link to the fable? Or was showing a seven-headed monster the only option? Either way, other characters from the fable were missing from the art: the fox wasn't present, nor the eagle. Not yet anyway.

Had Botticelli placed enough details to tie back to the *The Comedy*'s fable scene? That was the real question.

At times, I saw how the artist illustrated words directly from the poem. He covered the head of one of the satyrs so it would be assumed to have two horns, but also so it could be argued to only have one—fitting details Dante wrote. Sometimes the artist illustrated words in a literal sense, sometimes allegorically. Three satyrs were positioned carrying the lance ("three from the pole"), and one in the bottom, right corner of the art ("one from each corner"). Many of the connections weren't obvious at first, and some I didn't catch until I'd examined the art countless times. Sometimes, I wouldn't even catch various meanings for two or three years, when I would read something that would take me back to a specific painting. But like a detective who couldn't give up, I kept pondering, finding more and more clues—and once I did, it became obvious that the connections were there, such as the connection between the satyr's actions in the art, and the allusion to Christ when the painting was turned on its corner.

I don't know why I was so adamant in tracking down every single clue. Even when I eventually found enough ties to prove Botticelli's art had come from Dante's *Comedy*, it still wasn't enough to make me stop searching. I wasn't sure if it was a fascination or an obsession. Maybe I wasn't sure if anyone would believe what I was finding and wanted all the proof I could get. But the truth was right there in the art. Seeing was believing.

Botticelli included an abundance of ties to Dante's work, but the *The Comedy* itself referenced many people, events, and stories in its lines—from Medusa to Moses receiving the Ten Commandments to Homer's *Odyssey*. One reason I started reading a translation of the Latin Vulgate Bible that was used in the sixteenth century was to better understand not only Dante's story and references, but the Biblical stories to which Dante's writings so often referred. It helped deepen my appreciation of Botticelli's art even more, since I could see he not only referenced *The Comedy*, but also the stories referenced in the poem, like that of twins Jacob and Esau, mentioned in Genesis.

Jacob stole Esau's birthright by holding him back by his heel in their mother's womb in order to be born first.

Looking at Beatrice's left hand, it held an odd position, obscuring Dante's right foot—as if pinching something that wasn't there.

I pulled a Sharpie from a jar of markers on my desk, shaking my head in amusement. I dash-marked the outline of Dante's foot as if it could be seen, chuckling at the shape I drew.

Maybe I'd spent too much time with the art, and read too much into it. But the outline I drew of Dante's foot told another story. Beatrice was pinching Dante's heel—or really the outlined shape of his heel. After that, connections fell into place one after another, like dominoes.

It was as if the painting was a sort of game. Esau is described in the story as "hairy like a skin …"—not a far description of the satyrs. And in birth, Jacob came out holding Esau's foot: "Immediately the other coming forth, held his brother's foot in his hand, and therefore he was called Jacob" (Gen. 25.25).[18] Another reference to the heel appears in the story of Adam and Eve, when they eat from the tree: "I will put enmities between thee and the woman, and thy seed and her seed: she shall crush thy head, and thou shalt lie in wait for her heel" (Gen. 3:15).[19] Beatrice was pinching the outline of Dante's foot. And the satyrs looked like they were about to ram the lance and conch into Dante's skull ("crush thy head") while he laid there ("lie in wait").

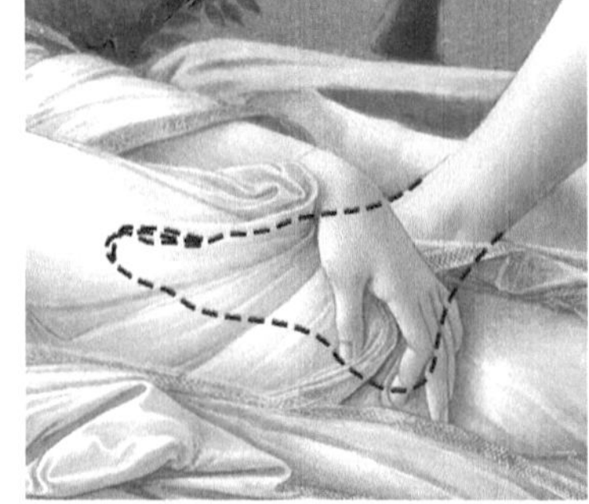
Outline of foot.

Every detail in that painting was suspicious. Every single detail. Like Dante's right hand, which seemed to be pointing at something. It looked innocent enough at first, but I didn't believe any detail was innocent of deceit.

Paradiso led me to an explanation later on, which would also explain Beatrice's expressionless face. She tells Dante that her smile would be so powerful to his mortal senses that he would be killed by seeing it, just as Semele was killed when she saw her lover Zeus in his god form. "... And [Beatrice] smiled not; but 'If I were to smile,' / She unto me began, 'thou wouldst become / Like Semele, when she was turned to ashes'" (*Par.* 21.4-6; Longfellow).[20]

Dante began his journey blinded by earthly concerns until Virgil and Beatrice helped him see the true importance in life. His growing purification along the way allows him to eventually receive the brilliance of Beatrice's brightening *smile*. Her *true* smile can only be seen by purified souls. Throughout the poem, the author makes it a point to progressively describe her increasing smile. When Dante's divine vision first improves, Beatrice offers him "somewhat" of a smile. Later, she smiles at him "a little." Her smile increases proportionally with Dante's divine vision. (That same smile would later lead me to *Mona Lisa*'s identity.)

I remembered having written something down about Semele. Checking back to my notes, I had written "Mortal mother of Dionysus" beside Semele's name. Dionysius, the only god with a mortal parent, was the god of fertility and wine. Zeus rescued the unborn Dionysius by sewing him into his thigh when Semele was killed. From the god's thigh, Dionysius was later born.

And there in Botticelli's painting was Dante—pointing to his thigh.

I had seen a Roman stone sarcophagus from around 260 A.D. in The Metropolitan Museum of Art with a carving showing the Triumph of Dionysius. Beside Dionysius was a small satyr. On the left end of carving is Mother Earth, reclining along the ground, similar to Beatrice's position. Two young figures were next to her. They were not satyrs, but at the carving's right end was an unknown male, reclined like Dante in *Venus and Mars*, next to two more youths.

Was that something Botticelli had seen?

My notes grew and grew. Botticelli seemed to make an amazing number of story and figure references in his painting. *Jacob and Esau. Semele and Zeus. Dionysius. Adam and Eve. Mars and Venus. Dante and Beatrice.*

And Christ.

The reference to Christ amazed me most, not only for the riddle-like clues Botticelli included, but also because the painting had to be rotated in order to realize the allusion. It was a dramatic change to how art could be looked at. I'd figured out that the tree Botticelli placed behind Dante—according to a scene in *The Comedy*—was the Tree of Knowledge of Good and Evil, where Adam and Eve picked the forbidden fruit. The tree against which Dante rested was damaged. I noticed the four sharp grooves in the lower of the two cut branches on the tree's right side. They looked like marks made by eagle talons—the eagle that attacked the Tree of Knowledge of Good and Evil and causing it to be "despoiled / Of blooms and other leafage on each bough" (*Pur.* 32.38-39).[21] That had to explain its crudely cut branches.

Legend states that Christ's cross was cut from that same tree. And Dante didn't seem to be just leaning against it. One of his legs crossed over the other. His hands were suspiciously turned so neither the fronts nor backs could be seen, and his feet were covered—so there was no way to see any signs of stigmata. Botticelli wanted that detail to go unnoticed—just as he had covered one of the satyr's heads.

Hidden clues that pointed to higher truths.

But the hidden clues—even the obvious clues like covered hands and feet—weren't the only hidden clues that helped me see that Botticelli's masterpiece was a representation of Christ.

Dante's position against the tree is similar to paintings depicting the Lamentation of Christ, such as Albrecht Dürer's and Alessandro Turchi's versions, painted in 1498 and 1645, respectively. Many show Christ's nude figure wrapped in the same white loincloth and lying on a large cloth.

Dante was usually shown wearing red. The cloth he's lying on in Botticelli's painting is red. Or perhaps it could be the Epitaphios (the religious cloth that can be seen in Dürer's and Turchi's painting). Or it can be portraying the scarlet robe Roman soldiers placed on Christ. The soldiers also gave Him a staff to hold, pretending it to be a scepter so they could mock the King of Kings before stripping the robe back off Him and using the staff to beat Him.

And against Dante's left hand? A small scepter.

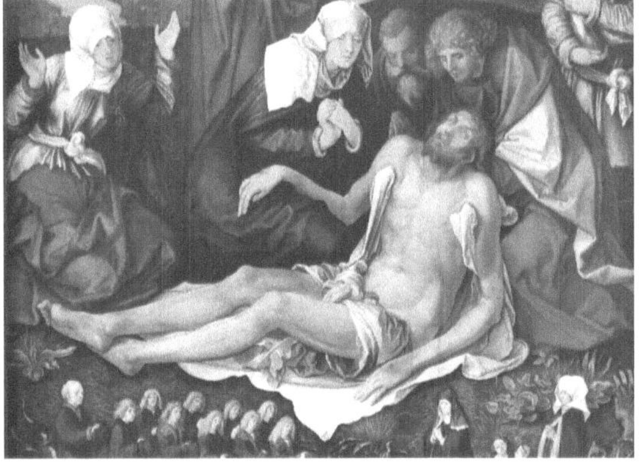

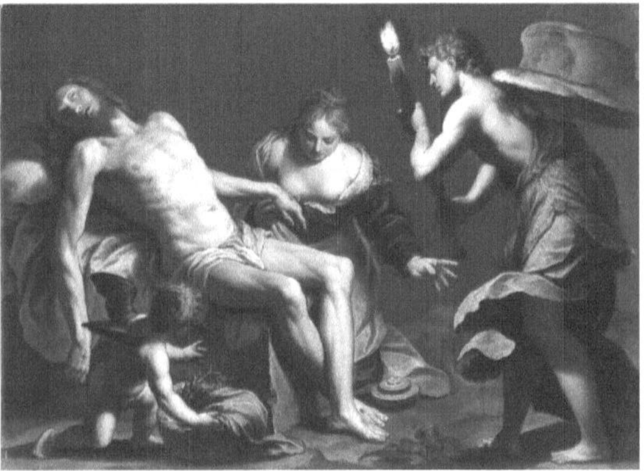

TOP: Albrecht Dürer, *Lamentation of Christ* (1498). **BOTTOM:** Alessandro Turchi, *Lamentation Over the Body of Christ* (1645).

And the satyr below him wears a mocking expression for a reason.

Botticelli was cunning. No sooner did I discover one disguised detail than I would also find that it was a detail that could support multiple meanings, such as three possible meanings of his loin cloth: a characteristic of Christ; the blank banner from the beginning of *Inferno*; the sexual innuendo experts explained as intimacy between Venus and Mars. I didn't doubt that other meanings existed.

There wasn't just one meaning. There were many. That was the key.

Beatrice offers less undeniable, yet more thought-provoking, clues to Christ's presence, some more arguable than others. Was the way she sat a reference to Mary sitting at the Lord's feet? Did the serious expression of her "countenance" refer to a line in *Purgatorio* pointing to Beatrice's similarity to Mary at the cross? "... And Beatrice, compassionate and sighing, / Listened to them with such a countenance, / That scarce more changed was Mary at the cross" (*Pur.* 33.4-6).[22]

In *Sandro Botticelli*, Zöllner points to the female figure's loosened braids of hair in determining why "Venus" is not nude as she is usually portrayed (even more unusual with the presence of a nude male), writing that "this arrangement suggests that loosening her braids would be tantamount to loosening her clothing."[23]

It wasn't an unreasonable linkage to make—if you remained only on the surface of the painting, and looked deliberately away from other, more Christian associations. But why do that when examining the work of a Christian painter in a Christian culture—a painter profoundly saturated in the work of the greatest Christian of the time? And if, as I had figured, the crucifixion of Christ was just one of the represented stories, was it plausible that her loosened hair points to the anointing of Jesus, when a woman wept her tears onto his feet and wiped them with her hair?

Even more sly in detail, could the lance be the *Holy Lance,* the one used to pierce Christ in the chest? The legend includes a centurion Roman soldier named Longinus, who, nearly blind, punctured Christ's chest as He hung on the cross. Blood fell into the soldier's eyes and miraculously cured his blindness. Could that explain the satyr positioned at the handle of the lance, blinded by his own helmet?

As I looked even closer, studying the satyr immediately to "Christ's" left and the one to his right side (below, when the art is in its normal position), I turned the painting almost onto its left side, searching for deeper layers of imagery. And there I caught something Botticelli must have enjoyed hiding.

Christ wasn't the only one to hang on a cross. Crucified to the left of him was one thief, and to his right, another. Known as the Two Thieves, one had joined the crowds in berating Jesus. The other, the penitent thief, rebukes the first thief and asks Jesus for mercy.

The two satyrs not only seem to help Dante form the shape of a crucifix, but also represent the two thieves. One of them (below the figure) seems to be mouthing off to him.

Again, a painting I had looked at so many times revealed something that never seemed to exist before. Was that idea possible with God? Would He appear only if I learned how to see Him? Like the crocodile behind Mona Lisa. Like everything I was finding. If that was the case, how could I be so sure about anything I saw? Or didn't see? How would I ever be able to tell that nothing else was hiding, waiting to be found? And what was Botticelli trying to point out?

The male figure in *Venus and Mars* represents Dante. The representation of Christ had been waiting to be found in the same image even though it existed separately *in context.* Maybe that idea of one image seen two different ways tied back to a line in a scene from *The Comedy* referencing the transfiguration of Jesus (an event in which Elijah and Moses appear out of thin air). "… And, still but little reassured, mine eyes / Saw Beatrice turned round towards the monster, / That is one person only in two natures" (*Pur.* 31.79-81).[24]

One person only in two natures. Perhaps Botticelli touched upon the idea that we had different sides to our personality, just as the painting showed Dante and a side of him that was naturally more divine.

I thought hard, trying to figure out my own nature. Did I have two sides? Or more? A spiritual side? A monstrous side? I hated to say I did. Looking back at the person I had been, I saw a man that at times had a beastly personality, naive, spiteful, unable to understand how to trust and love another person. I was ashamed at that part of me. But I also knew I had grown to be a kinder, more mature person, one who chose his words more carefully, someone who understood that spiteful actions caused by outrage were damaging to everyone.

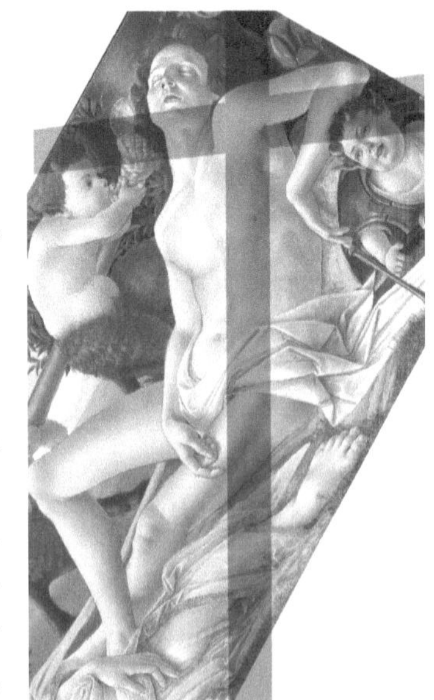

Venus and Mars, rotated, with overlay of Christian cross.

Botticelli was allowing viewers to experience his painting on a variety of levels, appropriate to their level of spiritual development. Pagans would see pagan gods and a sexual aftermath. Fans of *The Comedy* would see Beatrice and Dante in one of its defining scenes. Christians would see the presence of Christ, the Crucifixion, and Mary. Multiple meanings that could be interpreted literally or figuratively. Or first one and then another, or all at once. Or, like me, one could keep digging deeper, peeling layers of meaning away until, like Dante, you began to arrive at the vision of God.

It amazed me that so much could be taken from *The Comedy*, as though that poem had the ability to explain everything, which made it more than a story to me. It seemed to touch on endless possibilities, from religion to philosophy, to nature. Many of the scenes between Beatrice and Dante drove me to think about my own life. Maybe that was Dante's goal. One of them anyway. Beatrice tells Dante to take what he learned in his journey through the afterlife and spread his knowledge to the living world. He did. He wanted the world to understand how to live a better life. By incorporating philosophy and art and even the power of ancient stories and pagan religions, his writings put me on a personal and spiritual quest toward enlightenment.

Dante wrote *The Comedy* after his exile from Florence, resulting from a political struggle between two factions, the Guelphs and Ghibellines. Dante, part of the Guelph party, supported the Papacy, while the Ghibellines supported the Holy Roman Emperor. The Guelphs won, but soon they broke into two additional factions: Black Guelphs, who supported the pope, and White Guelphs, who wanted independence from the Papacy. Dante was a White Guelph, and eventually the Blacks condemned him to perpetual exile. Returning to Florence illegally would have meant being burned at the stake. (It wasn't until June 2008, nearly seven centuries after his death, that the city council of Florence passed a motion rescinding Dante's sentence.)

Believing there was a purpose for every tiny detail Botticelli put in his art, just as there was purpose or a point to every sentence in *The Comedy*, I tried to find an explanation to everything I saw in the art, even if it struck me as strange. Many things did. Two satyrs in *Venus and Mars* have white horns. A third satyr—the one below Dante—has black. Why? Was this a possible reference to the White and Black Guelphs that affected Dante's life? Having belonged to the White Guelphs, did Botticelli paint Dante holding down a Black Guelph while a White Guelph shouts in his ear?

Or does Dante leaning his arm on the satyr's head suggest something bigger, the location of Christ's crucifixion in relation to the scene? According to Gospel, Christ was crucified outside Jerusalem at Golgotha, also referred to as Calvary, translated from the Bible to *place of the skull.*

Or did it encompass both those ideas?

Every time I uncovered something new, I was euphoric. But the search for meaning can turn into an addiction. My own addiction began to put a strain on my relationship with Heather. No matter what we did or where we were, I couldn't stop thinking about famous Italian works of art. It consumed me, never fading as the months and years passed, and I never attempted to suppress my desires. If we watched television, I couldn't do it without an art book in my hand to examine other works. I even downloaded detailed images to my phone so I'd always have them with me—in case I had a few seconds in the car, or at a family event to look, and wonder.

Entire books could be devoted to examining every single one of Botticelli's masterpieces. I could spend a lifetime studying *Venus and Mars* alone. But I had to let it go—for the time being. I was sure I hadn't found every single story Botticelli referenced, and there was certainly a lot I discovered in Botticelli's art, but I couldn't put it all in my book on *Mona Lisa*. Unravelling Botticelli's art had sharpened my skills and deepened my knowledge. It would serve as a huge stepping stone for studying *Mona Lisa*, making it appear clearer and sharper, bringing Leonardo's achievement even more into focus. But it would become so much more than that too.

One of Leonardo's drawings came to mind: *Allegory of the Wolf and the Eagle*. It showed a boat being steered by what's been considered a wolf, heading toward a crowned eagle perched on a globe. Oddly, rooted in the center of the boat is a tree.

There have been numerous explanations to its meaning, yet it has remained elusive. One source interprets the wolf as Pope Leo X, and the eagle as King Francis, and the olive tree of peace, alluding to the King's desire to become Holy Roman Emperor.[25] Other interpretations include connections to "… St. John of Patmos whose symbols are the sea and the [crowned] eagle …" or to "the canalization of the Adda River financed by Francis I in 1515." The same source of the latter interpretations explains the drawing's wolf actually shows a dog since the "wolf has endless negative connotations in Italian lore."[26] It's even been presumed that the boat is sailing toward the German Empire.[27]

No interpretation mentioned *The Divine Comedy*. But just as scenes in *The Comedy* had brought me to *Primavera* and *Venus and Mars*, it also brought me

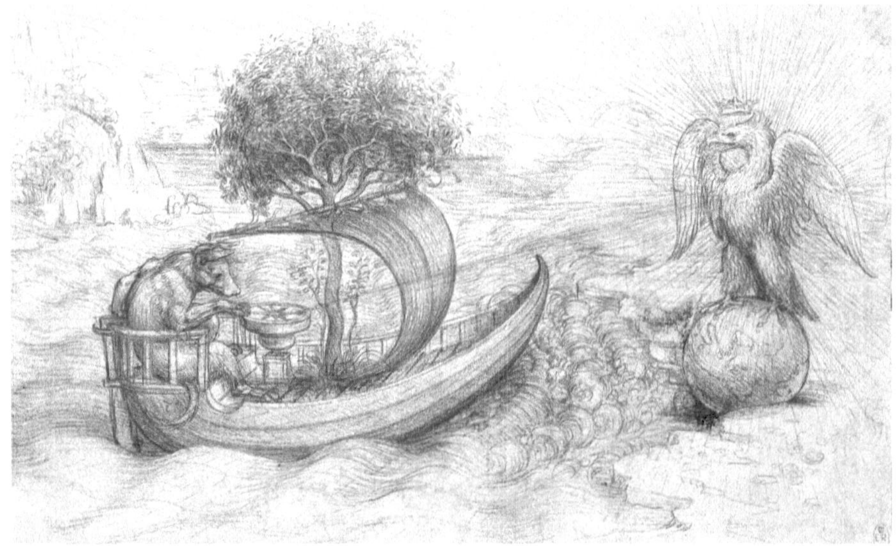

Allegory of the Wolf and the Eagle (c. 1516).

to Leonardo's drawings. Studying the drawing more closely, I wondered if the animal was a fox instead. Different species of wolves and foxes looked so much alike they could be confused for one another. A fox would have fit a fable from *The Comedy* in which a fox jumps into Beatrice's chariot after an eagle descends *through* a tree and attacks the vehicle, and a dragon smashes its tail through the vehicle's floor, leaving behind "… A fertile region … / Perhaps with pure intention and benign …" (*Pur.* 32.137), which might explain the olive tree symbolizing peace. I realized Leonardo's drawing showed a boat, but Dante used a metaphor to describe the chariot reacting like a boat in a windy storm, which Leonardo drew from:

> … As I beheld **the bird of Jove** descend
> **Down through the tree** …
> … And he with all his might **the chariot smote,**
> **Whereat it reeled, like vessel in a tempest**
> **Tossed by the waves, now starboard and now larboard.**
> Thereafter saw I leap into the body
> **Of the triumphal vehicle a Fox,**
> That seemed unfed with any wholesome food.
> But for his hideous sins upbraiding him …
> … Into the chariot's chest I saw the Eagle
> Descend, and leave it feathered with his plumes.
> … A voice from Heaven there issued, and it said:
> **"My little bark,** how badly art thou freighted!"
>
> (*Pur.* 32.112-13, 115-21, 125-26, 128-29, emphasis added)[28]

The drawing's connection to *The Comedy* became obvious to me, which also gave me some doubt about other interpretations to events that took place two centuries after Dante wrote his poem, such as that of the Pope and King Francis or the canalization of the Adda River. I also found very little discussing the drawing's interpretation of the German Empire, and didn't know enough about the empire's political power during Leonardo's time. But I did know about the German artist Hans Holbein the Younger and his painted illusion. Had Holbein seen Leonardo's drawing, or known about *Mona Lisa*'s illusions, and *seen* what I had seen? Did some mutual acquaintance introduce Holbein to Leonardo's anamorphosis technique? Or was the skill passed down through some other path?

Whatever the explanation, *The Ambassadors*, which displays a half-covered crucifix, two shelves filled with celestial objects, and a distorted skull, cried out for an explanation. The painting was almost as mysterious as *Mona Lisa* itself. But what did it all mean? I wasn't yet sure, but I couldn't help feeling that it would all lead back to Dante's writings.

37

The Banquet

Later on, toward the end of finishing my book in 2018, I'd come to realize that Renaissance artists not only secretly tied their art back to Dante's writings, but did it by following instructions Dante left behind. The realization would come to me like the apple falling onto Newton's head, an *Aha!* moment that felt like verification from Dante himself for everything I had found.

Dante's instructions addressed writers, explaining how to understand specific layers of meaning—some that were hidden—by a sort of way of *reading between lines* and *double entendres* in literature. It turned out that artists used these techniques to conceal story references in their art. The instructions would be found in *Il Convivo* (*The Banquet*), a set of books Dante left unfinished just before starting *The Comedy*.

Using the example of a dinner banquet to represent literature by its different *courses*, Dante explains how to properly pull different interpretations—*allegories*—through vernacular, linguistics, and philosophy. "I wish to show how it should be eaten" (bk. 2, ch. 1, par. 1; Hillard), wrote Dante.

As one of the last puzzle pieces, *The Banquet* would tie together all my findings. It would make sense of the multiple interpretations I came across in works of art—like how Botticelli's *Venus and Mars* showed one story on the surface, and less obvious stories as one looked for deeper meanings through more subtle details. Dante explains how "we should know that books can be understood, and ought to be explained, in four principal senses" (par. 2).[1] For artists, *books* would instead mean *art.* Readers—or viewers—were to understand the four meanings—or stories—in a specific order. The first meaning of narration in the hierarchy "is called *literal*, and this it is which goes no further than the letter ..." (par. 2), and "the literal sense should always come first ..." (par. 5).[2]

I initially realized how *Venus and Mars* showed a scene from *The Comedy*. The representation was literal: after a fainting spell in Purgatory, Dante lays along the grass with Beatrice. Botticelli's painting followed details of what took place.

Once the literal meaning is understood, the second message "is called *allegorical*, and this is the meaning hidden under the cloak of fables ..." (par. 2).[3] Once I realized *Venus and Mars* actually represented a *Purgatorio* scene, I was able to dig deeper to find that it also represented the fable of the eagle and fox Dante and Beatrice witness during the same scene. Although the painting showed no fox, no eagle, no chariot, and only a damaged tree trunk, subtle details alluded to the fable of the eagle's attack on Beatrice's chariot and the fox and the Tree of Knowledge of Good and Evil. *The Banquet* states that a fable represents

> a truth concealed beneath a fair fiction; as when Ovid says that Orpheus with his lute tamed wild beasts, and moved trees and rocks; which means that the wise man, with the instrument of his voice, softens and humbles cruel hearts, and moves at his will those who, having no rational life whatever, are almost like stones. … Theologians, however, take this meaning differently from the poets. … Because [Dante] intend[s] to follow here the method of the poets, [he] shall take the allegorical meaning. … (par. 2)[4]

Allegories were a common inclusion in art. Works like *Primavera* and *Venus and Mars* were even categorized as allegorical. Usually, artwork was believed to only have a literal and allegorical meaning, if not just literal. Even then, the allegorical seemed to be taken lightly, as if the artist added it spontaneously and not as part of the overall plan, but *The Banquet* showed the idea was real and tangible and part of an artist's original intention. "… This hidden thing (the allegorical meaning) may be found by the wise…" (par. 2), Dante wrote.[5] The presence of an allegory was always viewed as a big deal in art (and literature), which made Dante's description of a third and fourth meaning unexpected:

> The third sense is called *moral;* and this readers should carefully gather from all writings, for the benefit of themselves and their descendants; it is such as we may gather from the Gospel, when Christ went up into the mountain to be transfigured, and of the twelve apostles took with Him but three; which in the moral sense may be understood thus, that in most secret things we should have few companions (par. 3).[6]

In the most secret things we should have few companions?

Goosebumps climbed my back and neck as I read those lines. It felt like Dante was addressing me directly. There he was, not only writing about hidden things, but the "most secret things. …" That told me the images I found were not supposed to be seen by just anyone, but were meant to not be found. But what did "few companions" refer to? Readers willing to dig under the surface for deeper meanings? Artists inside their trusted circle?

Dante's example of Christ's Transfiguration couldn't be a coincidence. *Venus and Mars* included symbolism to what I had believed was Christ's Transfiguration, His Descent from the Cross, or His Crucifixion, or possibly all three!

I would become euphoric as I read *The Banquet*, feeling as though I was part of that Renaissance circle of painters and poets. But how did one become part of the group of *few companions* to share those secrets with? By breaking down those unseen clues in their art? Or were all artists and writers automatically accepted into their association?

Either way, the key was understanding how to unlock a work of art's secret layers of meaning. "... The literal sense should always come first," Dante explains, and

> without which it would be impossible and irrational to understand the others; and above all would it be impossible with the allegorical. Because in everything which has an inside and an outside, it is impossible to get at the inside, if we have not first got at the outside (par. 5).[7]

So once the literal is understood, the allegorical could then be figured out. And once the literal and allegorical meaning are known, the moral can then be pieced together.

Yet, there was more. There was never a clear explanation for some of the stories I found *Venus and Mars* alluding to, such as that of Jacob and Esau, Semele and Zeus, Dionysius, Adam and Eve, and whatever other tales were still hiding there. I had to wonder if I had been looking way too deep into the art, that its details were simply coincidental to the stories—at least in the layers of meaning that went beyond literal or allegorical. Yet, allusions had no way of providing a definitive answer to their presence. My belief was that Botticelli *did* allude to those stories through carefully placed details. And that belief would prevail upon reading *The Banquet*'s description to the fourth meaning of exposition:

> The fourth sense is called *anagogical* (or mystical), that is, beyond sense; and this is when a book is spiritually expounded, which, although (a narration) in its literal sense, by the things signified refers to the supernal things of the eternal glory; as we may see in that psalm of the Prophet, where he says that when Israel went out of Egypt Judæa became holy and free. Which, although manifestly true according to the letter, is nevertheless true also in its spiritual meaning—that the soul, in forsaking its sins, becomes holy and free in its powers (or functions) (par. 4).[8]

In reading *The Banquet*, I'd end up feeling validated and somewhat reassured about my findings. Perhaps I would have been just as satisfied to find an explanation showing that I was incorrect about the moral and mystical layers of meaning—at least then I would have certainty to what I found (or thought I had found). Either way, I'd finally have an answer.

Dante provided a clear understanding on how to excavate various meanings—messages meant to be extracted from literature, which Renaissance artists used as a guide in creating their art also. The literal would lead to the allegorical. Those two led to the moral. And the three would lead to a work's mystical meaning.

The Banquet also gave me new insight that would affect my own art by making it more meaningful. I thought of the portrait I painted after finding Botticelli's hidden story references inspired me. The portrait was of me and Heather together, side by side. Literally, it showed us along a path, which I also used to symbolize our journey together. She carries a rolled up yoga mat and sunflowers (a passion of hers and her favorite flowers). In my arms I hold my dog Pinch, some painting supplies, and a book. The book represents my future memoir (literally), but subtle details show that it is upside down—an homage (and allegory) to Leonardo da Vinci and the upside-down question mark that started it all. The painting's border shows a lilac flower, symbolizing Highland Park where Heather and I took our first walk together. The house we recently purchased is *on the horizon*. A plane flies overhead—a regular occurrence due to the nearby airport. I'd awe at the sight of their bellies ascending directly above our home on the street that divides us from Genesee Valley Park. But I also had Leonardo in mind when I added the plane. It's a symbol of his studies on man's flight.

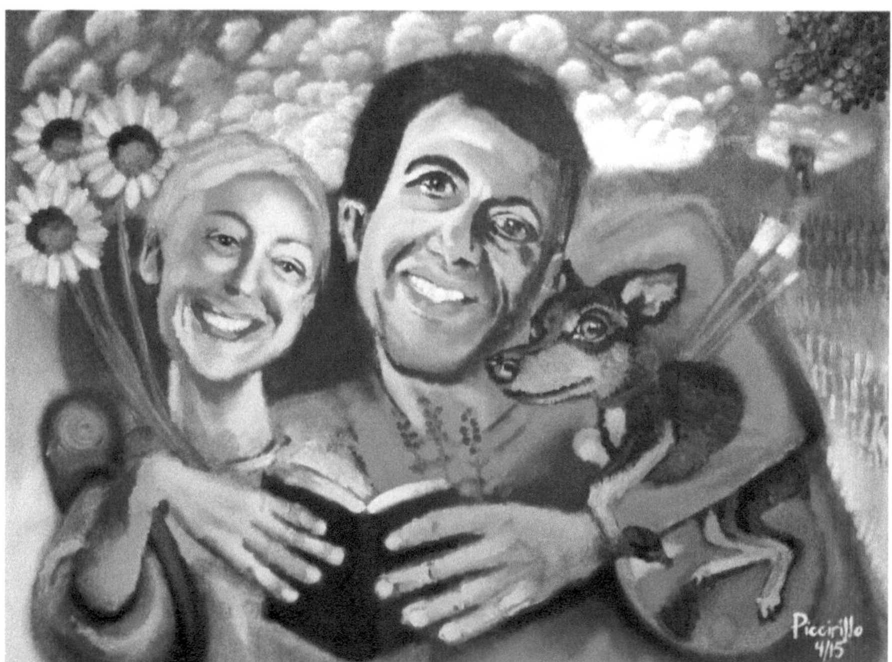

Ron Piccirillo, Self-portrait (2015).

I really enjoyed that art project, adding personal meanings throughout. Anyone could appreciate the art's *surface*, but the ideas *behind* the details made it a better work of art. *The Banquet* would show me how to be more expressive with my creations. It would also provide a way to deal with ideas that could be too hot to handle—in case I ever needed a method to hide messages in my art. Every society had something that couldn't be said easily. *The Banquet* provided a solution to help avoid offending audiences. Its approach was just plain *interesting*. Hidden images could add another layer of support to the surface, to mock or criticize the surface meaning, or create an entirely separate meaning, or simply to add a fun challenge for the viewer. No wonder it appealed to Renaissance artists. To be able to express anything they wanted was one thing. But saying it in a way that took their artistry to a whole new level was another, especially if it meant avoiding repercussions like the torture and executions that threatened lives throughout Renaissance Italy.

No wonder artists took Dante's words to heart. And so would I.

The Banquet would also make sense of the multiple stories I'd eventually discover in *Mona Lisa*. It would also help explain the animals I found throughout many famous artworks. Dante, stressing the importance of the ability to separate one's senses from one's reasoning, points out the *battle* of conflicting thoughts that occur from irrationality, stating that "he who gives up the use of his reason, and lives only the life of the senses, lives not as a man, but as a beast, …" which are different from "the lower animals, …" instead "those in human shape, with the spirit of a sheep or any other abominable beast" (bk. 2, ch. 8, par. 1-2; Hillard).[9]

To some degree, it was known that Renaissance artists read and drew inspiration from *The Comedy*, in some cases painting and sketching from the story. How difficult was it to believe that they were inspired by his other works as well? Somehow the real extent of Dante's importance to artists was missed by scholars. Maybe artists simply wanted their patronage to the poet to be missed. Or had it been overlooked, with most of the attention instead focused elsewhere, while any understanding of Dante's true importance diminished? And if artists portrayed *The Banquet*'s four categories of meaning, what was to stop them from adding more?

Further research into the vernacular and linguistics during Dante's time would lead me to Roger Bacon, an Oxford philosopher born around 1214, roughly fifty years before Dante. In *Roger Bacon in Life and Legend*, Evelyn Westacott explains that Bacon, in addition to astronomy, "devoted himself to chemistry, natural science, mathematics …" and that "experimentation … revealed to him the secrets of nature, …"[10] which also could be said of Leonardo two centuries later. Some of Bacon's and Leonardo's writings sounded eerily similar. Bacon wrote about such things as "flying machines

[that] can be constructed so that a man sits in the midst of the machine ... by which artificial wings are made to beat the air like a flying bird"; a pulley in which "one man can draw a thousand to himself by violence against their wills ..."; and a machine for safely "walking in the sea and rivers. ..."[11] Leonardo sketched concepts for flying machines, pulleys and gears, and a scuba suit.

What intrigued me most about Bacon were his ideas on seeking truth through experimentation—"the verification of knowledge through experience. ..."[12] Westacott draws on other works about Bacon which expressed the importance of philosophizing or understanding the vocabulary of a writing's original author and his background when it came to Scripture translations, that its "knowledge ... requires such aids as the mystery of tongues, grammar and history," and can "be interpreted literally, allegorically, metaphorically, or mystically and morally. ..." Accepting only the literal interpretation was ignorant, yet the Middle Ages was a very dangerous time for someone like Bacon to question how Scriptures were customarily understood, even if his intent was to seek greater knowledge of their meanings.[13]

The idea of layered interpretations and wordplay seemed to thread its way through history from as far back as biblical writings at least, so the idea was nothing new to Bacon or Dante or Leonardo and many others, whether applied to their writings or art.

Author Simon Singh, who discusses the history of encryption in *The Code Book*, wrote that Bacon was the first to describe cryptography to the European world. Bacon's *Epistle on the Secret Works of Art and the Nullity of Magic* "included seven methods for keeping messages secret, and cautioned: 'A man is crazy who writes a secret in any other way than one which will conceal it from the vulgar,'" Singh points out, a few lines later adding that

> By the fifteenth century, European cryptography was a burgeoning industry. The revival in the arts, sciences and scholarship during the Renaissance nurtured the capacity for cryptography, while an explosion in political machinations offered ample motivation for secret communication. Italy, in particular, provided the ideal environment for cryptography.[14]

It made me wonder if Dante was in any way inspired by Bacon when he wrote *The Banquet.* Unfortunately for Bacon, his studies and writings on sacred theology were condemned by many friars, and "the pope was asked to help suppress the dangerous doctrines. ..."[15] Bacon was then imprisoned for fourteen years until 1292. Initially, in his pursuit for knowledge, he had been allowed to write down his ideas, but prohibited from publishing them.[16] What would the same Church that imprisoned Bacon for his heretical views (and indirectly caused Dante's exile and the threat of being burned at the stake) think of artists secretly "publishing" their ideas in their art? Especially Christian art?

How much more dangerous could it have been to represent Dante's version of the spiritual realms, disgracing the Church and other political powers?

Whatever the consequences would have been, the artists still placed it there in their art—whether to publish their beliefs, provide deeper, philosophical layers of meaning, or simply as some sort of game. Writers had their history of using cryptography. And so did artists.

In *Brunelleschi's Dome*, Ross King (a favorite writer on the Renaissance subject with books like *Leonardo and The Last Supper*) discusses how Italian designer Filippo Brunelleschi (1377-1446) would inscribe "cryptic symbols and Arabic numbers: a secret code ..." similar to Leonardo da Vinci's reverse writings years later, and that scientists regularly used ciphers to protect their work from jealous rivals, even later ones such as Robert Hooke and Galileo who used anagrams. King even mentions Bacon's claim "that no scientist should ever write of his discoveries in plain language but must resort instead to 'concealed writing.'"[17]

Layered interpretations, secret messaging, and cryptic symbols seemed to be a part of everyday life. The more I would dig, the less unusual it would seem for Renaissance artists to place secret messages in their work. However, *The Banquet*'s explanations to understanding a work's various interpretations, nor the name Roger Bacon, nor my knowledge of Italy's long history with cryptography and secret codes would come into my possession until later, just before I would finish writing my book, after I would end up figuring out who and what *Mona Lisa* really was.

38

The Background

I had watched and studied *Mona Lisa* carefully over the years, obsessing over everything that was unknown about her, waiting for her to tell me more. Many theories crossed my mind as I tried to figure out what Leonardo painted. I carefully took my time dissecting each one. But any flaw I found, no matter how small, caused me to discard that theory and move on to another.

I needed answers, proof of who she was, not the mere speculation experts had been using as the basis of her alleged identity.

Giorgio Vasari's original description of *Mona Lisa*, assumed to be of the one with the current name, described that painting the least when I compared Vasari's exact words to Leonardo's female portraits. Aside from one arguable detail, each of the twelve features Vasari described fit Leonardo's *Lady with an Ermine*. *Mona Lisa* only matched two of the twelve, with four other details I considered questionable.

I wasn't out to claim that *Lady with an Ermine* was the real *Mona Lisa*—it had only been a test to see how accurate the information out there was, a test with surprising results. It caused me to really question and check everything I had been taught. It drove me to want real answers. Especially when no one ever noticed the animal faces that had been there all along.

So I knew I was on the right track.

Except, nothing explained the animals. Why were they mostly just the heads? I supposed it made sense in *Mona Lisa*. In the anamorphic image of the crocodile's domain, the animals were drowning, their bodies submerged in water.

But that didn't explain the heads in all the other paintings.

I laid out everything I knew about *Mona Lisa* before me in my attic, in piles of paper notes and printouts. During the winter months, the space was uncomfortably cold at times. But it gave me the privacy I wanted to become lost in my own world of thought, which allowed me to contemplate everything I examined from every single angle—both literally and metaphorically—even if I was already sure of its meaning—because multiple meanings were everywhere. Warmth came from my determination in solving what I set out to do. It reminded me of Michelangelo painting the Sistine Chapel ceiling in the winter months, his trembling hands dripping with cold paint in the bitter air as he worked, driven to finish his finest creation, feeling that nothing existed outside the walls containing his creation of the impossible.

Gradually, I began to notice a pattern to the multiple meanings in the paintings I studied. First, came the obvious details, like in Botticelli's *Venus and Mars*. By its name alone, it was known as a portrait of the god and goddess. But looking deeper, more layers of meaning appeared that pointed to stories of Jacob and Esau, Semele and Zeus, Dante and Beatrice, and Christ. It was already believed that Botticelli used parts of Ovid's writings in his art.

In fact, when I later began to read Ovid's works, I was caught by the first line of his *Metamorphoses*.

> My mind leads me to speak now of **forms changed**
> **into new bodies:** O gods above, inspire
> This undertaking (which you've changed as well)
> And guide my poem in its epic sweep
> From the world's beginning to the present day.
> (*Metamorphoses* 1.1-5; Martin, emphasis added)[1]

My mind had led me to speak—*to write*—of how Botticelli's figures did change into new bodies. When it came to the artistry of figures changing into new bodies—physically changing in their illusions or sometimes allusions, or changing in meaning from their surrounding context—Botticelli had been one of the best of them.

But before embracing Ovid's writings, Dante had all my attention.

I dissected each word in *The Comedy* for all possible interpretations. Who could deny that the art from that period was rich in allegories? Botticelli's *Primavera* even *pointed out* the allegory in its other given name: *Allegory of Spring*. Many works of art were referred to as allegoric, and they existed in Italy many years before and after Leonardo or Botticelli's time. There's the *Allegory of the Active and Triumphant Church* fresco (c. 1365), *the Allegory of Good and Bad Government* (1338), *Allegory of Fortune* (c. 1658). Leonardo himself sketched *Allegory of the Wolf and the Eagle* (c. 1516) and *Allegory of Statecraft* (c. 1490-94), along with another fittingly called *Two Allegories of Envy* (c. 1480).

The real surprise was how many more possible allegorical meanings were missed. The working world for Renaissance artists was awash in symbolism. But unless it came pre-labelled in the title, it was mostly assumed that the surface of the painting was all there was.

But there was more. One had to dig deep to see it, but it was there. Breaking through to the images and symbols was definitely difficult at times. Each deeper layer of meaning seemed harder to crack, like levels of security access into the minds of the great artists. Leonardo's writings had multiple meanings. Botticelli's paintings also, as did Dante's *Comedy*. Was it Dante's writings that inspired artists to create multiple layers of meaning? I wondered.

How many other artists learned the tricks of hiding private, additional imagery?

I came across passages Leonardo wrote comparing the skills of painters and writers, and I got the impression he set out to *prove* a painting could arouse the senses better than poetry:

> If you historians, or poets, or mathematicians had never seen things with your eyes you would be ill able to describe them in your writings. And if you, **O poet, represent a story by depicting it with your pen, the painter with his brush will so render it as to be more easily satisfying and less tedious to understand.** If you call painting 'dumb poetry,' then the painter may say of the poet that his art is 'blind painting.' Consider then which is the more grievous affliction, to be blind or to be dumb! (emphasis added)[2]

In fact, Leonardo wrote quite a bit about the comparison of the arts, practically ranting on as if there had been an ongoing argument between the poets and painters of his time:

> Truly were painters as ready equipped as you are to praise their own works in writing, I doubt whether it would endure the reproach of so vile a name. If you call [painting] mechanical because it is by manual work that the hands represent what the imagination creates, your writers are setting down with the pen by manual work what originates in the mind. If you call it mechanical because it is done for money, who fall into this error … more than yourselves? If you lecture for the Schools do you not go to whoever pays you the most? … [Yet] every labour looks for its reward. And if the poet should say, "I will create a fiction which shall express great things," so likewise will the painter also, for even so **Apelles made the Calumny.**[3]

Leonardo's unexpected mention of Apelles brought me back to Agostino Vespucci's note ("Apelles the painter. …"). Were the two mentions of Apelles directly related to each other? As if Leonardo planned to create *Mona Lisa* in order to prove painting's superiority over poetry, and Vespucci had known and therefore referenced it in his note?

One day, as I read for the umpteenth time passages I had highlighted from Leonardo's writings, a thought came to me. They were the same passages—*instructions*—that led me to discover *Mona Lisa*'s secret anamorphic illusion.

Leonardo's *d-Point* passage directed the viewer to see the illusions from the left. "Because that spot is least exposed to these reflected rays of light," he wrote, and so "you will get a good view of" the image. But I knew he wasn't really trying to teach the viewer how to avoid a painting's glare. Elsewhere he wrote that "The point of sight must be at the level of the eye of an ordinary man," and that "the farthest limit of the plain where it touches the sky must be placed at the level of that line where the earth and sky meet; excepting mountains, which are independent of it."

I looked over near my desk at the large printout of *Mona Lisa* I had pieced together to the size of 30 by 21 inches, the actual size of the original. I looked back down to his *Point-of-Sight* passage laid out in front of me, then glanced back at *Mona Lisa.* I had a sudden strong feeling about what existed behind the woman.

I pulled a marker from the mason jar on my desk and highlighted the words "an ordinary man" in the entry: "The point of sight must be at the level of the eye of **an ordinary man,** and the farthest limit of the plain where it touches the sky must be placed at the level of that line where the earth and sky meet; excepting mountains, which are independent of it."[4]

Three years had passed since seeing that upside-down question mark for the first time. It was 2014, and I had spent a lot of time rereading from his thousands of pages of notes. I came to have a good sense of how Leonardo worded his sentences. He was meticulous in how he used his words. *Ordinary man* was somehow off. I wondered if it meant something different. Something more since they weren't the best chosen words for the context? Leonardo had a way with words, and those two words—*ordinary man*—were awkward in his writing.

In *The Divine Comedy*, every character was a dead soul, a divine entity, a monster, an angel, or some other kind of unearthly being, each one unusual in their own way. Except for Dante. He wasn't a three-headed Cerberus, or a walking spirit, or a god, or in any way unusual. Except for his bizarre journey, he was just a normal human being. He was *The Comedy's* only "ordinary man."

I then highlighted the words "excepting mountains" in the *Point-of-Sight* passage.

Visions regularly appeared to Dante throughout his poem. On the Mountain of Purgatory, visions of encouragement and discouragement appeared to him, such as the execution of Haman for his hatred of the Jews. Each image related to the sin of each terrace. A spiraling clockwise path ascending around the mountain took Dante through each of the seven terraces where souls pay penance for one of the seven sins. The path was essentially a continuous cliff—the mountain wall along his right, the cliff along his left, where he could see out over its edge.

Approaching each terrace as he continuously veered right along the curving path, the visions always appeared to his right. To view the hidden *visions* in the art, I had to look right also, just like his *d-Point* explained.

Next to the word *mountains* I had highlighted, I wrote, *Purgatory?*

But I still wasn't one hundred percent sure about my hunch.

... *Excepting mountains, which are independent of it.*

In *The Comedy*, Purgatory existed as a mountain on an island in the ocean—a place where "Earthly life and glory, seen with new eyes from the hereafter, is despoiled of all its illusions, its vanity, and its fallacious appearances."[5]

... Illusions ... vanity ... fallacious appearances.

I unrolled a large banner-sized paper across the table.

On it was a web-shaped diagram I'd created showing everything new I found in *Mona Lisa.* I had sketched and noted items I found as I came across them over time. There were images drawn all over it—like a question mark and animal heads. Since then, I had come to think the buffalo also represented other creatures—possibly a frog or an ox. (When I originally compared different versions of *Mona Lisa*, I found no hidden images. But later, after developing a better sense of how to spot the images, I realized that the Prado version contained them. They just weren't as obvious as the ones in Leonardo's version. The animal heads in the Prado version shouldn't have been a surprise. They appeared in the same three spots as Leonardo's version when the painting stood on its right side. The lion and an ape head were there. But the third animal looked like an ox, its short horns turned downward. Because the Prado looked to be a copy of Leonardo's *Mona Lisa*, I had to assume the third animal in Leonardo's version was also an ox.)

I had printouts of the *Envy* passage and Leonardo's other writings taped along the banner, like the wall diagrams investigators created in those detective movies as they tried to piece together the elements to a puzzling mystery, lines connecting different crime scene photos and clues.

So what was it about the *Point-of-Sight* passage that bothered me so much? On the surface, they seemed to be directions about how to view a work of art. On a deeper level, they were directions on how to find and see anamorphic images.

But was there a third and even deeper level of meaning to the passage?

... Must be at the level of the eye of an ordinary man, ... excepting mountains, which are independent of it. I repeated the words to myself.

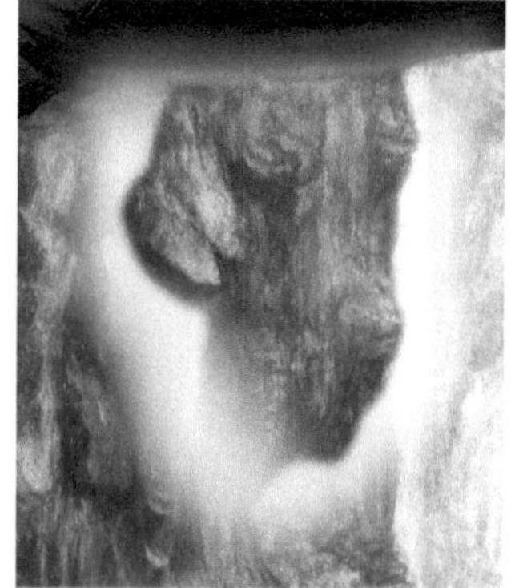

Anamorphic ox head in Prado's *Mona Lisa* (highlighted) when turned 90° clockwise.

I sat and raised my feet to rest them onto the table, reading the lines over and over. Then I tried to get at the core of what was really being said, applying the idea of Dante's story to what Leonardo wrote. I deleted unnecessary words. Crossed out "an ordinary man." In its place wrote *Dante*. Changed the words "point-of-sight" to the word *view*. And changed "at the level of" to *the same*. There was a sense of madness to what I was doing, but at the same time, I couldn't help feeling that it was perfectly reasonable. Nonetheless, I held up what I wrote:

> The ~~point of sight~~ *view* must be ~~at the level of~~ *the same as* the eye of ~~an **ordinary man,**~~ *Dante* and the farthest limit of the plain where it touches the sky must be placed at the level of that line where the earth and sky meet; **excepting mountains,** (*Purgatory?*) which are independent of it.

"The point of sight must be at the level of the eye of an ordinary man …" became "The view must be the same as the eye of Dante. …"

Would "view" pertain to what Dante literally saw, or his belief?

I considered Leonardo's secret imagery, the hidden meanings in his words, the vague portrait he created. I rubbed my temples at the thought of the danger artists could face in a time when torturing heretics was common. Dante had assigned Popes Nicholas III, Boniface VIII, and Clement V to the lowest depths of Hell in *Inferno*, along with figures from the highest elitist ranks in Florence. Had Dante become a subject of taboo more than a century after his exile from Florence?

Then I thought back to something silly I had noticed. It had no merit. At best, I found it amusing, but it did give me a strange idea. I spent a moment thinking back to when I noticed that the letters in MONA LISA could be arranged to spell out ANIMALS, except that the letter O had been left over. As I read Dante's poem, I realized that the O was not left over. How I didn't see it before, I wasn't sure, because it was used throughout the writings of both Leonardo and Dante. I had seen it in cases like "O' poet" and "O gods" (not always with an apostrophe). The O was vocative—showing a direct address to the pronoun that followed. "O poet" was like calling out "Hey, you poet." "O gods" equated to "Hey, you gods."

MONA LISA actually became an anagram for O ANIMALS. *Hey, you animals.* I passed it off as a big coincidence, especially as I considered that the painting's name was an Italian spelling that came from Giorgio Vasari. And the Italian word for ANIMALS was ANIMALI, which didn't work as an anagram. But it—along with what *Primavera* had showed me—left me with the idea that *Mona Lisa* was representing *The Comedy.*

Back when I was an artist at the agency, I worked closely with coworkers and clients. We learned a lot about each other over time. Sometimes that included religious beliefs. If the subject came up, I was honest in expressing my views. But what if I no longer could? What if I lived during Leonardo's time, and the only art commissions came from clients associated with the Church? Would I hide my beliefs and lie? Pretend to be someone I wasn't? Attend church just to keep anyone from questioning me? Or worse, allow others to force their beliefs down my throat? Would I chance being seen as a heretic? Would I choose torture over falsifying what I was sure was true? I'm sure I'd avoid physical punishment at any cost. Heck, I'd probably lie to avoid any kind of confrontation back then.

Or would I choose to slip my views into my work here and there, quietly, in ways visible only to those in the know, hiding them under a conformist surface, using ambiguous images that would give me "plausible deniability"?

Is that what the animal heads represented—secret criticisms of the Church? Of the corrupted popes and cardinals that deserved a place in the Hell Dante created? Were they the evil roaring lions of the powerful? The lustful and malicious apes? Were the images there to convey some mysterious underlying system of belief? Or unbelief?

I shook my head, unsure if I was just reading too much into it. But that didn't stop me from looking further into everything, no matter how unlikely an idea was.

With all the hidden meanings appearing everywhere with everything, I even checked to see if there was any significance to the size of *Mona Lisa*'s 30 by 21 inch wooden canvas, which had been cut specifically by Leonardo or an assistant. Everything appeared to have multiple meanings. Maybe the painting's size did too. That painting was hiding things no one had probably thought of ever checking. I didn't know if I was right, but if I was wrong, what turned out to be a very interesting coincidence appeared as I checked chapter 30, verse 21 in every book of the Bible (if that verse existed). Leonardo had a copy of the Book of Psalms in his possession. Interestingly, Psalm 30:21 read, "Thou shalt hide them in the secret of thy face, from the disturbance of men. Thou shalt protect them in thy tabernacle from the contradiction of tongues."[6]

Was it just coincidence? Or did *Mona Lisa* have some religious tie? If she was not a religious figure, why would Leonardo choose to show the painting along with *St. John the Baptist* and *The Virgin and Child with St. Anne* during a meeting involving Cardinal Luigi when he came to visit the artist in October 1517 at Leonardo's home in Amboise after he moved to France? Why show the cardinal two religious works of St. John and of the Virgin and include *Mona Lisa* if it was not also a religious work of art?

I wasn't an art historian or scholar, but I *was* a working artist. I *did* work for clients and organizations and project managers who let you know straight up what you could and couldn't say in the art that was created. Sometimes I didn't agree or like it, and sometimes I pushed the envelope. If I wanted to, I *could* slip things in, things invisible to the client and unnoticeable by the public.

As a rule, I didn't slip anything bad into my art. Ad clients don't commission lasting masterpieces. Selling a product is not on the same level as expressing your deepest feelings about the meaning of life. It didn't mean I didn't enjoy what I was doing. A good graphic design piece could be technically challenging, and meeting that challenge was satisfying. Very satisfying.

But helping to sell a decent product didn't compromise my beliefs. Nor was my life ever really threatened to do work I didn't want to do as Michelangelo's was by Pope Julius to paint the Sistine Chapel ceiling. What if I were forced to create art in support of things I strongly disagreed with, such as an ad for the annual Yulin Dog Meat Festival in China, or to promote a very corrupt politician? Would I find a way to rebel? I believed I would.

I wondered what disagreement the artists might share to make them hide animals and faces in their art.

The view must be the same as Dante's.

What was Dante's view? That he disliked sinners? Those lacking faith in God? Or was the view literal?

An idea suddenly came to me. Just as I had with Vasari's writings, I made a list of scenery descriptions from *The Comedy*, curious to see if any matched the details in *Mona Lisa*. I listed them verbatim, by order of appearance, starting in *Inferno*.

Mona Lisa seemed to offer no hint of its whereabouts—its *view*. There was only a woman and an obscure landscape.

But you gave us plenty of clues, didn't you, Leonardo?

I got to work.

My marker roamed over the printout of *Mona Lisa*. As I came across details in Leonardo's painting that matched what I read in Dante's *Comedy*, I wrote numbers over the areas that corresponded to the relevant parts of the poem.

I knew the poem well enough to spot some of the references right away. But sifting through fourteen thousand lines of complex meanings from Dante's poem was a way bigger job than going through Vasari's one-page description of *Mona Lisa*.

And the imagery Leonardo put into *Mona Lisa* was, in its own way, almost as complex. The Louvre Museum's website had an interactive link (which they named "A Closer Look") that allowed me to zoom into *Mona Lisa* as if she were right in front of me. Like studying her under a microscope. It made it possible to examine the painting down to the fine cracks in the oils. Every detail, every stroke could be seen on the surface.

Maybe *Mona Lisa* had nothing to do with Dante. But I would let Leonardo's imagery and Dante's words speak for themselves.

Renaissance artists had used Greek myths for the content of their art. They used biblical writings. In many cases that didn't include portraits, a written source was used. It wasn't unreasonable to think that Leonardo used a written source for *Mona Lisa*, or that, specifically, he had used *The Comedy*. The references to Beatrice's smile alone—a smile, which I learned, increased throughout the poem—made me believe in a possible connection between Beatrice and the woman in Leonardo's painting.

But belief wasn't enough. I needed evidence. And getting evidence that would tell me exactly where she was sitting was a good place to start. Like first obtaining the address of a crime scene, then figuring out who lives there—the location seemed to be as good a place to start as any.

Comparing Leonardo's imagery to Dante's writings immediately grabbed my attention. There were lines that made me think I was on the right track. "O ye who have undistempered intellects, / Observe the doctrine that conceals itself / Beneath the veil of the mysterious verses" (*Inf.* 9.61-63; Longfellow)![7]

Observe the doctrine that conceals itself? Veil of mysterious verses?

It took me months, but the list of corresponding details grew. There were *Comedy* lines Leonardo was sly to illustrate. I passed over them many times, too caught up in its story to notice at first, such as one describing *Mona Lisa*'s lion: "… A lion's aspect which appeared to me. // … With head uplifted, and with ravenous hunger, / So that it seemed the air was afraid of him" (*Inf.* 1.45-48).[8] It was exactly what Leonardo painted.

And there were many other descriptions I came across in Dante's poem that matched. What other painting could be described as "a place … where nothing shines" (*Inf.* 4.151), with a mountain in the middle of the sea, and "a path that strikes into a valley …" (10.135) that is *dark* and *vermilion*, with a plain with no vegetation because it "rejecteth every plant …" (14.9), and with "… The countenance of the Lady who reigns [there], / Ere thou shalt know how heavy is that art …" (10.80-81)?[9]

Were they simply vague details that fit any dark-looking art piece? It sure didn't describe any Goya or Warhol or Picasso artwork I knew of. I tried to think of others, but only one painting came to mind that fit that description.

Slowly, *Mona Lisa*'s strange, unearthly background began to reveal itself. My picture of *Mona Lisa* ended up covered in so many numbers corresponding to lines from *The Comedy* that I was running out of room to mark up the painting. *The Comedy* was decoding the art. Was I forcing Dante's poem into the painting? I didn't think so. Maybe if there was one accidental correspondence. Maybe even if there were two or three. But *dozens*, and counting?

Mona Lisa contained "mountains … where the valley terminated. …" "… Hidden is … a serpent." "… There in the valley I [could] discern / Vermilion," the color of the terrain near the "fat lagoon. …" "There is a mountain there, …" in the distance, "in the mid-sea. …" The mountain sat literally in the middle of the sea next to the figure's head. And the art was full of "high, hard bank[s] …" and crags, and along "the outer bank are little bridges …" (and I later discovered other bridges in the art). The whole painting was in a place "where nothing shines." Nowhere in the art was there a single shining object, not even a glint in the woman's eyes where a shine could almost always be found in portraits. Strangely, the painting appeared to be turning into some kind of map.

In fact, I was able to link more than 200 matching details before deciding to move on. There were more, but I had enough to be sure *Mona Lisa*'s background had been illustrated from *The Comedy*. Sometimes the match was literal, such as "there in the valley I discern Vermilion," which described the red valley. Sometimes it matched in the form of a double entendre, such as "many the animals with whom she weds,"—the figure wears a veil, an association to marriage ("weds"), and has animals hidden around her (*wed* can also mean *join*). My list included subtle details I knew were arguable, but in context, seemed to match, such as "how I a skillful ape of nature was," which I knew was a reference to the ape face, cleverly concealed ("skillful") as part of the natural ("of nature") landscape. I even got the impression that Leonardo illustrated details from metaphors like "As of the snow on Alp," (the icy-looking mountain right of the woman's head) in their literal meaning. Sometimes it involved a combination of different word plays from different sentences that took a bit to figure out. "There appeared to us a mountain, dim from distance, and it seemed to me so high" described the single-looking mountain in the farthest *distance* of the background. Of course, it was tall ("so high"), but was also positioned "so high" in the painting's composition. Specifically, it was the mountain along the painting's right border on top of the horizon, barely noticeable ("dim from distance").

But of all the lines describing *Mona Lisa*, one sent shivers down my spine: "… That dense and darksome atmosphere / I saw a figure swimming upward come, / Marvellous unto every steadfast heart …" (*Inf.* 16.130-32).[10] It reminded me of the first time the crocodile head revealed itself—which I believed symbolized Lucifer—facing me as if coming onto shore to make me its prey, "that in the sea is hidden, … // 'Behold the monster with the pointed tail, / Who cleaves the hills, and breaketh walls and weapons, / Behold him who infecteth all the world'" (16.135-17.3).[11]

I was starting to think the artists maybe wanted their work to be interpreted multiple ways, just as lines in *The Comedy* could be. It wasn't just a matter of including other possible meanings in their art, like the different stories Botticelli alluded to in *Venus and Mars* using subtle clues. Perhaps it was also about encouraging viewers to find new meanings of their own, while accepting the idea of ones they didn't see, that different viewpoints existed. I realized how ironic the idea was. There I was, out to prove with my memoir that all these images had been here all along even though no one else saw them. Funny, I thought, since I didn't believe in God for lack of proof, though some had tried to convince me that the Bible was proof enough.

Leonardo knew Dante's writings were allegoric. Was it really such a stretch to see he had used allegory for his own art? The correspondences spoke for themselves. In *Inferno* (near the souls of those who had denied God) was a line about disciple and his master:

"Philosophy," he said, "to him who heeds it,
  Noteth, not only in one place alone,
  After what manner Nature takes her course
From Intellect Divine, and from its art;
  And if thy Physics carefully thou notest,
  After many pages shalt thou find,
That this your art as far as possibles
  Follows, as the disciple doth the master;
  So that your art is, as it were, God's grandchild. (*Inf.* 11.97-105; Longfellow)[13]

In the story, Dante was the disciple, Virgil the master. In actuality, Leonardo was the disciple, Dante the master.

Follow my secret teachings through my verses, Dante was saying, practically shouting to readers to look deeper into his writings while artists wanted viewers to look deeper into their art: "O ye who have undistempered intellects, / Observe the doctrine that conceals itself / Beneath the veil of the mysterious verses" (*Inf.* 9.61-63)![14] Dante had written. Yes, his verses definitely were mysterious, yet, what was I observing? *Mona Lisa* in Hell? Dante's path in the afterworld? Both?

Details came from almost every canto in *Inferno*, and several from *Purgatory*. Of course, every time I went back to read them again, I found more. Some were straightforward, easy to pinpoint in *Mona Lisa*; other descriptions could pertain to more than one location in the painting. Some were visible only through non-standard or anamorphic angles. Eventually, I was finding images that could be seen from all different sides of the art.

Whatever the way—they matched. But there were constant surprises. It helped to know *The Comedy*'s layout of Hell and Purgatory. Both existed on opposite sides of the world from each other, like the South and North Pole. So, in a way, they were upside down in relation to one another. This made sense of all the upside-down images I was finding in *Mona Lisa*, starting with that question mark, which I thought, as one possibility, might refer to lines in *Inferno*: "the sudden question I proposed. // … And here have been in this way upside down …" (19.78, 80).[15]

Even more impressive was the way Leonardo could create multiple images out of the *same* image: the mountain became a lion when on its side. Led by Dante's writings, I found that upside down, the mountain also showed a wolf's head that was anamorphic.

I was amazed Leonardo could take a drawing like *Leonardo's Eye* and develop the idea of anamorphosis to such amazing and yet unrecognized heights.

Or was that not so surprising? If Leonardo's first anamorphic drawing were placed on a museum wall, how many viewers would even be allowed close enough to view it from the proper side angle? How many would be allowed

A few of the details in Leonardo's *Mona Lisa* depicting lines from *The Divine Comedy*

1 (*Inf.* 1.13-14) But after I had reached a mountain's foot, / At that point where the valley terminated • **2 (*Inf.* 1.100)** Many the animals with whom she weds • **3 (*Inf.* 3.19)** And after he had laid his hand on mine • **4 (*Inf.* 4.151)** … And to a place I come where nothing shines. • **5 (*Inf.* 7.84)** "… Which hidden is, as in the grass a serpent." • **6 (*Inf.* 7.106-08)** A marsh it makes, which has the name of Styx, / This tristful brooklet, when it has descended / Down to the foot of the malign gray shores. • **7 (*Inf.* 8.71-72)** "… Within there in the valley I discern / Vermilion, as if issuing from the fire" • **8 (*Inf.* 9.6)** … Through the heavy fog. • **9 (*Inf.* 9.28)** "… That is the lowest region and the darkest" • **10 (*Inf.* 9.62-66)** And now there came across the turbid waves / The clangor of a sound with terror fraught, / Because of which both of the margins trembled • **11 (*Inf.* 9.76-78)** Even as the frogs before the hostile serpent / Across the water scatter all abroad, / Until each one is huddled in the earth. • **12 (*Inf.* 10.80-81)** "… The countenance of the Lady who reigns here, / Ere thou shalt know how heavy is that art" • **13 (*Inf.* 10.135)** … Along a path that strikes into a valley • **14 (*Inf.* 11.70)** "But tell me, those within the fat lagoon" • **15 (*Inf.* 12.1-2)** The place where to descend the bank we came / Was alpine • **16 (*Inf.* 12.10-11)** … Even such was the descent of that ravine, / And on the border of the broken chasm • **17 (*Inf.* 12.40)** "… Upon all sides the deep and loathsome valley" • **18 (*Inf.* 12.86)** "… Me it behoves to show him the dark valley" • **19 (*Inf.* 14.8-9, 11)** … I say that we arrived upon a plain, / Which from its bed rejecteth every plant // … All round about, as the sad moat to that • **20 (*Inf.* 14.30)** … As of the snow on Alp without a wind. • **21 (*Inf.* 14.88-89)** "… Nothing has been discovered by thine eyes / So notable as is the present river • **22 (*Inf.* 14.94, 97, 99)** "In the mid-sea there sits a wasted land, // … There is a mountain there / … Now 'tis deserted, as a thing worn out." • **23 (*Inf.* 16.130-33, 135, 17.1-3)** … Athwart that dense and darksome atmosphere / I saw a figure swimming upward come, / Marvelous unto every steadfast heart, // Even as he returns who goeth down / … that in the sea is hidden, // Who upward stretches, and draws in his feet. // "Behold the monster with the pointed tail, / Who cleaves the hills, and breaketh walls and weapons, / Behold him who infecteth all the world." • **24 (*Inf.* 18.2-5, 7-9, 15-18)** … Wholly of stone and of iron color, / As is the circle that around it turns. // Right in the middle of the field malign / There yawns a well exceeding wide and deep // … Round, then, is that enclosure which remains / Between the well and foot of the high, hard bank, / And has distinct in valleys ten its bottom. // … Unto the outer bank are little bridges, // So from the precipice's base did crags / Project, which intersected dikes and moats, / Unto the well that truncates and collects them. • **25 (*Inf.* 19.133)** … Thence was unveiled to me another valley. • **26 (*Inf.* 21.1, 3)** From bridge to bridge / … We came along, and held the summit • **27 (*Inf.* 26.100, 133-34)** "… But I put forth on the high open sea // … When there appeared to us a mountain, dim / From distance, and it seemed to me so high" • **28 (*Inf.* 29.138-39)** "… Thou must remember, if I well descry thee, / How I a skilful ape of nature was." • **29 (*Pur.* 8.20)** … For now indeed so subtile is the veil[12]

THIS PAGE AND NEXT: Just a few of many lines from *The Comedy* that match details in the art. Though not shown, some lines can apply to more than one area of the painting, just as some areas can depict more than one line.

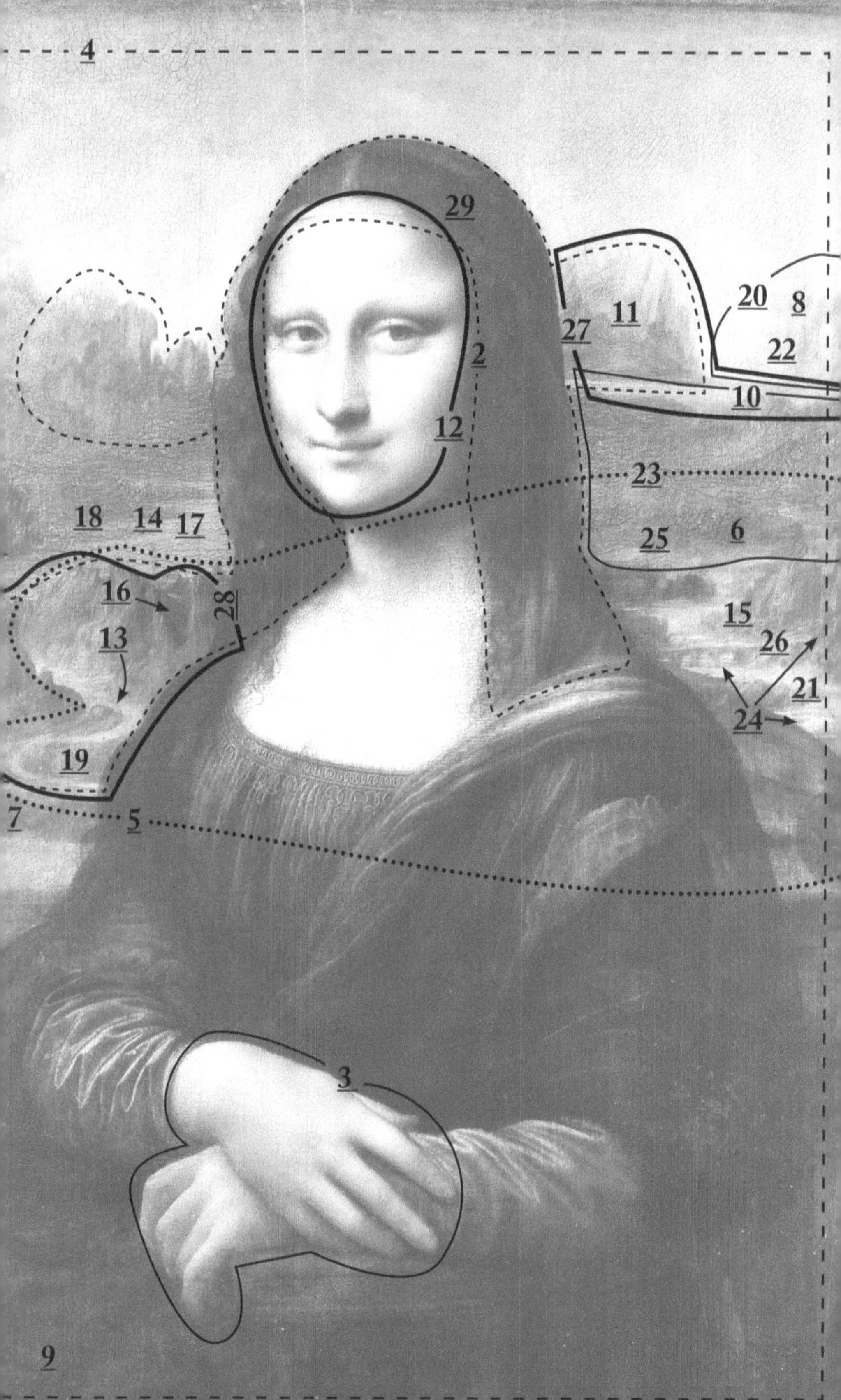

4
29
20
8
11
27
2
22
10
12
23
18
14
17
25
6
16
28
15
13
26
21
24
19
7
5
3
9

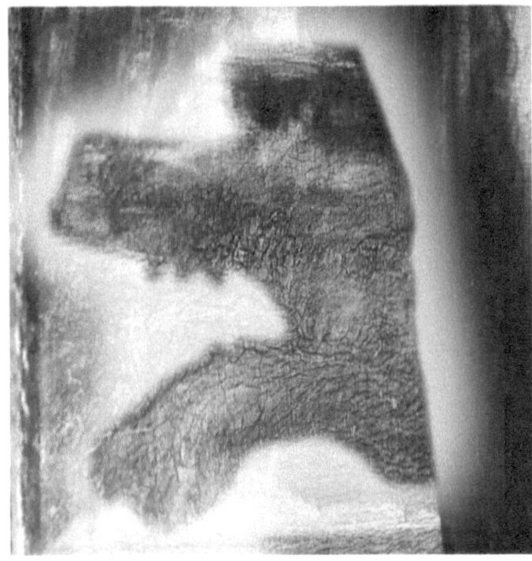

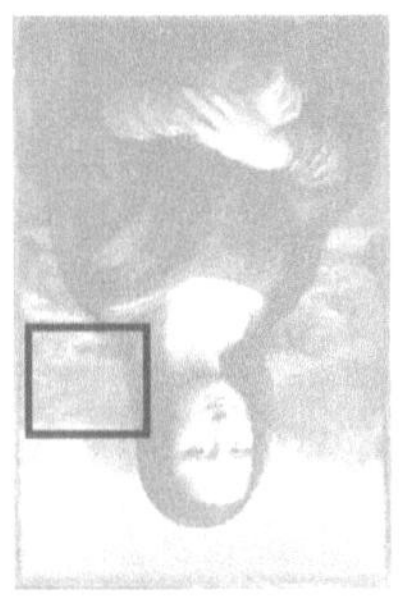

LEFT: Anamorphic view of possible wolf's head in *Mona Lisa*. **RIGHT:** Image key showing its location.

to take it off the wall, and turn it upside down? The most conventional way to see it was the way nearly everyone saw it. And so they could only see the most conventional things about it, when in reality, the art would have to slowly pivot around on the wall to give anyone a chance of seeing the more complex facets of the work. (For some images, a system of angled mirrors could be used.)

There were so many extra depths, so much writing I had to dig through, so many new images to spot. I chipped away at the details, excited, determined, and anxious, feeling that I was finally close to figuring it all out.

The third animal I thought was a buffalo or more likely an ox, for instance, may have been something else also. It came to me in the description fitting what Leonardo painted in the section just right of *Mona Lisa*'s head, where the ox head was:

> Mine eyes he loosed, and said: "Direct the nerve
> Of vision now along that **ancient foam,**
> There yonder where that **smoke is most intense."**
> Even as the **frogs before the hostile serpent**
> **Across the water** scatter all abroad,
> Until each one is **huddled in the earth.** (*Inf.* 9.73-78, emphasis added)[16]

It was an amphibian, a frog. Combined with a line that came later—describing souls bobbing their heads in and out of Lucifer's lake—mentioning that "frogs stand only with their muzzles out, / So that they hide their feet and other bulk ..." (*Inf.* 22.26-27),[17] I was able to decipher the image of the frog (that was also still an ox). It was time-consuming, but I enjoyed the challenge of matching art to poetry. Once I spotted what I thought were matching descriptions, I dissected the text. "... Direct the nerve / Of vision ... / There yonder where the smoke is most intense" (9.73-75)[18] led me to direct my vision to the area on the right of the painting at the horizon, where Leonardo concentrated the smoky, cloud-like detail.

Also hinting to the frog's location are the words "frogs before the hostile serpent / Across the water ..." (9.76-77).[19] The "hostile serpent" was obviously the crocodile or crocodile-looking creature, which I previously established. But the sentence also told me that literally across the water from the serpent were frogs. In that case, only one frog was present, as far as I was able to tell. "... Each one is huddled in the earth" (9.78)[20] was one explanation why only the head was showing. But nothing seemed to have just one reason or meaning.

A later part of *Inferno*—canto 22—mentions frogs again. The frogs from both cantos are technically not related. In canto 9, frogs are used in a simile to describe souls fleeing from an enemy. In canto 22, frogs are used to describe a different set of souls hiding in a ditch from some devils—"As on the brink of water in a ditch / The frogs stand only with their muzzles out, / So that they hide their feet and other bulk ..." (*Inf.* 22.25-27)[21]—but Leonardo combines both sets of descriptions into one image. "Only with their muzzles out" was another explanation why only the head was showing. "... They *hide* their feet and other bulk ..." explained why it is not only buried in the earth, but positioned in back of *Mona Lisa*'s figure, *hiding* behind her.

I never considered it to look like a frog because of what looked like textured fur wrapping around its head, but Dante also uses the analogy of frogs to describe some of the weeping souls, with the air so cold, their tears crystallize into a shield of ice around their eyes, "... Because the earliest tears a cluster form, / And, in the manner of a crystal visor, / Fill all the cup beneath the eyebrow full" (*Inf.* 33.97-99).[22] It explained why it didn't initially look like a frog—after reading that sentence, I realized that it did look like a frog with a layer of ice frozen around its eyes.

Leonardo, like Botticelli, used fragments of text from different parts of *The Comedy*, which added another layer of difficulty to figuring out what he did. It was as if the artist didn't want it to be easy to figure out the connections. Or did Leonardo want to fit in so many details that he stuffed as many as possible into each object in the art, such as one mountain showing multiple animal heads?

I thought again of how movie posters sometimes depicted scenes from a story. I began to wonder if Leonardo perhaps represented so many objects from Dante's story that he had no choice but to overlap several meanings to specific objects.

But it still didn't explain what the animal heads meant?

Frogs are referenced in *The Comedy*, mostly as a simile to some of the shades in Hell. The ape is mentioned only once in the whole book, in a conversation when Dante declares, "How I a skillful ape of nature was." The lion is used several times: as one of the three beasts blocking Dante's path in the woods, as a simile to a few characters, and as part of an emblem on a shield.

But why the lion, ape, and frog—which was possibly an ox also?

It was becoming clear that *Mona Lisa* showed many references to *The Comedy*. But was Leonardo only an illustrator of Dante? I found that hard to believe. In his own way, he was as much a genius as Dante Alighieri was. The woman in *Mona Lisa*, or at least her smile, suggested Beatrice, but a passage in his writings, the *Envy* passage, made it clear that the woman represented Envy. One interpretation didn't cancel out the other. Meaning could be anamorphic too.

If *Mona Lisa* was the only painting to show the animals, I would have thought they were simply detailing *The Comedy*, but there were many works of art that I felt sure did not represent the poem, yet still showed hidden animal heads. So there had to be some other meaning to them. Or were the animals some kind of half-reference to the Gospels themselves? Leonardo did own an Italian edition of the Bible. John was traditionally symbolized by the Eagle; Luke, as the winged Ox; Mark, the winged Lion; Matthew, the winged Man. Or were they related to Leonardo's friend, Niccolò Machiavelli, who I recently read about? In *The Prince*—a written philosophy on politics—he describes how a prince should rule with the qualities of a lion and a fox. Leonardo had worked with him, and had to be aware of Machiavelli's use of animal imagery to describe human nature. Was that a clue to the lion's meaning? If Leonardo knew Machiavelli had been tortured by the Medicis, was it reason enough to hide a Machiavellian image? But I then remembered that the animals started appearing in art that was created before Machiavelli was born. Although it was possible that their symbolism changed over time—that their meanings may have been altered by *The Prince*'s usage of animal association—I was convinced their meaning had remained consistent over time.

The more I read and researched, the more answers I found that seemed to fit. Although it brought me closer to an answer, it only made it harder to pinpoint. And seeing how multiple meanings was turning out to be a common theme in Renaissance art, was it possible that all the answers I was finding to explain the animals were correct—at least, in *Mona Lisa*?

39

The Envious Blind

On the table in front of me sat *Venus and Mars*, next to a spread of other images and writings. It was 2016, and my attic had become a crime scene. A case of mistaken identity, and there in plain sight were all the clues.

Lisa Gherardini? She had become a red herring, stealing everyone's focus away from where the real answers existed.

She *may* have been the sitter, though the evidence wasn't convincing enough. The sitter was believed to be a Florentine. Yet, Dante's real life acquaintance, Beatrice Portinari, was also from Florence. Still, even *if* Gherardini simply was the model for *Mona Lisa*, it had nothing to do with the actual meaning of the painting. She was not the answer.

Envy and Beatrice? *They* were the culprits. The d-point and anamorphic perspectives were how the artists got away with it. But I still hadn't unravelled the whole story. I needed a long break away from my research. *Give it a week, a month*, I'd tell myself. My eyes were constantly strained and overworked. My mind too. The problem was that I couldn't go two minutes without looking for more clues or details I may have missed.

Like an invisible barrier, whatever riddle Leonardo had painted kept my outside life out of focus. I felt distant from everything else around me. Whenever Heather came home from work, she would come up to the attic to see me. Pinch would be near my side, sleeping in her dog bed. Sometimes Heather would have to ask me more than once if I was done working for the day and ready to spend time with her. The question always caused me anxiety, the way a child might feel when pulled away from an addictive video game just before completing the final mission. There was no question that I loved Heather and wanted to spend my time with her. But I found it difficult to pull myself away from the unorganized books and drawings spread out across the tables. It had become more than an obsession. It consumed all my time, and until I could figure it all out, nothing else seemed to matter.

One day, it dawned on me—I had become careless in my approach somehow. Perhaps it was from staring too long at Dante's writings and Leonardo's art. To someone not immersed the way I was, the mistake I made would have been clear. The whole time, I assumed that Envy was a specific character. I had been so tunnel-visioned toward the idea.

Except, she wasn't really a woman, was she, Leonardo?

She was a thing. A representation of one of seven deadly sins. A representation of all the envious spirits from the Mountain of Purgatory.

So many times I had read over *Mona Lisa*'s description without realizing it. Many had, I was sure. How many millions of readers came face to face with the description of the woman in the world's most famous painting without realizing it? Sure, no one knew of the painting's connection to *The Divine Comedy*. But if readers came across the description of an unnamed figure like Abraham Lincoln or Christ or Elvis, wouldn't someone notice, even if they weren't looking for it?

It was all right there, right where the souls who were guilty of the sin of envy pay penance on the mountain's second terrace. As the two poets circle the path around the mountain, Virgil tells Dante of the envious souls they are approaching:

> And the good Master said: "This circle scourges
> The sin of envy, and on that account
> Are drawn from love the lashes of the scourge.
> **The bridle** of another sound shall be …
> But **fix thine eyes athwart the air right steadfast,**
> And people thou wilt see before us sitting,
> And **each one close against the cliff is seated."**
> Then wider than at first mine eyes I opened;
> I looked before me, and saw shades with mantles
> … **Not from the color of the stone diverse.**
> . . . .
> **Covered with sackcloth** vile they seemed to me,
> And **one sustained the other with his shoulder,**
> And **all of them were by the bank sustained.**
>
> (*Pur.* 13.37-40, 43-48, 58-60; Longfellow, emphasis added)[1]

Covered in sackcloth?

Seated close against the cliff?

Mantles the same color as the surrounding stone?

The description of the spirits matched the look of the woman in *Mona Lisa.* She—*Envy*—appeared to be representing the envious souls in *Purgatory.*

And so, as I studied *Mona Lisa* closer than ever before, I saw the answers to her identity forming—strong similarities between Dante's writings and that woman in the picture. More than similar.

On his climb up the Mountain of Purgatory, Dante dreams of an ugly, deformed woman with unhealthy, pale brown skin who transforms into "a beautiful and alluring damsel. …"[2] *Mona Lisa* had to be showing this transformation in her illusion. She looked slightly younger and alluring from the anamorphic d-point.

As I kept examining Leonardo's many drawings, I knew he had to be a fan of Dante more than was already believed. History's timeline made sense of Leonardo's exposure to the poet's work. Dante was known to be an inspiration to Renaissance artists, and the first copy of *La Comedia di Dante Alleghieri* was published in 1472 in Foligno, Italy,[3] and (with alternate titles) in Venice in 1477 and Florence in 1481. One of the first illustrated versions of *The Comedy* had an image of Lucifer in his frozen lake, filled with tortured souls, their heads just barely above the lake's surface—a concept showing strong resemblance to *Mona Lisa*'s animal heads.

Yet, I still wasn't sure why Leonardo chose those specific animals. And what determined why some illusions could be seen when facing the art directly, and others revealed themselves from the anamorphic d-point?

Without realizing it, I had some of the answers all along.

Back when I had met with Kristine about publicizing the discoveries, I told her they looked to be drowning in the crocodile's swamp. In a way it was true. But it wasn't a swamp. It was a lake of ice. And maybe the drowning victims symbolized the human race and the sins we practiced on Earth. It was at that lake that Dante completed his journey through Hell.

I had my suspicions that the crocodile was Lucifer, the prince of Hell, who flaps his wings to chill the water around him to ice. The swamp is a frozen lake, where the devil himself inhabited the realm of *Inferno,* where souls of the damned are submerged within the ice in correlation to their sin. Just as Dante described in the ninth and worst circle of Hell, those who lie in the frozen Lake Cocytus have only their faces poking out in Lucifer's realm.

Maybe that explained the cool-colored, icy-looking background too.

So why would a woman by the name of Envy be in front of it all?

Although no one knew that Botticelli's *Primavera* and *Venus and Mars* show scenes from *The Comedy*, it was known that he created illustrations of the story in the 1480s. He was a Florentine, as was Leonardo. They were associates who both belonged to Verrocchio's circle of artists, so they likely shared ideas with each other.

Or secrets.

As I looked over his drawings for connections to Dante's writings, I thought it was possible Leonardo not only sketched details from *The Comedy*, but did so as early as 1481—years before painting a portrait of a woman he called Envy (and we call *Mona Lisa*). There were drawings I felt could have come from the association of the seven deadly sins in *Purgatorio.*

One drawing that led me to think so was a sketch of two women, one with a sword and mirror, another with what could be either a mask or two faces, both seated on what looked like a cart. *Or is it Beatrice's chariot?* Included is a male figure with horns, and descending into the scene is an eagle. It was later titled *Allegory of Statecraft*, but it reminded me of Leah and her sister Rachel—who never leaves "her looking-glass"—and the fable that included an eagle and horned monster.

Leonardo also made a sketch of a nude woman holding a vase of flowers, armed with arrows, and riding a skeleton. It was on the same sheet where he wrote his *Envy* passage. The *Envy* passage describes the sketch, but I also believed it described *Mona Lisa*. The title of that drawing is *Two Allegories of Envy*. On the same sheet of paper is a second sketch, titled *Allegory of Ingratitude and Envy*. It's well-known that artists regularly sketched out their ideas before ever starting a painting. Maybe the sketch of Envy was an earlier idea that was never used.

I placed the drawings aside with others that looked to be connected. There were drawings of what have been called dragons, but to me, looked more like tweaked versions of *The Comedy*'s Griffin, a flying creature that was half lion, half eagle. There was also a drawing of what I thought were dancing maidens that reminded me of the ones in *Primavera*.

And as familiar as I thought I was with Leonardo's work, there were drawings from his notebooks I was still unfamiliar with. One was a muscle study called *The Anatomy of the Mouth*. It included a simple rendition, just a few strokes of pencil dividing the lips into a weak smile. The left side was marked with the letter *d*, which made me think of Leonardo's *d-Point* and how *Mona Lisa*'s true smile revealed itself when I looked at it from the *d*'s position as it was marked in Leonardo's diagram.

These clues would have been meaningless to me before the discoveries, as they must have been to experts who studied them. But those drawings suddenly stuck out like zebras on a horse farm.

Like Botticelli's paintings, it wasn't easy to find comparisons between *The*

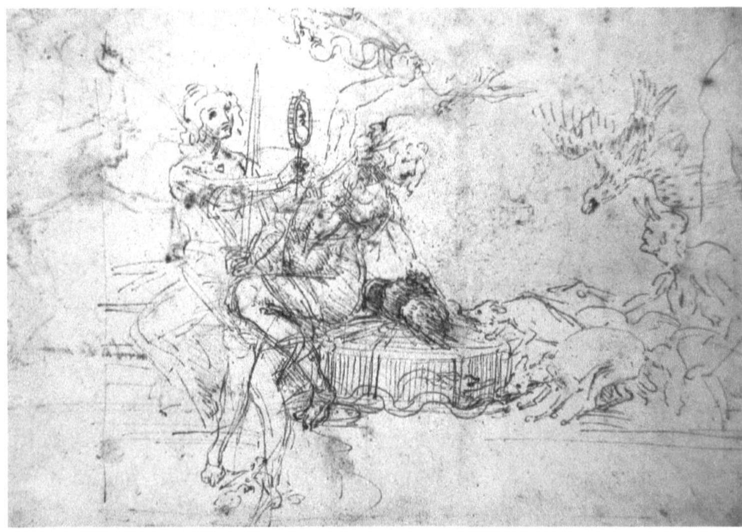

Allegory of Statecraft (c. 1490-94).

Comedy and Leonardo's art. At least, not until I knew *what* to look for and *how* to look. I felt like an archeologist brushing dirt off buried bones from a very large area with a very small brush: tedious work that demanded patience.

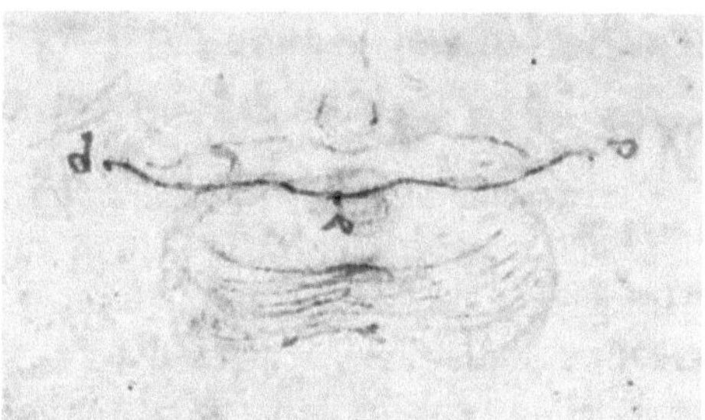

The Anatomy of the Mouth (c. 1506).

As I thought of it, *Mona Lisa* had two meanings. First, she was Envy, the woman we all have been familiar with. Second, in the illusion, where her smile has grown, and she becomes skinnier and younger-looking, she is Beatrice.

Even the background showed two versions. When viewed from the left d-point, the wide, rocky landscape behind her looked to be flooded with water, where the more attractive-looking Beatrice could be seen in the same transformation. Artists back then used objects to represent several things, like the male figure in *Venus and Mars* that represented more than just Dante.

Since I had a possible context to the environment they occupied, I went back to my book of symbols in hopes of finding specific meaning. I didn't have great luck, but I did start to get the idea the animals represented beastly characteristics, the catalyst that caused man to sin in Dante's story. It fit as the best explanation anyway.

Mona Lisa's smile—*Beatrice's* smile—became my focus. But she was also one of the envious shades. I became sure of it when I read the last line from Leonardo's *Envy* passage: "Sooner will there be a body without a shadow than Virtue without Envy." Just as a body couldn't exist without a shadow, and virtue couldn't exist without the envious, Beatrice couldn't exist without Envy.

One couldn't exist without the other. Like good and evil. Jekyll and Hyde.

But if she was Envy and Beatrice, how could the painting show Hell if the envious spirits existed in Purgatory, and Beatrice resided in Heaven? And why had Leonardo used a female figure to represent the envious? Maybe it had something to do with all evil stemming from envy.

As I thought more about it, I remembered that Dante encounters Beatrice for the first time in The Earthly Paradise—at the top of Mount Purgatory, six levels above the envious souls.

Reaching the group of envious spirits on the second terrace, Dante exchanges words with one specific person in the group—a female soul named Sapia.

The spirits in *Purgatorio* are dressed in dark brown clothing and mantles the same color as their immediate surroundings: "each one close against the cliff is seated [on the mountain], ... shades with mantles / Not from the color of the stone diverse" (*Pur.* 13.45, 47-48; Longfellow).[4] In fact, in the bottom portion of *Mona Lisa*, Leonardo didn't make it easy to distinguish the bottom part of the figure—from the waist down—from the surrounding details.

But there was also her position.

Historians had pointed out *Mona Lisa*'s aerial perspective.

Sapia, seated, looks up at Dante, who describes his approaching the spirit: "Among the rest I saw a shade that waited / In aspect, and should anyone ask how, / Its chin it lifted upward like a blind man" (*Pur.* 13.100-02).[5] Longfellow explains in his translation of *Purgatorio* that Sapia was a lady who was banished and living at Colle. To watch the battle between her townsmen and the Florentines, Sapia placed herself at the window of a tower, hoping for the destruction of her own people.[6] It made me wonder if, in addition to symbolizing the envious souls, *Mona Lisa* also represented Sapia? It could explain details of what could be argued as the figure's view from a balcony or tower—once again showing Leonardo's use of wordplay: he showed the *terrace* where the envious souls are, and may have also showed the *terrace* of a tower from which Sapia may have watched the battle.

Either way, the painting, first and foremost, shows the envious soul. Leonardo called her Envy. Beatrice seems like she is secondary—her smile increases in the illusion as the whole painting changes.

In essence, Dante seems to represent each one of us—at least in Leonardo's art—since we are actually the viewer of the painting, seeing the envious soul exactly as Dante did in his approach, standing in place where Dante would be standing to see her. History's first virtual reality painting.

After all those years studying her, it finally made sense. The envious souls live on the second terrace of Purgatory. The ascending terraces spiral around the mountain. There is no outer wall—only a view that shows everything below. An aerial perspective, as if we are standing on its continuous cliff.

It's not only a figure of Beatrice, her smile increasing as the anamorphic illusion reveals itself when you look right at the painting, approaching your view from the left—*the way Dante continuously turns right as he progresses up the mountain, and sometimes has visions.* Just as visions appeared in the painting! *Mona Lisa* had to be showing Beatrice and Envy, because even the envious souls had a virtuous side. *The Comedy*'s framework explained it all.

In *Purgatorio*, Dante describes the path they take through the mountains: "We mounted upward through the rifted rock, / Which undulated to this side and that, / Even as a wave receding and advancing" (*Pur.* 10.7-9).[7] To the left of *Mona Lisa* looked to be wavy-textured mountains that are split—or *rifted*. The rift is also the mouth of the ape head—just before the backward winding S-shaped path near her shoulder. Dante and Virgil then take the zigzagging path: "'Here it behoves us use a little art,' / Began my Leader, 'to adapt ourselves / Now here, now there, to the receding side'" (*Pur.* 10.10-12).[8]

With the mountains at their backs, they make their way toward the first terrace of Purgatory, "from out that needle's eye; / But when we free and in the open were, / There where the mountain backward piles itself, ... [where the poets] stopped upon a plain / More desolate than roads across the deserts" (*Pur.* 10.16-18, 20-21). Dante "perceive[s] the embankment round about, / Which all right of ascent had interdicted ..." (10.29-30).[9] On the *right* of the painting, between the figure's shoulder and the bridge, is a sloping side of a curved-faced plateau—a *round embankment.* At one level higher than the rest of the terrain, but still one level below the seated figure, that plateau had to be the first terrace!

But I also noticed another peculiar fracture in the mountains along the right edge of the art, on the opposite side of the *rifted rock* I had linked the text to. Just across the water from the round embankment in the art, on the side of the mountains, may have been where the poets passed through instead when they "mounted ... through a rifted rock // ... [and proceeded] forth from out that needle's eye ..." (*Pur.* 10.7, 16).[10] The fracture looked to be shaped like the opening of a needle—*out that needle's eye.* I wasn't sure which opening referred to the text. Perhaps Leonardo meant for both to be, humorously placing them on opposite sides of the art as a playful reference to the previous sentence: "'Here it behoves us use a little art,' / Began my Leader, 'to adapt ourselves / Now here, now there, to the receding side'" (10.10-12).[11]

Regardless, everything Leonardo placed in that painting tied back to *The Comedy.* No one clue was enough to prove anything. But the multiple details told the whole story.

Without any knowledge of Dante, and no awareness of the additional imagery Leonardo worked into the painting, there appeared to be no information about the portrait. But the information *had* always been there ...I was just blind to it. Millions had been, just as the envious were blind to what

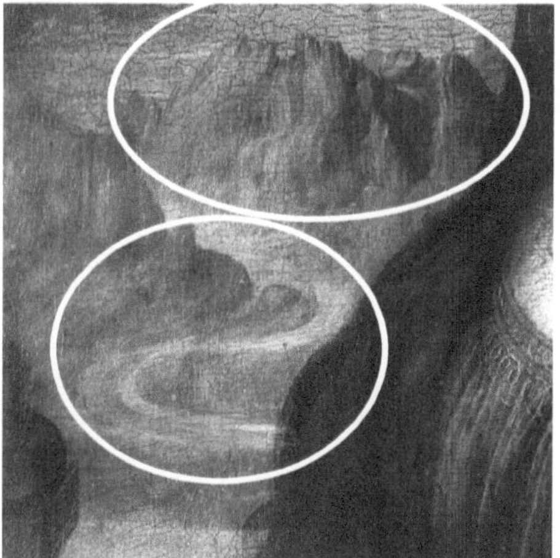

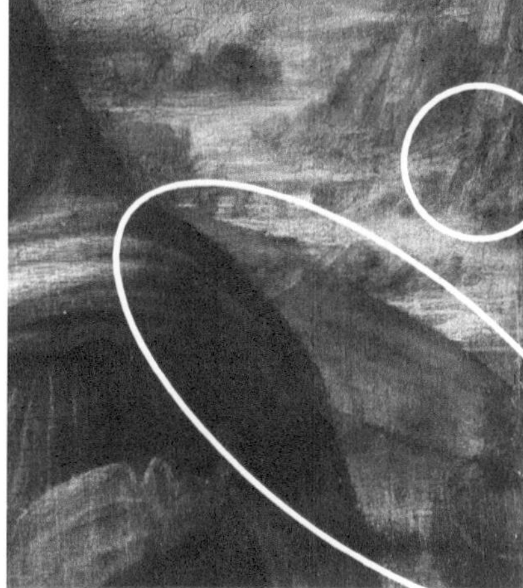

LEFT: Zigzagging path and rifted rock (circled). **RIGHT:** First terrace embankment and needle's eye (circled).

really mattered in life.

Was that it? Was that the whole point of the painting, Leonardo?

The woman was Beatrice, and also a representation of the envious souls. The background was literal in showing Dante's path toward Purgatory after leaving Hell, a sort of map of his journey.

As a scientist, Leonardo was usually made out to be some kind of secular humanist. But was that true? "There can be no denying the formal [similarity] between the *Mona Lisa* and depictions of the Virgin," Frank Zöllner points out, it's "something evident in many Renaissance portraits. …"[12] Some historians have said it's exactly what the portrait represents.

Details in both the painting and Dante's writings would soon tell me that historians may have been right. Leonardo turned out to be a master of combining multiple images. Why not multiple meanings in the same image as fellow artist Botticelli had done? It wasn't long before I realized *Mona Lisa* represented a third woman besides Beatrice and Envy—who turned out to be representing the envious souls.

40

Rome

"Hi, Professor," I called out when I saw Pasquale at the grocery store, where I had stopped to pick up a few items.

He gave me a big smile and shook my hand.

"Chasing me down while I'm shopping? What, you can't find information about the Renaissance on Google like everyone else?" He said, widening his smile to make it obvious he was joking.

"Your information's more interesting than Google, professor."

"How's your secret book coming along?"

"Still trying to figure out a few details," I said.

We slowly walked down one of the aisles together, looking at this and that as we talked.

"Something in the art you can't find?" he asked.

"Finding them isn't the problem—the problem is figuring out their meaning."

I was slightly entertained by how he looked at items in disgust as he took them off the shelf, like there was something wrong about the price or the product itself.

"I'm not a hundred percent sure about something I came across," I said, referring to Leonardo's painting of Envy and Beatrice, but not wanting to reveal it so that I could save the surprise for my book.

"It could be that whatever it is doesn't mean anything except to the artist. Or maybe the artist was just trying to spark a reaction or thought? Who was it—um, wait a minute," he said, squeezing his eyes closed for a moment. "Yes, T. S. Eliot. He wrote an essay in response to critics who said symbolism in his poetry was obscure. 'Better that it was obscure,' Eliot said, 'because that made the readers work out their own meaning from a consideration of the symbols.' Kind of like those Rorschach ink blots psychiatrists use to test the mind. You see my meaning?"

"I do. But ink blots are random. Artists don't spend years planning and executing those blots. The *ink blots* I've found," I said, gesturing my fingers in the quotation sign, "are described in the artist's writings."

"But maybe the same principle applies. It's possible the artist may be more interested in getting you to make your own interpretation. Maybe it's a little bit of both." He looked at a tomato, frowned slightly, and placed it back.

"Actually, I'm interested in learning more about Rome," I said.

"Roma?" He held up the tomato to see if I got the joke. *Roma tomatoes.* "Okay, what do you got?"

"What did people in Renaissance times think about Rome."

"Depends on which people, but an interesting question. There were mixed feelings about Rome. There were two Romes—the Roman Republic and the Roman Empire. And, of course, the Roman Catholic Church—really an extension of the Roman Empire in a lot of ways. They were very different, and people during the Renaissance had different feelings about them."

"Okay."

"Back around 500-something BC, Romans overthrew their king and set up a system that wasn't all that far from our own—annual elections, a senate, commoners allowed into the aristocracy, an aggressive military, a Justinian Code to set up legal and legislative structures. Rome expanded like America did at the start. Kind of a Democratic Golden Age. Some centuries later, Caesar becomes dictator for life. Some of the old republican ways persisted for a while, but the emperors were still dictators, some of them pretty bloody, and some, like Caligula, were outright nuts. Eventually, corruption and cultural decadence set in, and it all fell apart. At least in the West."

"So the Empire was bad news, then?"

"Oh, no. There were lots of good things about the Empire. It kept growing, for one thing. It moved into Africa, Asia, the Mediterranean. At its height, it ruled over 70 million people—a good chunk of the world's population at the time. It spread Western ideas about law and civic order across the known world. When Christianity came along, it spread like wildfire. After the Empire was established there were two hundred years of peace everywhere, more or less."

"So the Empire was a good thing?"

He smelled a cantaloupe and put it back.

"Bit of both. There was a kind of Imperial summer when everything looked good. Authoritarians like to point to it as an example of how well government works when you have a wise ruler dispensing good decisions from the top down. The truth is, the Empire was just way too big to manage, and while some of the emperors were genuinely good, some were clowns. It wasn't sustainable. When it fell apart—boom." Pasquale threw up his hands with raised eyebrows. "The Dark Ages for the next thousand years. But you want to know about the Renaissance, which came next. May I ask why?"

"I can't really say until my book comes out," I said. "Sorry."

He laughed. "OK. Well …the Renaissance didn't see massive empires, but independent political entities did exist. They looked to earlier models. The Florentine Republic looked to the Roman Republic. They wanted a state that was fairly democratic and kept tyrants and corruption out of the picture. Can't blame them for that. Folks that liked that style of government were very pro-

Roman Republic. On the other hand, would-be tyrants—as well as those who thought dictatorship had its good points, like speed and efficiency, and civic order and military strength—were all for the Imperial model. Kind of like in the *Star Wars* movies. Anyway, and then there was the Church!"

"What do you mean?" I asked.

"Well, with the Roman Empire's collapse, there was no government, no cops, no maintenance, no military. Only thing left standing was the Church. It wasn't the *government* exactly, but they were able to maintain whatever little order there was."

"I see."

"Where's the pasta in this store?" he asked.

"I'll show you."

"Leave it to an Italian."

We pushed our carts to the other side of the store together.

"You know about Constantine?" he asked. "Pagan Roman Emperor?"

"Not really," I said.

"One day he has a vision of a cross—and of conquering the world. And so that's what he does. He figured he owed it to the Christian God, and wasn't stingy when it came to payback."

"How so?"

"Constantine stopped the persecution of Christians—which was going on for centuries. He supported the Church financially, built basilicas, exempted clergy from taxes, promoted Christians to high office. All sorts of things. Christianity didn't become the official religion of the Empire 'til the Edict of Thessalonica in 380 AD, but it was pretty much on its way."

"So what's the connection to the Renaissance?"

"What Constantine did was take the Catholic Church out of the shadows and gradually make it a part of the Roman Imperial State. The Church began mimicking Imperial structure and practices. The Pope was no longer an underground leader, but a glorious Emperor of the Church, so to speak."

"So those who favored democracy and the Roman Republic probably didn't like that?"

Pasquale shook his head. "Popes and petty tyrants liked it. Once the Roman Catholic Church joined the Empire and became Imperial, freedom and civic liberties went out the window. There was plenty of corruption to go around after that. Mind you, there were good things about the Empire. Unity, stability. It was a high point of world culture in many ways. But personal freedom?" He shook his head again. "To those in the Renaissance who wanted to be free of uncontrolled dictatorship, Rome was Hell on Earth."

Hell on Earth.

I was trying to understand the complete mystery of it—why Leonardo spent so many years, practically until his death—painting a representation of

Dante's *Comedy*. It was where all the details pointed.

Among *Mona Lisa*'s many mysteries was the question of the actual location where she was sitting. Not the imaginary world of Hell and Purgatory as defined by Dante's writings, but the real-world location. People had searched throughout Italy, sure that Leonardo painted the scenery from an existing place.

I always thought the background wasn't real, that it only existed in the painting. *How could it? Leonardo made it up*, I figured. He had to, in order to show the animal heads.

But after my conversation with Pasquale, I was sure Dante provided that answer. The background was not just a collage of symbols put into an imaginary landscape, or even a general location signifying Dante's *Inferno* and *Paradiso*. It was a real-world location that Dante mentions.

What set me on the trail was that Dante set both his *Inferno* and his *Paradiso* in a real physical location. Dante's Hell is situated underneath the city of Jerusalem, which is at the center of the northern hemisphere, and extends all the way to the center of the Earth. The mountain of Purgatory is on the other side of the Earth, at the center of the southern hemisphere, exactly opposite Jerusalem.

It was showing details from Hell and Purgatory. *Mona Lisa*—Envy—was sitting on the second terrace of Purgatory, overlooking Hell. How would anyone know what those places looked like? According to *The Comedy*, Hell's location is under Jerusalem, which made the physical location impossible for Leonardo to access and paint from reality.

But if Leonardo followed Dante's writings as closely as it seemed, and Dante liked to use real-world locations, then the background *had* to exist somewhere.

In the years before the discoveries, I felt poisoned with the inner demons that haunted me. My divorce from Paige left me pessimistic about relationships. After meeting Heather, I learned the value of having a lover and companion, but I still didn't open myself fully to her. I didn't know how to invest everything I had into our life together the way I could with my art, or even my writing, in which everything I did was done to improve my book. And although I took steps to improve our relationship, it didn't feel like I was giving it every bit of effort. Many times, we did things like take a day trip to hike the gorges and waterfalls in nearby Ithaca, but as much as I enjoyed our trips and our time together, I never felt fully present. Part of my mind was always back on my writing table—as if I were emotionally cheating with the largest project of my life.

Still, I had come a long way. The relationships I had since Paige (and before Heather) were practically emotionless on my end. They were purely carnal. I wanted my emotions to be present, but they were too far out of reach. The best I could do was pretend to care. But the truth always revealed itself one way or another, causing the women I dated to feel hurt or become frustrated that I had wasted their time, and ultimately wanting to end our relationships.

There was also the distance I created between me and my father—stemming from our inability to respect one another. We were like two male rams who had butted horns too many times, both too stubborn to concede to the other. What did my refusal to patch things up with him say about me? I missed having a father, but I was also less anxious without him in my life.

By not accepting the existence of those inner demons, I had been dishonest to myself. It took a horrible divorce and witnessing a coworker's death to see the tormented feelings that had grown inside of me. From there, I was able to heal and embrace the life I had. I was no longer ashamed of who I was, admittedly dysfunctional in some key relationships.

Just like with *Mona Lisa*, I knew more about my life than anyone else in the world, yet there was still so much more to understand. I envied friends and family members who had healthy relationships with their fathers, and had happy families.

It took time to recognize the discoveries as a symbol of the spiritual vision Dante learned to develop. And that spiritual vision could be measured by the brilliance of Beatrice's smile. As Dante came closer to experiencing divine vision, Beatrice was able to offer a more expressive smile—which Dante was initially too mortal to experience.

Was that the test, Leonardo? Did seeing the anamorphic smile, seeing Envy turn into the virtuous Beatrice, represent Dante's divine vision?

Maybe we were all given that test in one form or another.

By following Dante's writings, Leonardo must have painted Purgatory's entrance behind Envy and Beatrice. Even though the view was *from* Mount Purgatory, the entrance to Purgatory was actually in the distant landscape below.

After journeying through Inferno, Dante and Virgil climb up Lucifer's back, where he stands in the center of the Earth, and they emerge (in a sort of teleportation) from an island where Mount Purgatory sits. Dante explains that the island is in the middle of the ocean—on the opposite side of Earth from Jerusalem. It's the mountain touching *Mona Lisa*'s head on the right.

The conundrum was that it meant Leonardo was showing the view *of* Mount Purgatory in the distance while also showing the view *from* the mountain's second terrace, where Envy is sitting. But it would fit what I eventually realized with Botticelli's paintings: the art is essentially a collage of chosen scenes from *The Comedy*, as is sometimes done in art, such as on movie posters.

Standing at the shore, Dante is told where the entrance to Mount Purgatory is: "… Whence I, who now had turned unto that shore / Where salt the waters of the Tiber grow, / Benignantly by him have been received" (*Pur.* 2.100-03; Longfellow).[1] He names the Tiber River in Italy where it meets the salt water—the sea. It's the Tyrrhenian Sea—on the west coast of Italy, (presently) about fifteen miles from Rome. It had to mean that behind *Mona Lisa*'s figure was the mouth of the Tiber.

The Tiber River passes southward through Rome, westward toward the sea, bends south, and then doglegs west in a 90-degree bend, splitting Isola Sacra (*Holy Isle*) to the north and Ostia to the south.

In *The Comedy*, the souls of those still worth being saved assemble on the shore of Ostia. A translation by Marcus Sanders made it clear: "So I went down to the shore ... / ... and he let me board. Now / he's heading back toward Ostia, down near // Tiber's river mouth. That's where all the dead meet" (*Pur.* 2.100-03; Sanders).[2]

Although Ostia's history was unclear, it was believed to be Rome's first colony.[3] Classical writings are important to its history.[4] In Virgil's *Aeneid*, "Ostia was founded at the place ... [where the story's hero] landed after his [Trojan War] adventures. ..."[5]

On the opposite side of the Tiber is Isola Sacra, containing remnants "of a great cemetery ..." that served the area slightly further north that was once called Portus.[6] In Ostia, during its decline in the fifth century, "the dead were buried in random graves."[7] It started to sound like a good place for Leonardo to paint a picture about dead souls. If he did use Ostia at the area of the mouth of the Tiber, I had to be sure.

I searched photos of Ostia's geography and the surrounding areas to match up to the painting—if that was possible at all, since the landscape had to have changed over the past five centuries. I was hoping that bridge on the right of the canvas was still standing. *The Comedy*'s Purgatory existed as "a huge mountain located on a small island in the middle of the ocean, ..."[8] so I needed to find an

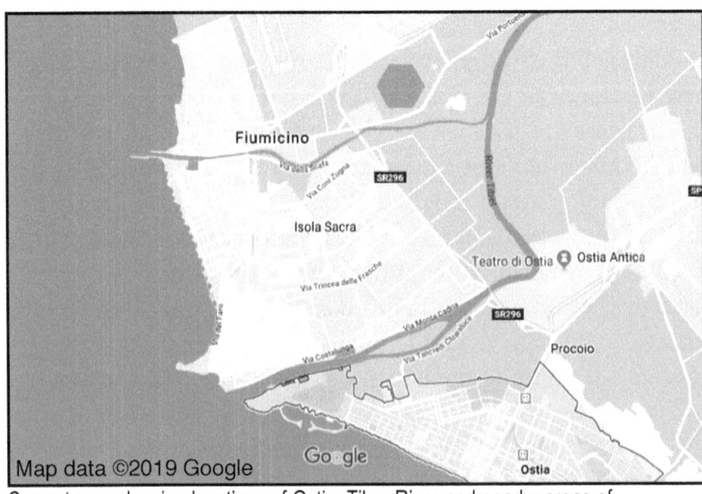

Current map showing locations of Ostia, Tiber River and nearby areas of Isola Sacra, Fiumicino, and Ostia Antica.

island just as the painting showed. At first, Isola Sacra didn't stand out as an island in the middle of the sea, but technically it was: surrounded by water on all sides, separated from the main land, partially by the Tiber.

Leonardo would have known the place. From 1513-16, he was in Rome, just miles away.

I got lost for a while looking at the geography of the area, imagining Leonardo there, studying the landscape next to the sea for what would become one of the most magical paintings in the world.

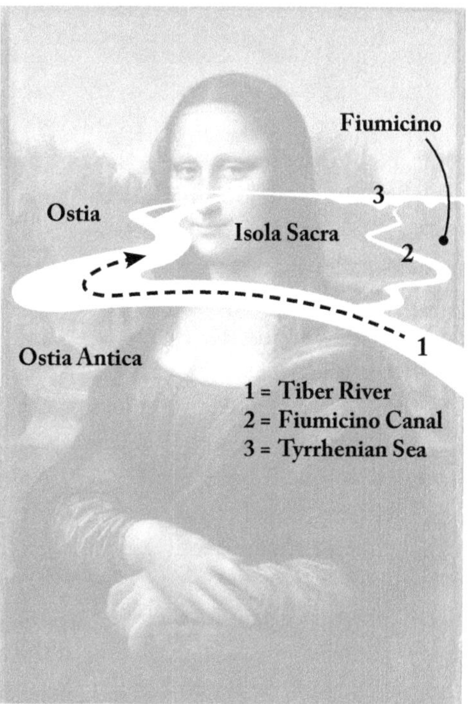

Mona Lisa with overlay showing approximate path of Tiber River and canal in background, location of Tyrrhenian Sea, and surrounding geography.

Although I spent a lot of time examining photos, old maps, and drawings of the area, I found no ancient bridge at that location. Also, there were no mountains in the area as the painting showed. While I didn't expect them to resemble animal heads, I assumed there would be some kind of mountainous landscape. This also included the mountain the figure was sitting on. My guess was that Leonardo added the animal-head-shaped mountains with the existing location just to match the scenery Dante described. But how could I be sure?

Leonardo had a way of leaving no question about what he did—even if nobody noticed it for centuries. It wasn't that I doubted the idea that he added mountains to the location. It was that I had to prove it to myself, otherwise my findings wouldn't feel absolute.

It was later, as I went back over my own notebooks, that I thought of a possible answer. His *Point-of-Sight* passage may have explained the added mountains. It wasn't just part of the set of instructions on viewing the illusions. It was also a clue to the location. No mountains existed there, but the passage read that the view must be "where the earth and sky meet; excepting mountains, which are independent of it."

Independent? As in *separate* or *not connected*?

I superimposed images of Isola Sacra, Ostia, and the surrounding area to *Mona Lisa*'s background. It took a bit to come up with an image fitting the exact angle Leonardo painted, but when I did, I just sat there, staring at the overlapping images on my computer screen. Except for its texture, the shape of the land and water matched up. It surprised me that after 500 years, even with the silting known to take place there, the geography was an incredible match.

I realized then that I mistook what was believed to be a river running underneath the bridge along the right side of the painting. It wasn't a river at all. The Tiber's snaking path does start on the right of the painting (it's barely noticeable), but splits off to the left side behind the sitter, then out and away from the viewer, and toward the Tyrrhenian Sea at the horizon. That river's sharp turn away from the viewer was the sharp dogleg just before reaching and splitting Ostia and Isola Sacra. That dogleg is the water on *Mona Lisa*'s left, just above the backward S-shaped trail near her right shoulder.

On the right, flowing underneath the bridge, was something much smaller. It was the Fossa Traiana—the Fiumicino Canal. But it still showed no ancient bridge that would have existed in Leonardo's time.

Ostia, it turned out, was on the far left of the painting behind the figure, which meant that directly behind the figure was Isola Sacra—on the other side of the cutting river. To the right is a place currently called Fiumicino, once known as Portus, which had been a harbor of ancient Rome. The figure—Envy/Beatrice—was likely sitting in the area called Ostia Antica—the land on the east side of the river that was closer to the viewer.

And in a way, I realized I was sort of wrong about the appearance of the mountains. I saw no trace of mountains in images of Ostia, Isola Sacra, Portus, or Ostia Antica, especially near the shore—as the painting showed. But matching the viewer's line of sight along a three-dimensional map of the Italian region's geography (with a little imagination) a different story was revealed. I suddenly saw what Leonardo added to make it appear as a single mountain next to the figure's head on the horizon. As part of *The Comedy*, it's supposed to look like Mount Purgatory. But in representing the actual geography of the area, he used something bigger to represent mountains. Again, it all came down to satisfying multiple meanings in the art. Not only did he paint details to fit *The Comedy*, but also in a way to keep the location's geography correct.

You were truly full of surprises, Leonardo.

The mountains—especially at the horizon's left—only *appeared* as part of the foreground's landscape. *The point of sight ... must be placed at the level of that line where the earth and sky meet; excepting mountains, which are independent of it.* It was obvious in the center mountain, but not in the set to the left or to the right. Still, all three sets of mountains were different areas of land altogether. And Dante mentions all three of them.

What sat behind *Mona Lisa*, roughly 150 miles out, was the Italian island of Sardinia—the second largest island in the sea. I wasn't sure if it could be seen from Ostia's shore, but it didn't matter. Leonardo used the general layout of the existing locations, whether they could be seen with the naked eye from shore or not. With Sardinia where it was, I then knew that the distant mountainous area to the left of the painting was Sicily—the sea's largest island. It only looked to be part of the foreground because the area of water in between could not be seen from the figure's position. That meant the faded mountainous area on the right had to be the French island of Corsica. And all three islands contained mountainous landscapes.

There was no longer any question of *Mona Lisa*'s location—her *real* life location. And having already found her location from *The Comedy*, it didn't seem like there was much more in the background to figure out.

But there was nothing simple about the painting's appearance, was there Leonardo?

Discovering her location suddenly left me with one question about her position. Looking at *Mona Lisa*, and having figured out where I was looking *from*, I realized what direction the figure was looking *toward.*

Why, Leonardo, was Envy facing Rome?

"You're saying Rome was to blame for the Papal and Church corruption?" I said to Pasquale, as we continued pushing our carts through the grocery store.

"That's an old story. The Church up and cut a deal with Emperor Constantine and received money and power and supporting Imperial dictators. Constantine's intent was good. He didn't expect the Church to abuse the power he entrusted in them. They sold out to good, old Satan and became the Antichrist or the Whore of Babylon, depending on which critic you want to listen to. Many a Catholic thought the Church made a really bad move when it went Constantinian."

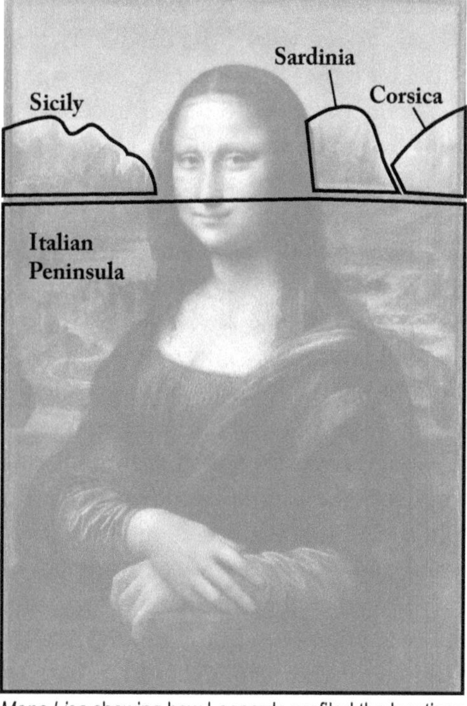

Mona Lisa showing how Leonardo profiled the locations of the islands of Sicily, Sardinia, and Corsica.

"What did Renaissance artists think about that history?" I asked.

"Can't say. If I were them—I wouldn't like being told what I could and could not paint. But, artistic license wasn't really a thing back then—at least not in commission work."

41

The Third Woman

It was no secret that religion played a big part in Italy's history,. Thinking of those persecuted for their beliefs made me feel like there was no place for religion in the world. There was good that came with religion, but I wasn't sure if it was worth the terrible things it historically led to, things like the Spanish Inquisition in Italy, where heretics (or those accused of heresy) were tortured beyond imaginable depths.

One of the many reasons I came to admire Leonardo was that he seemed to believe in science rather than religion, despite the works he painted, like *The Last Supper* and *The Annunciation.* But I saw that as no different than the graphic design work I did for clients. Sometimes, it was just about getting the bills paid rather than creating what we wanted to.

I remember the feeling of freedom I had after I was let go from the agency.

I had to be warned more than once to stop openly voicing discontent for the hours I worked and the pay I received. I was sort of a loudmouth, even unprofessional at times if I felt I was being taken advantage of. So when I was called down to the president's office in March of 2010, after working there for almost five years, I was sure that I was about to be fired. I brought my keys and my phone with me after taking time to look through my desk for anything I would later regret not grabbing. I had a strange mixture of fear and hope, but I began to think about how truly unhappy I had become in my career. I accomplished a lot, and learned so much ...and didn't have the courage to quit. Although I was frustrated at times, I enjoyed the challenge of the demanding work. On the way to his office, my worry started to feel strangely pleasant. I told myself that if I was about to be let go, I would keep my head held high. I wasn't going to try and talk anyone out of firing me.

Instead of the president, my account executive and creative director were the only other ones in the room when I walked in. They took turns explaining that one of the agency's larger clients took their business to another agency, and our agency had been forced to lay off some of the workers. I was sort of surprised, because I thought I was one of the better artists there, but my reputation probably preceded me.

I had been on close terms with my account executive and creative director, and I could see how difficult it was for them to give me the news.

I should have been worried that I no longer had a job, but I found myself glancing out the large office window behind them, one thought alone circling in my mind like the bird I caught sailing lazily in the summer sky: that I would get to leave early and spend more time oil painting. Even though oil painting was somewhat new to me at the time, it was all I really wanted to do.

I told them to keep me in mind if my position eventually reopened, but I already knew I'd never work for an agency again. That kind of life wasn't for me anymore.

I gave them each a hug, and told them how much I would miss working with everyone. One thing that always stuck with me was how much I enjoyed working with each person there.

The drive home was peaceful. Warm air curled in through the windows as the hairs on my arms danced. I looked in the rear view mirror at the agency—a world I once wanted to be a part of more than anything. I watched the building become smaller and smaller. And I saw that I was smiling. It wasn't a fake smile like the one I sometimes used around clients and in meetings. My smile was genuine.

That night, after taking Pinch and Ginger for a very long walk, I painted with such intensity, almost dancing in my shoes as the brushes moved across the canvas. I felt like a drunken wizard crazily waving his magical wand, no longer the struggling, aspiring artist I had been years before. I was different. I was free.

Even though I was out of a job, everything felt right about the situation. I had been so envious of artists who worked in the advertising world before I was one of them. What I didn't realize until after I was let go was that I had been focused on maintaining a glorified job rather than finding one that made me happy. I had tolerated the work until it became intolerable. Or maybe they had tolerated me until I became intolerable.

I was no different than the envious souls from Purgatory's second terrace until I learned to find what really made me happy. It wasn't about the job; it was about creating art, no matter how I went about it.

Years later, I found myself asking the question, *Was there something you envied, Leonardo?*

Though the *Envy* passage turned out to be describing the envious souls, and *Mona Lisa* showed the envious souls *and* Beatrice, I wondered if the *Envy* passage was also describing Beatrice—since one supposedly could not exist without the other. I thought that figuring out the answer might provide more insight about the painting.

In the *Envy* passage, Leonardo wrote, "Many thunderbolts should proceed her evil speaking." Prior to Beatrice's appearance in *The Comedy*, thunder claps the air. The tricky part was the allegoric meaning. *Evil speaking* could have meant some offensive language. But I thought it could reference Beatrice if I took it to mean that she was speaking *about* evil, as she does in first confronting

Dante about his sins.

Beatrice also wears a veil. Just as *Mona* does.

Through *Inferno,* Beatrice is mentioned only twice by name. There wasn't much description to easily bring Leonardo's painting to mind unless it was looked for. Although I found details of the background, they were mixed throughout other details of *Inferno* and *Purgatorio* like spots on a cheetah: none of them stood out on their own for any reason. And *Purgatorio* never seemed to get much attention from scholars compared to *Inferno*. If it did, maybe someone would have figured out *Mona Lisa*'s identity sooner.

Beatrice doesn't appear until after the well-known *Inferno*, toward the end of *Purgatorio*. She is described by the poet in all her glory, her chariot pulled by a Gryphon and surrounded by a parade of Elders, dancing maidens, animals in human form, and other creatures such as the four Beasts of the Apocalypse—described as cherubs with four faces and wings. I kept track of lines that described her as she looked in *Mona Lisa*—either literally or through wordplay. I constantly underlined words, highlighting sections of different scenes, flagging important pages with colored tabs.

> Although **the veil, that from her head descended,**
> … **Did not permit her to appear distinctly,**
> In attitude still **royally majestic**
> Continued she, like unto one who speaks,
> And keeps his warmest utterance in reserve:
> **"Look at me well; in sooth I'm Beatrice!**
> How didst thou deign to come unto the Mountain?
> Didst thou not know that man is happy here?"
>
> (*Pur.* 30.67, 69-75; Longfellow, emphasis added)[1]

Asked by the angels why she shames Dante, Beatrice tells how he chose to pursue false images in life—the reason he was then brought on the journey to see what might become of him in the afterlife if he continued his way of living.

> … So much more malignant and more savage
> Becomes the land untilled and with bad seed …
> Some time did **I sustain him with my look;**
> **Revealing unto him my youthful eyes,**
> I led him with me **turned in the right way.**
> As soon as ever of **my second age**
> I was upon the threshold and changed life …
> And **beauty and virtue were in me increased,**
> I was to him less dear and less delightful;
> And into ways untrue he turned his steps,
> Pursuing the false images of good
>
> (*Pur.* 30.118-19, 121-25, 128-31, emphasis added)[2]

The lines were suggestive of *Mona Lisa*: she revealed her second self in the anamorphic illusion when she was "turned in the right way" and looked at across the canvas from the left side. It was arguable if the land behind her looked "untilled and with bad seed," but the figure did seem to "sustain [us] with [her] look." And in the illusion, she did transform into a younger woman, her "second age," revealing her "youthful eyes" as her "beauty … increased. …"

Reading the lines gave me a sense of guilt and loneliness, as if Beatrice were directing her disapproval at me. I thought back to all the years I spent chasing my dream of working at an ad agency. It wasn't the effort in chasing that dream that I regretted, but what I sacrificed for it. I thought of an old girlfriend I was in love with in my twenties who wanted me to move in with her, but I had refused, afraid the relationship would derail me from focusing on my dream. I thought of my ex-wife, and how wrong I had been in resenting her because I felt she was getting in the way of my work. I thought of my family, who I never spent enough time with because I was always "too busy" painting, or "too busy" with work, or "too busy" to pick up the phone.

I looked at Pinch, resting in her bed near me, her eyes pointing up at me with a look of boredom. Then I shut down my computer for the day and took her for a walk in the park. It took a few hours to shake off that terrible feeling I had for having focused so much of my attention on my book. *The more things change …*

Late that night, as Heather and Pinch both slept, I tiptoed up to the attic to continue working. I read over the words again, as I did with many of the ones I marked, especially when it felt as if something was hiding in the text. A few lines later, Dante looking into Beatrice's eyes, sees the reflection of the Griffin as its features change, and addresses this to the reader directly: "Think, Reader, if within myself I marveled, / When I beheld the thing itself stand still, / And in its image it transformed itself" (*Pur.* 31.124-26). That the image *transformed itself* didn't stand out until I read what followed a few lines later: "In grace do us the grace that thou unveil / Thy face to him, so that he may discern / The second beauty which thou dost conceal" (31.136-38).[3] Something about those last few words threw me off. That the Griffin's *image transformed itself* into a *second beauty which thou dost conceal* was too much to ignore.

Mona Lisa showed Envy, the not-so-attractive version of the figure seen straight on. Beatrice, the younger, more attractive figure with the increased smile, appears in the anamorphic illusion. I didn't consider Envy as beautiful. And I didn't think Leonardo tried to show her that way except for in the illusion when she becomes Beatrice.

Think, Reader / … in its image it transformed itself. / … The second beauty. …

Envy wasn't a *second beauty*, which made me wonder if the painting was hiding something else. Of the two females of Envy and Beatrice, only the latter had beauty. So was there a third woman? I wondered. The idea should have sounded impossible, even after finding that the one figure was a portrait of two woman. But Leonardo's ability to amaze went beyond what I could ever realize.

... Unveil / Thy face to him, so that he may discern / The second beauty ... dost conceal.

I didn't think that text had anything to do with the animals, because they showed no beauty either. I kept studying the context of the line, looking for other key words or phrases Leonardo could have incorporated. What I ended up with were three additional groups of text that made me think back to *Venus and Mars* and how the male figure of Dante had alluded—*transformed itself*—into an image of Christ.

> "Turn, Beatrice, **O turn thy holy eyes"**
> . . . .
> ... He would not seem to have his mind encumbered
> Striving to paint thee as thou didst appear,
> Where **the harmonious heaven o'ershadowed thee,**
> When **in the open air thou didst unveil?**
> . . . .
> ... **Upon this side and that they had**
> **Walls of indifference, so the holy smile**
> **Drew them unto itself** with the old net
> When forcibly **my sight was turned away**
> **Towards my left hand by those goddesses**
> **... But to the less when sight reshaped itself**
>
> (*Pur.* 31.133, 142-45, 32.4-8, 13, emphasis added)[4]

I thought back to a line I read many pages before, back when Dante and Virgil approached the first circle of Purgatory containing the souls guilty of pride, back when I started to see Leonardo's use of wordplay from *The Comedy* to make *Mona Lisa*, just as I was realizing that her background resembled a sort of geography map of Dante's journey. When Dante and Virgil were in an open plain—which would have placed them on the left side of the *Mona Lisa*, just over the figure's right shoulder, with the mountains behind them—they saw "a human body three times told would measure ..." (*Pur.* 10.24)[5] at the top of a sizable bank.

The human body would turn out to be the *Mona Lisa* figure. As I read the scene over, I pictured Dante and Virgil, as if they existed in the painting, as if *Mona Lisa* was their stage, the poets in the far distance walking toward the front of the picture, but only able to view the back of *Mona Lisa*'s figure, *a human body three times told would measure.*

... Three times told. ...

It could have meant a person who could be described three different ways. Or as three separate figures. *Three times told.* I already knew who two of them were. And I would have bet anything that a third woman was hiding in that portrait. But who could it be?

I checked every part of the painting for ambiguous and anamorphic clues of another woman. Maybe something in the art symbolized her instead of showing her, the way Botticelli used the female figure in *Venus and Mars* to symbolize the Virgin Mary instead of literally showing her. An allusion instead of an illusion.

Of course, I assumed the third figure in *Mona Lisa* would be a female. Was a hidden male possible? Sure, I thought. Anything was possible.

I read the scene over and over countless times, as if it were a puzzle that needed to be figured out. In reality, it was. Every line in that book could have been part of the puzzle. I had learned to trust my instinct when a set of words felt peculiar. Usually, there was a good reason for it. The words that stuck out to me were "walls of indifference, so the holy smile." Something about that part of the sentence tapped me on the back, as if I had simply passed over it when it deserved more attention.

Walls of indifference, so the holy smile.

I remembered how author and art historian Frank Zöllner pointed out that "*Mona Lisa* bore a strong resemblance to many Renaissance depictions of the Virgin Mary." That got me thinking.

Just after seeing the large figure at the top of the bank, Dante and Virgil come to the embankment wall made of white marble and find three breathtaking carvings. One was of Emperor Trajan and his calvary, a poor weeping widow asking him for vengeance for the son she lost in war. But it wasn't her I was thinking of.

The second carving was of King David, dancing around the Ark of the Covenant as his wife gave him a scornful look. But it wasn't her I was thinking of either.

It was the carving of the Annunciation I was thinking of. Gabriel and the Virgin Mary, lifelike figures looking so real one could almost hear them speaking, Dante had explained.

I did more research into why some historians thought that she could have been the Virgin Mary, listing all the possible reasons for it in a notebook dedicated just for *Mona Lisa*. A second notebook was labeled *Divine Comedy Notes*. I accumulated more notebooks for specific paintings as time went on.

As someone who once hated research and essay writing, I dove into my research with incredible determination.

I didn't set out or expect my memoir to become any kind of great literary work—that wasn't its purpose. At best, I considered my writing to be mediocre. My purpose was to correct art history, to fix what we knew about *Mona Lisa* as Leonardo da Vinci would have wanted us to see it. I wanted to show everyone what was hiding under our noses. Just as art had inspired me in life, I wanted to inspire whoever I could, by showing how something could be right in front of our eyes, yet invisible, that sometimes we need to be shown what we're missing in order to see things more clearly. In doing so, I would have to preach how the same religious icons I never believed existed in real life, had been secretly living in some of the world's most famous paintings.

Regardless of how it would all play out, I started to recognize that *Mona Lisa* represents the Virgin Mary, as well as the envious souls and Beatrice. It wasn't like that "apparition" of the Virgin Mary I had seen on that glass building back in 1996 in Florida. I *knew* that "Christmas miracle" was just a random shape people threw their imaginations at. Maybe that was another reason that "walls of indifference so the holy smile" spoke to me. Was I reminded of the building's mirrored glass wall that some believed showed the apparition of the Virgin? And that I had felt indifferent to it and to everyone's belief in it?

Mona Lisa had plenty of reasons to be Mary. Just like Botticelli had personified the Virgin Mary and Christ in *Venus and Mars*. In fact, I noticed similarities between *Mona Lisa*'s dress and the *Annunciation's* Virgin that Leonardo painted. But if Leonardo wanted to obscure Mary's presence, he wouldn't have dressed her in the same exact clothing.

Or would you, Leonardo?

In *The Three Mona Lisas*, Rab Hatfield points out that her "hood-and-veil combinations [are often] in representations of nuns and female saints—especially the Virgin Mary. …"[6]

I noticed that aside from a difference in colors, *The Annunciation*'s Mary and the figure in *Mona Lisa* both wore mantles and a veil. They had similar hairstyles: parted down the center, straight on top of the head, then turning into curls down the length. Both showed barely any eyebrow hairs. I was actually so surprised at how close their hairstyles were that I superimposed them over each other to compare further. When I did, I noticed something funny that gave me that euphoric feeling I got whenever I realized something unbelievable that nobody had ever pointed out, but should have caught.

Were you playing with our minds, Leonardo?

If he did what I thought he did, then the answer was yes.

No matter how much I discovered, Leonardo continued to surprise me. Even from his grave, he was always steps ahead, allowing me to believe I was so close to figuring everything out until I would realize that I was still only scratching the surface.

Comparing the two figures I superimposed over each other, I saw that not only did he follow Dante's writings to show the Virgin in *Mona Lisa*, but he planted clues from his *Annunciation* scene of Gabriel and the Virgin.

The placement of the curls in their hair matched. The proportions of the facial features—nose, eyes, eyelids, lips—matched also. But it was the hand gestures that really started to give her away. I pictured Leonardo laughing as he painted them. It was as if he took Mary's position in *The Annunciation* and turned her around slightly to position her in *Mona Lisa*, pushing the viewer's angle to the right, then reversing some of the details, as if looking at a reflection in the mirror to throw the viewer off—just as he wrote backwards in his notebooks in his mirrored-writing style.

Or maybe the reversed image had something to do with the carving of the Virgin and the angel Gabriel that the poets come across in *The Comedy*, showing the story of the Annunciation shortly before seeing the envious souls.

Ascending the steps toward an angel who will carve seven P's on Dante's head—to be erased one at a time on each terrace of Purgatory—Dante describes the first step, "marble white, so polished and so smooth, / I mirrored myself therein as I appear" (*Pur.* 9.95-96).[7] The carving of the Virgin is made of the same white, polished marble Dante sees his reflection in right after. Or it could have something to do with Dante's pursuit of divine vision, in which he essentially sees the world through God's eyes. And God, as it's explained in *The Comedy*, sees futuristic events in his mind as if in a mirror. The mirror comparisons Dante used could explain why there are details in *Mona Lisa* that seem to match those in *The Annunciation*, but in reverse view.

Any depiction of the Virgin without Gabriel's presence would likely represent a time *after* the Annunciation since the Bible doesn't mention much about Mary before the event—making it highly unusual that an artist would illustrate her representing a moment before the Annunciation. Leonardo would have taken that into consideration when deciding that *Mona Lisa* would portray the Virgin Mary. So *Mona Lisa* would have to represent a future event after Gabriel's visit. And according to *The Comedy*, future events would be seen with divine vision, and appear as if reflected in a mirror as God would see it.

Maybe the anamorphic images were designed to be a way to test our own divine vision. Leonardo may have hinted at it in his *Last Supper*. In *Leonardo da Vinci*, Walter Isaacson points out that the artist hammered a nail in the wall at the center of the painting—where Christ's right temple is—to use as the painting's vanishing point. But I wondered if there was more meaning behind Leonardo's choice in concentrating the perspective point near Christ's right eye. Did it symbolize the idea of directing our view to the right in order to see some of the illusions in his art by way of this divine vision? In fact, Isaacson also mentions some of the distorted elements in Leonardo's painting of *The Annunciation*, and comments that the young Leonardo "was experimenting with the trick known as anamorphosis, in which some elements of a work may look distorted when viewed straight on but appear accurate when viewed from another angle."[8]

Either way, I continued to compare *The Annunciation* to *Mona Lisa* in search for clues. Although positioned at different angles, *Mona Lisa*'s left hand shares a similar gesture to Mary's right in *The Annunciation*. Each pinky and pointer finger are outward from the palm the most, with the ring finger extended outward the least.

Mona Lisa's right hand and Mary's left are just as similar. It looks like the same exact hand gesture, but Mary holds her hand up, while *Mona Lisa* is resting hers on her other arm. The curl of the fingers and spacing in between look exactly the same. The triangular points of the tips of the pointer, middle, and ring finger stand out, as if *Mona Lisa* had just held that odd position with her finger tips. I was so sure Leonardo did that to show both figures were in a sense the same—at least, for anyone who would look for clues. It was as if the scenes in the two paintings took place just seconds apart, the Virgin Mary reading in a book one moment, then bringing her arms together to rest them on the chair as she turns to her left, slightly wrapping her right hand (what would be *Mona Lisa*'s left hand) around the edge of the arm of the chair. Like Mary

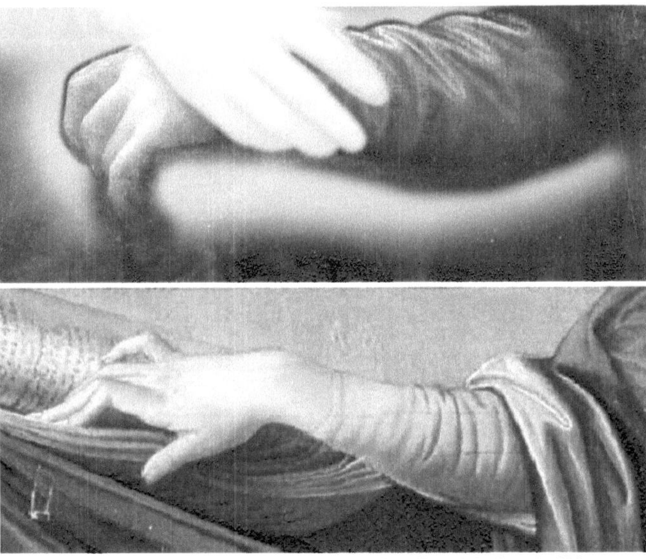

Comparison of left hand in *Mona Lisa* (highlighted) to right hand of Mary.

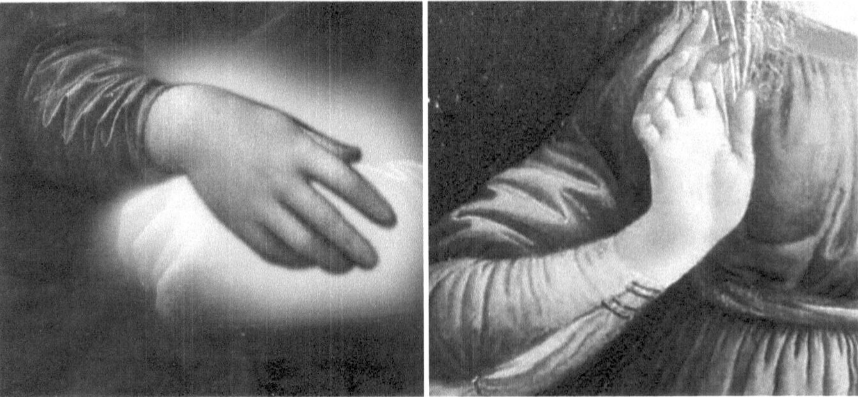

Comparison of right hand in *Mona Lisa* (highlighted) to left hand of Mary (image reversed).

was suddenly turning to face the viewer almost behind her at the building's entrance in *Annunciation,* therefore rotating the background to the right, which would place the similar zigzagging path behind Gabriel's right hand so it appears directly behind the figure in *Mona Lisa.*

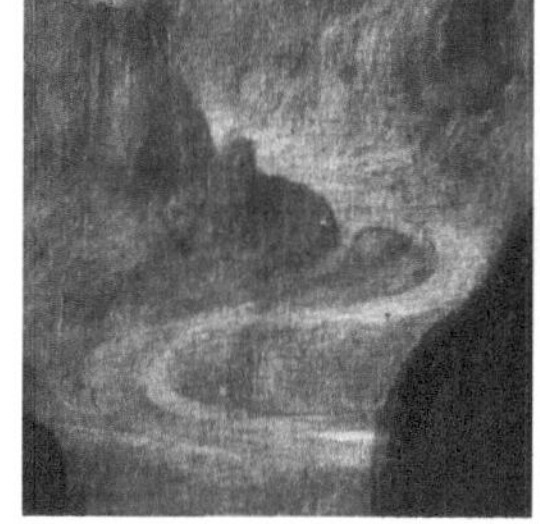
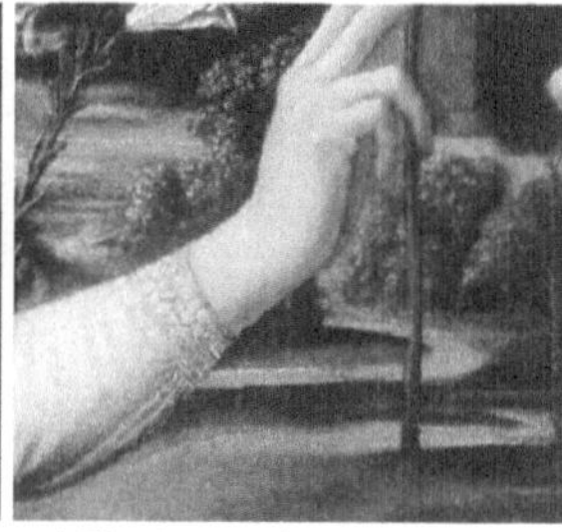

Zigzagging trails in *Mona Lisa* and *The Annunciation.*

They had to be clues Leonardo left behind. But he changed just enough details in the art to fool us.

At first, their sleeves look different. White stripes run underneath Mary's forearms. *Mona Lisa*'s are solid-colored. At least, it looked that way, until I realized Leonardo may have used Botticelli's trick—the one he used in preventing anyone from checking for signs of stigmata by positioning his *Venus and Mars* male figure so only the sides of his hands and feet could be seen. If *Mona Lisa* had the same white stripes under her forearms, Leonardo positioned her arms so the bottoms are hidden away from the viewer. It wasn't proof that the white stripes existed. It was the possibility that they could in order to serve Leonardo's purpose in leaving clues.

As always, the answers were right on the canvas.

The embroidery around her neckline may have been another clue. In *Signs & Symbols in Christian Art*, George Ferguson points out that the Virgin Mary "is sometimes represented teaching her companions to spin or to embroider. ..."[9] Could the embroidery on *Mona Lisa*'s neckline have been a hint of the Virgin's presence? And was that twisted cloth over her left shoulder the same twisted cloth Mary wears around her waist in *The Annunciation?* Girdles were worn both around the waist and over the shoulder. Did it point to the story of the Holy Girdle Mary takes off to give Doubting Thomas—a story that has been portrayed in Renaissance art?

I couldn't be sure either way. Still, considering the mirrored approach, in *The Annunciation*, the Virgin Mary wears her mantle on her right side. *Mona Lisa*'s is on her left. I was also very suspicious of the chairs they sit on, which would help identify *Mona Lisa* if the details of Mary's chair were not covered by her gown. But both chairs sure were shaped the same. In fact, Hatfield points out that the curve of the chair "appears in special photographs to

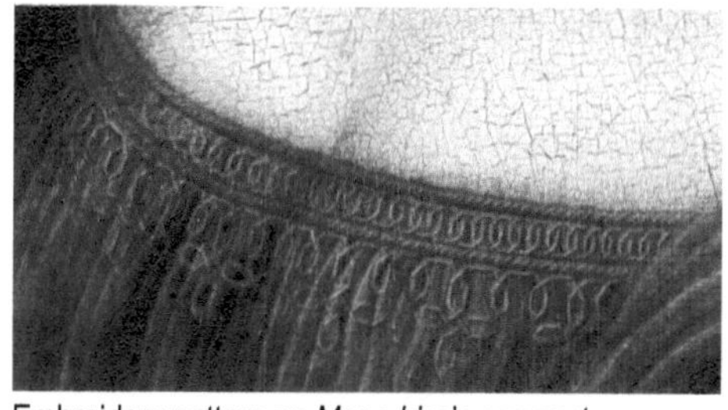

Embroidery pattern on *Mona Lisa*'s garment.

be slightly misdrawn."[10] I wondered if it was a coachman's seat instead, alluding to Beatrice's chariot, which to me would explain its *misdrawn* shape.

The more I compared the figures in the two paintings, the more *The Annunciation*'s Mary looked like *Mona Lisa*, as if she were being shown seated in Dante's Hell with its lack of sunlight, dressed just like the envious souls in their dark cloths.

Hanging on the wall over my bed was a poster-sized image of *Mona Lisa*. It was a puzzle I had put together and framed for that purpose. At the time, I was aware that she was both Envy and Beatrice, and I had no problem sleeping under the masterpiece for months. But, when I saw she also represented the Virgin Mary, I wasn't sure how to feel about it. Had the art been by another painter, I would have felt compelled to move it away from where it could fall onto my head. Because it was Leonardo, it felt okay to keep it where it was, although I began to look at her differently each night before I went to bed.

Maybe I felt Leonardo was so personally attached to the painting, that he understood what it was like to be envious of others—whatever he could have been envious about. Considered a bastard child, perhaps he envied those who had strong relationships with their fathers. I knew what that was like.

For years I wanted to be as great as the comic illustrators I studied as a child, artists like Todd McFarlane and Burne Hogarth. When I was older, I spent time trying to copy Van Gogh's style, eventually drawing from Leonardo's art. I too had been envious for what other artists could do, including those I worked with over the years in my career.

Maybe that was partly why Leonardo placed clues from *The Annunciation* into his painting of Envy. He was around twenty years old when he painted his first known painting, collaborating with his master, Verrocchio. Could the young Leonardo have been envious of other painters at the time? Perhaps the tie-back of clues to his first painting was a humble showing of the envy he may have felt at the time. I don't think anyone is immune to envy.

As time passed, I continued searching. And other clues showing the Virgin Mary appeared. The biggest clues yet were the lion, ape, and what I found to be both an ox and frog. It was their positioning that gave them away. The lion was farthest away from her, the ape to her right, and what was the ox—in this case—told the rest of the story.

Leonardo strategically placed them.

It all pointed to the presence of the Virgin Mary. She did turn out to be the third woman in the painting. The "second beauty" that had been concealed. What came next was a little difficult for me to accept, but I couldn't deny what I was sure I saw, because something miraculous appeared in the painting right after. Moses was there, too.

42

Water from a Rock

I thought Leonardo was a man of science, not religion, but the Virgin Mary and Moses appeared in *Mona Lisa*, and it made me question what I knew.

You didn't believe in them—or did you, Leonardo?

No doubt the artist was full of surprises, but something didn't feel right about the presence of the two biblical references in the art. (Although many of the books I read described Leonardo as having religious beliefs, I learned that wasn't true. Giorgio Vasari's original 1550 edition of *Lives of the Artists* had been censored and edited for the later edition most of us were accustomed to. In the original, Vasari wrote that "... Leonardo was of so heretical a cast of mind, that he conformed to no religion whatever accounting it perchance much better to be a philosopher than a Christian."[1] That text was removed for the edited version.)

I was 9 years old when *Indiana Jones and The Raiders of the Lost Ark* introduced me to the idea of the Ark of the Covenant. I later learned that it was based on biblical stories—much like *The Ten Commandments* movie our family watched around Easter time. I found it strange, but in its own way, kind of cool. (My parents insisted our family watch it.) Those kinds of movies made me want to read the Bible, simply so I could understand what was taking place in the film. Renaissance art was full of references to those stories. In a way, they were like the religious movies of their day. Like big-screen still images of biblical scenes.

Because *The Comedy* itself was rooted in religious stories, and because *Mona Lisa* represented *The Comedy*, I didn't completely doubt that the painting held substantial religious meaning—especially after finding that the third woman she represented was the Virgin Mary. I still wasn't sure if her 30 by 21 inch size was a deliberate connection to Psalm 30:21 ("Thou shalt hide them in the secret of thy face, from the disturbance of men. Thou shalt protect them in thy tabernacle from the contradiction of tongues."), but the scripture stayed in the back of my mind. I understood *tabernacle* from Psalm 30:21 to be a sort of shrine for the Ark.

Over time, I began to notice how the *Mona Lisa* fit the description of the Ark of the Covenant, just as the Bible describes it.

Around the same time he worked on *Mona Lisa*, Leonardo also illustrated apocalyptic scenes of the deluge—the biblical flood from the Book of Genesis. He created the drawings for himself, unlike art such as *The Last Supper* that were commission pieces. It wasn't hard to accept that Leonardo mixed biblical references into his *Comedy*-related illustration since Michelangelo, years later, mixed illustrations from Dante into his *Last Judgement* fresco illustrating the Second Coming of Christ. In fact, Vasari wrote in Giotto's biography that "scenes from the Apocalypse that [Giotto] made in [the Santa Chiara chapel in Naples] are said to have been inventions from Dante. ..."[2] I wondered if it had anything to do with Leonardo's decision to create his own apocalyptic scenes.

Nonetheless, I continued to discover more layers of meaning.

When I first studied the Bible, I watched documentaries to help me better understand its stories. Simcha Jacobovici's *Beasts of the Bible* explains that when Moses confronts the Pharaoh, and the staff is cast down onto the ground, it does not turn into a snake as generally told. The "... Hebrew word 'tannin' is mistranslated as 'snake' ..." from the original Hebrew text, explains Jacobovici, and that the actual translation of tannin is crocodile. He tells how a crocodile makes better sense of the scene "Since the Egyptians worshipped the crocodile god—Sobek [and that] Aaron's crocodile swallowed up the Egyptian crocodiles, ..." stressing God's power.[3] The mistranslation was a detail Leonardo may have been aware of, which would help explain his use of a crocodile.

Moses, lacking faith in God, is chosen to save his people from the Egyptian Pharaoh. Through God's commands, Moses builds the Ark out of wood and painted gold. After a long time spent crossing the desert with his people, he parts the Red Sea with the help of his staff, which is also used in a separate miracle of pulling water from a rock.

Although the Bible could never convince me that anyone had split the Red Sea apart, *Mona Lisa* would make sense of it. It all started when I spotted the cherubim.

Instead of describing the cherub himself, Dante tells the reader to search the writings of Ezekiel for a description. Translated from the Latin Vulgate, the prophet wrote: "And as for the likeness of their faces: there was the face of a man, and the face of a lion on the right side of all the four: and the face of an ox, on the left side of all the four: and the face of an eagle over all the four" (*Douay-Rheims*, Ezek. 1:10).[4]

At the figure's right side in *Mona Lisa* was a lion head. On her left was a frog that was also an ox. The "face of a man" could be the sitter's face, who was definitely human, or maybe the ape's head symbolized a man.

Until that moment, I was unsure about the eagle. Back when I looked through every animal mention in *The Comedy,* I spotted what looked like the head of a hawk. In *Purgatorio* XIII, the envious souls, guilty of allowing sight to lead them to wanting materialistic things others possess, discuss having to have their eyes wired shut as part of their penance. Dante compares it to what is done to the *sparhawk*, or sparrowhawk, its eyes sewn shut as a training technique: "... For all their lids an iron wire transpierces, / And sews them up, as to a sparhawk wild / Is done, because it will not quiet stay" (*Pur.* 13.70-72). Earlier, Dante used the simile of the falcon, "flying, upward he his breast directed; // Not otherwise the duck upon a sudden / Dives under, when the falcon is approaching, / And upward he returneth cross and weary" (*Inf.* 22.129-32),[5] which Leonardo likely followed to place the bird in his art.

I found what looked like a hawk's head when I placed the painting on its left side. The bird's head takes up the figure's upper left arm, shoulder, and part of the *breast.* Leonardo followed Dante's words in placing it there—"flying, upward he his breast directed. ..." Placing the hawk's beak just behind the lower part of her neck, it faces upward (toward *Mona Lisa*'s sky) since Dante describes its movement in that direction.

The bird, following the pattern of one object representing multiple objects or sections or scenes from *The Comedy*, is both the *sparhawk* and the falcon. Together, with the lion, ape, ox, and hawk around the figure, it forms a cherub.

St. John's description of the cherub also fits, the only difference being they are four separate creatures. The figure and its surrounding creatures can be considered one creature with multiple faces—to fit Ezekiel's description—or they can be considered separate creatures altogether in the painting—to fit St. John's description: "And the first living creature was like a lion: and the second living creature like a calf: and the third living creature, having the face, as it were, of a man: and the fourth living creature was like an eagle flying" (*Douay-Rheims*, Apoc. 4.7).[6]

And although hawks and eagles are not the same species, St. John's description says "*like* an eagle flying," which I accepted to include a hawk. I marked the page of the Bible containing St. John's description as I had marked so many other pages, and paced slowly back and forth across the attic, carrying the book, thinking. Countless articles on every continent had mentioned the animals I found. There were blogs and all sorts of online reports all over the world. Journalists had interviewed me. Television programs had discussed my findings. My YouTube video showing the animal heads and their positions had received over 400,000 views. Yet, not one single soul caught the idea that the specific animals I pointed out were

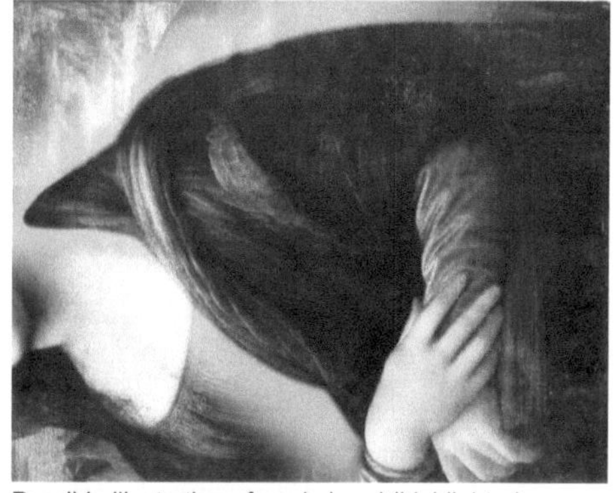
Possible illustration of eagle head (highlighted, facing left) when *Mona Lisa* is on its left side.

the same ones that formed a cherub.

How was it possible that, with so many people going over the image, no one had caught that? Yes, five years had passed since first seeing the animals before I realized it myself, but I was just one person. Still, as submerged as I had been in examining the art, how did it take me so long to realize the placement of the animals meant something more?

It made me wonder how much I really understood about my own life and beliefs. What was hiding in my life that I had not yet seen? Was I still too blind to see it all clearly?

The painting was a dark, endless pit of secrets. But I knew that secrets could be uncovered, even if it meant uncovering something that was difficult to believe. And the same could be said of my own life.

The cherub was just the beginning. Other clues were pointing to Moses. The crooked horizon line scholars had been unable to figure out was another clue. The horizon on the right side of the art didn't line up with the left. Even though nobody ever knew why before, I had faith that Leonardo did it for a reason. Eventually, I figured out why.

At first, I thought it had something to do with the anamorphic view, since Leonardo instructs the viewer to look at the illusion from the left side of the art at a level along the horizon. In a way, the horizon looks more distorted from that point. At the same time, the landscape becomes flooded with water to resemble the crocodile's swamp. I knew the crooked horizon couldn't be a mistake.

Then, one day, I came across an observation Leonardo wrote down in his notebooks that explained it. He describes how an earthquake caused the sea's bottom to split apart, swallowing enough water to expose the seafloor:

> In [fourteen hundred and] eighty nine there was an earthquake in the sea of Atalia near Rhodes, which opened the sea—that is its bottom—and into this opening such a torrent of water poured that for more than three hours the bottom of the sea was uncovered by reason of the water which was lost in it, and then it closed to the former level.[7]

In a different piece of writing, Leonardo wrote that "there are springs which suddenly break forth in earthquakes or other convulsions and suddenly fail; and this happened in a mountain in Savoy where certain forests sank in and left a very deep gap," and that "about four miles from here the earth opened itself like a gulf in the mountain, and threw out a sudden and immense flood of water which scoured the whole of a little valley of the tilled soil, vineyards and houses, and did the greatest mischief, wherever it overflowed."

The "sudden and immense flood" presented the same idea that *Mona Lisa*'s illusion shows—a sudden flooding.

In a way, the crooked horizon *did* have something to do with the anamorphic illusion. In it, the background changes from the rocky landscape we all know to what looks like a marsh or lake or sudden flooding of water in which the crocodile—Lucifer—appears. The reddish area of landscape on the left side of the painting makes it look as if the water around the crocodile's mouth is bloodied. (The reddish terrain might be explained by a richness in iron oxides. Italians even had a term for red soil—Terra Rossa. The red tint might also be explained by Malebolge—an area of Inferno's realm made "of stone and of an iron color." Rusted iron also becomes reddish.)

Leonardo was one of the first to scientifically study the movements of the Earth's crust—movements that created earthquakes.

It turned out that the horizon line wasn't crooked at all. It had to be showing one side of a fault line pressured against the other, causing the crust to rise on the right side of the painting—an earthquake was taking place.

Was there an earthquake in *The Comedy*? Yes. The first came after Dante enters Hell, as Charon ferries him across the River Styx to the shore of Acheron. And did earthquakes have any connection to Moses? Yes. One took place just before he spoke the Ten Commandments on Mount Sinai, when "all the mountain fearfully shook …" (*Wycliffe's Bible*, Exod. 19.18).[8] And was that Mount Sinai lying on *Mona Lisa*'s horizon? Possibly, in addition to showing Mount Purgatory, the mountain next to the female's head could allude to Mount Sinai.

Because nothing had only one meaning—did it, Leonardo?

And earthquakes on the mountain of Purgatory? Yeah, an earthquake "trembles here, whenever any soul / … [pays its penance and] Feels itself pure, so that it soars, or moves / To mount aloft, and such a cry attends it" (*Pur.* 21.58-60),[9] signaling its flight to heaven:

> "And I, who have been **lying in this pain**
> **Five hundred years and more,** but just now felt
> A free volition for a better seat.
> **Therefore thou heardst the earthquake, and the pious**
> **Spirits along the mountain rendering praise**
> **Unto the Lord, that soon he speed them upwards."**
>
> (*Pur.* 21.67-72, emphasis added)[10]

Having lived in western New York all my life, I never felt the occurrence of an earthquake, since they were never powerful enough for me to feel. Only when that truck had crashed into the side of the building where I worked back in 2005 did I experience what felt like a terrible quake. That day had changed my life—my soul had been shaken from its shell, similar to what *Purgatorio*'s souls may have felt "lying in … pain. …"

I thought about that day every so often, and still wondered if it had anything to do with God. I didn't know. Did I really know anything at all about the world? The discoveries taught me that what I saw and what I believed could be very different from the truth, that you can feel so sure of something your whole life, then one day have your mind changed by something unexpected.

The rocky landscape became water in the anamorphic illusion. Maybe the water was supposed to look like it was spreading in the viewer's direction—some kind of interactive symbolism, perhaps. Ingeniously, the mountains turn into the textured top of the crocodile's mouth as it prowls along the surface. Around the end of its snout on the left edge of the painting, the red-tinted landscape becomes blood-colored water.

It reminded me of the bloodied water of the marsh Styx, in which the wrathful are divided into three groups, which may explain the three groups of animals drowning in the crocodile's (Lucifer's) swamp. But did the blood-colored water also connect to Moses, alluding to the *Red* Sea?

The sitter in the picture was a symbol. But a composite symbol. She represented Envy, Beatrice, and the Virgin Mary. In Purgatory, Dante is shown the three wall carvings. The first is of Virgin Mary. "… In rear of Mary …" (*Pur.* 10.50)[11] is the sculpture of King David dancing around the Holy Ark. The third sculpture is of Emperor Trajan.

> … I moved mine eyes, and I beheld
> **In rear of Mary,** and upon that side
> Where he was standing who conducted me,
> **Another story on the rock imposed;**
> Wherefore I passed Virgilius and drew near,
> So that before mine eyes it might be set.
> There sculptured **in the self-same marble were**
> **The cart and oxen, drawing the holy ark**
> . . . .
> There the high glory of the Roman Prince
> Was chronicled, whose great beneficence
> Moved Gregory to his great victory;
> 'Tis of the Emperor Trajan I am speaking …
>
> (*Pur.* 10.49-56, 73-76; Longfellow, emphasis added)[12]

And if *Mona Lisa* showed the Virgin Mary, was "the cart and oxen" there "drawing the holy ark" behind her, symbolizing the Ark? The ox was already there where I had discovered it. An allusion to the Red Sea looked to be present also. God instructed Moses to build the Ark of the Covenant to hold the Ten Commandments. Moses was given specific details. Two cherubim were to be placed on the Ark. Combined with the animal heads, the Envy/Beatrice/Virgin Mary figure fit the description of a cherub. *Mona Lisa* shows two cherubim—Ezekiel's version along with St. John's.

There's also the earthquake Leonardo shows with the fault line in the art.

He had described how the bottom of the sea opened to swallow so much water that the seafloor became exposed.

The earthquake explained the bent horizon. But more importantly, it pointed to the story of Moses splitting the sea. I kept going over and over everything new I was seeing, as doubt and trust battled it out inside me. Allusions allowed no certainty, so I knew I could never be sure. But Leonardo already proved that he liked to play mind games with his art. All I could do was piece together what I knew. *The Comedy* mentions the Ark "in rear of Mary." So Leonardo must have alluded to the story of Moses if the clues were present. The prophet was mostly known for building the Ark of the Covenant, speaking the Ten Commandments, and splitting the Red Sea. *Mona Lisa* alluded to the presence of two cherubim, an earthquake (explaining the unaligned horizon), the Red Sea (reddish water), and the exposure of a seafloor after a flood (anamorphic background is flooded; normal view shows areas of dry landscape).

But how did Leonardo regard the story of Moses parting the Red Sea? Was he reasoning that if there was a man named Moses at all, it only *appeared* that he split the Red Sea? Was Leonardo showing us an alternate, scientific explanation of what actually took place in the biblical story?

Was his description of what took place in the sea of Atalia—an earthquake causing the sea's bottom to open, swallowing all its water before filling back up again—his explanation of how Moses seemed to part the sea, before it returned again to its former level, drowning the Pharaoh and his Egyptian army? A result of nature, not miracle? Pure luck?

What I knew for sure was that two scenes were taking place in *Mona Lisa.* From the d-point, the horizon was more distorted and the background became flooded with water, suggesting that an earthquake had taken place. And in Leonardo's note on Savoy, an earthquake caused a spring to break, throwing "out a sudden and immense flood of water which scoured the whole of a little valley." And from that same illusion, the figure was Beatrice, a symbol of virtue, sitting in front of it all.

The view straight on shows a less bent horizon, as if an earthquake was just starting to occur—the fault lines just starting to push against each other—but had not yet caused any springs to break open and flood the land. In that view sat Envy, or the envious souls.

It was as if Leonardo was not only presenting the idea of the miracle of Moses splitting the sea, but also presenting a scientific solution to explain it. Like he was offering possibilities to what may have actually taken place. And maybe the viewer would see what they wanted to believe—the faithful would see the divine miracle, atheists would see a natural phenomena, and the agnostics would be open to both interpretations. Or maybe Leonardo was fascinated with how details in his art were perceived. A philosophy of mind.

With so many references coming together, it was hard to consider them coincidences rather than allusions. What was *not* plausible was that Leonardo was too incompetent to paint the horizon correctly.

Whatever the reason(s), the line from the wall carvings scene in *The Comedy* said it all—"... Another story on the rock [was] imposed. ..."

As I read God's instructions to Moses, I noticed that strangely, detail by detail, *Mona Lisa* began to fit the Bible's description of the Ark. The connection seemed so unreal I was sure I was finally just seeing things, that I had lost my mind and was imagining it all.

Mona Lisa as *The Ark of the Covenant? Really?*

I was a working artist, not Harrison Ford playing Indiana Jones. I had to be kidding myself. But references were references. Did the painting really represent, in part, the Ark of the Covenant? It was Leonardo, after all. Sure, Leonardo, like he had done with *The Comedy*, used wordplay from Exodus to dress *Mona Lisa* with the same details describing the Ark. To carry the Ark, Moses is told to "let two rings be on the one side, and two on the other," and "make bars also of setim wood [to put] ... through the rings that are in the sides of the ark ..." (Exod. 25.12-14).[13] On each side of *Mona Lisa*, Leonardo painted a brown column with two decorated rings.

Facing each other on the Ark would also be "two cherubims of beaten gold, on the two sides of the oracle" (25.18).[14] Envy couldn't be an oracle, but Beatrice could be if Leonardo intended for that to help fit the description. At least one cherub was present—two, if both Ezekiel's and St. John's description were considered. Two versions, two cherubim.

I also thought that while Mona's face helped form Ezekiel's cherub, the ape face might fit the other cherub since St. John alludes to a face that is sort of like a man's, but not necessarily human. This made the idea of two cherubim more plausible since it showed the cherubim facing each other (the female figure and the ape face are close to facing each other), fitting the instructions Moses was given. And maybe the cherubim didn't look to be made of *beaten gold*, but the figure's sleeves are gold. And I knew from my years as a graphic designer at the jewelry store that real gold reflected colors of browns and reds.

The Ark was also to be covered in "curtains of fine twisted linen ... diversified with embroidery" (Exod. 26.1). The twisted fabric over *Mona Lisa*'s left shoulder looked like it could be *fine linen*. There were more details, like the curtains used to "cover the back parts of the tabernacle" (26.12).[15] *Mona Lisa*'s back seemed to be fully covered in curtain-like material—as far as I could tell, anyway.

Leonardo must have also used clues from the description of Aaron's vestment to help allude to Moses and the Ark, such as Aaron's "girdle of embroidered work," which is how Leonardo dressed *Mona Lisa*. The embroidered loop-pattern on her chest follows a description in Exodus of "loops of violet in the sides and tops of the curtains, that they may be joined one to another" (Exod. 26.4).[16] The painting shows a continuously joined loop pattern.

So much was going on in that painting. Clues alluding to the Ark's existence were there all along, yet, no one ever saw it. As I read the instructions given to Moses, I had to shake off the odd comparison of how the same could be said of God. *There all along, yet no one ever saw it.*

But I knew that was different—there really was no proof of God. Was there?

Just as there was no proof of Mona Lisa*'s identity? Until I knew how to look.*

I needed to cool off. I was only trying to understand the mysteries of a painting, not the mysteries of the universe. But I couldn't help my curiosity about it all.

There was one more thing I couldn't ignore if there really were two cherubim present. In Exodus, God tells Moses that he will speak to him from between the two cherubim on the Ark. Was *Mona Lisa* acting as the Word of God?

Moses was undoubtedly there in *Mona Lisa*, but Leonardo put a scientific twist on it by showing that an earthquake may have "split" the sea, not divine power.

I liked that thought. It was a realistic possibility. And it reaffirmed what I felt: that Leonardo's painting was an act of *self-expression*. He didn't spend all those years painting some plain Florentine wife with no eyebrows, as scholars had been preaching. It's why there was never any record that the painting existed as a commission piece. Because it wasn't a commission. It was something much greater.

The painting looked like a vague work of art at first, but it was exactly the opposite. Leonardo devoted so much of his life to making that portrait, and it seemed to express some of his most profound thoughts. Even if the Church and possibly his patrons preferred he stay quiet.

I wondered, did Leonardo and I share some of the same thoughts—that maybe there had been a woman named Mary and a man named Moses, but that their stories had been exaggerated over time, like legends eventually accepted as facts? That the truth had a scientific explanation? That Mary didn't ascend into heaven, and that Moses never parted the sea? Still, the stories and the painting built around them were beautiful and powerful. *Mona Lisa* became one of the most meaningful paintings I had ever seen. I couldn't get enough of it.

But there was still one thing missing in the painting.

Of the three marble carvings Dante is shown in Purgatory, two appeared in the painting—the first of the Virgin Mary, and the second showing the Ark of the Covenant. So where was Emperor Trajan? It was logical to think the third image of the Emperor on his horse with a widow crying for the son she lost to battle would be represented also. In fact, I had no doubt it *had* to be there somewhere.

For months I looked around the painting for clues of Emperor Trajan's presence. However, I found none. I researched Trajan's history, his accomplishments, his life. I looked for things that would connect him to the sin of envy. And to the Virgin Mary.

Still, nothing in *Mona Lisa* seemed to point to him.

But I knew Leonardo portrayed him in some way.

The more I saw into the subtlety, the complexity, the richness of his art, the more hungry I became to fully understand each and every detail, every allusion, every aspect. I was so sure Trajan was there, literally staring me in the face. I could almost *feel* the delight Leonardo must have felt creating his wonderfully complex puzzles. What a detective writer he could have been, hiding clues, leaving hints, knowing that one day people would come along and try to unlock it all.

And what was so important about Emperor Trajan anyway?

Would this be the toughest clue yet, Leonardo?

The thought made me smile. Never had I been so sure of my purpose in life.

43

The Hidden Background

Everyone assumed the painting's bridge had been standing over a river. It was also assumed that only one bridge could be seen in the painting. Both ideas turned out to be wrong. The waterway beneath the bridge turned out to be the Fossa Traiani—now called the Fiumicino Canal—which shortened the shipping distance along the Tiber River between Rome and the Tyrrhenian Sea.

To the right of the canal in the art, mostly out of view outside the picture's frame, is the town of Fiumicino, with a nearby airport—coincidentally called Leonardo da Vinci International Airport. What can still be seen there—off to the right, outside of the painting—is where the artificial harbor of Ancient Rome used to be. Around 42 AD, Emperor Claudius formed the extending harbor to Portus that opened up to the sea. It was the heart of Rome's trade, for centuries prosperous with the activity of ships transporting materials such as salt, corn from Alexandria,[1] animals from Africa, even supplies for the Colosseum entertainment.

What can still be seen at the ancient harbor's location is a 2,000-year-old, man-made, hexagon-shaped body of water that Emperor Trajan had added that was able to receive large ships.[2]

Leonardo used the area's history to allude to Emperor Trajan in the painting. After seeing the allusions to the stone carvings of the Virgin Mary and Moses mentioned in *Purgatorio*, I knew Leonardo had to leave a clue connecting Emperor Trajan from the third carving in *Purgatorio*. The Fossa Traiani, the artificial waterway built under Emperor Trajan's instruction, had to be it. Together with the Tiber and the sea, the waterways surround the area of land to create the man-made island of Isola Sacra, bordered by Ostia to the south and Portus to the north.

Ostia was once "… the most important town on its stretch of coast, … a cosmopolitan town … [filled] with particularly fine marble and mosaic work, sculptures, and inscriptions."[3] But in time, Ostia and Portus suffered from the Roman Empire's decline, from plague, attacks, and pillages. Life in Ostia deteriorated. Its population dwindled. Ostia and Portus received less attention from Roman authority, and eventually were exploited for building materials by Pisa. Later, around the Renaissance period, Romans would plunder art from Ostia and take apart existing building structures to reuse elsewhere.[4] I could imagine the disgust artists of the period must have felt hearing or even witnessing the events. And maybe, something about that history explained just why Envy, with her back to Ostia, was facing Rome.

These days—where Portus once existed—Trajan's geometrical-shaped lagoon is filled with swaying reeds and the sounds of passing planes from the nearby airport. But the place I once thought couldn't exist, thinking it must have been an invention of Leonardo's mind, turned out to be real. Once again, Leonardo had shown me how to seek the truth, despite whatever belief I held. But as enlightening as *Mona Lisa* had been, learning of the location's history also saddened me.

Thinking further of Trajan's history with Rome, I wondered if it had connection to the columns Leonardo placed on either side of *Mona Lisa*. They reminded me of a famous monument constructed for Trajan around 107 AD. The shape of the columns looked like that of Trajan's Column in Rome, portraying his victories in the Dacian wars.[5] It wasn't an exact match. And only one monument existed, compared to the two columns showing in the painting. But the monument did represent Trajan's *two* victories. Still, I didn't see any clues to provide me a definite answer either way. Yet, considering everything else he did, I couldn't completely disregard the idea.

Sometimes, what seemed obvious could turn out to be a trick of the eye. *Mona Lisa*'s bridge was one of those tricks. It was always "known" to be the one and only bridge in the painting. Fanatics had searched for it, sure that it would lead to answers about the art's mysteries. Some had even claimed to have identified the bridge. To my surprise, I stumbled upon two more bridges.

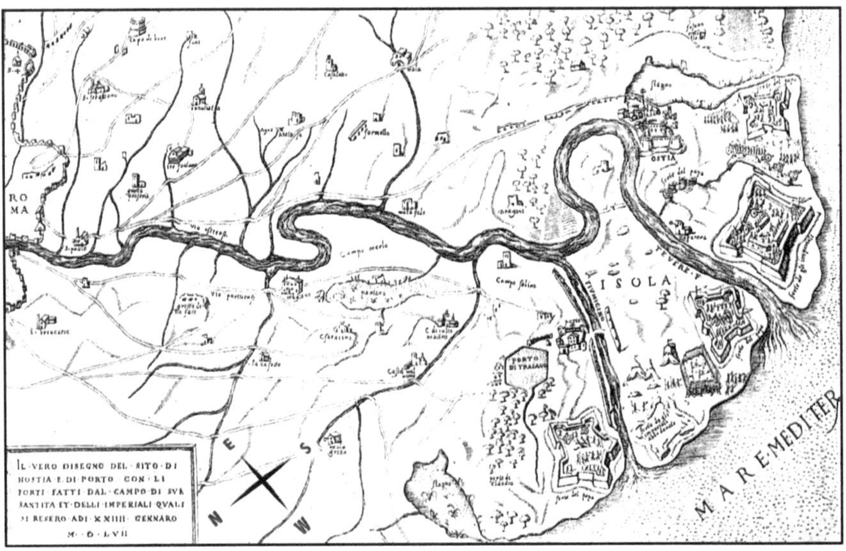

1557 map showing Portus, Ostia, Tiber River, and surrounding areas. Aerial view from the northwest. (Compass added.)

It wasn't something I was looking for, just something I realized when they appeared.

The second bridge was so obvious, it astounded me that it had never been seen before. Of everything I would find, it was probably the most shocking detail to have slipped by everyone's eyes. It wasn't even a hidden reference or allusion. It was literally right *there* for anyone to see. I noticed it as I was zoomed in very close to the painting's details. The structure, which had gone unnoticed (like so many other details), was part of the landscape, but too perfectly shaped to be formed naturally. It looked like part of a man-made wall, not too far from the first bridge, along the Fossa Traiani. What gave it away was its arch, barely visible, but visible nonetheless. Only half of the arch was showing, the other half disappearing off the canvas. Anyone could see the formation was man-made. Leonardo positioned it so that it would be missed unless looked at closely.

Just like everything else in the painting.

Why had no one ever seen this second bridge and pointed it out? I wondered.

Yes, it took me quite a few close examinations on a magnified version to catch it, but so many sets of eyes had seen the real painting up close. I thought maybe the frame had overlapped the painting's edge just enough to hide it from scholars, but that couldn't be the case. I remember seeing many images in old textbooks of the painting being studied without its frame. It was amazing that such an obvious detail had been missed.

So how would it connect back to *The Comedy*? After all, it had to come from the poem. After some searching, I saw that it did, taken from "the half arch of a bridge, ..." literally what Leonardo showed "... Between the two walls of the solid granite" (*Pur.* 19.42, 48; Longfellow).[6]

The third bridge wasn't easy to see. That bridge was alluded to.

In *Inferno*, the poets cross a series of bridges in Malebolge on their way through Hell. They are told by Malacoda, leader of the demons, that they "... Can no farther go / Forward upon this crag, because [the bridge] is lying / All shattered, at the bottom, ..." but "Near is another crag that yields a path" (*Inf.* 21.106-08, 111).[7] Sitting between the first and second bridge (*half arch*) was a neat pile of rocks. *Too neat.* The rocks rested like a set of fallen dominoes. It had to be the shattered bridge—*the sixth arch*—Malacoda pointed out.

Figuring out the bridges' connection to *The Comedy* was just part of it. Like the rest of the landscape, the bridges had to have existed at one time somewhere in the world, most likely Italy. *The Comedy*'s Beatrice was based on Dante's real-life love, Beatrice Portinari. Inferno's geography was based on real land. The Tyrrhenian Sea and the Tiber represented themselves from the real world and from *The Comedy.*

But the only bridge I could find along the Fiumincino Canal was built

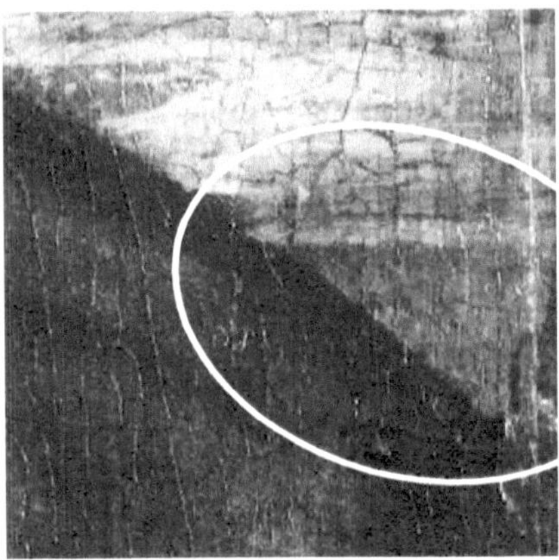
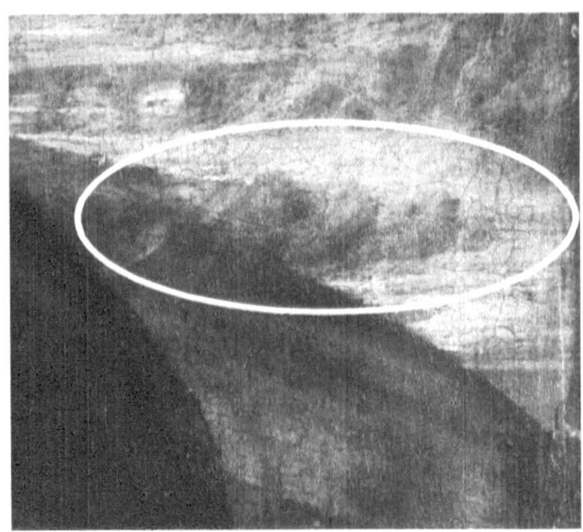

LEFT: Close-up of second bridge showing a half arch (circled). **RIGHT:** Possible fallen bridge (circled) from Inferno's Malebolge.

after Leonardo's time. So what bridge had he referenced?

I searched the surrounding area's history, but didn't find a definite answer. I was truly stumped. My best guess turned out to be a bridge called Pons Matidia (Bridge of Matidia) that one time crossed the canal.[8] It had been rebuilt in the fifth century after a fire destroyed it. But I also thought it was possible Leonardo took a bridge from another location. Either way, I had to move on. I knew that sooner or later, I'd come across the answer, just as many other answers had been revealed over time.

In addition to the second bridge (*the half arch*) were other details that went unnoticed. Above the bridge everyone was aware of looked to be the structure of a dome-shaped rock.

Its center was black and circular, which made it look hollow, like a cave, which is exactly what I thought it was. But a cave that led to where? Was it the entrance to Hell?

I wasn't sure, since I found no physical description of Hell's entrance in *The Comedy*. It later turned out the structure was instead Inferno's *exit*. To leave, the poets have to climb Lucifer's back, exiting the dark abyss by following the sound of a stream near the way out, "… Which not by sight is known, but by the sound / Of a small rivulet, that there descendeth / Through chasm within the stone, which it has gnawed …" (*Inf.* 34.129-31).[9]

They pass through the *chasm within the stone*, following the *hidden road* of a *small rivulet* until they are in reach of the exit, able to see Heaven's sky *through a round aperture* in the stone:

> The Guide and I **into that hidden road**
> Now entered, to return to the bright world;
> And without care of having any rest

We mounted up, he first and I the second,
Till I beheld **through a round aperture**
Some of the beauteous things that Heaven doth bear

(*Inf.* 34.133-38, emphasis added)[10]

The cave sat right along the canal (*small rivulet*) behind *Mona Lisa*'s figure, just above the bridge.

One bridge did appear along the Fiumincino Canal on a 1557 map, 50 years after *Mona Lisa* was painted. But what happened to it? Other bridges had also existed there at one time, but eventually collapsed or were destroyed somehow. It made sense that he'd use a bridge with more significance. Or one that was symbolic? A bridge from up the Tiber River on the way to Rome perhaps? Or could it have been an aqueduct, which Romans were ingenious in creating?

I looked to other works for help, but found nothing. I eventually narrowed it down to two strong possibilities. The first was that it could be Milvian Bridge, which Giulio Romano, with the assistance of Raphael, painted in *The Battle of the Milvian Bridge*. Dante references the battle in *Inferno*, in which the bridge marked Constantine's conversion to Christianity. Professor Pasquale had pointed out that Constantine entrusted his power to the Church, which, under an Empire, made Rome feel like Hell on Earth. I couldn't be sure, but considering the battle's importance in history, it felt like a decent guess, especially when I noticed that the painting's bridge forms the eye of the crocodile-serpent's head in the anamorphic illusion. The eye felt symbolic of the envious. After all, envy is derived from the sight of desired objects.

My second guess at the bridge's identity was the Ponte Sant'Angelo in Rome. In *Inferno*, Dante references the Roman bridge when he reaches Malebolge and sees that "filling the first ditch / along both banks, new souls in

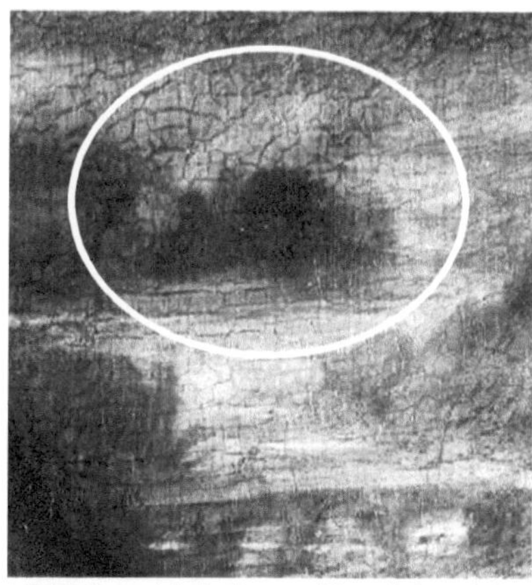

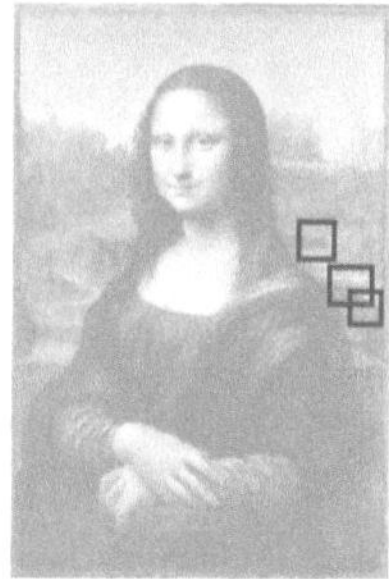

LEFT: Cave (circled), possible exit from Inferno. **RIGHT:** Image key showing locations of second bridge, fallen third bridge, and cave.

pain appeared, / new torments, and new devils black as pitch" (*Inf.* 18.22-24; Ciardi).[11] He compares the naked sinners to pilgrims visiting Rome "in the year of the Jubilee …" (18.29),[12] proclaimed by Pope Boniface VIII in the year 1300—the same year *The Comedy*'s story takes place. The souls are compared to how pilgrims visited Rome to be granted indulgences, traveling "so that all face the Castle as they go / on one side toward St. Peter's, while on the other / all move along …" (18.31-33)[13] to exit the Ponte Sant'Angelo.

Studying photos of the bridge, I saw that *Mona Lisa*'s bridge did resemble Ponte Sant'Angelo, except for the tall statues of angels that currently decorated the length of the bridge. But further research showed they were added in the seventeenth century—after Leonardo's (and Dante's) time.

The more I considered it, the more sure I was that I had figured out the identity of that bridge. What Dante witnesses in Hell's Malebolge (when he references the Ponte Sant'Angelo), in which he sees "new souls" with "new torments" held a strong comparison to the idea of Christian pilgrims—*new souls*—crossing the Ponte Sant'Angelo to visit St. Peter's to be granted indulgences for their sins—*new torments*—during the Jubilee. A Roman bridge with history of a pilgrimage to reduce one's punishment in Purgatory couldn't be any more perfect for the painting Leonardo made.

Of course, there was always a possibility of another explanation to the bridge's identity.

44

Beasts

Pasquale asked if he could meet with me again. He had a thought he wanted to share about why Renaissance artists were hiding images.

"So what Leonardo was *really* saying was that her boyfriend was a weasel," Pasquale said, chuckling.

I thought about it for a moment. "Maybe *she* was the weasel? Or her boyfriend—the weasel—was in the palm of her hands? Who knows?"

We met at the same Starbucks as our first meeting. Pasquale drank from a lidless cup of coffee—black, as far as I could tell.

We were looking at *Lady with an Ermine* on my phone—a portrait Leonardo painted of Cecilia Gallerani, mistress to Ludovico Sforza, Duke of Milan. In the portrait, Cecilia was holding a weasel in her arms as if it were a pet. What sat in the back of my mind was that *Lady with an Ermine* had fit Giorgio Vasari's description of *Mona Lisa* better than any of Leonardo's other works when I had checked many months before. Some scholars thought Vasari was describing another painting rather than the *Mona Lisa* that was now in Paris, but I had more important things to figure out.

"I still don't see how they used obvious imagery like this weasel without getting in trouble," I said. "If Leonardo was caught calling the Duke's mistress a weasel, there'd be hell to pay. Maybe a public torturing. How could the Duke miss such an obvious symbol?"

"That's why I asked to meet. You know," he said, "maybe you shouldn't be looking to Italian history for your answer."

"Where should I look?"

"Soviet history."

"What's the connection to Italy?" I said, confused.

"Nothing. But in a lot of ways artists there faced the same kind of situation."

"How so?"

"Solzhenitsyn. The writer and dissident. You've heard of him, right?"

"Not really," I said.

"He was critical of the government. Brutal, actually. He was exiled."

Exiled like Dante was from Florence, I thought.

"Because of his political view?" I asked.

"My point is that even though Solzhenitsyn was exiled, no one would talk about his work or mention him by name out of fear of the penalties they'd receive. But, everyone in the USSR knew his name. You could even buy his books—under the table. There was no mystery about what he had to say. He was a very popular author in the country. Even people in power read his work and knew about him."

"So you think everyone knew about the secret images and what they meant, but no one wanted to talk about it?"

"I wouldn't find it hard to believe."

Feeling like I could trust Pasquale to keep it quiet, I decided to tell him about Dante's connection to the hidden images. Without telling him too much, I thought he might be able to offer valuable information. Plus, I enjoyed our discussions. He seemed just as intrigued as I was. He wasn't surprised at all when I mentioned how everything seemed to tie back to Dante's *Comedy.*

"It would make sense that they wouldn't want to openly acknowledge Dante," I said, "since he was throwing popes and corrupt patrons into Hell. Maybe it was taboo, in the same way most people would never mention anything about assassinating a political leader, no matter how they felt. Except, everyone seemed to know about Michelangelo's fascination with reading Dante. Especially since he placed a scene from *The Divine Comedy* in his *Last Judgement* fresco. And Botticelli did a whole series of Dante illustrations. I don't think that was a secret."

"Maybe the boy had guts. Maybe he was pulled aside and told to cut it out. Who commissioned the illustrations anyhow?"

"I think he drew them for himself."

"He create a lot of Dante art?"

"Just Dante's portrait, a map of Hell, and the illustrations I think was all."

Pasquale shrugged. "The thing is, Renaissance Italy wasn't a totalitarian state. It wasn't like the Church tried to control *everything.* Savonarola may have leaned in that direction. But mostly, the Church and Mob wanted you to look like you were going along with the program. Not rock the boat."

"Some artists like rocking the boat."

"Which is why some paintings ended up in Savonarola's bonfire. The rest got the message."

I thought of what it would be like to destroy my own art, but knew I wouldn't be able to do it. Any art I created but didn't like went into storage, where no one else could see it. Destroying my work would be like taking a sledgehammer to my own car, or burning down my own house. Once, a girl I dated found out about a portrait of an ex-girlfriend I had made, and it caused several arguments between us. She couldn't understand what the painting meant to me and why I still had it hanging in my living room, that it had nothing to do with my ex, and that I felt nothing for the girl in the picture. It was a token of the heart and soul I put into creating it, and also a physical substance of how much better I had gotten since my previous work, a reminder of what I had learned in the experience of that particular painting.

I knew destroying the portrait would resolve the issue of our fights (I wouldn't be able to simply throw it away for someone to find—it would probably require some ceremonial destruction by my own hands), but I couldn't bring myself to consider the idea. So I wrapped the painting to conceal the image and hid it deep in the back of my attic, hoping it would never be seen.

"I could never destroy my own art. Between Savonarola and the Church, I'm not sure what I'd do. Those hidden images are making more sense though. I hate to admit this, but in the famous portrait of Pope Julius II, I found that Raphael painted the folds of his skirt in a way so it forms a female body part. The Pope looks like he's having fun with himself, *if* you know what I mean." *Which explained why scholars thought his expression looked a little odd.*

Pasquale laughed. "I'll bet that isn't the only painting out there like that."

"Believe me, it's not."

I was almost embarrassed to admit how artists of the high Renaissance painted such childish and daring images, but it became pretty obvious once I spotted them. In one of his anatomical drawings of the female genitalia, Leonardo had drawn what I could only call *The Screaming Vagina*, which made sense considering his assumed preference for men.

Pasquale looked thoughtful for a second.

"You know," he said, "There was some animal symbolism in those days that we are aware of."

"That we know of?"

"I should have thought of this earlier, but the Four Evangelists were commonly symbolized by a lion, ox, bull, and winged man," he said.

"You mean like the cherubs in the Bible?"

"Not exactly, although there are similarities. Anyway, the Pope you mentioned, with the vagina skirt—maybe he *did* notice it in his portrait, but couldn't get angry because he didn't want to bring attention to it. Kind of like the story of *The Emperor's New Clothes*."

"Never heard of it."

"Really? Well, a couple tailors convince the Emperor that the clothes they've made for him are invisible to anyone unfit to be

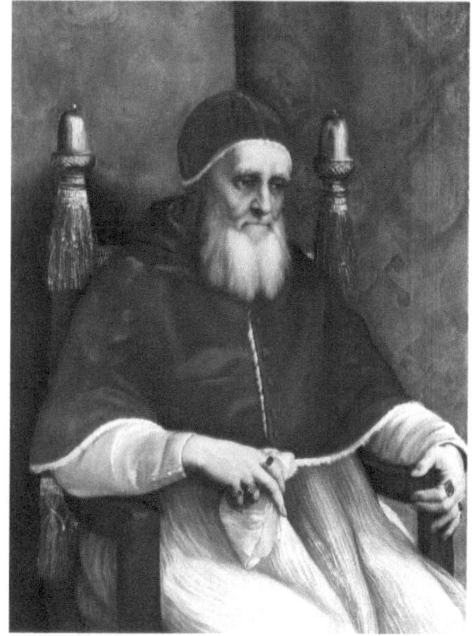

Raphael's *Portrait of Pope Julius II* (1511-12).

Emperor, so he has no choice but to pretend he can see them. In reality, he ends up walking around naked, too dignified to admit he can't see he's wearing anything at all."

"Sounds like an idiot."

"Maybe. People may pretend not to see what they do see because it's just easier that way," Pasquale said. "For the Pope to be mocked by an artist like Raphael would have been a true embarrassment. If you started layering those symbols one on top of the other you could make some very subtle … statements. Or maybe 'creations' would be a better word. People in the know would have fun trying to figure out their meanings. Sort of like those British mysteries."

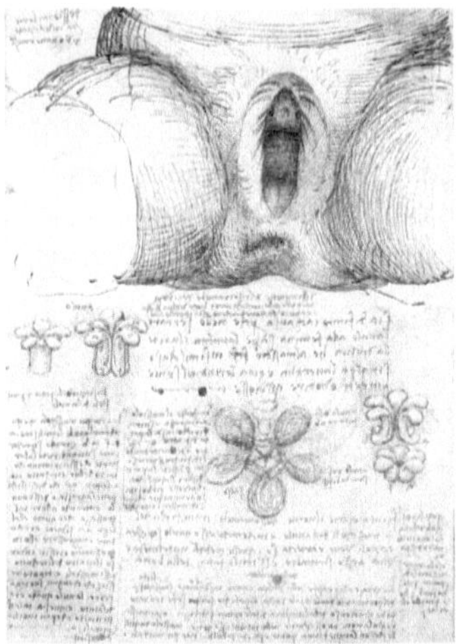

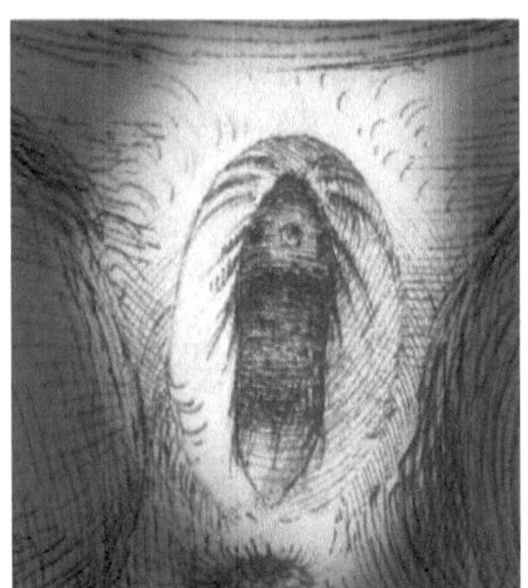

TOP: Leonardo's sketch of female reproductive system (c. 1508-09). **BOTTOM:** Close-up showing Leonardo's humorous side.

"You think people besides artists knew about the hidden pictures?"

He shrugged again. "Some probably did. Some may have even protected the artists. If a pope thought one of his cardinals was a jackass, he might give an artist a bonus to hide a jackass head into the Bishop's portrait. Plenty of people in power disliked each other. Florence wasn't a totalitarian sort of place back then. It wasn't *1984.* Half the art historians writing about art nowadays call our time period 'Late Capitalism,' but Renaissance Florence was more like Late totalitarianism. The Church *had* been in control, and *had* tried to compel total agreement, internal agreement, on its essential beliefs. But, like the USSR, leadership became lazy and corrupt, and criminal organizations were becoming new power groups all their own, and states were preparing to break away. Like Protestant states preparing to break from Catholicism. There were real similarities.

"Near the end, Soviet artists and writers could say a lot, but there were things they couldn't say. They would write novels about World War II and denounce fascist oppression. Except, they would describe it in ways that perfectly described Soviet oppression. Or they'd write science fiction and criticize brutal dystopias in other worlds—that looked a lot like the one they were living in. You could *suggest.* You could *slip things in.* But you had to camouflage it enough to get it under official radar."

"After the government fell, why didn't writers point all this out?"

"Not every Communist government fell," Pasquale said. "To this day, you still can't mock the Communist leadership in China and North Korea. And once they *did* fall, why go back and point out the hidden criticism you were making back then when you could finally criticize it out loud?"

He sipped his coffee and gave me a look. "You really think they were hiding stuff left and right?"

"If they weren't, then I'm as nuts as that Emperor with his new clothes."

He thought about it for a minute, and laughed. "That's why people hide things—they don't want them to be found."

"Sometimes they hide things so they can be found," I said.

As a graphic designer, it was sometimes difficult to keep up with the amount of revisions I received from clients. Over the years, as I learned what the client wanted exactly, creating the art became less of a challenge, at times making me feel like I knew them better than they knew themselves. The amount of revisions they requested seemed to decrease over time, and I began to receive minor comments about microscopic details. I was sure I was supplying the client exactly what they wanted, but that they still felt the need to provide some kind of feedback.

Surprisingly, I began to miss the challenge of my earlier days when impossible deadlines hung over my head like a guillotine. The pressure forced me to create my best work, like a clutch player with seconds left on the clock. Eventually, I hit a plateau, no longer growing as an artist. I no longer felt challenged. I was no longer questioned about my concepts the way I had been earlier in my career. Bosses, such as creative directors and account executives, were putting more trust in my ideas. But I no longer felt like I had anything to prove to myself. I had mastered the skills to artistically satisfy clients. Everything became the same old, same old. My only concern was keeping clients from interfering with my artwork (as if it was *my* art even though they were paying to have it made).

I didn't think clients were capable of approving designs without altering them out of personal taste or emotions instead of objectively considering the purpose of the art (usually to promote a product or service). In my career, I had my share of frustration from clients who thought they knew more than they did about what their art should look like.

So I tried to manipulate their thoughts. My objective was to keep them from ruining my designs with meaningless revisions. Once I got the art to a point I thought looked best, I would add extra imagery or alter colors I knew the client would request to be changed or removed. It was a way of satisfying their need to request some kind of revision to the art—which I believed they needed in order to feel some kind of control over the art—so I would end up with the art the way I wanted it.

I couldn't help snickering one day when my account executive explained the revisions the client wanted.

"What's so funny, weirdo?" she asked me. (We bantered regularly.)

"I knew they would request that change," I said proudly.

"Well then, why didn't you do it before sending it to everyone?" she scoffed.

I explained my plan as if it was an ingenious idea no one had thought of before.

"You mean dead-dogs?" she said.

"What?"

"Adding things you know the client will take out," she said. "You think you're the first to think of that idea, silly bird?"

Actually, I did think that until she corrected me.

"Why do you call it a dead-dog?" I asked.

"What would you do if you saw a dead dog on your property?"

"Remove it."

After Pasquale left, I sat there with my coffee, watching students come and go, thinking of all the puzzle pieces I had so far, and how they fit together.

There were references to creatures in *The Divine Comedy*, the Bible, in writings like those of Machiavelli; there was hidden imagery going back as early as the Middle Ages with Giotto, and stretching centuries later—yet I wasn't sure if there was any kind of connection to later artists like Ingres that came after the seventeenth century or if it was purely coincidence that Ingres had anamorphic imagery in his art. But one day, I had a real breakthrough about what the animals might be. It came in a scene in *Inferno*, where the punishment of the Hypocrites is to wear beautiful, glimmering coats lined on the inside with heavy lead, making it difficult for them to move around.

The coats reminded me of the two men in Holbein's *Ambassadors*, both stylishly dressed in full, thick-looking coats. Referenced in the scene is a fable like that of the fox and eagle I had come across, except that it involves a frog and mouse, which Dante is reminded of after seeing two demons fall into a boiling pond as they fight over an escaping sinner.

My mind went back to *The Ambassadors* at the mention of the fable. It wasn't just the painting's images I had found of what looked like a rodent or mink in the first figure's coat and an amphibian in the second figure's that reminded me of Holbein's artwork. It was also the coats that the Hypocrites' are forced to wear.

Dante only references the fable, but I was quick to look it up, leaving no stone unturned. In the tale, a frog invites its mouse-friend over for a meal across the pond after the rodent offered to share its food supply with the frog. Unable to swim, the mouse is guided by the frog across the water after they tie themselves together. But the treacherous frog decides to drown the mouse halfway across in order to take its food supply. The commotion made while drowning catches the attention of a kite, who swoops down to capture it as food. But the frog, bound to the mouse, is carried off to share the same fate: "Upon the fable of Aesop was directed / My thought, by reason of the present quarrel, / Where he has spoken of the frog and mouse …" (*Inf.* 23.4-6; Longfellow).[1] It's the fable's writer who was the real breakthrough, who Dante credits as Aesop. I learned that he had been a Greek storyteller and also a slave who told fables using animals and inanimate objects with human characteristics. Born in 620 BC, his fables have been shared for over two millennia.

His stories would end with a moral lesson. I knew of such fables as *The Tortoise and the Hare*, *The Boy Who Cried Wolf*, and *The Goose that Laid the Golden Egg*, but never realized that they originated with Aesop. Even though he lived long ago, I thought of how we still sometimes described one another as beasts: a wicked *dog*; a cold-blooded *snake*; a dirty *pig*.

Was that the answer? Animals with human characteristics? Or rather humans with animalistic traits?

Considering the analogies in Dante's writings, I strongly believed it had to be the meaning behind all the animal heads. It made sense why I kept spotting mostly just the heads—I believed it symbolized the corrupted minds—the psyche—of the sinful. But were they also representing virtuous qualities at times? I couldn't be sure since not all of the characters in Aesop's stories had evil intent, such as the innocent mouse who wanted to share its food supply with the frog.

To help answer the question of why I was finding mostly images of heads, I looked to the *Dictionary of Symbols.* By then, I had a better understanding of the context of the images. One of the examples it gives is of the statue in Notre Dame showing the first Bishop of Paris, martyr St. Denis. In Christian iconography, the depiction of a saint carrying its own head would

> symbolize the belief that the executioner has been unable to deprive his victim of life, that St. Denis continues to live and move spiritually and that through the spirit he masters the power of death. The victim's spirit, symbolized by his or her head, not only lives, but continues to be carried on Earth by those who share the same faith as it was by the martyr.[2]

Maybe the idea also applied to the souls in Hell and Purgatory who carried their sinful characteristics with them from the living world and continued "to live and move spiritually" in those realms of the dead.

Yet, although Aesop's fables, along with the description in the *Dictionary of Symbols*, seemed to help explain the heads of animals, I wasn't sure if it applied to the human-like heads I found. In *Aesop, Five Centuries of Illustrated Fables*, John J. McKendry explains that the fables, "sometimes told with no comment, …" are meant to teach a moral lesson, warning the reader "either to emulate or to beware of the behavior of the actors when faced with a similar situation," and that the actors are sometimes "inanimate objects given the power of speech, but most often they are animals."[3] In *Mona Lisa*'s case, inanimate mountains became the heads of animals, possibly representing spirits from *The Comedy* that were likened to creatures like the ape, frog, and ox. I came to believe that artists chose to hide faces within the garments of figures since the elaborate amounts of folds (characteristic of Renaissance art) offered an ideal place to disguise images, and because folds could be manipulated to hide objects while still maintaining a natural look to what figures wore, though I didn't yet understand the symbolism of their location in the clothing.

"There are seldom more than three characters, … [and] the illustrations do not explain themselves …" without a story, McKendry explains, adding that "[Aesop's] talent for telling fables enabled him to make fools of his masters. …"[4] It's possible artists were mocking or shaming figures in power, such as political officials or religious leaders, but I still wasn't sure what the animals specifically meant or who they represented. Still, I felt confident that their broad meaning was Aesopic.

Interestingly, his fables were first published in Italy and Germany "between 1476 and 1479 … [and included] simply drawn [animals] with a minimum of background, a tree perhaps, or a cluster of buildings if the setting is urban."[5] *Or a vague, rocky background of mountains, water, and a bridge behind the portrait of a mysterious woman*, I thought to myself.

In Titian's case, I found that trees were literally used to hide animals like the elephant and ape head in his *Pastoral Concert*.

The earliest concealed animal heads I found in Leonardo's art—specifically horse heads—were drawn in the late 1470s, making sense of the timeline when printed editions of Aesop's fables were available to him (although he may have been aware of the stories beforehand). In fact, a book on Aesop's fables was listed in Leonardo's possessions. Leonardo even wrote his own fables, and his notebooks contain bestiary writings taken from ancient books he owned, such as the peaceful beaver, the angry bear, and the greedy toad. In his notes are adaptations taken from Pliny's *Natural History*, comparing animal traits to those of mankind:

> The great elephant has by nature qualities which are rarely found in man, namely honesty, prudence, a sense of justice, and of religious observance. … And when they are ill they throw themselves upon their backs and toss up plants toward heaven as though they wished to offer sacrifice. [And] they bury their tusks when they drop out from old age.[6]

The description reminded me of the elephant shrouded in Michelangelo's *Fall and Expulsion from Garden of Eden*, lying on the ground as if dead, its upward pointed tusk made from the tree branch buried in the ground.

It made sense that artists like Leonardo and Michelangelo were aware of Aesop. But I wondered how Giotto knew about the fables when he lived a couple centuries before books on Aesop were available in Italy. He was a "very great friend ..." of Dante,[7] who was obviously familiar with Aesop. Surely, as friends, they could have discussed the fables. Was it possible the artist and the poet together came up with the idea of hiding images? It was just a guess. Although, in relation to the wordplay technique I was sure artists used to create secret images from Dante's writings, Giotto may have been the pioneer.

Vasari described Giotto as "sharp-witted, ... always ready with a witty remark, ..." pointing out the dialogue of the time in which "we can be reminded of the phrases and modes of speech used in those days."[8] In a separate story involving Giotto, Vasari tells of the king of Naples, who was very fond of Giotto, and "wanted to make him the first man in Naples. ..." Responding to the king, "... Giotto retorted that he was already the first man in Naples, since he was living at the very gates of the city by the Porta Reale." In another banter, the king also said to the artist: "If I were you I would leave off painting for a while, now it's so hot," to which "Giotto answered: 'And so would I, if I were you.'"[9] It wasn't difficult to imagine a man like Giotto, getting together with Dante, developing the idea of secret wordplay in art.

In Gustave Doré's illustrations of Aesop's fables, McKendry points out, "the animals move in a murky sinister world, very like the world of his *Inferno* illustrations. ..."[10] The version of *The Comedy* I had been mostly referring to had been illustrated by Doré. It looked like I finally had my answer to the heads' meanings—at least one that sounded convincing and left me satisfied.

Maybe each artist had his own reason for hiding them. Maybe Michelangelo thought his art would be completely seen and understood by God alone—and that was enough. Maybe he gloried in the use of anamorphic techniques simply because he was Michelangelo, and wanted to prove to himself that he could do any technique better than any competitor. Maybe because Leonardo was in love with secret codes and puzzles, he arranged clues for someone to connect the dots between his writings about the d-point and his paintings. Maybe Holbein—a Protestant free from the Church—painted his anamorphic skull to demonstrate that he was free from the popes and the Church, and didn't have to fear hiding images, even though he still did that too. Or perhaps he couldn't shake off concealing images in *The Ambassadors*, simply as a tribute to the Italian Renaissance artists who inspired him.

Maybe the technique of hidden anamorphosis eventually died out after the Renaissance. Or perhaps the images simply weren't hidden anymore as the fear of being persecuted had dissipated. Painters like Ingres were now free to openly reference the technique or the era in plain sight. Or was it that a new technique had been developed to replace that of hidden anamorphosis?

45

The Ambassadors

In its own way, Holbein's *Ambassadors* is as enigmatic as *Mona Lisa*, baffling historians with its mysteries. I felt the two masterpieces were connected somehow, particularly because of the anamorphic skull and other images that Holbein hid in the art—like the frog and mouse from Aesop's fable. In addition, King Francis was known to have connections with both Leonardo and Holbein.

Why did Holbein make the skull so obvious, dragging the technique 'out of the closet' and throwing it in everyone's face? He never gave a reason, and no one could explain its meaning with certainty, but there were too many coincidental links to *The Comedy*.

Holbein wasn't from Florence like many of the other artists hiding illusions. In fact, he wasn't even Italian—he was a German painter.

Leonardo spent the last part of his life in a small chateau in France working for King Francis. The two apparently became such close friends that Vasari wrote of how the King held Leonardo in his arms when the artist died. The story is said to be only a legend, but French artist Jean-Auguste-Dominique Ingres used it to create *The Death of Leonardo da Vinci*. Coincidentally, that had been the first painting I noticed containing the hidden anamorphic illusion of an *entire* horse—which was completely different from just the heads I had spotted in Italian Renaissance works of art. Ingres's painting was created in 1818, exactly three hundred years after Leonardo's death—the number caught my attention since the number three had such divine significance in *The Comedy*.

It's likely Holbein never met Leonardo, but Holbein *was* thought to have visited France before 1533, and was believed to be looking for work in the court of King Francis. Whether he did or not, one of the two men pictured in *The Ambassadors* is believed to be Jean de Dinteville—who had been an ambassador for France while Francis I was king. The other man in the portrait, Georges de Selve, was Bishop of Lavaur of France.

So how did Holbein learn of the secret illusions?

Could the King's ambassador have known about Leonardo's anamorphic techniques? Could other people in the King's court have known or spoken with Leonardo about his techniques, and passed the secrets on to Holbein? Or had Holbein, one of the greatest artists of the age, simply studied Leonardo's work and seen the subtle hidden images his legendary predecessor left behind?

Did he somehow see Dante's references and inspiration because he read and knew Dante's work also? I thought Holbein's skull may have tied back to several scenes in *The Comedy*, and it was also possible that it contained several meanings from several stories, as was the case with *Mona Lisa* and *Venus and Mars*.

The more I saw the mysteries deepen, the more connections I found between what were believed to be unrelated works of art. And the more intent I was to know the truth.

What exactly caused Leonardo to paint a portrait of Envy and Beatrice (and the Virgin), and Hell and Purgatory? Was it Pope Alexander VI—believed to be one of the most cruel and corrupt popes in history—that soured Leonardo's view? Was it Alexander's son, Cesare Borgia, who expanded his power by war, and had forced Leonardo into service as his chief military engineer? Working for Borgia, the peaceful artist had been exposed to the horrific acts of violence and murder Borgia was famous for.

In *The Artist, the Philosopher, and the Warrior*, author Paul Strathern explains that "something within [Leonardo] had changed forever during his eight months working for Borgia. … [A] more profound psychological change … had taken place as a result of his terrifying experiences with [the general]."[1]

Strathern's words sent such a chill through me. Sometimes I'd think back and wonder how my life would be if John had never died that day at work many years before, if I had never found myself standing over his contorted, lifeless body, if instead the day was just like any other. Would I have learned to value just how precious life was? Would I have been able to move on from my marriage and subsequent divorce? Or would I have remained too weak and naive to understand how short life could be, and struggled to fix our relationship as our months or years on Earth wasted away? Would I have moved on from the job I dreaded, where the parking lot reminded me only of that cold February day, time marked by the days, weeks, and months that had passed since the accident? As I fought through depression, that scene served as the catalyst that later drove me to leave my pessimistic view of the world around me behind, vowing never to use that lens again. I had previously blamed my general negativity on my father because of all the hopeless heart-to-heart conversations we'd had in which he would seem to show discontent for the choices I made toward my career, or the friends I hung out with, or how I spent my money, along with comments about how he loathed women, especially Ma. I later realized I had only myself to blame for any negativity I felt. It took time to break from the mold that had formed me since my childhood, and to adjust to an optimistic approach in life. The idea felt forced, but eventually my mind accepted it, and over the next few years, the lens I was so accustomed to using slowly changed—the world began to look different, brighter. I found peace within myself. I no longer prioritized my job over my family, my friends, my sanity and health. And through all that was my love of art, and the importance of finding someone to share all of that with. My empathy for others grew. Sad stories of other's misfortunes, which once left me indifferent, suddenly would leave me weeping, even those of strangers. Materialistic things I never cared much for appealed to me even less, as I *saw* that the real pleasures in life were the friends and family and people around me. But it was in oil painting where I found a truly magnificent new joy.

And then *Mona Lisa* entered my life. Working to figure out the answers to her mysteries caused me to examine my own life, one in which Leonardo helped me realize the true meaning as well. I felt like I truly understood him. So it pained me to read about his experiences under Cesare Borgia.

Leonardo was stuck with horrible memories after working for Borgia, Strathern explains, "the massacre he had witnessed at Fossombrone ..."[2] where "soldiers proceeded to pillage the town and massacre its inhabitants."[3]

In 1503, the following year, Leonardo began his sketches for *Mona Lisa*.[4] I began to understand exactly why Leonardo focused his painting on the sin of envy, and Hell with its corrupt souls. Images related to Borgia must have been on his mind as he painted its beasts, its crocodile-devil, hidden, like the dark side Borgia possessed, such as his ability to deceive enemies.

No question Renaissance Italy wasn't an easy place to live. So in 1516, when a young, twenty-something King Francis invited Leonardo, in his sixties, to leave Italy for the first time in his life and move to France,[5] Leonardo may have seen it as a way to live out the rest of his life in peace, away from the political darkness of the Italian Renaissance. The artist may have viewed the King as exceptionally tolerant of religious differences, a man with a desire for knowledge, and someone to share his views on life with, perhaps as a young Alexander the Great had with an older and wiser Aristotle.

Did Leonardo become so close with the King that he entrusted him with the secrets of what Italian artists were hiding, possibly showing him *Mona Lisa*'s illusions and how it was inspired by Dante? And did the king later pass the secrets on to artists like Holbein?

Less than seventeen years later, anamorphic art began to appear outside of Italian art for the first time, and with connections to King Francis. In 1533, Hans Holbein would display a skull as the first openly visible anamorphic image in a painting—one of a French ambassador and a French bishop. Two years later, a fellow German artist named Erhard Schön created two woodcut anamorphic picture puzzles, one that included a portrait of King Francis. Other German artists began using anamorphosis in the following years.[6]

Leonardo began *Mona Lisa* during some of the most dangerous years in Renaissance history. Holbein created *The Ambassadors* during some of the bloodiest years of the court under King Henry VIII. Both created works that were more *careful*, more rich in symbolism and ambiguity, and—aside from

Holbein's skull—concealed with hidden imagery. I sensed a connection there. Yet, Holbein's painting wasn't hiding the skull, and the piece practically invited the viewer to search for more hidden images. Both learned to conceal imagery. If not through some connection to King Francis, Holbein may have learned it by studying Leonardo's work closely. It was possible, anyway. Yet, I felt there had to be a more convincing answer.

Regardless, my intent was to figure out the meaning of *The Ambassadors*, beginning with the skull. I wondered if Holbein was showing his respect to the deceased Leonardo da Vinci. Oddly positioned and very close to the edge, the skull's shadow extends beyond the bottom of the canvas. Could it be some homage to Leonardo, who by then was lying in his grave? It seemed like a stretch, but I considered it a starting point.

John Ciardi explains in his translation of *The Comedy* that "Dante writes in depth. Though his language is normally simple, his thought is normally complex. But if the gold of Dante runs deep, it also runs right up to the surface. A lifetime of devoted scholarship will not mine all that gold. … [The reader] need only follow the vein as it goes deeper and deeper into the core of things."[7] The same seemed true of certain painters portraying *The Comedy*. The poem was a key to understanding many Renaissance artworks. In turn, the art was key to better understand *The Comedy*.

Starting with the use of the word "skull," I found that (in Longfellow's translation) Dante uses the word only twice—both at the end of *Inferno*. (I also searched synonyms like "brain" and "head," which appeared more than seventy times, but I strongly felt the artist would depict a skull from a line using that exact word.)

One scene references a story of Archbishop Ruggieri, who imprisoned Count Ugolino and his four sons and left them to starve to death. Unable to bear the pain of starvation, his son Gaddo begs his father to end his and his two brothers' lives by eating them, but the Count is unable to bring himself to murder his own sons. "And there [Gaddo] died; and, as thou seest me, / I saw the three fall, one by one …" (*Inf.* 33.70-71; Longfellow).[8] The Count can do nothing as they die one by one, his vision blinded from his own starvation. Desperate and dying from hunger, the Count eventually starts gnawing like a dog on his son's head: "When he had said this, with his eyes distorted, / The wretched skull resumed he with his teeth, / Which, as a dog's, upon the bone were strong" (33.76-78).[9] It was a possible connection to the painting's *distorted* view of the skull.

Just a few pages later, in a second scene using the word "skull," Dante is warned not to step on the exposed faces of the souls lying frozen in the ice. Holbein seemed to paint ambassador Jean de Dinteville, the left figure, close to stepping on the skull. Dante does end up kicking one of the heads, and learns it is a friar who had committed such a crime that his live body was stripped of its soul and taken over by a devil: "… Know that as soon as any soul betrays // As I have done, his body by a demon / Is taken from him, who thereafter rules it …" (*Inf.* 33.129-31).[10] The friar's soul was pulled to Hell—rushed down "into such a cistern …" (33.133), [11]while his old body in the living world above appeared to still be alive: "… And still perchance above appears the body / Of yonder shade, that winters here behind me. // … And still above in body seems alive!" (33.134-35, 157).[12] Could the skull symbolize the sinking of a soul into Hell, especially when described as if rushing down a cistern? The skull's downward-facing made me think so.

The scene also tells how "the sinners stand out in the cold" (*Inf.* 32.117),[13] which comes after the mention of the Hypocrites with their lead-heavy coats. Was that why Holbein painted the two men in their coats, with one holding a pair of gloves in his hand? Was he secretly calling them hypocrites for some reason?

The year Holbein created the painting—1533—stood out as a significant date to me because of *The Comedy*'s specific use of the number three. Three was also the number of the Trinity, a particularly significant number in Christian Europe. Still, I took the date at face value.

The real question looked to be why there wasn't a mystery like the other paintings—why wasn't the skull hidden at all? Was Holbein drawing attention to the skull in order to pull attention away from other hidden images and meaning in the painting? Sure enough, when I looked closer, plenty of anamorphic images were there. And like *Mona Lisa*, like *Venus and Mars*, like *Primavera*, like many other paintings, *The Ambassadors* revealed its story through Dante's *Comedy*.

There was the mouse and frog I previously found. The mouse hung lifelessly off Jean's coat, within its white fur. Georges's robe shows the head of a large frog, its puffy lips made from the lapel, wrapping around the man's neck, as if swallowing or licking the figure.

There was also the crocodile head edging downward toward Jean's right shoulder. Another head also appeared. Facing downward at Georges's right elbow is what I was sure was a duck head, its green head hidden in the pattern of the drapery, its gold bill made from the gold disk-like torquetum. It faced downward.

A duck just didn't seem to belong since it wasn't threatening like a lion or ape or even a hawk, yet *Mona Lisa* contained a duck along with a hawk. It seemed to verify the idea that, like the mouse the frog attempted to drown before becoming prey to a kite in Aesop's tale, not all the creatures represented sinful traits of mankind. The duck was mentioned just before Dante references Aesop: "Not otherwise the duck upon a sudden / Dives under, when the falcon is approaching, / And upward he returneth cross and weary" (*Inf.* 22.130-32).[14]

When I read that same canto again, that time with more focus on *The*

Ambassadors, a comparison of the souls to frogs in a ditch seemed to also describe Georges's robe: "... The frogs stand only with their muzzles out, / So that they hide their feet and other bulk, // So upon every side the sinners stood ..." (*Inf.* 22.26-28).[15] It's as if Holbein used those details to position the figures. Georges, on the right, holds his robe closed, hiding his *feet and other bulk* of his body. If he followed Dante's writings as Leonardo did, Holbein may have alluded to the figures as sinners—*upon every side the sinners stood.* Looking for hidden art, the d-point had previously revealed the large head of a mechanical-looking beast, which looked ready to attack Georges. Including a saddened man's face in the red of Jean's right sleeve, there were images hiding all over *The Ambassadors* painting.

Careful examination of the pattern in the green drapery while looking straight at the painting revealed not only the duck, but also a lion's head above the celestial globe, an ape head just to the right, then a horse head, and near the right edge, what looked like a woman's face.

It became obvious that the painting's meaning was linked to *The Comedy.* Items along the shelves, that no one had been able to explain, were alluding back to *Inferno*, *Purgatorio*, and *Paradiso.*

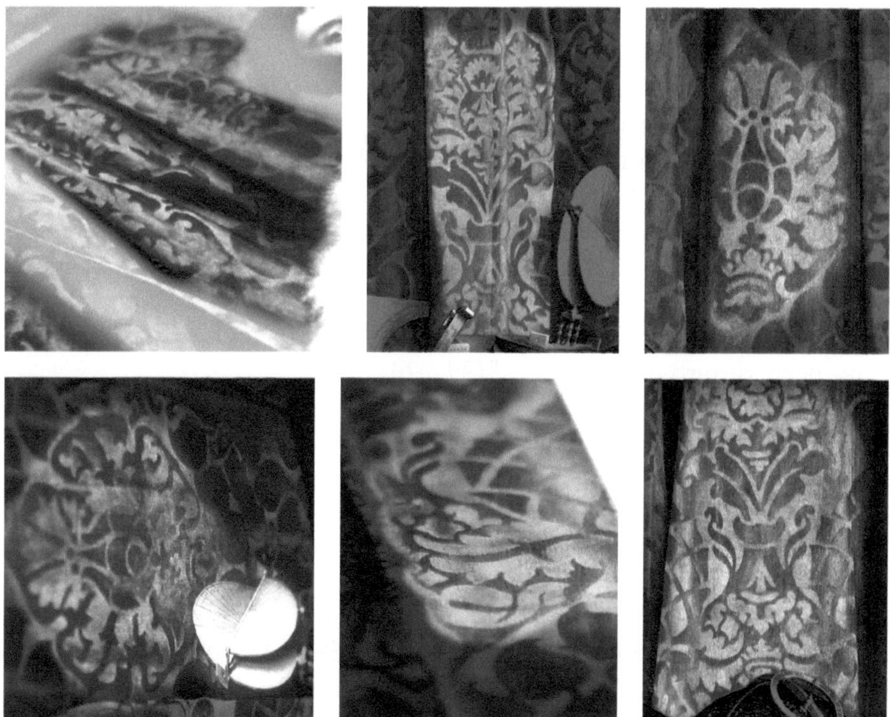

Hiding in *The Ambassadors*. **TOP ROW:** Anamorphic reptilian head, ambiguous illusions of a horse head and what could be the head of an ape. **BOTTOM ROW:** Anamorphic illusions of a duck head and female head, and an ambiguous illusion of lion head. All images highlighted.

Details from *Inferno* were used to create the wood shelves—details that came just after Dante accidentally kicks the friar's skull and sees two souls frozen close together in the icy lake. It took me some time to figure out Holbein's subtle clues. "Ye who so strain your breasts together, tell me, / … who are you …" (*Inf.* 32.43-44),[16] Dante calls to them, curious of their identity. "… Why dost thou so mirror thyself in us?" (32.54)[17] another responds. *The Ambassadors* figures not only were pressing their breasts against the shelves, but mirrored each other's posture. Like the other works of art, no one clue was a sure connection to *The Comedy*. But the assortment of many details, pieced together, linked the two. Dante poetically describes the two souls frozen in the ice: "Clamp never bound together wood with wood / So strongly; whereat they, like two he-goats, / Butted together …" (32.49-51).[18]

In Holbein's art, the two figures, or *he-goats*, were positioned like a set of clamps pressing together against each side of the wood shelves. How funny the idea was, I thought, like many of the clues artists used. It was all about wordplay. And who could have been more creative with wordplay than the brilliant minds of Renaissance artists?

Objects along the top of the *wood with wood* shelf were used to study the heavenly bodies. The lute with a broken string on the floor, and the case of flutes with one missing might symbolize Dante's mortality, at times unable to hear music in Purgatory for lack of divine vision.

Luckily, there were easier details to help reference it back to the story later in *Paradiso*. The celestial globe in the art, supported by little brass *ram heads*, was one of them, as was its *scale*, near the globe's *zenith*: "… Surmounted by the Ram and by the Scales, / Together make a zone of the horizon, // As long as from the time the zenith holds them …" (*Par.* 29.2-4).[19] The ram heads also were placed at the globe's horizon, holding the *girdle* that separated one *hemisphere* from the other. Holbein painted the globe exactly as Dante worded his lines: "… In equipoise, till from that girdle both / Changing their hemisphere disturb the balance …" (29.5-6).[20]

Making & Meaning Holbein's Ambassadors points out that the globe's latitude incorrectly shows Italy or Spain instead of correctly showing that of London.[21] Though, I was sure Holbein was pointing out Italy or Spain for a reason. He could have been displaying the place of origin of the secret images, or Dante's or Leonardo's homeland, or both Italy and Spain since, at the time, the southern half of Italy—the Kingdom of Naples—was controlled by the Spanish Empire.

The authors also point out that the shepherd's dial appears to show April 11. I realized that in 1533, April 11 fell on Good Friday. *The Comedy* began on Good Friday.

They also point out that the quadrant—which determines the sun's position from the horizon—appears to be upside down. I knew right away that it had to be a reference to *Inferno*, where Hell is an upside-down realm where no sun shines.

Comparing Holbein's painting to *The Comedy*, the clues fell like rain.

In the upper left of the painting, the half-covered crucifix likely ties back to a Dantean scene Botticelli also pointed to in *Venus and Mars.* In Paradise, "those who believed Christ was to come" are seated on one side. On the other "are those who looked to Christ already come."

Every detail had meaning. Even the floor's design. There were nine sets of circles—the amount of circles that divided Dante's Hell. Of course, that alone could be considered nothing but a possible coincidence by itself. So I looked further at the details to either confirm or reject the idea. If there was a connection, I knew I'd find it through wordplay. At first, I didn't think much about the figures' feet. Not until I came to the last canto of *Paradiso*, where Dante, captivated by the Eternal Light, is granted the vision of God. Within the Light are *three circles*, all *one dimension* and of slightly different colors:

> Within the deep and luminous subsistence
> Of the High Light appeared to me **three circles,**
> **Of threefold color and of one dimension,**
> And by the second seemed the first reflected
> As Iris is by Iris, and the third
> Seemed fire that equally from both is breathed.
>
> (*Par.* 33.115-120; Longfellow, emphasis added)[22]

In one of the circles Dante sees, the image of a man appears: "Seemed in Itself of Its own coloration / to be painted with man's image. I fixed my eyes / on that alone in rapturous contemplation" (*Par.* 33.130-32; Ciardi).[23] Both figures in *The Ambassadors* have their front foot set in the series of circular patterns on the floor. Arguably, four circles were showing, but only three were similar in dimension—made of curved lines, which technically are one-dimensional; mathematically, the center circle, or dot, has a dimension of two—the amount of points to describe its position. Holbein likely understood this concept since Nicholas Kratzer, a good friend he had painted a portrait of, was a mathematician and astronomer.[24]

In any case, I believed the position of Jean's foot in the exact center of the first circle was an allusion to Dante seeing a circular formation of lights in Heaven in which a man's image appeared.

Georges's foot is in the second circle from the center, where "the circles are diviner / As they are from the center more remote ..." (*Par.* 28.50-51; Longfellow).[25] The measurement of divinity between the two figures, determining where their feet would be placed in the circles on the floor, seemed to be described later in the canto: "The three Divine are in this hierarchy, / First the Dominions, and the Virtues next; / And the third order is that of the

Powers" (28.121-23).[26]

A description after the scene describes a river of light made of angels that spark with their movements, that "Out of this river issued living sparks ..." (*Par.* 30.64).[27] On part of the floor, inside the square, Holbein created a continuous pattern of gold sparks. Within the area of gold sparks are two lines of a yellow and black checkerboard pattern, linking back to Dante's chess game reference in describing the enormous amount of sparks—the sphere of angels flying around: "Their coruscation all the sparks repeated, /And they so many were, their number makes / More millions than the doubling of the chess" (*Par.* 28.91-93).[28]

I was amazed at Holbein's ingenuity. By that point, practically every page in my copy of *The Divine Comedy*—14,233 lines of poem—was highlighted or marked in some way with a note connecting a line or more to some Renaissance artwork—more than I could possibly write about. I knew I could spend months or *years* trying to figure out all the tiny, but deeply meaningful details in Holbein's painting alone. I felt a heavy obligation to continue studying that painting, and had to force myself to move on. It slightly frustrated me as I thought of all the scholars out there who could have helped to analyze the art's full complexity. But I was also torn, selfishly wanting to do it myself. I was eager to share with them what I knew, but only once my book was out. If any were willing to listen.

Art historian Martin Kemp, first interviewed about my discoveries back in 2011 on *The Today Show*, would later again try to refute the animal heads in his book, *Living with Leonardo*, which he would release in 2018. Included in his book was an image I sent him of *Mona Lisa* and the highlighted animal heads. Although I didn't expect praise from Kemp when his publisher emailed me requesting the image for his book, the idea of being mentioned in a book for the first time was very exciting. Maybe I was guilty of pride. Maybe I felt a sliver of validation in his request, no matter what he would end up writing.

Kemp would write that my "'discovery' was widely reported by journalists who should have known better, but who realized that the story would gain them some column inches."[29]

Did I have the right to be upset about his comments? Sure. But, instead, I saw it with a tinge of hidden compliment. (I would also be stupidly captivated at seeing "Piccirillo, Ron" in the book's index, right between "Picasso, Pablo" and Leonardo's father, "Piero, Sen.") I didn't know Kemp personally, but of the videos I had seen of him, he struck me as a man who, deep down, wanted to know the truth about *Mona Lisa* more than he let on. I was always driven by other people's doubt. And a world-renowned art historian would be no different. I pictured him reading my book one day, filled with doubt at the first pages, but eventually giving in to the possibility that the ideas it presented would deserve more consideration.

In his book, Kemp would admit to once mistakingly believing *Salvador Mundi* was painted by someone other than Leonardo, that it looked like "a drug-crazed hippy ..." and dismissing it as one of Leonardo's "nastier copies." But his mind was changed about *Salvador Mundi*'s originator after it was cleaned and retouched, and he concluded that it was indeed painted by Leonardo, later admitting that "We should have looked more carefully."[30] That admittance would give me hope for Kemp and other historians to one day see what *Mona Lisa* and many other paintings had been hiding from them all along.

(As for *Salvador Mundi*, I examined images of the art after it sold for a record-breaking $450 million in 2017, but I found no hidden imagery like I had in Leonardo's other religious works. Although I wasn't an expert at determining a painting's originator, there seemed to be inconsistencies in *Salvador Mundi* that I felt were uncharacteristic of Leonardo. For one, the figure's body language was too stiff. But the misaligned eyes were an even bigger problem, which couldn't have come from someone who studied dissected bodies and exhaustively filled his notebooks with sketches of human anatomy and writings on its proportions. So I actually found myself agreeing with Kemp's *original* impression that the painting probably came from another artist.)

But I welcomed criticism from historians like Kemp, even if I wasn't graceful at handling it. There was no doubt in my mind about what I continued to find, including one of the last lines of *The Comedy*, which I also believed helped to explain the meaning of *The Ambassadors*. But more importantly, it would help explain one of Leonardo's most iconic drawings.

Dante sees the divine image of man encircled by light in the sphere of Heaven.

> As the geometrician, **who endeavours**
> **To square the circle,** and discovers not,
> By taking thought, the principle he wants,
> Even such was I **at that new apparition;**
> I wished to see how **the image to the circle**
> **Conformed itself,** and how it there finds place;
> But **my own wings** were not enough for this,
> Had it not been that then my mind there smote
> A flash of lightning, wherein came its wish.
> Here **vigour failed the lofty fantasy**
>
> (*Par.* 33.133-42; Longfellow, emphasis added)[31]

As I read the last canto of *The Comedy*, Leonardo's drawing of *Vitruvian Man* came to mind. It showed a "vigour"-looking man with arms stretched outward, almost in motion of flapping his "wings," centered into the shape of a square and circle. Leonardo, "as the geometrician," included proportional measurements of the human body around the drawing. The drawing is explained to be referencing ancient architect Vitruvius. Maybe so, but it certainly was referencing *The Comedy*. *Vitruvian Man* had to be Leonardo's artistic solution to an old geometric puzzle of squaring the circle, his reflection on *Paradiso*'s last canto, where a human image appears in one of the heavenly circles. The human image—just as Leonardo would later draw it—is described by Dante as the same color as the circle. In the scene, Dante, with his divine vision, is fascinated at seeing the image of a man surrounded by a heavenly circle, but his "own wings" are not enough to bring him closer. Perhaps, Leonardo's wing-flapping *Virtruvian Man* is playing off an earlier prayer of hope for mortals to the Virgin Mary:

> … among the mortals,
> You are a living spring of hope. Lady,
> you are so high, you can so intercede,
> that he who would have grace but does not seek
> your aid, **may long to fly but has no wings.**
>
> (*Par.* 33.11-15; Mandelbaum, emphasis added)[32]

Nevertheless, Dante can't make sense of the image he sees, like the "geometrician, who endeavours / To square the circle, and discovers [it can] not …" be done.

In his notebooks, Leonardo had written, "Let no man who is not a Mathematician read the elements of my work."[33] It was based on what Plato wrote a thousand years before at the entrance of his academy: "LET NO ONE IGNORANT OF GEOMETRY ENTER HERE!" Roger Bacon, (who I'd later learn about) considered geometry the first step to understanding the Bible, since one must first be able to comprehend the physical appearance of objects such as Noah's Ark before understanding the Bible's hidden meanings.[34] It was also common belief at the time that numbers contained mystical meanings and associations—one reason Dante structured *The Comedy* on this idea.[35] Leonardo's writings show an obvious regard for detail pertaining to the success of the whole. A painter must achieve perfection in every universal aspect of painting in "all that the eye can see, …" he explained, and that "all these things ought to be regarded as of equal importance and value, by the man who can be termed a good painter."[36] I believed Leonardo was also speaking of details others might find insignificant, such as a painting's size.

When I had noticed a pattern early on that seemed to make use of the number 3, it was hard to ignore, especially because of its importance in *The Comedy*'s structure: 3 realms, 33 cantos, 3 days to journey through the 3 divisions of Hell, taking place in the year 1300, and so on.[37] The examples that stood out most were *The Ambassadors* having been painted in 15*33*, *Mona Lisa*'s *30* inch height, and the 33.3 centimeter height of Leonardo's (alleged) self-portrait. At

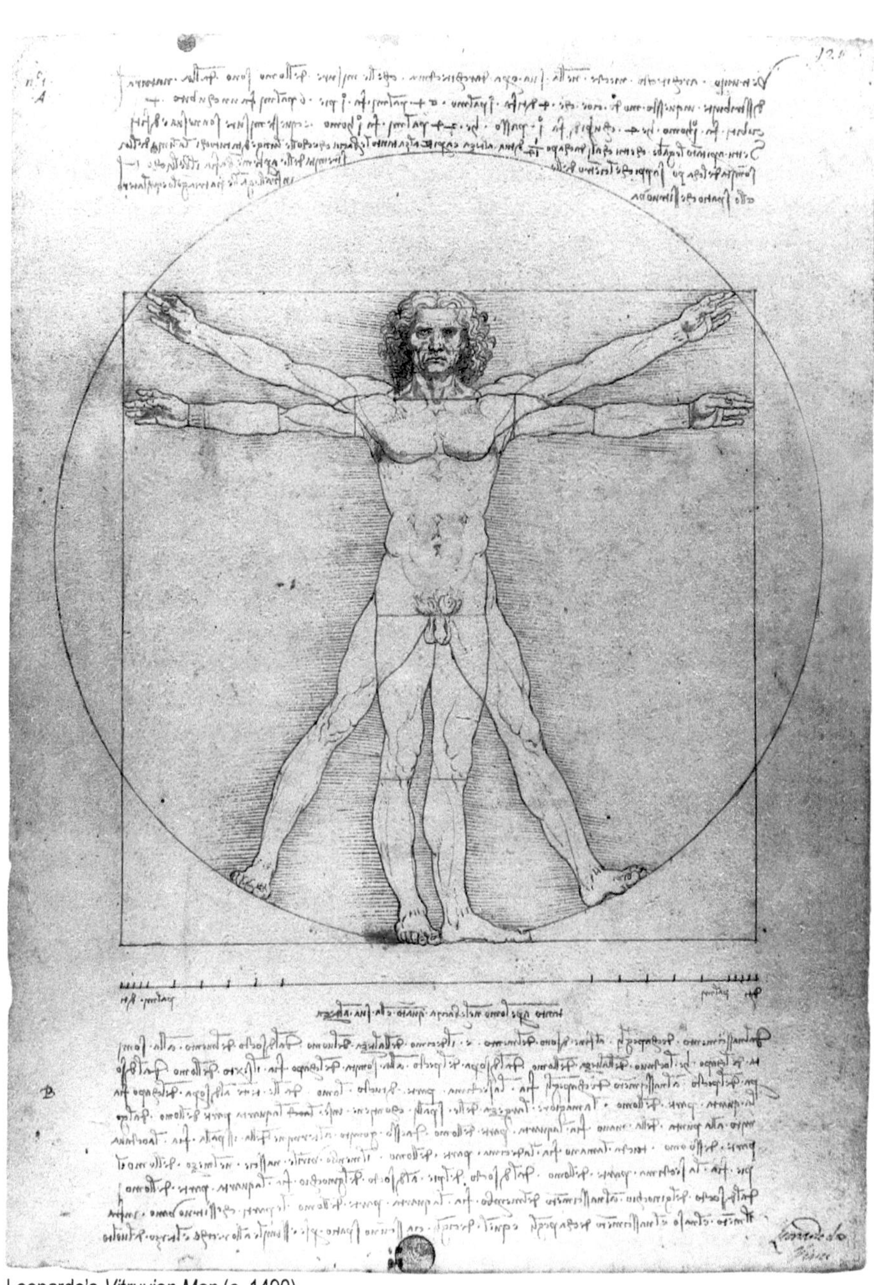

Leonardo's *Vitruvian Man* (c. 1490).

times, an artwork's size seemed to contain some hidden association to the work. The alleged self-portrait's 33.3 centimeter height could have meant nothing. But I couldn't help thinking of *Inferno*, *Purgatorio*, and *Paradiso* with 33 cantos each (ignoring *Inferno*'s first canto, considered an introduction). If symbolic, it wasn't done consistently enough to fully convince me, but I found it more than coincidental.

Could artists have been alluding to the Holy Trinity? Possibly. Perhaps my constant suspicion led to reasoning out everything I came across, no matter how coincidental it seemed at first.

Yet, after all that *Mona Lisa* revealed, one thing I felt a little more certain about was Leonardo's decision to make *Mona Lisa*'s canvas 30 by 21 inches as an association to Psalm 30:21: "Thou shalt hide them in the secret of thy face, from the disturbance of men. Thou shalt protect them in thy tabernacle from the contradiction of tongues."[38] Leonardo owned a book of Psalms, and too much had been stressed on geometry and mathematics for me to believe otherwise. That scripture fit that painting too perfectly.

After studying *The Ambassadors* so closely, I believed Holbein played his part in the numbers game also. Revealing his anamorphic painting in 1533 seemed ...calculated. If Holbein learned about anamorphic images indirectly from Leonardo or King Francis as I had guessed, he may not have learned about them until at least 1516 when Leonardo moved to France, where he possibly revealed that knowledge before his death three years later. If three was significant, then 1533 would have been a symbolic date to reveal a painting full of Dantean symbolism and openly displaying an anamorphic illusion.

46

Mona's Black Dress

In 2015, I was four years into writing my book. Heather and I had been living in our house for a year. I continued to keep the book's contents a secret from the world, but shared everything I knew with Heather. We'd discuss the mysteries, and I'd bounce my findings off of her at times to make sure they sounded coherent. I was also excited to have someone I could talk about the discoveries with, someone who I trusted and who was also intrigued with what the artists had kept quiet about. I knew I was so immersed in trying to answer too many questions at the same time, that I had to make sure what made sense in my mind made sense to someone hearing them for the first time without sounding problematic.

She knew how passionate I was about getting the book out, but was also blown away by the whole story behind *Mona Lisa.*

Her support helped to strengthen my feeling of purpose with my work.

Because we regularly watched documentary mysteries like *Forensic Files* and whodunit programs, it was fun taking on the art world's great mysteries together like two couch-detectives. Heather even helped me unravel a few of the details.

One night we were in the living room watching a documentary on Rome's history. I was sitting on the floor against the couch, looking through some books on Ancient Rome. Heather was reclined on the couch with her iPad researching the life of Cesare Borgia. I had told her my theory that Leonardo painted the envious *Mona Lisa* because of the evil things he saw while working for Borgia.

One of the things that had been puzzling me was *Mona Lisa*'s dark hair and clothing. In *Venus and Mars* and *Primavera*, Botticelli primarily portrayed Beatrice, therefore painting auburn hair and bright white clothing. I figured Leonardo wanted his figure to primarily resemble the envious souls first on the dark terrace of Purgatory, and portray Beatrice second. It seemed to explain her dark clothing, the color of the surrounding rocks as described by Dante. Yet, Dante never described the envious as clothed in black.

Leonardo appeared to follow Dante's writings word for word. So where did he come up with the idea to use such dark colors for her hair and wardrobe?

I knew the painting's varnish darkened over time, that her clothes' true colors were not as dark as they seemed, but they were still never pure white like in Botticelli's figures.

Why deviate from colors Botticelli used, Leonardo?

Maybe the answer was that simple, that the envious souls had clothing the color of their rocky surroundings. But it still felt like something was missing. Leonardo created every detail by following specific words from *The Comedy.* There seemed to be a reason for every piece of scenery, for the position of each element, for every color he used. So I wondered why her wardrobe was slightly darker than her surrounding landscape?

Then Heather found something that gave me a reason to think there was more meaning to Cesare Borgia's connection with *Mona Lisa.*

As an artist, my best work always happened with projects that had a lot of personal meaning. The ability to pour my feelings onto a canvas or drawing always gave the art more life—a luxury I gladly took advantage of. Over the years, I learned to use my art to cope with some of life's unpleasant events. A heartbreaking event or death of a loved one would send me to my painting easel, where I let my feelings out, letting them swoop over me, controlling my mind, my arms, and the movement of my brushes. In the process, I realized what a better painter I was during those instances, and began to welcome (but not wish for) those kind of experiences. As an experiment, I once created a series of self-portraits based on specific moods I felt at the time of the painting's creation: once after an argument that left me infuriated, another time when I was close to being drunk, and once just after intercourse. I was surprised to see how differently I portrayed myself each time. It taught me that art didn't just come from talent, but from one's emotional state.

When I first started oil painting, I made several attempts to paint a girlfriend of mine at the time, but was unsuccessful in drawing up the right feelings I needed to paint her. I just couldn't find motivation and eventually stopped trying. Then she revealed something about her past that touched me deeply—that she had been in an abusive relationship in which her ex-boyfriend had beaten her close to death. It was after hearing her emotional story that I suddenly had that missing ingredient to be able to paint her with the passion and determination I was searching for. It was similar to how a poet could describe a lover with such clarity and purpose.

I believed Leonardo had his own purpose in creating *Mona Lisa*, that he had poured his soul into the project. As an artist, I was sure of it. How else could he have spent so many years working on it?

Paul Strathern's *The Artist, the Philosopher, and the Warrior* gave me better insight and a stronger belief in Leonardo's personal connection with the painting. Witnessing the evil acts men in war were capable of doing had altered his view on human nature. Also spending time traveling closely with Leonardo and Borgia during the Romagna Campaigns was Niccolò Machiavelli (*the Philosopher)*—the same Machiavelli who later wrote about the beastly qualities of man in *The Prince*, stating that a prince should act and rule with characteristics of both a lion and a fox. Borgia—who was suspected of murdering his brother Juan out of jealousy (envy?) and throwing him into the Tiber River—had been Machiavelli's inspiration for the book.

Strangely, Machiavelli was known to have a smile described as *enigmatic*—a word regularly used to describe *Mona Lisa*'s smile.

I didn't think Machiavelli's enigmatic smile had anything to do with *Mona Lisa*'s (although it was possible that inspiration for the idea could have sprung from Leonardo's time spent with Machiavelli—as ideas sometimes come to artists from unexpected places). I imagined the two of them talking about Borgia and how evil his tactics could be. I was sure there was no coincidence that Leonardo started work for *Mona Lisa* not long after the months he spent traveling with Borgia and Machiavelli. Leonardo had even made three sketches of Borgia—one I found containing the hidden head of a fox.

What Leonardo saw had to have some effect on his decision to depict *Inferno* and *Purgatorio* in *Mona Lisa.* Other details had been percolating in my mind over time that added to the idea. Borgia and his family (including his father, Pope Alexander VI), were despised by Cardinal della Rovere for desecrating the Holy Church. Rovere would eventually become Pope Julius II and delegate Michelangelo to paint the Sistine Chapel ceiling. He also made Borgia's life a living hell. Pope Julius II despised the Borgias so much that once he became Pope, he had Cesare Borgia hunted down and imprisoned in a castle in Ostia—an area which made up part of the left side of the landscape in *Mona Lisa.*

"Did you know Pope Julius ordered the Borgia Apartments to be sealed closed?" Heather said to me from the couch, reading from her tablet. The Borgia Apartments were a suite of rooms in the Vatican used by Pope Alexander VI.

"What do you mean?" I asked, quickly looking up from an art book when I heard the two names together.

"Listen to this," she said, smiling with delight as she read a line from a website she had been looking at. "On the day of his election, Julius declared that 'all paintings made of the Borgias or for them must be covered over with black crepe.'"

"Wait," I said, with a sudden flash of revelation, "Black crepe?"

My eyes widened as Heather continued to read out the Pope's full quote.

> I will not live in the same rooms as the Borgias lived. [Alexander VI] desecrated the Holy Church as none before. He usurped the papal power by the devil's aid, and **I forbid under the pain of excommunication anyone to speak or think of Borgia again.** His name and memory must be forgotten. It must be crossed out of every document and memorial. His reign must be obliterated. **All paintings made of the Borgias or for them must be covered over**

> **with black crepe.** All the tombs of the Borgias must be opened and their bodies sent back to where they belong—to Spain. (emphasis added)[1]

... *Paintings ... covered over with black crepe.*

I immediately thought of *Mona Lisa*'s clothing, especially on her chest (not necessarily black, but appearing black, or possibly covered in a translucent black fabric—which would give her clothing that dark, muddy look), filled with intricate wrinkles and folds—as the crimped texture of *crepe* would look. (Other versions, such as the Prado *Mona Lisa*, showed a see-through material that was definitely black. The *Isleworth Mona Lisa* was also covered in black clothing, but hers didn't look to be translucent.) I thought about a detail from Leonardo's *Envy* passage, the words "covered by a mask of fair seeming." In an instance in Ostia, Borgia was said to have worn a mask to cover his "blotched and disfigured" face when "he seemed to be suffering from the French disease [syphilis]."[2]

I wasn't sure, but I had a hunch those details contributed to Leonardo's inspiration—at least, in writing about Envy.

"Can I see that?" I said to Heather, needing to read the Pope's words again myself. Was it possible, even if just a tiny bit, that he was thinking of Cesare Borgia while he painted Envy? "That *has* to be why she looks like she's wearing black."

The Pope had made it a crime to speak Borgia's name because "his name and memory must be forgotten." It made me think of all the secrets tying back to *The Comedy*. Was it possible the same had happened to Dante—that it became a crime to "speak or think" of Dante after he was exiled? Could that have been the reason for all the secrecy? That artists wanted to keep his name alive, but on a grander scale than just the occasional portrait or illustration? In a sonnet about Dante, Michelangelo begins with a line that seemed to suggest there was something forbidden about discussing Dante: "No tongue can tell of him what should be told, for on blind eyes his splendor shines too strong; 'Twere easier to blame those who wrought him wrong, than sound his least praise with a mouth of gold."[3] Of course, I had to think part of that line was referencing the secret illusions, that they were unseen by *blind eyes*, even as *his splendor [shined]* to those aware and able to see them.

Whether it was true or not, it was certainly one possibility. In time, I found other possible reasons for her dark clothing.

One that seemed more plausible came from Ovid's *Metamorphoses*. It was already believed that Botticelli used Ovid's writings to illustrate parts of *Primavera*, and known that Dante was inspired by Ovid's work, but I realized Leonardo may have used Ovid's writings also. Envy's character is mentioned in full detail in "The House of Envy" from *Metamorphoses*: "... Envy's squalid quarters, / black with corruption, hidden deep within / a sunless valley where no breezes blow ..." (2.1049-51; Martin)[4] seemed to describe the mood of *Mona Lisa*'s surroundings pretty well, as did "... a sad and sluggish place, richly frigid, / ...and fog that never lifts embraces all" (2.1052, 54).[5] The painting certainly looked like a *sunless valley* that was *squalid* and *black with corruption.* Ovid's Envy "... only smiles at sight of another's grief ..." (2.1073),[6] and "sluggishly / arises from the ground where she'd been sitting ..." (2.1062-63)[7] when a visitor comes to her quarters.

Although Leonardo painted Envy sitting in some sort of seat, and was primarily guided by Dante's description of the envious souls who were sitting along the ground, I still felt he was somewhat guided by Ovid's description of Envy. And I found other details from Ovid that Leonardo must have pulled from.

But if Leonardo depicted Cesare Borgia in any way within the various layers of meaning *Mona Lisa* had, it was difficult to prove. For me, it would always be no more than a strong hunch. One thing was for certain—he portrayed *The Comedy*, first and foremost. Details from *Metamorphoses* were likely portrayed too, yet the importance of Ovid's writings seemed secondary to Dante's.

47

The Question

I was still riddled by *Mona Lisa*'s upside-down question mark. My assumption was that the mark represented a specific question in *The Comedy*, but I couldn't find a way to match it to a specific scene. I tried, but a lot of questions were asked in the story. And none stood out more than the rest. In fact, the word itself—*question*—was used over thirty times. The truth was that anything could have explained it. It was too vague to pinpoint.

Still, like every other detail, I spent a lot of time contemplating it. Because it stood out to me before anything else, it seemed unusually important. I thought about the possibility that I was wrong about its shape, that the shape was random and appeared as a question mark only by coincidence. But that thought lasted only a short time. I was sure Leonardo placed it there. I just didn't think I would ever figure out why.

It was something author Stephen King wrote that gave me an idea. Trying to improve my writing (and I thought I could use all the help I could get), one of the books I read was King's *On Writing*. In it, King discusses how writers should *read a lot, write a lot,* and carry a book wherever they go—waiting rooms, checkout lines, the john. He writes that if he has "to spend time in purgatory before going to one place or the other," he prefers to have some kind of book to pass the time.[1]

It was that line that brought me back to *Mona Lisa*'s question mark.

Dante is originally bound for Hell, but his journey, guided by Virgil then Beatrice, alters his destination when he learns to hop back onto the righteous path using his newly earned divine vision and changing his ways. I wondered if that was the meaning to Leonardo's question? A question for each and every person who saw that painting.

Are you destined for Hell, Purgatory, or Paradise?

Maybe I wasn't on the path to Hell with corrupt popes and politicians, but there were things I wanted to change to avoid my own personal Purgatory. Dante's story inspired me. I didn't have a sudden belief of the afterlife that included Hell and its boiling rivers or its three-headed Lucifer, but I did view the world differently after reading his writings. What I believed was that our choices in life lead us to happiness or despair. To me, it was life itself that could at times feel like Hell, or Purgatory, or Paradise.

Looking back at the times in my life when it did feel like I was in some sort of Hell, such as during some of the relationships I was in, I realized the core of the problem was me, not the women I dated. Paige's reaction in becoming distant from me was as an effect of how I acted toward her. By not projecting enough love outward—afraid that doing so made me look weak—I practically forced her into another man's arms. Looking back, I had been afraid. What I considered my strength, my *pride*, was an evil kind of weakness. It must have made her feel alone, as if on a journey with no guide. Dante's writings taught me that it is better for two people to receive guidance from one another. That one should not make the journey alone. What I wanted was to live a good, passionate life, and I realized that I needed someone to share that life with.

Toward the end of *Paradiso*, while in one of the celestial spheres, Beatrice directs Dante to look back on the journey he has taken so far:

> "... Look down once more, and see how vast a world
>   Thou hast already put beneath thy feet;
> So that thy heart, as jocund as it may,
>   Present itself to the triumphant throng
>   That comes rejoicing through this rounded ether."
> I with my sight returned through one and all
>   The sevenfold spheres, and I beheld this globe
>   Such that I smiled at its ignoble semblance" (*Par.* 22.128-35; Longfellow)[2]

I spent a few minutes on *Mona Lisa*'s scenery, reminiscing over the physical part of Dante's journey that Leonardo had painted. I thought of how strange and mysterious that landscape had once been, and how familiar and sadly comfortable every detail had become to me over the years, how I had grown as I learned so much about that painting and about myself.

As for the question mark, because other upside-down imagery in the painting had become so significant, I continued giving it serious thought.

But why upside down, Leonardo?

I revisited the illusion many times, studying the painting while it stood upside down. At one point, I thought the figure in *Mona Lisa* seemed to be shaped like Botticelli's *Mappa dell'Inferno* (Map of Inferno). The similarity was subtle, but knowing his *Mappa dell'Inferno* illustrated Dante's Inferno, I wondered if Leonardo used the figure's shape to represent Inferno's funnel-shaped realm. Forgetting that it was the figure of a woman, an argument could be made that she sort of resembled a spiraling funnel, with the darkest part of the painting at her abdomen—what looked like the pit of the funnel-shaped structure of Inferno. It may tie back to a line in *Inferno*, when Dante, scared he would never leave Hell, asks Virgil if he knows the way through. Virgil assures him that he once returned from the "... lowest region and the darkest, / And farthest from the heaven which circles all" (*Inf.* 9.28-29).[3]

Because that funnel-shaped portion of the art is wrapped by the shape of the question mark, I wondered if Leonardo's mark pertained to Dante's worry about leaving the realm of Hell? The curve of the question mark "circles" around "the darkest" part of the painting. And if it is purposely funnel-shaped to represent the Inferno, the darkest area would lead downward toward the deepest level of Hell—which would make it "farthest from the heaven." I was aware of how deep I was looking into things, but trying to get into the mind of some of the artists, I had to question everything. Artists from that time were the brainiacs of the art world, and so I didn't think it was possible to overanalyze their work. In fact, I wondered if I was analyzing it enough. It was worth a guess anyway. A mind as clever as Leonardo's probably possessed abyss-like depths of thoughts that many of us wouldn't comprehend. Still, I examined further, chipping away like an archaeologist who was in search of deeply buried bones that may or may not exist, but had to dig in order to find out.

Examining the question mark further, I pondered the idea that it was showing a letter *P* also.

It came to me as I noticed how a strip of weaker highlights almost connected the beginning of the question mark with its tail, closing off its shape—as if it were a *P* that was in the middle of being wiped away. *A partially erased letter P.* Dante had one of seven P's wiped from his forehead after exiting each terrace in Purgatory. Maybe it was showing a question mark *and* a partially erased letter P.

Just as numbers had played a role in *The Comedy*'s structure, so did certain letters. *P* was one of them. Another was *M.*

In *Paradiso*, in a scene taking place in the sphere of Jupiter, a flock of souls come together to form the letter M before shaping into an eagle. Academic material I referred to explained that the "*M* signifies monarchy" and that "the eagle was the emblem of Rome," and also "stands for imperial unity and dominion." It went on to explain that "the transformation of the M into the eagle is presumably the emblem of Florence and its ruling Guelph party."[4]

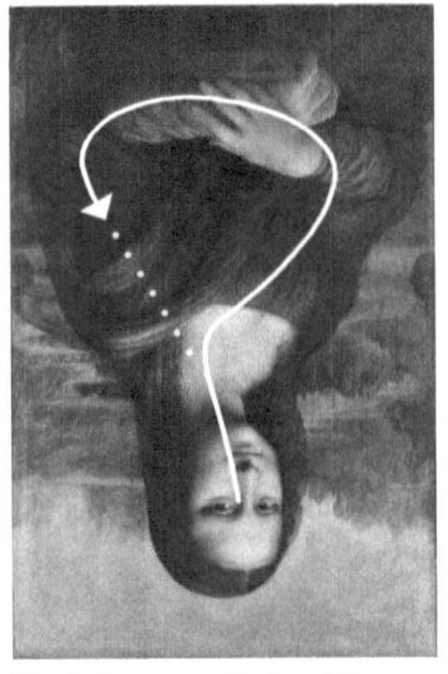
Partially erased letter P?

Before coming to that scene, I had noticed odd M-formations in several of Leonardo's works. Again, I was unsure if I was looking too deep into it at first, but in *Virgin and Child with St. Anne and St. John the Baptist*, three of the legs form the M-shape. In *The Annunciation*, when turned upside down, the unnecessary amount of robe on the seated Virgin Mary also forms an M. Since it was upside down—realistically a W—I tried to pass it off as

Some of the possible M-formations (highlighted) in Renaissance art like *The Annunciation* (upside down), *The Last Supper*, Sistine Chapel ceiling, and *The Ambassadors*.

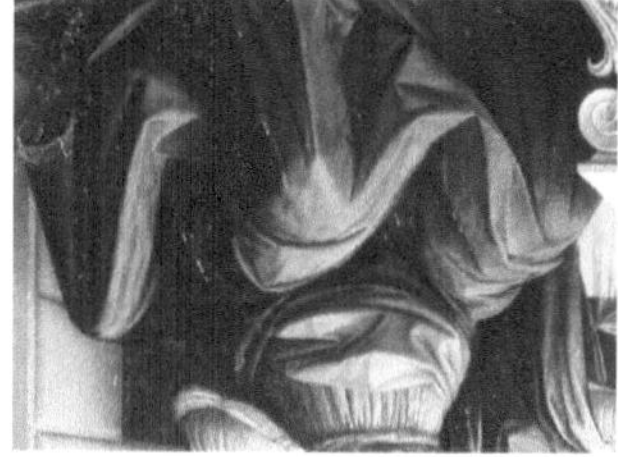
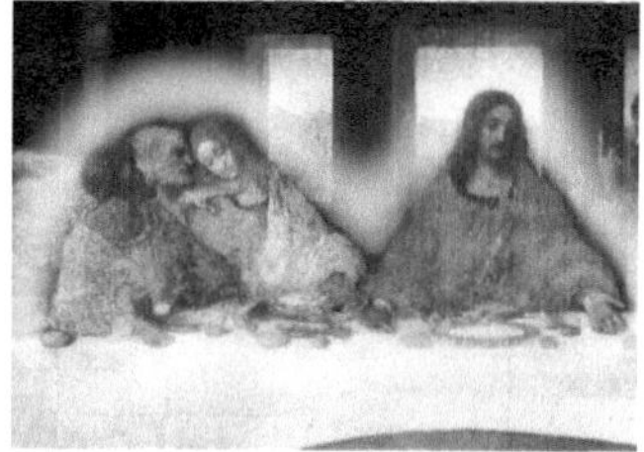
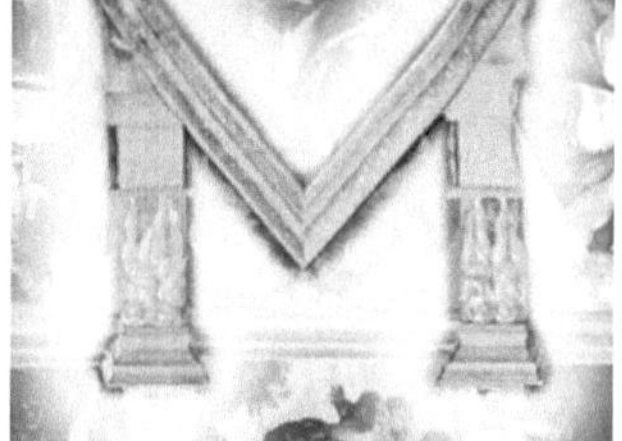
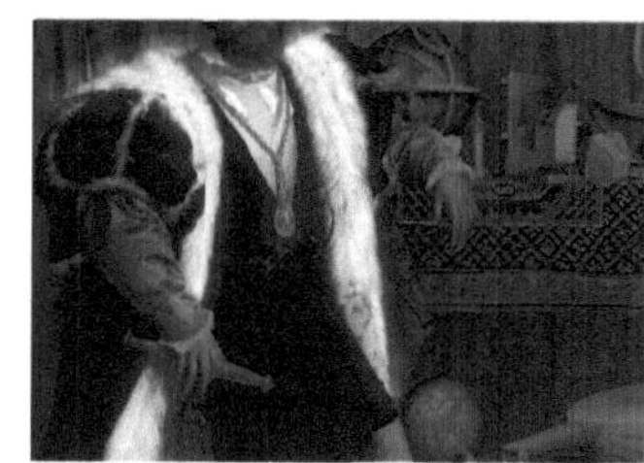

a coincidence. But a Renaissance painting-coincidence was an oxymoron. Renaissance artists were meticulous, and sometimes took years planning and executing their work. It was difficult to believe anything was accidental—such as an intricately shaped M-shape I was finding everywhere—especially in *The Annunciation* where there was way too much extra robe showing.

True, one could look almost anywhere to find the shape of an *M*, but these *M*-shapes were at times so prominent. Plus, there were plenty of paintings in which I didn't find them. In *The Last Supper*, the four figures from Judas to Christ form an *M*. Michelangelo's Sistine Chapel ceiling is practically dominated by *M*-shapes—produced by details of the stone molding. The artists seemed to put such care into the details of the letters. It looked like the consistency that could be found in each letter of a font family. They just seemed to be related.

Could the M have been a symbol in favor of the Republic, or against a monarchy?

The idea took me back to *The Ambassadors*, where I had also noticed the shapes of letters in each of the men's clothing. The lapel around Georges' neck is P-shaped. And he seems to be holding the end of the P's tail for some reason. More obvious was the large M formation in Jean's coat from the white fur and red clothing of his chest. What also stuck out was the pattern around the edge of the rug sitting on the top shelf. The pattern looked to be shaped just like the examples I came across in study guides that described the eagle's transformation into the letter *M* in *Paradiso*. Or was I really looking too deep at the details?

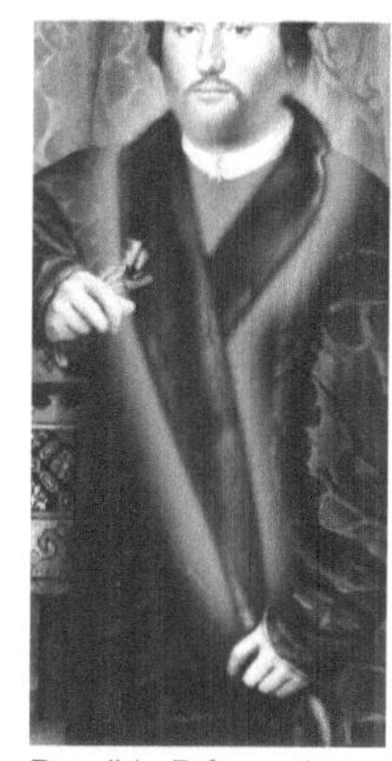
Possible P-formation (highlighted) in *The Ambassadors*.

48

Another World

It started out with the questions: Who was she? Where was she? Why the animal heads? And the illusions? The answers gave me a better understanding of paintings like *Mona Lisa*, *Mars and Venus*, and *The Ambassadors.* I had built up a collection of notes that felt like they could stretch to the ceiling—some of which would be put into a book. But no matter what became of the book, seeing those masterpieces in their true depth had been worth everything I sacrificed.

Still, there was one last thing to do. So I turned to the greatest masterpiece of all, the anamorphic creation that overwhelmed all others the way an ocean overwhelms a pond.

I unfolded the largest photographed version of Michelangelo's Sistine Chapel ceiling art and laid it out in front of me on the coffee table. There was still something I had to see. Having originally found a few illusions there, and knowing how much time I would need to examine such a large work of art, I originally had to put it aside, on hold, in order to focus on Leonardo's art, knowing I would return to it later. But with *Mona Lisa*'s age-old mysteries finally solved (but causing new questions to emerge), I then returned my focus to Michelangelo—not just his ceiling, but also *The Last Judgement*, which he painted thirty years later.

For several hours, rather than rotating the art in my hands as I had with all the other paintings, I crawled around the poster image of the ceiling. The illusions emerged one at a time, like ghosts out of the darkness. There were many. As I saw what Michelangelo had done, the entire ceiling came alive, its movement like that of an aquarium. It was like looking through a portal, the art on the ceiling the same, but also completely different, as if I had awakened it to appear as it had in Michelangelo's mind. The figures no longer looked as though they were still, instead seeming to move as each image magically appeared, one after another, each one breathtaking and beautiful. They came from every direction.

The first anamorphic ones appeared in each of the prophets and sibyls along the ceiling's perimeter. They became visible as I looked from the outside inward—what Michelangelo would have seen when positioned at the outer walls and looking underneath and across each ceiling image. Each prophet and sibyl morphed into something different when I viewed them from a d-point below their feet (treating the bottom side of the panel art as the left side in the illusion, and the right side in the panel art as the bottom of the illusion). In most of the sections, the figures morphed into large heads the size of the main figures themselves. They appeared as though I were looking over the shoulder of the figures that the heads belonged to, as if I were standing *behind* them.

The first to stick out at me was the *Cumean Sibyl*, in which appeared eyes and a mouth with an evil smirk, its neck stretched forward, its head reaching toward the ceiling's center panels. The sibyl and putti behind her emerged into a large head of a hideous monster, the sibyl's clothed head becoming the bandaged nose of the creature in the illusion.

In the image of *Daniel*, the prophet's head became the eyebrow of another large head illusion. The peeking figure behind the prophet became its nose; Daniel's left shoulder formed its cheekbone. It looked human, unlike the creature from *Cumean*'s illusion, but it was also looking toward the center of the ceiling art, like it was *watching*. It appeared as if I were positioned just behind it, catching the side of its face, which had on blue and white face armor.

Erythraean Sibyl also turned into a head covered in head armor. *Prophets Zechariah* and *Ezekiel* became the heads of bearded, old men. *Persian Sibyl* became a hooded woman carrying a baby in a blanket. *Prophet Isaiah* revealed a head with a snobbish and unamused expression.

Even if I wanted to, I wouldn't be able to pull myself away, afraid I would miss something if I turned my attention away for a second. The prophets and sibyls that morphed into large heads were facing the art panels running down the center illustrating the Book of Genesis. But why? I couldn't make sense of it. And why was there a secret image of a woman with a baby? And armored knights or soldiers or whatever they were in two of the other panels?

I didn't need to understand them in order to be amazed at the art's complexity, its technical mastery, its ingenuity. One could be amazed at Michelangelo's work without understanding exactly what he did or how he had done it.

There were more illusions. Some were unmistakable, while in others, I wasn't sure what I was looking at, but could only tell something was definitely there, hiding. Some figures formed additional illusions when turned in a different direction. On its right side, *Zechariah* first turned into an anamorphic head of a bearded, old man, but rotated 90 degrees counter-clockwise and looked at straight on, he became the head of a gargoyle in perfect profile—an ambiguous illusion. Zechariah's head formed the nose; the young, male figures at his back formed the gargoyle's puckered lips; and the folds of teal drapery created a large ear that looked anatomically correct. *Delphic Sibyl* also morphed into a gargoyle (or possible goblin) head when on its left side.

I wasn't sure why the large faces in the prophets and sibyls appeared to be watching the story of Genesis in the center panels, as if watching God in a

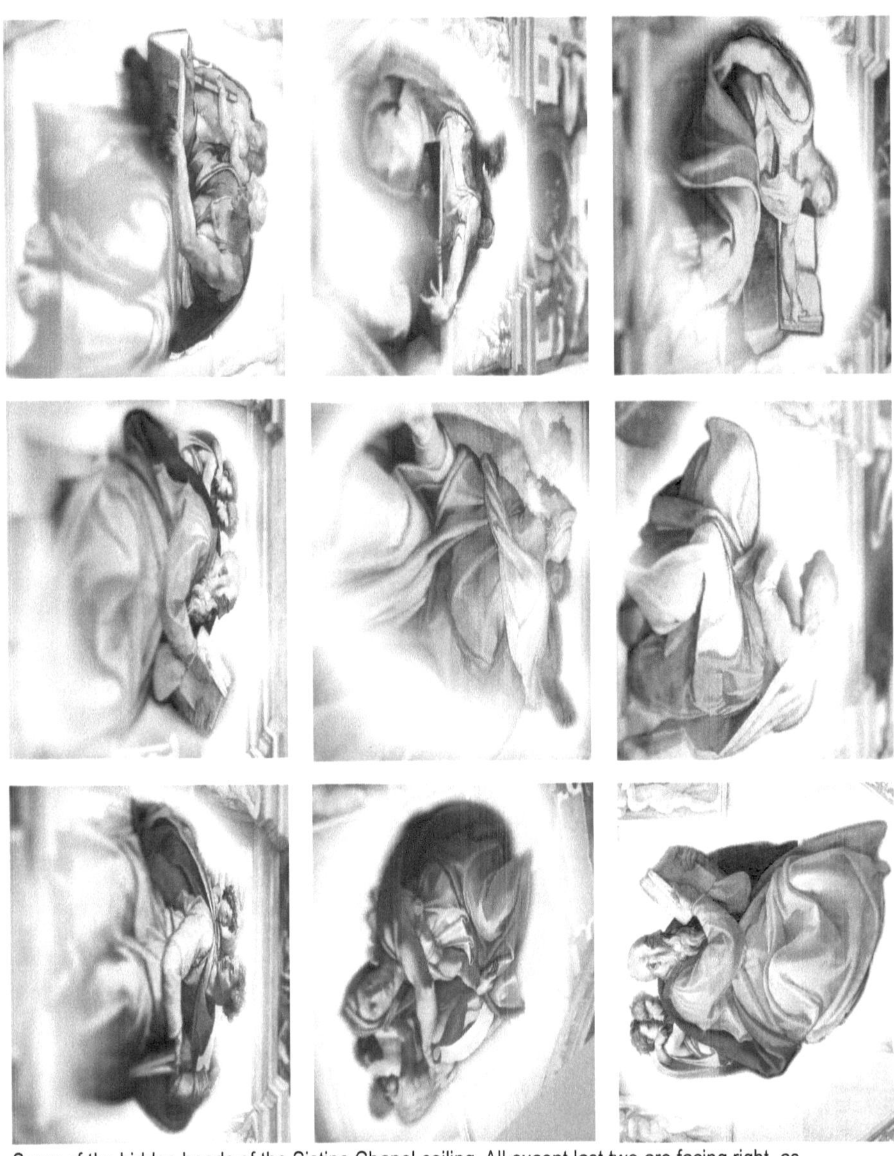

Some of the hidden heads of the Sistine Chapel ceiling. All except last two are facing right, as if viewer is looking over the figures' right shoulders. Last two face left. **TOP ROW:** Anamorphic illusions of a hideous monster head in *Cumean Sibyl*, heads with what looks like military barbute helmets in *Daniel* and *Erythraean Sibyl.* **MIDDLE ROW:** Anamorphic illusions of the heads of bearded men in *Zechariah* and *Ezekiel*, and a woman carrying baby in *Persian Sibyl*. **BOTTOM ROW:** Anamorphic illusion of unamused-looking face in *Isaiah* and the head of a gargoyle or goblin in *Delphic Sibyl.* Also a gargoyle or goblin head in *Zechariah*, but an ambiguous illusion when rotated left. All face inward toward the story panels of Genesis. All heads are highlighted.

documentary about the creation of life.

There was *so much* to explore all over the ceiling, so I returned to spend whatever free time I had, day after day, even hanging sections of the art around my attic so I could sneak glances as I came and went, giving me a chance to catch something I may have missed. I hung multiple images of figures by themselves, some on their sides, or upside down, as I routinely searched for multiple illusions within the same figure. It was like being in a room full of never-before-seen Michelangelo illustrations with so many things to discover that it was difficult to focus on one single image.

Whenever I had the chance, I'd spend time circling the poster, checking and rechecking illusions while also looking for new ones. The Sistine Chapel art was a nice break from the years I had spent focusing most of my attention on *Mona Lisa*, but I also spent time scrolling through many other Renaissance artworks as a whole, more focused on the bigger picture rather than individual paintings and drawings.

Everywhere I looked, obscure faces regularly appeared. I kept finding hidden faces where faces didn't belong. Not just animal faces, but human-like faces. Sometimes they were more beastly in nature, more monstrous. There seemed to be three kinds of faces. There were the obvious animal heads, like the lions and apes, then there were faces that were beastly, not quite animal or human. Then were the human faces. There was no way I was imagining the faces—once I spotted them, the images were too clear, too obvious. Although hidden animal heads many times appeared in the folds of figures' clothing, they also appeared in naturalistic settings of the art, especially rocks. I was sure they were *meant* to look like faces, especially when I referred back to Ovid's *Metamorphoses*, which included stories of transformations—*illusions*. Its stories included gods and goddesses that were sometimes turned into animals as punishment, and also stories of animals born from the Earth itself. "My mind leads me to speak now of forms changed / into new bodies" (bk. 1.1-2; Martin)[1] was the very first line.

Ovid wrote of figures being turned *to* stone, and also of the goddess Themis who created figures *from* stones. I felt that there was a link to many of the human-looking faces in illustrated sections of landscape. Botticelli's *St. Jerome* was the most obvious to show one. The cave's rocky exterior around St. Jerome showed a man's face in profile, looking right, with a perfectly shaped eye, a jutting lower lip, chin, and hair made from the dark green grass. In one of Leonardo's chalk drawings of mountains—*Snow-capped Peaks*—was the profile of a man's face, when the artwork was turned onto its left. In the landscape of *Virgin and Child with St. Anne* and both versions of *Virgin of the Rocks* are also faces that can be seen. In *The Annunciation*, a face made of white lilies looks directly back at Gabriel.

Although I didn't think much of it when I first saw them in *Mona Lisa*, the first three animal heads were carved into the rocky landscape for a reason. The connection to Ovid's writings were apparent, and made the location of the heads camouflaged into the art more significant.

Years after the Renaissance, artists became more obvious, creating anthropomorphic landscapes—nature resembling human faces on a grander scale, taking up whole canvases rather than hidden in small areas—until, over time, artists seemed to stop hiding them altogether—as Holbein had originally done with the skull in *The Ambassadors* many years before.

Dating back to the seventeenth century, Flemish artist Joos de Momper, in *Winter*, shows a known image of an anthropomorphic scene. Shaped in the profile of a human face, the ragged landscape forms a beard, a building structure creates an ear, and the irregular terrain shows a nose, mouth, and eyes.

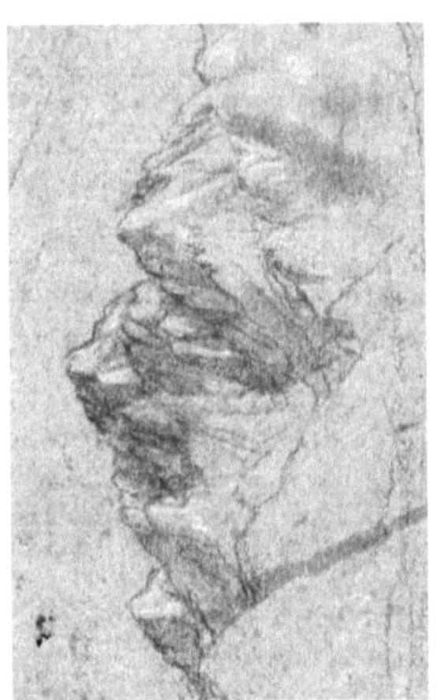

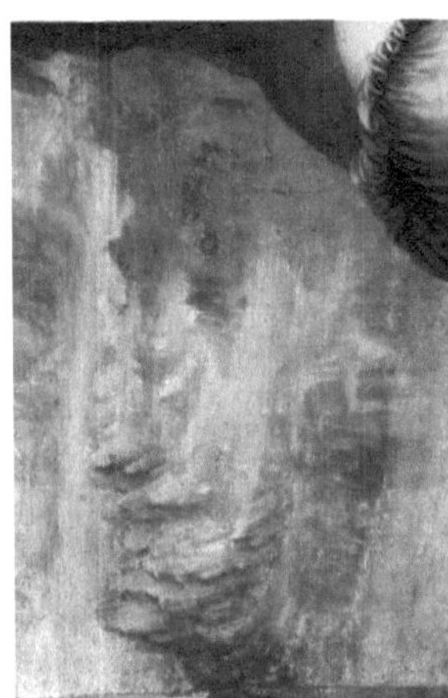

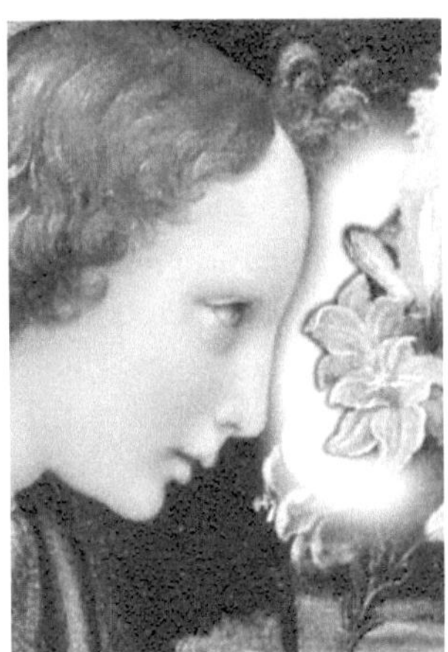

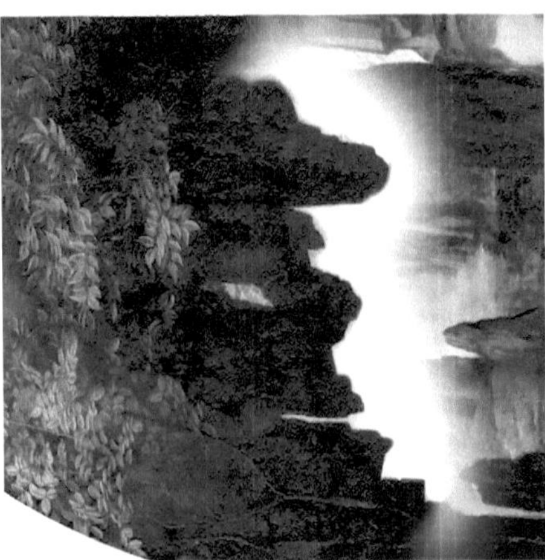

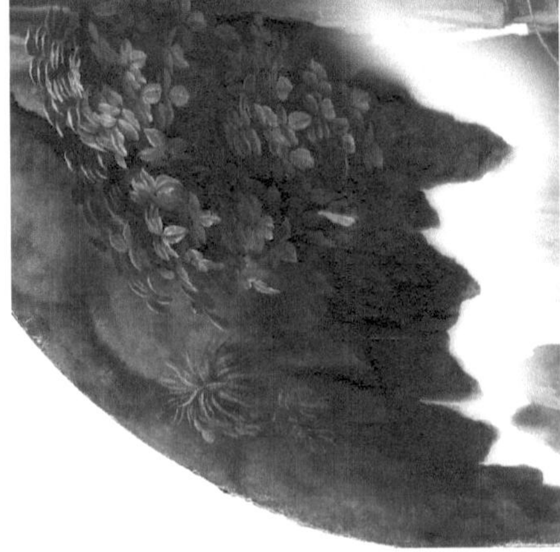

TOP ROW: Rotated counter-clockwise, faces (facing left) can be seen in the landscapes of Leonardo's *Snow-capped Peaks* (c. 1511) and *Virgin and Child with St. Anne* (c. 1503). The shape of a face profile (highlighted) formed from the flowers faces Gabriel eye to eye in *The Annunciation.* **BOTTOM ROW:** Silhouettes of faces (facing right, highlighted) in Paris and London versions of *Virgin of the Rocks* when rotated onto their left sides.

In Marcus Gheeraerts the Elder's *Allegory of Iconoclasm*, created just decades after Leonardo's and Botticelli's time, is a face-shaped scene. A less obvious example is *Coastal Landscape with Anthropomorphic Rocks*, in which Simon de Vlieger created the subtle images of several faces of men and also what looks like animals. But earlier, more subtle images of faces from the Renaissance continued to remain unnoticed—even after it became obvious in later artworks displaying face illusions out in the open.

Scholars had already found that Botticelli created imagery from Ovid's *Fasti*, but I believed *Metamorphoses* played a more important role than anyone realized. (I had already found that Leonardo may have pulled details from *Metamorphoses* for *Mona Lisa* from a section called *The house of Envy*.) I later learned that "the artists of the Renaissance used [*Metamorphoses*] as a veritable handbook for artistic themes."[2] Ovid's story of the Great Flood may have also provided the idea of combining faces and nature, as he unifies elements of the Earth with human form:

> ... his awful face concealed in pitchy blackness;
> his beard is utterly suffused with rain
> that runs in channels down his streaming locks;
> Upon his forehead gather clouds of gloom,
> And his flowing robes are—literally—flowing.
>
> (*Metamorphoses*, 1.367-71; Martin)[3]

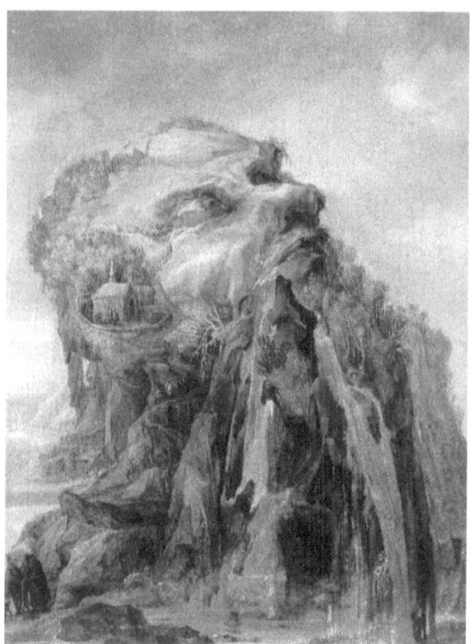

Allegory of Winter by Joos de Momper (early 17th century).

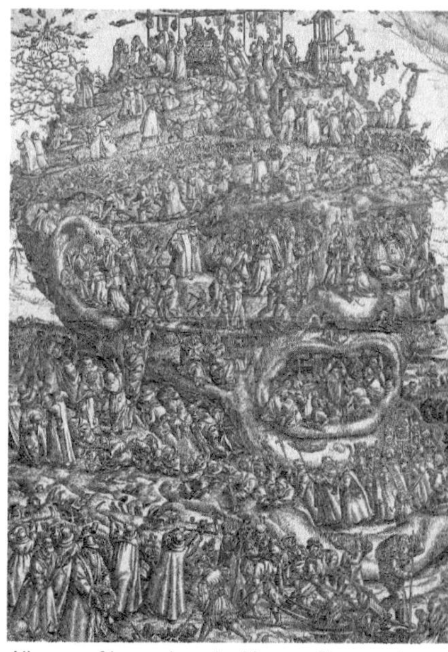

Allegory of Iconoclasm by Marcus Gheeraerts the Elder (c. 1566-68).

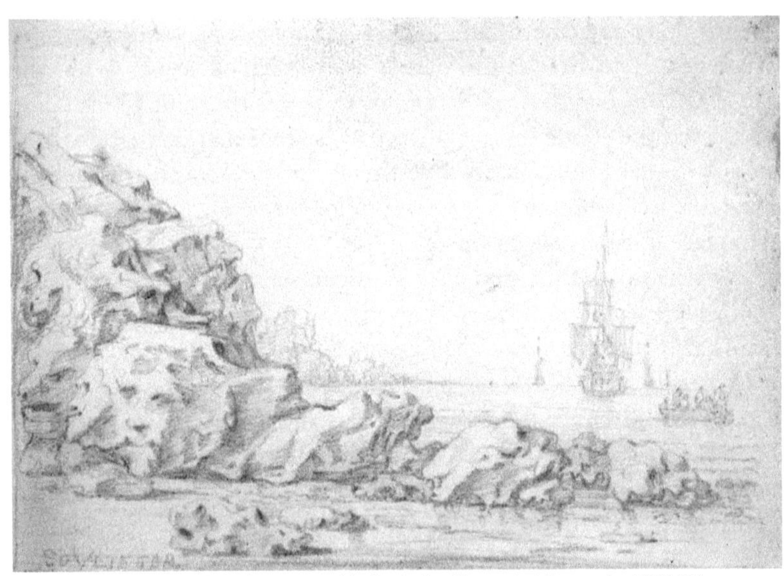

Coastal Landscape with Anthropomorphic Rocks by Simon de Vlieger, (c. 1634-38).

It later tells how "the earth spontaneously generated / the varied forms of other animals" (1.578-79).[4]

And when the goddess of justice grants Deucalion and his wife Pyrrha the ability to create men from stones, the two are confused by her words, so "they repeat the oracle's / Obscurities, those words whose sense is hidden, / Turning them over in their puzzled minds, / Until at last the son of Prometheus / Spoke" (1.536-40),[5] interpreting its hidden meaning.

The scene points to the actual meaning of the oracle's words, that if taken literally, will be misinterpreted, and how Deucalion figures out the oracle's real sense by finding the hidden meaning of her words—which leaves Pyrrha excited, but doubtful of her husband's interpretation.

It reminded me of some of the reaction I initially received attempting to convince experts about the secret meanings behind Leonardo's words and art. I had felt like Deucalion, presenting the real hidden meaning of the oracle's words when others (his wife in this case) doubted his interpretation. At least Pyrrha was excited and willing to give Deucalion's translation a try:

> Though Pyrrha was excited by her husband's
> interpretation of the oracle,
> it seemed a rather doubtful hope at best,
> for neither of them had much confidence
> in heaven's admonitions—still, what harm
> could come from trying it? (1.547-52; Martin)[6]

I considered myself lucky though. Unlike Pyrrha, Heather showed no doubt about anything I shared with her. Maybe that was because I was able to supply explanations I wasn't in possession of during my publicity a few years earlier. I suspected she would have been supportive either way.

Nonetheless, I wasn't going to pick apart *Metamorphoses* line by line as I had with Dante's *Comedy*. I had a feeling that if I did, another few years would pass before I finished my book. And what if it didn't stop with Ovid? The paintings represented stories from various writers—likely including authors and works I hadn't yet realized. Even if I made it through Ovid's writings, where would it end? Each time I thought I'd figured out each meaning or story to a painting, another seemed to appear—some so subtle or skillfully hidden I had the impression there were others that might never be found. Even if I were wrong, it would take me years to be sure, as I would have to examine each line in writings from Plato, Aristotle, Virgil, Ovid, Homer, Petrarch, Chaucer, Machiavelli, and on and on.

For the time being, I was satisfied in discovering that *The Comedy* had been the (main) explanation behind many Renaissance mysteries. My intent was to eventually pursue works by the other poets and writers, but I had to focus on getting my book out first. It was causing a strain in my relationship with Heather and in my social life—which pretty much became nonexistent. I began to gain weight from not exercising. It was difficult to focus on things not associated with my book. Maybe one day I'd get the chance to start up some organization to study those other writings and the art they inspired. But it would have to wait. I had to march on and complete my book and move on with my life.

What amazed me most was Michelangelo's ability to create multiple anamorphic and ambiguous illusions within single figures, and with such complexity, seen from different directions on such a large scale. His brush was like the wand of some unbelievable wizard. On a smaller scale, other artists had done the same, but, with the Sistine Chapel, Michelangelo had done it over such an impossibly large area. What made it more amazing was that he didn't want to paint that ceiling in the first place. How did he find the will to create such a world of optical illusions? According to Vasari, artist Raphael was jealous of hearing the Pope praise Michelangelo's work, and saw an opportunity to sabotage Michelangelo's reputation. Michelangelo, a sculptor with no experience painting fresco, was forced to use the technique—a skill other artists refused to use due to its difficulty. Raphael expected—*wanted*—Michelangelo to fail big time, which could give Raphael the upper hand with future commissions. That's why he persuaded Pope Julius II to have Michelangelo paint the ceiling.

Not only did it become one of the greatest works of all time, gigantic images were hidden throughout. To miss hidden images in paintings that sometimes had to be turned upside down or on their sides was one thing, but the Sistine Chapel ceiling was different. Millions observed that ceiling, walking in different directions, facing this way and that. Many looked at the sibyls and prophets upside down and sideways as they roamed the floor below. Why didn't anyone else see what was hidden beneath the surface?

If, before the discoveries, I'd been asked if Michelangelo had placed any kind of secret art up there, I probably would have rolled my eyes doubtfully, pretty sure nothing was hiding because I had seen images of that ceiling my whole life and never noticed anything. *Was I wrong to doubt God's existence also because I had never seen evidence of Him either?* Why hadn't I spotted Michelangelo's illusions when a book was turned this way or that? Was it simply a matter of seeing what we expected to see? Or had I been looking at it *all* the wrong way?

That thought kept me awake one night. I laid in bed, listening to the sounds of the city through the open windows. Pinch was asleep in her bed nearby. Heather was asleep next to me. One hour passed, then two hours, until it was early in the morning, and I still hadn't fallen asleep. I couldn't stop thinking about Michelangelo, high up on his scaffold, as he worked all those years ago, planning and painting, painting and planning, creating what the whole world would eventually see and what they wouldn't see. In a way, he would create the image of God better than God had created the image of him. Michelangelo was a brilliant artist. Yet, God had been an artist first. According to the story of Genesis, He "created the heavens and the earth." Michelangelo, in turn, painted God creating the heavens and the Earth. *And the artist saw that it was good.* But it was better than good.

And since all those years ago—centuries—was it possible I had been the first to see what was hiding up there since the artist last saw it with his own eyes? As I stared into the blackness of the room from my bed, I was moved by the thought. Unable to sleep, I lifted the covers off me, quietly got out of bed, and tiptoed barefoot to the attic, needing to see the ceiling art once again. Some time passed as I remained hunched over the art, straining my tired eyes over its details, my back stiffening from all the hunching over I had done over the previous weeks. There were images I couldn't figure out. I could tell something was there, but they were harder to distinguish than others.

One amazing illusion I kept returning to came from Jonah, the most expressive of the prophets. Jonah looks upward, withdrawing in his seat as if cowering from something above—an expression that never made sense to me. And yet, he points a finger from each hand down to his right. In Leonardo's portrait of St. John, the saint was pointing to the place from which the viewer needed to look to see an anamorphic illusion hidden within the figure of St. John. The illusion had revealed a coiled viper, as if about to strike with its fangs.

And why was there so much pointing taking place in Renaissance art anyway? No one had ever explained it, but it was always there. Only in Renaissance art were pointing gestures so regular that it seemed like a fashion statement.

I had scrunched my face many times trying to make sense of it. Leonardo's writings again seemed to answer the question. He wrote that "The action by which a figure points at anything near, either in regard to time or situation, is to be expressed by the hand. …"[7] But it didn't explain what the object being pointed at was. His portrait of St. John had shown a snake. In *The Virgin and Child with St. Anne and St. John the Baptist* was a crocodile, and again it was St. John that was pointing to it. In *The Last Supper*, Leonardo painted St. Thomas with a finger pointing up toward heaven. In *The School of Athens*, Raphael supposedly used Leonardo's features to depict the figure of Plato, whose right hand points upward with practically the same exact gesture.

More subtly was the finger-pointing in art such as Raphael's portrait of his mistress, *Woman with the Veil*. Her middle finger aims at the illusion of a pig head, while she points another finger at herself. Was the pointer finger some sort of secret sign?

I thought I was getting carried away, yet, the idea didn't seem so far-fetched. Although Leonardo wrote secret instructions on how to view illusions from the d-point on the left, other artists sometimes contradicted his writings. His *St. John the Baptist*, which revealed a viper that can be viewed from above the art, did not follow it exactly.

Many works of art came to mind as I considered other hidden illusions, also containing figures pointing in a certain direction. Art pieces marched through my mind as if through a spotlight in a darkened room, a forming pattern beginning to make sense of the pointing gestures.

Where there's a figure pointing, there's also an illusion hiding.

Was it possible that the unexplained gesture was a sign for the viewer looking at the art? The most iconic pointing finger in the world suddenly came to mind: *The Creation of Adam*, which exists near the center of the Vatican ceiling, and represents the moment God reaches out a finger to breathe life and knowledge into Adam.

Or was He clueing Adam in on a secret?

I'd seen the image used on everything from screen savers to dish towels. If there was an iconic image used more than *Mona Lisa*, it was the fingers of God and Adam. With everything I had learned, I had to wonder if God was telling Adam to look for the pointing finger?

Was it some kind of key, Michelangelo? The hands telling the observer where to view the illusion from?

Jonah was just a few panels away, pointing a finger from each hand. But why? I swallowed, already knowing the answer before looking. If it was true, then it made sense why God was looking directly at His and Adam's fingers about to touch. God's eyes focused not on Adam, but on the finger pointing itself, the point of impact, like two electric cables about to connect and

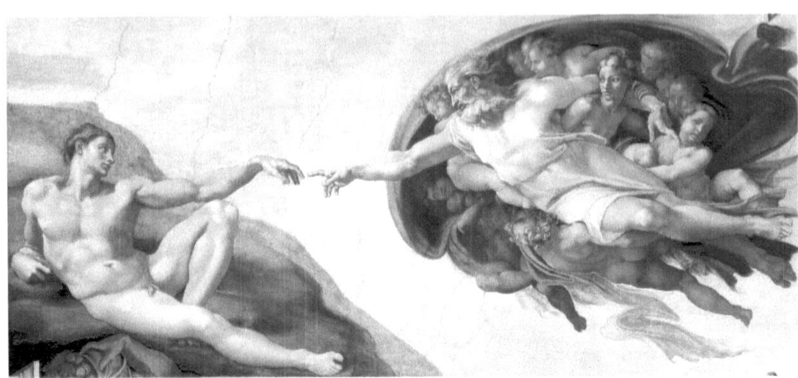

Michelangelo's *Creation of Adam* (c. 1512).

discharge a powerful current. The anticipation of what would happen next was electric. God creating Adam, God touching life into his body: "And the Lord God formed a man of the slime of the earth: and breathed into his face the breath of life, and man became a living soul" (*Douay-Rheims*, Gen. 2:7).[8] And even though Michelangelo had painted the image of God, Michelangelo had become a god himself to art fans all over the world.

I revisited the illusions I previously found on the chapel ceiling, examining and comparing the fingers of each figure's hands. In the painting of Daniel that showed a face dressed in armor, the prophet's finger pointed downward—*where the anamorphic face could be seen from.*

In the *Cumean Sibyl* that revealed a creature's face, even as the figure held a book with her hands, a left pointer finger was aimed subtlety downward, also pointing to where the anamorphic face would reveal itself from.

Rotated onto its right side, *Prophet Zechariah*, showing the anamorphic face of a bearded old man, has one of the two putti behind him pointing downward—the point from which to view the bearded man's anamorphic face.

I felt light-headed, oblivious to everything else around me, uncertain if even an earthquake would be able to shake me from my trancelike state. I had unlocked something big. The realization was both beautiful and terrifying—terrifying because it meant I would one day have to revisit hundreds of paintings, including ones I found nothing in, but might still reveal something once I paid attention to any finger pointing. Potentially, it could have meant ten different directions if a figure showed each of their fingers. An open hand with the fingers spread open could signal five different directions. Some paintings contained many figures.

Had Michelangelo provided a clue all along? I carefully followed where Adam and God each pointed to, tilting my head to study their possible d-points to see if anything could be seen. It wasn't long before I got my answer. "Yes," Michelangelo seemed to say through his art, "*The Creation of Adam* is a key."

49

The Point

If Michelangelo had illustrated *The Creation of Adam* as a key to literally point out the illusions, how could it be? The woman in *Mona Lisa* wasn't pointing to anything. The transformation of the woman and the background is seen from the d-point. So were fingers only pointing out anamorphic illusions when those illusions appeared from somewhere other than the d-point?

Shuffling through various paintings, I began to see that it wasn't always an obvious pointing gesture. Many times it was the position of relaxed fingers that very subtly indicated secret imagery. "What do you see from over there?" figures seemed to ask. At times, there was no hint at all. I couldn't figure out exactly what determined this, but it seemed to differ from one artist to another. Yet, when finger pointing was apparent, many times, illusions did reveal themselves.

The Creation of Adam had to be a visual instruction from Michelangelo, telling viewers to look from where fingers pointed to. *The Creation of Adam* also showed two fingers pointing—one from Adam, and one from God. So if one finger potentially signified an illusion, could multiple pointing gestures in the same picture possibly reveal multiple illusions?

I followed the direction of Adam and God's finger pointing to their prospective d-points, examining every bit of the panel for a long time, and from every possible direction. Never would I have expected what I saw.

What I would realize—at least on Michelangelo's ceiling art—was that whatever figure was pointing out the secret viewing point to look from was sometimes the same figure that contained the illusion. So God was pointing out where to look from in order to see whatever secret anamorphic picture the figure of God was hiding. And Adam was pointing out where to look from to see whatever anamorphic image the figure of Adam was hiding.

From where Adam was signaling to look from (below him to the right), I made out the image of a smushed human face protruding from his rib cage. His right hand is almost in a pinching motion, like he's pulling out his own rib. Perhaps a reference to the taking of Adam's rib to create Eve?

Where God points his iconic finger reveals something much more complicated. What appeared first was a mouth, beady eyes, and head from his torso and upper legs. The head had a wide, meaty nose, like that of a bull. God's biceps created the appearance of horns, and His beard became a tuft of hair on the creature's head. An evil looking thing, and definitely not human. It looked like a Minotaur.

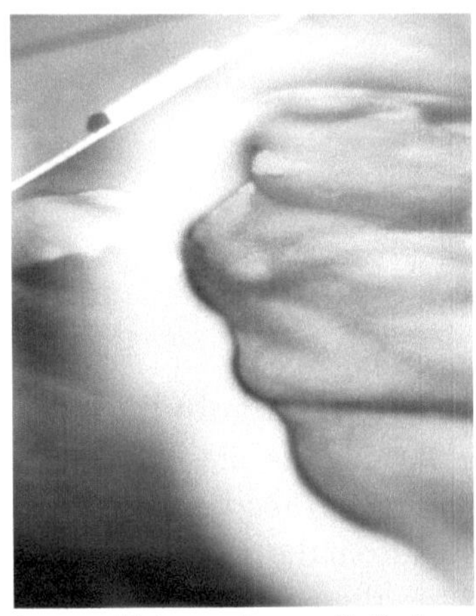
Anamorphic human face profile (facing left, highlighted) in Adam's torso.

From below, where his left thumb points, God's legs and those of the putto directly beneath Him form a crocodile head. The eye looked to be in the area above God's left thigh. In the putti below him there looks to be a head of what could be an ape. Oddly, the creatures had a babyish look to them, almost cute instead of creepy, like most of the others I came across.

Months later I would realize exactly what was taking place in the scene. It began with the red cloth surrounding God and the figures around him—which always looked unusual for being there at all. Renaissance artists had a reason for every detail they added, even if it was simply a personal preference. So I questioned it, like anything else.

One day, I was lost in thought. Another birthday had just passed and I was then in my 40s, thinking back to years earlier, how my marriage had ended in divorce. I had been hesitant about the idea of marriage or having children ever since. Still, I imagined what it would be like to have children at my age, what it would be like to have a wife who was pregnant, to watch her give birth, to raise that child together, me acting like the goofy father I imagined I would be, pretend-fighting with light sabers if it were a boy, or sitting down for pretend teatime with a girl, wearing a silly hat and talking with a fake English accent. Would I ever make a good father? I wondered. My relationship with my father had made me hesitant about wanting to be a father myself. I never had the kind of relationship in which my father and I played catch or talked one-on-one like two close friends. Our relationship always felt distant and without empathy. He was a hard worker who took on many overtime hours in order to provide a house for our family. Our fridge and cupboards were always filled with food. But the concept of a nurturing relationship was alien. Growing up, I accepted our relationship for what it was, reasoning that it was how all traditional Italian fathers were with their sons. He was simply there—present, but in a way that felt unavailable.

In past arguments, girls I dated would criticize me in a way that sounded to me as if they were describing my father, who they usually never met. No matter what, we were of the same blood. He was the tree and I was the apple. The idea of being a father scared me. Human behavior could be changed, but heredity could not.

The idea of children was percolating in my mind as I was looking at that large cloth surrounding God in *The Creation of Adam*. There had been a story of

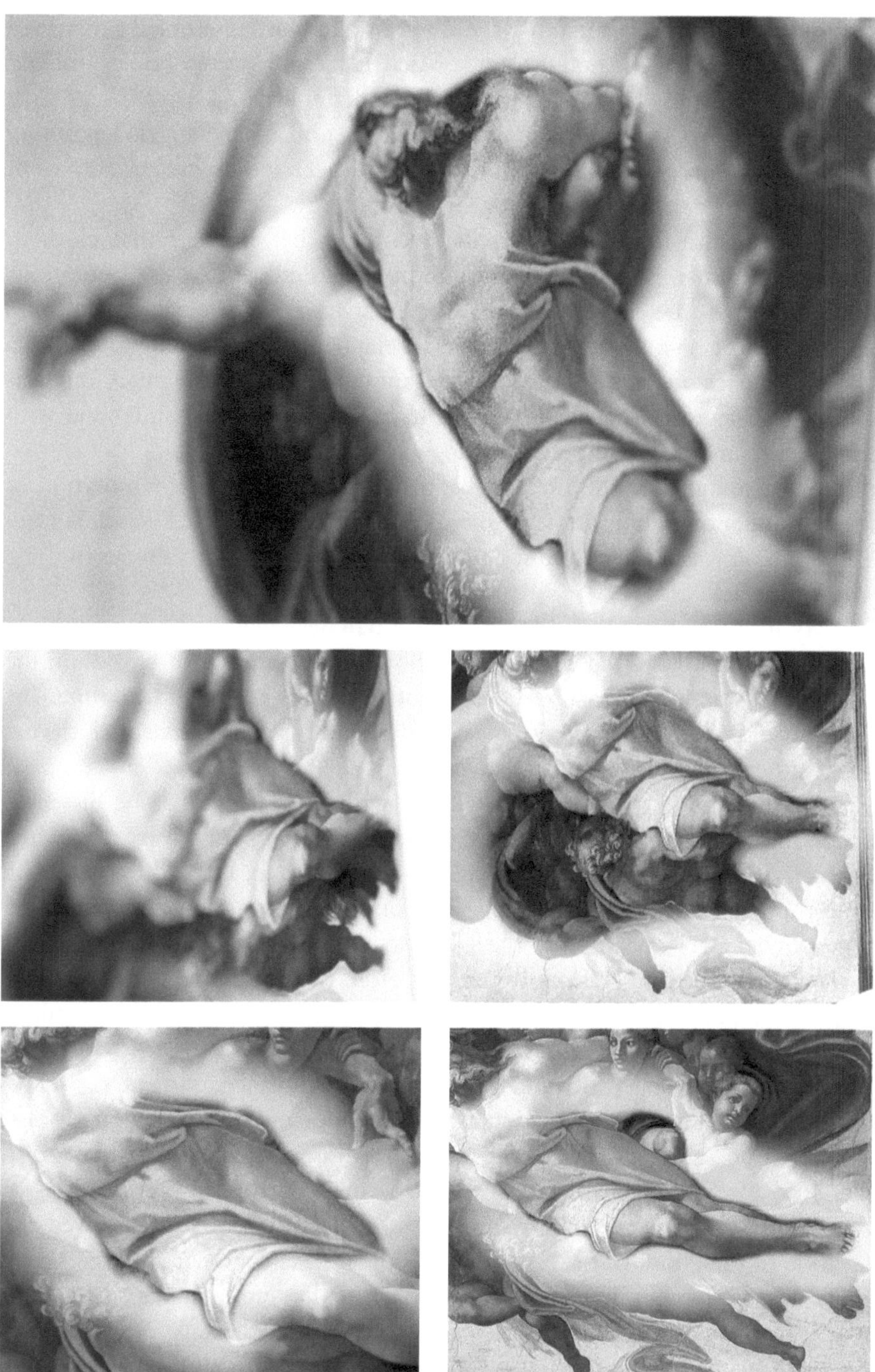

Creation of Adam illusions (highlighted). **TOP:** Anamorphic minotaur head in figure of God. **MIDDLE ROW:** Anamorphic view of what looks like a young wolf head and elephant head. **Bottom row:** Ambiguous illusions of possible bird head and crocodile head, both youthful in appearance.

a brain surgeon who claimed that the shape of that cloth resembled a dissected brain.[1] "It's possible," I thought, since Michelangelo dissected bodies—as did Leonardo—to study human anatomy, to be a better artist.

The idea of all those hidden animal heads and Michelangelo's pointing figures really got me thinking. No longer had I been looking at the surface of artworks, but more at what artists were trying to say.

I wasn't sure that Michelangelo meant for the shape of that cloth to resemble a human brain, but I didn't completely doubt it. At the same time, there seemed to be other creatures hidden within God's cloak, what could be the head of a lion, and maybe even an elephant. I wasn't sure about them like I had been in seeing other hidden animals. What really stuck out was the babyish features they each seemed to have. Smooth and undefined with adolescent, innocent qualities. Its strangeness confused me.

I kept going over the meaning of Adam's creation—a representation of the beginning of mankind. Man's *birth.* Which brought me back to a line from Leonardo's *Envy* passage: "No sooner is Virtue born than Envy comes into the world to attack it."

My intuition screamed. I wasn't sure if Michelangelo had a human brain in mind when he painted that maroon cloth around the set of figures on the right, but I was suddenly sure he had another organ in mind at the time. The anatomy of its round, maroon shape, and that odd turquoise piece of cloth that hung out of place became a dead giveaway.

The air around me seemed to vibrate with energy. Because he dissected bodies, he could draw the anatomy of virtually any organ or body part. So when I looked up images of the human placenta and uterus, I was dumbfounded, even though I shouldn't have been. I shook my head in awe, as it registered that Michelangelo positioned the cloth to look like a uterus, even with its correct color. The long, teal cloth hanging from the bottom looked even more suspicious, until I searched images of umbilical cords. There were plenty online, some shown in a bright teal color.

I found that I wasn't the first to notice the resemblance to the uterus shape, but nobody had noticed that Michelangelo had portrayed the birthing process. The cloth on the right side of the art had a more dramatic movement to it, like an explosion, or burst. *Or birthing.* It explained the babyish qualities of the creatures that were possibly present. On the surface, the art showed the creation of mankind. But secretly, as I put the images together, *The Creation of Adam* signified something dark. Leonardo wrote that "no sooner is Virtue born than Envy comes into the world to attack it," and Michelangelo had painted the birth of mankind, and that with it, came the genesis of the cardinal sins deriving from mankind's animalistic traits—pride, greed, lust, gluttony, wrath, sloth, and envy.

And maybe God was to blame.

And perhaps the only redemption was God warning Adam that artists would point out mankind's evil traits in their creations with simple finger gestures.

Besides Adam and God, Jonah had the most obvious pointing gesture of all. Originally, it took a moment to see what Jonah was looking at. I used the anamorphic view below Jonah, from the spot he was pointing to. I expected to see a large head, like in all the other prophets and sibyls, but there was no illusion at all, even though all the other prophets and sibyls hid images. I looked all around the prophet, but it wasn't until, from the secret viewing spot he pointed at, that I also noticed his eyes. His eyes seemed to be telling me what area to look *to*. Jonah was looking above his head.

It didn't appear immediately, but when it did, I nearly recoiled as Jonah did, understanding why he looked so scared!

In the scene above him, *Separation of Light from Darkness*, where God separates night from day, the Ignudi formed not one, but two giant, human-like figures looking down onto Jonah. Pronounced chins. Thick cheekbones. Tight, powerful lips. And not just heads, but partial torsos also, each one extending an arm and hand that seemed to reach out toward me! In actuality, they were actually reaching for Jonah, as if about to pick him up and out from his seat.

At first, the figure of God didn't seem to play any part in the illusion. But as I stared in wonder, He appeared to be trying to stop the two giants, like a referee separating two opposing players, His arms stretched out defensively toward one of the large figures. He didn't look scared like Jonah, but He did look a little nervous—the giants were much bigger than the figure of God.

I rotated the illusion back and forth, watching the giants appear and disappear, studying Michelangelo's technique in awe. I noticed how highlights and bright colors were placed to stand out, to make the images appear, and how the Ignudi were posed to create the effect, certain details falling out of focus when viewed from the anamorphic angle, and others becoming more dominant. The figures had to take on certain poses for images to appear. It made sense why so many figures in Renaissance art were overdramatic.

There was also something very odd going on with Jonah. Something completely new took place. Jonah *himself* was reacting, not to the art first seen, but to the hidden illusion. Although Jonah looked like he could be reacting to the image of God above, it never made complete sense to me until the giants appeared. It was the first time I noticed a figure in the painting doing so, as if he could see the illusion himself. Up until then, I didn't notice any figures reacting to the hidden images around them.

I thought only the viewer was supposed to see the secret images. Jonah was "breaking the fourth wall," and I had no idea why. It made it feel as though Jonah were alive, rather than just a painted character.

Was that your intention, Michelangelo?

Every so often, I found myself returning to that magical image of two large giants reaching for Jonah. Were they the same giants from Genesis: "Now giants were upon the earth in those days" (*Douay-Rheims*, Gen. 2:7)?[2] Or maybe the race of human-shaped in Ovid's *Metamorphoses*: "So that the skies above might be no more / secure than earth, the race of Giants plotted / (we hear) to rule in heaven by themselves" (1.205-07; Martin)?[3] It might have explained why God looked to be frightening them off. Or maybe they represented the giants from both stories. I couldn't be sure.

Either way, I observed other illusions along the ceiling. Above the giants, in the very next panel—*The Creation of the Sun, Moon and Vegetation*—more heads appeared. God points to his right with one hand, and to the left with the other, his arms spread like wings. On the surface, He commands the sun and moon to their positions, but I realized He was secretly signaling, "Look from here, and look from there," like an orchestra conductor. From one side, an old, bald man appeared to be crying. I could feel his agony as I made out his long, white beard, his heartbroken face, his eyes squeezed shut, his mouth open in a sorrowful expression. I couldn't tell if it was God Himself or someone completely different, but I was curious why he was weeping.

The figure's expression reminded me of the old man who drove the vehicle that killed John. The expression that had been seared into my mind was the same—their wide, open mouths and that painful look on their faces.

In the opposite figure of God, to the left, I made out the heads of an ape and a roaring lion. From the other side, exactly where that figure of God facing the viewer points, appeared something else. His body became a head, not really human-looking, with a long nose, prominent chin, shallow eyes, and two long, bull-like horns made from God's extending arms. A tuft of devilish hair from God's beard hangs

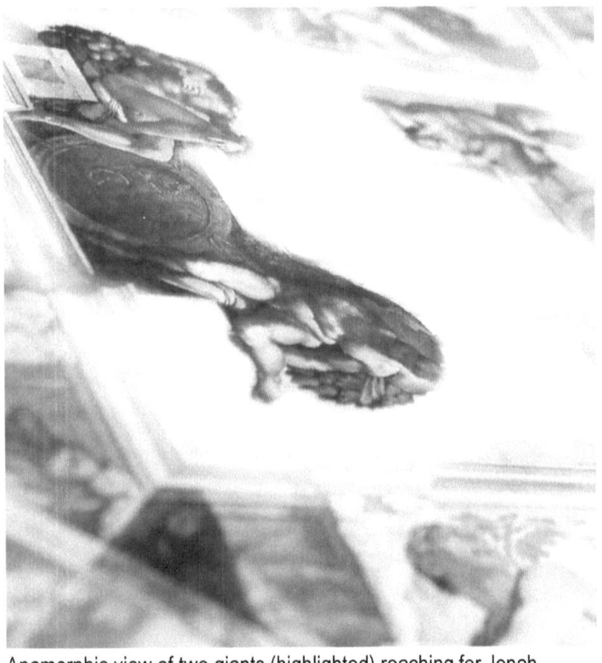

Anamorphic view of two giants (highlighted) reaching for Jonah.

over the forehead of the creature. Michelangelo would have been crucified if the Pope ever saw it, because it looked like the head of a goofy looking devil.

Was it all just a private joke among masters? *Hey, Botticelli! Top this one!* Or was it a safe way of giving patrons and clients the finger? Like artists slipping a snake behind the Pope, or a weasel behind a Bishop, because they knew the Pope *was* a snake and the Bishop *was* a weasel? Or was there something more?

I made sure to constantly document what I found, worried that I would eventually lose track of some of the secret details.

> *"The Creation of the Sun, Moon and Vegetation"—Second figure of God facing viewer, when rotated 90 degrees clockwise, forms the face of a man with beard. A d-point isn't needed, but seems to help the illusion stand out if you look upward across the art of what has become the bottom side. The perspective of the head is from slightly below, as a child's view. Eyes, nose, forehead, cheekbone, beard are clearly detailed. Drapery around God's legs form the beard and lower lip. Darker shading above creates the open mouth. Dark folds between the arm and the leg of the nude youth next to God form an eye.*
>
> *With panel still positioned 90 degrees clockwise, opposite figure of God (with back to viewer) forms an animal head in profile. It faces left and looks like an ape head, but is difficult to tell. The bottom left tail of drapery forms the mouth, the circular curl of drapery tail creates the nostril. God's right foot gives us the bottom jaw.*
>
> *A possible roaring lion is formed from same view and figure, but placed slightly higher than head of ape, but again, difficult to tell. The left foot forms a tongue. Curls of drapery tail (that formed the nostril of the ape) create the bottom jaw of lion. Cloth wrapping resembling a cuff around God's left calf forms the upper jaw. Wrinkles above that form nose and eyes.*

The faces made me think of the sorts of illusions Salvador Dali painted. In his 1938 work, *The Image Disappears* (what I thought could be a suitable name for many Renaissance works), the painting shows a female figure reading a letter. Its clever shadowing also forms the portrait of Diego Velázquez. A double-image, two scenes sharing the same canvas, but one stands out more than the other, depending on how closely the image is viewed.

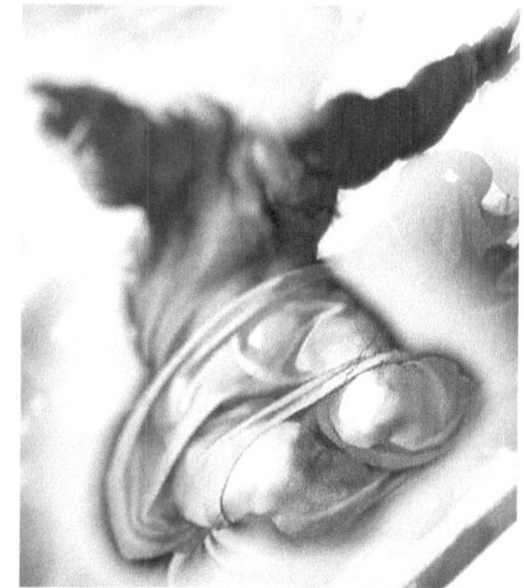

Anamorphic view of goofy, devil-like head (highlighted).

I looked down at the poster showing the whole ceiling, realizing that even at

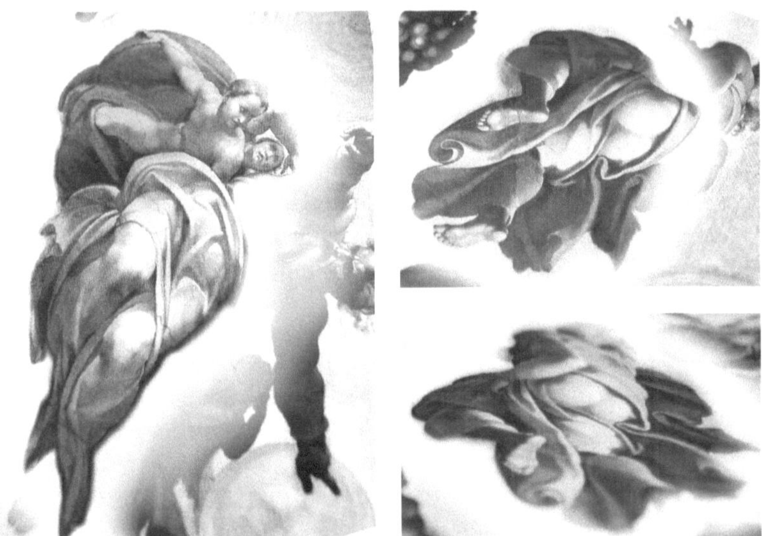

Images of various heads (highlighted) in *Creation of the Sun, Moon and Vegetation* when rotated right. **LEFT:** Anamorphic head of bald, bearded man. **RIGHT:** Possible ape head, facing left and possible head of lion, facing left.

its large size, the figures in the panels were still pretty small. And I wondered if, like the style of illusion Dali later used, the small panels were the only reason I was seeing some of the illusions, in the same way a cloud can't be seen unless from a far distance—up close, it would only appear to be like a thin fog.

Just as anthropomorphic landscapes began to show their illusions out in the open, no longer hiding them in the art, later artists like Dali made art that showed multiple images without needing any secret viewpoint. I wasn't sure if there was any connection between artists like Dali and Renaissance artists since they lived hundreds of years apart, but Arcimboldo in the sixteenth century used a similar concept in which multiple items combined to show a larger, completely different image.

The illusions in Renaissance art were not only more difficult to see than later works, but practically impossible to see at times without knowing exactly how to look. So what were the *real* illusions? I wondered. The imagery on the surface that kept everyone filled with so much admiration and awe that no one thought to look past the surface for anything hidden? Like a mansion that was so large and so breathtaking, no one thought to look for secret passages? Or was the secret imagery the real illusion? Were the incredible-looking figures and fake columns and stonework Michelangelo painted on the chapel ceiling all just a bunch of distractions? A deterrent? "Look at the wonderful ceiling. Masterfully painted, isn't it?" he seemed to say, like a magician diverting our attention away from what was really going on.

50

Facing Judgement

More than twenty years after finishing his ceiling masterpiece, Michelangelo painted *The Last Judgement* on the altar wall of that same church, in a way extending the magic and beauty and sheer size of the ceiling onto the wall. It represented the Second Coming of Christ, and included over three hundred eighty figures, by my count. He started the fresco in 1536, three years after Holbein publicly displayed the distorted anamorphic skull in *The Ambassadors.* In Michelangelo's *Last Judgement*, also front and center is Charon and his boat from Dante's *Inferno.*

After Michelangelo's death, another artist was commissioned to paint loincloths over the offensive nudity he included—details that nearly got him accused of heresy. The new artist also repainted St. Catherine and St. Blasius, altering their postures as well as adding clothing.

Way before my obsession with Renaissance art began, the art style in *The Last Judgement* fresco always looked different to me from his ceiling art. Compared to the art on the ceiling, its structure was more chaotic, less elegant. The figures on the wall fresco seemed to have shorter necks, wider body frames and more muscle mass—almost as if the whole wall had been stretched sideways. There was an odd sense to the composition, especially in how the patches of blue sky clumsily broke up the groups of figures around the wall. It gave the entire wall the appearance of large goggle-like eyes at the top arches and a triangular mouth below, like a Halloween pumpkin.

I spent plenty of time examining images of the fresco wall. My plan was to one day, after finishing my book, take a trip to see it (and visit other parts of Italy for its art), although there was no way to look at the wall from all the different angles the way I could with printouts.

His *Last Judgement* was hiding plenty. The images were more subtle, more technically brilliant, more thought-provoking than the ones he created on his ceiling two decades before. My stack of notebooks continued to grow taller, and so were my binders of art images, their secret illustrations marked in detail. The sheer artistry of it all continued to amaze me. How far it all was from the surface's flat portrayal everyone was used to. To think that so much continued to be missed by those who appreciated the art, and that the world still saw *Mona Lisa* as just some unknown homely woman, and that the Sistine Chapel ceiling plainly showed scenes from the Book of Genesis was awful. It saddened me—there was so much more, and I wanted everyone to see it.

At the time he was creating the wall fresco, Michelangelo was in his sixties. Leonardo had passed away more than sixteen years earlier. To me, his notebooks made it obvious that Leonardo had been a man of science, while Michelangelo was a man of God. *The Comedy* was arguably his favorite book, and he would recite its lines and write poems honoring Dante. There were stories of Michelangelo and Leonardo disliking each other. I thought back to the famous taunt between the two near the Palazzo Spini when Leonardo, as he passed by with friend Giovanni di Gavina, was called over by several notables to come and explain a passage from Dante the men were discussing. Michelangelo also happened to be passing by, and so Leonardo called out:

> "Michelangelo will be able to tell you what it means," to which the latter, thinking this had been said to entrap him, replied, "Nay, do thou explain it thyself, horse-modeller that thou art—who, unable to cast a statue in bronze, wast forced with shame to give up the attempt." So saying, he turned his back upon them and departed.[1]

I would come to wonder if their disdain had anything to do with an incredibly large illusion on *The Last Judgement* wall that I found (although *found* didn't seem like the appropriate word since the illusion was so large that it maybe was more fitting to say that it practically fell on top of me). It jumped out at me as I examined a small printout, just a few inches tall, in one of my binders. I wasn't sure if patrons would be able to stand back far enough in the chapel to see it. It appeared for the same reason *Mona Lisa*'s question mark appeared when I stood far back from the art, except that *The Last Judgement* wasn't upside down. It was easier to see on a shrunken image as was the case with many other secret images of its kind—the equivalent effect of standing at a distance so it would appear smaller. Even then, I was a little unsure of what I was looking at.

I took out a marker to trace outlines of what I thought I was seeing. With anticipation, I started at the top of the printout, with the arch on the left connected to the ceiling, tracing the top half of the circle of what looked like the top of a head. Then I continued the line down along the shape of what became a forehead, moving downward to create the shape of a nose, then mouth, then further down to draw the chin, and finally ending the line toward the bottom of the fresco around the bearded jaw. Had I drawn it on the actual wall of the chapel, the outline would have measured thirty feet high. I then repeated the same shape on the right half of the wall, but in reverse, as if in a mirror, and without a beard, so the two outlines faced each other.

Superimposed on my printout of the altar wall were two large shapes of faces in profile, not so different from the kinds of faces that hid in the figures on the ceiling—faces like those in the prophets and sibyls that were as large as the figures themselves—except the two in *The Last Judgement* were the size of the whole altar wall, each face made from roughly half of all the characters in the art. The two heads faced each other, angled downward, nose to nose, foreheads touching as if butting heads in a heated argument. The head on the left had a long, cartoonish nose of mocking quality and the shape of a beard. On the right was a man with a crooked nose.

The facial shapes were a little easier to see when looking at the whole wall from its anamorphic angle underneath. It seemed to explain the patchy composition, which helped create the shape of the heads.

The faces made me think of Leonardo and Michelangelo, back near the Palazzo Spini, arguing about Dante. Leonardo looked to be on the left with a beard, Michelangelo on the right with his crooked nose (a broken nose that never healed properly after Pietro Torrigiano, a jealous sculptor, had punched

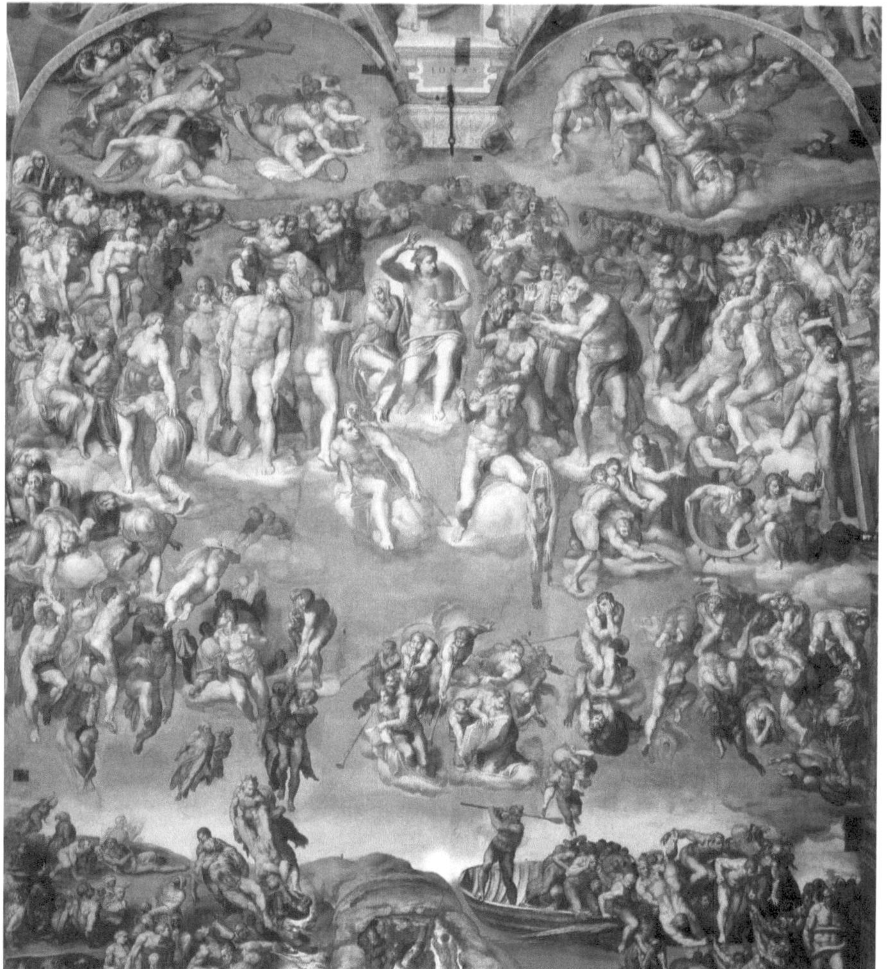

The Last Judgement (1536-41) by Michelangelo.

him in the face). Yet, I couldn't be sure it was them. As far as I could tell, no clues were pointing to them specifically.

Examining the shapes further, I noticed how the different groups of figures throughout the wall were positioned to create the effect of facial features. To the left of Christ, in the center of the art, closely grouped figures formed the nose, cheek, and forehead. Two horizontal clouds made the upper and lower lips. Another larger group of figures made the hair and beard. Oddly, inside the head on the left where the brain would be positioned were the figures carrying the cross on which Christ was crucified. Where the brain on the right head would be were figures carrying the pillar against which Christ had been flogged, as if Michelangelo was providing a view inside their minds. If that was the case, why hide such a meaningful idea?

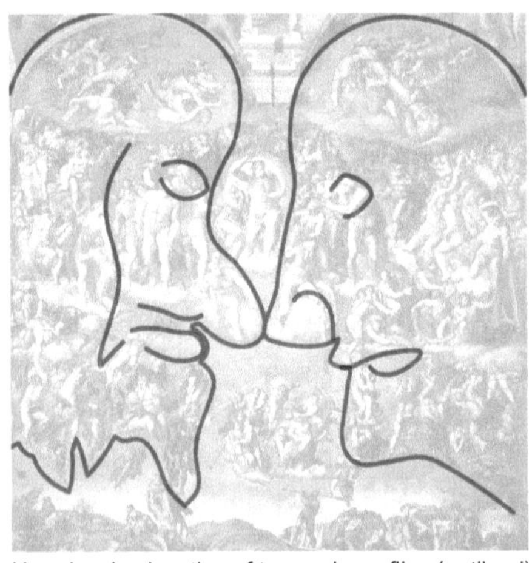

Key showing location of two male profiles (outlined) facing each other in Michelangelo's fresco.

In between the two butting heads was the dramatic figure of Christ, standing in the line of sight between them. He was not just standing between them, he was holding up an arm as if dramatically signaling "Enough!" Like Jonah's reaction on the ceiling, the figure of Christ appeared to be interacting with the illusion. But who did the two faces represent? If so, what drove Michelangelo to portray that in the Vatican? What feelings did he harbor against Leonardo to have dedicated years of hard work to a potential illusion of him when he was in his sixties? Or were they both showing someone else?

I thought of Leonardo's long, flowing beard, but the face on the wall outlined a beard that looked short and bushy. Maybe it wasn't Leonardo. Maybe it wasn't a man at all. Could it be God? Did Michelangelo show himself butting heads with the Almighty? It was hard to imagine the faithful artist doing so. He was a loyal Catholic whose greatest works of art (on the surface, anyway) supported and celebrated the Catholic Church in an age when entire nations broke away from the Catholic faith. But he had also been frustrated and angry at the Church. Was he frustrated with his Maker about the cruel world He created? Did he resent the years of hardship he went through as an artist, constantly pulled in different directions by different patrons, temporarily having to abandon jobs at times to complete other jobs for other patrons when all he wanted was to chisel marble into the shapes of man? Was it more than just a fresco of Judgement Day? Did he secretly portray the day in which *he* would be judged?

I thought of the self-portrait he was known to have placed with the figure of St. Bartholomew, believed to have been flayed alive for spreading his faith. The figure is shown holding out an organ of skin as if it were his costume. Experts note that Michelangelo painted his own face on the skin.

Considering what he put on that ceiling, I already viewed Michelangelo as godlike. At the same time, I felt a connection with the artist, his experiences making me think of my own life. Michelangelo struggled to please his father—who didn't want his son to become an artist and shame the family name. Growing up, I didn't feel that my father was proud of me pursuing a career in art. He didn't show much interest in seeing my work, probably wasn't ever aware that for years some of the most prominent billboards he drove by in the city had been designed by me. But I also never shared that kind of information with him, having felt that he had no interest in my art. Like in the stories I read of Michelangelo's relationship with his father, my father would inquire about the money I made as if that was all that mattered. Like Michelangelo, I made just enough to get by, happy for the most part that I was able to get paid for practicing what I was passionate about.

Perhaps Michelangelo had been upset with God because he was kept away from his true passion as a sculptor. Unlike Michelangelo, I didn't believe in God, even though there were times in life I wished He existed, moments in which I had questions I felt no one else could answer. *Why did John have to die that day? Why was I put through that hell when my world was already falling apart, my marriage with Paige tumbling, and barely any strength left in my body? Why did things have to be the way they were with my father?*

Though his harsh comments were not unusual, I couldn't disrespect my father. "You're the only one to treat me with respect," he once said to me after complaining about other family members.. Many times, he'd share opinions I didn't agree with, but I'd pretend to agree to avoid confrontation, even when he criticized me. There were plenty of times when I wanted to voice my disagreement, but he had that fatherly power over me I think most dads had over their children which sometimes kept them from talking back. In rare moments when I opposed his view, he would sometimes laugh as his face took on an expression that made me feel naive and idiotic and ashamed. So I learned to keep my mouth shut. Nothing in the world gave me more regret than that reaction of his.

But, over the years, I became less patient with him, less quiet, less respectful, more bold. My "boldness" amounted to letting myself become more distant from him. I gave up trying to keep what we had intact, and I eventually began avoiding him altogether instead of confronting him about the resentment I held. I didn't know if that made me a coward, or a bad son, or both, but the increasing lack of interaction between us made me less anxious than I had been.

I looked back on that time in my life, when there was also the stress of my divorce, and how I became depressed, and dreaded my job. I felt like a worthless, untalented graphic designer stuck in the life I had. I could barely get through the day. It was as if bags of sand were always tied to my feet, each step requiring great amounts of energy. Then came the death of my coworker. My desire to go on practically vanished. I remembered how I stood in the pew at John's funeral, defeated, angered, wishing, daring, for God to meet me face-to-face so I could scream out my hatred to Him. I had been pushed past the edge, but, like the times I needed Him, He never came.

And there I was years later with the image of *The Last Judgement*, when I thought I had gotten over trying to figure out if God was real. The discoveries had taken over my life, and again my mind went back to wondering about Him. There was something I needed to know, something that had been eating away at me, a question to which the need for an answer had only been growing stronger. Why had I been burdened with the discoveries?

I had become obsessed with finding answers to explain it all, unable to pull myself away from my work, obligating myself to years of research and writing when I could have been trying to live a normal life like everyone else around me. I knew I couldn't just do the job to get it done. I had to do so much more. I had to find answers to every mystery. And I had to do it all myself. I was too *proud* to ask for help, too *greedy* to share any credit. Just as Michelangelo put everything into creating the greatest work of art on that ceiling. He had to prove to himself that he could do something so great. And I had to prove to myself that I could understand those artists better than anyone, that I was worthy as an artist, that all along, I had made the right decisions to become an artist. That I was destined to do something that would impact the art world.

The image of the two butting heads in *The Last Judgement* struck me hard, touching me deep down. All those centuries ago—had Michelangelo felt the anger that I felt?

What I never would have—*could have*—expected, then happened. Spellbound by the fresco, I was suddenly imagining my own profile up on the wall. In place of the head on the right with the pronounced nose I envisioned my own profile and large, Italian nose. It wasn't anything one could call evidence—at best one could argue it was a sign, depending on the religious belief of who was asked. Whatever it was, for the first time, I saw myself face to face with the image of God. It was me up there butting heads with the Almighty. For a long while, I stared at the shaped outlines on the altar wall, stinging with mixed emotion, not resisting the feeling as I would have in the past. I submitted myself, knees weakening slightly as I lowered myself onto a cold chair in the attic where I stood. With that came one final question. There was no way to ever be sure if solving *Mona Lisa* had been in my future all along, placed there by some higher power, or if all the discoveries had been the result of some big fluke. Had everything in my life all been part of one big plan to lead me to that image of *The Last Judgement*, facing God, facing me?

Something else then disrupted those thoughts. Perhaps it was the pronounced nose that stopped me, but I was thankful for the interruption. I had been sure it was Michelangelo's profile up on the right side of that wall. Compared to the long, droopy one on the left, the crooked nose appeared to be a clue. Could it be another person known to have a distinguishable nose? Was a poet butting heads with God? *Dante?* But there was no way to be sure. The identities of the two men would have to remain unknown. For all I knew, it could have been anyone, and everyone. Maybe Michelangelo intended for every person to look up at that altar wall and imagine themselves facing God with whatever thoughts they had for the Almighty.

Whenever strangers asked about the book I was working on, I hesitated to respond. I didn't expect anyone to believe what I had discovered without giving them specific details I wanted to keep secret—at least until my memoir was released. If in a gutsy mood, I'd say that I figured out who *Mona Lisa* actually was and wanted to share the experience of my discoveries with the world. On occasion, the eyes of inquisitors widened with fascination or bewilderment (a source of motivation for me at times). Questions followed. *Who is she? Is it a man? A self-portrait?* "You'll have to wait for the book," I'd say, and hint at how secretive Renaissance artists were. Usually, they were left somewhat intrigued by the animals that news stories had already reported on. But the eyes of those who were doubtful would become narrow, and their lips would tighten. Questions were still asked, but in a way that made it sound like an interrogation. *You an art professor or something? How can you know why she's smiling?* The question always put a grin on my face. "How do we know the thoughts of the figures in *The Last Supper*?" I'd ask, hoping to get my point across that it's because Leonardo based his art on an existing story, as was the norm for many paintings. *Have you seen the actual painting?* others would ask, at times insinuating that I couldn't possibly have figured out her identity without having seen the actual *Mona Lisa.* A silly misconception.

Some hid their doubt better than others. Either way, I couldn't blame them. I also couldn't help talking about it. Asking me about the discoveries was like asking a child to talk about their favorite cartoon—I'd trip over my own words, excited over the topic. Succeeding to turn one's expression to a look of surprise and wonder as I danced around the discoveries gave me great pleasure. There's something so magical about the idea of secret images hidden in front of our eyes for so long. Seeing people's faces transform with just a few movements of facial muscles said so much. Leonardo studied this by carving up cadavers and drawing anatomical details in his notebooks. That faces were so revealing was why I loved studying people's expressions and painting portraits. The eyes always drew me in. Leonardo wrote that "the eye … is called the window of the soul. …"[2] I wondered what people would see if they looked into my soul. Could my eyes reveal my past? Secrets long forgotten? An artist too passionate for his own good?

What did your eyes hide, Leonardo? Would we see the genius we all portrayed you as? Or someone much different? Did the man behind those eyes struggle to convince others about certain ideas, such as man one day being able to fly? Or perhaps that Moses was lucky and that an earthquake caused the sea to split open rather than by some divine event? Considered brilliant even in his own time, Leonardo had a way with words, but I wondered what resistance he might have received in speaking of such possibilities. No one ever called me brilliant, and I was certainly no Leonardo da Vinci. My speech was often clumsy, so I envied those capable of opening minds to new ideas. It was a trait that would come in handy if I ever faced publicity again.

Seeing the world through the eyes of an artist can be challenging. Some things have to be experienced. A true artist understands what it's like to lose sleep over their work, that inspiration and determination can become so tightly balled inside of us, the only cure is to cover a canvas in paint, or paper with charcoal, or a computer screen with a finished design, that there's no sacrifice too large, that it's okay to ignore that sense of self-destruction we sometimes face when it comes to pursuing that perfect creation, and that perfect creation—if ever reached—could never leave us satisfied for long. Perhaps Michelangelo felt that same way at times while at the top of his scaffolding, an arm's reach from the ceiling as he sacrificed his health—strained eyes, aching back, perhaps a distressed mind—in pursuit of the perfect artistic creation.

Some of those who may have lacked artistic vision, incapable of seeing the illusions, have accused me of only imagining what I found. The cloud analogy seemed to be a favorite go-to comparison. One person told me it was like seeing "the face of Christ on burnt toast." I got used to not rolling my eyes, but defending my work became tiring. Some were so set on their opinion, no matter how much I explained that optical illusions were not unusual at all in Renaissance times, that aside from what I found, there was in fact an existing history to optical illusions even then. One could argue that the birth of optical illusions occurred in Renaissance times.

In *Hidden Images: Games of Perception, Anamorphic Art, Illusion*, Fred Leeman points out that in 1584, painter Giovanni Paolo Lomazzo wrote of an image hidden in a work "by Gaudenzio [Ferrari], a Christ in profile, whose hair resembles the waves of the sea," that from a specific view through a constructed hole, "appeared a very beautiful head of Christ" and that Francesco Melzi[3], Leonardo's pupil and heir to his manuscripts[4], "related that in the same fashion Leonardo made a dragon that fought with a lion—a wonder to behold" and "similarly constructed the horses that he gave to Francis I, king of France."[5]

In a way, all art revolved around the idea of illusions, such as taking a blank two-dimensional surface and illustrating a three-dimensional world. I thought back to my childhood when I started pencilling images like Spider-Man and Doctor Octopus battling it out on blank pages of drawing paper.

But there was a difference between seeing imaginary images in real clouds and those an artist placed in their work. Art historians couldn't deny the face of a devil hidden in the clouds in *Death and Ascension of St. Francis* that went seven hundred years without being noticed until it was spotted by experts in recent years. No one could deny that Leonardo knew about anamorphic perspective, because he was known to create the first illusion of its kind with *Leonardo's Eye.*

Giorgio Vasari, who wrote (in describing Michelangelo in a scene with a naive critic) "that no one can be a better judge than a man with experience of what he is criticizing,"[6] became the world's first art historian when he wrote *Lives of the Most Excellent Painters, Sculptors, and Architects.* And he knew about the illusions. Maybe he learned of them as a friend of Michelangelo, but he was aware of the illusions because his art contained them. I believed it may have been why Vasari mysteriously inscribed **CERCA TROVA** in his *Battle of Marciano* in Florence's Palazzo Vecchio. It was another mystery with no convincing explanation. Translated to *seek and find*, experts were unsure why Vasari placed the words in his fresco. Some believed it referred to the location of a missing Leonardo da Vinci painting—*The Battle of Anghiari*. **CERCA TROVA** was considered a clue from Vasari, hinting that Leonardo's painting existed on a separate wall behind Vasari's fresco. Experts (foolishly) drilled holes through Vasari's fresco in search of Leonardo's lost art. Drilling through a 500-year-old fresco was controversial. I opposed the defacing of Vasari's art, even if there was a Leonardo work hiding behind it. The story left me a little angered. I didn't even like the idea of art restoration in which someone other than the original artist sometimes touched up an original painting. Even seeing photos of experts handling *Mona Lisa* without gloves upset me. It sickened me to think about the greasy oils from their bare hands being spread onto Leonardo's masterpiece.

In any case, I wondered if **CERCA TROVA** was instead Vasari's way of telling the viewer to "seek and find" illusions in his *Battle of Marciano.* Or in any other painting, for that matter. Was it a clue like the written ones Leonardo left in his notebooks, or the illustrated clue Michelangelo put in *The Creation of Adam*? I had checked Vasari's fresco, and I did find illusions of faces, but they weren't as noticeable as some of those from other artists. Vasari's were very subtle, almost too subtle, but like their art, the styles in which the illusions were created varied from artist to artist.

Spotting hidden faces became second nature as I wrote my story. They were everywhere. Some were more beastly looking than others—which I was confident tied back to the animal-like qualities in humans Aesop's fables stemmed from, and that Dante referred to. Many appeared when I turned the

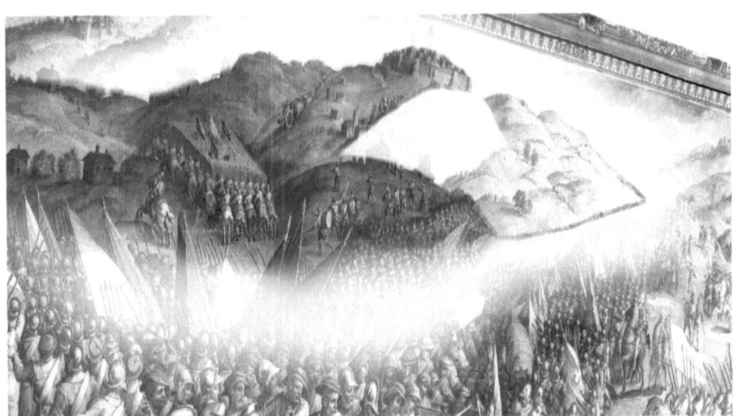

Section of Giorgio Vasari's *Battle of Marciano* (1554). Anamorphic illusion of a crocodile and the head of an animal on its side (highlighted).

artwork upside down, some when the art was on its side. Most were ambiguous rather than anamorphic. And many were easier to see when viewed from a distance. The more I shrank the artwork, the more prominent hidden faces became. As the art was made smaller and more difficult to see, details making up the secret faces (such as contrasting areas of color and shading or thick lines) would stand out more. Shrinking the art also helped to disconnect the mind from the art it was trained to see, or had memorized. The art usually camouflaged the illusion.

Like other images, there was a range of difficulty in spotting the faces. One of the easier ones included an upside-down lion head in Leonardo's *Five Grotesque Heads.* It looks straight at the viewer. In one of his water studies hides an upside-down face that looks to be smoking or perhaps chewing something. In *Virgin and Child with St. Anne and St. John the Baptist* is a head on its side spanning the drawing's width. It shows a stupefied expression. In a Michelangelo sketch for *The Last Judgement* is a bearded face in profile that looks like a self-portrait, and in the *Madonna and Child with Infant St. John* there is also a face comparable to the characters I used to see in comic books. Titian's *Portrait of a Man with a Quilted Sleeve* also hides a face. Even *Mona Lisa* hides a woman's face when on its left side.

Compared to the original animal heads I spotted, the human-like heads were more difficult to see, more faint, as if the artists wanted them to be even more subtle.

FOLLOWING PAGE: Ambiguous illusions of faces (some highlighted) in works of art turned upside down. **TOP ROW:** What looks like a lion head in Leonardo's *Five Grotesque Heads* (c. 1494) and a ghostly face in *Virgin and Child with St. Anne and St. John the Baptist* (c. 1500). **MIDDLE ROW:** Anamorphic face in one of Leonardo's water studies (c. 1512-13). Ambiguous facial profiles in Michelangelo's sketches for *The Last Judgement* (1536-41) and *Madonna and Child with Infant St. John* (c. 1533). **BOTTOM ROW:** Face in Titian's *Man in a Quilted Sleeve* (c. 1510) and section of Leonardo's *Mona Lisa* (turned onto its left side).

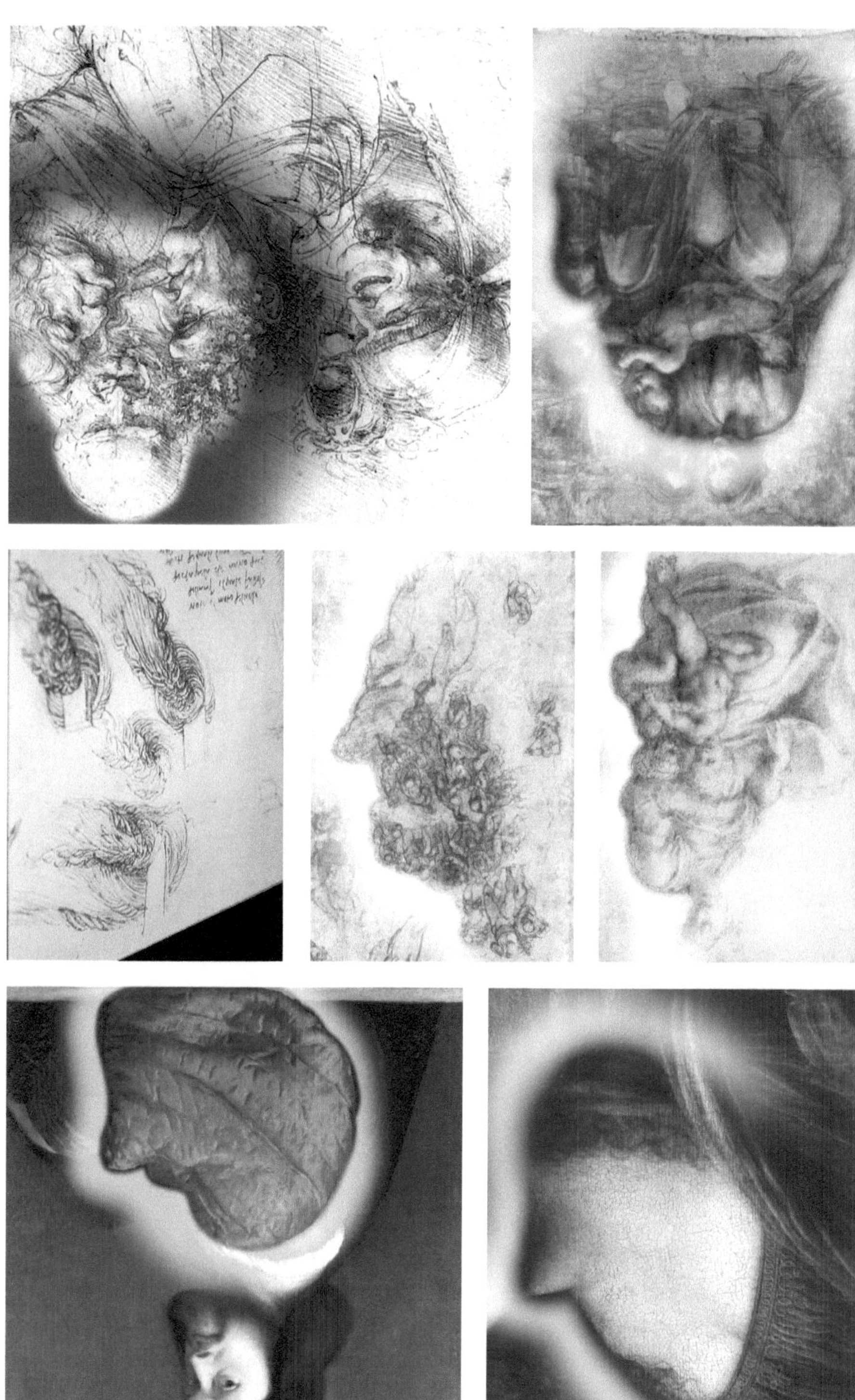

The idea of intertwining images of faces into the art was not as odd as it sounded. Arcimboldo's *The Cook* and *The Gardener* were both considered "double paintings," what Al Seckel in his book *Masters of Deception* refers to as "topsy-turvy" images: paintings created to portray two different images when inverted. The bowl of turnips in *The Cook* is inverted to reveal a portrait of a cook (made from vegetables). Seckel explains that "topsy-turvy portraits were popular on coins of that period that made fun of the Pope, whose image when inverted would turn into the devil."[7] So the idea that popes were sometimes made fun of in their own portraits wasn't such a crazy concept (which explained why Pope Julius II, in a portrait by Raphael, appeared to be sexually entertaining himself, as I had pointed out to Pasquale).

Although the animal heads had to be Aesopian, I wasn't so sure about the more human-looking ones, but I had an idea where I would find an answer. And eventually, I did. In *Paradiso*, Dante questions the faint images he sees in the higher regions of Heaven: "... There appeared a vision," said Dante, "which withdrew me / So close to it, in order to be seen" (*Par.* 3.7-8).[8] They turn out to be the faces of spirits, though Dante second-guesses himself as to what he is seeing, because they are difficult to perceive:

> Such as through polished and transparent glass,
> Or waters crystalline and undisturbed,
> But not so deep as that their bed be lost,
> Come back again **the outlines of our faces**
> **So feeble,** that a pearl on forehead white
> Comes not less speedily unto our eyes;
> Such saw I many faces prompt to speak,
> So that I ran in error opposite
> To that which kindled love 'twixt man and fountain.
>
> (*Par.* 3.10-18; Longfellow, emphasis added)[9]

A female spirit who was related to the poet says to him, "if thy mind doth contemplate me well, / The being more fair will not conceal me from thee ..." (*Par.* 3.47-48).[10] Dante responds: "... In your miraculous aspects / There shines I know not what of the divine, / Which doth transform you from our first conceptions" (3.58-60).[11]

In planning the illusions of human-like faces, artists might have considered the words *first conceptions* to mean the art first noticed on the surface. To "transform you from our first conceptions" might apply to visualizing the illusions as secondary to the surface art, but only if "thy mind doth contemplate me well." In his explanatory notes to the scene in *Paradiso*, Longfellow explains Dante's reference to Narcissus, who "mistook his shadow for a substance, [while] Dante, falling into the opposite error, mistakes these substances for shadows."[12] Beatrice assures Dante that the hazy apparitions are actually spirits.[13] Artists likely meant for the hazy-looking faces hidden in their art to go unnoticed except by the most perceptive eyes. "In the higher regions of heaven, the bodily forms of the spirits are entirely indistinguishable,"[14] one study guide explained. It seemed to make sense of the range of difficulty in seeing some of the art images—some that were practically indistinguishable.

Looking further, *The Dictionary of Symbols* explains "the face is there to be gazed at by God,"[15]—which I thought clarified why they usually appeared upside down, seen from *above* the art, from heaven's position. "The face is the symbol of the divinity in each human being," it continued to explain, that it "symbolizes human evolution out of darkness and into light," and "such a vision anticipates the state of bliss." It provided the biblical example of when Moses cried out, "I beseech thee, shew me thy glory" (*King James*, Exod. 33.18), longing to see God, but that no one was capable of seeing His face and living.[16] Perhaps the artists wanted viewers to experience God's vision as Dante had temporarily in the story.

The idea of faces seemed to play a big part in the illusions Renaissance artists created. In October of 2017, I spotted something I wasn't supposed to see. I had taken a break from writing to enjoy a movie and give my tired mind some time to rest. I laid in bed, hovering an iPad over my face. The movie I was about to watch was the 2016 version of *The Magnificent Seven* starring Denzel Washington, Chris Pratt, and Ethan Hawke. At the beginning of the movie appeared an image full of clouds. In them, I noticed a pair of eyes, a nose, and mouth. And it was smiling.

I'm overworking myself, I thought. *I'm imagining faces all over the place.*

After replaying the first few seconds over and over, I stopped the movie to research the origin of the movie art. The image originally came from a painting, but was created many years after the Renaissance. In fact, the artist had been born in 1956—less than twenty years before me, so I didn't see a reason for spotting faces in art made centuries after the Renaissance. At least, not in the same way Renaissance artists hid them. It actually appeared in the introduction of the production company. I must have seen the scene thousands of times before in some of my favorite movies—films like *The Karate Kid*, *Shawshank Redemption*, and *The Pursuit of Happiness.* It was the Columbia Pictures logo. Each time, a woman posing on a set of stairs—positioned almost like the Statue of Liberty—appeared in front of a sky full of clouds, then floated to the center of the logo and the screen. The cloud-face appeared just next to what has been called the Torch Lady. The first movie I saw in a theater, back in 1984 when I was ten, was *The Muppets Take Manhattan*, and it contained that same set of clouds (before Tristar Pictures became Columbia Pictures). It reminded me of Giotto's devil face.

I paused and replayed the opening of *The Magnificent Seven* several times, but unlike imaginary images in real clouds, this face didn't look accidental. It looked too real, too purposeful. Its features were proportionally correct—or correct enough to make it look to be created on purpose. An online search showed that I was not the first to notice it. Many links referenced the same smiling face. A couple links even pointed out a second cloud face in a different section of the clouds.

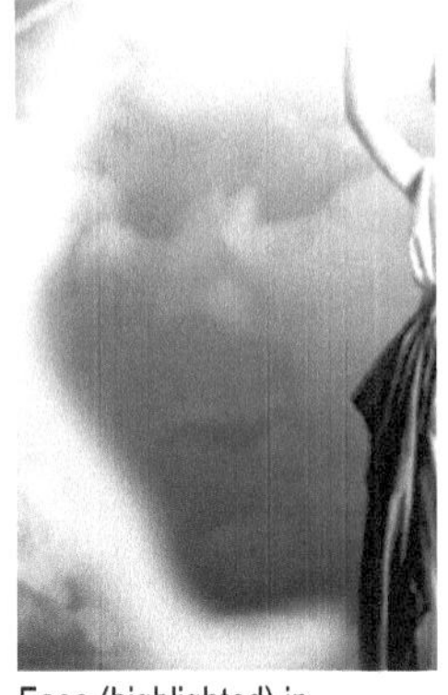
Face (highlighted) in Columbia Pictures logo intro, directly left of Torch Lady.

I knew the artist placed it there, but had to make sure. The problem as I looked even closer was that I saw more than just the two faces. One or two might have been questionable. But rotating an image of the intro produced many other ambiguous illusions of faces. By the time I was done examining the logo, I counted over 40 profiles. Many faces can be seen appearing then disappearing during the movie's intro through the clouds subtle movements. Characteristic of what some Renaissance artists did, parts of some faces formed parts of others. In fact, the image's characteristics were strangely close to what Renaissance artists had done. Some were in profile, others angled. Smaller faces created features of bigger faces. They faced all different directions. Practically every single cloud in that sky turned out to be a human face.

I'd seen the Columbia Pictures logo play on television many times without ever noticing them, yet I would never look at it the same way again. But was I seeing a technique I assumed had died out in the centuries after the Renaissance—at least, in the way it was secretly hidden? The name of the artist who created the painting for the Columbia Pictures logo was Michael J. Deas. And according to his website, he was an American living in Virginia.

I didn't believe there was a connection between Italian Renaissance artists and a Virginian who was currently living just a few states south of me. But still that strange thought was there. And it grew stranger when I saw a face hidden in the folds of the female figure's toga, anamorphic style, when the painting was on its right side. From the other side, there looked to be a bird's head—its beak wide open, resembling something like an eagle or falcon—*similar to the bird head Michelangelo hid in* The Creation of Adam*!* Neither of the images were obvious in Deas' art, but after all the practice examining I had by that point, they didn't need to be.

Yet, I realized that even though the Columbia Pictures intro revealed faces in the animation of the clouds on-screen, they did not appear in an image of the actual painting Deas had created—at least, not the exact same ambiguous faces I had spotted in the movie intro. It seemed that whoever used Deas' painting to create the intro must have added the cloud faces in the process. Still, his painting did reveal different sets of faces. But the ones I saw in the

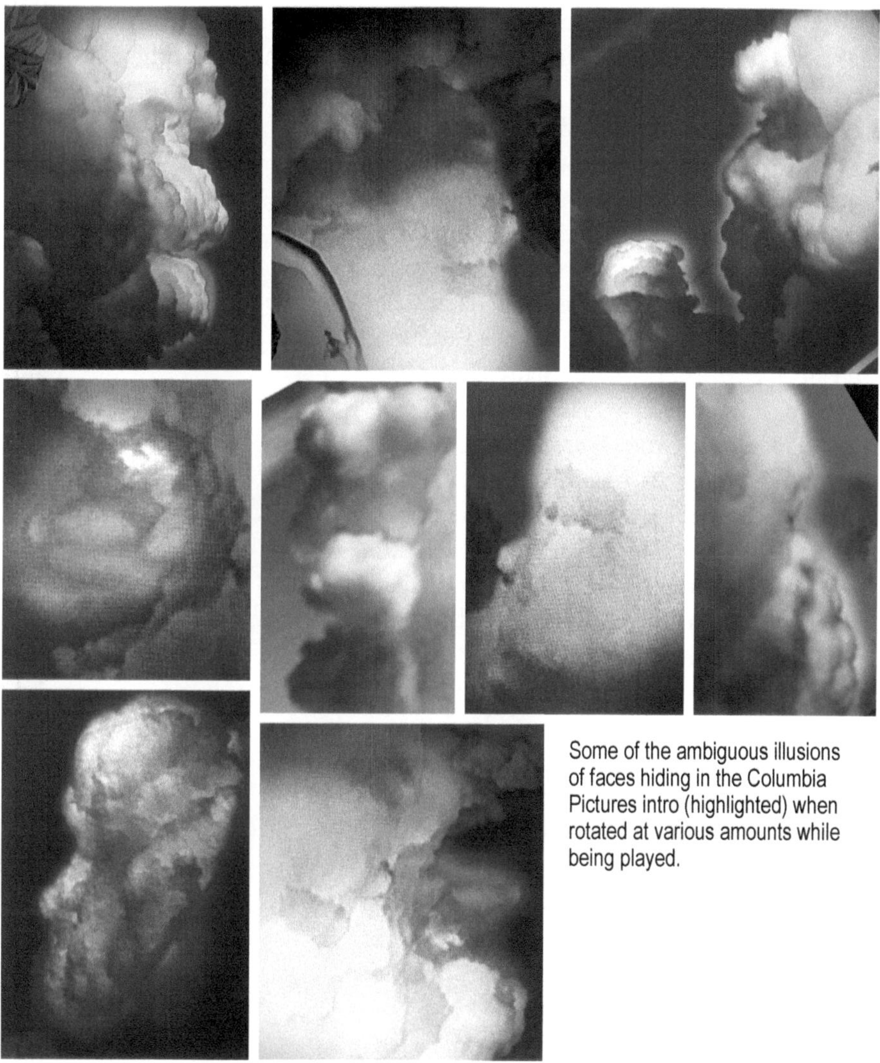

Some of the ambiguous illusions of faces hiding in the Columbia Pictures intro (highlighted) when rotated at various amounts while being played.

painting were anamorphic, and therefore, a lot harder to spot.

Since the Renaissance, there were artists like Dali who created double-image paintings like *The Great Paranoiac* and *Man/Couple with Sleeping Dog* that showed ambiguous faces that were subtle enough for the viewer, but were still meant to be seen. It looked to me like Deas (and whoever animated the Columbia Pictures intro) tried to hide the faces in their art, just as European artists had hundreds of years before. At least, I felt pretty sure about it.

I enjoyed spending time examining Deas' art online. His talent was incredible. And his ability to hide images would have made Renaissance artists proud. But I was more puzzled when I found something else in a painting called *Aguirre, the Wrath of God.* In the rocky cliffs behind the figures of two soldiers, another face was hiding along with the large head of a crocodile. *A crocodile!* In his portrait of Benjamin Franklin there looked to be an anamorphic illusion of a face in the figure's sleeves! An anamorphic face also stood out in another set of clouds in a piece called *The Empty Window.*

Did Deas know about the Renaissance illusions? Was he somehow connected to them? Had all those *years* I spent on my work caused me to hallucinate and imagine secret symbols where there were none? Was I finally experiencing pareidolia as I had originally been accused of? I wanted to call Deas. There were many questions I would have liked to ask Leonardo and Michelangelo, but they were long gone. The idea that Deas had possibly been part of some long line of secrets that stretched back hundreds of years sounded crazy. But what if it was true? What if it was the only chance I'd get to find out the truth once and for all? Had I been right about Envy and Beatrice? About Dante and Aesop? About Moses and the Ark? About the large face of God?

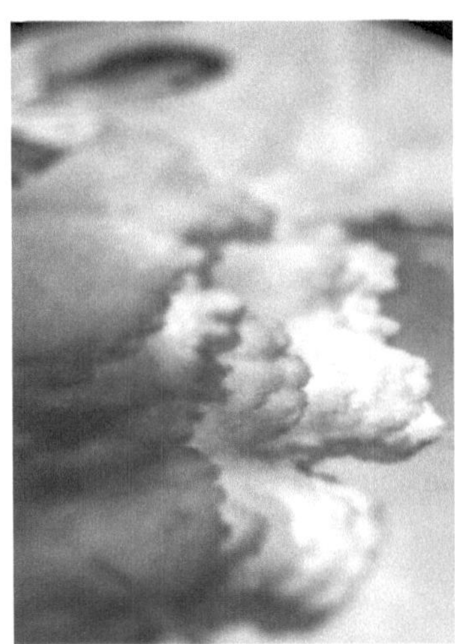

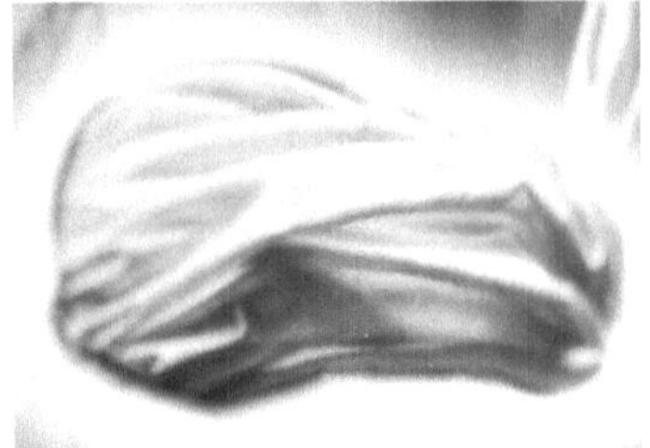

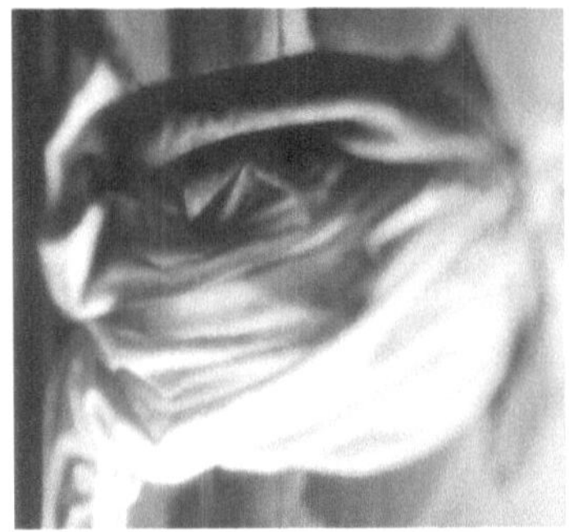

TOP: A group of at least three anamorphic faces can be seen in original *Columbia Pictures Logo* painting by Michael J. Deas. **MIDDLE:** Also hiding is an anamorphic bird head (highlighted) and **(BOTTOM)** a head facing left in folds of figure's toga.

I had Deas's phone number. So I made a list of questions to ask him. *Why hide all those faces in Columbia Pictures? What did they mean? Where did the idea come from?*

I would tell him I was writing a book, but I would feel out our conversation before asking anything crazy-sounding—in case he wasn't aware of what the other artists hid. For the same reason, I didn't want to spoil what my book was going to reveal. If he admitted to what he hid, then I would ask if he was aware of other artists who did the same, as I guided the conversation to Leonardo's work, then I would wait for a reaction. I knew how I would do it too. Although Deas first painted an updated version of the logo with hidden faces in 1992, versions of the logo existed since the 1920s. After I got him to open up about the Columbia Pictures faces, I'd ask him the history behind its details, leading him to the Torch Lady—an image that was suspiciously based on Roman history. *Why does she wear a Roman toga? Why portray her like a classical sculpture? Why was the original 1920s logo based on a Roman soldier?*

Was I going mad to even humor a connection between the Columbia Pictures art and Leonardo da Vinci's? Although, wouldn't I be naive to ignore the logo's original use of a Roman soldier, that the Torch Lady wore a toga and cloak filled with the same kinds of folds Renaissance artists used to camouflage secret images, that it contained heads that were practically undetectable and faced all different directions, and was painted by an artist who somehow came up with the same secret idea Renaissance artists practiced that no one else in the world supposedly knew about? And why the crocodile head in the rocky background of one of the paintings?

I stared at the number I retrieved from Deas's contact page online. All I had to do was pick up the phone and dial the ten digits. On the other end would be someone who could know the answers to some of the most famous paintings in the world, someone who might be able to confirm everything I found, maybe even things I wanted to know about Leonardo and Michelangelo that no one else knew, things that may not have been caught yet. The six-plus years I spent figuring out riddles and chasing down answers could be verified with one simple question to Deas: *Was it all true?*

I bit my nails as the keypad lit up when I pressed the phone icon. I touched the first number, then the second, and hesitantly the third, suddenly feeling a little uncertain. Something didn't feel right as I hovered my finger over the fourth number in the sequence.

Living with those secrets for so long had done something to me. Having done everything in my power to find answers made the mysteries personal. In the process, it gave me a better perspective to who I was. Although the journey at times had worn me down, it also left me feeling enlightened. It taught me that just because something couldn't be seen, it didn't mean it wasn't there. There was more to what appeared on the surface, if one just knew how to look.

Did I really want to be *told* the answers? The best part of those years was the fascination in making the discoveries. Like a great road trip, sometimes the journey becomes more meaningful than the destination.

Yes, I wanted to be sure of my answers. But I also wanted to be left with the wonder of it all. Had my search only been about getting answers? Or was it all about the possibilities? I thought long and hard about it.

Philosophy played an important role in Renaissance art, and artists showed this by presenting multiple meanings in their works—choices for viewers to contemplate once they obtained vision to see the possibilities. Because of that, artists like Leonardo and Botticelli showed me how to make my art more interesting. Contemplation is what leads us to new possibilities, to our beliefs, and for some of us, our faith. *The Comedy* stressed the importance of this contemplation with a scene between Beatrice and Dante—a scene Botticelli portrayed in *Venus and Mars.* Auguste Rodin's *The Thinker*, created in 1880, is a bronze sculpture of a sitting figure, shown in deep thought—in contemplation. Originally, it was named *The Poet*, believed by some scholars to depict Dante at the Gates of Hell.

That same idea of open-mindedness that *The Comedy* points out is what led me to the writings of Dante, Ovid, and even those in the Bible—works I may have never taken the time to read otherwise. It was all about philosophy.

In *The Banquet*, Dante told of how ancient Greek philosopher Pythagoras, who when asked, "said that he was not wise, but a lover of wisdom." Dante then explained "that all students of wisdom were called *lovers of wisdom*, that is, philosophers; for *philo* and *sophia* in Greek are equivalent to *love* and *wisdom*," which make up the name *philosopher*, which "is not a term of arrogance, but of humility." (bk. 3, ch. 11, par. 2; Hillard)[17].

The more I discovered in my journey, the more I wanted to know. And as I realized how much more there was to learn, and, ironically, the more knowledgable I became, the more ignorant I felt. Maybe that was why Leonardo filled thousands of pages of notebooks with some of the greatest knowledge from any one mind, created some of the most beautiful works of art man has known, and yet, in the last hours of his life expressed "how much he had offended God and mankind in not having worked at his art as he should have done."[18]

I knew what I did with *Mona Lisa* would likely be my greatest accomplishment. Yet, somehow, I didn't feel it was good enough. It's why I kept taking so long to finish *Solving Mona Lisa*. I was regularly side-tracked, trying to chase down answers to unresolved questions to paintings that were sometimes unrelated to *Mona Lisa*—simply because I was too curious and intrigued to ignore them. I needed to remember that it was not all about the answers, that it was never really about the answers. That it's the journey I needed to cherish most.

Did I ever end up calling Deas? No. I just couldn't do it. It just didn't feel right to do so. I believe it's how artists like Leonardo da Vinci would have wanted it. As for everything I would write in my book—it was there to be contemplated, just like the art it discussed. But if, by some crazy chance, I happen to run into Deas one day, maybe I'll ask him my questions. Or perhaps I'll ask without wanting him to answer, just so I could study the expression on his face, and be left wondering what he is thinking.

51

Never Ending

As the final draft of my book came to a close, I found myself looking over the whole long road, asking myself what it all really amounted to. Just what *had* I discovered exactly? It wasn't just about animal heads. That was just one tree in a forest. It began there, but then came the anamorphic images, then keys in Leonardo's own writings, like *The d-Point*, and Michelangelo's pointing fingers in his *Creation of Adam*.

Everything hidden seemed to stem from the willingness to say what couldn't be said—whatever the reasons: Scandal? Shame? Salvation? But aimed at who? ...or what? Although artists—on the surface of their art—appeared to be inspired by classical literature, Christian and pagan stories, or even storytellers like Aesop, there seemed to be a deeper meaning from Ovid than was believed. But behind the imagery, artists had risked their lives by hiding messages from the writings of Dante Alighieri. There were too many obvious links to deny it. Dante provided the true framework for understanding Renaissance art.

Life during the Renaissance seemed much more dangerous and cruel for artists than is usually presented. Perhaps it was the brutal politics and religious fanaticism of the time that led artists to be so secretive. Putting those same images out in the open would have been an act of self-destruction. But allegory, symbolism, and especially the use of secret illusions provided a safety net for speaking out.

The Inquisition was also something for artists to worry about. In 1573, Renaissance artist Paolo Veronese was questioned by inquisitors for including "buffoons, drunken Germans, dwarfs" in his version of *The Last Supper*.

The methods I uncovered—which inquisitors thankfully never caught—added profound meaning to the art. It almost didn't matter that Leonardo *had* placed anamorphic images and *had* used material from Dante to create *Mona Lisa*. What really mattered was that he greatly expanded the meaningfulness and power of self-expression in that work of art. And he did so with a technique that, now uncovered, future artists could use. But the technique came before Leonardo's time, during Dante's. I had found similar types of imagery in the works of Giotto. Further research suggested that Dante and Giotto could have formed the idea of hidden images and meanings in both art and in poetry together. The poetry helped make sense of the art, and the art helped make more sense of the poetry.

It was a little shocking to see how experts discussed the paintings without being able to tie them directly to Dante, which changed the entire meaning of the art. I was not a scholar, or historian, or professor. Yet, I believed I was sitting on a time bomb by presenting my discoveries. I imagined that sooner or later, the knowledge I had come across would cause a frenzy of disagreements that would involve reevaluating many works of art not only from the Renaissance, but spanning hundreds of years after. I considered that to be a good thing, as it would provide the art world a better understanding of its own history, and of every Renaissance piece. The disguised imagery expanded each work's meaning in new and previously unknown ways. New connections between paintings could be revealed, such as that between Leonardo's *Mona Lisa* and Botticelli's *Venus and Mars*—two works that primarily stemmed from *The Comedy*, one created with a darker approach to the story, but were previously considered unrelated in subject matter.

A new, dark, picture of the Renaissance emerged: not liberating, but repressive and cruel. Dante's role in the Renaissance had been undervalued, almost ignored, when it deserved to take center stage. Even those *deliberately refusing* to admit that these secret images occurred in Renaissance art would have to admit that the idea of such images could now be used by painters to expand the meaning of their work. In addition, it provided the art world a means of applying another version of a signature, or style, in which to figure out the true creators of artworks by unknown artists. Because it wasn't common practice for artists to sign their work (considered a form of vanity), historians occasionally struggled to match artworks to their creators, at times misinterpreting their true originators.

But the discoveries kept coming.

In solving *Mona Lisa*, I felt I made a good case as to who she was, and why the painting's centuries-long puzzles and mysteries were what they were. Leonardo's notebook reference to *Mona Lisa*'s anamorphic picture left no doubt that he called her Envy. On the surface, it's what the figure represented. References in the painting made it clear that her smile was that of Beatrice. And that they sat in a place mostly showing *Purgatorio* and *Inferno*. I no longer had to question the meaning to her smile, her location, or where she was sitting exactly. In the process, I figured out a lot about myself. In a way, *Mona Lisa* helped me solve the meaning of my own life.

I couldn't pretend the exact meaning wasn't debatable. Images were not literal statements. Undiscovered illusions still existed. But I had uncovered new underlying visuals and the stories which they referenced. Likely, it would be debated for as long as the art and their secret images lasted. The world of Renaissance art was vast. There were lots of pointing fingers throughout the art from that period. Michelangelo's art showed me that at times, the pointing fingers of figures (and where figures eyes were sometimes directed) acted as clues telling viewers where to look from to see the illusions. The pointing fingers in *The Creation of Adam* was his biggest clue.

And still, there were plenty more secrets hiding. My book could only mention a fraction of what I came across. There were things I found that I still shook my head at—things I wasn't sure anyone would believe. More time was needed to examine these findings, such as the hidden imagery that seemed to appear in some of the statues I studied. They too contained gestures of pointing fingers. Unlike paintings and drawings, I'd have to study the statues in person to be sure, since they were three dimensional. Michelangelo's poetry and letters and sketches would have to be restudied, and I would look at the Sistine Chapel again, and take more notes in order to figure out what all his hidden imagery meant. However, I would have to save that for another book.

The discoveries never seemed to stop. And I realized something about the questions that followed them: answers only caused more questions to surface. And I had asked enough questions for the time being. As an artist, I wanted to observe and create. It's what I've always done. The months and years of examining and researching and writing had taken enough precious time away from me. The exact meanings behind other famous works of art were important, but I had my own life to live. Let experts track down their meanings and figure out all those other answers. Maybe some wouldn't even bother. But I had a feeling others eventually would. The great artists of the Renaissance called on us to *see.* They knew some would, just as they knew some wouldn't.

I wanted the whole story to be told. I wanted all the details out there to explain what couldn't be explained otherwise in news reports. My quest to write it all down was almost over. Would the media only be interested in covering the answers to *Mona Lisa*? Perhaps. But a much larger picture existed out there of what had been going on. I had to admit my fear that it would be ignored.

For me, there was no doubt about what I uncovered. Yet, each person would have to make their own judgement.

Did my connection to it all have anything to do with faith? I couldn't say. Maybe my purpose was to spread the word of what I witnessed, just as Dante brought the story of his journey back to those in the living world. Yes, things can exist whether everyone can see them or not. *Funny how that idea was similar to my loss of faith so long ago.* I couldn't ignore how I placed my faith in art when the one I had in God disappeared, only to be brought back to the idea of God's existence through that art. Had I been wrong about Him all along?

About ten years back, Ma had asked me why I no longer attended Sunday Mass. I was sitting on her couch, watching some scene from a Charles Bronson movie, studying the way the wrinkle shadows moved on his jacket. Two thieves were trying to rob him, but they didn't know about the gun in his pocket. His smile said it all.

"I don't know," I said, scared by her question. "I haven't gone in months."

"But why?" she asked.

She was a devout Catholic. And I thought I would break her heart if I told her the truth, but I knew I had to be honest with her.

"I don't believe in going to church anymore," I said after a long pause. It felt as though that were the most courageous thing I had ever said to her.

"I don't understand," she said.

"I don't believe in God."

She said nothing. She just pouted her lips with straining thought, her eyes disappearing from the room then back again. The silence was impenetrable. Then she nodded her head once, like a pitcher understanding the catcher's call.

"Tell me something," she then said. She always wanted me to *tell her something*. "Did your wife believe in God?"

"Ex-wife, ma. Yes, she believed in God. Why?"

"*Ex*-wife. Sorry." She waited a moment. "I don't know. I just was wondering *why* you don't believe." Maybe she thought I had been somehow convinced by another person. Perhaps I should have talked more with her of my past experiences to make her understand my view better.

"Because there's no proof," I told her.

I struggled to make eye contact with her, but had to see her reaction. She seemed to contemplate my answer for a moment. I thought she was going to try and convince me on why I should have faith in God and go back to church. Growing up, it was a Sunday morning family event.

"Well," she finally said, "as long as you believe in something."

Her answer was unexpected, and it took me a moment to register her acceptance. A great sense of weight was lifted from me. Her understanding surprised me, even if it shouldn't have. Despite all the years she attended Mass, she never tried to convince me of God's existence. Nor would I ever have attempted to convince her that He didn't exist.

Looking back, I'm not exactly sure why she decided to ask me that question. I had to guess that as a mother, she was more focused on the path I had chosen rather than the one I had left. If I were to look deep into her mind and see her memories of my childhood, I believe it would include me sitting at the drawing table every night before bed, or sketching in front of the television as Saturday morning cartoons played, or me carrying large art projects home from school—memories of a son dedicating his life to what he loved to do.

Perhaps it was more important to her that I, rather than have faith in God, pursue the path that allowed me to live a joyful life.

As long as you believe in something, Ma had said.

And I did believe in something, Ma. I believed in it all along.

That art has the power to affect our lives.

Epilogue

Science Center

Heather and I visited the Rochester Museum and Science Center one day. It was to see an exhibit I couldn't miss on *Mona Lisa*. Pascal Cotte, a French scientist, had used a special technology to photograph different layers of the painting as if with an x-ray machine, magically removing some of the top layers. Somehow, he managed to show how the painting progressed and changed as Leonardo worked on it, and even how it looked when Leonardo last touched it, before the paint colors slowly changed and the varnish darkened over time. It showed the painting as it was originally intended, as if the original colors had been restored. Looking at some of the images, I imagined it as Leonardo stood back to see his finished creation just after applying the very last brush strokes.

On the museum walls hung other large versions of the painting—cropped sections and full versions—some over ten feet high. The special camera equipment used to process the x-ray-like imagery showed details with a clarity I had never seen. A clarity even Leonardo probably never saw.

I still hadn't come across the fourth animal category Leonardo mentioned in his animal passage. I had found three of the four categories from his *Anamilia* passage, and assumed from the beginning that the fourth—the horse head—had to be hidden somewhere in the art. But it was never found.

For a long time, I didn't notice that I had misinterpreted the word "bridle" in Leonardo's *Envy* passage, incorrectly connecting it to *Mona Lisa*'s veil, as what a bride might wear. I was thrown off by the context he used—"... hand full of flowers ... Make her bridle, ..." and I mistook its meaning as that of *bridal*. I should have caught my mistake sooner. Bridle is the headgear a horse wears to help a rider control it. Leonardo, using the term *bridle* to describe his version of Envy, must have taken the term from Dante's description of the envious souls, writing that:

> "... The sin of envy, and on that account
> Are drawn from love the lashes of the scourge.
> The bridle of another sound shall be;
> I think that thou wilt hear it, as I judge,
> Before thou comest to the Pass of Pardon." (*Pur*. 13.38-42; Longfellow)[1]

From *The Comedy*, I concluded that the hidden horse heads symbolized guidance through a life without corruption, in the sense that man uses the horse to journey.

The Banquet helped define this. In discussing the noble nature of the horse and a virtuous rider, Dante asserts that the horse's bridle conveys "temperance, and shows us how far we may pursue," and that the good rider's spur is "fortitude, or magnanimity, which virtue shows us where we should stop," and so we use the spur "when [the horse] flees, to turn its back to the place" of the righteous path, resisting evil.[2]

Yet, I wasn't able to come up with an exact meaning to what the specific species—lion, ape, ox—meant in *Mona Lisa*, even though I strongly believed their concept was Aesopian. Leonardo's notes included studies on animal habits, such as with the lion, which "never feels fear, ... [but] fights with a stout heart in fierce combat against the crowd of hunters, always seeking to injure the first who has injured him,"[3] and the crocodile, which he compares to the hypocrite, "showing himself thus to have the heart of a tiger, [who] rejoices in his heart over another's misfortunes with a face bedewed with tears."[4] I couldn't be sure or even feel confident about their application to what he hid in his art—especially since I found no useful description of the habits of apes, oxen, or frogs in his notes.

At the exhibit, I was overcome by seeing Leonardo's artistry so large, as if with a sudden telescopic vision, my eyes right up to the painting through its stages. There was so much beauty. So much to explore underneath the surface. Literally.

The actual *Mona Lisa* sat protected behind thick, bulletproof glass in Paris. No harm would come to her. Over the years, she had been attacked by vandals and lunatics. The mark from a thrown rock can be seen near her eye. And at the bottom right of the painting, top layers of paint were distorted from an acid spill. Along with the varnish that darkened over time, areas of the painting were more difficult to make out than others. But Cotte's photos showed how the painting looked before it had been vandalized, and without the darkened varnish, making details of those areas clearer to see.

Heather and I took our time strolling through the exhibit, taking in every detail of every display. There were re-creations of some of Leonardo's famous inventions: an armored tank, a diving suit, large bat-inspired wings designed to allow a man to take flight. We held hands as we walked around, took a photo in his mirror room, tested out some of the interactive pulley systems created from his sketches, and eventually sat down to have coffee and share our impressions of what we had seen. In one room was a replica of *Mona Lisa*, positioned so it could be walked around in order to see both its front and aging back. For me, it was a great way to see the painting from any angle. I wanted to take the replica home. We sat on a backless bench and studied the large replicas hanging around the room. A few were as tall as the wall itself.

I sat quietly, studying the different images and stages of *Mona Lisa* around the room.

No one had ever used such advanced technology to photograph the different layers of paint in *Mona Lisa* as Cotte had. His work showed details that had been previously unseen. But what did those details *tell* us? I had seen things others didn't normally see also, but I wanted to know more. I always wanted to know more.

Of course, something caught my eye. It took a moment to notice it. On one of the wall-sized banners showing a grayscale image of *Mona Lisa* without her layer of darkened varnish, and without the distorted effect caused by the spilled acid, something appeared. It was a clean, clear painting, just as Leonardo had seen it at that stage. *Something only today's technology could see.*

I pointed it out to Heather, the warmth of her body at my side as we sat closely next to each other.

In the painting, toward the bottom, in the area hit by acid in 1956, I could see it. For the first time since that assault, that section of the art was clearly visible. For years I had looked for it, even beginning to think that it didn't exist. Maybe Leonardo simply left it out, I thought. Or maybe I just couldn't see it. Until that moment, it puzzled me.

As I studied the wall portrait, it made sense why I'd never been able to see that specific animal. The top layer, destroyed by acid, had concealed it. But there it was—the long, subtle shape of the horse's head. It was as if the figure—whether Envy, or Beatrice, or the Virgin Mary, or perhaps all three—was embracing the head of a small, young horse in her arm, by the neck. Embracing its existence. *A symbol of the righteous path. A symbol showing that deep down, each of us had the ability to be a better person in the world.*

And in that moment, I smiled.

Notes

1 "Anamorphosis." Apple's Dictionary App. New Oxford American Dictionary. Accessed August 1, 2018.

What You See Isn't What You Get

1 McMullen, Roy. *Mona Lisa: The Picture and the Myth*. Houghton Mifflin, 1975, pp. 187-8

2 Livingstone, Margaret. *Vision and Art: The Biology of Seeing*. Harry N. Abrams, 2014, pg. 73

3 Goldin, Dina Q. "*Mona Lisa's Secret Revealed.*" 1 Nov. 2002. www.cse.uconn.edu/~dqg/papers/monalisa.htm

Chap. 1. The First Clue

1 Ferguson, George. *Signs and Symbols in Christian Art.* Oxford University P, 1961, p. 37.

2 King, David J. "Who was Holbein's Lady with a squirrel and a starling? Ever since it was acquired by the National Gallery, London, in 1992 this celebrated English portrait by Holbein has remained tantalisingly anonymous. A detective trail has led David J King to East Harling in Norfolk, where clues in stained glass and a tomb reveal the sitter's identity.." The Free Library. 2004 Apollo Magazine Ltd. 12 Apr. 2019. www.thefreelibrary.com/Who+was+Holbein%27s+Lady+with+a+squirrel+and+a+starling%3f+Ever+since+it...-a0116733377

3 Zöllner, Frank. *Leonardo da Vinci: The Complete Paintings and Drawings*. Taschen, 2003, p. 37.

Chap. 2. The Mountain

1 DeFalco, Tom. *The Amazing Spider-Man. Unmasked!*, no. 276, Marvel, May, 1986.

2 "Riddles." *Bat-Mania*. www.66batmania.com/guides/riddles/

Chap. 4. Animals

1 Cronin, Brian. "Comic Book Legends Revealed #289." *CBR,* 3 Dec. 2010, www.cbr.com/comic-book-legends-revealed-289/

2 Isaacson, Walter. *Leonardo da Vinci.* Simon & Schuster, 2017, p. 4.

3 Kuruvilla, Carol. "Mormon Church Drops $35 Million On Printer's Manuscript Of The Book Of Mormon." *Huffington Post,* 22 Sept. 2017, www.huffingtonpost.com/entry/mormon-church-drops-35-million-on-printers-manuscript-of-the-book-of-mormon_us_59c42a12e4b06ddf45f6b427

4 Dean, Katrina. "Keeping books of nature: An introduction to Leonardo da Vinci's Codices Arundel and Leicester." *The British Library Board,* www.bl.uk/ttp2/pdf/leonardodean.pdf

5 Vinci, Leonardo da. *The Notebooks of Leonardo da Vinci*. MacCurdy, Edward, editor and translator. Konecky & Konecky, 2003. p. 91.

6 Ibid., 201.

7 Ibid., 887-88.

8 Ibid., 191.

Chap. 5. Those Who See

1 Ibid., 58.

2 Dickens, Emma, editor. *The Da Vinci Notebooks.* Arcade Pub., 2005, p. 75.

3 Ibid., 77.

Chap. 7. Anamorphosis

1 Kleiner, Fred S. *Gardner's Art through the Ages: The Western Perspective.* Cengage Learning, 2016. vol. 2, p. 512.

2 "Third Bull." *Lascaux.* Ministère de la Culture, 2018. archeologie.culture.fr/lascaux/en/mediatheque/third-bull

Chap. 8. Ah, You See?

1 Morgan, Charles Hill. *Life of Michelangelo.* Weidenfeld & Nicolson, 1960, p. 28

Chap. 11. Not Alone

1 No author. No title. No publisher, No date, No p. #.

Chap. 13. The Art Gallery

1 Chevalier, Jean, and Alain Gheerbrant. "Crocodile." *T he Penguin Dictionary of Symbols,* translated by John Buchanan-Brown, Second Edition, Penguin Books, 1994, p. 245.

2 Aesop. "A Short History of the Aesopic Fable." *Aesop: The Complete Fables* (The Greatest Writers of All Time), Kindle, Book House Pub, 2016, 443-4.

Chap. 17. The Crocodile

1 *Beasts of the Bible.* Amazon Prime. Directed and written by Graeme Bell, starring Simcha Jacobovici, narrated by Maurice Dean Wint. Associated Producers, Ltd. 1 April, 2010.

2 Vinci, Leonardo da. *The Notebooks of Leonardo da Vinci.* MacCurdy, Edward, editor and translator. Konecky & Konecky, 2003. pp. 890-91.

Chap. 22. Fame

1 Levato, Ray. "Hidden Animal Images in Da Vinci's Mona Lisa." 12 Dec. 2011, www.youtube.com/watch?v=fIWaWJurK5k
---. Interview with Ron Piccirillo. *News 10NBC,* 1 Dec. 2011, www.mpnnow.com/x1622880782/Rochester-artist-designer-claims-new-discoveries-about-Mona-Lisa-including-hidden-horse-head-crocodile

2 Ibid., Lomax, Janet

3 Fiorica, Holly Ingram. "WOW...so AWESOME Ron! Good for you...what

an amazing discovery. I was so intrigued watching your video and reading the blog. Congratulations!!!" *Facebook*, 30 Nov. 2011

4 Tomer, Ellen. "Nicely done, Ron!! Truly." *Facebook*, 30 Nov. 2011

5 Monacelli, Julianna. "How amazing, Ron!! Congrats on all the great media coverage!!!" *Facebook*, 30 Nov. 2011

6 Tausch, Jim. "Have you googled yourself today? Close to 500 references to your story out there!" *Facebook*, 1 Dec. 2011

Chap. 23. Distorting the Picture

1 "Secrets of a Masterpiece: Is Da Vinci's "Mona Lisa" Hiding Animal Images?" The Today Show. National Broadcasting Company. NBC, New York City, 3 Dec. 2011. Television.

Chap. 24. Deeper Distortions

1 Bates, Daniel. "Artist finds animals hidden in Mona Lisa." *The Sun,* 5 Dec. 2011, www.thesun.co.uk/archives/news/953482/artist-finds-animals-hidden-in-mona-lisa/

2 Wikipedia, European Bison, en.wikipedia.org/wiki/European_bison

3 Bigi, Daniele, and Alessio Zanon. *Atlante delle razze autoctone: Bovini, equini, ovicaprini, suini allevati in Italia* (in Italian). Milan: Edagricole, 2008, p. 92–5.

Chap. 26. Exposure

1 Muscato, Lyndsey. "Here I am ...workng hard... and I come across what's trending on Yahoo! YUP!!! YOUUUUUU AREEEEEE!!!! So excited I get to say "I knew him when..." LOL." *Facebook,* 7 Dec. 2011.

2 Aaro n. Comment on "Solving The Mona Lisa Mysteries." *The Hidden Horse Head,* 9 Dec. 2011, 2:33 a.m. www.thehiddenhorsehead.com/solving-the-mona-lisa-mysteries

Chap. 28. Pride

1 "Serpent." Apple's Dictionary App. New Oxford American Dictionary. Accessed August 1, 2018.

2 *The Holy Bible.* Douay-Rheims Version, Saint Benedict Press. Charlotte, NC, 2009.

3 Ferguson, George. *Signs & Symbols in Christian Art.* Oxford University Press, 1961, p. 16.

Chap. 29. Religious?

1 Blumberg, Antonia. "Elephant Mosaic In 5th Century Synagogue Uncovered." *Huffington Post*, 9 Aug. 2014, www.huffingtonpost.com/2014/08/09/galilee-elephant-mosaic_n_5658512.html

2 King, Ross. *Michelangelo & the Pope's Ceiling.* Walker & Company, 2003, p. 27.

Chap. 30. Scene From Above

1 Harris, Elena. "Crow Spirit Animal." *Spirit Animal*, www.spiritanimal.info/crow-spirit-animal/

2 Mariani, Valerio. *Michelangelo The Painter.* Harry N. Abrams, Inc., NY. 1964, p. 51.

3 Simons, Daniel J. "The Monkey Business Illusion." 8 Apr. 2010, www.theinvisiblegorilla.com/videos.html

4 Vinci, Leonardo da. *Treatise on Painting*. Translated by John Francis Rigaud. George Bell & Sons, 1897, p. 63

5 Ibid., 60.

Chap. 31. Research

1 Kemp, Martin. "Navis Ecclesiae: An Ambrosian Metaphor in Leonardo's Allegory of the nautical Wolf and imperious Eagle," *Bibliotheque d'Humanisme et Renaissance*, p. 257. philpapers.org/rec/KEMNEA

2 Vasari, Giorgio. *Lives of the Most Eminent Painters Sculptors and Architects,* vol. 9. Translated by Gaston Du C. De Vere. Philip Lee Warner, 1912-15, pp. 16-17.

3 Vasari, Giorgio. *Lives of the Artists,* vol. 1. Translated by George Bull. Penguin Books, 1965, pp. 266-7.

4 Ibid., pp. 230, 270.

5 According to the German translation given on *Probst, Veit. "Rätselhafte Mona Lisa." Heidelberg University Library (in German). University of Heidelberg. Archived from the original on 7 June 2011. Retrieved 2011-05-25.*

6 Altrocchi, Rudolph. "*The Calumny of Apelles in the Literature of the Quattrocento.*" Modern Language Association, Vol 36, No. 3, Sep. 1921, p. 455.

Chap. 34. Dante

1 Longfellow, Henry Wadsworth. *Longfellow's Poetical Works.* Fall George Routledge and Sons, 1883. p. 297.

2 Vasari, Giorgio. *Lives of the Most Eminent Painters Sculptors and Architects,* vol. 3. Translated by Gaston Du C. De Vere. Philip Lee Warner, 1912-14, p. 250.

3 "Plot Overview." SparkNotes on *Inferno* by Dante Alighieri. Spark Publishing, 2007. Print.

4 "Analysis of Major Characters." SparkNotes on *Inferno* by Dante Alighieri. Spark Publishing, 2007. Print.

5 "Summary & Analysis." SparkNotes on *Inferno* by Dante Alighieri. Spark Publishing, 2007. Print.

6 "Themes, Motifs & Symbols." SparkNotes on *Inferno* by Dante Alighieri. Spark Publishing, 2007. Print.

7 Vasari, Giorgio. *Lives of the Artists, vol. 1.* Translated by George Bull. Penguin Books, 1965, p. 259

8 "Canto 11." CliffsNotes *The Divine Comedy: Purgatorio.* 1996. Print.

9 Alighieri, Dante. *The Divine Comedy of Dante Alighieri.* Translated by Henry Wadsworth

Longfellow. Houghton, Mifflin & Co., Boston and New York, 1884. *Pur.* 11.91-96. p. 283. Print.

10 Vasari, Giorgio. *Lives of the Artists, vol. 1.* Translated by George Bull. Penguin Books, 1965, p. 58. Print.

11 Vasari, Giorgio. *Lives of the Most Eminent Painters Sculptors and Architects,* vol. 3. Translated by Gaston Du C. De Vere. Philip Lee Warner, 1912-14, pp. 251-53.

12 Ibid., 252.

13 Vinci, Leonardo da. *Treatise on Painting.* Translated by John Francis Rigaud. George Bell & Sons, 1877, p. 149.

14 Zöllner, Frank. *Sandro Botticelli.* Prestel, 2005, pp. 66-67.

15 Ibid., 67.

16 *The Holy Bible.* Douay-Rheims Version, Saint Benedict Press. Charlotte, NC, 2009.

17 Ibid., 70-2.

18 Ovid. *Fasti.* Translated and edited by Boyle, A.J. and R.D. Woodard. Penguin Books, 2000. bk. V, 193-94. p. 119. Print.

19 Ibid., bk. V, 201-14.

20 Ovid. *Metamorphoses.* Translated by Charles Martin. W. W. Norton & Company, 2004. Print.

Chap. 35. Between The Lines

1 Alighieri, Dante. *The Divine Comedy of Dante Alighieri.* Translated by Henry Wadsworth Longfellow. Houghton, Mifflin & Co., Boston and New York, 1884. *Pur.* 27.97-108. Print.

2 Ibid., *Pur.* 28.52-57.

3 Ibid., *Pur.* 28.90.

4 Ibid., *Pur.* 28.54-55.

5 Kemp, Martin and Giuseppe Pallanti. *Mona Lisa: The People and the Painting.* Oxford University Press, 2017, pp. 146-47.

6 Alighieri, Dante. *The Divine Comedy of Dante Alighieri.* Translated by Henry Wadsworth Longfellow. Houghton, Mifflin & Co., Boston and New York, 1884. *Pur.* 29.121-22, 132. Print.

7 Ibid., *Pur.* 29.127-29.

8 Ibid., *Pur.* 30.31-32.

9 Ibid., *Pur.* 33.55-57.

10 Ibid., *Pur.* 33.61-63.

11 Ibid., *Pur.* 31.16-18.

12 Ibid., *Pur.* 30.25-33.

13 Ibid., *Pur.* 30.57.

14 Chevalier, Jean, and Alain Gheerbrant. "Crocodile." *The Penguin Dictionary of Symbols,* translated by John Buchanan-Brown, Second Edition, Penguin Books, 1994, pp. 244-6.

Chap. 36. Venus and Mars

1 Deimling, Barbara. *Sandro Botticelli 1444/1445-1510: The Evocative Quality of Line,* Edited by Michael Claridge, TASCHEN, 2014, p. 49.

2 Zöllner, Frank. *Sandro Botticelli.* Prestel, 2005, p. 125, 129-30

3 Ibid., 125.

4 Alighieri, Dante. *The Divine Comedy of Dante Alighieri.* Translated by Henry Wadsworth Longfellow. Houghton, Mifflin & Co., Boston and New York, 1884. *Pur.* 32.61-69. Print.

5 Ibid., *Pur.* 32.86-88, 94-98.

6 Ibid., *Par.* 1.46-47.

7 "Canto 32." CliffsNotes *The Divine Comedy: Paradiso.* 1972. Print.

8 Alighieri, Dante. *The Divine Comedy of Dante Alighieri.* Translated by Henry Wadsworth Longfellow. Houghton, Mifflin & Co., Boston and New York, 1884. *Par.* 32.22-27, 39. Print.

9 Ibid., *Pur.* 32.3-8, 106-7.

10 Alighieri, Dante. *The Divine Comedy: The Inferno, The Purgatorio, The Paradiso.* Translated by John Ciardi. New American Library, New York, NY, 2003. *Pur.* 32.80-81. Print.

11 Alighieri, Dante. *The Divine Comedy of Dante Alighieri.* Translated by Henry Wadsworth Longfellow. Houghton, Mifflin & Co., Boston and New York, 1884. *Inf.* 3.63. Print.

12 Ibid., *Inf.* 3.52-57, 64-67.

13 Alighieri, Dante. *A New Life/La Vita Nuova.* Edited and translated by Stanley Appelbaum. Dover Pub., 2006, p. 5.

14 Alighieri, Dante. *The Divine Comedy of Dante Alighieri.* Translated by Henry Wadsworth Longfellow. Houghton, Mifflin & Co., Boston and New York, 1884. *Par.* 31.1-2, 7. Print.

15 Alighieri, Dante. *The Divine Comedy of Dante Alighieri.* Translated by Henry Wadsworth Longfellow. Houghton, Mifflin & Co., Boston and New York, 1884. *Par.* 32.85-87. Print.

16 Ibid., *Pur.* 32.116-17.

17 Alighieri, Dante. *The Divine Comedy: The Inferno, The Purgatorio, The Paradiso.* Translated by John Ciardi. New American Library, New York, NY, 2003. *Pur.* 32.142-147. Print.

18 *The Holy Bible.* Douay-Rheims Version, Saint Benedict Press. Charlotte, NC, 2009.

19 Ibid.

20 Alighieri, Dante. *The Divine Comedy of Dante Alighieri.* Translated by Henry Wadsworth Longfellow. Houghton, Mifflin & Co., Boston and New York, 1884. *Par.* 21.4-6. Print.

21 Ibid., *Pur.* 32.38-39.

22 Ibid., *Pur.* 33.4-6.

23 Zöllner, Frank. *Sandro Botticelli.* Prestel, 2005, p. 125

24 Alighieri, Dante. *The Divine Comedy of Dante Alighieri.* Translated by Henry Wadsworth Longfellow. Houghton, Mifflin & Co., Boston and New York, 1884. *Pur.* 31.79-81. Print.

25 *Circa 1492: Art in the Age of Exploration*. Edited by Levenson, Jay. A. and National Gallery of Art. Yale University Press, 1991, p. 287.
26 Emboden, William A. *Leonardo da Vinci on Plants and Gardens*. Dioscorides Press, 1987, p. 157-60.
27 Harris, Elena. "Allegory of Boat, Wolf, and Eagle by Leonardo da Vinci." *Leonardo da Vinci Paintings, Drawings, Quotes, Biography*, www.leonardodavinci.net/allegory-of-boat-wolf-and-eagle.jsp
28 Alighieri, Dante. *The Divine Comedy of Dante Alighieri*. Translated by Henry Wadsworth Longfellow. Houghton, Mifflin & Co., Boston and New York, 1884. *Pur.* 32.115-20. Print.

Chap. 37. The Banquet

1 Ibid., par. 2.
2 Ibid., par. 2, 5.
3 Ibid., par. 5.
4 Ibid., par. 2.
5 Ibid., par. 2.
6 Ibid., par. 3
7 Ibid., par. 5.
8 Ibid., par. 4.
9 Ibid., bk. 2, ch. 8, par. 1-2.
10 Westacott, Evalyn. *Roger Bacon in Life and Legend*. Folcroft Library Editions, 1974, p. 18.
11 Thorndike, Lynn. *A History of Magic and Experimental Science*. Folcroft Library Editions, vol. 2, 1974, p. 654-5.
12 Westacott, Evalyn. *Roger Bacon in Life and Legend*. Folcroft Library Editions, 1974, p. 114.
13 Ibid., 87-91.
14 Singh, Simon. *The Code Book. The Science of Secrecy from Ancient Egypt to Quantum Cryptography*. Anchor Books, 1999, pp. 26-7.
15 Thorndike, Lynn. *A History of Magic and Experimental Science*. Folcroft Library Editions, vol. 2, 1974, p. 628-30.
16 "Bacon, Roger" *Oxford Encyclopedia of World History*, compiled by Market House Books, Oxford UP, vol. 2, 1998, p. 19.
17 King, Ross. *Brunelleschi's Dome: How a Renaissance Genius Reinvented Architecture*. Penguin Books, 2000, pp. 24-5.

Chap. 38. The Background

1 Ovid. *Metamorphoses*. Translated by Charles Martin. W. W. Norton & Company, 2004. Print.
2 Vinci, Leonardo da. *The Notebooks of Leonardo da Vinci*. Edited by Edward MacCurdy. Konecky & Konecky, 2003. p. 852.
3 Ibid., 853.
4 Dickens, Emma, editor. *The Da Vinci Notebooks*. Arcade Pub., 2005, p. 75.
5 "Plan of Dante's Purgatory." CliffsNotes *The Divine Comedy: Purgatorio*. 1996. p. 23. Print.
6 *The Holy Bible*. Douay-Rheims Version, Saint Benedict Press. Charlotte, NC, 2009.
7 Alighieri, Dante. *The Divine Comedy of Dante Alighieri*. Translated by Henry Wadsworth Longfellow. Houghton, Mifflin & Co., Boston and New York, 1884. *Inf.* 9.61-63. Print.
8 Ibid., *Inf.* 1.45-48.
9 Ibid., *Inf.* 4.151, 10.135, 14.9, 10.80-81.
10 Ibid., *Inf.* 16.130-32.
11 Ibid., *Inf.* 16.135-17.3.
12 Ibid., *Inf.* 1.13-14, 100; 3.19; 4.151; 7.84, 106-08; 8.71-72; 9.6, 28, 62-66, 76-78; 10.80-81, 135; 11.70, 12.1-2, 10-11, 40, 86; 14.8-9, 11, 30, 88-89, 94, 97, 99; 16.130-33, 135, 17.1-3; 18.2-5, 7-9, 15-18; 19.40, 133; 21.1, 3; 26.100, 133-34, 142; 29.138-39; *Pur.* 8.20.
13 Ibid., *Inf.* 11.97-105.
14 Ibid., *Inf.* 9.61-63.
15 Ibid., *Inf.* 19.78, 80.
16 Ibid., *Inf.* 9.73-78.
17 Ibid., *Inf.* 22.26-27.
18 Ibid., *Inf.* 9.73-75.
19 Ibid., *Inf.* 9.76-77.
20 Ibid., *Inf.* 9.78.
21 Ibid., *Inf.* 22.25-27.
22 Ibid., *Inf.* 33.97-99.

Chap. 39. The Envious Blind

1 Alighieri, Dante. *The Divine Comedy of Dante Alighieri*. Translated by Henry Wadsworth Longfellow. Houghton, Mifflin & Co., Boston and New York, 1884. *Pur.* 13.37-40, 43-48, 58-60. Print.
2 "Canto 19." CliffsNotes *The Divine Comedy: Purgatorio*. 1996. p. 71. Print.
3 Kleinhenz, Christopher, "Foligno" *Medieval Italy: An Encyclopedia*, Routledge, 2004, vol. 1, p. 360.
4 Alighieri, Dante. *The Divine Comedy of Dante Alighieri*. Translated by Henry Wadsworth Longfellow. Houghton, Mifflin & Co., Boston and New York, 1884. *Pur.* 13.45, 47-48. Print.
5 Ibid., *Pur.* 13.100-02.
6 Ibid., Longfellow, Henry Wadsworth. "Notes on Purgatorio." p. 403.
7 Ibid., *Pur.* 10.7-9.
8 Ibid., *Pur.* 10.10-12.
9 Ibid., *Pur.* 10.16-18, 20-21, 29-30.
10 Ibid., *Pur.* 10.7, 16.
11 Ibid., *Pur.* 10.10-12.
12 Zöllner, Frank. *Leonardo da Vinci: The Complete Paintings and Drawings*. Taschen, 2003, p. 160.

Chap. 40. Rome

1 Alighieri, Dante. *The Divine Comedy of Dante Alighieri*. Translated by Henry Wadsworth Longfellow. Houghton, Mifflin & Co., Boston and New York, 1884. *Pur.* 2.100-03. Print.
2 Alighieri, Dante. *Dante's Purgatory*. Translated

by Marcus Sanders. Chronicle Books, 2005, *Pur.* 2.100-105. p. 11.

3 *International Dictionary of Historic Places: Southern Europe*, edited by Trudy Ring. Fitzroy Dearborn, 1995, vol. 3, p. 498.

4 Meiggs, Russell. *Roman Ostia.* Oxford University Press, 1973.

5 *International Dictionary of Historic Places: Southern Europe*, edited by Trudy Ring. Fitzroy Dearborn, 1995, vol. 3, p. 498.

6 Ibid.

7 Ibid., 503.

8 "Structure of Purgatory." CliffsNotes *The Divine Comedy: Purgatorio.* 1971. p. 21.

Chap. 41. The Third Woman

1 Alighieri, Dante. *The Divine Comedy of Dante Alighieri.* Translated by Henry Wadsworth Longfellow. Houghton, Mifflin & Co., Boston and New York, 1884. *Pur.* 30.67, 69-75. Print.

2 Ibid., *Pur.* 30.118-19, 121-25, 128-31.

3 Ibid., *Pur.* 31.124-26, 136-38.

4 Ibid., *Pur.* 31.133, 142-45, 32.4-8, 13.

5 Ibid., *Pur.* 10.24.

6 Hatfield, Rab. *The Three Mona Lisas.* Officina Libraria, Milan, 2014, p. 52

7 Alighieri, Dante. *The Divine Comedy of Dante Alighieri.* Translated by Henry Wadsworth Longfellow. Houghton, Mifflin & Co., Boston and New York, 1884. Print.

8 Isaacson, Walter. *Leonardo da Vinci.* Simon & Schuster, 2017, p. 58

9 Ferguson, George. *Signs & Symbols in Christian Art.* Oxford University Press, 1961, p. 73.

10 Hatfield, Rab. *The Three Mona Lisas.* Officina Libraria, Milan, 2014, p. 57

Chap. 42. Water from a Rock

1 Richter, Irma A, editor. *The Notebooks of Leonardo da Vinci.* Oxford University Press, 1988, p. 288.

2 Vasari, Giorgio. *Lives of the Most Eminent Painters, Sculptors, and Architects by Giorgio Vasari,* Translated by Gaston du C. De Vere, vol. 1, London: Macmillan and Co., Ld. & The Medici Society, Ld. 1912-1914, p. 82. Print.

3 *Beasts of the Bible.* Amazon Prime. Directed and written by Graeme Bell, starring Simcha Jacobovici, narrated by Maurice Dean Wint. Associated Producers, Ltd. 1 April, 2010.

4 *The Holy Bible.* Douay-Rheims Version, Saint Benedict Press. Charlotte, NC, 2009.

5 Alighieri, Dante. *The Divine Comedy of Dante Alighieri.* Translated by Henry Wadsworth Longfellow. Houghton, Mifflin & Co., Boston and New York, 1884. *Pur.* 13.70-72; *Inf.* 22.129-32. Print.

6 *The Holy Bible.* Douay-Rheims Version, Saint Benedict Press. Charlotte, NC, 2009.

7 Leonardo Da Vinci. The Notebooks of Leonardo Da Vinci - Complete Edition: By Leonardo Da Vinci - Illustrated (p. 451). Kindle Edition.

8 biblehub.com/wycliffe/exodus/19.htm

9 Alighieri, Dante. *The Divine Comedy of Dante Alighieri.* Translated by Henry Wadsworth Longfellow. Houghton, Mifflin & Co., Boston and New York, 1884. *Pur.* 21.58-60. Print.

10 Ibid., *Pur.* 21.67-72.

11 Ibid., *Pur. 10.50.*

12 Ibid., *Pur.* 10.49-56, 73-76.

13 *The Holy Bible.* Douay-Rheims Version, Saint Benedict Press. Charlotte, NC, 2009. p. 88.

14 Ibid., 88.

15 Ibid., 89.

16 Ibid., 89.

Chap. 43. The Hidden Background

1 *International Dictionary of Historic Places: Southern Europe*, edited by Trudy Ring. Fitzroy Dearborn, 1995, vol. 3, p. 501.

2 Ibid., 501.

3 Ibid., 500-01.

4 Ibid., 498-503.

5 Rodgers, Nigel. *Roman Empire.* Metro Books, 2016, p. 34.

6 Alighieri, Dante. *The Divine Comedy of Dante Alighieri.* Translated by Henry Wadsworth Longfellow. Houghton, Mifflin & Co., Boston and New York, 1884. *Pur.* 19.42, 48. Print.

7 Ibid., *Inf.* 21.106-08, 11.

8 Petriaggi, Roberto. "*Isola Sacra—1 Bridge of Matidia.*" Ostia The Harbour District: Portus, 4 Apr. 2019. www.ostia-antica.org/portus/s001.htm.

9 Alighieri, Dante. *The Divine Comedy of Dante Alighieri.* Translated by Henry Wadsworth Longfellow. Houghton, Mifflin & Co., Boston and New York, 1884. *Inf.* 34.129-31. Print.

10 Ibid., *Inf.* 34.133-38.

11 Alighieri, Dante. *The Divine Comedy: The Inferno, The Purgatorio, The Paradiso.* Translated by John Ciardi. New American Library, New York, NY, 2003. *Inf.* 18.22-24. Print.

12 Ibid., *Inf.* 18.29.

13 Ibid., *Inf.* 18.31-33.

Chap. 44. Beasts

1 Alighieri, Dante. *The Divine Comedy of Dante Alighieri.* Translated by Henry Wadsworth Longfellow. Houghton, Mifflin & Co., Boston and New York, 1884. *Inf.* 23.4-6. Print.

2 John Buchanan-Brown, translator. *The Penguin Dictionary of Symbols.* The Penguin Group, 1996, p. 477-478.

3 McKendry, John. J. Introduction. *Aesop, Five Centuries of Illustrated Fables.* The Metropolitan Museum of Art, 1964, p. 5.

4 Ibid., 6.
5 Ibid., 8.
6 Vinci, Leonardo da. *The Notebooks of Leonardo da Vinci.* Edited by Edward MacCurdy. Konecky & Konecky, 2003. p. 1084.
7 Vasari, Giorgio. *Lives of the Most Eminent Painters, Sculptors, and Architects by Giorgio Vasari,* Translated by Gaston du C. De Vere, vol. 1, London: Macmillan and Co., Ld. & The Medici Society, Ld. 1912-1914, p. 72. Print.
8 Vasari, Giorgio. *Lives of the Artists, vol. 1.* Translated by George Bull. Penguin Books, 1965, p. 78. Print.
9 Vasari, Giorgio. *Lives of the Artists, vol. 1.* Translated by George Bull. Penguin Books, 1965, p. 69. Print.
10 McKendry, John. J. Introduction. *Aesop, Five Centuries of Illustrated Fables.* The Metropolitan Museum of Art, 1964, p. 292.

Chap. 45. The Ambassadors

1 Strathern, Paul. *The Artist, the Philosopher, and the Warrior.* Bantam Books, 2009, pp. 234-35.
2 Ibid., 243.
3 Ibid., 139.
4 Ibid., 243.
5 Isaacson, Walter. *Leonardo da Vinci.* Simon & Schuster, 2017, pp. 495-7.
6 Leeman, Fred. *Hidden Images: Games of Perception, Anamorphic Art, Illusion.* Translated by Allison, Ellyn Childs and Margaret L. Kaplan. Harry N. Abrams, Inc., 1975, pp. 12-13.
7 Ciardi, John. "How to Read Dante." *The Divine Comedy: The Inferno, The Purgatorio, The Paradiso.* Translated by John Ciardi. New American Library, New York, NY, 2003. p. ix. Print.
8 Alighieri, Dante. *The Divine Comedy of Dante Alighieri.* Translated by Henry Wadsworth Longfellow. Houghton, Mifflin & Co., Boston and New York, 1884. *Inf.* 33.70-71. Print.
9 Ibid., *Inf.* 33.76-78.
10 Ibid., *Inf.* 33.129-31.
11 Ibid., *Inf.* 33.133.
12 Ibid., *Inf.* 33.134-35, 157.
13 Ibid., *Inf.* 32.117.
14 Ibid., *Inf.* 22.130-32.
15 Ibid., *Inf.* 22.26-28.
16 Ibid., *Inf.* 32.43-44.
17 Ibid., *Inf.* 32.54.
18 Ibid., *Inf.* 32.49-51.
19 Ibid., *Par.* 29.2-4.
20 Ibid., *Par.* 29.5-6.
21 Foister, Susan, and Ashok Roy and Martin Wyld. *Making & Meaning Holbein's Ambassadors.* National Gallery Publications, 1997, pp. 36-7
22 Alighieri, Dante. *The Divine Comedy of Dante Alighieri.* Translated by Henry Wadsworth Longfellow. Houghton, Mifflin & Co., Boston and New York, 1884. *Par.* 33.115-120. Print.
23 Alighieri, Dante. *The Divine Comedy: The Inferno, The Purgatorio, The Paradiso.* Translated by John Ciardi. New American Library, New York, NY, 2003. *Par.* 33.130-32. Print.
24 Foister, Susan, and Ashok Roy and Martin Wyld. *Making & Meaning Holbein's Ambassadors.* National Gallery Publications, 1997, p. 37
25 Alighieri, Dante. *The Divine Comedy of Dante Alighieri.* Translated by Henry Wadsworth Longfellow. Houghton, Mifflin & Co., Boston and New York, 1884. *Par.* 28.50-51. Print.
26 Ibid., *Par.* 28.121-23.
27 Ibid., *Par.* 30.64.
28 Ibid., *Par.* 28.91-93.
29 Kemp, Martin. *Living with Leonardo: Fifty Years of Sanity and Insanity in the Art World and Beyond.* Thames & Hudson, 2018, p. 297.
30 Ibid., 297.
31 Alighieri, Dante. *The Divine Comedy of Dante Alighieri.* Translated by Henry Wadsworth Longfellow. Houghton, Mifflin & Co., Boston and New York, 1884. *Par.* 33.133-42. Print.
32 Alighieri, Dante. *The Divine Comedy.* Translated by Allen Mandelbaum. Everyman's Library, 1995. *Par.* 33.11-15. Print.
33 Vinci, Leonardo da. *The Notebooks of Leonardo da Vinci.* MacCurdy, Edward, editor and translator. Konecky & Konecky, 2003. p. XXX.
34 Westacott, Evalyn. *Roger Bacon in Life and Legend.* Folcroft Library Editions, 1974, p. 91.
35 "The Structure of the Poem." CliffsNotes *The Divine Comedy: Inferno.* 2001. p. 7. Print.
36 Leonardo Da Vinci. The Notebooks of Leonardo Da Vinci - Complete Edition: By Leonardo Da Vinci - Illustrated (p. 185). Kindle Edition.
37 "The Structure of the Poem." CliffsNotes *The Divine Comedy: Inferno.* 2001. p. 8. Print.
38 *The Holy Bible.* Douay-Rheims Version, Saint Benedict Press. Charlotte, NC, 2009.

Chap. 46. Mona's Black Dress

1 Cawthorne, Nigel. *Sex Lives of the Popes: An Irreverent Exposé of the Bishops of Rome from St. Peter to the Present Day.* Prion, 1996, p. 219.
2 Strathern, Paul. *The Artist, the Philosopher, and the Warrior.* Bantam Books, 2009, p. 337.
3 Symonds, John Addington, translator. *The Sonnets of Michael Angelo Buonarroti.* Portland, ME.: Printed for Thomas B. Mosher, 1895, p. 27.
4 Ovid. *Metamorphoses.* Translated by Charles Martin. W. W. Norton & Company, 2004. Print.
5 Ibid., bk. 2.1052, 54.
6 Ibid., bk. 2.1073.

7 Ibid., bk. 2.1062-63.

Chap. 47. The Question

1 King, Stephen. *On Writing: A Memoir of the Craft.* Scribner, 2000, p. 104
2 Alighieri, Dante. *The Divine Comedy of Dante Alighieri.* Translated by Henry Wadsworth Longfellow. Houghton, Mifflin & Co., Boston and New York, 1884. *Par.* 22.128-35. Print.
3 Ibid., *Inf.* 9.28-29. Print.
4 "Canto 18." CliffsNotes *The Divine Comedy: Paradiso.* 1972. p. 74. Print.

Chap. 48. Another World

1 Ovid. *Metamorphoses.* Translated by Charles Martin. W. W. Norton & Company, 2004. 1.1-2. Print.
2 "Introduction." MAXnotes *The Metamorphoses of Ovid.* 2005. p. 4. Print.
3 Ovid. *Metamorphoses.* Translated by Charles Martin. W. W. Norton & Company, 2004. 1.367-71. Print.
4 Ibid., bk. 1.578-79.
5 Ibid., bk. 1.536-40.
6 Ibid., bk. 1.547-52.
7 Vinci, Leonardo da. *Treatise on Painting.* Translated by John Francis Rigaud. George Bell & Sons, 1897, p. 60.
8 *The Holy Bible.* Douay-Rheims Version, Saint Benedict Press. Charlotte, NC, 2009.

Chap. 49. The Point

1 Meshberger MD, Frank Lynn. "An Interpretation of Michelangelo's Creation of Adam Based on Neuroanatomy." JAMA Network, num. 14, 10 Oct. 1990, pp. 1837-41. jamanetwork.com/journals/jama/article-abstract/383532
2 *The Holy Bible.* Douay-Rheims Version, Saint Benedict Press. Charlotte, NC, 2009.
3 Ovid. *Metamorphoses.* Translated by Charles Martin. W. W. Norton & Company, 2004. 1.205-07. Print.

Chap. 50. Facing Judgement

1 Richter, Jean Paul. *Leonardo.* Scribner and Welford, 1881, p. 75.
2 Vinci, Leonardo da. *The Notebooks of Leonardo da Vinci.* Edited by Edward MacCurdy. Konecky & Konecky, 2003. p. 852.
3 Leeman, Fred. *Hidden Images: Games of Perception, Anamorphic Art, Illusion.* Translated by Allison, Ellyn Childs and Margaret L. Kaplan. Harry N. Abrams, Inc., 1975, p. 11.
4 Ibid., 15.
5 Ibid., 11.
6 Vasari, Giorgio. *Lives of the Artists, vol. 1.* Translated by George Bull. Penguin Books, 1965, p. 372. Print.
7 Seckel, Al. *Masters of Deception.* Fall River Press, 2004, p. 31.
8 Alighieri, Dante. *The Divine Comedy of Dante Alighieri.* Translated by Henry Wadsworth Longfellow. Houghton, Mifflin & Co., Boston and New York, 1884. *Par.* 3.7-8. Print.
9 Ibid., *Par.* 3.10-17.
10 Ibid., *Par.* 3.47-48.
11 Ibid., *Par.* 3.58-60.
12 Ibid., Longfellow, Henry Wadsworth. "Notes on Paradiso." p. 613.
13 "Canto 3." CliffsNotes *The Divine Comedy: Paradiso.* 1972. p. 42. Print.
14 Ibid., 43.
15 John Buchanan-Brown, translator. *The Penguin Dictionary of Symbols.* The Penguin Group, 1996, p. 367-368.
16 Ibid.
17 Alighieri, Dante. *The Banquet* (*Il Convito*) *of Dante Alighieri.* Translated by Katharine Hillard. Kegan Paul, Trench & Co., 1889. bk. 3, ch. 11, par. 2, Print.
18 Vasari, Giorgio. *Lives of the Most Eminent Painters Sculptors & Architects by Giorgio Vasari,* Translated by Gaston du C. De Vere, vol. 4, London: Macmillan and Co., Ld. & The Medici Society, Ld. 1912-14, p. 104. Print.

Epilogue. Science Center

1 Alighieri, Dante. *The Divine Comedy of Dante Alighieri.* Translated by Henry Wadsworth Longfellow. Houghton, Mifflin & Co., Boston and New York, 1884. Print. *Pur.* 13.38-42.
2 Alighieri, Dante. *The Banquet* (*Il Convito*) *of Dante Alighieri.* Translated by Katharine Hillard. Kegan Paul, Trench & Co., 1889. bk. 4, ch. 26, par. 4, Print.
3 Vinci, Leonardo da. *The Notebooks of Leonardo da Vinci.* MacCurdy, Edward, editor and translator. Konecky & Konecky, 2003. p. 1078.
4 Ibid. 1083.

Bibliography

Apple's Dictionary App. New Oxford American Dictionary.

According to the German translation given on *Probst, Veit. "Rätselhafte Mona Lisa." Heidelberg University Library (in German). University of Heidelberg. Archived from the original on 7 June 2011. Retrieved 2011-05-25.*

Aesop. "A Short History of the Aesopic Fable." *Aesop: The Complete Fables* (The Greatest Writers of All Time), Kindle, Book House Pub, 2016

Alighieri, Dante. *A New Life/La Vita Nuova.* Edited and translated by Stanley Appelbaum. Dover Pub., 2006

Alighieri, Dante. *Dante's Purgatory.* Translated by Marcus Sanders. Chronicle Books, 2005

Alighieri, Dante. *De Monarchia by Dante.* CreateSpace Independent Pub. Platform, 2015. Print

Alighieri, Dante. *The Banquet (Il Convito) of Dante Alighieri.* Translated by Katharine Hillard. Kegan Paul, Trench & Co., 1889. Print

Alighieri, Dante. *The Divine Comedy I: Hell.* Translated by Dorothy L. Sayers. Penguin Classics, 2004

Alighieri, Dante. *The Divine Comedy II: Purgatory.* Translated by Dorothy L. Sayers. Penguin Classics, 2004

Alighieri, Dante. *The Divine Comedy III: Paradise.* Translated by Dorothy L. Sayers and Barbara Reynolds. Penguin Classics, 2004

Alighieri, Dante. *The Divine Comedy of Dante Alighieri.* Translated by Henry Wadsworth Longfellow. Houghton, Mifflin & Co., Boston and New York, 1884

Alighieri, Dante. *The Divine Comedy: The Inferno, The Purgatorio, The Paradiso.* Translated by John Ciardi. New American Library, New York, NY, 2003

Alighieri, Dante. *The Divine Comedy.* Translated by Allen Mandelbaum. Everyman's Library, 1995. *Par.* 33.11-15. Print.

Altrocchi, Rudolph. "*The Calumny of Apelles in the Literature of the Quattrocento.*" Modern Language Association, Vol 36, No. 3, Sep. 1921

"Bacon, Roger" *Oxford Encyclopedia of World History*, compiled by Market House Books, Oxford UP, vol. 2, 1998

Bates, Daniel. "Artist finds animals hidden in Mona Lisa." *The Sun*, 5 Dec. 2011, www.thesun.co.uk/archives/news/953482/artist-finds-animals-hidden-in-mona-lisa/

Beasts of the Bible. Amazon Prime. Directed and written by Graeme Bell, starring Simcha Jacobovici, narrated by Maurice Dean Wint. Associated Producers, Ltd. 1 April, 2010

Bigi, Daniele, and Alessio Zanon. *Atlante delle razze autoctone: Bovini, equini, ovicaprini, suini allevati in Italia* (in Italian). Milan: Edagricole, 2008

Blumberg, Antonia. "Elephant Mosaic In 5th Century Synagogue Uncovered." *Huffington Post*, 9 Aug. 2014, www.huffingtonpost.com/2014/08/09/galilee-elephant-mosaic_n_5658512.html

Bo, Carlo. *Botticelli.* Rizzoli International Pub., 2005

Bramly, Serge. *Leonardo: Discovering the Life of Leonardo da Vinci.* Harpercollins, 1991

Burstein, Dan. *Secrets of the Code.* Vanguard Press, 2004

Cahill, Thomas. *Heretics and Heroes.* Anchor Books, 2013

Cahill, Thomas. *Mysteries of the Middle Ages.* N.A. Talese, 2006

Cawthorne, Nigel. *Sex Lives of the Popes: An Irreverent Exposé of the Bishops of Rome from St. Peter to the Present Day.* Prion, 1996

Chubb, Thomas Caldecot. *Dante and His World.* Little, Brown and Company, 1966

Ciardi, John. "How to Read Dante." *The Divine Comedy: The Inferno, The Purgatorio, The Paradiso.* Translated by John Ciardi. New American Library, New York, NY, 2003

Circa 1492: Art in the Age of Exploration. Edited by Levenson, Jay. A. and National Gallery of Art. Yale University Press, 1991

CliffsNotes *The Divine Comedy: Inferno.* 2001. Print

CliffsNotes *The Divine Comedy: Purgatorio.* 1996. Print

CliffsNotes *The Divine Comedy: Paradiso.* 1972. Print

CliffsNotes *Virgil's The Aeneid*. 1990. Print

Cohen, Simona. *Animals as Disguised Symbols in Renaissance Art*. Brill's Studies on Art, Art History, and Intellectual History, vol 2, book 169. Brill Academic, 2008

Cronin, Brian. "Comic Book Legends Revealed #289." *CBR*, 3 Dec. 2010, www.cbr.com/comic-book-legends-revealed-289/Harris, Elena.

Da Vinci, Leonardo. *Leonardo's Notebooks*. Edited by H. Anna Suh. Black Dog & Leventhal, 2005

Da Vinci, Leonardo. The Notebooks of Leonardo Da Vinci - Complete Edition: By Leonardo Da Vinci - Illustrated. Kindle Edition.

Da Vinci, Leonardo. *Prophecies*. Hesperus Press, 2002

Dean, Katrina. "Keeping books of nature: An introduction to Leonardo da Vinci's Codices Arundel and Leicester." *The British Library Board*, www.bl.uk/ttp2/pdf/leonardodean.pdf

DeFalco, Tom. *The Amazing Spider-Man. Unmasked!*, no. 276, Marvel, May, 1986

Deimling, Barbara. *Sandro Botticelli 1444/1445-1510: The Evocative Quality of Line*, Edited by Michael Claridge, TASCHEN, 2014

Dickens, Emma, editor. *The Da Vinci Notebooks*. Arcade Pub., 2005

Emboden, William A. *Leonardo da Vinci on Plants and Gardens*. Dioscorides Press, 1987

Ferguson, George. *Signs and Symbols*. Oxford University P, 1961

Foister, Susan, and Ashok Roy and Martin Wyld. *Making & Meaning Holbein's Ambassadors*. National Gallery Publications, 1997

Goldin, Dina Q. "*Mona Lisa's Secret Revealed.*" 1 Nov. 2002. http://www.cse.uconn.edu/~dqg/papers/monalisa.htm

Harris, Elena. "Crow Spirit Animal." *Spirit Animal*, www.spiritanimal.info/crow-spirit-animal/

Hatfield, Rab. *The Three Mona Lisas*. Officina Libraria, Milan, 2014

Hibbard, Howard. *Michelangelo*. Harper & Row, Publishers, 1974

biblehub.com/wycliffe/exodus/19.htm

International Dictionary of Historic Places: Southern Europe, edited by Trudy Ring. Fitzroy Dearborn, 1995, vol. 3

Isaacson, Walter. *Leonardo da Vinci*. Simon & Schuster, 2017

Isbouts, Jean-Pierre and Christopher Heath Brown. *Young Leonardo: The Evolution of a Revolutionary Artist*. Thomas Dunne Books, 2017 John Buchanan-Brown, translator. *The Penguin Dictionary of Symbols*. The Penguin Group, 1996

Kemp, Martin and Giuseppe Pallanti. *Mona Lisa: The People and the Painting*. Oxford University Press, 2017

Kemp, Martin. "Navis Ecclesiae: An Ambrosian Metaphor in Leonardo's Allegory of the nautical Wolf and imperious Eagle," *Bibliotheque d'Humanisme et Renaissance* philpapers.org/rec/KEMNEA

Kelly, J. N. D. *The Oxford Dictionary of Popes*. Oxford University Press, 1986

Kemp, Martin. *Living with Leonardo: Fifty Years of Sanity and Insanity in the Art World and Beyond*. Thames & Hudson, 2018

King, Ross. *Brunelleschi's Dome: How a Renaissance Genius Reinvented Architecture*. Penguin Books, 2000

King, Ross. *Leonardo and The Last Supper*. Bloomsbury, 2012

King, Ross. *Michelangelo & the Pope's Ceiling*. Walker & Company, 2003

King, Stephen. *On Writing: A Memoir of the Craft*. Scribner, 2000

Kleiner, Fred S. *Gardner's Art through the Ages: The Western Perspective*. Cengage Learning, 2016. vol. 2

Kleinhenz, Christopher, "Foligno" *Medieval Italy: An Encyclopedia*, Routledge, 2004, vol. 1

Kuruvilla, Carol. "Mormon Church Drops $35 Million On Printer's Manuscript Of The Book Of Mormon." *Huffington Post*, 22 Sept. 2017, www.huffingtonpost.com/entry/mormon-church-drops-35-million-on-printers-manuscript-of-the-book-of-mormon_us_59c42a12e4b06ddf45f6b427

Lascaux. Ministère de la Culture, 2018. archeologie.culture.fr/lascaux/en/mediatheque/third-bull

Lass, Abraham H. and David Kiremidjian. *The Wordsworth Dictionary of Classical & Literary Allusion*. Wordsworth Editions Ltd, 1994

Leeman, Fred. *Hidden Images: Games of Perception, Anamorphic Art, Illusion*. Translated by Allison,

Ellyn Childs and Margaret L. Kaplan. Harry N. Abrams, Inc., 1975
Leonardo da Vinci Paintings, Drawings, Quotes, Biography, www.leonardodavinci.net/allegory-of-boat-wolf-and-eagle.jsp
Levato, Ray. "Hidden Animal Images in Da Vinci's Mona Lisa." 12 Dec. 2011, www.youtube.com/watch?v=fIWaWJurK5k
Livingstone, Margaret. *Vision and Art: The Biology of Seeing*. Harry N. Abrams, 2014
Longfellow, Henry Wadsworth. *Longfellow's Poetical Works*. Fall George Routledge and Sons, 1883
Machiavelli, Niccolo. *The Prince and Other Writings*. Translated by Luigi Ricci and E. R. P. Vincent. Barnes & Noble Classics, 2003
Mariani, Valerio. *Michelangelo The Painter*. Harry N. Abrams, Inc., NY. 1964
MAXnotes *The Metamorphoses of Ovid*. 2005. Print
McKendry, John. J. Introduction. *Aesop, Five Centuries of Illustrated Fables*. The Metropolitan Museum of Art, 1964.
McMullen, Roy. *Mona Lisa: The Picture and the Myth*. Houghton Mifflin, 1975
Meiggs, Russell. *Roman Ostia*. Oxford University Press, 1973
Meshberger MD, Frank Lynn. "An Interpretation of Michelangelo's Creation of Adam Based on Neuroanatomy." JAMA Network, num. 14, 10 Oct. 1990, pp. 1837-41. jamanetwork.com/journals/jama/article-abstract/383532
Morgan, Charles Hill. *Life of Michelangelo*. Weidenfeld & Nicolson, 1960
News 10NBC, 1 Dec. 2011, www.mpnnow.com/x1622880782/Rochester-artist-designer-claims-new-discoveries-about-Mona-Lisa-including-hidden-horse-head-crocodile
Ovid. *Fasti*. Translated and edited by Boyle, A.J. and R.D. Woodard. Penguin Books, 2000. bk. V, 193-94. Print.
Ovid. *Metamorphoses*. Translated by Charles Martin. W. W. Norton & Company, 2004. Print.
Richter, Irma A, editor. *The Notebooks of Leonardo da Vinci*. Oxford University Press, 1988
Richter, Jean Paul. *Leonardo*. Scribner and Welford, 1881
Rodgers, Nigel. *Roman Empire*. Metro Books, 2016
Seckel, Al. *Masters of Deception*. Fall River Press, 2004
Simons, Daniel J. "The Monkey Business Illusion." 8 Apr. 2010, www.theinvisiblegorilla.com/videos.html
Singh, Simon. *The Code Book. The Science of Secrecy from Ancient Egypt to Quantum Cryptography*. Anchor Books, 1999
SparkNotes on *Inferno* by Dante Alighieri. Spark Publishing, 2007. Print
Stone, Irving. *The Agony and the Ecstasy*. Doubleday, 1961
Stone, Irving, editor. *I, Michelangelo, Sculptor*. Doubleday & Company, 1962
Strathern, Paul. *The Artist, the Philosopher, and the Warrior*. Bantam Books, 2009
Symonds, John Addington, translator. *The Sonnets of Michael Angelo Buonarroti*. Portland, ME.: Printed for Thomas B. Mosher, 1895
The Holy Bible. Douay-Rheims Version, Saint Benedict Press. Charlotte, NC, 2009
Thorndike, Lynn. *A History of Magic and Experimental Science*. Folcroft Library Editions, vol. 2, 1974
Vasari, Giorgio. *Lives of the Artists, vol. 1*. Translated by George Bull. Penguin Books, 1965. Print.
Vasari, Giorgio. *Lives of the Most Eminent Painters Sculptors & Architects by Giorgio Vasari*, Translated by Gaston du C. De Vere, vol. 4, London: Macmillan and Co., Ld. & The Medici Society, Ld. 1912-14. Print.
Vasari, Giorgio. *Lives of the Most Eminent Painters Sculptors and Architects*, vol. 9. Translated by Gaston Du C. De Vere. Philip Lee Warner, 1912-15.
Vasari, Giorgio. *Lives of the Most Eminent Painters Sculptors and Architects*, vol. 3. Translated by Gaston Du C. De Vere. Philip Lee Warner, 1912-14
Vasari, Giorgio. *Lives of the Most Eminent Painters, Sculptors, and Architects by Giorgio Vasari*, Translated by Gaston du C. De Vere, vol. 1, London: Macmillan and Co., Ld. & The Medici Society, Ld. 1912-14. Print.
Vasari, Giorgio. *Lives of the Most Eminent Painters, Sculptors, and Architects by Giorgio Vasari*, Translated by Gaston du C. De Vere, vol. 1, London: Macmillan and Co., Ld. & The Medici Society, Ld. 1912-14. Print.

Vergil. *The Aeneid.* Translated by Christopher Pearse Cranch. Barnes & Noble Classics, 2007
Vinci, Leonardo da. *The Notebooks of Leonardo da Vinci.* Edited by Edward MacCurdy. Konecky & Konecky, 2003
Vinci, Leonardo da. *Treatise on Painting.* Translated by John Francis Rigaud. George Bell & Sons, 1877
Vinci, Leonardo da. *Treatise on Painting.* Translated by John Francis Rigaud. George Bell & Sons, 1897
Westacott, Evalyn. *Roger Bacon in Life and Legend.* Folcroft Library Editions, 1974
Wikipedia, European Bison, en.wikipedia.org/wiki/European_bison
Zöllner, Frank. *Leonardo da Vinci: The Complete Paintings and Drawings.* Taschen, 2003
Zöllner, Frank. *Sandro Botticelli.* Prestel, 2005

www.ingramcontent.com/pod-product-compliance
Ingram Content Group UK Ltd.
Pitfield, Milton Keynes, MK11 3LW, UK
UKHW040242300726
14061UKWH00002BD/115

9 781733 037242

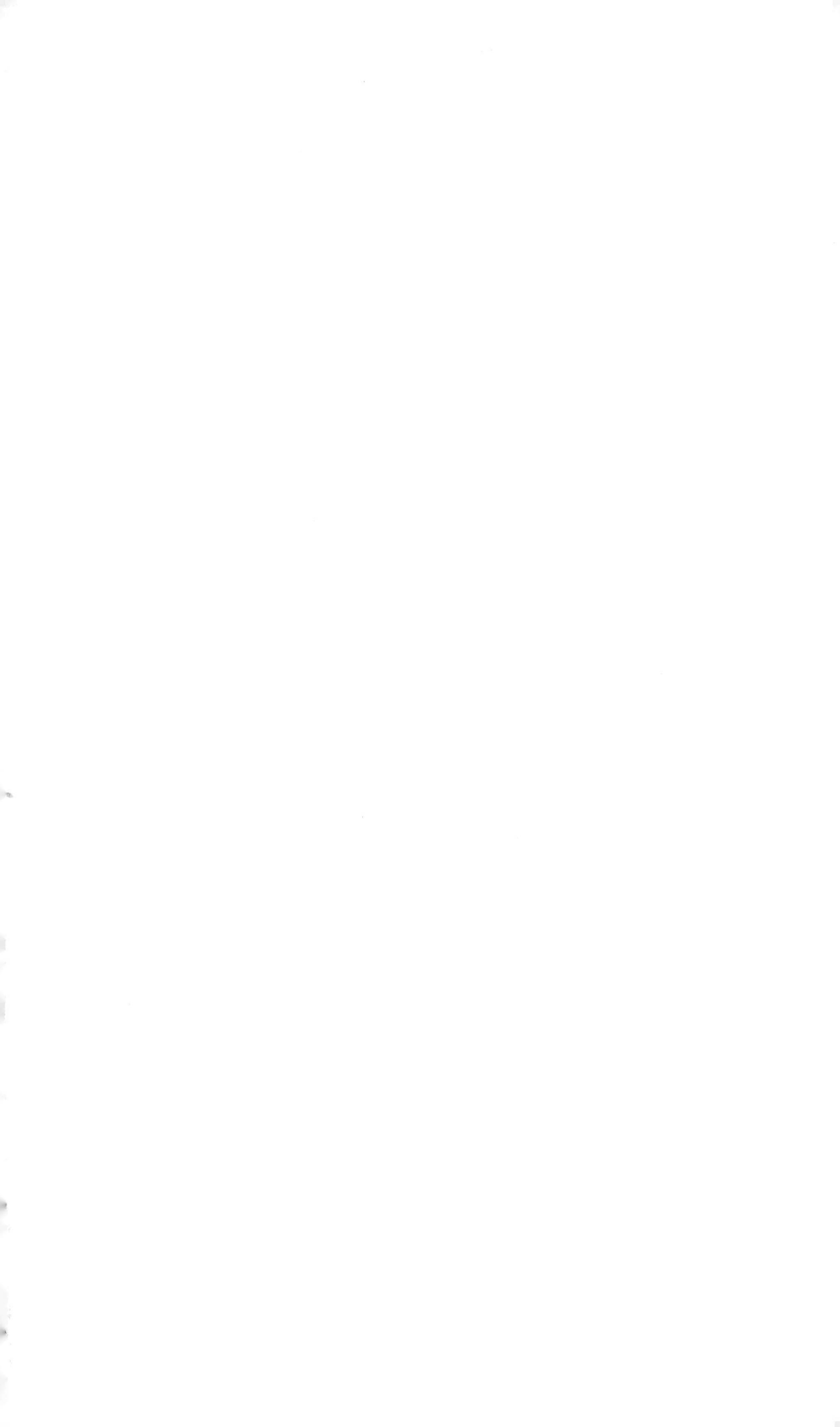